OLD PERSIAN

GRAMMAR   TEXTS   LEXICON

BY
ROLAND G. KENT
Professor Emeritus of Indo-European Linguistics
University of Pennsylvania

AMERICAN ORIENTAL SOCIETY
NEW HAVEN, CONNECTICUT
1950

The University of Pennsylvania's Committee on the Publication of Research has supported the publication of this volume by an appropriation from the Ella Pancoast Widener Fund.

Copyright 1950
By American Oriental Society

MADE IN UNITED STATES OF AMERICA

Waverly Press, Inc., Baltimore, Maryland

AMERICAN ORIENTAL SERIES

VOLUME 33

EDITOR

MURRAY B. EMENEAU

ASSOCIATE EDITORS

SCHUYLER CAMMANN   JAMES B. PRITCHARD

AMERICAN ORIENTAL SOCIETY
NEW HAVEN, CONNECTICUT

1950

AMERICAN ORIENTAL SERIES
VOLUME 33

OLD PERSIAN

PLATE 1

The Inscription and Sculptures of Darius the Great at Behistan
Copyrighted by George G. Cameron, by whose courtesy it appears here

THIS VOLUME IS GRATEFULLY DEDICATED TO THOSE STUDENTS, COLLEAGUES, AND FRIENDS
WHOSE GENEROUS CONTRIBUTIONS MADE ITS PUBLICATION POSSIBLE
AND WHOSE NAMES ARE HERE INSCRIBED:

Anonymous in memory of
   A. V. Williams Jackson
Anonymous
Joseph H. D. Allen Jr.
Helen Cheyney Bailey
Philip L. Barbour
Clarence L. Barnhart
Erminnie H. Bartelmez
George Bechtel
Ruth Moore Bechtel
Charles E. Bidwell
J. David Bishop
Chauncey J. Blair
George J. Bobrinskoy
Morrison C. Boyd
Abraham J. Brachman
J. E. Bresnahan
Helen C. Stock Brown
Charles D. Buchanan
Carl Darling Buck
Florence Buckley
Rhys Carpenter
Bernard F. Cataldo
Charlotte H. Child
James R. Child
Ethel L. Chubb
Edith Frances Claflin
Frank L. Cloud
Henry H. Collins
J. Milton Cowan
Orlando D'Amato
William F. Diller
Isidore Dyen
John M. Echols
Murray B. Emeneau
Charles A. Ferguson
Robert A. Fowkes
Sarah E. Gallagher
John J. Gavigan
James A. Geary

William Gerber
S. Colum Gilfillan
Harold W. Glidden
Mildred Gooding
Louis H. Gray
E. Adelaide Hahn
Frederic S. Hall
Katharine M. Hall
Robert A. Hall, Jr.
Ruth Maynard Hall
Walter Hauser
Mildred M. Hayward
John L. Heller
J. Raymond Hendrickson
Carleton T. Hodge
Henry M. Hoenigswald
Hartley Howard
James F. Irwin
May L. Keller
Gertrude Hall Kent
Harold V. King
George S. Lane
Imelde Langebartel
William W. Langebartel
Erma Renninger Learned
Henry Dexter Learned
Adrián F. León-Márquez
Harry L. Levy
Elizabeth Yarnall Maguire
Emile Malakis
Eugene S. McCartney
Ernest M. McCarus
William C. McDermott
Mary B. McElwain
John C. Mendenhall
Ellen Wyatt Milliken
Christine C. Morley
Harry G. Nickles
Merle M. Odgers
Charles J. Ogden

Robert B. Palmer
Alexander E. Pearce
Ruth Lilienthal Pearce
Herbert Penzl
Frances E. Peters
Horace I. Poleman
Helen Pope
Rachel Hall Potter
James W. Poultney
Edith M. Proctor
Mabel Quay
Horace Abram Rigg Jr.
Kimberley S. Roberts
Jessie A. Rodman
Harold Rosen
Norman P. Sacks
Susan Savage
Philip Scherer
Erich F. Schmidt
Edward H. Sehrt
Alfred Senn
Henry V. Shelley
Lucius R. Shero
George J. Siefert Jr.
Mehmed A. Simsar
Patrick W. Skehan
Maria Wilkins Smith
Friedrich Solmsen
E. A. Speiser
Edgar H. Sturtevant
Robert G. Thompson
University of Notre Dame
Ralph L. Ward
Evelyn Wardle
James R. Ware
Royal M. Weiler
Edwin B. Williams
Francis Wolle
L. Kent Wyatt
Mary Kent Wyatt
Elizabeth G. Zenn

v

FOREWORD

This volume has been prepared to meet the need for a comprehensive treatment of the Old Persian inscriptions; neither the latest collections of texts, nor the latest lexicon of their vocabulary, nor the latest grammatical treatment represents the evidence of all the material, a considerable portion of which is of very recent publication.

In matters of etymology it has seemed desirable to give a goodly representation to cognates outside the Indo-Iranian; not all those interested in Old Persian are primarily specialists in Avestan and Sanskrit. For greater clarity, stems of nouns and adjectives ending in -i- and -u- have been cited with -i- and -u-, rather than with the strong grade -ay- and -av- customary among Iranists; but verbs of OP and Avestan are cited in the strong grade, though Sanskrit verbal roots are cited in the form fixed by the Hindu grammarians and customary among Sanskritists. The English translations of words and passages in the Grammar, especially in the Chapter on Syntax, frequently vary from the translations which accompany the texts in Part II; this variation is intentional, to bring out more clearly the point for which the word or passage is being cited.

Published views of my own on any of the problems involved, so far as they are inconsistent with the views presented in this volume, are to be considered as abandoned even though not explicitly renounced; at times I have considered it desirable specifically to condemn such older views of my own. References to my own printed articles are normally by the name of the journal only, unless there might be ambiguity.

To the American Oriental Society I give my hearty thanks for the opportunity of publication in its American Oriental Series, and to the Society's Editor, Dr. Murray B. Emeneau, and its Secretary-Treasurer, Dr. Ferris B. Stephens, for their labors upon the manuscript and the business management of the volume. To Mr. A. Eric Parkinson, of the University Museum in Philadelphia, I am indebted for the skillful drawing of the cuneiform characters which are reproduced on pages 12 and 215. My grateful appreciation is also expressed to those numerous friends who during the preparation of the volume have shown their interest in it and have urged that it be completed without undue delay. My special thanks are extended to Dr. Erich F. Schmidt, leader of The Persepolis Expedition sponsored jointly by the Oriental Institute of the University of Chicago, the Boston Museum of Fine Arts, and the University Museum in Philadelphia, for generous permission to include new texts found by The Expedition and to use the evidence of The Expedition's photographs of inscriptions already known as well as of those newly discovered. This indebtedness is acknowledged in many places, not infrequently being made by the statement that data have been furnished by Dr. Schmidt or by Dr. George G. Cameron, formerly his colleague at the Oriental Institute, and now Chairman of the Department of Near Eastern Studies at the University of Michigan. Dr. Cameron has for years given me in every way the benefit of his direct acquaintance with the inscriptions and of his rich scholarship, and recently has transmitted to me the chief results of his examination in 1948 of the Behistan Inscription, with permission to use them although he had himself as yet not placed them in printed form before the public; to him, for all these favors, my profound gratitude is here expressed, though any such expression must needs fall far short of his deserts.

Finally, my unending thanks are here given to a small group of those who have studied with me, who—when the American Oriental Society found that it did not have at its command funds adequate to publish the volume—undertook to secure the financial support necessary to see it through the press, and carried their plan through to successful completion: Ruth Lilienthal Pearce, Alfred Senn, Maria Wilkins Smith, E. A. Speiser.

I must add that to Dr. Maria W. Smith is due also much of the typographical accuracy of the book; for to her the Editor of the Series, first because of absence in Europe and then because of press of work, delegated the task of proofreading in his stead. Her repeated skillful readings caught numerous misprints that had escaped me; yet with all our care I dare not think that perfection has been attained, and I shall be grateful to any reader who sends me a list of such misprints and errors as he may discover.

R. G. K.

Wynnewood, Pa.,
March 21, 1950.

CONTENTS

GENERAL BIBLIOGRAPHY 1
   Abbreviations . . 2
   Symbols for Designating Inscriptions and Locating Words .. 4

PART I. GRAMMAR

CHAPTER I. THE LINGUISTIC SETTING

§1. Old Persian .. 6
§2. The Iranian Languages 6
§3. Old Iranian . 6
§4. Middle Iranian 6
§5. New Iranian . .. 7
§6. Dialect Mixture in the Old Persian Inscriptions . . 8
§7. The Median Dialect 8
§8. Median Phonetic Developments . 8
§9. OP Words showing Median Peculiarities... 8
§10. Dialect Mixture in the OP Forms 9
§11. Dialect Mixture in the OP Vocabulary. 9
§12. Aramaic Influence 9

CHAPTER II. THE SCRIPT

§13. The Script of the Old Persian Inscriptions.... . . . 9
§14. Early Steps in the Decipherment 10
§15. G. F. Grotefend.. . 10
§16. The Completion of the Decipherment. 11
§17. Summary of the Decipherment . 11
§18. The Old Persian Syllabary . 11
§19. The Syllabic Characters of OP 12
§20. The Alphabetic Order of Normalized Old Persian.. . .. 12
§21. The Representation of a in OP Writing 13
§22. The Representation of i and u in OP Writing 13
§23. Written Indication of Length of i and u. 13
§24. The Diphthongs. 14
§25. Postconsonantal y 14
§26. Postconsonantal v. 14
§27. The Combination h^ai 14
§28. The Combination h^au 15
§29. The Persistence of Vowel r 15
§30. Old Persian r. 15
§31. Old Persian ar 16
§32. Old Persian ara 16
§33. Old Persian ra after consonants .. 16
§34. Old Persian graphic ar of uncertain value . 16
§35. Old Persian ar before y and v 16
§36. Old Persian final $\check{a}$ 17
§37. Old Persian final i 17
§38. Old Persian final u 17
§39. Old Persian Nasals before consonants 17
§40. Old Persian Reduced Final Consonants 18
§41. Repetition of the Same Consonant-Sign 18
§42. The Ideograms 18
§43. Numerals 19
§44. The Separation of Words . 19
§45. The Normalization of OP Texts . 19
§46. The Reduction of OP to Writing 20
§47. Irregularities and Errors in OP Writing 20
§48. Medial ay and av . . . 21
§49. Variations in Consonants . 21
§50. The Errors of Writing. 21
§51. Metathesis of Characters . 21
§52. Omissions of Characters 22
§53. Addition of Characters.. 22
§54. Alteration of Characters by omission or addition of a stroke..... 23
§55. Miscellaneous Errors of Writing 23
§56. Errors in Syntax......... 23
§57. Neologisms in the Later Inscriptions. . 24

CHAPTER III. PHONOLOGY

§58. The pIE Sounds . 24
§59. The Old Persian Sounds 25
§60. The Position of Sounds and Sound-Clusters in OP Words . 25
§61. pIE e o a 25
§62. pIE $\bar{e}$ $\bar{o}$ $\bar{a}$ 26
§63. pIE Reduced Vowels 26
§64. pIE i and u. 26
§65. pIE $\bar{\imath}$ and $\bar{u}$ 26
§66. pIE r and l 27
§67. pIE m and n 27
§68. pIE $\bar{r}$ $\bar{l}$ $\bar{m}$ $\bar{n}$ 27
§69. The pIE Short Diphthongs in i 27
§70. The pIE Short Diphthongs in u 28
§71. The pIE Short Diphthongs ∂i and ∂u 28
§72. The pIE Long Diphthongs.. 28

§73. The pIE Stops in Proto-Aryan	28
§74. The pIE Stops in Proto-Iranian.	29
§75. The pIE Labial Stops in OP	29
§76. The pIE Dental Stops in OP	30
§77. pIE *t* before consonants	31
§78. pAr. *tr*	31
§79. pAr. *tr* after spirants	31
§80. pIE *ti̯*	32
§81. pIE *tu̯*	32
§82. pIE *tn*	32
§83. Other Developments of Non-Final Dental Stops	32
§84. Final Dentals	32
§85. The Dental Clusters *tst(h)* and *dzd(h)*	32
§86. The pIE Palatal Stops	33
§87. pIE *k̂* before vowels	33
§88. pIE *ĝ* and *ĝh*	33
§89. pIE *k̂i̯*	34
§90. pIE *k̂u̯*	34
§91. pIE *ĝhu̯*	34
§92. pIE *k̂s*	34
§93. pIE *k̂t*	34
§94. pIE *k̂l*	34
§95. pIE *k̂m* and *ĝhm*	35
§96. pIE *k̂n ĝn ĝhn*	35
§97. pIE *sk̂*	35
§98. The pIE Velars and Labiovelars in pAr.	35
§99. pAr. *k* and *ć*	35
§100. pAr. *kh*	36
§101. pAr. *g* and *ǵ*, *gh* and *ǵh*	36
§102. OP *xš*	36
§103. pAr. *k* and *g* before consonants	37
§104. pAr. *ći̯*	37
§105. The Cluster *-s-ć-*	37
§106. pIE *r*	38
§107. pIE *l*	38
§108. The pIE Nasals	38
§109. pIE *m*	38
§110. pIE *n*	39
§111. OP Unwritten Medial Nasals	39
§112. OP Final *n*	39
§113. pIE *i̯*	39
§114. pIE *u̯*	39
§115. pIE *s*	40
§116. pIr. *s*	40
§117. pIr. *š*	40
§118. pIr. *h*	41
§119. pAr. *h̭*	41
§120. pIE *z*	41
§121. The Ablaut Grades of the Vowels	42
§122. Ablaut Variation within the Root	43
§123. Functional Ablaut Variation within the Verbal Root	43
§124. Functional Ablaut Variation within the last Stem-Syllable of Nouns	43
§125. Guna and Vriddhi	44
§126. Vriddhi as a Formative	44
§127. Epenthesis	45
§128. Anaptyxis	45
§129. Haplology	45
§130. Shortening of Long Consonants	45
§131. Contraction of Vowels	46
§132. Consonantal Variation	46
§133. Enclisis	46
§134. The Phonetics of Enclisis	47
§135. The *-ă* before enclitic	47
§136. The *-iy* before enclitic	47
§137. The *-uv* before enclitic	47
§138. Consonants before enclitics	47
§139. Contraction of Vowels in Sandhi	47
§140. Sandhi in Connection with Prefixes	47
Appendix to Chapter III. The Origins of OP Sounds	48

CHAPTER IV.

FORMATION OF NOUN AND ADJECTIVE STEMS

§141. Noun and Adjective Stems	49
§142. Root Nouns and Adjectives	50
§143. Noun and Adjective Stems with thematic *-a-*	50
§144. Noun and Adjective Stems with suffix *-(i)i̯a-*	50
§145. Noun and Adjective Stems with suffix *-ta-*	51
§146. Noun and Adjective Stems with suffix *-ka-*	51
§147. Noun and Adjective Stems with suffix *-na-*	51
§148. Noun and Adjective Stems with suffix *-ra-*	51
§149. Noun and Adjective Stems with suffix *-ma-*	51
§150. Noun and Adjective Stems with suffix *-u̯a-*	51
§151. Noun and Adjective Stems with miscellaneous *-a-* suffixes	52
§152. Noun and Adjective Stems ending in *-ĭ-*	52

§153. Noun and Adjective Stems ending in -ū-	52
§154. Noun and Adjective Stems ending in -r-	52
§155. Noun and Adjective Stems ending in -n-	52
§156. Noun and Adjective Stems ending in -s-	52
§157. Adjective Stems with suffix -vant-	52
§158. Other Noun and Adjective Stems ending in consonants	53
§159. Noun and Adjective Compounds in OP	53
§160. Determinative Nouns and Adjectives	53
§161. Possessive Adjectives	54
§162. Participial Compound Adjectives	54
§163. Names of Persons	54
§164. Personal Names of Iranians	55
§165. Names of Months	55
§166. Names of Places	55
§167. Province Names and Ethnics	56

CHAPTER V.

DECLENSION OF NOUNS, ADJECTIVES, PROUNOUNS

§168. Declension in OP	57
§169. The Case-Endings of -o- Stems in pIE	57
§170. The Case-Endings of -o- Stems in Aryan	58
§171. Case-Forms of -o- Stems in OP	58
§172. The Development of the -o- Declension in OP	59
§173. The Case-Endings of -ā- Stems in pIE	59
§174. The Case-Endings of -ā- Stems in Aryan	60
§175. Case-Forms of -ā- Stems in OP	60
§176. The Development of the -ā- Declension in OP	60
§177. The Case-Endings of -i- and -ī- Stems in pIE and in Aryan	60
§178. Case-Forms of -i- and -ī- Stems in OP	61
§179. The Development of the -i- and -ī- Declensions in OP	61
§180. The Case-Endings of -u- Stems in pIE and in Aryan	62
§181. Case-Forms of -u- Stems in OP	62
§182. The Development of the -u- Declension in OP	62
§183. The -ū- Stems and u-Diphthong Stems in OP	62
§184. The Case-Endings of Consonant-Stems in pIE and in Aryan	63
§185. The -s- Stems in OP	63
§186. The -r- Stems in OP	64
§187. The -n- Stems in OP	64
§188. The Stems in Stops, in OP	65
§189. The Dual Case-Forms of OP	65
§190. Adjectives in OP	65
§191. The Adverbs of OP	66
§192. The Pronouns of OP	67
§193. The First Personal Pronoun	67
§194. The Second Personal Pronoun	67
§195. The Enclitic Pronouns of the Third Person	67
§196. The Third Personal Pronoun *hauv*	68
§197. The pIE Relative Pronoun *i̯o-	68
§198. The OP Relative and Article *hya hyā tya*	68
§199. The Demonstrative Pronoun 'this'	68
§200. The Demonstrative Pronoun 'that'	69
§201. The Interrogative-Indefinite pIE *q^{u}o- *q^{u}i-	69
§202. The Demonstrative *aita-* 'this'	69
§203. Semi-Pronominal Adjectives	69
§204. The Numerals	69

CHAPTER VI. STEMS AND FORMS OF VERBS

§205. The Verb in Old Persian	70
§206. Verbal Prefixes	70
§207. The Present-Tense Formations	70
§208. The Present-Tense System (type, Skt. *ásti*)	70
§209. The Present-Tense System (type, Skt. *dádhāti*)	71
§210. The Present-Tense System (types, Skt. *kṛṇóti, krīṇā́ti, vénati*)	71
§211. The Present-Tense System (type, Latin *jungit*)	71
§212. The Present-Tense System (type, Skt. *pṛccháti*)	71
§213. The Present-Tense System (types, Skt. *bhávati, rudáti*)	72
§214. The Present-Tense System (types, Skt. *náhyati, drúhyati*)	72
§215. The Present-Tense System (types, Skt. *pātáyati, patáyati*)	72
§216. The Present-Tense System with suffix -i̯e-/-i̯o-	73

§217. The Present-Tense System of Denominative Verbs .. 73
§218. The Aorist-Tense Formations 73
§219. The Perfect Tense 73
§220. The Passive-Voice Present Stem 73
§221. The Finite Moods of the Verb in OP. 74
§222. The Subjunctive Formations 74
§223. The Optative Formations 74
§224. The Injunctive Formations 74
§225. The Personal Endings of the Verb 74
§226. The Personal Endings of the First Singular Active 75
§227. The Personal Endings of the Second Singular Active 75
§228. The Personal Endings of the Third Singular Active 75
§229. The Personal Endings of the Third Dual Active 76
§230. The Personal Endings of the First Plural Active 76
§231. The Personal Endings of the Second Plural Active 76
§232. The Personal Endings of the Third Plural Active 76
§233. The Personal Endings of the First Singular Middle 76
§234. The Personal Endings of the Second Singular Middle 77
§235. The Personal Endings of the Third Singular Middle 77
§236. The Personal Endings of the Third Plural Middle 77
§237. The Personal Endings of the Imperative 77
§238. The Infinitive 77
§239. The Participles found in OP 78
§240. The Present Active Participle 78
§241. The Present Middle Participle 78
§242. The Perfect Passive Participle in *-to-* 78
§243. The Perfect Passive Participle in *-no-* 79
§244. The Future Passive Participle in *-eto-* 79

CHAPTER VII. SYNTAX AND STYLE

§245. The Syntax of OP 79
§246. The Syntax of the Noun in OP 79
§247. The Nominative Case 79
§248. The Vocative Case 79
§249. The Accusative Case 79
§250. The Genitive Case 80
§251. The Locative Case 81
§252. The Instrumental Case 81
§253. The Ablative Case 82
§254. Syncretism of the Cases 82
§255. Number 83
§256. Grammatical Agreements 83
§257. Appositives 83
§258. Agreements of Pronouns 83
§259. Agreement of Predicates 83
§260. The Pronouns of OP 84
§261. The Relative-Demonstrative 84
§262. The Articles in OP 85
§263. The Demonstrative *hauv* 85
§264. The Demonstrative *ava-* 85
§265. The Demonstrative *iyam* 85
§266. The Demonstrative *aita-* 85
§267. The Pronouns in Relative Clauses 85
§268. The Prepositions and Postpositions 86
§269. Prepositions with the Accusative 86
§270. Prepositions with Other Cases 87
§271. Prepositions with Two or More Cases 87
§272. The Voices of the Verb 87
§273. The Active Forms 87
§274. The Middle Forms 87
§275. The Passive Forms 88
§276. The Verb 'to be' with Passive Participle 88
§277. The Indicative Mood 88
§278. The Subjunctive Mood 89
§279. The Optative Mood 89
§280. The Imperative Mood 90
§281. The Injunctive Mood 90
§282. The Infinitive 90
§283. The Participles 90
§284. The Tenses 90
§285. The Present Tense of the Indicative 90
§286. The Imperfect and Aorist Tenses of the Indicative 90
§287. Tense Aspect 91
§288. The Perfect Tense 91
§289. The Future 91
§290. Coordination and Subordination 91
§291. The Coordinating Conjunctions 91
§292. The Negative Adverbs 92
§293. The Subordinating Conjunctions 92
§294. The Conjunction *yātā* 92
§295. The Conjunction *yaθā* 92
§296. The Conjunction *yadātya* 93
§297. The Conjunction *yadiy* 93
§298. The Conjunction *yāvā* 93
§299. The Conjunction *tya* 93

CONTENTS

§300. Subordinate Clauses . 93
§301. Relative Clauses 93
§302. Substantive Clauses 93
§303. Conditional Clauses 94
§304. Temporal Clauses 94
§305. Miscellaneous Adverbial Clauses 94
§306. The Position of Adjectives 95
§307. The Position of Predicate Nouns and Adjectives . . . 95
§308. The Position of Appositives 95
§309. The Position of the Genitive 95
§310. The Word-Order in the Sentence 96
§311. The Position of Enclitic Words 96
§312. The Naming Phrases 97
§313. The Artaxerxes Genealogies 98
§314. Anacoluthon 99
§315. Features of OP Style 99
§316. Stylistic Omissions 100
§317. Chiasmus . . 100
§318. Riming Phrases 100
Index of Passages Cited in Chapter VII . 100

PART II. THE TEXTS

Description and Bibliography of the Inscriptions 107
AmH 107; AsH 107; CMa etc. 107; DB 107; DPa etc. 108; DN 109; DSa etc. 109; DZ 111; DE 111; DH 111; XPa etc. 112; XSa etc. 113; XE 113; XV 113; XH 113; A¹Pa etc. 113; D²Sa etc. 113; A²Sa etc. 113; A²Ha etc. 114; A?P 114; A³Pa etc. 114; Wa etc. 114; SD etc. 115; XVs etc. 115; Spur. 115.

The Texts with Notes and Translation . 116
AmH 116; AsH 116; CMa etc. 116; DB I 116, II 121, III 124, IV 128, V 132, minor 134; DPa etc. 135, e 136; DNa 137, b 138, minor 140; DSa etc. 141, f 142, g etc. 144, m etc. 145; DZ 146; DE 147; DH 147; XPa 147, b 148, c etc. 149, g etc. 150, i etc. 152; XSa etc. 152; XE 152; XV 152; XH 153; A¹Pa 153; A¹I 153; D²Sa etc. 154; A²Sa etc. 154; A²Ha etc. 155; A?P 155; A³Pa 156; Wa etc. 156; SD etc. 157; XVs etc. 157.

Historical Appendix. 158
I, The Achaemenian Dynasty 158; II, Smerdis and Gaumata 159; III, The Helpers of Darius 160; IV, The Persian Calendar and Behistan I–IV 160; The Accession of Xerxes 163.

PART III. LEXICON 164

Lexicon and Concordance 164; Numerals 215; Defective Passages 215.

ADDENDA 216

ILLUSTRATIONS

I The Inscription and Sculptures of Darius the Great at Behistan . . . Frontispiece
II The Gold Tablet of Hamadan . . . facing page 10
III The Daiva Inscription of Xerxes. . . . facing page 151

GENERAL BIBLIOGRAPHY

Bibliography of OP studies is to be found in the following:

Chr. Bartholomae, Die altpersischen Inschriften, in Geiger und Kuhn's Grundriss der iranischen Philologie 2.54-75, Strassburg 1896-1904.

Chr. Bartholomae, Altiranisches Wörterbuch, Strassburg 1904; with bibliography in the notes attached to the caption words.

H. C. Tolman, Ancient Persian Lexicon and Texts 59-134, Nashville 1908; where references are attached to the words in the lexicon.

F. H. Weissbach, Die Keilinschriften der Achämeniden, Leipzig 1911; which lists and evaluates virtually all the previous literature.

Indogermanisches Jahrbuch, in the appropriate section, beginning with 1912, but lacking some items, notably from 1914 to 1920.

J. H. Kramers, A Classified List of the Achaemenian Inscriptions, pp. 12, reprinted from the Annual Bibliography of Indian Archaeology for 1931 (Leiden 1933), containing bibliography of the separate inscriptions from 1911 to 1932.

R. G. Kent, The Present Status of Old Persian Studies, in JAOS 56.208-225 (1936), with bibliography from 1912 to 1936.

R. G. Kent, Old Persian Jottings, in JAOS 58.324-30 (1938), with continuation of the preceding bibliography.

There are the following historical grammars of OP:

E. L. Johnson, Historical Grammar of the Ancient Persian Language, New York 1917.

A Meillet, Grammaire du Vieux Perse, 1915; 2d ed., entirely revised by É. Benveniste, Paris 1931.

The following items might be listed here:

W. Foy, KZ 35.1-78 (1899); a preliminary sketch of the phonology.

H. C. Tolman, Cuneiform Supplement, Nashville 1910; pp. vii-xxv give a summary of the phonology and morphology.

T. Hudson-Williams, A Short Grammar of Old Persian, Cardiff 1936; pp. 1-19 give a brief and inaccurate account of the phonology and morphology.

Sukumar Sen, Old Persian Inscriptions, Calcutta 1941; pp. 259-88 give an essentially descriptive grammar, inaccurate in many points.

A concordance of the OP vocabulary is found in E. L. Johnson, Index Verborum to the Old Persian Inscriptions, published with Tolman's Cuneiform Supplement (see above).

A glossary of the OP vocabulary is to be found in W. Hinz, Altpersischer Wortschatz, Leipzig 1942; including bibliographical references and concordance.

On the names of persons and places, reference may be made to the entries in our lexicon, and to the following:

F. Justi, Iranisches Namenbuch, Marburg 1895.

G. Hüsing, Die iranischen Eigennamen in den Achämenideninschriften, Soltau 1897.

A. Hoffmann-Kutschke, Persische Eigennamen, in OLZ 9.439-44, 604-6 (1906); Iranisches bei den Griechen, in Philologus 66.173-91, 320 (1907).

F. H. Weissbach, Die Keilinschriften der Achämeniden 136-58, Leipzig 1911.

A. H. M. Stonecipher, Graeco-Persian Names, New York 1918.

The difficult problem of the chronology of the Behistan inscription has evoked a voluminous literature on the OP calendar; it will be adequate here to refer to a recent discussion by A. Poebel, in the American Journal of Semitic Languages and Literatures 55.130-65, 285-314 (1938); see Historical Appendix IV.

There are the following complete collections of the OP inscriptions; I omit those before the reading of the Rock of Behistan by Rawlinson:

H. C. Rawlinson, JRAS 10.187-349 (1847); text, translation, notes.

Theodor Benfey, Die persischen Keilinschriften, mit Uebersetzung und Glossar, Leipzig 1847.

J. Oppert, Les Inscriptions des Achéménides, Paris 1851; text, translation, notes.

Fr. Spiegel, Die altpersischen Keilinschriften, Leipzig 1862; 2d ed., 1881; text, translation, grammar, glossary.

C. Kossowicz, Inscriptiones Paleo-persicae Achaemenidarum quot hucusque repertae sunt, Petropolis 1872; cuneiform and transliterated text, Latin translation, glossary.

F. H. Weissbach und W. Bang, Die altpersischen Keilinschriften, fasc. 1, Leipzig 1893; fasc. 2, 1908; text, translation.

H. C. Tolman, Ancient Persian Lexicon and Texts, Nashville 1908; text, translation, lexicon.

H. C. Tolman, Cuneiform Supplement to the preceding, Nashville 1910; autographed cuneiform texts.

F. H. Weissbach, Die Keilinschriften der Achämeniden, Leipzig 1911; OP, Elam., Akk. texts, with translation and glossary of proper names; the bibliography to the separate inscriptions, pages x–xxx, is especially valuable.

More recently discovered inscriptions were for the most part published in the following:

V. Scheil, Inscriptions des Achéménides à Suse, in Mémoires de la Mission Archéologique de Perse, tome xxi; Paris 1929. The inscriptions, with English translation and partial vocabulary, are repeated by J. M. Unvala, The Ancient Persian Inscriptions of the Achaemenides found at Susa, Paris 1929.

V. Scheil, Inscriptions des Achéménides, pp. 105–29, in Mémoires etc., tome xxiv; Paris 1933.

Ernst Herzfeld, Altpersische Inschriften, Berlin 1938.

Collected editions of these inscriptions, so far as already published, are found in the following:

R. G. Kent, JAOS 51.189–240 (1931).

Wilhelm Brandenstein, WZKM 39.7–97 (1932), with F. W. König, Der Burgbau zu Susa, Leipzig 1930: OP, Elam., Akk.

All OP texts to date are contained in the following:

Sukumar Sen, Old Persian Inscriptions of the Achaemenian Emperors, Calcutta 1941; text, Sanskrit and English translations, notes, glossary, grammar (inaccurate and unreliable).

Two other volumes must be noted here, in the publications of the Oriental Institute of the University of Chicago:

George G. Cameron, Persepolis Treasury Tablets, Chicago, 1948 (Or. Inst. Publ. vol. 65); containing all Elamite inscriptions found in the Treasury Halls of Darius, Xerxes, and Artaxerxes I at Persepolis. An important feature is the collection and discussion of the words borrowed from OP, many of them not found in the OP texts themselves.

Erich F. Schmidt, Persepolis, shortly to appear; containing reproductions of photographs of all inscriptions attached to reliefs at Persepolis and Naqš-i-Rustam.

The literature on the individual inscriptions is given at the beginning of Part II, before the texts; but no references are there given to Unvala's Ancient Persian Texts, since it has no value. Nor, in general, are citations made to volumes which appeared before KT's volume. The present location of the inscriptions is given according to available records, but may have been changed by the events of the Second World War.

ABBREVIATIONS

The following periodicals are referred to in abbreviated form:

AbkSGW = Abhandlungen der philosophisch-historischen Klasse der königl. sächsischen Gesellschaft der Wissenschaften.

Acta Or. = Acta Orientalia.

Acta Sem. Phil. Erlangen = Acta Seminarii Philologici Erlangensis.

AfOF = Archiv für Orientforschung.

AJP = American Journal of Philology.

AJSLL = American Journal of Semitic Languages and Literatures.

Arch. Anz. = Archäologischer Anzeiger.

BB = Beiträge zur Kunde der indogermanischen Sprachen, herausgegeben von Ad. Bezzenberger.

BIFAO = Bulletin de l'Institut français de l'archéologie orientale.

BSLP = Bulletin de la Société de Linguistique de Paris.

BSOS = Bulletin of the School of Oriental Studies, London.

GGA = Göttingische Gelehrte Anzeigen.

GN = Nachrichten von der königlichen Gesellschaft der Wissenschaften zu Göttingen.

IF = Indogermanische Forschungen.

ABBREVIATIONS

IFA = Indogermanische Forschungen, Anzeiger.
JAOS = Journal of the American Oriental Society.
Jb. DAI = Jahrbuch des deutschen archäologischen Instituts.
JCOI = Journal of the Cama Oriental Institute.
JNES = Journal of Near Eastern Studies.
JRAS = Journal of the Royal Asiatic Society.
KZ = Zeitschrift fur vergleichende Sprachforschung, begrundet von A. Kuhn.
Lg. = Language.
MSLP = Mémoires de la Société de Linguistique de Paris.
MVAG = Mitteilungen der vorderasiatisch-aegyptischen Gesellschaft.
OLZ = Orientalistische Literaturzeitung.
PAPA = Proceedings of the American Philological Association.
Rec. Trav. = Recueil de Travaux relatifs à la philologie et à l'archéologie égyptiennes et assyriennes.
Rev. d'Assyr. = Revue d'Assyriologie.
RHRel. = Revue de l'Histoire et des Religions.
Riv. Stud. Or. = Rivista degli Studi orientali.
SbPAW = Sitzungsberichte der königlich. preussischen Akademie der Wissenschaften.
TAPA = Transactions of the American Philological Association.
TPS = Transactions of the Philological Society (London).
Ung. Jrb. = Ungarische Jahrbücher.
WZKM = Wiener Zeitschrift für die Kunde des Morgenlandes.
ZDMG = Zeitschrift der deutschen morgenlandischen Gesellschaft.
ZfA = Zeitschrift für Assyriologie.
ZII = Zeitschrift für Indologie und Iranistik.

The following authors and works are referred to in abbreviated form:

Bthl. = Chr. Bartholomae.
Bthl. AF = Bthl., Arische Forschungen; 3 vols., Halle 1882–7.
Bthl. AiW = Bthl., Altiranisches Worterbuch; Strassburg 1904.
Bthl. Stud. = Bthl., Studien zur indogermanischen Sprachgeschichte; Halle 1890–1.
Bthl. zAiW = Bthl., Zum altiranischen Wörterbuch; Strassburg 1906.
Brd. = Wilh. Brandenstein.
Brugmann, Gdr. = Karl Brugmann, Grundriss der vergleichenden Grammatik der indogermanischen Sprachen, 2d ed.; Strassburg 1897 ff.
Bv. = É. Benveniste.
Bv. Gr. = A. Meillet, Grammaire du Vieux-Perse, 2d ed., revised by Bv.; Paris 1931.
Bv. Origines = Bv., Origines de la Formation des Noms en Indo-européen; Paris 1935.
Cowley, AP = A. Cowley, Aramaic Papyri of the Fifth Century B.C.; Oxford 1923.
Gdr. IP = Grundriss der iranischen Philologie, herausgegeben von W. Geiger und A. Kuhn; Strassburg 1895–1906.
Hinz = W. Hinz, ZDMG 93.364–75.
HK = A. Hoffmann-Kutschke.
HK 1 or HK ApKI 1 = HK, Die altpersischen Keilinschriften des Grosskönigs Dārajawausch des Ersten am Berge Bagistān; Stuttgart 1908.
HK 2 or HK ApKI 2 = HK, Die altpersischen Keilinschriften des Grosskonigs Dārajawausch des Ersten bei Behistun; Stuttgart und Berlin, 1909.
Hz. = Ernst Herzfeld.
Hz. AMI = Hz., Archäologische Mitteilungen aus Iran; Berlin 1929 ff.
Hz. ApI = Hz., Altpersische Inschriften; Berlin 1938.
Jn. = A. V. Williams Jackson.
Jn. Iran. Rel. = Jn., Iranian Religion, in Zoroastrian Studies; New York 1928.
Johnson, Gram. = E. L. Johnson, Historical Grammar of the Ancient Persian Language; New York 1917.
Johnson, IV = E. L. Johnson, Index Verborum to the Old Persian Inscriptions; in Tm. CS (q.v.).
Justi, INB = F. Justi, Iranisches Namenbuch; Marburg 1895.
Kg. = Fr. Wilh. König.
König, Burgbau = Kg., Der Burgbau zu Susa nach dem Bauberichte des Konigs Dareios I; in MVAG 35.1, Leipzig 1930.
König, RuID = Relief und Inschrift des Koenigs Dareios I am Felsen von Bagistan; Leiden 1938.
KT = [L. W. King and R. C. Thompson,] The Sculptures and Inscription of Darius the

Great on the Rock of Behistûn in Persia; London 1907.
MB Gr. = Mt. Gr. (q.v.) and Bv. Gr. (q.v.).
Mt. Gr. = A. Meillet, Grammaire du Vieux Perse; Paris 1915.
Nyberg, Rel. = H. S. Nyberg, Die Religionen des alten Iran, deutsch von H. H. Schaeder; Leipzig 1938.
Oppert, IdA = J. Oppert, Les Inscriptions des Achéménides; Paris 1851.
Oppert, Mèdes = J. Oppert, Le Peuple et la Langue des Mèdes; Paris 1879.
Prašek, GMP = J. V. Prašek, Geschichte der Meder und Perser, vol. II; Gotha 1910.
PW = Paulys Real-Encyclopädie der classischen Altertumswissenschaft, Neue Bearbeitung herausgegeben von Georg Wissowa; Stuttgart 1894 ff.
Rawlinson = H. C. Rawlinson, JRAS vol. 10.
Reichelt, Aw. Elmb. = Hans Reichelt, Awestisches Elementarbuch; Heidelberg 1909.
Rl. = Rawlinson (q.v.).
RV = Rigveda.
Sachau, AP = E. Sachau, Aramäische Papyrus und Ostraka aus einer jüdischen Militär-Kolonie zu Elephantine; Leipzig 1911.
Scheil 21 = V. Scheil, Inscriptions des Achéménides à Suse, in Mémoires de la Mission archéologique de Perse, tome XXI, Mission en Susiane; Paris 1929.
Scheil 24 = V. Scheil, Inscriptions des Achéménides, supplément et suite, in Mémoires etc., tome XXIV; Paris 1933.
Sen = Sen, OPI (q.v.).
Sen, OPI = Sukumar Sen, Old Persian Inscriptions of the Achaemenian Emperors; Calcutta 1941.
Spiegel = Fr. Spiegel, Die altpersischen Keilinschriften im Grundtexte, Uebersetzung, Grammatik, und Glossar; Leipzig 1862, 2d ed. 1881.
Sturtevant, IH Laryngeals = E. H. Sturtevant, The Indo-Hittite Laryngeals; Baltimore 1942.
Tm. = H. C. Tolman.
Tm. CS = Tm. Cuneiform Supplement; Nashville 1910.
Tm. Lex. = Tm. Ancient Persian Lexicon and Texts; Nashville 1908.

Tm. VS or Vdt. Stud. = Tm. The Behistan Inscription of King Darius, Vanderbilt University Studies vol. I; Nashville 1908.
Vd. = Vendidad, originally Vīdaēvadāta (a book of the Avesta).
Wb. = F. H. Weissbach.
Wb. Grab = Wb. Die Keilinschriften am Grabe des Darius Hystaspis; AbkSGW vol. XXIX, no. 1.
Wb. KIA = Wb. Die Keilinschriften der Achämeniden; Leipzig 1911.
Wb. Symbolae Koschaker = Wb. in Symbolae Paulo Koschaker Dedicatae; Leiden 1939.
WB = F. H. Weissbach und W. Bang, Die altpersischen Keilinschriften in Umschrift und Übersetzung, 1. Lieferung; Leipzig 1893.
WBn = WB, 2. Lieferung, Nachträge und Berichtigungen; Leipzig 1908.

Other abbreviations are readily understood; they include those for modern scholars and their works when only slightly shortened, for Greek and Latin authors and their works, for names of languages, for grammatical terms.

SYMBOLS FOR DESIGNATING INSCRIPTIONS AND LOCATING WORDS

The inscriptions are referred to by abbreviations on the following plan:

First symbol		Second Symbol	
Am	= Ariaramnes		
As	= Arsames	B	= Behistan
C	= Cyrus the Great	P	= Persepolis
D	= Darius the Great	N	= Naqš-i-Rustam
X	= Xerxes	S	= Susa
A¹	= Artaxerxes I	Z	= Suez
D²	= Darius II	E	= Elvend
A²	= Artaxerxes II	V	= Van
A?	= Artaxerxes II or III	H	= Hamadan
A³	= Artaxerxes III	M	= Murghab
W	= Weight of Darius	I	= incerto loco
S	= Seal	Vs	= Vase
SD	= Seal of Darius		

Further symbols, if any:
An immediately following small letter indicates a particular inscription or part of an inscription already designated.

SYMBOLS FOR DESIGNATING INSCRIPTIONS

A second small letter indicates a particular copy of the inscription.

A small v indicates a copy with variant orthography.

A Roman numeral after a gap indicates a special part of the inscription.

Phrases or words are designated after a gap:

By two numerals, indicating column and line.

By one numeral, indicating line.

By 0, indicating a line preceding those previously known and numbered.

By f after the line-number, indicating that the phrase or word runs over into the next line.

Note also the following indications:

The lack of a number where it is expected indicates that the inscription consists of one line only.

° at the end of the reference means that the entire word is restored.

[ ] mark the enclosed word or words or part of a word as restored; but in the complete texts of the inscriptions in Part II the restorations are indicated only by italics.

PART I. GRAMMAR

CHAPTER I. THE LINGUISTIC SETTING OF OLD PERSIAN

§1. OLD PERSIAN is the name applied to the Persian language used in the cuneiform inscriptions of the Achaemenian dynasty; it can be localized as the language of southwestern Persia, or Persis in the narrower sense, and was the vernacular speech of the Achaemenian rulers. The OP inscriptions are commonly accompanied also by translations into Elamite and Accadian, engraved in other types of cuneiform writing, and sometimes by an Aramaic version or an Egyptian hieroglyphic version. Linguistically, OP belongs to the Iranian branch of Indo-Iranian or Aryan, which is one of the main divisions of the Indo-European family of languages.

§2. THE IRANIAN LANGUAGES[1] are, like many other sets of languages, divisible on a chronological basis into three periods: Old Iranian, Middle Iranian, and New[2] Iranian. They were spread in ancient times over the territory bounded by the Persian Gulf on the south, by Mesopotamia and Armenia on the west, and by the Caucasus Mountains; to the east of the Caspian Sea they extended considerably to the north of the present boundary of Iran and Afghanistan, into the Pamir plateau of Turkestan, and thence approximately along the course of the Indus River to the Gulf of Oman. This is even today approximately the area of Iranian-speaking peoples, although at all periods there have been islands of non-Iranian speech within it, and islands of Iranian speech outside it.

§3. OLD IRANIAN includes two languages represented by texts, Old Persian and Avestan, and a number of other dialects which are but very slightly known.

I. Old Persian is known by inscriptional texts found in Persis, at Persepolis and the nearby Naqš-i-Rustam and Murghab (Pasargadae); in Elam, at Susa; in Media, at Hamadan and the not too distant Behistan and Elvend; in Armenia, at Van; and along the line of the Suez Canal. They are mainly inscriptions of Darius the Great (521–486 B.C.) and Xerxes (486–65); but others, mostly in a corrupted form of the language, carry the line down to Artaxerxes III (359–38).

II. Avestan is the language of the Avesta or sacred writings of the Mazdayasnians, known also as Parsis (i.e. Persians) and as Zoroastrians or followers of Zoroaster, the prophet who proclaimed the religion. It consists linguistically of two parts: an older part containing the Gāθā's or metrical sermons of Zoroaster himself, and the Later Avesta, differing in a number of linguistic features from the Gāθā's. Zoroaster himself came from the northwest, but his successes in converting to his faith were made in the northeast, in Bactria; it is therefore disputed as to whether Avestan is a northwestern or a northeastern language. It is noticeable that it agrees rather with Median than with OP, but this is not decisive.

III. Among the less known Old Iranian languages the most important was Median, known only from glosses, place and personal names, and its developments in Middle Persian, apart from borrowings in OP, which are of considerable importance for the understanding of OP itself. Others were the language of the Carduchi, presumably the linguistic ancestor of modern Kurdish; Parthian, the language of a great empire which contended against Rome in the time just before and after the beginning of the Christian era; Sogdian in the northeast, the ancestor of the medieval Sogdian; Scythian, the language or languages of the various tribes known in OP as *Sakā*, located to the east of the Caspian and north of Parthia and Sogdiana, but also to the west of the Caspian on the steppes north of the Euxine Sea.

§4. MIDDLE IRANIAN includes the Iranian dialects as they appear from about 300 B.C. to about 900 A.D. They are in general called Pahlavi, which is only the regular development of a deriv-

---

[1] Cf. Meillet et Cohen, Les Langues du Monde 34–42; MB Gr §5–§6, Kieckers, Die Sprachstamme der Erde 6–7; E W West, Gdr IP 2 75–81; W. Horn, Gdr IP 1 2 412–23 [2] New is preferable to Modern, which leads to an abbreviation identical with that for Middle.

ative of the OP word *Parθava* 'Parthian'. It is clearer to discuss the dialects partly by dialects and partly by the extant remains.

I. Arsacid Pahlavi was the official language of the Arsacid dynasty of Parthia, which ruled from 250 B.C to 226 A.D.; it did not die out with the dynasty. It is represented in some bilingual inscriptions alongside the Sasanian Pahlavi, where it is often called Chaldaeo-Pahlavi or Parthian; by the parchment manuscripts of Auromān; and by certain Manichaean texts from Turfan (IV). It is also called Northwest Pahlavi, and apparently was developed from a dialect which was almost or quite identical with that of Media.

II. The Sasanian or Southwest Pahlavi was the official language of the Sasanian dynasty, which ruled from 226 A.D. until the Mohammedan conquest in 652. It is known from some rock-inscriptions of the kings in the general region of Persepolis, datable in the 3d and 4th centuries, some being accompanied by a translation into Arsacid Pahlavi or even by a second translation into Greek; from some texts on Egyptian papyri, of about the 8th century; from many religious texts preserved by the Zoroastrians (III); and from some of the Manichaean texts found at Turfan. In inscriptional form it can be observed in legends on coins, seals, and gems, until near the end of the 7th century. It appears to have developed from Old Persian or from a very similar dialect.

III. The 'Book-Pahlavi' includes the writings preserved by the Zoroastrians of Persia and India, forming a very considerable body of literature divisible into (1) translations of parts of the Avesta, with commentary, (2) texts on other religious subjects, (3) texts on other than religious topics. They represent both Sasanian and Arsacid Pahlavi. They are written in an alphabet derived from that of Aramaic, and, like all the early Pahlavi writings and inscriptions, contain an extremely high percentage of Semitic words; but many of these were to be read with the Iranian equivalents, even as we write *id est* and say 'that is', *viz.* and say 'namely'.

IV. The manuscripts found at Turfan, in the early years of the 20th century, give us texts that are mostly of the 8th and 9th centuries, though some of them go back almost to the beginning of the Christian era. These texts represent several dialects, including the Arsacid and the Sasanian types, the Sogdian (known also from a trilingual inscription of Kara-Balgassūn), and a dialect known as 'Eastern Iranian', perhaps a derivative of northeastern Scythian, in which there are texts of the Buddhists of Khotan. The notable peculiarity of these Turfan texts is that they are written in relatively pure Iranian, without the Semitic writings for the words which are to be spoken by the Iranian equivalent.

V. Among the earliest traces of Pahlavi, however, are certain legends in Greek characters on coins of Indo-Scythic rulers of the Turuška dynasty in northwestern India, belonging to the first two Christian centuries.

§5. NEW IRANIAN includes the Iranian languages from about 900 A.D. onward; its greatest monument is the national epic of Persia, the Shāh Nāmăh or Book of Kings, composed by Firdausi about the year 1000. The languages of this period are the following:

I. Persian, the national language of Persia to this day, spoken in numerous varying dialects throughout the empire; some of the aberrant dialects may go back to different dialects of antiquity, but the language as a whole seems to come from the general types of the Old Persian and the Avestan. The most highly esteemed literary Persian is the dialect of Shiraz.

II. Pushtu, sometimes called Afghan, the national language of Afghanistan.

III. Baluchi, the language of Baluchistan.

IV. The dialects of the Pamir, in the northeast.

V. The Caspian dialects, to the south and west of the Caspian Sea; probably derived from ancient Scythian.

VI. The Kurdish dialects, apparently derived from the ancient Carduchian; now spoken by various tribes in western Persia and in the neighboring parts of the Turkish Republic.

VII. The Ossetic dialects, in the general region of the Caucasus; derived from the Scythian of Southern Russia.

VIII. The Yagnobi or dialect spoken in the valley of the Yagnob, in the northeast; apparently derived from ancient Sogdian.

All but the last division consist of varying dialects. Throughout the territory of the New Iranian languages there is competition with other languages, such as Arabic, Turkish, Armenian,

Mongol. The Persians in Bombay and its vicinity, usually called Parsees, speak the Indic language known as Gujrati (or Gujerati).

§6. DIALECT MIXTURE IN THE OLD PERSIAN INSCRIPTIONS. Like most or perhaps all other series of documents, the OP inscriptions are not in pure OP dialect, free from admixture from outside.[1] They contain the expected borrowings of names of persons and places, and presumably of some cultural materials. Thus *Aθurā* 'Assyria', *Bābiruš* 'Babylon', *Mudrāya* 'Egypt' are from Semitic; *Izalā* (a district in Assyria), *Dubāla* (a district in Babylonia), *Labanāna* 'Mt. Lebanon', *Haldita-* (name of an Armenian) betray their non-Iranian character by the *l*; a few words lack a convincing IE etymology, such as *si*ⁿ*kabruš* 'carnelian', *θarmiš* 'timber', *yakā* (a kind of wood), *skauθiš* 'weak, lowly', or are obvious borrowings, such as *maškā-* 'inflated skin' from Aramaic. But the main outside influence is that of the Median dialect, seen in phonetic and lexical differences, perhaps also in variant grammatical forms. Aramaic also seems to have had a certain influence on the phrasing and the syntax. There is no evidence that OP itself, at the time of the inscriptions, possessed a literature of any kind apart from these inscriptions themselves.

§7. THE MEDIAN DIALECT was the language of the great Median Empire, which at the death of Cyaxares in 594 extended from the Indus to the Aegean Sea; the last Median ruler was Astyages, son of Cyaxares, who in 559 was conquered and deposed by his grandson Cyrus, son of Cambyses King of Persis and of Mandane daughter of Astyages. The new ruler naturally took over the Median chancellery and the Median royal titles, and their influence is still seen in the language of the OP inscriptions of Darius and his followers.

§8. MEDIAN PHONETIC DEVELOPMENTS which can be identified in the language of the OP inscriptions are the following; they are discussed in the phonology, with complete lists of examples:

pIE $\hat{k}$ became Med. *s*, Av. *s*, OP *θ*; §87.
pIE $\hat{g}$ and $\hat{g}h$ became Med. *z*, Av. *z*, OP *d*; §88.
pIE $\hat{k}y$ became Med. *sp*, Av. *sp*, OP *s*; §90.
pI $\hat{g}^hy$E became Med. *zb*, Av. *zb*, OP *z*; §91.

[1] MB Gr. §5–§18.

pAr. *km* became Med. *xm*, Av. *xm*, OP (*h*)*m*; §103.II.
pIE *sq*ᵘ before front vowel became pAr. *šc*, then Med. *šc*, Av. *šč*, OP *s*; §105.
pIE -*s qᵘ*- and -*d qᵘ*- in sandhi, before front vowel, became Med. *šc*, Av. *šč*, OP *s* (shown by Pahlavi only) and remade *c*; §105.
pIE *tr* and *tl* became pAr. *tr*, then Med. *θr*, Av. *θr*, OP *ç*; §78.
pAr. *tr* after Iranian spirants or sibilant became Med. *tr*, Av. *tr*, OP *ç* or perhaps *š*; §79.
pIE *ty* became Med. *θy*, Av. *θy*, OP *šy*; §80.
pIE *sy* became Med. *f*, Av. *hv* and *xᵛ*, OP (*h*)*y*; §118. IV.

§9. OP WORDS SHOWING MEDIAN PECULIARITIES are the following, which are here listed in groups, according to their meanings and uses; fuller discussion will be found in the phonology and in the Lexicon, s.vv.:

I. Place-Names:

Asagarta 'Sagartia', a district of Media, with *s* in *asa-* from $\hat{k}$ if it means 'stone'.

Sikayauvatiš, a Median fortress, with *s-* from $\hat{k}$ if, as is probable, the first part is identical with OP *θikā* 'broken stone'.

Two East Iranian names, outside the Median territory, show non-OP phonetics identical with those of Median:

Bāxtriš 'Bactria', with *tr* retained after a spirant.
*Zra*ⁿ*ka* 'Drangiana', with *z* from $\hat{g}$ or $\hat{g}h$.

II. Personal names:

taxma- 'brave', with *x* retained before *m*, in the names of the Mede *Taxmaspāda* and of the Sagartian *Ciçataxma*.[1]

Xšaθrita, the name assumed by the Mede *Fravartiš*, with *θr* from *tr*.

Uvaxštra 'Cyaxares', a king of the Median line, with *tr* retained after a sibilant.

Vištāspa 'Hystaspes', father of Darius, with *sp* from $\hat{k}y$.[2]

Aspacanā, one of Darius's helpers, with *sp* from $\hat{k}y$.

---

[1] Note that *Ciça-* in this name has the OP form and not the Median *Ciθra-*. [2] *Vištāspa*, *Aspacanā*, and *Vidafarnā*, despite the Median phonetics, are specifically Persians; but personal names often belong to other dialects or languages than that of the locality to which the owner of the name belongs. Cf. also note 1.

Vi^n dafarnā, one of Darius's helpers, with *f* from *sṷ*.

III. Words in the official titles:
xšāyaθiya 'king', with *θi̯* from *ti̯*.
vazraka 'great', with *z* from *ĝ*.
vispa-zana- 'having all men', with *sp* from *k̑ṷ* and *z* from *ĝ*.
paru-zana- 'having many men', with *z* from *ĝ*.
uvaspa- 'having good horses', with *sp* from *k̑ṷ*.

IV. Technical words of the religion:
zūra 'evil', with *z* from *ĝh*.
Varka-zana- '(month) of the Wolf-Men', with *z* from *ĝ*; but the entire word is merely restored after the Elamite.

V. Names of cultural materials:
asan- 'stone', with *s* from *k̑*.
kāsaka 'semi-precious stone', with *s* from *k̑*.

VI. Miscellaneous:
masc. *kašciy*, nt. *cišciy, avašciy, aniyašciy*, with *šc* from *-s qᷓ-* and *-d qᷓ-* respectively, in sandhi; no specific reason can be assigned for the borrowing by OP of this type.
Pārsa 'Persia', with *s* from *k̑*, cf. *Parθava* with *θ*; the name seems to have been imposed by an outside source.
patiyazbayam 'I proclaimed', with Med. *-zb-*, but *hᵃzānam* (acc.) 'tongue' with OP *-z-*, both from IE *ĝhṷ*; see also §91.
vasiy 'at will, greatly', with *s* from *k̑*; but see §87 for another explanation of the form.
Mitra Mᵗθra, divine name borrowed from Indic; see §78.

§10. DIALECT MIXTURE IN THE OP FORMS may be regarded as uncertain, though in the verbs there are alternative forms used apparently without distinction of meaning: thus impf. 3d pl. *abara^n abaraha^n abara^ntā*. Only the peculiar plural *aniyāha bagāha* 'the other gods', with double endings (like Vedic Skt. *devā́sas* for *devā́s*) seems to come from the language of religion, for a normal OP *aniyaiy bagā* (pl. *bagā* happens not to occur).

§11. DIALECT MIXTURE IN THE OP VOCABULARY: it is difficult at times to decide what is genuinely OP and what is borrowed. Of the two words for 'good', *naiba-* is a religious term, and *vaʰu-* is found only in proper names. Of the two for 'earth', *zam-* (which would have Med. *z*) appears only in the form *zm-*, which is phonetically OP as well as Median, and occurs in one proper name and in an official term for execution with torture; *būmi-* occurs chiefly in phrases of official character, but is used also in DSf to denote the earth which was excavated for the palace of Darius. On some other points, the usages of Pahlavi seem to inform us: nom. *hauv* 'he', *iyam* 'this', prep. *hadā* 'with' belong to Pahlavi of the Northwest and not to that of the Southwest, and thus are shown to be borrowings from Median.[1]

§12. ARAMAIC INFLUENCE. Aramaic, a Semitic language, was the international language of southwestern Asia from the middle of the eighth century B.C.; speakers of Aramaic were in charge of all archives for some centuries thereafter. As OP had no developed literary style at the time of the inscriptions, it is to be expected that the style of the inscriptions should reflect the style of Aramaic; and it does. Notable are the short sentences, with repetition of all essential words (§290); certain of the official titles (§309); and the anacoluthic definition of place and personal names (§312).

---

[1] P. Tedesco, Le Monde oriental 15.248; Bv. Gr page 4 infra

CHAPTER II. THE SCRIPT OF OLD PERSIAN

§13. THE SCRIPT OF THE OLD PERSIAN INSCRIPTIONS is, as we have said, of the cuneiform type: that is, the characters are made of strokes which can be impressed on soft materials by a stylus having an angled end. The OP inscriptions, being on hard materials, must have been made with engraving tools with which the strokes impressed on soft materials were imitated. There was no tradition from antiquity as to the significance of the characters, nor was any OP inscription accompanied by a version in a previously known system of writing; modern scholars were therefore obliged to start from the very beginning in the task of decipherment.

§14. EARLY STEPS IN THE DECIPHERMENT. OP inscriptions and writing are mentioned in a number of ancient authors, from Herodotus onward, and are remarked upon and described by certain modern travelers early in the seventeenth century, who published parts of inscriptions from Persepolis in the accounts of their travels. The first inscription to be published in complete form was DPc, given by Chardin in 1711. Better copies of several were given in 1778 by Carsten Niebuhr, who recognized that the inscriptions were composed in three systems of writing, and that the writing ran from left to right: the direction of the writing was shown by two copies of XPe with somewhat differing line-divisions. O. G. Tychsen in 1798 discovered that the three systems of writing represented three different languages, and that a recurring diagonal wedge in the simplest of the three types was a word-divider; but he wrongly assigned the inscriptions to the Parthian period. Friedrich Munter in 1802 independently identified the word-divider, and thought that a frequently recurring series of characters must be the word for 'king'; he assigned the inscriptions to the Achaemenian period.[1]

§15. G. F. GROTEFEND of Frankfurt in 1802 applied himself to the problem of the decipherment, and by a comparison of DPa and XPe (in Niebuhr's copies) he made the first real progress. He assumed that the inscriptions were inscriptions of the Achaemenian kings, that they consisted essentially of the names and titles of the kings, and that those in the simplest type of writing were in Persian, closely resembling the language of the Avesta. He was helped by Silvestre de Sacy's recent decipherment of the royal titles in Pahlavi, '. . ., great king, king of kings, king of Iran and non-Iran, son of . . ., great king,' etc., which guided him as to what to expect. To facilitate the exposition, we set the two inscriptions in parallel columns:

DPa
Dārayavauš ·
xšāyaθiya : vazraka

XPe
Xšayārša :
xšāyaθiya : vazraka :

[1] A detailed account of these matters and of the further steps of the decipherment is given by Weissbach, Gdr IP 2 64–72; by E L. Johnson, Gr 1–16; by R W Rogers, History of Assyria and Babylonia, vol. 1, chapters 1–2.

DPa
xšāyaθiya :
xšāyaθiyānām :
xšāyaθiya : dahyūnām :
Vištāspahyā :
puça : Haxāmanišiya :
hya : imam : tacaram :
akunauš

XPe
xšāyaθiya :
xšāyaθıyānām ·
Dārayavahauš :
xšāyaθiyahyā :
puça : Haxāmanišiya :

Grotefend recognized correctly that the names of two different kings were followed by titles, 'great king, king of kings', and then a third similar title in the one which was lacking in the other; that then followed the name of the king's father, who was the same person in one inscription as the king in the other, and that in the other the father did not bear the title king. He decided upon Darius, whose father Hystaspes had not been king, rather than upon Cyrus, since Cyrus and his father Cambyses had names beginning with the same letter[1] whereas the corresponding two names in the inscriptions began with different characters; he thought the name of Artaxerxes to be too long. Thus he saw in the three names Hystaspes, Darius, Xerxes, in the transliteration of which he used the later Iranian pronunciations:

Grotefend	Correct
g o sch t a s p	vı i ša ta a sa pa
d a r h e u ` sch	da a ra ya va u ša
kh sch h a r sch a	xa ša ya a ra ša a

Thus he had identified, for all but the inherent *a*, the characters *a, u, x* (his *kh*), *t, d, p, r, s, š* (his *sch*), and elsewhere he identified *f*. But his reliance on the later pronunciations misled him sorely, and of the 22 different signs in DPa and XPe he got only 10 correctly, and even for two of these he admitted two values each (*a* and *e*, *p* and *b*). Apart from the three names, 'king' and 'great' were the only words which he identified correctly; later (1815) he identified the name 'Cyrus' in CMa. But the remainder of his read-

[1] As it happens, Cyrus and Cambyses do not begin with the same letter in OP, but with k^u and k^a respectively, but Grotefend could have dismissed the Cyrus line on the ground that Cyrus's father and Cyrus's son were both named Cambyses, but the first and the third of the dynasty in these inscriptions bore different names.

PLATE II

THE GOLD TABLET OF HAMADAN
The Limits of the Empire of Darius the Great
showing the three systems of writing of the three versions
Old Persian (top), Elamite (middle), Akkadian (bottom)
Reproduced by courtesy of the Oriental Institute of the University of Chicago

ings, even in these inscriptions, is sorry stuff, and he could never realize in later years that the foundations which he had laid had been built upon and improved.

§16. THE COMPLETION OF THE DECIPHERMENT. After a gap of twenty-one years other scholars took up the task, but progress was mainly in identifying individual characters and single words. The notable steps in the decipherment were the following: Lassen in 1836 supplied the vowel *a* after many consonants; that is, he realized that these consonants had an inherent *a*. Lassen in 1839 noted that some characters were used only before *ı* and others only before *u*; Rawlinson in 1846, Hıncks in 1846, and Oppert in 1847 independently realized that these consonants had inherent *i* and inherent *u*. Oppert at the same time discovered that diphthongs were indicated by *i* or *u* after a consonant with inherent *a*, and that *n* and *m* were omitted before consonants.

§17. SUMMARY OF THE DECIPHERMENT. The detail of the decipherment can best be portrayed in tabular form. For simplicity in composition, I use *c* and *j* rather than *č* and *ǰ*, and as a better representation of the sound I use *ç* rather than *θr*.

The scholars who participated in the decipherment are indicated by the following abbreviations; the dates of their publications are also given:

B	Beer 1838	L	Lassen 1836 '39 '45
Bf	Burnouf 1836	M	Munter 1802
Br	Brandenstein 1932	Op	Oppert 1847 '51 '74
E	Evetts 1890	Rk	Rask 1823
G	Grotefend 1802	Rl	Rawlinson 1846
H	Hincks 1846	Sc	Scheil 1929
Hl	Holtzmann 1845	SM	Saint-Martin '23 '32
Hz	Herzfeld 1931	Ty	Tychsen 1798
J	Jacquet 1838	W	Windischmann 1845

Number	Present Orthog.	Progress of Decipherment
1	a	a G 02
2	i	y SM 23, i SM 32
3	u	u G 02
4	k^a	k Bf-L 36
5	k^u	k G 15, k^u L 39, ku Rl-H 46
6	x^a	kh G 02
7	g^a	g L 36
8	g^u	gh Bf 36, g' L 36, gu Rl-H 46
9	c^a	k' J 38
10	j^a	z J 38, j Hl 45
11	j^i	g' L 36, ji Rl 46
12	t^a	t G 02
13	t^u	t' L 36, t^u L 39, tu W 45, Rl 46
14	$θ^a$	$ṣ$ L 36, th J 38, $θ$ L 39
15	$ç^a$	t' L 36, thr L 45, $tř$ Rl 46
16	d^a	d G 02
17	d^i	d' Hl 45, di Rl-H 46
18	d^u	d' L 36, du Rl-H 46
19	n^a	n Rk 23
20	n^u	nu Rl 46
21	p^a	p G 02
22	f^a	f G 02
23	b^a	b Bf-L 36
24	m^a	m Rk 23
25	m^i	$'m$ L 36, m^i L 39, mi Rl-H 46
26	m^u	mu Rl 46
27	y^a	y B-J 38
28	r^a	r G 02
29	r^u	sr G 15, r^u J 38, ru Rl 46
30	l^a	l Op 51
31	v^a	w L 36, va Rl-H 46
32	v^i	v SM 23, vi Rl-H 46
33	s^a	s G 02
34	$š^a$	sch G 02
35	z^a	z Bf-L 36
36	h^a	h B-J 38
		Ideograms and Ligature
37	XŠ	'König' M-G 02
38	DH	'Land' L 45
39	BU	'Erde' L 45
40	AM	'Ahuramazda' Op 74, E 90
41	BG	baga 'god' Sc 1929
42	AMha	Auramazdā Sc 1929, Auramazdāha Br 1932 (cf. Hz 1931)
		Word-divider
43	:	Ty 1798

§18. THE OLD-PERSIAN SYLLABARY. The inscriptions composed in the Old Persian language are inscribed on various hard materials in a syllabary, each character having the value of a vowel or of a consonant plus a vowel. To the 36 characters of this nature must be added 5 ideograms (§42), one ligature of ideogram and case ending (§42), the word-divider (§44), and numerical symbols (§43).

This syllabary quite obviously goes back to

Syllabary

𒀀	a		j^a		n^a		r^a
	i		j^i		n^u		r^u
	u		t^a		p^a		l^a
	k^a		t^u		f^a		v^a
	k^u		θ^a		b^a		v^i
	x^a		$ç^a$		m^a		s^a
	g^a		d^a		m^i		$š^a$
	g^u		d^i		m^u		z^a
	c^a		d^u		y^a		h^a

Ideograms

XŠ = xšāyaθiya   BU = būmiš

DH = dahyāuš   AM = Auramazdā

BG = baga   AMmaiy

Word Dividers

the cuneiform syllabary of Akkadian, but its simplicity as compared with its parent syllabary shows that it has been specially drawn up for its present purpose. There is no conclusive evidence how the Akkadian characters were utilized and how the new characters received OP values; though several scholars have advanced theories.[1]

It is uncertain also when this Old Persian system of writing was invented. The extant inscriptions are largely those of Darius I and of Xerxes, and it is tempting to ascribe the invention to the orders of Darius when he wished to record the events of his accession, on the Rock of Behistan; but there are three inscriptions of Cyrus, as well as one each purporting to be of Ariaramnes and of Arsames. These last two may have been set up as labels to small monuments or other objects of a later period;[2] the orthography points to approximately the time of Artaxerxes II.[3] Of the inscriptions of Cyrus, one is very fragmentary, and the other two are brief labels; yet as they were inscribed in the palace which belonged to Cyrus,[4] at Pasargadae (Murghab), they show that the OP cuneiform syllabary existed and was in use in Cyrus's time.[5]

§19. THE SYLLABIC CHARACTERS OF OP number 36, including the following:

3 vowel-signs: $a\ i\ u$

22 consonant-signs with inherent a:

$k^a\ x^a\ g^a\ c^a\ j^a\ t^a\ \theta^a\ ç^a\ d^a\ n^a\ p^a\ f^a\ b^a\ m^a\ y^a\ r^a\ l^a\ v^a$
$s^a\ š^a\ z^a\ h^a$

4 consonant-signs with inherent i:

$j^i\ d^i\ m^i\ v^i$

7 consonant-signs with inherent u:

$k^u\ g^u\ t^u\ d^u\ n^u\ m^u\ r^u$

A close transcription of the cuneiform, when desirable, will be given by keeping the inherent vowels as raised letters; but for most purposes a normalized transcription (§45) will be satisfactory.

§20. THE ALPHABETIC ORDER OF NORMALIZED OLD PERSIAN, as employed in this volume, is the following: $ă\ ĭ\ ŭ\ k\ x\ g\ c\ j\ t\ \theta\ ç\ d\ n\ p\ f\ b\ m\ y\ r\ l\ v\ s\ š\ z\ h$. The transcription here used differs in

---

[1] For a critique of these theories, see Wb KIA lv–lx
[2] Ariaramnes was great-uncle of Cyrus and great-grandfather of Darius I; Arsames was son of Ariaramnes and grandfather of Darius Note that the two inscriptions are both on gold tablets and found at or near Ecbatana (Hamadan) in Media; though the two kings are spoken of in them only as 'king in *Pārsa* = Persis', which was quite distinct from Media. They may have been set up in the time of Artaxerxes II as part of an anti-Cyrus propaganda, since Cyrus the Great had dethroned Arsames, and Cyrus the Younger came very near defeating and killing Artaxerxes II at Cunaxa (cf. JAOS 66.206–12) The gold tablet A²Hc may have been a third in the same series; all three are in Old Persian only. [3] Cf. especially Schaeder, SbPAW 1931 636–42.
[4] They are hardly to be ascribed to Cyrus the Younger, despite Wb. ZDMG 48 653–65 (cf. also KIA lxvii–lxix) on CMa, which alone was known to him; for the opposing view, cf. Hz. Klio 8.1 ff [5] Though perhaps not much used by him The other three known inscriptions of Cyrus the Great are in Akkadian; but Strabo 15.3.7–8 (page 730), on the authority of Onesicritus, states that the tomb of Cyrus at Pasargadae bore at least two inscriptions, one being bilingual, Greek and Persian. We need attach no importance to the identification of the languages by Onesicritus, but the account indicates that Cyrus had inscriptions engraved in more than one language; in which case it is unlikely that his own vernacular was omitted Cf. JAOS 66.206–12; but also Hinz, ZDMG 96.343–9

some points from that used by certain other scholars in recent years, as follows:

ā   also â (KT, Scheil).
ī ū   i u without mark of length (KT, Wb., Scheil, Mt., Bv.).
x   kh (KT), ḵ (Wb.), ḥ (Kg., Brd.), ḫ (Hinz).
c or č   k̂ (Wb.).
j or ǰ   ǧ (Wb., Scheil), ž (Hz., Hinz).
θ or þ   th (KT), ṭ (Wb., Hinz), ṯ (Scheil).
ç   tr (KT), θʳ (Tm., Hz.), ř (Wb.), s͟s (Bv.),[1] ś (Kg., Brd., Hinz).
f   p̱ (Wb.).
y v   j w (Kg., Brd.).

Some scholars also regularly indicate omitted h and n by raised letters or by letters in parenthesis, or the omitted n by a tilde over the preceding vowel. A few other variations are found, but it is hardly worth while to list them.

§21. The Representation of a in OP Writing. The character a at the beginning of a word represents either ă or ā, and decision must be made on etymological and morphological grounds. Elsewhere in the word the character a is used only after an a-inherent character, the value being ā; thus nᵃamᵃa = nāmā. When the a-constant is immediately followed by another consonant, or is final, the a of the consonant either represents ă or has no value at all; thus dᵃrᵃšᵃmᵃ = daršam. For a or ā in diphthongs, see §24: for final ă written ā, see §36.

§22. The Representation of i and u in OP Writing. OP i is normally represented by the character i initially, and medially by the character i preceded by an i-consonant, or, if there is no special i-consonant character for the consonant sound, by the a-consonant; thus imᵃ = ima, jⁱivᵃ = jīva, pⁱitᵃ = pitā.

OP u is similarly represented; utᵃa = utā, kᵘurᵘuš ᵃ = Kūruš, pᵃuçᵃ = puça.

Thus the difference of short and long in i and u is not represented in the script, except in the way indicated later (§23), of rare occurrence; and where there is no special i-consonant character or u-consonant character, there was no means of indicating the difference between ĭ and the diphthong ai, and between ŭ and au (§24).

---

[1] Bv. Gr. §105 uses this transcription to indicate a strong sibilant; not a long sibilant, since Iranian shortened all long consonants (§130).

The i is occasionally omitted after an i-inherent consonant, and the u after a u-inherent consonant; there are the following examples, in the normalization of which we indicate the omission by printing the inherent vowel as a raised character:

vⁱθbiš DB 1.65 and other forms of the same word; so always in DB, but vθ- in other inscriptions.

Vⁱštās-pa -pam -pahyā, always in DB, in some DS inscriptions, and in those of Artaxerxes II and III; but Vištāspa etc. elsewhere.

Armⁱniyaiy four times in DB; also -min-.

jⁱva-diy A²Sd 3; but jīva, jīvahyā, ajīvatam, jīvā twice each, in inscriptions of Darius and Xerxes.

Mⁱθra, Mⁱtra, and also Mit[ra], in late inscriptions.

[Uvāra]zmⁱya A?P 8; Vahyavⁱšdāpaya Sd.

Nabukᵘdracara DB 1.78f, 84, 93; but more often Nabukudracara.

Kudᵘruš DB 2.65.

Sugᵘda DPe 16; but Suguda DB 1.16, DNa 23, Sugudā DSf 38, and Sugda XPh 21, Sugdam DPh 6, DH 5. With sᵃugᵃdᵃ alongside sᵃugᵘudᵃ, cf. fᵃrᵃhᵃrᵃvᵃmᵃ = fra-haravam DB 1.17, alongside the usual hᵃrᵘuvᵃ = haruva (DB 1.40, etc.).

The i is omitted after an a-inherent consonant, three times in inscriptions of Darius, and four times in those of Artaxerxes II; we may indicate this by a raised a:

Bābᵃrauv DBi 11; elsewhere Bābirauv.

baratᵃy DB 5.22f; but baratiy DNa 42.

Haxāmanišᵃya DSa 2f, A²Sd 2 (copies a and c); Haxamānᵃšiya A²Sa 3; for the common Haxāmanišiya.

abᵃyapara A²Sa 4, for *abiyaparam.

apanᵃyākama A²Sa 3, and presumably [nᵃyā]kama A²Sa 4.

§23. Written Indication of Length of i and u was at most sporadic, and is not absolutely certain even where it seems to be meant. Since final i and u were written -iyᵃ and -uvᵃ, whether long or short (§§37–8), it is only in other positions that indication of length can be sought.

I. Apparently -iya- in the interior of words contracted to -ī-; there are the following examples:

niyašādayam DNa 36, and nīšādayam XPh 34f.

niyaštāya DSn 1, XPh 50, XV 21, and nīštāya XPh 52f.

abiyajāvayam XPg 9, and *abījāvayam* XPf 40.

nīyasaya DNb 5, 46, 49, probably for *nıyayasaya.

[*a*]*tīya*[*si*]*ya* DB 4.91, perhaps for *atıyayasıya.

marīka- DNb 50, 55, 59°, cf. Phl. *mērak*, Skt. *maryaka-*; see Lex. s.v.

Perhaps in the verbs the longer writings should be normalized *nīyjāvayam*, etc., with -*iyᵃ*- = -*īy*- graphic for -*ī*-; but this cannot be definitely proved, for the uncontracted forms of these verbs may have survived alongside the contracted forms, by the analogy of the uncompounded forms *ajāvayam, etc., where contraction was impossible.

II. For *uvᵃ* = *ū*, there is better evidence; cf. the following:

ūvnarā DNb 45, 51, *ūvnaraibiš* DNb 48, cf. Skt. *sūndra-*.

uvᵃjᵃ uvᵃjⁱiyᵃ = *Ūvja Ūvjiya* many times, alongside *ujᵃ ujᵃiyᵃ* = *Ūja Ūjaiy*; cf. later *Huž*.

dahyūvnām DPh 2, DH 1f, alongside many occurrences of *dahyūnām*.

parūvnām DNa 6, 7, DSe 6, 7, A³Pa 6, 7, alongside many occurrences of *parūnām*.

The last word gives the clue to the origin of this usage: asn. *paruv* for *parŭ was the source of the orthography in the wrongly divided *paruv : zanānām* (§44; five occurrences), as well as in the undivided *paruvzanānām* (XPb 15f, XPd 11), alongside the correct *paruzanānām* (DE 15f, XE 15f), with *ŭ*; thence this script passed into the gen. pl. *parūnām*, where the *ū* was long, giving *parūvnām*; whence also the gen. pl. *dahyūnām* became *dahyūvnām*. But initially, in *Ūvja* and *ūvnarā*, the usage must rest on an over-pronunciation in the process of analysis for reduction to writing (§46).

§24. THE DIPHTHONGS were indicated initially by the *a*-character + the *i*- or *u*-character; medially and final, by the *a*-consonant + the *i*- or *u*-character (for final diphthongs, see §§37–8): *aivᵃmᵃ* = *aivam*, *aurᵃa* = *Aurā*; *dᵃivᵃa* = *daivā*, *tᵃumᵃa* = *taumā*; *nᵃiyᵃ* = *naiy*, *hᵃuvᵃ* = *hauv*.

Long diphthongs could not be indicated initially, as distinct from short diphthongs, but were indicated in non-initial position by the writing of the *a*-character to show length: *aišᵃ* = *āiš*, but *fᵃrᵃaišᵃyᵃmᵃ* = *frāišayam*, *dᵃhᵃyᵃaušᵃ* = *dahyāuš*.

Ambiguities of interpretation are present where there are no special characters for the *i*-inherent or *u*-inherent consonants:

cᵃišᵃpᵃišᵃ = nom. *Cıšpıš* and gen. *Cišpaıš*, whence for distinction also a writing *cᵃišᵃpᵃaıšᵃ* = *Cišpāiš* is found for the gen.

-*tᵃiyᵃ* = act. -*tıy*, mid. -*taıy*, personal ending of the third singular.

pᵃuçᵃ = *puça*, but would represent also *pauça* if such a word had to be written.

§25. POSTCONSONANTAL *y* was written as -*iy*-; thus *anᵃiyᵃ* = *anıya*, Skt. *anyás*; *dᵘušᵃiyᵃarᵃmᵃ* = *dušıyāram* 'famine', from *duš- + *i̯ār*- 'year'. But *hy* was not written *hıy*, since *i* was not normally represented after *h* (§27, where a few variant writings are listed).

An important regular exception is the relative pronoun and article *tya-*, always written *tᵃyᵃ*- = *tya-*, and never *tᵃiyᵃ*- = *tıya-*. The reason for this is that the nom. sg. masc. and fem. were *hya* and *hyā* (Skt. *syás syā́*), in which an *ı* could not be written (§27); and the other forms, using the stem *tya-*, followed their model in this point: thus nom. masc. *hya*, fem. *hyā*, nt. *tya*; acc. *tyam tyām tya*; etc.

§26. POSTCONSONANTAL *v* was written -*uv*-: thus *hᵃrᵘuvᵃ* = *haruva*, Skt. *sárvas*; *θᵃuvᵃamᵃ* = *θuvām*, Skt. *tvām*. In *fᵃrᵃhᵃrᵃvᵃmᵃ* = *fraharavam* (for *fra-haruvam*) there is an exceptional orthography. But as *h* was not written before *u*, the *huv* from *hv* was written merely *uv* (§28).

§27. THE COMBINATION *hᵃi* was peculiar, since it could normally be used only for the value *haı*, not for *hi*. In representing *hi*, whether the *ı* was an etymological vowel or only a part of *hıy* for *hy* (§25) or for final -*hi* (§37), the *ı* was normally omitted in writing: *anᵃhᵃtᵃ* = *Anahᵃta*, Av. *Anāhitā-*; *dᵃhᵃyᵃaušᵃ* = *dahyāuš*, Skt. *dásyu-*; *hᵃyᵃ* = *hya*, Skt. *syás*; *pᵃrᵃibᵃrᵃahᵃyᵃ* = *pari-barāhy*, Skt. *bhárāsi*; *hᵃzᵃanᵒmᵃ* = *hᵃzānam* DB 2.74, Av. *hizvā-*. Before an enclitic, the -*y* of -*hy* for -*hi* disappeared: *paribarāh-diš* DB 4.74, cf. *paribarāhy* 78; *vikanāh-diš* DB 4.77, cf. *vikanāhy* 73. Rarely, the *hᵃ* is omitted and the *i* is kept: *aišᵃtᵃtᵃa* = *aⁱštatā* DB 1.85, cf. Av. pres. *hištaᵢte*. Both types of writing are exemplified in *maniyāhay* DPe 20, *maniyāıy* XPh 47, for *maniyāhaıy*.

By exception, *hᵃi* is written in the value *hi* normally in the place name *hᵃidᵘušᵃ* = *Hınduš* and its forms, and in its ethnic $h^aid^uy^a$ = Hi^n-$duya$; and once in $an^ah^ait^a$ = $Anahita$ A²Sd 3f. Occasionally there are writings with h^aiy^a for -hiy- in words which are normally written h^ay^a: such are:

$aθ^ah^aiy^a$ = $aθahiya$ XPh 18; elsewhere $aθahya$.

$d^ar^ay^ah^aiy^a$ = $drayahiyā$ XPh 23; elsewhere $drayahyā$.

$ah^aiy^ay^a$ = $ahiyāyā$ XPb 17, XPd 12, XE 17, and in some copies of XPj; elsewhere $ahyāyā$.

$XŠy^ah^aiy^a$ = $XŠyahiyā$ apparently in some copies of XPj; elsewhere $XŠyahyā$.

§28. THE COMBINATION h^au also was peculiar, since it could be used only in the value hau, as in h^auv^a = $hauv$. In indicating hu, the h^a was always omitted, and only the u written: $ub^ar^at^am^a$ = $^hubartam$; $p^at^aip^ay^auv^a$ = $patiyapaya^huvā$, cf. Skt. -$yasva$; $an^aiy^aauv^a$ = $aniyā^huvā$, cf. Skt. $anyāsu + ā$; $d^ar^ay^av^ah^uš^a$ = nom. $Dārayava^huš$, $d^ar^ay^av^ah^auš^a$ = gen. $Dārayavahauš$.

§29. THE PERSISTENCE OF VOWEL $r̥$ into OP[1] makes difficulties in the normalization. The normalized form of some words containing r^a is certain: thus $g^ar^am^a$- in the month-name $Garmapada$- might theoretically be $grama$- or $garama$- or $gr̥ma$-, but is actually $garma$-, a form assured by etymological cognates. The name $ar^aš^am^a$ is $r̥šāma$, though the characters might equally well stand for $Aršāma$; and those who would normalize with r as a vowel, write '$ršāma$, using the sign for the glottal stop to represent the character which elsewhere has the vowel value a. But in $θ^ar^am^iš^a$ we have no clue to the vowel of the first syllable; it may be $θarmiš$ or $θaramiš$ or $θr̥miš$ (though hardly $θramiš$, since $θr$ became $ç$). To avoid the necessity of making decisions in cases where there is no evidence, the normalization here employed is ar alike for phonetic ar and for phonetic $r̥$, and for those instances where we do not have proof of the value, which may also be ara or ra.

The problem confronts us wherever we find three successive consonants of which the first has inherent a and the second is r^a; wherever we find initial $a + r^a +$ a consonant; and wherever we find at the end of a word the r^a preceded by an a-inherent consonant. The evidence which may determine the phonetic value consists of the following kinds:

I. The evidence of etymological comparison: since OP $r̥$ comes only from older $r̥$, it is testified to by correspondence with $r̥$ or its products in other languages; notably (1) with Skt. $r̥$, (2) with Av. $ərə$ (Av. $arə$ normally represents earlier ar from pIE er or ar, el ol al).

II. The evidence of later Iranian: the development of the sounds into Pahlavi and into Modern Persian and its dialects may show the distinction between older ar and $r̥$. Thus $r̥$ appears as NPers. ir after dental and guttural sounds, and as ur after labials, but ar regularly keeps the a-quality, and does not become ir or ur.

III. The evidence of borrowed words: OP words appear in Elamite with ir or ur for $r̥$, and with ar for ar; but there are occasional inconsistencies. There are also some borrowed words in Armenian, and a few in Arabic (from Pahlavi), which have differences reflecting the distinction in OP between $r̥$ and ar.

IV. But sometimes the various items of evidence contradict one another, and then a decision must be made as to which line of evidence is stronger.[2]

§30. OLD PERSIAN $r̥$ seems to be established in the following words, in many instances, fuller listing of evidential forms will be found in the Lexicon:

$artācā$ = $r̥tācā$, Elam. ir-ta-ha-ci; so also in $artāvā$, $Artaxšaçā$, $Artavardiya$, by the Elamite transcriptions.

$Aršāma$ = $r̥šāma$, Elam. ir-$ša$-ma and ir-$ša$-um-ma; so also in $Aršaka$, $Aršādā$.

$arštām$ = $r̥štām$ by etymology, see Lex. s.v.

$arštiš$ = $r̥štiš$, Skt. $r̥ṣṭí$-, Av. $aršti$- ($r̥$ > Av. ar before $št$), NP $hišt$ (h- is a later accretion); so also $arštibara$.

$avahar[da]$ = $avahr̥da$, Skt. ava-$sr̥jat$.

$uvāmaršiyuš$ = -$mr̥šiyuš$, Av. $mərəθyu$-, Skt. $mr̥tyú$-.

---

[1] On this subject, MB Gr. §93, on the development of $r̥$ into Avestan, see Reichelt, Aw. Elmb §109.2.

[2] Greek ερ is not conclusive evidence for $r̥$, despite κέρσα = $karša$- and Σμέρδις = $Bardiya$, both with $r̥$ (§30); cf Ἰνταφέρνης = $Vi^ndafarnā$, with -ar-, and Ἀρσάμης = $Aršāma$ and Ἀρταξέρξης = $Artaxšaçā$, both with $r̥$ by the Elam testimony, despite Gr. αρ-. Several Greek transliterations of place-names have αρ for Persian ar Παρθία = $Parθava$, Σαγαρτία = $Asagarta$, etc.

karta- = *kr̥ta-*, Skt. *kr̥tá-*, Av. *kərəta-*; NPers. *kard* has -*ar*- by analogy to other forms of the verb *kar-*.

karnuvakā = *kr̥nuvakā*, cf. Av. present stem *kərənv-*.

karša- = *kr̥ša-*, Elam. *kur-ša-um*.

agarbāyam, āgarbīta = -*gr̥b-*, Skt. *agr̥bhāyat*, Av. *gəurvayat̰*.

Θāṷgarcaiš = -*gr̥c-*, Elam. *sa-a-kur-ri-ṣi-iš*.

Dādaršiš = -*dr̥š-*, Skt. *dādhr̥ṣi-*, Elam. *da-tur-ši-iš* (once *da-tar-ši-iš*).

adaršnauš = -*dr̥š-*, Skt. *ádhr̥ṣṇot*.

parsāmiy = *pr̥sāmiy*, Skt. *pr̥cchámi*, Av. 3d sg. imf. *pərəsat̰*; and other forms of the same verb.

Bardiya = *Br̥d-*, Elam. *bır-ti-i̯a*.

Parga = *Pr̥ga*, NPers. *Purg*, Arab. *Furǰ*; despite Elam. *par-rak-qa*.

marta- and -*barta-*, ptcc. to roots *mar-* and *bar-*, = *mr̥ta-* and -*br̥ta-*, Skt. *mr̥tá-* and *bhr̥tá-*, Av. *mərəta-* and *bərəta-*.

vi-mardatiy, Skt. *mr̥dáti*.

varnavatām and other forms, = *vr̥n-*, Skt. *vr̥ṇo-*, Av. *vərənav-*.

Varkāna = *Vr̥kāna*, Elam. *Mi-ir-qa-nu-i̯a-ip* 'Hyrcanians', Phl. MPers. *Gurgān*, Gk. Ὑρκᾱνίᾱ.

vardanam = *vr̥j-*, GAv. *vərəzəna*, LAv. *varəzāna-*, Skt. *vr̥jána-*; see Lex. s.v.

ardata- 'silver', Av. *ərəzata-*; Yezdi *ālī* 'silver', from earlier *ard-*, is not necessarily evidence for OP, since Yezdi is a Kurdish dialect; Skt. *rajatá-* also has a different initial.

partara- 'battle', Av. *pəšana-*, Skt. *pr̥tana-*.

§31. OLD PERSIAN *ar* seems to be established in the following:

By the Elam. writings: *Arxa* (or *Araxa*), *Arbairā-*, *Armina, Asagarta, Parθava, Fravartiš* (also Phl. *fravartīkān*), *Marguš, Marduniya*, -*vard-* in *Artavardiya, Vıdafarnā* (also Av. *xᵛarənō*), *Vidarna, Sparda, haumavargā*: many of these confirmed also by Greek forms, etc.

By the Avestan and Skt. cognates: *atar*, Skt. *antar*; *garma-* in *Garmapadahya*, Skt. *gharmá-*; *θard-*, Av. *sarəd-*; *darga-*, Av. *darəga-*, Skt. *dīrghá-*; *baršnā*, Av. instr. *barəšna*; *martiya*, Skt. *mártya-*.

ardastāna- 'window-frame', Elam. *har-da-iš-da-na*.

tarsatıy with Iran. *tars-* because of NPers. *tarsað*, despite Av. *tərəsaiti*, from *tr̥s-*, both with IE suffix -*sk̂e-*; but Skt. *trásati* from *treseti*.

cartanaiy: the *c* shows that a front vowel formerly stood immediately after it; therefore *car-* from *cer-* from *ker-*.

Karkā, Gk. Κᾶρες, Κᾶρικοί; Elam. *kur-qa-ap* seems to have no evidential value.

[*va*]*rtaiyaiy*, if identical with Skt. *vartaye*; see Lex. s.v. *vart-* for reff.

§32. OLD PERSIAN *ara* seems to be established in the following:

By cognates in Skt. and Avestan: *apataram, aparam, para, hamarana-, partaram*, and the verbal nouns -*kara-* and -*bara-* as second elements of compounds.

By Elamite and other transcriptions: *Arakadriš* (or *Ark-* ?), *Arabāya*, the final of *Nabukudracara*.

arasam impf. of pres. stem *rasa-* (-*sa-* from *-sk̂e-*), NPers. *rasam*; despite Skt. *r̥ccháti* from *r̥-sk̂eti*.

arašaniš, Skt. *aratnı̄-*; see also Lexicon.

daraniya-, Av. *zaranya-*, Skt. *híraṇya-*.

§33. OLD PERSIAN *ra* AFTER CONSONANTS seems to be established in the following:

After *f θ x*, since *p t k* in Iranian became the corresponding voiceless spirants before another consonant (θr became OP *ç* but remained in Median, §78): *fra-* as prefix, Skt. *pra*, and all words beginning with *fra-*; *Miθra; xraθum*.

By transliterations: *Patigrabanā*; -*dra-* in *Nabukudracara*; *Zraka*, Gk. Δραγγιᾱνή.

fraštam in *u-fraštam u-frastam*, ptc. to root seen in Lt. *precor*, keeping strong-grade vowel.

brazmaniya, Elam. *pir-ra-iš-man-ni-i̯a*.

vazraka, a disputed word; see reff. in Lexicon.

§34. OLD PERSIAN GRAPHIC *ar* OF UNCERTAIN VALUE. OP graphic *ar* cannot be evaluated with certainty in the following:

Ablaut grades uncertain: *Ardumaniš*, for which the Elam. transcription is lacking; *duvarθim*; [*da*]*rtanam*, in which the restoration and formation are both uncertain.

Adequate cognates lacking: *arjanam, θarmiš*.

§35. OLD PERSIAN *ar* BEFORE *y* AND *v*. In this position OP *r̥* cannot be demonstrated with certainty. In all instances, graphic *ar* is followed by *iy* or *uv*, precisely as though the *r* were a consonant. In some words there is testimony to the value *ar*.

I. The sequence *-ariy-* is found in *Ariya* (and compounds), where Elam. has *har-ri-ia*, proving phonetic *ar* and not *r̥*: and in the middle *amariyatā* to root *mar-* 'die', the passive *abariya* to root *bar-* 'bear', and the passives *akariya akariyatā kariyaiš* to root *kar-* 'do, make'. The corresponding Skt. forms, in the 3d sg. impf., are *amriyate, abhriyate; akriyate*; but the OP forms from root *kar-* cannot have this vocalism, since the product would be **axriya-*. In this verb then there was in these forms a vowel between the *k* and the *r*: either a full vowel or the reduced vowel (shwa secundum or *ъ*), which assumed the full value of a short vowel in Indo-Iranian. It is likely that the other two verbs had the same formation. Thus there is no sure support for the sequence *r̥i* in OP.

II. For OP *-aruv-* we find the following examples:

haruva-, once written *fra-haravam*; Skt. *sárva-* shows that this has a full vowel, as does also Gk. ὅλος.

paruvam (and derivatives), corresponding to Skt. *pūrva-*, which had *r̥*; this became *ar* in Avestan, so that here there is Iran. *arv*.

aruvāyā and *aruvastam* probably have *arv-*, since the Elam. transcribes *aruvastam* with *har-va-as-tam*.

Gaubaruva = *barv-*, on the evidence of Elam. *kam-bar-ma*, or *-baruv-* on the added evidence of Akk. *gu-ba-ru-'*, Gk. Γωβρύης.

§36. OLD PERSIAN FINAL *ă*.

I. OP final *ă* was written with the sign of length, that is, with addition of the separate character for *a*: *ut^aa* = *utā*, Skt. *utá*; *-c^aa* = *-cā*, Skt. *ca*; *m^ar^at^aiy^ah^ay^aa* = *martiyahyā*, Skt. *-asya*.

II. But graphic final *ā* represents regularly also any absolutely final *ā* or any *ā* followed by an unwritten minimal final consonant (§40): *pⁱt^aa* = *pitā*, Skt. *pitá*; *napā* = *napā^t*, Skt. *nápāt*; abl. *Pārsā* = *Pārsā^d*, Skt. abl. *-ād*; npf. *tyā* = *tyā^h*, Skt. *tā́s*.

III. Any graphic final *ă* represents the *ă* with an unwritten minimal final consonant: *ab^ar^a* = *abara* for *abara^t*, Skt. *ábharat*, or *abaraⁿ*, Skt. *ábharan*; *h^ay^a* = *hya* for *hya^h*, Skt. *syás*; *t^ay^a* = *tya* for *tya^d*, Skt. *tyád*; *p^aic^a* = *piça* for *piça^h*, Gk. πατρός.

IV. Occasionally a graphic final *ă* represents final *ă* without a following consonant, especially if there is close syntactic connection with the next word; this is almost confined to the genitive ending *-ahyā* = Skt. *-asya*:

a. Regularly in the *-ahyā* genitive of the month name, before *māhyā*: *Viyaxnahyă māhyā* DB 1.37; other examples 1.42, 96; 2.26, 36, 41, 56, 61, 69, 98, 3.7f, 18, 39, 46, 63, 68; and restored in 1.89, 3.88.

b. Sometimes in other genitives standing before the nouns on which they depend: *Uvaxštrahyă taumāyā* DB 4.19, 4.22, e.7, g.9f (but *-hyā* DB 2.15f, 2.81), *Nabunaitahyă puça* DB 3.81, 4.14, 4.30, d.5f, i.7f (but *-hyā* DB 1.79); *Halditahyă puça* DB 3.79; or with which they agree: *Aurahyă Mazdāha* XPc 10 (cf. §44); *haruvahyāyă būmiyā* DSb 8f (but probably *-yāyā* DSf 16, 18).

c. Four times before an initial vowel, all in one short passage (DB 3.38–51): *Vahyazdātahyă aja* DB 3.38f, 3.46; *āhată agarbāya* DB 3.49, *āhată Uvādaicaya* DB 3.51 (*āhatā* often); in none of which the syntactic connection is close.

§37. OLD PERSIAN FINAL *i* was always written with added *y^a* (§46): *amⁱiy^a* = *amiy*, Skt. *ásmi*; *as^at^aiy^a* = *astiy*, Skt. *ásti*; this includes the diphthong *-ai*: *v^ain^at^aiy^a* = *vainataiy*.

But final *-hi*, which would be expected to give *-h^aiy^a* = *-hiy*, must be written *-h^ay^a* = *-hy*, since *h^ai* is almost never written for *hi* (§27): *am^ah^ay^a* = *amahy*, for **as-masi*; *v^ain^aah^ay^a* = *vaināhy*.

§38. OLD PERSIAN FINAL *u* was always written with added *v^a* (§46): *p^ar^uuv^a* = *paruv*, Skt. *purú*; *an^uuv^a* = *anuv*, Skt. *ánu*; *b^ar^at^uuv^a* = *baratuv*, Skt. *bháratu*; *h^auv^a* = *hauv*.

§39. OLD PERSIAN NASALS BEFORE CONSONANTS were omitted in the writing, except before *y* and *v*; such omitted sounds may be represented by raised letters in the normalized transcription, when desirable: *h^at^aiy^a* = *haⁿtiy*, Skt. *sánti*; *k^ab^aujⁱiy^a* = *Ka^mbūjiya* 'Cambyses', see Elam., Akk., Gk. transcriptions in Lexicon, *b^ad^ak^a* = *baⁿdaka*, Phl. *bandak*; *k^ap^ad^a* = *Ka^mpaⁿda*, Elam. *qa-um-pan-taš*.

Before enclitics, a final nasal which would otherwise be written, is retained: $g^a\iota\theta^a am^a c^a a$ = $gai\theta\bar{a}m$-$c\bar{a}$; $x\check{s}a\varsigma am$-$\check{s}im$, $paruvam$-ciy, $adam$-$\check{s}im$.

For -ny- and -nv-, -niy- and -nuv- are written (§§25–6): $an^a iy^a$ = $aniya$, Skt. $any\acute{a}s$; $t^u un^u\text{-}uv^a t^a m^a$ = $tunuva^n tam$, for *$tunvantam$.

§40. OLD PERSIAN REDUCED FINAL CONSONANTS were omitted in writing: these were s (after $\breve{a}$), t, d, n, nt; s had become h and nt had been reduced to n in pAryan. That they were still pronounced, though with a minimal value, at least after short $\breve{a}$, is shown by the fact that they prevented the representation of a preceding $\breve{a}$ by a long vowel (§36.III): thus voc. $martiya$ for -$y\breve{a}$, Skt. -ya; but nom. $martiya$ for -ya^h, Skt. -yah. The unwritten consonants may be represented by raised letters in normalized transcription, when desirable: thus hya^h, tya^d, $abara^t$, $abara^n$ (for -nt), $n\bar{a}ma^n$; nom. pl. $martiy\bar{a}^h$, abl. sg. $P\bar{a}rs\bar{a}^d$. There is one example of such a reduced consonant after i:[1] enclitic -ciy, = Av. -$c\bar{\iota}t$, Skt. cid, Lt. $quid$. There is no example of the reduced final consonants after u.[2]

§41. REPETITION OF THE SAME CONSONANT-SIGN is permitted only when the inherent vowel of the prior character is a pronounced vowel: $ad^a d^a a$ = $adad\bar{a}$, $\iota m^a m^a$ = ιmam. Any long consonants which had developed by assimilation had been shortened in Iranian; even the doubles that came from enclisis were graphically reduced to singles: $\bar{a}p\iota\check{s}\iota m$ DB 1.95f = $\bar{a}pi\check{s}$-$\check{s}im$, $taumani\check{s}aiy$ DNb 25f = $taumani\check{s}$-$\check{s}aiy$, [$n^a y\bar{a}$]$kama$ A²Sa 4 = $niy\bar{a}kam$-$maiy$ (§52.I). An error in cutting the characters, or in the drafting of the model copy, has given a repeated m^a in $c^a iy^a ak^a r^a m^a\text{-}m^a c^a\iota y^a$, twice in DNb 51–2, for -$m^a c^a m^a\iota y^a$, = $ciy\bar{a}karamcamaiy$.

§42. THE IDEOGRAMS are five in number, standing respectively for $x\check{s}\bar{a}ya\theta iya$ 'king', $dahy\bar{a}u\check{s}$ 'province', $b\bar{u}mi\check{s}$ 'earth', $Auramazd\bar{a}$ 'Ahuramazda', and $baga$ 'god'; they are transcribed by $X\check{S}$, DH, BU, AM, BG. In DSk 4 there is what seems to be a ligature for AM-ha.

The ideograms, without addition of syllabic characters, stand for the nominative singular; other forms are indicated by writing after the ideogram the last character or characters of the full word. Thus acc. $x\check{s}\bar{a}ya\theta iyam$ is written $X\check{S}$-m^a or $X\check{S}$-$y^a m^a$ = $X\check{S}m$ or $X\check{S}yam$; gen. $x\check{s}\bar{a}ya\theta iyahy\bar{a}$ is written $X\check{S}$-$y^a a$ $X\check{S}$-$h^a y^a a$ $X\check{S}$-$y^a h^a y^a a$ = $X\check{S}y\bar{a}$ $X\check{S}hy\bar{a}$ $X\check{S}ahy\bar{a}$; but $X\check{S}$-$ah^a y^a a$ A²Sd 2 is a misspelling, since this should mean $X\check{S}ahy\bar{a}$ rather than the intended $X\check{S}\bar{a}hy\bar{a}$.

The use of ideograms had its limitations in time and place, to judge by the extant inscriptions. Darius I used no ideograms at Behistan, Naqš-i-Rustam, Elvend, and on the weights; Xerxes used none at Elvend and Van. Darius I used only $X\check{S}$ at Suez, and varied between $X\check{S}$ and none at Persepolis; Xerxes also varies between $X\check{S}$ and none at Persepolis, but in XPj has $X\check{S}$ and DH, but not BU. At Susa, Darius I varied from the use of none to the use of $X\check{S}$ only, and that of $X\check{S}$ DH BU AM, so far as they occur (on DSe DSf DSm DSt, see below); Xerxes in his two short inscriptions gives no proof of using any ideogram, but Darius II seems to have used all five, including BG which appears only in D²Sa; Artaxerxes II certainly used four ideograms, but may also have entirely avoided their use in another inscription. At Hamadan, Ariaramnes has no ideogram, Darius I has only $X\check{S}$; Xerxes has only $X\check{S}$, but happens not to use the other words; Artaxerxes II has four (but see below on A²Hc), but writes $baga$ in full in A²Hc. The other texts are too brief or defective to warrant special remark.

In general, then, more ideograms appear in later texts, and they were more used at Susa than elsewhere. Further, $X\check{S}$ was the ideogram of most widespread use, and the order of introduction into texts was DH, BU, AM, BG. Few texts have any irregularity in this respect, and few use both ideogram and full writing for the same word; there are the following exceptions: DSe contains all five words, with a regular use of $X\check{S}$, and the rest in full, except that after four occurrences of $Auramazd\bar{a}$ and its forms AM is found in line 50 (restored but certain). DSf has both $b\bar{u}mim$ and BU $BUy\bar{a}$; otherwise $X\check{S}$ and DH, but $Auramazd\bar{a}$ and $baga$ in full. DSm, as restored by Brandenstein, WZKM 39.55–8, has $X\check{S}$ and $x\check{s}\bar{a}ya\theta iyam$, $DHn\bar{a}m$ and $dahy\bar{a}va$, $b\bar{u}miy\bar{a}$, $AMh\bar{a}$ and $AMmaiy$; it is probable that all the words should be written

---

[1] Final s after $\bar{\imath}$ and $\bar{u}$ became $\check{s}$ in pAryan, and this final $\check{s}$ is written in OP. [2] The final t was analogically replaced by $\check{s}$ in such forms of 3d sg $akunau\check{s}$ (= Skt. $ak\d{r}not$); §228 III.

in full, but in presenting the text it seemed hardly worth while to make the alterations, since only a few slight fragments are preserved.

DSt, as restored, has *XŠ* and *xšāyaθiyam* (both entirely restored), and *būmim Auramazdā bagaibiš*; this should not be, but I fail to see any alternative.

A²Sc seems to have *XŠ* and *xšāyaθiya*; but this is a much mutilated text, and also the inscriptions of Artaxerxes II are not accurately written.

A²Hc agrees with DSf; it has *būmim* and *BUyā*, otherwise *XŠ* and *DH*, but *Auramazdā* and *baga*.

A³Pa has *xšāyaθiya*, *DH*, *būmām* (sic) and *BUyā*, *Auramazdā*, *baga*; a state of variation which is attributable to the inaccuracy of OP writing at this period.

§43. NUMERALS: The cardinals are not written in full (except *aiva-* 'one' in a formulaic phrase), but are indicated by signs: 1, a single long vertical wedge; 2, two short vertical wedges, one above the other; 3, two short verticals with a long vertical to the right, and so on; 10, an angle with point to the left; 20, two small angles, one above the other; 100, two short horizontal wedges meeting at their points, above a single vertical wedge. Smaller units are placed to the right of larger units. But the ordinals are written in full, with the regular characters.

The cuneiform characters for the numerals are given at the end of the Lexicon, where their occurrences also are listed.

§44. THE SEPARATION OF WORDS is made in OP by a word-divider, which in the Behistan text has the form of an angle with the point to the left, and in other texts is a single slanting wedge running from upper left to lower right. The divider stands at the beginning of each column and of each section and each smaller inscription at Behistan, and at the end of Behistan a–g, i–j; elsewhere it does not stand at the beginning, but it stands at the end of DPd, of some copies of XPd, of A³Pa, and of some of the items in A?P. It is frequently lacking between words in Scheil's texts from Susa, notably in DSa, DSc, DSd, DSg, DSi, DSj, DSy, A²Sd; these texts have been published not in mechanical reproductions, but only in hand-drawn copies, but the reliability of the copyist is confirmed by similar omissions in DSy, our text of which has been read from a carbon rubbing of the original.[1] In other inscriptions omission of the divider is extremely rare: examples are *yadimaniyāiy* XPh 47 = *yadi(y) : maniyā(ha)iy*, and *upā Artaxša-[çām]* Sf. The gen. *Auramazdāha* is replaced in XPc 10 by *Aurahyā Mazdāha*, with declension of both parts of the compound, but no divider.[2]

The emphatic adverb *apiy* is sometimes attached to the preceding as an enclitic, and sometimes separated from it by a divider. The enclitic pronoun *diš* is preceded by a divider in DB 4.34, 35, 36. At DB 5.11, *utā : daiy : marda* is probably to be emended to *utā : viyamarda*, with wrongly inserted divider;[3] other peculiarities in connection with enclitics are given in §133.

Two compound words are sometimes cut by the divider; these are *Ariya : ciçā* and *Ariyaciçā*, *paruv : zanānām* and *paruvzanānām paruzanānām*. There is also variation between the phrasal adverb *paradraya* and the prepositional phrase *para : draya*. But in Fragment Theta of DSf, the . . .]*yᵃ- :-kᵃ-*[. . . supposed to belong to *dāraniyakarā* 49 should be read . . .]*yᵃ-:-sᵃ-*[. . . as part of *avaiy : Spardiya* 51–2.

§45. THE NORMALIZATION OF OP TEXTS.[1] The first step is to make a close transcription of the text, representing the inherent vowels of the consonantal characters by raised letters. Then in normalizing:[2]

---

[1] Cf. JAOS 67.32–3. [2] For possible haplography of the divider with the angle-sign of the adjacent character, see notes on DB 4 71 and 4 83. [3] So Wb. ZfA 46 55, for KT's reading; cf. Lex. s.vv. *-di-* and *mard-*.

§45.[1] The normalized text is not necessarily a phonetic text, but only an approximation to such a text. Especially note the normal writings
(a) final *-ā -iy -ŭv* for phonetic *-ă -ĭ -ŭ*.
(b) *iy* and *uv* for postconsonantal *y* and *v*.
(c) *hᵃ* or rarely *ι* for *hi*, and especially *hy* for (phonetic) *hy* or *hiy* or final *hi*.
(d) *u* for *hu*, and especially *uv* for (phonetic) *hv* or *huv* or final *-hu*.

[2] This system of normalization for Old Persian texts has become standard among scholars; it is the outcome of a long series of attempts to reach sound conclusions, made by the earlier workers in the field (§16; §14.n1, citing Weissbach's article in which earlier literature may be traced). The proof of its correctness lies in the fact that it works, enabling us to make cogent comparisons with cognates in other IE languages and with

A. The vowel character *a* initial becomes (normalized) *ă* or *ā*, or the prior part of a diphthong *ăi* or *ău*: medial, *ā* or the prior part of *āi āu*: final, *ā*.
B. The vowel characters *i* and *u* become *ĭ* or *ī*, *ŭ* or *ū*; or the second part of a diphthong.
C. The consonantal characters with inherent *i* and *u*, if standing before *ı* or *u*, lose the inherent vowel.
D. The consonant characters with inherent *a*
   (a) keep the *a* to show the vowel sound before a medial consonant, or as part of the diphthongs *ai* and *au*, or final before an unwritten minimal consonant (*t d n ḥ*);
   (b) lose the *a* when the consonant sound is immediately followed by another consonant, or by the character *a* (= *ā*), or when the consonant is final in the word (-*š* -*m* -*r* -*y* -*v*), or when the *a*-inherent character functions for an *i*- or *u*-inherent character before the characters *i* or *u*.
E. Raised *i u a* are used in the normalized text to show:
   (a) *i* and *u*, to show *i*- and *u*-inherent characters after which the *ı* and *u* failed to be written.
   (b) *a*, to show *a*-inherent characters functioning for *i*-inherent characters after which *i* failed to be written.
F. Raised *n* and *h* medial, *t d n ḥ* final, may optionally be supplied to mark sounds not indicated in the writing:
   (a) medial *n*, before a consonant not *y* nor *v*.
   (b) medial *h*, before *u* and rarely before *i* and *m*.
   (c) final *t d n ḥ*, after *ă* and *ā*.

§46. THE REDUCTION OF OP TO WRITING. The scribes, in analyzing the OP words into sounds, must have spoken the words slowly, prolonging them until the sound-units could be clearly distinguished and receive each a symbol. This procedure was, apparently, responsible for the most conspicuous of the peculiarities of the syllabary, notably the following: every consonant which stood before a consonant or final was equipped with the common vowel *a*; postconsonantal *y* and *v* became *iy* or *uv* (§25, §26); final *ă* was prolonged to *ā* (§36), though the reduced final consonants, even though they were never written, checked the prolongation and caused the keeping of *ă* (§40): final *i* and *u* were prolonged to *iy* and *uv* (§37, §38; after *i* and *u* the reduced final consonants seem to have been entirely lost, §40); anteconsonantal *ī* and *ū* were occasionally prolonged to *īy* and *ūv* (§23); medial *ay* and *av* occasionally became *aiy* and *auv* (§48).

This procedure, however, does not explain the peculiarities in the writing of *h* before *ı* and *u* (§27, §28), nor the omission of the anteconsonantal nasal and of certain reduced final consonants (§39, §40); the most that we can say is that they were disregarded in writing because they were weak sounds, yet most of them survived into later periods of Persian.

§47. IRREGULARITIES AND ERRORS IN OP WRITING are, of course, to be found, in the preceding sections we have listed the examples of the following irregular phenomena:

Lack of *i* or *u* after a consonant with inherent *i* or *u*, to denote *i* or *u*; §22.

Lack of *i* after a consonant with inherent *a*, to denote *i*; §22.

Lack of *a* final, to mark absolutely final *ă* as *ā*; §36.

Writing of *hi* by *hᵃ* or by *i* or by *hᵃi*; §27.

Writing of *tya*- and its forms by *tᵃyᵃ*- instead of by *tᵃɩyᵃ*-; §25.

Occasional writing of *iyᵃ* and *uvᵃ* to denote *ī* and *ū*; §23.

Variation between ideograms and full writing in the same inscription; §42.

---

borrowed words in non-IE languages. Although some scholars use other symbols to represent certain OP syllabic characters (§20), there is no important disagreement in method, and there is no gain in using those other characters A goodly amount of ambiguity still remains in connection with initial *a* and with *a*-inherent characters (§21, §22), and with the value of (normalized) *ar*, which is phonetic *ar* or *r̥* (§29–§35); such problems must be settled by etymological comparison or by comparison with borrowings in other languages; but these are only problems relating to individual words or forms, not affecting the general method of normalization On these, one should consult the Lexicon, where divergent views are cited under the words concerned. Some scholars, it is true, normalize or rather 'interpret' OP *aı* and *au* as *e* and *o*, but the only result is to obscure the relation between the word and its cuneiform representation, it is quite simple, if one so desires, to regard *ai* and *au* as symbols for the sounds *e* and *o*

Irregularities in word division and in the use of the word-divider; §44.

Other irregularities and errors will be discussed in §48–§57.

§48. MEDIAL *ay* AND *av* were occasionally prolonged in the analysis for reduction to writing, so that they became *aiy* and *auv* (cf. JAOS 62.271–2); the examples are the following:

adāraya DB 1.85, 2.9, 3.23, DNa 41; *adāraiya* DNa 22.

amānaya DB 2.48, 2.63, *amānaiya* DB 2.28.

paradraya DNa 28f; *paradraiya* A?P 24 (cf. *draya*, *drayahyā*, *drayahiyā*).

Perhaps [*va*]*rtaiyaiy* DB 4.44, for *vartayaiy*.

Cf. also the sandhi phenomena of *dūraiapiy* DNa 12, *dūrayapiy* DNa 46, and the same as two words, *dūraiy apiy*.

bavatiy DNb 14, *bauvatiy* DNbv 14.

gāθavā DB 1.62f, etc.; *dahyauvā* DB 1.34.

tauvīyā DSe 39, cf. Skt. *sthavīyas-*.

yauvīyā DZc 8f, 10; cf. Skt. *yavyà*.

hauvam DB 1.29, for **hav-am*, from *hauv* + enclitic *-am*.

§49. VARIATIONS IN CONSONANTS sometimes appear in the writing, though this can usually be explained as the product of special causes: lateness, dialect, borrowing from other languages.

(a) *t/d*, in the late *Ardaxcašca* AVsa, for *Artaxšaçā*.

in borrowed *tacaram* DPa 6, XPj, and *dacaram* DSd 3.

(b) *c/š*, in late inscriptions:

haša A²Sdc 4, for the usual *hacā*.

Xšayārcahyā A²Sa 2 bis, for *Xšayāršā* etc.

[*usta*]*canām* A²Sc 5f, for *ustašanām* A³Pa 22.

Ardaxcašca AVsa for *Artaxšaçā*.

(c) *ç* and variants: in late *Ardaxcašca* AVsa, for *Artaxšaçā*.

in late *Mit*[*ra*], *Mᵗra*, *Mᶿra* (see Lexicon), and the Persian personal name *Vau-misa* DB 2.49 etc.

Other variants are explained in the phonology as being due to admixture of Median forms; cf. §8.

§50. THE ERRORS OF WRITING can be divided into the following heads:

1. Metathesis of characters; §51.
2. Omission of characters and of groups of characters; §52.
3. Addition of characters or of groups of characters; §53.
4. Alteration of characters by omission or addition of a stroke; §54.
5. Miswritings less easily classified; §55.
6. Syntactical misuse of forms; §56.
7. Creation of new incorrect forms; §57.

Some examples might be classified under more than one of these headings, but will be arbitrarily assigned to the places which are most appropriate. As will be seen, most of these errors belong to late inscriptions, that is, after those of Xerxes. For by this time the development to Middle Persian was under way; sounds were undergoing changes, new words and meanings were coming in, the final syllables were being lost. OP had ceased to be a vernacular, and the scribes who composed the inscriptions had no experience of the language as it had been. They were thrown back upon the use of words and forms found in the older records, the use of which they often failed to understand. The result was inevitably an inaccurate orthography, most notably in the final syllables.

§51. METATHESIS OF CHARACTERS. The examples are the following:

ciyākarammᵃcᵃiyᵃ DNb 51, 51f, for *-cᵃmᵃiyᵃ*, = *ciyākaram-ca-maiy*.

imᵃyᵃ A?P 22, for *iyᵃmᵃ*, = *iyam*.

Dārayavahauš nom. XPf 25, *Dārayavauš* gen. XPf 28: the original copy had *-vᵃušᵃ* in both places, and the corrector, finding the error in 28, made the insertion in the word where it stood in 25.

Skudrā XPh 27, *Kūšiya* XPh 28: a similar error; the lacking *a* should have been added to *kᵘušᵃiyᵃ*, but was actually added to *sᵃkᵘudᵃrᵃ*, which stood just above it.

šarastibara DNc 2, written *šᵃrᵃsᵃtᵃibᵃrᵃ*: the original copy had *arᵃsᵃtᵃibᵃrᵃ* = *arstibara*, and in endeavoring to change to *arᵃšᵃtᵃibᵃrᵃ* = *arštibara*, the scribe altered the first character instead of the third.

Haxamānᵃšiya A²Sa 3, with *-xᵃmᵃanᵃ-* for *-xᵃamᵃnᵃ-*.

daivadāvam XPhb 37f for the correct *-dānam* in copy a; the *vᵃ* for *nᵃ* stands at the end of line 37, and is copied from line 36, where the last character is *vᵃ*.

§52. OMISSIONS OF CHARACTERS: The omissions fall into several classes.

I. The characters iy^a at the end of a word are sometimes omitted after an a-inherent consonant: $t^ay^a = tya(iy)$ XPh 23; $an^aiy^a š^ac^a = aniyašc(iy)$ XPh 41f; $p^ar^aiy^ait^a = pariyait(iy)$ XPh 52. $ap^an^ay^ak^am^a = apan^ayākama(iy)$ A²Sa 3; $[n^ay^a]k^am^a = [n^ayā]kama(iy)$ A²Sa 4. $p^ar^as^a =$ (loc.) $Pārsa(iy)$ AsH 3. $a[v^a]m^ac^a = a[vā]mc(iy)$ DB 5.2f (probable restoration).

II. The -i- may be omitted in final -aiy: $Auramazdā$-tay DB 4.58, for -$taiy$. $maniyāhay$ DPe 20, for -$haiy$. uta-may A²Sdc 4, for uta-$maiy$ (which is in db). Cf. forms of $dūraiy$, with enclitic $apiy$ (§136).

III. The character a was sometimes omitted where it marked length: $XŠyănām$ DPh 1, DH 1, $xšāyaθiyănām$ A²Sc 2f, A³Pa 10, for -$yānām$. $avaθă$ XPf 30, for the common $avaθā$. $Auramazdăhā$ XPf 34, 43, XPh 14, 33, 37, 44, A¹Pa 18f, for -$āhā$. $ahăniy$ XPh 47, 48 (1st sg. subj.) = Skt. ásāni; unless the ă is analogical to the ă in other forms, such as 3d sg. $ahatiy$. $stūnăyă$ D²Sa 1, A²Hb, perhaps 1sf. for -$āyā$. $framătāram$ A³Pa 8, for the common $framātāram$. $Anăhită$, $Anăh^ată$, in A²Sa, A²Sd, A²Ha, for (Av.) $Anāhitā$-. $hyă uvaspā$ AmH 6, for $hyā$. $tyă ukārām uvaspām$ AsH 9f, for $tyām ukārām uvaspām$ (cf. §56. V).

IV. The character a, represening the augment, seems to be lacking in $avăhar[da]$ DB 2.94. On an apparently unaugmented $marda$ DB 5.11, cf. §44 and Lex. s.v. $mard$-.

V. Final m is lacking in iya DB 4.90; $tuva$ XPh 46; $XŠyānā$ A²Sb; $apadāna$ A²Sa 3, A²Ha 5; $ab^ayapara$ A²Sa 4. For all but the last, the forms with -m are found in other passages. Cf. also tya AsH 9, 13°, for $tyām$ (§52. III, §56. V).

VI. Miscellaneous characters are lacking as follows; for brevity we put the omitted value in the word, in parenthesis: $Auramaz(d)ām$ DB 1.54f; $u(t)ā$ DB 3.77; perhaps $ava(θ)ā$ DB 4.51; $i(ya)m$ DB 4.91; in $U]tā[na : n]āma$ DB 4.83, according to KT, the gap is inadequate for $n^a : n^a$; im^a DB 4.89 (Cameron), for $i(mā)m$; $Nabuku(d)racara$ DBi 5f.

$Auramazdā(ma)iy$ DNa 50; $ayāu(ma)iniš$ DNb 59. $y^ad^im^an^aiy^aaiy^a$ XPh 47, for $yadi(y :) maniyā$-$(ha)iy$. $ahyā(yā)$ A²Sdc 1 = $ahyāya$ A²Sdb 1. $utamaiy$: $kartam$ A²Sdb 4 (-may dc), for $ut(ā : tya)maiy$: $kartam$. $Dārayava(u)šahyā$ A²Ha 2, 2°, 4, 4°. $marti(ya)hyā$ A³Pa 4f; $aθaga(i)nām$ A³Pa 22.

VII. A serious haplography occurs, according to Bv. MSLP 23.182–3, in DB 1.66, where he would read $adīnā$: $adam$: ($patiyābaram$: $adam$:) $kāram$; but his assumption is not necessary for an interpretation.

§53. ADDITION OF CHARACTERS: in almost all examples the addition is of the character a: $avājaniyā$ DB 1.51, 52, perhaps for $avajaniyā$; cf. JAOS 62.274. $patiyābaram$ DB 1.68, perhaps for $patiyabaram$; cf. JAOS 62.275. $Hāxāmanišiya$ XPa 10f, for $Haxāmanišiya$. $āhām$ XPh 15f, for $āham$. $akunauuš$ XSab 2, for $akunauš$, as in XSaa 2. $Artaxšaçāhyā$ A²Sa 2 bis, for $Artaxšaçahyā$ (or as in §172). $XŠah^ay^a = XŠāhyā$ A²Sd 2, for $XŠh^ay^a = XŠhyā$ or $XŠy^ah^ay^a = XŠyahyā$. $akunavām$ A²Sdb 3, for $akunavam$. $gāstā$ A²Sda 4, db 4, for $gastā$ (as in A²Sdc, and elsewhere). $puçā$ A²Hb, for $puça$ (after $napā$, acc. to Brd. WZKM 39.92). $Pārsā$ AmH 5, for $Pārsa$. $asmānām$ A³Pa 3, for $asmānam$.

Doublet forms, one with and the other without the character a, sometimes occur, where doubt may exist as to whether two pronunciations actually existed, or one of the two writings is erroneous: $uvăipašiyam$ DB 1.47, but $uvăipašiyahyā$ DNb 15. $ciyākaram$ DNb 50, 51, 51f, but $ciyăkaram$ DNa 39. gen. $Cišpāiš$ DB 1.5f, but $Cišpăiš$ DBa 8, AmH 3; cf. §179. IV, Lg. 19.222. acc. $dahyāum$ DPd 15, 18, DNa 53; but -y^aum^a = -$yaum$ or -yum, in $visadahy^aum^a$ XPa 12, DHy^aum^a A³Pa 26.

In A²Sb an extra $XŠ$ is inscribed after $XŠyānā$; unless indeed the engraver has omitted the word

SCRIPT

DHyūnām immediately after the apparently extra *XŠ*.

§54. Alteration of Characters by omission or addition of a stroke sometimes occurs, altering the value; the error may be either in original engraving, or in the reading by the modern observer:

I. The stroke is lacking; the corrected form is given first:

[*A*]*tamaita* DB 5.5, formerly read]$m^am^ait^a$; see Lexicon.

θadayātaiy DSa 5, formerly read -m^aiy^a = miy; cf. Hz. ApI 156–8.

utava DB 4.71f, for KT's $d^at^as^a$.

abaraha XPh 17, inscribed $ab^ar^an^a$.

θatagudaya, perhaps to be read for *θataguiya* A?P 11; see Lexicon.

II. The stroke is in excess:

agaubatā DB 3.55, inscribed $ag^aur^at^a$, acc. to KT.

abara DB 3.67, inscribed ar^ar^a, acc. to KT.

akariyatā DB 3.92, inscribed as^ar^a- acc. to KT.

vikanāhy DB 4.71, 73, inscribed v^is^a- acc. to KT.

vikanāh^{a}diš DB 4.77, inscribed v^is^a- acc. to KT.

pasāva : had]*ā : k*[*ārā* DB 5.21, correction from KT's *hadā : kār*]*ā : Sa*[*kām*.

$f^ar^aš^am^a$ = *frašam* DSa 5, rather than $f^ar^aš^at^a$ = *frašta*; cf. Hz. ApI 156–8.

§55. Miscellaneous Errors of Writing are in the following:

I. The word is recognizable, but is considerably changed from the writing known in other passages:

$š^ak^aur^aim^a$ = *škaurim* DB 4.65, for $s^ak^auθ^aim^a$ = *skauθim*.

$y^ad^iy^aiš^a$ = *yadaiyaiša* XPh 39, for $y^ad^iy^aiš^a$ = *yadiyaiša*.

$y^ad^ay^a$ = *yadāyā* XPh 39, apparently for *yadātya*.

$v^as^ap^a$ = *v^{i}āspā* A²Sdb 4, for $v^is^ap^a$ = *vispā* (so A² Sda, dc 4).

$b^aum^am^a$ = *būmām* A³Pa 2, for $b^um^im^a$ = *būmim*.

$š^ay^at^am^a$ = *šāyatām* A³Pa 4, for $š^iy^at^im^a$ = *šiyātim*.

$ak^un^am^a$ = *akunām* XSc 3 and A²Ha 5f (only *ām* visible), A²Sa 4 and 5 (restored); ak^un^a = *akunā* A²Ha 7; $ak^uv^an^aš^aš^a$ = *akuvanašāša* A²Sdc 3 (and $ak^un^av^am^a$ = *akunavām* A²Sdb 3, see §53); all for $ak^un^av^am^a$ = *akunavam*.

$ak^un^aš^a$ = *akunaš* A²Sa 3f, D²Sbb 3, for $ak^un^auš^a$ = *akunauš*.

II. The word is itself problematic or obscure:

$a+t^aa+$ DB 4.89, as read by KT; see now Cameron's reading.

$am^ax^am^at^a$ DB 4.92, as read by KT; perhaps *hamaxmatā* (JAOS 62.269).

$af^auw^ay^a$ DNb 38, perhaps for *aruvāyā* (JNES 4. 44, 52).

$b^at^uug^ar^a : s^iy^am^am^a$ = *bātugara : siyamam* A¹I; uncertain words.

$j^iv^ad^iy^a : p^ar^ad^ay^ad^am^a$ = *j^{i}vadiy : paradayadām* A²Sd 3; uncertain words.

All the words on Seals b, c, d, e; uncertain.

§56. Errors in Syntax may be either the product of an intentional writing of a form other than that called for by the use of the word in its context, or the product of a fortuitous miswriting which accidentally yields a form not called for by the context. Those occurring in the OP inscriptions may be classified as follows:

I. The nominative form, in a group of two or more words, is used as appositive or as predicate to a noun in another case or to an adverb; see §312, §313, §247E.

II. The nominative is apparently misused for the genitive, or the genitive for the nominative, in genealogies of Artaxerxes I–II–III; these misuses are explainable as examples of anacoluthon; see §313.

III. The labels of the throne-bearers in DN and A?P are sometimes written with the plural of the ethnic, or with the province-name for the ethnic; we give the examples, with a literal translation:

DN xv *iyam : Sakā : tigraxa*[*udā*] 'this is the Pointed-Cap Scythians'.

DN xxix *iyam : Maciyā* 'this is the men of Maka'.

A?P 9 *iyam : Zrakā* 'this is the Drangians'.

A?P 14 *iyam : Sakā : haumavargā* 'this is the Amyrgian Scythians'.

A?P 15 *iyam : Sakā : tigraxa*[*ud*]*ā* (as above).

A?P 23 *iyam : Yaunā* 'this is the Ionians'.

A?P 24 *iyam : Sakā : paradraiya* 'this is the Scythians across the sea'.

A?P 26 *iyam : Yauna : takabara* 'this is the Ionian (sg.), petasos-wearers (pl.)'.

DN xvi [*iyam : Bā*]*biruš*, A?P 16 *iyam : Bābiruš* 'this is Babylon'.

IV. The use of masculine plural pronouns with

collective antecedents either masculine or feminine, exemplifies the constructio ad sensum rather than syntactical error; examples in §258.III.

V. Miscellaneous errors concerned with cases and genders:

AmH 2 *Pārsā* for loc. (§314.b); 5 *tya* as asf. (= *tyām*); 8f *iyam dahyāuš*, nom. for loc. (§314.b).

AsH 2 *Pārsa*, nsm. for lsf. (§52.I); 9f *tya ukāram uvaspam*, nt. for fem. *tyām ukārām uvaspām* (possibly by imitation of the phrasing seen in DSf 11, where the agreement is with nt. *xšaçam*).

XPh 33 *ava* (for *avām*) *dahyāvam*.

A¹I *hya* (nsm. for gsm.) *imam* (asm. for nsm. *iyam*) *bātugara siyamam* (asm. for nsm. *-ma*).

A²Sc 4f [*i*]*mām* (asf. for asn. *ima*) *hadiš*; 6 *tya* (for asf. *tyām*) *aθagainām*.

A²Sd 3 *imām* (asf. for nsn. *ima*) *hadiš*.

A²Ha 7 *imam* (asm. for asn. *ima*) *tya*; so also A²Sa 5 (restored).

A³Pa 22f *imam uštašanām aθaganam* (for nom. *iyam uštašanā aθagainā*) *mām* (perhaps for *manā*) *upā mām kartā*.

A³Pa 26 *tya mām kartā* (perhaps for *manā kartam*).

§57. NEOLOGISMS IN THE LATER INSCRIPTIONS, that is, after Xerxes, may perhaps be counted as errors, though susceptible of explanation. There are the following, all new formations for the genitive—presumably after the gen. *xšāyaθiyahyā*, with which the genitives of the royal name were constantly associated, and gen. *Artaxšaçahyā*:

Haxāmanišahyā AmH 3f.

Dārayavaušahyā in A¹I, A²Sa, A²Hc, and restored in A²Sc; *Dārayavašahyā* in A²Ha.

Xšayāršahyā in A¹Pa, A¹I, A²Ha; *Xšayārcahyā* (§49b) in A²Sa; *Xšayāršāhyā* (§187) in A²Hc.

CHAPTER III. PHONOLOGY

§58. THE pIE SOUNDS, whose history will be traced down into OP, were the following:

I. Vowels:

	pure	semi-consonantal
short:	e o a	i u r̥ l̥ m̥ n̥
reduced:	ъ ъ ə	
long:	ē ō ā	ī ū r̥̄ l̥̄ m̥̄ n̥̄

II. Diphthongs:
short: *ei oi ai əi   eu ou au əu*
long: *ēi ōi āi   ēu ōu āu*

III. Consonants:

	voiceless		voiced		
	non-asp.	aspirate	non-asp.	asp.	
Stops					Nasals
labial	p	ph	b	bh	m
dental	t	th	d	dh	n
palatal	ḱ	ḱh	ĝ	ĝh	ñ
pure velar	q	qh	g	gh	ŋ
labiovelar	qᵘ	qᵘh	gᵘ	gᵘh	

Clusters

| dental | tst | tsth | dzd | dzdh |

Continuants (voiced, except *s*)

sibilants	s	z
liquids		l r
semivowels		i̯ u̯

Remarks on the list of pIE sounds:

A. I have omitted from this list (a) Brugmann's *þ þh ð ðh*,[1] sounds of problematic nature which are posited to explain the occurrence of dental stops in Greek corresponding to sibilants in other IE languages; (b) Sturtevant's *z* and preaspirated continuants,[2] which also explain only certain peculiarities of development in Greek; (c) Brugmann's *sh* and *zh*,[3] from *s* after voiceless and voiced aspirated stops, no distinctive product of which appears in any IE language; (d) short and long vocalic *ñ* and *ŋ*, since they were nonphonemic, and so rare that they seem not to occur in the extant words of OP.

B. Not all the sounds in the list were phonemic: *ñ* and *ŋ* developed only from a nasal standing before palatal and velar stops respectively; *z* developed only from *s* before voiced stops and after voiced aspirated stops, and in the voiced dental clusters.

C. There is no need for a special symbol to denote velar *g*, since the Aryan developments (§73.I–III) distinguish velar *g* from palatal *ĝ*.

D. The dental clusters were clusters consisting

---

[1] Brugmann, Gdr.² 1.790–3; cf. §102. [2] Sturtevant, IH Laryngeals §80b, §73–§77. [3] Brugmann, Gdr.² 1.721, 724.

of three phonemes each, but of such peculiarity in their developments in the separate languages as to deserve places in the list; they originated in pre-Indo-Hittite from the following combinations:

tst < t-t d-t
tsth < th-t th-th t-th d-th
dzd < t-d d-d
dzdh < dh-t dh-th dh-d dh-dh th-d t-dh th-dh d-dh

The most important of these are the combinations of *t d dh* with *t* of a suffix.

E. Of the 'reduced vowels', ъ is a reduction of *e*; ъ is a reduction of *o*; ə is a reduction of *ē ō ā*.

§59. THE OLD PERSIAN SOUNDS are represented, in the normalized orthography, by the following equipment of graphic signs:

Vowels: a i u ā ī ū
Diphthongs: ai au āi āu
Stops and corresponding Spirants and Nasals:
　Labial　p　b　f　m
　Dental　t　d　θ　n
　Palatal　c　j
　Velar　k　g　x
Sibilants　s š ç z
Other Continuants　r l y v h

The sounds represented by these symbols cannot be defined with entire precision; but in general they may be said to be those usually represented by these symbols, with the following limitations:

(a) *b d g* were probably voiced spirants when intervocalic, rather than voiced stops.[1]

(b) *c j* were not stops, but the affricates *č* and *ǰ* (as in Eng. *church* and *judge*); but *j* represented also *ž* (as in *azure*).

(c) *f θ x* were voiceless spirants.

(d) *ç* appears to have been a voiceless sibilant between dental *s* and alveolar *š*.

(e) *v* was the voiced labial semivowel, as in Eng. *we*.

(f) The sound *r̥* was indicated by *r* preceded by the character *a* or an *a*-inherent consonantal character, and is indistinguishable graphically from phonetic *ar*; see §29.

(g) For other sounds present in the spoken language and not represented in the writing, see §27, §28, §39, §40, §103.II, §118.II.

---
[1] On the phonetic value of *b d g*, see MB Gr. §§127–9.

(h) Other details will be presented in connection with the history of the sounds concerned.

(i) There is no evidence as to the position and nature of the syllabic accent of OP, except that the presence of enclitic words shows that there was an accent.

§60. THE POSITION OF SOUNDS AND SOUND-CLUSTERS IN OP WORDS.

I. The vowels *ă ā ĭ ī ŭ ū r̥* and the diphthongs *ăi āi ău āu*, may occur anywhere in the word; there are extant examples initially of *ă ā ĭ ŭ r̥ ăi ău*, medially of all, final of *ă ā ĭ ī ŭ ăi ău*.

II. All the consonants occur initially before vowels, except *f*; all occur medially intervocalic.

III. The following clusters of two consonants occur initially before vowels: *xr xš dr dv fr br sk st sp zr hy*; *ty* only in the stem *tya-* (see Lex. s.v.). The only initial cluster of three is *xšn*.

IV. The following clusters of two consonants occur medially between vowels: *xt xθ* xn xm* xr xš, gd gn gm gr, jy, tp* tr*, θb* θm θr*, dr dv, ny nv, fr, br, mn my, rk rx rg rc rj rt rθ rd rn rb rm ry rv rs rš, ld*, st sp sm, šk šc št šd* šn šp šm šy šv, zd zb* zm zr, hy*. In the clusters *nk nx* ng nt nd mp mb hm hv*, all of which actually occur, the prior sound is omitted in the writing. Of those marked with *, *θb* occurs by analogical formation; *xθ* only in an uninterpretable word; *xm, θr*, and *zb*, only in Median words; *nx* only in a Scythian name; *tp, tr, ld* only in non-Iranian names of persons and places; *šd* only in apparently corrupt writings.

V. Clusters of three or four sounds occur medially intervocalic, as follows: *xšn*, transferred from the initial position (III); *xtr* and *xštr*, which are Median; *ngm*, written *gm*; *ršt, ršn, ršy*; *rvy*, unless this is phonetically *rviy*.

VI. In final position only single consonants are found, and of these only *m r š* are written; but peculiarities of the script show that final *t, d, n* (from *n* and *nt*), *h* (from *s* after pAr. *ă*) survived in the speech as faintly pronounced (i.e., minimal or reduced) sounds.

§61. pIE *e o a* fell together into one sound *a* in pAr., and this situation remained unchanged in pIr. and OP:[1]

---
[1] Some scholars argue that OP *a* was pronounced *e* and *o* before *y* and *v* respectively, and that the OP diphthongs *ai* and *au* were pronounced *ē* and *ō* respec-

*ebherom, OP abaram, Skt. ábharam, Gk. ἔφερον.
*ek̑yom, OP asam, Skt. áśvam, Lt. equom.
*pro, OP fra-, Skt. prá, Gk. πρό.
*apo, OP prefix apa-, Skt. ápa, Gk. ἀπό 'from', Lt. ab.
*ak̑mōn-, OP acc. asmānam, Skt. áśmānam, Gk. nom. ἄκμων 'anvil'.

In many words it is impossible to determine from what pIE vowel the OP ă has developed; a cognate outside Aryan, from a language which preserves the distinctions among the original vowels, is necessary, except where a pIE front vowel has palatalized a preceding velar stop and has thus indicated its own original quality (§73. III).

Absolutely final ă in OP was written -ā; that is, with addition of the character a, as though it were lengthened. This does not apply where the -ă was protected by a following unwritten minimal consonant. See §36.I, §40.

For -ay- becoming -aiy- and -av- becoming -auv-, see §48; for contraction of ahah to āh after dissimilative loss of the prior h, see §131.

§62. pIE ē ō ā, like the corresponding short vowels, fell together in pAr. in the one quality ā, and remained in this value in OP:

*e-dhē-t, OP adā 'he made', Skt. ádhāt, Lt. fē-cit.
*mātē[r], OP -mātā, Skt. mātá, Gk. (Dor.) μάτηρ.
root *dō-, OP dadātuv 'let him give', Skt. dádātu, cf. Gk. δίδωμι 'I give'.
subj. *ĝnō-sk̑ē-ti, OP xšnāsātiy 'he shall know', Lt. (fut.) nōscet 'he will learn'.
*bhrātēr, OP brātā, Skt. bhrátā, Gk. φράτηρ 'clan-brother'.

§63. pIE Reduced Vowels.

I. pIE ƀ was the reduction of full-grade e, and ʊ the reduction of full-grade o; in the remains of OP they are convincingly seen only as the vowel remaining before liquid or nasal + vowel, in situations in which the liquid or nasal might be expected to assume merely vocalic value. Examples are given of ƀ in connection with vocalic l and r, and vocalic m and n (§66.II, §67.I–II);

---

tively; cf. MB Gr. §88, Hz. ApI 116, König Burgbau 62. These views are not supported by the OP orthography (cf. §48), and rest on the transliterations into Elamite and Akkadian, which sometimes stand in opposition to each other, and on the developments in Middle Iranian, which are not necessarily to be pushed back to the period of the OP inscriptions.

there are the following probable examples of ʊ, where other languages, notably the Skt. u, seem to indicate that the reduction is from o rather than from e:

*pʊros, OP para, Skt. purás, Gk. πάρος.
*pʊlu-, OP paru-, Skt. purú-, Gk. πολύς.

II. pIE ə was the reduction of ē or ō or ā; it became i in pAr., but a in all other IE branches.[1]

*pətē[r] 'father', OP pitā, Skt. pitá, Gk. πατήρ.
*sedəs, OP hadiš 'abode', but *sedos, Gk. ἕδος 'seat'.
*menəs, OP -maniš in personal names, but *menos, Gk. μένος 'vigor (of spirit)'.

In hadiš and -maniš the ə varies with a short vowel, which indicates another origin; the problem is too complicated for adequate discussion here.

But before i̯ or u̯ of the same or the next syllable, pIE ə became a even in pAryan; see §71.

§64. pIE i AND u have undergone very few changes in the various languages; they appear unchanged in OP:

*qᵘid, OP -ciy, Skt. cid, Gk. τί 'what', Lt. quid.
*peri, OP pariy, Skt. pári, Gk. περί 'around'.
*esisteto, OP aʰištatā, cf. Skt. átiṣṭhata.
*su- 'good, well', OP u-fraštam, Skt. su-, Gk. ὑ-γιής 'healthy'.
*putlo-, OP puça, Skt. putrá-, Osc. puclo-.
*susko-, OP ʰuška-, Skt. śúṣka-, Lith. saũsa-s 'dry'.

Final -i was in OP always followed by the character yᵃ, and final -u by the character vᵃ; this was true whether the i and u were monophthongal or in diphthongs. See §37, §38.

For the method of writing i and u in OP, and irregularities therein, see §22; for the method of writing hi and hu, see §27, §28.

§65. pIE ī AND ū survived into most IE languages, including OP, without change; but because of the nature of the OP system of writing they can with rare exceptions be distinguished from ĭ and ŭ, only by etymological considerations:

*gᵘīi̯os 'living', OP jīva, Skt. jīvás, Lt. vīvos.
*dhī-dhi (§129), OP imv. dīdiy 'see', cf. NPers. dīdan 'to see', Skt. root dhī- 'think'.

---

[1] To identify pIE ə, it is necessary to have two cognates, one in Aryan and the other outside, or to have a cognate with the long-vowel grade.

*bhūmi-, OP acc. būmim 'earth', Skt. bhū́mim.
pAr. *dūra-, OP adv. dūraiy 'afar', Skt. dūrá- 'far'.

For the occasional use of $uv^a = uv$, and possibly of $iy^a = iy$, to denote $ū$ and $ī$, see §23.

§66. pIE r AND l fell together in pAr. in the sound r, which remained unchanged in Skt., and so apparently in OP, though its written representation is by r^a preceded by a or by an a-inherent consonant: thus $k^ar^at^am^a$, normalized kartam, is kr̥tam, Skt. kr̥tám; ar^at^a-, normalized arta-, is r̥ta-, Skt. r̥tá-. For details, see §29–§35.

I. Apparently pIE r became OP u before n, though this value is seen only in forms of kar- 'make, do'; and this peculiar development is rather to be attributed to the influence of other verbs with u in the root before the -nau- suffix:[1]
pAr. *kr̥nauti, OP kunautiy, Skt. kr̥nóti; so also other forms of the present and imperfect, such as 1st sg. imf. akunavam, 1st sg. subj. mid. kunavānaiy, etc.; and by extension in the strong aorist: 3d sg. mid. akutā, etc.

II. When r (of either origin) is expected to stand before a vowel, it must be either as consonant r, or as the reduced vowel + consonant r. The latter combination[2] appears in OP as -ar-:
pIE *ĝhr̥l-eni̯o-, OP daraniya- 'gold', Skt. híraṇya-.
pIE *e-kr̥ri̯onto, OP akariya^ntā, cf. Skt. ákriyanta.[3]

Before $i̯$ and $u̯$ there seems to have been the same development as before a vowel; it is possible that OP akariya^ntā is based rather on *ekr̥ri̯onto.

§67. pIE $m̥$ AND $n̥$ became pAr. a before consonants.

*m̥bhi, OP abiy, Skt. abhí, oHG umbi (but see Lex. s.v. abiy).

*ḱm̥tom '100', in Θata-guš (uncertain etymology, see Lex. s.v.).

*bhn̥dh-to-, OP basta- (§85), Skt. baddhá-, cf. Eng. bound.

negative prefix *n̥- in a-xšaina-, a-xšata-, etc.

*sm̥-dhe, OP hadā, Skt. sahá 'with'.

I. Before a vowel or $i̯$ or $u̯$, pIE $n̥$ and $m̥$ must, like $r̥$ (§66.II), appear as $ən$ and $əm$, which became OP an and am:

*g^u̯əm-i̯ēt, Skt. gamyāt, OP ā-jamiyā 'may it come' (with analogical j, §101).

neg. prefix *ən- in An-āhitā (never so written, see Lexicon) 'The Spotless Goddess'.

In a-yāu(ma)iniš, negative of yāumainiš, the prefix has been generalized in the anteconsonantal form.

II. When final in the word, pIE $n̥$ and $m̥$ became pAr. a, which of course was written $ā$ in OP (§36.I):
acc. *nōmn̥ 'name', OP nāmā, Skt. nā́ma, Lt. nōmen.

But if -m̥ was the ending of the acc. sg. of a noun or of the 1st sg. of a verb, the value -am for -əm which was proper before an initial vowel of the next word, was generalized: doubtless this -am was fixed as normal by the concurrent influence of the -am in the acc. sg. of -ŏ- stems and in the 1st sg. of the imperfect of thematic verbs:
acc. viθ-am, asmān-am; cf. kāra-m, martiya-m.
*ēs-m̥ 'I was', OP āh-am, Skt. ā́s-am, Gk. (Hom.) ἦ-α; cf. OP abara-m, Skt. ábhara-m, Gk. ἔφερο-ν.

§68. pIE $r̥̄$ $l̥̄$ $m̥̄$ $n̥̄$ relate to the corresponding pIE short vowels as $ī$ $ū$ to i u; the first two became OP ar, Skt. īr or ūr, the latter two became $ā$ in OP and Skt. alike. A few examples only can be recognized with some probability, on the basis of the Skt. equivalents:

*dl̥gho- 'long', OP dargam, Skt. dīrghá-, Gk. δολιχός.

*g^u̯m̥̄-tu- 'place', OP gāθu-, Skt. gātú- to the root *g^u̯em- 'come'.

*e-ĝn̥̄-nā-t 'he knew', OP adānā, Skt. ájānāt, to root *ĝnō-; unless this tense-formation really be *ĝnō-nā-, with pAr. dissimilative loss of the prior n.

*pr̥̄u̯om, OP paruvam 'formerly', Skt. pū́rvam.

§69. THE pIE SHORT DIPHTHONGS IN i, namely ei oi ai,[1] all became pAr. ai, which remained in OP,[2] but became Av. aē or ōi, and Skt. e; they remained distinct in Greek, with virtually no change, and in Latin, where they became respectively $ī$, oe or $ū$, ae. The ambiguity of OP

---

[1] Lg. 18.79–82 [2] Phonetically proper when the r was preceded by two consonants, or by one consonant which was itself preceded by a long vowel or a diphthong. Edgerton, Lg 10 257 [3] The OP must not be normalized akr- (like the Skt), since kr became xr in Iranian; §103.I.

---

[1] No certain examples of pIE ai can be identified in the OP vocabulary, for pIE əi, see §71. [2] On the theory that OP ai was sounded ē, see §61.n1.

writing makes considerable difficulty in their identification; but $j^a\ d^a\ m^a\ v^a + i$ show diphthongs, since there are special characters $j^i\ d^i\ m^i\ v^i$ which are used before the monophthongal i. Further, kai and gai mark original oi or ai; for cai and jai result if the original diphthong was ei (§98).

*$eitiy$ 'he goes', $aitiy$, Skt. *éti*, Gk. εἶσι.

*ne-id 'not', OP $naiy$, Av. *nōiṯ*, Skt. *néd*, cf. Lt. *ne*- in *nescio* 'I don't know'.

*$oiu̯os$ 'one', OP asm. $aivam$, Av. nsm. *aēvō*, Gk. (Hom.) οἶος 'lone'.

*moi 'to me', OP $maiy$, Skt. *me*, Gk. μοι.

Also $vainā̆hy$, Skt. ind. *vénati*; $hainā$, Skt. *sénā*; $aita$, $duvaištam$, $gaiθām$, $naibam$, -$taiy$, -$šaiy$, $tyaiy$.

For ai graphic for a before y, see §48; for -aiy graphic for final -ai, see §37; for $h^ai = hai$ and not hi, §27.

§70. THE pIE SHORT DIPHTHONGS IN u, namely $eu\ ou\ au$,[1] all became pAr. au, which remained in OP,[2] but became Av. ao or $əu$, and Skt. o; they remained essentially unchanged in Greek, and appeared in Latin as $ū\ ū\ au$ respectively. These diphthongs are less frequent of occurrence than the i-diphthongs, and the distinction of them from one another is more difficult because of the lack of obvious evidence. But in OP, a diphthong is definitely proved by the use of an a-inherent consonant before u, if there is a corresponding u-inherent consonant ($k\ g\ t\ d\ n\ m\ r$); and as k and g would be palatalized before original e (§98), the au after k or g must be from pIE ou or au.

suffix -neu- in OP $kunautiy$ 'he makes', Av. *kərənaoiti*, Skt. *kr̥ṇóti*.

*$leukes$-, OP $rauca$ 'day', Av. *raočō*, Skt. *rocas*- 'light'.

*$dhroughos$, OP $drauga$ 'Lie', Av. *draoγō*, Skt. *drógha-s*.

OP $kaufa$ 'mountain', Av. *kaofō*; $gauša$ 'two ears', Av. *gaoša*; $tau^hmā$ 'family', Av. *taoxman*-; $hauv$ 'this one', cf. Gk. οὗ-τος.

For au graphic for a before v, see §48; for -auv graphic for final -au, see §38, for $h^au = hau$ and not hu, §28. An apparent au is often for a^hu, as in $A^huramazdā$, Av. *Ahurō Mazdå*, Skt. *ásura-s*; nom. $Dārayava^huš$, but gen. $Dārayavahauš$.

§71. THE pIE SHORT DIPHTHONGS $əi$ AND $əu$ always develop like pIE ai and au, from which they can be distinguished only by etymological considerations; they originated only as zero-grades of long diphthongs. Similarly, pIE $ə$ became pAr. a before $i̯$ or $u̯$ of the next syllable. An almost certain example is seen in the present stem $paya$- ($apayaiy$ 'I protected'; $pati$-$payauvā$ 'do thou protect thyself') as a variant of $pā$- ($pātuv$ 'may he protect', etc.); since $pā$- seems to be the normal grade (on the testimony of Sanskrit also), then $paya$- must be for *$pə$-$i̯e$-. Similarly, if the $xšnau$- of $ā$-$xšnautiy$ 'he satisfies' (cf. further zero-grade in $xšnuta$ 'satisfied') is an extension of root $xšnā$- 'learn' (from *$ĝnō$-; see Lex. s.v. $xšnav$-), it must stand for *$ĝnəu$-.

§72. THE pIE LONG DIPHTHONGS appear in OP as $āi$ and $āu$, corresponding to the short diphthongs ai and au; they are easily identified by their writings, except when they are initial, in which position they are ambiguous with the short diphthongs. There are the following occurrences:

$uvāipašiyam$ 'his own', cf. $uvaipašiyahyā$ with the short diphthong (see Lex. s.v.).

root *ei- 'go', augmented in $āiš$ 'he went', where $āi$ is proved by the compound $atiy$-$āiš$ 'he went past'.

root *eis- 'hasten', augmented in causative $frāišayam$ 'I sent forth', from *fra-$āišayam$.

$Θāigarcaiš$, gen. sg. of month-name, with vriddhi (§§125-6) in the first syllable; etymology uncertain.

nom. $dahyāuš$, acc. $dahyāum$ 'province', with lengthening of the diphthong of the stem in these case-forms.

But $āi$ in gen. $Cišpāiš$ and $Cicixrāiš$ is only graphic, cf. §179.IV; $aniyāuvā$, $maškāuvā$ are for -$ā^huvā$, = Skt. -$āsu$ + enclitic -$ā$; $Paišiyāuvādāya$ is probably for $Paišiyā$-$^huvādāya$.

§73. THE pIE STOPS IN PROTO-ARYAN: The pIE stops underwent certain general changes in the passage into Proto-Aryan, as follows:

I. The pIE palatal stops became pAr. sibilants ($ś\ śh\ ź\ źh$).

---

[1] For pIE $əu$, see §71. [2] For possible pronunciation of OP au as $ō$, cf. §61 n1.

II. The pIE labiovelars lost their labialization, and with the pIE velars formed a new series of velars (q qh g gh).

III. The new series of velars split into two series, according to the nature of the following sounds: palatal ($ć$ $ćh$ $ǵ$ $ǵh$), if standing before pIE $ĕ$ $ĭ$ $i̯$; velars (k kh g gh), if standing before other sounds.

IV. In pInd. (and also separately in Proto-Greek), the prior of two aspirated stops standing in the same word and separated by at least one vowel lost its aspiration; this formulation is known as Grassmann's Law. Examples are to be found in §75.III, §76.III, §101. Though this change did not take place in pAr. nor in Iranian, it is cited here to facilitate the proper understanding of Sanskrit words and forms in which it has operated.

V. It is to be remembered that at virtually all times the old general process which worked in pIE continued to operate: that voiced stops and z became voiceless if they came to stand before voiceless stops or s, and voiceless stops and s became voiced if they came to stand before voiced stops or z.

VI. From the pIE stops, therefore, pAr. had the following stock of sounds:

Labial Stops	p	ph	b	bh
Dental Stops	t	th	d	dh
Palatal Sibilants	$ś$	$śh$	$ź$	$źh$
Palatal Stops	$ć$	$ćh$	$ǵ$	$ǵh$
Velar Stops	k	kh	g	gh

§74. THE pIE STOPS IN PROTO-IRANIAN: In the passage from pAr. to pIr., the products of the pIE stops underwent certain additional general changes:

I. The voiceless stops p t $ć$ k, if standing before a consonant, became voiceless spirants f $θ$ $š$ x, unless an Aryan sibilant preceded.

II. The voiceless aspirates, if standing after a sibilant, lost their aspiration and became p t $ć$ k respectively; otherwise they became voiceless spirants f $θ$ $š$ x.

III. The voiced aspirates lost their aspiration, and became identical with the voiced non-aspirates: b d $ǵ$ g.

IV. Details, including the developments of the palatal sibilants and the additions to and exceptions from these general formulations, will appear in the following paragraphs; it is to be noted that $i̯$ is the only consonant before which the pAr. palatals can develop.

§75. THE pIE LABIAL STOPS IN OP: By the formulations in §73 and §74, pIE p will appear as OP p usually, f before consonants; pIE ph will be OP f, but p after s; pIE b and bh will be OP b. The common representations of these sounds in other languages are:

pIE p, Skt. p, Av. p and f, Gk. $π$, Lt. p, Gmc. f, BS p.

pIE ph (a rare sound), Skt. ph, Av. f and p, Gk. $φ$, BS p.

pIE b, Skt. b, Av. b, Gk. $β$, Lt. b, Gmc. p, BS b.

pIE bh, Skt. bh, Av. b and w, Gk. $φ$, Lt. f- and -b-, Gmc. b, BS b.

I. OP p:

pIE *$peri$, OP $pariy$, Av. $pairi$, Skt. $pári$, Gk. περί.

pIE *$pətē$ and *$pətēr$, OP $pitā$, Skt. $pitā́$, Gk. πατήρ, Lt. $pater$.

pIE *$putlo$-, OP $puça$-, Av. $puθra$-, Skt. $putrá$-, Osc. $puclo$-.

pIE *apo, OP apa-, Skt. $ápa$, Gk. ἀπό.

pIE *$nepōt$-s, OP $napā$, Skt. $nápāt$, Lt. $nepōs$.

OP gen. $xšapa$ 'by night', Av. $xšap$-, Skt. $kṣap$-.

II. OP f from pIE p before consonant:

pIE *pro, OP fra- as prefix, Skt. $prá$, Gk. πρό.

pIE *$prek̂$- in OP ptc. u-$fraštam$ 'well punished', cf. Lt. $precor$ 'I ask', and pIE *$pr̥k̂$-$sk̂ō$, OP $parsā$-miy, Skt. $pr̥cchá$-mi, Lt. $poscō$.

There is no identifiable example of OP f from pIE ph; OP $kaufa$- 'mountain', Av. $kaofa$-, seems to have no cognates outside Iranian.

III. OP b is mostly from pIE bh; for pIE b was an extremely rare sound, and its only probable occurrence in OP is in $ā$-$biǵ$-na-, second component of $Bagābigna$-, if this is a participle to the root in Skt. $bīja$- 'seed' (see Lex. s.v.).

pIE *$ebherom$ 'I bore', OP $abaram$ 'I esteemed', Skt. $ábharam$, Gk. ἔφερον.

pIE *$bhrātē$ and *$bhrātēr$, OP $brātā$, Skt. $bhrā́tā$, Lt. $frāter$.

pAr. *$abhi$,[1] OP $abiy$, Skt. $abhí$.

pIE *u-$bhō$ and -$bhōu$ 'both', OP $ubā$, Skt. $ubhā́$ $ubhā́u$, Gk. ἄμφω, Lt. am-$bō$.

---

[1] Conflux of pIE *$m̥bhi$ and pIE *$obhi$, see Lex. s.v. $abiy$.

In some words OP *b*, though from pIE *bh*, corresponds to Skt. *b*, because Grassmann's Law (§73.IV) operated in Indic:

pIE **bhendh-* 'bind', in OP *baⁿdaka-* 'subject', cf. Skt. *bandhá-* 'bond', and the *b-* in Eng. *bind, bond*, from pIE *bh-*.

pIE **bherĝh-* 'be high', in *Bardiya-, baršan-, brazmaniya-*; see Lex. s.vv.

IV. Combinations of the labials with following consonants, other than *r*, chance to be rare in OP; there is however **ap-bhis* > **abbhiš* > OP *abiš* 'with the waters' (JAOS 62.269–70; §73.V, §130). For *p* in *sp* from pIE *ku̯*, §90; for *b* in *zb* from *ĝhu̯*, §91; for *f* from *su̯* in *Viⁿdafarnah-*, §118.IV.

V. OP *p b f* are in some instances not traceable to pIE forebears or are definitely borrowings from outside sources; such are *piru-* 'ivory', *siⁿkabru-* 'carnelian', *naiba-* 'good' (only in Iranian), and many place and personal names, such as *Pirāva* 'Nile', *Putāya-* 'Libyan', *Bābiruš* 'Babylon', *Arabāya* 'Arabia', *Arbairā-* 'Arbela', *Ufrātu-* 'Euphrates', *Naditabaira* 'Nidintu-Bel', *Nabukudracara* 'Nebuchadrezzar'.

§76. The pIE Dental Stops in OP: By the formulations in §73 and §74, pIE *t* appears as OP *t* usually, but as *θ* before consonants; pIE *th* becomes OP *θ*, but *t* after *s;* pIE *d* and *dh* become OP *d*. But *θ* from pIE *t* before consonants underwent additional changes in some combinations, which will therefore be reserved for §77–§82. The usual correspondences of the pIE dentals in other languages are the following:

pIE *t*, Skt. *t*, Av. *t* and *θ*, Gk. τ, Lt. *t*, Gmc. *þ*, BS *t*.

pIE *th*, Skt. *th*, Av. *θ* and *t*, Gk. *θ̇*, Lt. *f- -d- -b-*.

pIE *d*, Skt. *d*, Av. *d* and δ, Gk. δ, Lt. *d*, BS *d*.

pIE *dh*, Skt. *dh*, Av. *d* and δ, Gk. θ, Lt. *f- -d- -b-*, BS *d*.

I. OP *t* from pIE *t:*

pIE **eti*, OP *atiy*, Skt. *áti* 'beyond', Gk. ἔτι 'yet', Lt. *et* 'and'.

pIE **ute*, OP *utā*, Skt. *utá*, Gk. Hom. ἤ-ύτε 'like'.

pAr. **tanū-*, OP *tanū-* 'body', Av. *tanū-*, Skt. *tanū́-*.

pAr. **tuvam*, OP *tuvam*, Skt. Ved. *tuvám*, cf. Lt. *tū*.

pIE **pətē*, OP *pitā*, §75.I; pIE **bhrātē*, OP *brātā*, §75.III.

pIE **qrto-*, OP *karta-*, Skt. *kr̥tá-*.

II. OP *θ* from pIE *th*:

pIE **pn̥thi-*, OP acc. *paθim* 'path', Skt. *paθí-*.

pIE **rotho-*, OP *u-raθa-* 'having good chariots', Av. *raθa-* 'wagon', Skt. *rátha-*, cf. Lt. *rota* 'wheel' (with pIE *t*, not *th*).

pAr. **i̯athā*, OP *yaθā*, Skt. *yáthā*; so also OP *avaθā*.

OP *mauθ-, Āθiyābaušna-, gaiθā-, fraθara-, miθah-*, see Lex. s.vv.

OP *raxθatuv*, an imv. of entirely unknown connections.

OP *t* from pAr. *th* after *s*, in OP *stā-* (see Lex.), Av. *stā-*, Skt. *sthā-*, from pAr. *sthā-* (evidence for the aspirate is lacking outside Indic; cf. Gk. Dor. ἴ-στᾱ-μι, Lt. *stā-re*, oCS *sta-ti*).

III. OP *d* from pIE *d*:

pIE **deii̯o-* 'deity', OP *daiva-* '(evil) god', Av. *daēva-*, Skt. *devá-*, Lt. *dīvos deus*.

pIE **ped-* 'foot', loc. in OP *ni-padiy*, Skt. *padí*, Lt. abl. *pede*, Gk. dat. ποδί; pIE **pedo-m*, OP *pati-padam* 'on its base', Skt. *padá-* 'step', Gk. πέδον 'ground'; pIE **pōdo-* 'foot', OP inst. dual *pādaibiyā*, Skt. *pā́da-*, cf. Gt. *fōtu-*.

pIE **dō-* 'give', OP *dadātuv* 'let him give', Skt. *dádātu*, cf. Gk. διδότω.

pIE **sed-* 'sit', OP *had-iš* 'seat, abode', Gk. ἕδος 'seat'; causative in OP *niy-ašādayam* 'I established' (on -š-, §117), Skt. *ásādayam*.

pIE insep. prefix **dus-* 'ill', OP *duš-*, Av. *duš-*, Skt. *duṣ-*, Gk. δυσ-.

pIE **du̯itīi̯o-* 'second', OP *duvitīya-m*, Skt. *dvitīya-*.

OP *d* from pAr. *dh* from pIE *dh*:

pIE **dhē-* 'put', OP *adā* 'he created', Skt. *ádhāt*.

pIE **dher-* 'hold', OP *dārayāmiy* 'I hold', Skt. *dhāráyāmi*.

pIE **dhu̯or-* 'door', in OP loc. *duvarayā*, Av. *dvar-*, Skt. *dhvar-*, cf. Gk. θύρᾱ.

OP *baⁿdaka* 'subject', to pIE **bhendh-*, §75.III.

OP *hadā* 'with', Skt. *sahá*, from pIE **sm̥-dhe*; same suffix in *avadā, idā, ada-kaiy*.

With Skt. *d* from pIE *dh* by Grassmann's Law (§73.IV):

pIE **dhrugh-i̯e-* in OP *adurujiya* 'he lied', Skt. *drúhyati* 'he deceives', Gm. *trugen*; pIE **dhrougho-* in OP *drauga-* 'Lie', Skt. *dróha- drógha-* 'injury'.

pIE **dhiĝhā*, OP *didā* 'wall', cf. Skt. *dehī́-*, Gk. τεῖχος.

pIE *dhugh- in OP ha-dugā- 'inscription', see Lex. s.v.

Reduplicated forms of pIE *dhē-, OP adadā, Skt. ádadhāt.

Reduplicated personal name, Dādarši- = Skt. adj. dā́dhṛṣi- 'bold', to pIE *dhers- seen in OP adaršnauš 'he dared', Skt. ádhṛṣnot.

IV. On pIE *t* before a consonant, §77–§82, on other special developments of non-final dental stops, §83; on final dentals, §84; on dental + dental, §85; on OP θ and d from pIE palatal stops, §§87–8.

V. There are also numerous instances of OP *t θ d* which are not traceable with certainty to IE origins, or are demonstrably borrowings from non-IE sources. Among these are *taka-* 'shield, round hat' in *taka-bara-*, *tacara-* 'palace', *dipi-* 'inscription' (see Lex. s.v.), *spāda-* 'army' (only in Iranian), imv. *raxθatuv* of uncertain meaning; and personal and place names such as *Atamaita-* (Elamite), *Naditabaira* (Semitic), *Ufratu-* 'Euphrates', *Katpatuka* 'Cappadocia', *Tigrā-* 'Tigris', *Putāya-* 'Libyan', *Dātuvahya-*, *Daha-*, *Dubāla-*, *Mudrāya-*, *Aθurā*, etc.

§77. pIE *t* BEFORE CONSONANTS became the voiceless spirant θ in pIr.; but further changes also took place, cf. §78–§82.

§78. pAr. *tr*, from pIE *tr* and *tl*, became (except after a spirant, §79) pIr. θr, which persisted in Av. and in Med., but became a sibilant in OP; it is transcribed by ç, and apparently was a sound intermediate between pure dental *s* and palatal *š*. Examples:

pIE *putlo-, OP puça- 'son', Av. puθra-, Skt. putrá-, Osc. puclo-.

pIE *pətr-os (not original, but a later remade form), OP piça, Av. piθrō, Gk. πατρός; gen. of OP pitā 'father'.

pAr. *kšatram 'kingdom', OP xšaçam, Av. xšaθrəm, Skt. kṣatrám; but Med. θr in Xšaθrita, the name assumed by the Median rebel Phraortes.

pIE *tritii̯o- 'third', OP çitīyam, Av. θritya- (graphic for θritīya-), cf. Skt. tṛtīya-, Lt. tertius.

Av. ātar- āθr- 'fire', seen in the OP month-name Āçiyādiya- and probably in the personal name Āçina (despite the fact that Āçina was an Elamite).

Av. čiθra- 'seed, lineage', OP çiça-.

OP vaça- 'bow', of uncertain etymology, in vaça-bara- 'bowbearer'.

Skt. mitrá- 'friend', borrowed into Iranian as epithet of a divinity, and eventually his name; in OP, written Mitra- Mⁱtra- Mⁱθra-, miça- in derivative ha-miçiya- 'united (in conspiracy)', misa- in personal name Vaʰu-misa- (= Skt. *vasu-mitra-; see below). The variant orthographies represent in part differences of dialect, and in part the variant pronunciations of a foreign word incompletely assimilated to the phonetic pattern of the dialects in which it was being used.

That the product of pIr. θr was in OP a sibilant is shown by the orthography of borrowed words. Thus the ç of Ciçantaxma- is represented by š in Elam. ši-iš-ša-an-tak-ma (the tr of Akk. ši-it-ra-an-tah-ma is based on the Median form of the name, since he was a native of Sagartia in Media). Note also the following:

OP *Ciça-farnā, Gk. Τισσα-φέρνης, Lycian cizza-prñna.

OP Arta-xšaçā, Elam. ir-tak-ša-aš-ša, Akk. ar-ta-ak-ša-as-su (Vases b and c; ar-tak-šat-su in longer inscriptions), Aram. (Elephantine) 'rtxšsš, Lydian artakśassa.

OP Vau-misa for -miça (see above), Elam. ma-u-mi-iš-ša, Akk. ú-mi-is-si; while Akk. mi-it-ri corresponds to the non-OP Mitra- or Mⁱθra-.

OP Āçina, Elam. ha-iš-ši-na, Akk. a-ši-na.

OP Āçiyādiya-, Elam. ha-iš-ši-i̯a-ti-i̯a-iš.

OP Çūšā-, from Elam. šu-ša-an, whence also Akk. šu-ša-an.

On ç from pIE k̂l in niy-açārayam 'I restored', see §94.

§79. pAr. *tr* AFTER SPIRANTS (including the sibilants) appears unchanged in Avestan. This seems to have been the development also in Median, as in the name of the Mede Uvaxštra- 'Cyaxares', Elam. ma-ak-iš-ta-ra, Akk. ú-ma-ku-iš-tar. The name of the northeastern province Bactria, Gk. Βάκτρα, likewise shows a non-OP form in Bāxtriš, Elam. ba-ik-tur-ri-iš, Akk. ba-aḫ-tar; but a pure OP *Bāxšiš or *Bāxçiš is attested by the alternative Elam. ba-ak-ši-iš. Finally, OP uša-bāri- 'camel-borne', by comparison with Av. uštra- 'camel', shows that in OP, even after a spirant or a sibilant, tr became θr and then ç, and that after š the ç was assimilated to that preceding š.

§80. pIE *tı̯* became regularly (§77) pIr. *θı̯*, which survived in Avestan and in Median, but became *šı̯* in OP:

OP *xšāyaθiya* 'king', from pAr. **kšāi̯ati̯a-*; a word of the Median officialdom.

OP *hašiyam* 'true', Skt. *satyám*.

OP *uvā-maršiyuš* (see Lex.), Skt. *mr̥tyú-* 'death'.

OP *uvă-pašiya-* 'belonging to one's self', from pAr. **pati̯a-* (see Lex.).

OP *anušiya-* 'follower', from **anu-ti̯o-*.

The preposition *aθiy* seems to be a sandhi doublet of *atiy*; see Lex. s.v.

For the retention of *t* in *tya-* and its forms, see Lex. s.v.

§81. pIE *tu̯* became regularly (§77) pIr. *θu̯*, which remained in OP with the writing *θᵃuvᵃ* = *θuv*:

pIE **tu̯ē* + acc. -*m*, OP *θuvām*, Av. *θwąm*, Skt. *tvā́m*.

pAr. **gātu- gātu̯- gātav-*, Skt. *gātú- gātv- gātav-*, Av. *gātu- gāθw- gātav-*, OP (with generalized *θ*) acc. *gāθum*, loc. *gāθavā*.

pAr. *kratu-* etc., Skt. *krátu-* etc., Av. *xratu- xraθw- xratav-*, OP (with generalized *θ*) acc. *xraθum*.

§82. pIE *tn* became regularly (§77) pIr. *θn*, which remained in Avestan but became OP *šn*; thus the pAr. **aratn- aratan-* gave Av. dual *arəθnå*, but OP *arašn-* and (with extension of the *š*) *arašan-* 'cubit', in inst. pl. *arašaniš* (see Lex. s.v. *arašan-*). For *vašnā* and *baršnā*, see §96, §120.

§83. OTHER DEVELOPMENTS OF NON-FINAL DENTAL STOPS.

I. pIE -*d-n-* became pIr. -*n-* (shortening of -*nn-*, §130), as in pIE **u̯eid-ne-*, OP *vaināmiy* 'I see', Av. 3d sg. *vaēnaiti*; cf. the same root with nasal infix (instead of nasal suffix) in Skt. *vindáti* 'he finds', and in OP *Viⁿda^t-farnah-* 'Intaphernes' (see Lex. s.v.; -*n-* proved by Gk., Elam., Akk. transliterations).

II. In two words *θ* is found where *d* is expected: OP *θanuvaniya* 'bowman', where Skt. has *dh* in *dhánvan-* 'bow';

OP *spāda-* 'army', in the name of the Mede *Taxmaspāda*, but with *θ* in its apparent derivative *spāθmaida-* 'camp, war'. No likely solution of this variation has as yet been suggested.

III. The province name *Katpatuka* shows an unassimilated -*tp-*, established by the Elam. and Akk. equivalents; the name is non-Iranian and has not been remodeled to the Iranian or Persian pattern of clusters.

§84. FINAL DENTALS were weakened and did not appear in the writing of OP. After *ă* they remained in the pronunciation sufficiently to prevent the writing of the vowel as long (§36.III): OP *abara* 'he bore', Skt. *ábharat*; OP 3d pl. *abara*, Skt. *ábharan*, for **ebheront*. After *ā*, it is likely that they disappeared entirely;[1] for *hyāparam* seems to be abl. **hyād + aparam*, and the crasis indicates a previous loss of the -*d*.

Final -*d* disappeared after *i*, as in the encl. OP -*ciy*, Skt. *cid*, pIE *q^uid*; OP *naiy* 'not', Av. *nōit̰*, from **ne + id*. After *u* the final *t* seems to be retained as *š* in OP *akunauš* 'he made', *adaršnauš* 'he dared', Skt. *ákr̥ṇot ádhr̥ṣṇot*; but this *š* is better taken as an extension of the *s* of the aorist, after which -*t* would be lost. The prefix *ud* 'up', which appears unchanged before a vowel in *ud-apatatā* 'he rose up (in rebellion)', suffers complete assimilation of the *d* in *uzma-* 'stake' (from **ud-zma-*), and became *us-* in *us-tašanā-* 'staircase' in the dental cluster (§85).

For the sandhi combination of final *d* with initial *c*, see §105.

§85. THE DENTAL CLUSTERS *tst(h)* AND *dzd(h)* (§58.D) properly lost the prior dental by dissimilation, and in fact do have this development in Iranian and in Greek; but in Indic they in most instances lost the sibilant and in Italic the second dental, through analogies of various kinds.[1] Thus their usual developments are the following:

pIE *tst*, Av. OP *st*, Skt. *tt*, Gk. στ, Lt. *ss*.

pIE *tsth*, Av. OP *st*, Skt. *tth*, Gk. σθ, Lt. *ss*.

pIE *dzd*, Av. OP *zd*, Skt. *dd*, Gk. ζ, Lt. (no certain examples).

pIE *dzdh*, Av. OP *zd*, Skt. *ddh*, Gk. σθ, Lt. *ss*.

Further changes of analogical nature took place in a number of these combinations, especially that the participle to a root in *dh*, which has -*dzdh-* from -*dh-t-*, often remade this in

---

[1] Cf the similar difference in development in Latin, where -*d* was kept after short vowels, as in *ad*, *sed*, *id*; but was lost after long vowels, as in *suprā*, *sē*, *Gnaeō*, Old Latin *suprād*, *sēd*, *Gnaivōd*.

§85.[1] Cf Kent, Lg 8.18–26; Emeneau, Lg. 9.232–6.

Iranian and Greek, to the more familiar -tst- (from -t-t- and -d-t-).

There are the following examples in OP:

pasti- 'foot-soldier', from **patsti-* from **ped-ti-*.

ustašanā- 'staircase', from **utst-* from **ud-te-*.

aruvastam 'activity', in form an abstract **arvattam* (becoming -tst-); but see Lex. s.v.

basta 'bound', ptc. to pIE root **bhendh-*; therefore **bhṇdh-to-* > **badzdha-* (Skt. *baddhá-*), replaced by **batsta-* in Iranian.

gasta- 'evil', ptc. to pIE root in Av. *ganti-* 'stench', Skt. *gandhá-* 'odor', with similar replacement of -dzdh- by -tst-.

azdā adv. 'known', Skt. *addhá* 'thus, truly', from pAr. **adzdha-*.

Aura-mazdā 'Ahuramazda', from **ma(n)dzhā-s*, see Lex. s.v.

§86. THE pIE PALATAL STOPS k̂ k̂h ĝ ĝh became sibilants in pAr., ś[1] śh ź źh; the voiceless aspirate was very rare and may be omitted from the following discussion. pAr. ś ź źh appeared in Skt. as ś (often transcribed ç), j, h; in Av. as s, z, z, since voiced aspirates lost their aspiration in pIr. There was a double representation in OP: θ and d in pure OP, s and z in words borrowed from Median (other developments in some clusters, §89–§97). In the *centum* branches of IE, these sounds developed precisely like the pure velars (§98).

§87. pIE k̂ BEFORE VOWELS, unless preceded by s, became OP θ, Med. s:

pIE **k̂ens-* in OP *aθaham*[1] 'I said', Av. root *saŋh-*, Skt. *śaṣ-*, Lt. pres. *cēnseō*.

pIE **nek̂-* 'destruction', in OP *vi-nāθayatiy* 'he injures', Lt. *nocet*, Skt. *nāśáyati*.

pIE **mak̂-* in OP *maθišta* 'greatest', Av. *masišta-* 'longest', Gk. μήκιστος.

pIE **ak̂-* in OP *aθaⁿga-* 'stone', Av. *asəⁿga-*; cf. *asan-* 'stone' with Med. s, in nom. *asā*, and possibly in *Asa-garta-* (see Lex. s.v.). Cf. also acc. *asmānam* 'sky', Av. *asman-* 'sky, stone', Skt. *áśman-* 'stone', Gk. ἄκμων 'anvil' (*sm* from *k̂m* is probably OP as well as Med.; §95).

pIE **u̯ik̂-*, OP *viθ-* 'house, royal house', Av. *vīs-* 'noble's residence', Skt. *viś-* 'dwelling place', cf. Gk. οἶκος 'house'; OP inst. pl. *viθbiš* keeps θ by influence of the stem. Deriv., OP adj. *viθa-* 'belonging to the royal house'.

OP *θikā* 'rubble, broken stone', see Lex. s.v.; probably from the same, with Med. s, the name of the Median fortress *Sikayahuvatiš*.

Parθava 'Parthia' and *Pārsa* 'Persia', where the θ and the s seem to reverse the local values of k̂; both provinces were apparently named by rulers of non-local origin.

vasiy 'at will, greatly', with Med. s if loc. to a root-noun, **u̯ek̂-i*, rather than *vasaiy*, loc. to **u̯ek̂-sk̂o-* (see Lex. s.v.).

kāsaka 'semiprecious stone', with Med. s if correctly referred to the same root as Skt. *kaś-* 'shine'.

Other examples of OP θ from pIE k̂ are to be seen in *θakata-, θard-, θaⁿd-, θuxra-, θūravāhara-*, and perhaps in *θāigarci-, θatagu-, θarmi-*; see Lex. s.vv.

§88. pIE ĝ AND ĝh before vowels and r (from pIE r and l) became OP d, Med. z:

pIE **ĝrei̯os*, OP *draya* 'sea', Av. *zrayō*, Skt. *jráyas* 'expanse'.

pIE **ĝī-* in OP *adīnam* 'I took by force', Av. *zināiti* 'he harms', Skt. *jáyati* 'he overpowers'.

pIE **i̯aĝetai*, OP *yadataiy* 'he worships', Av. *yazaite*, Skt. *yájate*.

pIE **r̥ĝn̥to-*, OP *ardata-* 'silver', Av. *ərəzata-*, Lt. *argentum*, cf. Skt. *rajatám*.

pIE **ĝeus-* in OP *dauštar-* 'friend', Av. *zaoš-* 'enjoy', Skt. *juṣ-*.

pIE **u̯eĝ-* in OP *vazraka-* 'great', in the royal title and as epithet of the Earth, cf. Av. *vazra-* 'club', Skt. *vájra-* 'Indra's thunderbolt'; with Med. z.

pIE **ĝono-*, OP *zana-* 'man' with Med. z, Av. *zana-*, Skt. *jána-*; in OP *vispa-zana-, paru-zana-*, and (restored month-name) *Varka-zana-*, OP d is seen in **visa-dana-* '*vispazana-*', inferred from the Elamite *mi-iš-ša-da-na*.

pIE **eĝhom*, OP *adam* 'I', Av. *azəm*, Skt. *ahám*.

pIE **ĝhosto-*, OP *dasta-* 'hand', Av. *zasta-*, Skt. *hásta-*.

pIE **ĝhl̥-* in OP *daraniya-* 'gold', Av. *zaranya-*, Skt. *híraṇya-*, cf. Eng. *gold*.

pIE **dhiĝhā*, OP *didā* 'wall, fortress', cf. Skt. *dehī-*, Gk. τεῖχος.

pIE enclitic particle **ĝhi*, OP *-diy*, Av. *zī*, Skt. *hi*.

---

[1] Except before s; see §92.

§87.[1] Perhaps lacking the nasal in the OP present-tense stem; see reff in Lex s v. *θah-*.

pIE *ĝhūros, OP zūra 'wrong', Av. zūrō, cf. Skt. hváras- 'deceit'; the OP has Med. z.

OP Zraⁿka 'Drangiana', name of an eastern province, with non-OP z from ĝ or ĝh; cf. Gk. Σαράγγαι, and also Δραγγιανή, with OP d.

Other examples of OP d from pIE ĝ are seen in ardastāna-, Ardumaniš, avahar[da], uradana-, dan- in adāna, vardana-; from pIE ĝh in gaud-, Bardiya; from pIE ĝ or ĝh in yaud-. For materials on these words, see Lex. s.vv.

§89. pIE ḱi̯ became pAr. śi̯, and then OP θi̯ and finally ši̯, since θ before i̯ became š in OP (§80); the only example is a dubious one, paišiyā- 'written text', from *peiḱ- or *poiḱ- + i̯ā-, in nsf. pai[š]iyā DB 4.91, and perhaps as the first element of the place-name Paišiyā^huvādā- (see Lex. s.vv.).

§90. pIE ḱu̯ became pAr. śu̯, and then Av. sp, Med. sp, OP s, Skt. śv:

pIE *eḱu̯o- 'horse', OP asa- in acc. asam and in asabāra-; OP aspa- (with Med. sp) in uvaspa-, Aspacanah-, Vištāspa-; Av. aspa-, Skt. áśva-, Lt. equos.

pIE *u̯iḱu̯o-, OP visa- 'all', also in visadahyu-; OP vispa- (with Med. sp) in vispazana-; Av. vīspa-, Skt. víśva-.

pIE *ḱu̯ā- in Av. spā- 'throw, set down', OP sā- 'erect, build', in s-aor. pass. frāsah[ya] DSf 27 (etymology not certain!).

§91. pIE ĝhu̯ became pAr. ẑhu̯, and then Med. and Av. zb,¹ Skt. hv, but OP z; the OP texts have one example of the Median value and one of the OP value:

pIE ĝhu̯- in OP patiy-azbayam 'I proclaimed', Av. root zba-, Skt. pres. hváyati.

OP h^azānam for acc. hizānam 'tongue', Av. hizvā-, Skt. jihvá-; see Lex. s.v. for details.

§92. pIE ḱs became pAr. čš and reverted in Indic (Skt.) to kṣ,¹ but became pIr. šš, shortened to š:

pIE aor. *e-peiḱ-s-m̥, OP niy-apaišam; cf. other forms in Lex. s.v. paiθ-.

---

¹ For the phonetic value of -b- in -zb-, see discussion by Debrunner, IF 56.176-7.

§92.¹ If pIE ḱ in ḱs had become the usual pAr. sibilant ś, it is difficult to see how the ś could have yielded the stop in Skt kṣ. Some other development of ḱ in pAr. before s must therefore be assumed.

§93. pIE ḱt (from ḱ or ĝ + t) became pAr. št, and then pIran. št, OP and Av. št, and Skt. ṣṭ; these clusters are seen in derivatives with a t-suffix:

pIE *piḱ-to-, OP ni-pišta- 'engraved'; *peiḱ-t- in inf. ni-paištanaiy; for cognates, see Lex. s.v. paiθ-.

pIE *u̯iḱ-to- 'entered', OP višta- 'ready' in Vištāspa-, see Lex. s.v.

pIE *preḱ-to-, OP ^hu-frašta- 'well punished'; for cognates, see Lex. s.v. fraθ-.

pIE *r̥ĝ-ta-tā- (with haplology) or fem. ptc. *r̥ĝ-tā-, OP aršta- 'rectitude'; from the root *reĝ-r̥ĝ- 'direct, hold upright', cf. rāsta- below.

Sometimes OP has st instead of št; this is probably analogical to the -st- of dental stems, such as basta- to pIE *bhendh-, gasta- 'evil' to pIE *gendh- (cf. §85), since pIE ḱ and ĝ(h) gave OP θ and d in other forms of the paradigm.¹ The examples are:

^hu-frasta-, varying with ^hu-frašta-, see above.

pIE *r̥ĝ-to-,² OP rāsta- 'straight, right', Av. rāšta- 'directed', Lt. rēctus 'directed, ruled, straight'.

pIE *neḱ-to-, OP vi-nasta- 'damage'; for cognates, see Lex. s.v. naθ-.

§94. pIE ḱl became pAr. and pIr. śr, then OP θr, whence ç; the only example is niy-açārayam

---

¹ This interpretation of the st from ḱt now seems to me preferable to that which I formerly maintained (as in Lg 21 58, following a suggestion of Bv. Gr. §125), that št was Median and st was OP; for the borrowing by OP of the words and forms which contain št can hardly be motivated. Tedesco, Le Monde Oriental 15 203-4 (referred to by Bv., l.c), thinks st merely a later development from št (of any origin, including št from st, §115, §117), found in many Phl words but not in all, and more extensively in SW Phl (derived from OP, §4.II) than in NW Phl. (derived from Median, §4.I). His conclusion is based on the spellings in the Turfan Phl. (§4.IV); but the Turfan documents are of the 3d century A.D , about 700 years after the time of Darius and Xerxes, in whose inscriptions the -st- forms of OP are found. With such a gap in time the variation seen in OP can hardly be considered valid testimony to a preliminary stage of the development seen in the Turfan texts. ² The length of the vowel, which is not in point here, is probably due to analogical extension from the s-aorist active, where the long ablaut-grade was a regular formation in pIE, but may not have extended to the participle until pIE had split into the separate branches.

'I restored', in which the root is that seen in Lt. *clīnō* 'I lean'; for details, see Lex. s.v. *çay-*.

§95. pIE *k̂m* and *ĝhm* gave respectively in OP *sm* and *zm* (not *θm* and *dm*, so far as we can tell[1]):

pIE **ak̂mōn-* in OP acc. *asmānam* 'sky', Skt. *áśmānam* 'stone', cf. OP *aθa^nga-* 'stone' and (with Med. *s*) *asan-* 'stone', §87.

pIE **ĝhem-* in Lith. *žẽmė* 'earth', Lt. *humus*, but **ĝhm-* in OP *u-zma-* 'stake' and in the province-name *Uvāra-zmī-*; see Lex. s.vv.

pIE **bhreĝh-* in OP *braz-man-iya-* 'prayerful'; see Lex. s.v.

§96. pIE *k̂n ĝn ĝhn* became pAr. *śn źn źhn*, then all became pIr. *śn* since sibilants became voiceless before *n* in Iranian (§120); initial *śn* took a prothetic *x*. This *xśn* remained unchanged initial in Av. and OP, and was sometimes analogically extended to medial positions.

pIE **ĝnōsk̂ēti*, OP 3d sg. subj. *xšnāsātiy* 'he may know', Lt. *gnōscet* 'he will learn', Skt. root *jñā-* 'know'; the *ĝ* is clearly shown in the *z*- of Av. *zixšnåŋhəmnā*, reduplicated ptc. npf. of the desiderative (for reduplication, cf. Skt. perf. *jajñáu*, Gk. pres. γιγνώσκω). See Lex. s.v. *xšnā-*.

pIE **ĝnu-to-*, OP *xšnuta* 'satisfied', Av. *xšnūtō*; medial *-xšn-* in the compound OP *ā-xšnautiy* 'he satisfies'. See Lex. s.vv. *xšnav-*, *uxšnav-*.

pIE **u̯ek̂-* 'wish' + suffix *-no-*, OP *vašna-* 'favor';[1] see Lex. s.v.

pIE *ĝhn* in medial position is found in the *šn* of *baršnā* 'by height' and probably in *ašnaiy* 'near';[1] see Lex. s.vv.

§97. pIE *sk̂* became pAr. *śś*, then pIr. *śś*, *ss*, shortened to *s*, which is seen in Av. and OP; but pAr. *śś* developed in Indic to Skt. *(c)ch*.[1] This cluster is seen especially in the present-tense suffix of certain verbs:

pIE **pr̥k̂-sk̂e-*, in OP *parsāmiy* 'I punish', Av. *pərəsaiti* 'he asks', Skt. *pr̥cchāti*, Lt. *poscit*.

---

[1] A somewhat differing view by Nyberg, Studia Indo-Iranica W. Geiger 213–6, does not convince me.

§96.[1] On Avestan *-sn-* for expected *-šn-*, as in *vasna* 'by the favor', *asne* 'near', see Bthl. Gdr. IP 1.§33.1.

§97.[1] On the relation of Skt. *ch* with *c* on the one hand and with a sibilant on the other, see J Wackernagel, Altindische Grammatik 1.153–8; A. Thumb, Handbuch des Sanskrit 1.113.

pIE **tr̥-sk̂e-ti*, OP *tarsatiy* 'he fears', Av. *tərəsaiti*.

pIE **ĝnōsk̂ēti*, OP *xšnāsātiy* 'he may know', Lt. *gnōscet* 'he will learn'.

pIE **i̯m̥-sk̂e-* in OP *āyasatā* 'he took as his own', Av. pres. *yasaiti*, Skt. *yácchati*.

pIE **r̥-sk̂eti*, Skt. *r̥cchāti* 'he moves'; but OP imf. *arasam* 'I went off' from **re-sk̂e-*.

pIE **u̯ek̂-skoi*, if *v^aš^iy^a* is to be normalized *vasaiy* rather than *vasiy*; see Lex. s.v. *vasiy*.

§98. THE pIE VELARS AND LABIOVELARS IN pAr. fell together into one set of velar stops (§73.II), which then split into two series by the Aryan Law of Palatalization (§73.III): palatals *ć ćh ǵ ǵh*, before pIE *ĕ ĭ i̯*; velars *k kh g gh*, elsewhere. The sounds therefore reached the following stage in pAr. (in Skt. the aspirates were subject to the dissimilation known as Grassmann's Law, §73.IV; and *gh* and *ǵh*, where not so changed, often became Skt. *h* rather than *gh* and *jh*):

pIE Velars and Labiovelars		pAr. Velars	pAr. Palatals
q	q^u	k	ć
qh	q^uh	kh	ćh
g	g^u	g	ǵ
gh	g^uh	gh	ǵh

The voiceless aspirates are so rare that in the main they may be disregarded from now on. In pIr., the voiced aspirates lost their aspiration; the voiceless non-aspirate *k* before consonants became the voiceless spirant *x*, and the voiceless non-aspirate *ć* before *i̯* (the only consonant before which it could originate) became *š*.

Examples of these developments will be given in the following sections; but while words containing these sounds are of frequent occurrence in OP, it is often impossible to distinguish between original velars and original labiovelars, because we have no cognate in a non-Aryan language where alone they are distinguished. Not infrequently also the words occur only in Iranian, where we cannot distinguish between original voiced non-aspirates and original voiced aspirates.

§99. pAr. *k* AND *ć* are found without further change in OP, in the following:

pIE *q-*, in OP *kāra-* 'people, army', cf. Lith. *kāras* 'war', Gm. *Heer* 'army'.

pIE *q^uos-q^uid, OP kaš-ciy, Skt. ka-s, Lt. quo-, and Skt. (particle) cid, Lt. quid.

pIE *$ul q^u$o- 'wolf' in Skt. vŕka-s, OP Varkāna- 'Hyrcania', Eng. wolf.

pIE *$seq^u ē$, OP hacā 'from', Skt. sácā 'with', to root in Lt. sequor 'I follow'.

pIE *leuq- 'shine' in OP rauca 'day', Skt. rócas- 'light', Gk. λευκός 'white'.

pAr. root kar- 'make, do', OP pres. kunautiy, imf. pass. akariya, zūra-kara- 'evil-doer'; but *ker- in pres. inf. cartanaiy, *kēr- in ucāram 'well-done, successful', *ke-kr- in perf. opt. caxriyā.

OP Maka, a province, but ethnic Maciya, with palatalization because the suffix began with the palatal sound.

OP Ākaufaciyā 'men of *Ākaufaka', similarly.

pAr. kāma-, OP kāma 'desire', Skt. kā́ma-.

So also other instances of k and c in OP, though many of them are in words with very scanty etymological parallels, and others are obvious borrowings from other languages, such as maškā- 'inflated skin', Katpatuka 'Cappadocia', Kūša- 'Ethiopia'.

Where pAr. k stood before varying vowels, there may be variation in the products (as in the forms from root kar-), or one value may be generalized: OP rauca from nom.-acc. pIE *leuqos, with c from oblique cases, where pIE had *leuqes- (cf. Gk. γένος γένεος, Lt. genus generis).

§100. pAr. kh seems to appear in a few words, which have no far-reaching etymological connections:

xaudā- 'cap', also in tigraxauda- 'wearing the pointed cap', cf. Av. zaranya-xaoδa- 'wearing a golden helmet'.

mayūxa- 'door-knob', Skt. mayūkha- 'peg'.

haxā- 'friend' in Haxā-maniš 'Achaemenes', Skt. nom. sákhā.

Also the place-name Raxā, personal names Arxa and Sku^{n}xa, and the doubtful words Xaršadašya and Hadaxaya; see Lex. s.vv.

For OP x from k before consonants, see §102 and §103. Corresponding to Skt. khánati 'he digs' we have OP akaniya 'it was dug', Av. kan- 'dig', and Av. xā̊ 'well', with unexplained variation between aspirate and non-aspirate.

§101. pAr. g and ǵ, gh and ǵh, appearing in OP as g and j; there is the same difficulty in determining precisely the pIE origin, as has been met in the preceding sections.

pIE root *g^uem- 'come', Lt. veniō, in OP ptc. pl. parā-gmatā 'gone forth', ha^{m}gmatā 'assembled', but with palatalization pres. opt. ā-jamiyā 'may it come', Skt. (without palatalization) gamyāt.

pIE *$g^u ī̯o$- 'living', OP jīva, Skt. jīvá-s, Lt. vīvos; pIE *g^uoi- in OP acc. gaiθām 'cattle'.

pIE stem *g^uou- 'cow' in personal names Gaubaruva, Gau-māta; see Lex.

pAr. *ghauša-, OP gauša- 'ear', Skt. ghóṣa- 'noise'.

pIE *dḷghos 'long', OP adv. dargam, Skt. dīrghá-s, Gk. δολιχός.

pIE *bhago-, OP baga 'god', Skt. bhága- 'dispenser', Gk. -φαγος 'eater'; with palatalization, OP bājim 'tribute'.

pIE *dhrougho-, OP drauga 'the Lie', and with palatal suffix -eno-, draujana- 'follower of the Lie'; adurujiya 'he lied', denominative verb to the stem seen in Av. (acc.) Druǰ-im 'Devil'.

pIE *g^uhormo- 'heat', Skt. gharmá-s, OP month-name Garma-pada-, cf. Lt. formus 'hot'.

pIE root *g^uhen- 'strike', OP ja^{n}tiy, Skt. hánti; OP 3d sg. imf. aja^n, Skt. áhan; pIE *g^uhṇdhí (imv.), OP jadiy, Skt. jahí (Skt. j by Grassmann's Law, §73.IV).

Other examples of g and j could be added, but these are adequate.

The pIE roots *g^uem- and *g^uhen- have in OP generalized the palatalized value of the velar consonant, except where it stands before a consonant.

On -j- in nijāyam, see §120.

§102. OP xš is of various sources, and should be discussed in association with š from similar clusters. The origins which call for discussion, and the correspondences, are the following:[1]

pIE qþ, Av. OP xš, Skt. kṣ, Gk. κτ.

pIE qs, Av. OP xš, Skt. kṣ, Gk. ξ.

pIE ḱþ, Av. OP š, Skt. kṣ, Gk. κτ.

pIE ḱs, Av. OP š, Skt. kṣ, Gk. ξ.

pIE root *qþei-, OP -axšayaiy 'I ruled', Skt. kṣáyati 'he possesses', Gk. κτάομαι 'I acquire'; with derivatives, see Lex. s.v. xšay-.

pIE root *qþen-, OP axšata- 'unhurt', Skt. kṣaṇóti 'he injures', Gk. κτείνω 'I kill'.

pIE *aug-, *u̯eg- 'increase', Lt. augeō etc.; with

---

[1] For pIE þ, cf. §58.Aa.

added -s-, *auks- *u̯eks-, in Gk. αὔξω, Gm. wachsen, Skt. vakṣati, OP U-vaxš-tra- 'Cyaxares'.

pAr. *baug- 'free', in Av. bunǰainti 'they rescue' (with nasal infix); with added -s-, -buxša- in Baga-buxša- (see Lex.); *baug-s-na-, becoming pIr. *bauxšna-, and losing the -x- in later OP, in Āθiyābaušna- (see Lex.).

Origin uncertain (no sure cognates outside Aryan): OP xšap- 'night', Skt. kṣap-; OP axšaina-, Av. axšaēna- 'dark-colored', xšaēta- 'shining'.

pIE *tek̂p- 'cut', Av. tataša 'he has created', Skt. tákṣati 'they fashion'; in OP us-tašanā- 'staircase'.

pIE *tek̂p- and *tu̯eqp-, contaminated in OP taxš- 'be active', pres. ha-taxšataiy (see Lex., s.v. taxš-).

pIE *qek̂-s-, probably in OP caša-m 'eye', cf. Av. cašman- 'eye', Skt. cákṣas- 'eye' (see Lex. s.v. caša-).

pIE *peik̂-s- in OP (aor.) niy-apaišam 'I engraved', cf. Skt. piśáti 'he cuts, adorns'.

For OP xšn- from pIE ĝn-, see §96.

§103. pAr. k AND g BEFORE CONSONANTS (other than s, §102) in OP: there are the following examples:

I. pAr. kr became pIr. xr (§74, I):

OP xraθu- 'wisdom', Av. xratav-, Skt. krátu- 'power'.

OP Θuxra- (man's name), Av. suxra- 'red', Skt. śukrá- 'bright'.

OP perf. opt. caxriyā, Skt. cakriyāt, to root kar- 'make, do'.

II. pAr. km became pIr. xm, remaining in Av. and Median, but becoming hm in OP (the h omitted in writing):

OP taxma- 'brave', with Med. -xm- in the name of the Mede Taxmaspāda- and of the Sagartian Ciçataxma-; Av. taxma- 'brave'.

OP tauʰmā- 'family', cf. with different suffix Av. taoxman- 'seed', Skt. tókman- 'green blade of barley'.

Perhaps in OP amaxmatā (see Lex. s.v. amaxamatā), where the relation to other forms from the root kam- (if this etymology be correct) prevented the further change of xm to hm.

III. Other examples of earlier k before consonants are found in the province-name Bāxtri- 'Bactria', the month-name Viyaxna-, and the imv. raxθatuv, of uncertain meaning and connections.

IV. Earlier g before consonants, other than s and t, seems to remain unchanged in the extant examples:

Patigrabanā, a town in Parthia, perhaps to OP grab- (pIE *ghrebh-), which elsewhere appears in OP only as garb- (graphic for both garb- and gr̥b-).

tigra- 'pointed', also in tigraxauda-; Tigra-, a fortress in Armenia; Tigrā- 'Tigris', borrowed from Semitic.

-gmata- 'gone', to root gam-, in parāgmatā hagmatā Hagmatāna-.

Bagābigna- a man's name, see Lex. s.v.

Sugda- a Persian province, also Suguda with anaptyxis (§128).

But pIE -gh-to-, becoming -gdho-, pIr. -gda-, was in OP replaced by -kt- (analogical to -gt- becoming -kt-): duruxtam 'false', ptc. to pres. stem durujiya-, cf. drauga- 'the Lie' (palatalization only in the present stem, where there is the suffix -i̯o-).

§104. pAr. ći̯ became ši̯ in Av. and OP (graphic -šiy- in OP, §25):

pIE *qᵘi̯ēto-, OP šiyāta- 'happy', GAv. šyāta- 'joyous', Lt. quiētus.

pIE *qᵘi̯ēti-, OP šiyāti- 'happiness', cf. Lt. quiēs, gen. quiēt-is.

pIE *qi̯eu̯-, OP ašiyava 'he set forth', Skt. ácyavat, Gk. (Hom.) aor. ἔσσευε 'he put into motion'.

§105. THE CLUSTER -s-ć- appears in OP with reduction to s in pasā 'after', from pIE *po-sqᵘē: cf. Av. pasča, Skt. paścā. The evidence of Sasanian Pahlavi shows that this value alone is phonetic in OP (Bv. Gr. §114), and that the -šc- which is seen in some sandhi combinations, belongs rather to Median: OP kašciy 'anyone' from pIE *qᵘos-qᵘid; manaš-c[ā] DNb 32 from *menos-qᵘe. On zūra-kara 'evil-doer' from *zuraḥ-kara-, see §119.

The sandhi product of -d ć- has a similar variation: OP s (not attested) and remade c (§130), Med. šc; there are the following examples:

pIE *ed-qᵘid, OP aciy 'then', Av. aṱčiṱ.

pIE *i̯od-qᵘid, OP yaciy 'when', Av. yaṱčiṱ.

pIE *qᵘid-qᵘid, OP cišciy 'anything', with Med.

šc; so also OP *avašciy* from earlier **avad-cid*, OP *aniyašciy* from earlier **aniad-cid*.

§106. pIE *r* remained unchanged in most IE languages, down into the recorded forms of the languages; exceptional combinations in which it suffered change in OP, are mentioned below.
pIE **reĝto-* 'directed', OP *rāsta-* 'straight', Av. *rāšta-* 'upright', Lt. *recto-*.
pIE **pro*, OP *fra-* (in cpds.), Av. *frā*, Skt. *pra*, Gk. πρό.
pIE **enter* 'inside', OP *aⁿtar*, Av. *antarǝ*, Skt. *antár*, Lt. *inter*.
pIE **su-preĝ-to-*, OP *ufrašta-* 'well punished', cf. Skt. *pṛcchāmi* 'I ask', Lt. *precor* 'I ask'.
pIE **proterom*, OP *frataram*, Skt. *pratarám*, Gk. πρότερον.
pIE root **dhreugh-* in OP *drauga-* 'the Lie', Skt. *drúhyati* 'he deceives', Gm. *trugen* 'to deceive'.
pIE **mortiio-*, OP *martiya-* 'man', Skt. *mártya-*, cf. Lt. *mortālis*.
pIE **ebheront* 'they bore', OP *abaraⁿ*, Skt. *ábharan*, cf. Lt. *ferō*.

OP *r* may come also from pIE *ṛ* *ṝ* (§66, §68, cf. §§30–35), and from pIE *l* *ḷ* *ḹ* (§107, §66, §68); but there are many ambiguities, since pIE *r* and pIE *l* can be distinguished only if we have a cognate outside the Aryan branch of IE. It is also difficult in many instances, to distinguish the original vocalic *r* and *l* from the original consonantal *r* and *l* (§30–§35).

For OP developments of pAr. *tr*, see §§78–9; of pAr. *sr*, see §118.II. In borrowed names of persons and places, *r* is of frequent occurrence; e.g. *Aθurā* 'Assyria', *Arabāya* 'Arabia', *Ufrātu-* 'Euphrates', *Armina* 'Armenia', *Karkā* 'Carians', in which the forms in other languages assure the *r* as original at the time of borrowing.

§107. pIE *l* became pAr. *r*, and therefore was indistinguishable from pIE *r* in the Aryan languages, unless a cognate from another IE branch can be adduced.
pIE **soluo-* 'all', OP *haruva-*, Av. *haurva-*, Skt. *sárva-*, Gk. Ion. οὖλος, Att. ὅλος.
pIE **pṛlu-*, OP *paru-*, Skt. *purú-*, Gk. πολυ-.
pIE **leuqos*, OP *rauca*, Skt. *rócas*, cf. Gk. λευκός 'white'.
pIE **suel-nos*, OP *-farna* in *Viⁿda-farnā*, Av. *xᵛarǝnō* 'royal splendor', cf. Gk. σέλας 'brightness' from **suel-ns*.

pIE **qᵘel-* in OP *car-* in *abicariš* 'pasture land', cf. Skt. *cárati* 'he goes', Lt. *colit* 'he tills'.
Also *l* or *ḷ* in OP *Varkāna-*, *Varkazana-* (see Lex.), *ḷ* in *darga-* (§68).

In borrowings, an original *l* became OP *r* if the words were really assimilated into the OP: thus *Arbairā-* 'Arbela' = Akk. *ar-ba-'-il*; *Tigrā-* 'Tigris' = Akk. *di-iq-lat*; *Nadiⁿtabaira-* 'Nidintu-Bel' = Akk. *ni-din-tú-ⁱˡᵘbēl*; *Bābiru-* 'Babylon' = Akk. *bab-ilu*. In others that received less use, the *l* remained: *Haldita-* an Armenian, *Labanāna-* 'Mt. Lebanon', *Dubāla-* a district in Babylonia, and *Izalā-* a district in Assyria.

For the development of pIE *tl*, see §78; for pIE *ĝl*, §94; for pIE *ḷ*, §66; for pIE *ḹ*, §68.

§108. THE pIE NASALS in general remained unchanged in the various IE languages, except that they changed to agree with the position of a following stop or spirant; but this shift is hardly evidenced in OP, since nasals before homorganic stops or spirants[1] were not written in the OP syllabary (§39).

§109. pIE *m* remained *m*, in general, in all the languages.
pIE **mā* 'not', OP *mā*, Skt. *mā́*, Gk. μή.
pIE **moi* 'of or to me', OP *maiy*, Skt. *me*, Gk. μοι.
pIE **mṛto-* 'dead', OP *marta*, Skt. *mṛtá-*, Lt. *mort-uos*.
pIE **somo-* 'same', OP *hama-*, Skt. *samá-*, Gk. ὁμός.
pIE **nōmṇ* 'name', OP *nāmā*, Skt. *nā́ma*, Lt. *nōmen*.
pIE **eĝhom* 'I', OP *adam*, Skt. *ahám*, cf. Gk. ἐγών.

OP *m* remains before *n* and final, and before enclitics: *kamnam, jiyamnam*, acc. *nāham, adam-šim, avākaram-ca-maiy, paruvam-ciy*. On [nᵃyā]-*kama* =]*kam-ma*, see §130. On pIE *ṃ*, see §67; on pIE *ṃ̄*, §68: on failure to write *m* before stops and spirants, §111.

M occurs in non-Iranian proper names and in *maškā-* 'inflated skin', from Aramaic.

---

[1] In pIr., nasals before spirants were reduced to a mere nasalization of the preceding vowel (so also in Indic, cf. Wackernagel, Altindische Grammatik 1.§224); the OP writing fails to show whether the nasalization persisted in OP (as it did in Av.) or was entirely lost. Thus OP *aθaha* may agree with Skt. *asqsat* in having a nasalized vowel, or may be from a form of the root lacking the nasal; cf ref. in Lex. s.v *θah-*.

PHONOLOGY

§110. pIE *n* remained *n*, in general, in OP, Av., Skt., Gk., Lt.

pIE *nās-* 'nose', OP acc. *nāham*, Skt. *nās-*, Eng. *nose*.

pIE *nepōt-s* 'grandson', OP nom. *napā*, Skt. *nápāt*, Lt. *nepōs*.

pIE *nōmn̥* 'name', OP *nāmā*, Skt. *nā́ma*, Lt. *nōmen*.

pIE *ĝnōsk̑ēti* 3d sg. subj., OP *xšnāsātiy*, Lt. fut. *(g)nōscet*.

pIE *egʷhen-m̥*, OP *ajanam* 'I smote', Skt. *áhanam*, cf. Lt. *dē-fen-dō*.

OP *n* was of frequent occurrence in personal and place names, some at least being non-Iranian. For *n* before stop or spirant, see §111; for *n* final, see §112. For pIE *n̥*, see §67; for pIE *n̥̄*, §68. For *ni̯*, written *niy*, §25; for *nu̯*, written *nuv*, §26.

§111. OP UNWRITTEN MEDIAL NASALS. OP nasals were not expressed in writing before stops and spirants (except *m* before enclitics, §39), but the presence of the sounds is indicated by the transliterations into other languages, or by the evidence of etymological comparisons.

Kaᵐpaⁿda a district in Media, Elam. *qa-um-pan-ta-š*.

Kaᵐbūjiya 'Cambyses', Elam. *kan-bu-ṣi-i̯a*, Akk. *kam-bu-zi-i̯a*.

Viⁿdafarnā 'Intaphernes', Elam. *mi-in-da-par-na*.

Skuⁿxa a Scythian rebel, Elam. *iš-ku-in-qa*.

Hiⁿduš 'Sind', Elam. *hi-in-du-iš*, Av. *Hindu-*, Skt. *síndhu-*.

aθaⁿga- 'stone', Av. *asənga-*.

baⁿdaka 'servant', Phl. *bandak*, NPers. *bàndah*.

aⁿtar 'inside', Skt. *antár*, Lt. *inter*.

§112. OP FINAL *n*. OP *n* was not written when final: loc. *nōmen*, OP *nāma* (see Lex. s.v.); 3d pl. imf. *ebheu̯ont*, OP *abava*, Skt. *ábhavan*. On *abaran* miswritten for *abaraha*, see §54.I.

§113. pIE *i̯* appears unchanged in OP, as well as in Skt., when initial and intervocalic; but in Av. it is subject to many graphic alterations:

OP *yaθā*, Skt. *yáthā*.

OP *yadataiy* 'he worships', Skt. *yájate*, Gk. ἅζεται (pIE *i̯-* > Gk. *h-*).

OP *dārayatiy* 'he holds', Skt. *dhāráyati*.

OP *vayam* 'we', Skt. *vayám*.

OP *draya* 'sea', Av. *zrayō*, Skt. *jráyas-*.

After consonants also, pIE *i̯* remains unchanged in OP and in Skt., but it is regularly written *-iy-* (§25):

root *kan-* 'dig' + pass. *-ya-*, in *akaniya* 'was dug'.

**dušː* 'ill' + *yār-* 'year', in *dušiyāram* 'famine'.

uvāmaršiyuš nsm. 'by self-death', Skt. *mr̥tyú-š* 'death', cf. *-tii̯o-* in OP *martiya* 'man'.

adurujiya 'he lied', cf. *drauga* 'the Lie'.

ašiyava 'he went forth', Skt. (mid.) *ácyavata*.

Note pAr. *ki̯* > pAr. *ći̯* > OP *šy*, §104; pAr. *ti̯* > pIr. *θi̯* > OP *šy*, §80. OP *Maciya-* to the province-name *Maka* must be for **maki̯os*, or a late formation in which **maki̯os* did not make the second phonetic change; similarly *Ākaufaciyā* to **Ākaufaka*.

But *hy* was normally written *hy* and not *hiy*, §27; on *tya*, with retention of *t* and failure to write *tiya*, see Lex. s.v.

At the end of a word, *y* was added in OP to a final *i*: thus OP *pariy*, Skt. *pári*, Gk. περί; OP *ciy*, Skt. *cid*, Lt. *quid* (§37; §84 for failure to write final *d* in OP); OP encl. *-maiy*, Skt. *me*, Gk. μοι.

Occasionally medial *-ay-* was written *-aiy-*; see §48. Very rarely *-i-yᵃ-* = *-iy-* was used to indicate length of *ī*, see §23.

§114. pIE *u̯* appears unchanged in OP and in Skt., while in Av. there are numerous changes, essentially only graphic: OP *v* was the semivowel as in Eng. *we*, not the spirant as in Eng. *eve*:

acc. **u̯ik̑-m̥*, OP *viθam* 'house', Skt. *víśam*, cf. Lt. *vīcus* 'village'.

pl. **u̯ei* 'we', OP *vayam*, Skt. *vayám*, Gt. *wei-s*.

pIE *deiu̯o-*, OP *daiva-* 'demon', Skt. *devá-* 'god', Lt. *dīvos*.

pIE *gʷīu̯o-* 'living', OP *jīva*, Skt. *jīvá-s*, Lt. *vīvos*.

After consonants also, pIE *u̯* remains unchanged in OP and in Skt., but is regularly written *-uv-* in OP (§26):

OP *haruva-* 'all', Skt. *sárva-*.

OP loc. *duvarayā* 'at the door', Skt. *dhvar-*.

OP acc. *θuvām*, Skt. *tvā́m*; but dissyllabic OP *tuvam*, Skt. *tuvám*.

OP *θanuvaniya* 'bowman', cf. Skt. *dhánvan-* 'bow'.

But pIE *u̯* was lost after labial stops:

OP 2d sg. opt. *biyāʰ*, 3d sg. *biyāⁱ*, from **bhu-ii̯ē-*, to root **bheu-*, see Lex. s.v. *bav-*.

Note pAr. *tu̯* > pIr. *θu̯* > OP *θv*, §81; pAr. *su̯* > pIr. *hu̯* > OP *hv*, written *uv* for *ʰuv*, and Med. *f* in *farnah-*, §118.IV; pAr. *ru̯* and *r̥u̯*, §35.

At the end of a word, *v* was added in OP to final *u*: OP *paruv* 'much', Skt. *purú*, Gk. πολύ; OP loc. *Margauv Hiⁿdauv Bābirauv* (§38). Occasionally medial *-av-* was written *-auv-*, see §48. Very rarely *-u-vᵃ-* = *-uv-* was used to indicate length of *ū*, see §23.

§115. pIE *s* remained unchanged in pAr. except as follows: (1) pIE *s* became pAr. *š* if preceded by pAr. *i*-vowel or *u*-vowel (including long and short vowels and diphthongs), or by pAr. *r* or *r̥* (also from pIE *l* or *l̥*), or by a pAr. palatal or velar stop; and (2) pIE *s* became a weak *h*-sound, indicated by *ḥ* (called in Skt. visarga), when final after pAr. *ă* and immediately followed by a pause between phrases or at the end of a sentence.

pAr. *s* remained in pIr. before pAr. *p t k* (and presumably before pAr. *ph th kh*, but of these there are no certain examples in OP); but in other positions it became pIr. *h*.

Final *s* was subject in Aryan to various sandhi developments other than *-š* and *-ḥ*; these are best seen in Sanskrit. But Iranian generalized *-š* and *-ḥ* and shows only these values and their direct phonetic developments, except for a few combinations with enclitics (the OP examples are in §105). Skt. words and forms will be cited with *-ṣ* and *-ḥ* in order to show clearly their relation to the OP words and forms with which they are compared.

The developments of pIr. *s š h ḥ* in Iranian and in OP will be discussed in the following sections.

§116. pIr. *s* from pIE *s* in pIr. *st sp sk* remained in OP without change:

st in pIE **esti* 'he is', OP *astiy*, Skt. *ásti*, Lt. *est*; pIE **ĝhosto-* 'hand', OP *dasta-*, Av. *zasta-*, Skt. *hásta-*. OP *avāstāyam* 'I restored', cf. Lt. *stāre*; OP *stānam* 'place', Skt. *sthánam* (it is uncertain whether the Iranian as well as the Skt. goes back to pIE *sth-*, but if so the aspiration was regularly lost in Iranian after a sibilant; other languages have the products of the non-aspirate).

sp in *spāda-* 'army', in *Taxmaspāda-* (name of a Mede); in *Vāyaspāra-* (name of a Persian): but the ultimate origin of these words is not clear.

sk in *skauθi-*, *Skuⁿxa-*, *Skudra-*: all non-Persian words by origin, and given here only as evidence for the occurrence of the sound cluster.

OP *s* is more commonly of other origins: (Med.) *s* from pIE *k̂*, §87; from clusters containing pIE *k̂*, §90, §93, §95; from pIE dental stop + *t*, becoming *tst*, §85; and in words of uncertain etymology or borrowed from other languages: *Saka-*, *Sug(u)da-*, *Nisāya-*, *siⁿkabru-*, and the dubious *siyamam*.

§117. pIr. *š* from pIE *s* after certain sounds (§115) remained unchanged in OP:

OP *maθišta-* 'greatest', Av. *masišta-*, Gk. μήκιστος 'longest'.

OP *frāišayam* 'I sent', Skt. *eṣayati* 'he brings'.

OP *uška-* 'dry', Av. *huška-*, Lith. *saũsa-s*.

OP *gauša-* 'ear', Skt. *ghóṣa-* 'noise'.

OP *adaršnauš* 'he dared', Skt. *dhr̥ṣṇóti* 'he dares'.

OP *arša-* 'male' in *Aršāma-* 'Arsames', Skt. *r̥ṣa-bhá-* 'bull'.

pIE **sed-əs-* in OP *hadiš* 'seat', cf. Gk. ἕδος (from pIE **sedos*).

pIE **e-si-ste-to*, OP *aʰištatā* 'he stood', cf. Gk. ἵσταται 'he stands' (from **sistətai*).

pIE **r̥sti-*, OP nom. *arštiš*, Skt. *r̥ṣṭí-ṣ* (cf. §115).

OP nom. *tanūš* 'body', Skt. *tanū-ṣ*.

For *ks* and other clusters giving *xš*, see §102; for *k̂n* and *ĝn* giving initial *xšn* and medial *šn*, §96; for *-šc-* as a sandhi product, §105; for pAr. *ći̯* giving OP *šy*, §104; for pAr. *ti̯* giving OP *šy* §80; for pAr. *tn* giving OP *šn*, §82.

The verbal prefix *ni-* affects an initial *s* of the verbal root; thus *ni-štā-* from *ni-* + *stā-* and *ni-šad-* from *ni-* + *sad-* (Iran. *had-*), and the value *š* is extended to positions where the *š* is separated from the *i* by the augment: *niyaštāyam* 'I commanded' (but *avāstāyam* 'I restored'), *niyašāda-yam* 'I commanded'. So also the enclitic pronoun *-šaiy -šim -šām -šiš* is generalized in the form which developed after a final *i* or *u* of the word to which it was attached; cf. Av. *hōi hīm hīš*, showing the generalization of initial *h*, which was regular after most finals.

For *št* from pIE *k̂t*, §93. The sound *š* also occurs in borrowed words, such as *maškā-* 'inflated skin' (from Aramaic); and in proper names, the origin of which is not always clear (here only after *i* and *u*): *Kāpišakāni-, Kūša-, Cišpi-, Patišuvari-, Adukanaiša-, Çūšā-,* etc.

§118. pIr. *h* from pIE *s*, §115.

I. pIr. *h* remained in OP.

pIE **soluo-* 'all', OP *haruva*, Skt. *sárva-*.

pIE **snt-iom*, OP *hašiyam* 'truth', Skt. *satyám*, cf. Eng. *sooth*.

pAr. **sainā-* 'army', OP *hainā-*, Skt. *sénā-*.

OP *vāhara-* 'spring' in Θūra-vāhara-, Skt. *vāsará-* 'bright', Lith. *vãsara* 'summer'.

pIE gen. *-osio*, OP *martiy-ahyā* 'of a man', Skt. *márty-ahya*.

pIE acc. **nās-m̥*, OP *nāham*, Skt. *nā́sam*.

II. Before *r* and *m* the *h* was not written in OP:

OP *rauta* 'river', Skt. *srótas-* 'current, river'.

OP *amiy* 'I am', LAv. *ahmi*, Skt. *ásmi*, from pIE **esmi*.

OP *amāxam* 'of us', Av. *ahmākəm*, Skt. *asmā́kam*.

OP *taumā* 'family', for **tauhmā* from **tauxmā*, §103.II.

III. OP *hai* was written with *h^a i*; OP *hi* initial or medial was written by *i* or by *h^a*; OP written *h^a iy^a* = *hiy*, which we expect for non-final *hy* and *hiy* and for final *hi*, is normally written without the *i*; OP final *h^a y^a* = *-hy* (for *-hi*) loses the *y^a* if it is followed by an enclitic. For examples, and a complete list of exceptions, see §27.

IV. The writing *h^a u* was normal for *hau*, as in *hauv, hauvam, haumavarga-, Vahauka-*, but was not used for *hu*; to express *hu*, with vocalic *u*, the single character *u* was used, and to express *huv* for *hu* (from *su*), *uv^a* was written—the *h^a* being omitted in both situations:

Nom. *Dārayava^h uš*, gen. *Dārayavahauš*.

Nom. *Hara^h uvatiš*, Skt. *sárasvatī*.

Loc. pl. *aniyā^h uv-ā*, Skt. *anyā́su*.

^h uva- 'own', Av. *x^v a-*, Skt. *sva-*.

^h uvaspa- 'having good horses', Skt. *sv-áśva-*.

In the name *Vi^n da-farnah-* 'Intaphernes', the second element is identical with Av. *x^v arənah-* 'royal splendor', from pIE **suel-nos-*, cf. Skt. *svar-* 'sun', Lt. *sól*; the *f* instead of OP *hu* from *su* seems to be a Median peculiarity, although Intaphernes was one of the Persians who aided Darius to overthrow the false Smerdis.

V. There are other words with *h*, which are of uncertain etymology or are borrowed from other languages: *Anāhitā*, usually written *Anahata*, the name of a goddess with apparently an Iranian name based on an unidentifiable root; *Haldita-*, an Armenian; *Hi^n duš*, a province-name from Indic, but with Iranian development of the initial *s*.

VI. For the loss of *h* in the sequence *ahah*, and subsequent contraction of the vowels, see §131.

§119. pAr. *h* developed from pIE *s* after pAr. *ă* when final in the phrase or sentence; it was not written in OP, but its presence as a sound is indicated by the fact that final *ă* remains *ă* in the writing if it is followed by *h*, but is written *ā* if it is absolutely final. When it is desirable to indicate this unwritten *h*, we use a raised *h* or a raised *s*,[1] as may be more convenient.

OP nom. *martiya^h*, Skt. *mártyaḥ*, from pIE *-os*.

OP nom. pl. *bagāha^h* 'gods', cf. Skt. Ved. *devā́saḥ* 'gods'.

But OP *abara^n tā*, Skt. *ábharanta*; OP *agarbāyatā*, Skt. *agr̥bhāyata*.

After *ā*, there is no evidence of the survival of *h* as an unwritten sound in OP:

OP gen. *taumāyā* 'family', Skt. gen. *-āyāḥ* in *-ā-* stems.

OP npf. *kartā* 'done, made', Skt. *kr̥tā́ḥ*.

The inst. pl. *raucabiš*, to *rauca^h* 'day', raises a problem. The corresponding declension of neuter *-os/es-* stems is, with partial use of Skt. *mánas-* 'mind' and Av. *manah-* 'mind, sense':

	pIE	Skt.	Av.	OP
Nom. sg.	**menos*	*mánaḥ*	*manō*	*rauca^h*
Ins. pl.	**menez-bhis*	*mánōbhiṣ*	*manə̄bīš*	*raucabiš*
Loc. pl.	**menes-su*	*mánaḥsu*	*raocōhv-a*

Apparently the suffix *-as-* or *-az-* was in some forms replaced by *-ah-* where *-ah-* yielded an easier phonetic development. We may assume that *raucabiš* is from *raucah-bhiš*, that the *h* became voiced before the voiced stop and was lost in OP, but in Av. and Skt. was lost with an attendant change of the preceding vowel to *ō*. A similar replacement is seen in *zūra^h -kara-* 'evildoer', where the *h* is lost before the voiceless stop; cf. Skt. *manaḥ-pati-* 'Lord of the Mind'.

§120. pIE *z* developed in pIE only (1) from *s* which in word-formation came to stand before a voiced stop; (2) from *s* which in word-formation

---

[1] The *s* indicates more clearly the etymological origin; similarly, we quote Sanskrit words with either *-ḥ* or *-s*.

came to stand after a voiced aspirated stop (of this there are no examples in OP); (3) in the voiced clusters *dzd* and *dzdh* which developed from certain combinations of dental + dental (§85).[1] There are only a few examples:

Personal name *Vahyaz-dāta-* '(Follower of) the Better Law', with *vahyas-* 'better' (Skt. *vásyas-*) + *dāta-* 'law'.

azdā and *Aura-mazdāh-*, with -*dzdh*-, see §85; for *basta-* and *gasta-*, with participial -*tst-* replacing -*dzdh*-, see §85.

The Aryan prefix **niš-*, from pIE **ni + s* (§115), became *niž* before voiced stops, as in Av. *niž-bərəta-* 'carrying off' (nt. sb.), and is written *nij-* in OP *nij-āyam* 'I went forth'.

Other instances of *z* are largely the product of pIE *ĝ* and *ĝh* in Median (§88, §91), or in OP before consonants (§91, §95); such a *z* became *s* and then *š* before *n*:

pIE *ĝ*: *paruzana-, vispazana-, Varkazana-, vazraka-*.

pIE *ĝh*: *brazmaniya-, Uvārazmī-, uzma-, zūra-, zūrakara-*.

pIE *ĝ* or *ĝh*: *Zraⁿka-*.

pIE *ĝhu̯*: *patiyazbayam, hᵃzānam*.

Names of non-Iranian places: *Zazāna-, Zūzahya-, Izalā-*.

It is to be noted that OP *z* remained unchanged before *m*, as in *brazman-*, though it became voiceless (and was further changed) before *n*, as in *baršnā*. But the *zm* which was retained in GAv. became *sm* in LAv.

§121. THE ABLAUT GRADES OF THE VOWELS: The pIE variation of the vowels, known as ablaut gradation, is well represented in OP, though it is obscured by the pAr. changes: pIE *e o a* became pAr. *a*, pIE *ē ō ā* became pAr. *ā*, and the diphthongs similarly were reduced to pAr. *ai āi, au āu*. Further, the reduced ъ before liquid, nasal, or semivowel, became *a* in pAr.; cf. also the development of the long vocalic liquids and nasals, §68. In general, then, the pIE series assumed the following forms in OP:

---

[1] As in §58 Ab, I intentionally omit Sturtevant's pIE *z* coming from pIH *s* with a preceding γ (the third laryngeal, which was voiced).

	pIE				OP		
Series I							
e o	nil ъ ъ	*ē ō*	*a*	nil	*a*	*ā*
ei oi	*i²*	*ēi ōi*	*ai*	*i²*	*āi*
eu ou	*u²*	*ēu ōu*	*au*	*u²*	*āi*
er¹ or	*r²* ъr ъr	*ēr ōr*	*ar*	*r²*	*ar*	*ār*
en³ on	*n²* ъn ъn	*ēn ōn*	*an*	*a,n*	*an*	*ān*
Series II[5]							
a⁴ o	nil	*ā ō*	*a*	nil	*ā*
Series IV and V							
ē⁷ ō	ə		*ā*	*i,a⁶*
ā ō	ə		*ā*	*i,a⁶*

Notes to the Table: (1) Similarly, pIE *el* etc., which became pAr. *ar* etc. (2) Either consonantal or vocalic, according to the nature of the neighboring sounds (3) Similarly, pIE *em* etc., which gave pAr. *am* etc. (4) There are diphthongal varieties of this series, as of Series I, but few if any examples of this series can be identified in extant OP (5) Series III, consisting of *o o* nil etc., and Series VI, consisting of *ō ō* ə, may be merely varieties of Series I and IV lacking extant examples of grades *e* and *ē* respectively. (6) The value *a* developed before *i* and *u*, *i̯* and *u̯*. (7) There are diphthongal varieties of Series IV and V, with zero-grades əi or ī, əu or ū, etc.

Apart from details, the vowel grades in the first two columns of the pIE belong by origin to accented syllables, those in the first to primarily accented syllables and those in the second to secondarily accented syllables; they are known as normal grades or accented grades. Those in the next three columns of the pIE belong by origin to unaccented syllables; those in the third column are known as zero grades, and those in the fourth and fifth as reduced grades. Those in the last two columns of the pIE have acquired length through special circumstances, such as contraction of the initial vowel of a verb with the vocalic augment, the marking of a derivative noun from a verbal root, the indication of the causative stem of a verb, or the indication of the nominative singular of a noun (sometimes extended to the accusative singular and the nominative plural); they are known as long grades, and originally bore respectively the primary and the secondary accent. But such a schematic distribution of the grades could not be thoroughgoing, since it would result in the alteration of related forms beyond the possibility of recognition, and analogy therefore interfered to preserve a useful similarity in related forms.

In the following lists, an attempt will be made to differentiate *e* and *o* grades; where this is impossible, the pre-form will be given with pAr. vocalism. For the most part, only examples will be given which show two different grades in OP itself.

§122. ABLAUT VARIATION WITHIN THE ROOT: examples from OP:

*es- in *as-tiy* 'he is', *s- in *h-a*ⁿ*tiy* 'they are', *ēs- augmented) in *āh-am* 'I was'.

*ped- or *pod*- 'foot' in *ni-padiy pati-padam Garma-pada*-, (Ar.) *pād- in *pādaibiya* 'with the two feet'.

*sed- 'sit' in *had-iš* 'seat, abode'; (Ar.) *sād- in *niyašādayam* 'I established'.

*neḱ- 'perish', in *vi-nas-ta*- 'damage', (Ar.) *nāś- in *viy-anāθaya* 'he injured'.

*ei- 'go' in *aitiy* 'he goes', *i- in *-idiy* 'go thou' (*para-idiy, parīdiy* from *pari-idiy) and *-itā* 'gone' (*para-itā*); *ēi- (augmented) in *upāyam* (from *upa-āyam) 'I arrived', *upariy-āyam* 'I behaved', *atiy-āiš* 'he went past'.

*perḱ- 'cut' in *ni-paištanaiy* 'to inscribe'; *piḱ- in ptc. *ni-pištam* 'inscribed'.

*teu- in *taumā* 'power', *u-tava* 'having good strength', *tauvīyā* 'stronger' (for *tavīyā*, §48); *tu- in *tunuvā* 'powerful'; (Ar.) *tāu- in *tāvayatiy* 'he is strong'.

*dhrouĝh- in *drauga* 'Lie', *dhruĝh- in *duruxtam* 'false'.

*gᵘou- in *Gau-māta, Gau-baruva*; *gᵘu- in *θatagu-š* (but see Lex. s.v.); (*gᵘōu- in Skt. *gāúṣ* 'cow').

*bheu- 'become' in *bavatiy* 'he is'; **bhu̯*- in *biyā* 'may he be'.

*bher- 'bear' in *bara*ⁿ*tiy* 'they bear'; *bhor- in *aršti-bara* 'spear-bearer'; **bhr̥*- in *u-bar-tam* 'well uplifted'; *bhōr- in *asa-bāra*- 'horse-borne', *uša-bāri*- 'camel-borne'.

*qer- 'make, do' in *cartanaiy* 'to do'; *qor- in *zūra-kara* 'evil-doer'; *qr- in *ca-xr-iyā* 'he might make', **qr̥*- in *kartam* 'made'; *qᵊr- in *akariya* 'it was done'; *qēr*- in *u-cāram* 'successful'.

*mer- 'die' in *marīka*- 'menial person' (see Lex. s.v.), *mor- in *martiya* 'man' (see Lex. s.v.), **mr̥*- in *marta* 'dead', *uvā-maršiyuš* 'by self-death' (see Lex. s.v.); perhaps *mᵊr- in *amariyatā* 'he died' (cf. Av. *miryeite* 'he dies').

*bhendh- or *bhondh- in *ba*ⁿ*daka* 'subject', **bhn̥dh*- in *basta* 'bound'.

*gᵘhen- in *ajanam* 'I smote', **gᵘhn̥*- in *jadiy* 'do thou smite', *-jata* 'slain'.

*dher- or **dhr̥*- in *adaršiy* 'I held'; *dhr- in *duruva*- 'firm'; (Ar.) *dār- in *dārayatiy* 'he holds'.

*gᵘem- 'come' in *ā-jamiyā* 'may it come', *gᵘm- in *parāgmatā* 'gone forth' (see §244).

*ap- 'water' in inst. pl. *abiš*, *āp- in nom. *āpiš*, loc. *āpiyā*.

*bhag- in *baga* 'god', *bhāg- in *bāji*- 'tribute'.

*gᵘoi- in *gaiθām* 'cattle' (*oi* proved by the lack of palatalization of the *g*), *gᵘī- in *jīva* 'living'.

*preḱ- in *ufraštam* 'well punished', **pr̥ḱ*- in *aparsam* 'I punished'.

*reĝ- 'direct, rule' or *roĝ- in *uradanām*; **r̥ĝ*- in *arštām, Ardu-maniš*; *rēĝ- in *rāstam* 'right' (cf. §93.n2).

*stā- 'place' in *stānam, avāstāyam, niyaštāyam*; reduced to *st- with thematic vowel, instead of *stə-, in *aʰištatā*.

(Ar.) *pā- 'protect' in *pādiy, pātuv, pāta*; *pə- in *apayaiy, patipayauvā* (§214).

*ĝnō- in *xšnāsātiy*; *ĝnə-u- in *ā-xšnautiy*, cf. *ĝn-u- in *xšnuta* (§208).

*dhē- 'put', only in this grade: *adā* 'he made', *dātam* 'law'.

*dō- 'give', only in this grade: *dadātuv* 'let him give'.

§123. FUNCTIONAL ABLAUT VARIATION WITHIN THE VERBAL ROOT: examples are found in the preceding section; they include
(1) strong grade varying with zero or reduced inside the regular paradigm, with long grade where there is contraction with the augment;
(2) long grade in causative formations, where other languages show the *-ŏ-* grade: *vināθaya-*, Lt. *noceō*; *dāraya-, mānaya-, çāraya-, -šādaya-, tāvaya-, jāvaya-*.
(3) long grade in substantives from the verbal root: *asa-bāra-, uša-bāri-; u-cāram, bāji-*.

§124. FUNCTIONAL ABLAUT VARIATION WITHIN THE LAST STEM-SYLLABLE OF NOUNS:
(1) In *-ŏ-* stems: nom. *-os* as in *martiya*, and *-o-* in several other forms; voc. *-e* in *martiyā*; see §169.
(2) In *-u-* stems: (Ar.) *-au* in loc. sg. *dahyauv-ā*, *-u-* in loc. pl. *dahyu-šuvā*, *-āu-* in nom. sg. *dahyāu-š*, see §180. Nom. sg. *Dārayava*ʰ*uš* and acc. *-va*ʰ*um* with *-u-*, gen. *-vahauš* with (Ar.) *-au-*. Perhaps *Pirāvā* 'Nile' with *-āv-*, to *piruš* 'ivory', cf. Lex. s.v.

(3) In -*i*- stems: -*i*- in nom. *Cišpiš*, (Ar.) -*aı*- in gen. *Cišpaiš*; see §177.

(4) In -*s*- stems: -*nos* in nom.-acc. nt. *manaš-cā*, -*nes*- in instr. *manahā*, -*nēs* in nom. masc. *Vida-farnā*, -*nəs* in *Haxā-maniš*, *Ardu-maniš*; see §185.

(5) The long grade as marker of the nom. sg. of consonantal stems: -*t*- stem *napā*, -*r*- stems *pitā* -*mātā brātā dauštā*, -*n*- stems *asā artāvā xšaçapāvā*; see §188, §186, §187. Of the long grade -*tē*[*r*] in *pitā*, the zero-grade -*tr*- is seen in gen. *piça* from *pə-tr-os. The -*u*- stem *dahyāuš* (see above, 2) also belongs here.

(6) The long grade as marker of the acc. sg. of these same classes: *asmānam framātāram nāham hᵃzānam dahyāum dahyāvam*, see §184.

(7) The long grade as marker of the nom. pl. of these same classes: *dahyāva*; see §183.

§125. GUNA AND VRIDDHI: The Hindu grammarians recognized a variation of vowels within the same root or formative element. The vowels which they recognized in their system of roots were taken by them as the fundamental vowels, prefixation of *ă* gave to each the guna-form (Skt. *guṇa*); lengthening of the guna-form gave the vriddhi-form (Skt. *vṛddhi* 'growth'). But '*ă* was its own guna'; that is, *ă* unchanged was also the guna of *ă*. Thus they got the following correspondences; note that to the Hindu grammarians the *e* and *o* were diphthongs *ai* and *au* (as they really were!).

Fundamental: *a ā i ī u ū r̥ l̥*
Guna: *a ā e o ar al*
Vriddhi: *ā ā āi āu ār āl*

In the main, this scheme represents the development of the pIE ablaut series in Aryan, where pIE *e o a* became *a* and pIE *ē ō ā* became *ā*; and it would be unnecessary to introduce it here, if it were not that in both branches of Aryan, and in no other branch of Indo-European, the alteration to vriddhi-vowels was an important method of word-formation. In this use, *ī* and *ū* sometimes functioned as the vriddhi-vowels corresponding to *i* and *u* (instead of the *āi* and *āu* in the table given above).

§126. VRIDDHI AS A FORMATIVE. Vriddhi or lengthening of the vowel was in Aryan a much-used method of forming derivatives; many adjectives, for example, are in Skt. distinguished from the nouns from which they come, only by the vriddhi-vowel in the initial syllable. There are a number of certain examples in OP (apart from those in which the long-grade vowel may be considered a direct inheritance from pIE or from a pIE system of formation):

dāraniya-kara- 'goldsmith', to *daraniya-* 'gold'.
Bāga-yādi- 'God-worship (month)', to *baga-* 'god'.
uvārštika 'good spearsman' (**hvār-*), to *arštiš* 'spear', Skt. *r̥ṣṭi-* 'spear'; this leaves it uncertain whether *ārštika* 'spearsman' agrees in vocalism with *uvārštika*, as we have taken it, or is *arštika*, with *arštiš*. Cf. the next item.
uvāsabāra 'good horseman' (**hv-āsa-*), to *asa-* 'horse'; *asabāra* with *ă* is rendered probable by the unlengthened vowel in *ušabāri-* 'camel-borne'.
uvāmaršiyuš 'having his own death' (see Lex.), to **hva-* 'own'.
uvāipašiya- 'own', with **hvāi-* in relation to *uvaipašiya-* 'own', unless the writing with -*āi*- is an error.
xšāyaθiya 'king', to -*axšayaiy* 'I ruled'.
Θāıgarci- a month-name, of uncertain etymology.
yāumainiš 'skilled', derivative of **yau-man-*.
māniya- 'personal property', see Lex. s.v.
ūnarā 'skills', to **hu-nara-* (here *u* is vriddhied to *ū*).
Mārgava 'Margian', to *Marguš* 'Margiana'.
Pārsa 'Persia', to *Parθava* 'Parthia'.

Vriddhi is probable or possible as a formative in the first syllable of the following:

The month-names *Adukanaıša-*, *Anāmaka-*, *Viyaxna-*; for two other month-names certainly have it (see above).
The personal names *Vāyaspāra-*, *Frāda-*.
The ethnic *Pātišuvaris* (to *patiy* ?).
The place name *Kāpišakānı-*.
aθagaina- or *āθagaina-* 'of stone', adj. to *aθaga-* 'stone'.
Ariya- or *Āriya-*,[1] *aruvastam* or *āruvastam*, *arjanam* or *ārjanam*.
kāsaka-, kāsakaina-.

Vriddhi as a factor in the second component of a compound is seen in the following:

---

[1] Tedesco, ZII 2 46–7, argues for *ārya-* (OP graphic *ārıya-*) exclusively, on the ground that Skt *ărya-* is merely a later form derived from the earlier *ārya-*, which then is alone original.

yād- in *Bāga-yādi-* and *Āçi-yādiya-*, month-names.

vāhara- in *Θūra-vāhara-* a month-name, cf. Lith. *vāsara* 'summer' with earlier *ă*.

Perhaps *uvā-dā-* (for **hvā-dā-*), in *Paı̯śıyā-uvādā-*; see Lex. s.v.

Perhaps *ʰU-vāra-zmı̄y*, *Vi-vāna*, *ʰU-tāna*, *Vāya-spāra-*.

-bāra-, *-bāri-*, *-cāra-*, as second elements of compounds.

Possibly nouns and adjectives formed on the root with the long vowel should be listed here: *kāma-*, *pāda-*, *bāji-*, *rāsta-*. See also the long-vowel forms in §143.

§127. EPENTHESIS is the insertion in a syllable, of *i* or *u* or other vowel by the influence of a sound in the following syllable, the result being a modification of the sound of the vowel in the syllable suffering epenthesis. It is frequent in Avestan, as in *paiti* for **pati*, OP *patiy*, or *pouru* for **paru*, OP *paruv*. The only certain example in OP is *yāumainiš* for **yāumaniš* and its compound *ayāu(ma)ınıš* DNb 40, 59. It is less likely that *Paı̯śiyāuvādā-* is for **paśı̯-ā-hvādā-*, for **patı̯-*, with epenthesis (see Lex. s.v.).

§128. ANAPTYXIS is the development of a vowel between two consonants which the speaker finds it difficult to pronounce without an intervening vowel; cf. the common pronunciation of *athletic* as *athəletic*. OP has anaptyxis in the cluster *dr* when it is followed by *u*: *duruva* 'firm', Skt. *dhruvá-s*; *duruxtam* 'false', Skt. *drudham*; *adurujiya* 'he lied', cf. Av. acc. *drujım* 'devil'. The only other cluster which suffered anaptyxis in OP was *gd*, which we find in the name of Sogdiana in its various writings: *sᵃugᵘudᵃ* = *Suguda*, *sᵃugᵘdᵃ* = *Sugᵘda*, but also *sᵃugᵈdᵃ* = *Sugda*, so that here the pronunciation was a shifting one.

There is a possibility that there was anaptyxis in the clusters *dr br fr zr* before *a*, but OP writing can give no evidence on this point. NPers. has *durōγ* = OP *drauga*, *birādar* = OP *brātā*, *farmān* = *framānā*; but the anaptyxis may be later than the OP period. For *Zraⁿka*, Greek has Ζαράγγαι (in Arrian) and Σαράγγαι (in Herodotus) with anaptyxis, but Greek has no initial *sr-* or *zr-*, and there is also the form Δραγγιανή (in Diodorus) without anaptyxis, when the initial cluster is one which is normal in Greek. To these words we may add *draya* 'sea', and *Nabukudracara*. The assumption that the anaptyxis seen in the NPers. words is later than the OP times, facilitates the derivation of NPers. *buzurg* from *vazraka* (rather than from *vazarka* or *vaẓrka*, see Lex. s.v.).

§129. HAPLOLOGY is the loss of one of two similar sequences of sounds, each containing at least one consonant and one vowel, or one vowel and at least one consonant: thus English *mineralogy* from **mineralology*. OP has one certain example, *hamātā* from **hama-mātā* 'having the same mother', cf. *hama-pıtā* 'having the same father', where no haplology is possible. A second example, probable but less certain, is *duvarθim* from **dvar-varθim* 'door-cover', = 'colonnade'. Possibly also *arštā-* 'rectitude' from **aršta-tā-*, but cf. Lex. s.v.; and *dı̄diy* 'see thou', if reduplicated pres. imv. **dhi-dhī-dhi* rather than aor. imv. **dhī-dhi*.

§130. SHORTENING OF LONG CONSONANTS. Long consonants frequently developed in word formation, either by juxtaposition of two identical consonants or by assimilation of one consonant to a contiguous consonant. All long consonants of earlier origin were shortened in pIr., and long consonants of later origin were shortened in pIr. or in OP. There are the following examples in OP:

pIE *sḱ* > pAr. *śś* > pIr. *ss* > *s* in the *-sḱe-* present-stems, such as OP *parsāmiy*, Skt. *pṛcchāmi*, Lt. *poscō*; §97.

pIE *ḱs* > pAr. *ćš* (§92) > pIr. *šš* > *š* in OP aor. *niy-apaišam* to pIE root **peiḱ-*; §102.

pIE *str* (after *u*) > pAr. *štr* > pIr. *štr* > OP *šθr šç šš š* as in OP *uša-* 'camel', Av. *uštra-*; §79.

pIE *dn* > pAr. *nn* > pIr. *n* as in OP *vaināmiy* 'I see' to pIE **u̯eid-*; §83.I.

pIE *pbh* > pIE pAr. *bbh* > pIr. *bb* > *b*, as in *abiš* from **ap-bhis* (§75.IV).

This shortening took place in most languages before and after consonants; OP example: *uzma-* 'stake' from **ud-zma-*, §84.

The shortening of the sandhi combination *-d c-* to *-c-* in *aciy yaciy* (§105) is probably by way of assimilation of the weak *-d* (§84) to the following *c-*, whereupon the long consonant was shortened; but the shortening of sandhi combinations may be merely graphic when free enclitics were attached in OP, as in *āpišım* = *āpiš-šim*, *tau-*

manišaiy = taumaniš-šaiy, [nᵃyā]kama = -kam-maiy, §138.

§131. CONTRACTION OF VOWELS took place in OP (or in pre-OP) when in word formation or composition two vowels came into immediate contact. There are the following examples:

ă + ă > ā: *ava-arasam > avārasam, *xšaya-aršā > Xšayāršā; *upa-āyam > upāyam, *fra-āišayam > frāišayam; *parā-arasam > parārasam; *ā-āyaⁿtā > āyaⁿtā; *pasā-ava > pasāva; *ariya-āramnā > Ariyāramnā.

ă + i > ai: *parā-itā > paraitā; *parā-idiy > paraidiy.

ă + āi > āi: *fra-āišayam > frāišayam.

ă + u > au: pAr. masc. *sa and fem. *sā + *u + OP masc.-fem. hauv.

ĭ + ĭ > ī: *pari-idiy > parīdiy.

-iya- in the interior of words > -ī-, see §23.I.

The view has been expressed that h was lost between two a-vowels which then contracted to ā; but this is true only if the sequence is -ahah-; note fraharavam, avahar[da], Auramazdāha -dāhā -dahā, nāham, aniyāha bagāha, āvahanam, Θūravāhara-, āham and other forms of the tense, aθaham aθaha etc., maniyāhaiy, frāhaⁿjam. The examples of ahah > āh are the following:

*ahahy > āhy 'thou mayst be', cf. ahatiy 'he may be'.

*θahāhy > θāhy 'thou mayest say'.

*θahahy > *θāhy 'thou sayest', whence by analogy *θahatiy > θātiy 'he says'.

*māhahyā > māhyā 'of the month' (not loc., see Lex. s.v.).

Vivāna is hardly *vi-vah-ana-, with the same prefix and root as Av. Vī-vah-vant-, Skt. Vi-vás-vant-; apariyāya is not *ahap-, see Lex. s.v. ay-.

For the sequence ăhă there are some wrong writings in XPh: ahᵃamᵃ = āhām for ahᵃmᵃ = āham 'I was', ahᵃnᵃiyᵃ = ahaniy for *ahᵃanᵃiy = *ahāniy 'may I be', (gen.) aurᵃmᵃzᵃdᵃhᵃa = Auramazdahā (4 occurrences; also twice in XPf) for -dᵃahᵃ = -dāha or -dᵃahᵃa = -dāhā; but these miswritings, some of them probably explainable (§52, §53, §222.I), do not controvert the views expressed above.

§132. CONSONANTAL VARIATION occurs in OP words as a result of (1) internal sandhi in word formation, (2) pAr. phonetic developments, (3) pIr. phonetic developments, (4) dialect mixture of OP and Median.

(1) Neg. a- before consonants, an- before vowels, from *ṇ-; prefix ha- and ham- similarly (= Skt. sa- and sam-). Root final before dental suffixes: pIE gh and gh-t > gdh, replaced by the product of gt in OP: adurujiya and duruxtam (§73.III, §242). pIE dh and dh-t > dzdh, replaced by the product of tst in OP: baⁿdaka and basta (§85, §242).

(2) pAr. palatalization of velars before palatal vowels, giving an alternation in OP k/c, g/j (§73.III): Maka Maciyā, kunautiy kartam cartanaiy, kašciy cišciy, drauga draujana adurujiya, parā-gmatā haᵐgmatā ā-jamiyā.

(2–3) pAr. split of pIE s into s š h, and pIr. split of pAr. s into s and h (§115): stānam avāstāyam niyaštāyam aʰištatā; hadiš niy-ašādayam; aθaham θastanaiy; nom. ending in baga-ʰ pasti-š piru-š.

(3) pIr. change of p t k to f θ x before consonants (§74.I): parā but fra-, aparsam but -fraštam, tuvam but acc. θuvām, akariya but caxriyā, drauga adurujiya but duruxtam.

(4) On the differences between OP and Median consonantism, see §8.

§133. ENCLISIS is a frequent phenomenon in OP. The enclitics are the following:

Pronouns: 1st sg. acc. -mā, gen. -maiy, abl. -ma.
2d sg. gen. -taiy.
3d sg. acc. -šim, gen. -šaiy, abl. -ša;
    pl. acc. -šiš, gen. -šām.
acc. -dim; pl. acc. -diš.
pl. acc. -tā (dubious; only in avaθāša-tā DB 4.72).

Coordinating conjunctions: -cā 'and', -vā 'or'.
Postpositions: ā, patiy; both also as separate words before or after their nouns.
Adverbs and particles: -am, -kaiy, -ciy, -diy, never separately.
    -apiy, -patiy both also separately.

Miscellaneous: tya in mātya DB 4.43, 48, 71; yadātya XPh 35f (miswritten yadāyā XPh 39), cf. yaθā : tya XPh 29.

mām, elsewhere orthotone, in mātyamām DB 1.52.

rādiy in avahya-rādiy DB 1.6f, etc.; also separately.

Double enclisis: mā-tya-mām DB 1.52; rauca-pati-vā DB 1.20; nai-pati-mā DNb 20; avā-

karam-ca-maiy DNb 27f; *ciyākaram-ca-maiy* DNb 51, 51f.

Exceptions: *diš* is written as a separate word (i.e. with a preceding divider) in DB 4.34, 35, 36; so also *taiy* in DNb 58. But *daiy* in DB 5.11 is a wrong reading, cf. §44. Other variations are noted above.

§134. THE PHONETICS OF ENCLISIS has certain effects on the writing of words with enclitics. Thus the addition of an enclitic normally prevents the prolongation of -ă -ĭ -ŭ to -ā -ĭy -ŭv in the reduction to writing; and there are a few examples in which other results take place. These are discussed in the following paragraphs.

§135. THE -ă BEFORE ENCLITIC normally reverts to its true value, and the indication of length disappears: thus

manā but *mana-cā*; *avākaram-ca-maiy*; *avahya-rādiy*; *fra-haravam*.

avadā but *avada-ša*, *avada-šim*, *avada-šiš*; but *avadā-sim* DB 3.74.

ada-kaiy; *dūrada-ša*.

utā but *uta-maiy* (often), *uta-šim* XPh 34; but more often the *utā* keeps the *ā*: *utā-maiy*, *utā-taıy*, *utā-šaiy*, *utā-šim*, *utā-šām*, *utā-diš*. The retention of the *ā* is by analogy to the separate word.

§136. THE -ĭY BEFORE ENCLITIC normally reverts to its true value, without the -*y*; but occasionally analogy of the separate word causes its retention:

nai-mā, *nai-maiy*, *nai-šim*, *nai-pati-mā*, *pati-maiy*, *tyai-šaiy*, *imai-vā*, *yadi-patıy*, *yadi-vā*, [*uš*]*ī-cā*; similarly in phrasal compounds, *pati-padam*, *ni-padiy*. By analogy, *naiy-diš* DB 4.73, 78.

dūraiy + *apiy*, which is most often two words, appears as *dūraiapiy*, without the *y*, and also as *dūrayapiy*, showing the development of intervocalic *i* to *y*.

Locatives with postpositive *ā*: -ăi(y) became -ăy- before the *ā*, as in *duvarayā* from **dvaraı + ā*, *Aθurāyā* from **Aθurāı + ā*. But the script does not show whether locatives in -*i* changed the *i* to *y* before *ā*, or kept the vowel by analogy: *drayahyā* (once -*hiyā*) may represent either -*hı̯*- or -*hiı̯*-.

Final -*hy* written for -*hiy* (§37) was reduced to *hᵃ* before an enclitic: *vikanāhy* and *vikanāhᵃ*-

diš DB 4.73, 77; *paribarāhy* and *paribarāhᵃ-diš* DB 4.78, 74.

§137. THE -*uv* BEFORE ENCLITIC normally reverts to its true value, without the -*v*; but sometimes analogy of the separate word causes its retention:

hauv, but *hau-maiy hau-šaiy hau-dim hau-diš*; also *hauv-maiy hauv-taiy hauv-ciy*.

anuv, but *anu-dim*.

When -*am* is added, -*auv* should become -*av*-, but remains by analogy in *hauv-am*; -*ū* became -*ŭv*- before -*am*, in *tuvam* from **tū + -am*.

When *ā* is added to locatives, -*au*(*v*) becomes -*av*- as in *gāθavā*, or remains by analogy as in *dahyauvā*; -*u*(*v*) + *ā* becomes -*uvā*, which is ambiguous after consonants, representing either -*uv*- or -*v*-, as in *dahyušuvā*, *aniyā*ʰ*uvā* (cf. Skt. loc. pl. ending -*šu* -*su*).

§138. CONSONANTS BEFORE ENCLITICS show few changes.

I. Doubled consonants are written single: *āpiš* + *šim* = *āpišim* DB 1.95f; *taumaniš* + *šaiy* = *taumanišaiy* DNb 25f; -*kam* + *maiy* in [*nᵃyā*]*kama* A²Sa 4. In DNb 51f *ciyākaramᵃmᵃcᵃiyᵃ* is twice written for -*mᵃcᵃmᵃiyᵃ*, = *cıyākaram-ca-maiy*.

II. The reduced final consonants which are not written at the ends of words rarely reappear in sandhi; the examples are of -*s c*-, -*s k*-, -*d c*-, and are given in §105.

§139. CONTRACTION OF VOWELS IN SANDHI is to be expected in combination with enclitics, but the situations which produce it rarely occur in OP; there is one probable instance, *vašnā*[*pi*]*y* XPg 7f, for *vašnā* + *apiy*.

§140. SANDHI IN CONNECTION WITH PREFIXES shows the same phenomena as with enclitics.

I. Graphic -*ā* -*iy* -*uv* for -*ă* -*ĭ* -*ŭ* revert to -*ă* -*ĭ* -*ŭ* before consonants:

Prep. *upā*, but *upa-stām*; prefix *fra*- (not occurring separately in OP) in *fra-mātāram*, *fra-haravam*.

Prep. *patiy*, but *pati-padam*; *pariy*, but *pari-barāmiy*; prefix *ni*- (not found separately in OP) in *ni-padıy*, *ni-rasātıy*.

Nt. adj. *paruv*, but *paru-zanānām*; also *paruv-zanānām* and *paruv : zanānām*, after separate *paruv*.

II. Final -*ă* contracts with following initial *ă*- *ĭ*- *ăi*- *ŭ*-; final -*ĭ* contracts with initial *ĭ*-; -*i* of prefix seems to have contracted with verbal augment a-, unless prevented by analogy; examples in §131.

III. Final -i before initial ă- keeps the writing iyᵃ; the script does not show whether the -i is consonantized before the vowel, since it has no machinery for the distinction; but pati- never becomes *pašiy- (= pašy-) in compounds, though -ty- becomes OP -š(i)y-: patiy-āvahyaiy, patiy-āršaⁿ, patiy-ajatā; pariy-ait(iy), niy-apaišam, viy-atarayam.

The sequence -iya- seems in some instances to contract to -ī-; all the examples are in augmented forms of compound verbs, in some of which the uncontracted forms also appear, in which the analogy of the separate uncompounded form is the cause of the failure to contract:

abī-jāvayam, also abiy-ajāvayam.
nī-šādayam, also niy-ašādayam.
nī-štāya, also niy-aštāya and niy-aštāyam.
nī-yasaya for *niy-ayasaya; perhaps [a]tīya[siya] for *atiy-ayasiya.

IV. Final -u before initial ă- is similarly ambiguous in its writing; but probably the prefix Aryan *su-, pIr. *hu-, became hv- before a vowel, as in uvaspa-, cf. Av. hvaspō, Phl. hvasp. Other examples of this prefix can be found in the Lexicon, under ʰu-.

V. Final m of the prior element was of course not written before an initial consonant of the second part:

haᵐ-gmatā, haᵐ-karta-, haᵐ-dugā, but ham-aranam.
haᵐ-taxšataiy, but ham-ataxšatā.

VI. The initial s- of the second element appears as š after a final -i or -u of the preceding element, according to the Aryan phonetic variation (§115):

pAr. *sad-, pIr. *had-, but pAr. ni-šad-, unchanged in Iranian: generalized in niy-ašādayam, contracted nī-šādayam.
*ni-stā-, pAr. ni-štā-, unchanged in Iranian and generalized: niy-aštāyam, niy-aštāya, contracted nī-štāya.
Skt. sam-araṇam, OP hamaranam; but with prefix, ušhamaranakara, with double writing of the initial, š being the value after u, and h being the value when initial in the separate word. Perhaps also OP Pātišuvariš for Pāti-šʰuvariš, see Lex. s.v. Cf. Reichelt, Aw. Elmb. §103, for the same phenomenon in Avestan.

For the initial š- of the enclitic pronoun -šaiy -šim -šām -šiš, see §117.

VII. Initial y- after a final consonant of the prior element must of course appear as -iy-, as in dušiyāram, from duš- + yāram.

APPENDIX TO CHAPTER III

The origins of OP sounds, as expressed in the normalized transcription, may be traced from the following data (some references to Chapter II are included):

a < pIE e o a §61, cf. §36; pIE ǝ ǝ §63.I, §66.II, §67.I–II; pIE m̥ n̥ §67; pIE ə §71; graphic for i §22; see also ar below.

i < pIE i §64; pIE ə §63.II.

u < pIE u §64; analogical for r̥ §66.I.

ā < pIE ē ō ā §62, §36; pIE m̄ n̄ §68; by contraction of ă + ă §131, of ăhă §61, §131; graphic for -ă §36.I, §135; by vriddhi §126.

ī < pIE ī §65; by contraction of ĭ + ĭ §131, of ĭ + ă §131, §140.III; by vriddhi §126.

ū < pIE ū §65; by vriddhi §126.

ai < pIE ei oi ai §69; pIE əi §71; by contraction of ă + i §131; from a with epenthesis §127; graphic for a before y §48; cf. §136.

au < pIE eu ou au §70; pIE əu §71; by contraction of ă + u §131; graphic for a before v §48, and for ahu §70.

āi < pIE ēi ōi āi §72; by contraction of ā + ăi §131; graphic for ai §72, §179.IV; by vriddhi §126, cf. §136.

āu < pIE ēu ōu āu §72; graphic for āhu §72; by vriddhi §126.

ar §29–§35.
  = r̥ < pIE r̥ l̥ §66, §29, §30.
  = ar < Iran. ar §31–§33; pIr. ʋr ʋr §66.II; pIE r̄ l̄ §68.

k < pIE q qᵘ §98, §99; by borrowing §99.

x < pIE qh qᵘh §100; pIE q §102; pAr. k §103.I–III; pAr. gh §103.IV; by borrowing §100.

g < pIE g gh gᵘ gᵘh §98, §101, §103.IV.

c < pIE q qᵘ §98, §99, §105; pIE d + qᵘ §105.

j < pIE g gh gᵘ gᵘh §98, §101; pIE s §120.

t < pIE t th §76, §76.I–II; pIE dh §103.IV; pIE t(h) in tst(h) and d(h) in dzd(h) §85; by borrowing §76.V, §83.III.

θ < pIE th §76, §76.II; pIE t §77–§81; pIE k̑ §86, §87; for d(h) §83.II; by borrowing §76.V.

NOUN STEMS

ç < pIE *tr tl* §78, §79; pIE *k̂l* §94; by borrowing §78.

d < pIE *d dh* §76, §76.III; pAr. *d* from pIE *dh* §76.III; pIE *d(h)* in *dzd(h)* §85; pIE *ĝ ĝh* §86, §88, by borrowing §76.V.

p < pIE *p ph* §75, §75.I; pIE *u̯* §75.IV, §90; by borrowing §75.V.

f < pIE *ph p* §75, §75.II; pIE *su̯* §75.IV, §118.IV; by borrowing §75.V.

b < pIE *b bh* §75.III; pAr. *b* from pIE *bh* §75.III; pIE *u̯* §75.IV, §91; pIE *p + bh* §75.IV, §130; by borrowing §75.V.

n < pIE *n* §110, cf. §67.I–II; pIE *dn* §83.I, §130; by borrowing §110.

m < pIE *m* §109, cf. §67.I–II; pIE *m + m* §130; by borrowing §109.

y < pIE *i̯* §113.

r < pIE *r l* §79, §106, §107; part of pIE *r̥ r̄ l̥ l̄* §66, §68; by borrowing §106.

l < by borrowing only, §107.

v < pIE *u̯* §114.

s < pIE *s* §115, §116; pIE *ts* of *tst(h)* and *dz* of *dzd(h)* §85; pIE *k̂* §86, §87, §90, §93, §95; pIE *k̂u̯* §90; pIE *sk̂* §97, §130; pAr. *sć* §105; by borrowing §116.

š < pIE *s* §102, §105, §115, §117, §140.VI, pIE *k̂* §89, §93, §96, §120; pIE *g gh* §93, §96, §120; pIE *k̂s* §92, §102, §130; pIE *þ k̂þ* §102; pAr. *ć* §104; pIE *t* §80, §82; pIE *str* §79, §130; pIE *d* §105; *š + š* §130; by analogical extension §84; by borrowing §117.

z < pIE *ĝ ĝh* §86, §88, §91, §95; pIE *ĝhu̯* §91; pIE *s* §120, pIE *d + ĝh* §130; pIE *dz* in *dzd(h)* §85; by borrowing §120.

h < pIE *s* §118, §140.VI; by borrowing §118.V.

There are also certain losses and increments which could not be included in the preceding; these are merely graphic except when specified as phonetic:

Losses:

i after *h* §64, §27, §38; after *a*-consonant §22.

h before *i* §27, §64, §118.III; before *u* §28, §70, §118.IV, §140.IV; before *m r* §103.II, §118.II; (phon.) in *āh* from *ăhăh* §131.

y final before enclitics §118.III, §136.

v final before enclitics §137.

t final §40, §84.

d final §40, §84.

n final §40, §84, §112; medial §39, §108, §111; (phon.) by dissimilation §68.

m medial §39, §108, §111, §140.V.

pIE *u̯* (phon.) after labials §114.

pAr. *t* (phon.) in *-nt* §40, §84.

pAr. *h* (phonetic in some positions) §40, §105, §119.

syllables by haplology (phon.) §129.

Increments:

i after consonants §25, §140.VII.

u after consonants §26, §114; (phon.) by anaptyxis §128.

y after *-i* §37, §64, §113; after *ī* §23.I, §65.

v after *-u* §23.II, §38, §64; after *ū* §23.II, §65, §114.

x (phon.) before *š +* consonant §96.

CHAPTER IV. FORMATION OF NOUN AND ADJECTIVE STEMS

§141. NOUN AND ADJECTIVE STEMS may be either the bare root, nominal or verbal (§142), or the same with a thematic vowel *-a-* (§143), or the same with suffix ending in *-ă-* (§144–§151) or in *-ĭ-* (§152) or in *-ŭ-* (§153) or in a consonant (§154–§158). A noun or adjective suffix attached directly to a verbal root is called a primary suffix; one attached to a noun or adjective stem is called a secondary suffix. Many stems have two or more suffixes, or are compounds of two elements, the prior of which is or becomes invariable. A fuller treatment of the stems than that given in the following sections will normally be found in the Lexicon s.vv. The suffixes and the antecedent stems will here be presented not in pIE form, but in their pAr. or even Iranian or OP values, as convenience may dictate.

The following noun and adjective stems are not dealt with here or are dealt with only in part, because of uncertainty in their formation or because they are loan-words; possible interpretations of their formation will in some instances be found in the Lexicon:

-a- stems: *fraša-, spāθmaida-, Ainaira-, Autiyāra-, Atamaɩta-, Adukanaiša-, Arabāya-, Arxa-, Armina-, Ū(v)ja-, Uvādaicaya-, Katpatuka-, Ka*ᵐ-

paⁿda-, Karka-, Karmāna-, Kūša-, Gaⁿdāra-, Gaⁿdutava-, Tigra-, Dātuvahya-, Daha-, Dubāla-, Naditabaira-, Nabukudracara-, Nabunaita-, Nisāya-, Parga-, Pirāva-, Frāda-, Maka-, Mudrāya-, Yauna-, Labanāna-, Sug(u)da-, Skuⁿxa-, Skudra-, Sparda-, Zazāna-, Zūzahya-, Zraⁿka-, Haraiva-, Haldita-.

-ā- stems: Aθurā-, Arbairā-, Aršādā-, Izalā-, Uyamā-, Kuganakā-, Tāravā-, Tigrā-, Çūšā-, Yautiyā-, Yadā-, Raxā-, Ragā-.

-ĭ- stems: Arakadri-, Kāpišakāni-, Cicixri-, Cišpi-, Pātišuvāri-, Višpauzāti-.

-ŭ- stems: Abirādu-, Kuⁿduru-, Bābiru-, Māru-.

§142. ROOT NOUNS AND ADJECTIVES, some of them only in derivatives or in compounds, are found as follows:

ăp- 'water', xšap- 'night', xšnau- in u-xšnau- 'well satisfied', gau- 'cow' in compounds, θard- 'year', duvar- 'door' in duvara-, nar- 'man' in ūv-nara-, nāv- 'ship', nāh- 'nose', pad- 'foot' in nipadiy etc., vas- 'wish' in adv. vasiy, viθ- 'house', stā- in upa-stā- 'aid', zam- 'earth' in u-zma- etc.; perhaps napāt- 'grandson', an old pIE word, probably a compound; possibly dā- in ʰuvādā- as element of Paišiyā-uvādā-, and vaǰ- in gen. āθaha-vaǰa.

§143. NOUN AND ADJECTIVE STEMS WITH THEMATIC -a- occur as follows:

I. Attached to a verbal root, the ablaut grade of the root varying: kara- in compounds, u-cāra-, kāma-, karša-, gauša-, raga-, adv. daršam, drauga-, baga-, bara- and bāra- in compounds, zana- in compounds; less certain formations in ā-θaha- in āθaha-vaǰa, caša-, U-tāna-, u-tava-, gara- in bātu-gara-, Vī-vāna-, varga- in hauma-varga-.

II. Extending a non-verbal stem: ūv-nara- to nar-, ʰuvăi-pašiya- to pati-, pada- pāda- to pad-, Mārgava- to Margu-, duš-iyāra- to yār-, vazra- in vazra-ka- to *vaẓṛ-, vāhara- in Θūra-vāhara- to *vasṛ-, u-zma- to zam-, hama- to ham-; perhaps Gau-baruva- to baru-, māha- to māh-, viθa- to viθ-.

III. With no obvious simpler nominal or verbal form: ama- in Aršāma-, asa- aspa-, u-ba-, poss. ʰuva-, kaufa-, kāra-, daiva-, darga-, naiba-, Pārsa- pisa-, Māda-, raθa- in u-raθa-, varka- in Varkāna- and Varka-zana-, Saka-, spāda- in Taxma-spāda-, spāra- in Vāya-spāra-; the restored hana- in hana-tā-; mayūxa-, of uncertain etymology; the possible vāra- in ʰU-vāra-zmī-.

IV. Corresponding feminine formations in -ā-: isuvā-, xaudā-, θikā-, didā-, yakā-, Sakā-, haᵐdugā-, hᵃzā- in hᵃzānam, the uncertain paradayadām, the borrowed maškā-; the feminines to adjectives in masc.-neut. -a-.

V. These formations have varying meanings, including the following:

Abstracts: kāma- 'desire'.

Agents: baga- 'dispenser, god'; drauga- 'deceiver, the Lie'; aršti-bara- 'spear-bearer'; zūra-kara- 'evil-doer'; dāraniya-kara- 'gold-worker, goldsmith'.

Passives: haᵐ-dugā- 'im-pressed' = 'inscription'; pati-kara- 'made thereto' = 'sculptured figure'; asa-bāra- 'horse-borne'.

Adjectives of relation: Mārgava- 'related or belonging to Margu-, Margian'; ūv-nara- 'good belonging-to-a-man, skillfulness'.

VI. The vocalism of the root varies in these formations, being either -a- (pIE -e- or -o- or -a-), as in baga-, bara-, daiva-; or a zero grade, as in karša-, u-zma-, darga- (see Lex. s.vv.); or a vriddhied or lengthened grade (§126), as in kāma-, asa-bāra-, Mārgava-.

§144. NOUN AND ADJECTIVE STEMS WITH SUFFIX -(i)i̯a-: these are adjectival formations which may acquire substantival use; before the suffix a stem-final -a- regularly, and -ā- sometimes, disappears. The OP examples are the following:

I. Perhaps primary, in ariya-.

II. In words of numerical value: -i̯a- in an-iya-; -ii̯a- in duvit-īya-, çit-īya-, to pAr. *dui̯ta- *trita-.

III. Forming ethnics: Ākaufac-iya- to *Ākaufaka-; Aθur-iya- to Aθurā-; Armin-iya- to Armina-; Asagart-iya- to Asagarta-; Ū(v)ǰ-iya- to Ū(v)ǰa-; Uvārazmi-ya-; Kūš-iya- to Kūša-; Gaⁿdāra-ya- (possibly error for -riya-) to Gaⁿdāra-; Θatagu-iya- (error for -uviya- or -udaya- or -udiya-?) to Θatagu-; Putā-ya-; Bābiruv-iya-; Mac-iya- to Maka-; Spard-iya- to Sparda-; Haxāmaniš-iya-; Harauvati-ya-; Hiⁿdu-ya (error for Hiⁿduv-iya- ?).

IV. Other formations, including some personal names: agr-iya- to agra- (§148.I), θanuvan-iya-, daran-iya-, brazman-iya-, mart-iya- to marta-, haš-iya- to hat- (§240), ha-miç-iya- to miθra-; Artavard-iya-, Kaᵐbūǰ-iya-, Bard-iya-, Mardun-iya-.

V. Corresponding feminine forms as abstracts, which may become concretes: yauv-iyā 'course, canal'; nāv-iyā 'navigability'; perhaps paiš-iyā 'writing, document'.

VI. With suffix -ti̯a-, becoming Med. -θi̯a- in xšāyaθiya-, and OP -ši̯a- in anušiya-.

§145. NOUN AND ADJECTIVE STEMS WITH SUFFIX -ta- found in OP are mostly participles (§242), superlatives (§190.II), and ordinal numerals (§204). The remaining examples are aruvasta-, a neuter abstract seemingly formed upon an adjective *aru̯ant- (see Lex. s.v.); Xšaθrita-, a hypocoristic to a compound personal name; ardata- 'silver', perhaps an -a- extension of a participle in -ṇt-, cf. Lat. arg-ent-um; dasta- 'hand', which cannot be related to any simpler extant root; and three feminine abstracts aršta-, hanatā-, avastā-, the last two of which are dubious and the third is taken as having acquired concrete meaning.

§146. NOUN AND ADJECTIVE STEMS WITH SUFFIX -ka- are adjectives which may assume substantival meanings. This -ka- may be attached directly to a stem, nominal or verbal; it may appear as -aka- or -ika-, in which it can often not be determined whether the vowel belongs to the suffix or to the basic stem. Only when -ika- is attached to an -a- stem is it clear that the -i- belongs to the suffix. The OP examples are:

I. Perhaps primary: uš-ka-, karnuv-aka-.

II. Secondary: *Ākaufa-ka- in Ākaufaciya-; Anāma-ka-; aʰr-ika-, to pAr. *asra-, LAv. aṷra-; Arša-ka-, hypocoristic to a compound name; āršti-ka-, probably with vriddhi; kapauta-ka-; kāsa-ka-; baⁿda-ka-; vazra-ka-; Vahau-ka-, hypocoristic to a compound name.

III. Of somewhat uncertain analysis: niyāka-, apa-niyāka-, marī-ka- (see Lex. s.vv.).

§147. NOUN AND ADJECTIVE STEMS WITH SUFFIX -na-, varying with -ana-, are not infrequent in OP; there are also extensions of the -na- to -ina- and -mna-.

I. Primary -na-, added to the root or to the thematic verbal stem (often not distinguishable from verbal nouns!), making nouns of various meanings:

Expressing place: apa-dā-na-, daiva-dā-na-, ā-yada-na-, fem. us-taša-nā-, ā-vaha-na-, stā-na-, varda-na-.

Expressing abstracts (actions): fem. fra-mā-nā-, loc. adv. aš-naiy, adj. ʰu-rada-na-, yā-na-, vaš-na-, ham-ara-na-; possibly fem. Pati-graba-nā-, becoming a place-name.

Expressing concretes: arja-na-, fem. stū-nā-, fem. hai-nā-.

Expressing adjectival actor, as personal name: Vi-dar-na-; name of month, Vi-yax-na-.

Forming adjectives: a-xšai-na-.

Forming passive participles, see §243.

II. Secondary -na-, forming adjectives: para-na-, perhaps here kam-na; as masc. sb., drauja-na-, as nt. abstract pariy-ana-; forming hypocoristic personal name, Āçi-na-; perhaps Marduna- in Mardun-iya-; forming place names, with lengthening of preceding vowel, Varkāna- to varka-, Haᵐ-gmatāna- to haᵐ-gmata-; with -na- of uncertain origin, ʰazāna- (see Lex. s.v.).

III. Secondary -ina-, forming adjectives: aθaⁿ-ga-ina-, kāsaka-ina-, nauca-ina-.

IV. -mna- in present middle participles, see §241.

V. For the dubious neuter abstract dar-tana-, see §238.

§148. NOUN AND ADJECTIVE STEMS WITH SUFFIX -ra- occur in OP as follows:

I. The suffix -ra-, sometimes primary and sometimes secondary, appears in agra- whence agriya-, Aʰu-ra-, tig-ra-, personal name Θux-ra-, θū-ra- in Θūra-vāhara-; adj. dū-ra-, whence adv. nū-ram; the uncertain ʰu-raθa-ra-. Problematic, and perhaps not Iranian, tacara- dacara-. On vazra- in vazra-ka-, vāhara- in Θūra-vahara-, partara-, see §154.I.

II. Comparatives in -(a)ra-, -tara-, -θara-, see §190.III.

III. Primary suffix -tra- appears in ci-ça-, xša-ça-, pu-ça-, va-ça- in vaça-bara-; ʰŪ-vāxš-tra- (with Med. tr after s); loanword Mitra- Miθra-, also in ha-miç-iya- and Vaʰu-misa-.

§149. NOUN AND ADJECTIVE STEMS WITH SUFFIX -ma-.

I. Primary, in the following: dar-ma- in personal name Upa-darma-, gar-ma- in month name Garma-pada-, fem. tau-mā-, adj. tax-ma- in personal names (see Lex.), hau-ma- in hauma-varga-. On dubious siyamam, see Lex.

II. Secondary, in ordinal nava-ma- (§204.IV).

§150. NOUN AND ADJECTIVE STEMS WITH SUFFIX -u̯a- are a miscellaneous group. They include ai-va- 'one'; adjective duru-va-, to verbal root dar-; adj. par-uva-; ethnic Parθa-va-, cf. Pārsa-; yā-va-, to relative ya-; har-uva-; visa- and (Med.) vispa-, from pIE *u̯iḱ-u̯o-; jī-va- 'living', unless the v is somehow radical (cf. §216). On Gau-baruva-, see Lex. s.v.; on fem. aruvā- as abstract, see Lex. s.v.

§151. Noun and Adjective Stems with miscellaneous -a- suffixes, not already given, include the following:
-θa- in fem. gai-θā-.
-ga- in aθaⁿ-ga-, cf. asan-.
-sa- in bux-ša-, in personal name Baga-buxša-.

§152. Noun and Adjective Stems ending in -ĭ-, apart from some names of persons and places listed in §141, are the following; stems in -ĭ- and those in -ī- cannot be distinguished except by correspondences in other languages, which sometimes are lacking (§22):

I. Stems in -ĭ-: acc. paθ-im, bāj-im; āθi- in personal name Āθiy-ābaušna-; dip-i-; uša-bār-i-; Āçi- extended from *ātr- in hypocoristic personal name Āçi-na- and in month name Āçi-yādiya-; personal names Dādarš-i-, month names Θāigarc-i-, Bāga-yād-i-; secondary in adjective yāuman-i-; loanword skauθ-i-.

II. Stems in -ī-, some of which may have been transferred to -i- stem declension (§179.I): āp-ī- (see Lex. s.v.); dual uš-ī-; fem. adjj. to stems in -vant-, as place names, Sikayaʰ-uvat-ī-, Haraʰ-uvat-ī-; fem. ptc. yau[daⁿtim], to masc. -ant-; to stem in -tar-, Bāx-tr-ī-; ʰUvārazm-ī-; adj., aθaⁿgain-ī- in npf. -iya, to masc. aθaⁿgaina-.

III. Suffix -ti-: arš-ti-, iš-ti-, pa-ti- in ʰuvāipa-šiya-, šiyā-ti-, pas-ti- to pad- 'foot', mar-ti- (pIE *mr̥-ti-) 'death' in uvā-maršiyu-, Fravar-ti-, perhaps ni-piš-ti-.

IV. Miscellaneous: -thi- in duvar-θi-; -mī- in bū-mi-; perhaps -mi- in θar-mi-.

§153. Noun and Adjective Stems ending in -ŭ-, apart from some place names listed in §141, are as follows:

I. Stems in -ŭ-: adj. par-u-, ard-u- in personal name Ardu-maniš-, vaʰ-u- in personal names Dāraya-vau- Vau-misa- Vahau-ka-; substantives baru- in Gau-baruv-a-, maršiy-u- 'death' in adj. uvā-maršiyu-, mard-u- in Marduniya, Mag-u-, Hiⁿd-u-, Marg-u-, Kūr-u-, uncertain bāt-u- in bātu-gara-; loanwords pir-u-, Ufrat-u-; restored loanword agur-u-; uncertain as to stem, Θatag-u-, sikabr-u-.

II. Stem in -ū-; tan-ū-.

III. With suffix -tu-: gā-θu-; xra-θu- (unless the -t- is in this word radical rather than suffixal). For θ, see §81.

IV. With suffix -i̯u-: dah-yu-, with uncertain root.

§154. Noun and Adjective Stems ending in -r-, as found in OP, consist of two classes of nouns.

I. Neuter nouns with nom.-acc. ending in -r, replaced by -n- in other case-forms; in OP, only in derivatives: pAr. *u̯az-r̥, in OP vazr-a-ka-; pAr. *u̯as-r̥ in OP Θūra-vāhar-a-; pAr. *pr̥t-r̥ in OP par-tara-. An extension of the -n- form of the suffix -tr̥/-tn- is probably to be seen in the OP infinitive (§238), perhaps also in [da]rtanayā (§238).

II. Nouns with suffix -tar-, including agents jaⁿtar-, fra-mā-tar-, dauš-tar-; words of relationship pi-tar-, mā-tar-, brā-tar-; also ā-tar- 'fire', in derivative personal names.

§155. Noun and Adjective Stems ending in -n- are of several kinds in OP:

I. Stems in -an-: as-an- and its derivative aθaⁿ-ga-, arš-an- varying with arš-a-, barš-an-.

II. Stems in -tan-: ara-šan- (for -š-, §82).

III. Stems in -man-: as-man-, tau-man-, nā-man-, braz-man- in adj. brazman-iya-, yāu-man- in adj. yāuman-i-.

IV. Stems in -van-: artā-van-, xšaça-pā-van-, θan-uvan- in θanuvan-iya-.

V. Stem in -vin-: adj. manaʰ-uvin-.

§156. Noun and Adjective Stems ending in -s- are of several kinds in OP:

I. Stem in -s-: Maz-dā-h-, also in Aʰura-mazdāh-.

II. Neuters in -as-: dray-ah-, man-ah, miθ-ah-, rauc-ah-, zūr-ah-, har-ah- in Haraʰ-uvatī-; can-ah- assuming masc. forms in cpd. personal name Aspa-canah-; suffixal -tas- in rau-tah-; suffixal -nas- in far-nah- assuming masc. forms in cpd. personal name Viⁿdaᵗ-farnah-.

III. Stems in -i̯as-: sika-yah- in place name Sikayaʰ-uvati-; comparatives tauvī-yah-, vah-yah- in personal name Vahyaz-dāta (§120); zero grade -is- in superlative ending -iš-ta-, in maθ-išta-duva-išta-, §190.II.

IV. Stems in -is-: neuters abi-cariš, had-iš; becoming masc. in personal names Ardu-man-iš, Haxā-man-iš.

§157. Adjective Stems with suffix -vant- are found in OP only in derivatives; the OP syllabary does not make clear whether these derivatives are formed on -vant- (pIE -u̯ent-) or on zero grade -vat- (pIE -u̯n̥t-), more probably they are made upon vat-: ar-uvant- in aruvas-ta-, sikayaʰ-uvant- in Sikayaʰuvat-i-, haraʰ-uvant- in Haraʰuvat-i-.

§158. OTHER NOUN AND ADJECTIVE STEMS ENDING IN CONSONANTS are to be found listed among Root Nouns and Adjectives, §142.

§159. NOUN AND ADJECTIVE COMPOUNDS IN OP, apart from phrasal adverbs (§191.IV), may have as prior element an inseparable adverb as in *a-xšata-*, *ʰu-cāra-*, *duš-iyāra-*, *ham-arana-* (§268); or a prepositional adverb, as in *apa-dāna-*, *patı-kara-* (§268); or a noun or adjective stem.[1] They have as second element a noun or adjective stem, which may receive an additional suffix.

Only compounds of stem + stem will be here discussed. Either stem may itself be a compound; either stem may already have one or more suffixes. The initial syllable of the first element, especially in adjectives, may show vriddhi or lengthening of the vowel, as in *dāraniya-kara-* 'gold-worker' to *daraniya-* 'gold'; less often this appears in the second part, as in *Bāga-yādi-* 'god-worshipping (month)', where it is seen in both parts, and in *asa-bāra-* 'horse-borne', where it indicates passive meaning.

Compound adjectives with second elements of a specific gender assume the genders of their derived meaning and use, with change of form if necessary. Thus the masc. name *Haxā-maniš* 'Having the mind of a friend, Achaemenes' has a neuter stem as its second element, used without change in the masculine adjective as noun; the masc. adjective *tigraxauda-* 'wearing a pointed cap' has as second element the fem. *xaudā-* 'cap'.

Derivative adjectives to compounds may be made by the addition of suffixes: *Haxāmaniš-iya-* 'Achaemenian' to *Haxāmaniš-*, *Asagart-iya-* 'Sagartian' to *Asa-garta-*.

Compounds of stem + stem, so far as they occur in OP, may be divided into (1) Determinative Nouns and Adjectives, dependent and descriptive; (2) Possessive Adjectives, dependent and descriptive; (3) Participial Adjectives, the prior element governing the second. Adjectives of all these classes may become nouns as names of persons and places.

The following will not be dealt with here, because of uncertainties or difficulties in their interpretations; but some information may be found in the Lex. s.vv.:

Common nouns: *āθahavaja*, *ʰuvādā-*.
Personal names: *Kaᵐbūjiya-*, *Gaumāta-*, *Cišpi-*.
Place names: *Uvādaicaya-*, *Uvārazmī-*, *Paišiyāuvādā-*.

Personal and place names of Elamite, Akkadian, and Armenian origin also cannot be discussed among OP compounds.

§160. DETERMINATIVE NOUNS AND ADJECTIVES, compounded of stem + stem; the prior element determines or limits the second.

I. Dependent determinatives, the prior element standing in some case relation to the second:

a. Accusative:

hamarana-kara- 'battle-making'; *zūra-kara-* 'evil-doing'; *dāraniya-kara-* 'gold-working'; *ciyā-kara-* 'doing how much', *avā-kara-* 'doing that'.

aršti-bara- 'spear-bearer'; *vaça-bara-* 'bow-bearer'; *taka-bara-* 'petasos-wearing'.

xšaça-pāvan- 'kingdom-protecting, satrap'; *du-varθi-* (for **duvar-varθi-*) 'doorway-covering, colonnade'; *hauma-varga-*, *maz-dāh-*, *bātu-gara-*, see Lex. s.vv.

Arta-vardiya- 'Justice-worker'.

b. Genitive:

arda-stāna- 'place of light'; *daiva-dāna-* 'holder of demons'.

Xšayāršan- (from **xšaya-aršan-*) 'Hero of Kings'; *Gau-baruv-a-* 'Lord of cattle'; *Vaʰu-misa-* 'Friend of the good'.

c. Instrumental:

asa-bāra- 'borne by horses'; *uša-bari-* 'borne by camels'; *[dasta]karta-* 'done by hand'.

Baga-buxša- 'Freed by God'; *Bagābigna-* perhaps 'Begotten by God'.

d. Ablative: *Āθiy-ābaušna-* 'Freed from misfortune'.

e. With idea of specification: *Ciça-taxma-* 'Brave in lineage'.

II. Descriptive determinatives,[1] the prior ele-

---

[1] In *Ciça-taxma-* the prior element is not the bare stem, but the stem with an added nasal, attested in the transliterations into Elam., Akk., and Greek This nasal can hardly be the acc. case-ending (as tentatively suggested by Bthl. AiW 587); it seems unexplainable except as a transfer from some other cpd. in which a nasal in this position was justified (Schulze, KZ 33.216 n3; Richter, IF 9.203-4, Foy KZ 37.504-5). Cf Gk Ἀρτεμ-βάρης (Hdt. 1.114-6, 9.122; Aesch. Pers. 29, 302, 971) = OP **Artam-bara* 'Arta-upholder', where the prior element seems to be in the accusative (cf Stonecipher, Graeco-Persian Names 27).

[1] The greatest part of this class consists of those whose first part is an inseparable adverb or a prepositional prefix; under our plan these are not here considered (§159).

ment directly modifying the second as adjective or appositive:

A^hura-mazdāh- 'Ahuramazda', lit. 'Lord Wise'; cf. Lex. s.v.

§161. POSSESSIVE ADJECTIVES, often differing from the preceding only by a shift of accent which can be observed in accented Sanskrit words, but cannot be determined in OP or Avestan.

I. Determinative compounds (cf. §160.I); the OP examples are all names of persons or of places or of months:

a. Accusative: *Aspa-canah-* 'Having love of horses'; *Bāga-yādi-* '(Month) marked by the worship of the *bagas*'.

b. Genitive: *Arta-xšaça-* 'Having a kingdom of justice'; *Aršāma-* (from **arša-ama-*) 'Having the might of a hero'; *Haxā-maniš-* 'Having the mind of a friend'; *Garma-pada-* '(Month) having the place of heat'; *Asa-garta-* '(Land) having caves of stone'.

II. Descriptive compounds (cf. §160.II.):

a. The prior element is an adjectival modifier: *paru-zana-* 'having many men'; *vispa-zana-* 'having all (kinds of) men', *visa-dahyu-* 'containing all lands'; *hama-pitar-* 'having the same father'; *ha-mātar-* 'having the same mother'; *tigra-xauda-* 'wearing pointed caps'; *uvā-maršiyu-* 'having one's own death' (see Lex.).

Ariya-çiça- 'Having Aryan lineage'; *Ardu-maniš-* 'Having an upright mind'; *Taxma-spāda-* 'Having a brave army'; *Vahyaz-dāta-* 'Following the better law'; *Vištāspa-* from **višta-aspa-* (see Lex. s.v.) 'Having ready horses'; *Θata-gu-* '(Land) having hundreds of cattle' (but see Lex. s.v.); *Θūra-vāhara-* '(Month) having vigorous spring-time'.

b. The prior element is appositive to the second:
Varka-zana- '(Month) belonging to the wolf-men'. *uvāi-pašiya-* 'having self as lord', with adjectival suffix.

c. The second element is predicate to the prior: *Ariyāramna-* from **ariya-āramna-* 'Having the Aryans pacified'; so to be interpreted because the *-na-* participles are passive.

§162. PARTICIPIAL COMPOUND ADJECTIVES, the participle as prior element of the compound governing the second; all the OP examples are personal names:[1]

---

[1] *Xšayāršā* is taken by Bv. Gr. §315 as an *-āh-* stem like *Auramazdāh-*, based on a contraction of *xšayaⁱ* 'rul-

Dārayaⁱ-vaʰu- 'Holding firm the good'.
Vⁱⁿdaⁱ-farnah- 'Finding the Glory'.
Vāyaⁱ-spāra- 'Weaving shields', = 'Maker of wicker shields'; unless *vāya-* is not a participle, but a noun of action (*-a-* stem), and the name is a possessive adjective (§161.I.b.), 'Having a shield of weaving, = wicker shield'.

§163. NAMES OF PERSONS in the OP inscriptions must be divided according to nationalities, which in the main show the linguistic nature.

I. Names of Persians are far the most numerous, but some show Median phonetics, indicated by a following M in parenthesis:

a. Names of the Achaemenian dynasty: *Ariyāramna-*, *Artaxšaça-*, *Aršāma-*, *Uvaxštra-* (M), *Kabūjⁱya-*, *Kūru-*, *Xšayāršan-*, *Gaubaruva-*, *Cišpi-*, *Dārayavau-*, *Bardiya-*, *Vištāspa-* (M).

b. Names of other Persians: *Artavardiya-*, *Ardumaniš-*, *Aspacanah-* (M), *Utāna-*, *Θuxra-*, *Dātuvahya-*, *Dādarši-*, *Bagābigna-*, *Bagabuxša-*, *Marduniya-*, *Vaumisa-* (with *-s-* which is not Persian nor Median), *Vāyaspāra-*, *Vahauka-*, *Vahyaz-dāta-*, *Vidafarnah-* (M), *Vidarna-*, *Vivāna-*, *Haxāmaniš-*.

II. Names of Medes: *Xšaθrita-*, *Gaumāta-*, *Taxmaspāda-*, *Fravarti-*, and the Sagartian *Çiçataxma-*.

III. Names of other Iranians: the Margian (Bactrian) *Frāda-*; the Scythian *Skuⁿxa-*; unspecified *Āθiyābaušna-*, *Aršaka-*.

IV. Names of Armenians: *Arxa-*, *Dādarši-*, *Haldita-*.

V. Names of Elamites: *Atamaita-*, *Cicixri-*, and four which have the appearance of IE names: *Āçina-*, *Upadarma-*, *Martiya-* (see Lex. s.vv.), which may have been more or less etymologized when transcribed into OP; and *Imaniš-*, the name assumed by the Persian Martiya as usurping king of Elam, with *-maniš-* reminding of *Haxāmaniš-* and *Ardumaniš-*.

VI. Names of Babylonians: Akkadian *Ainaira-*, *Naditabaira-*, *Nabukudracara-*, *Nabunaita-*.

VII. Uncertain writings, probably corrupt: *Xaršādašyā* (= *Xšayāršā*?), *Ardaxcašca* (prob-

---

ing' and *arša-* 'just', and therefore meaning 'Ruling with justice'. But there is no example in which contraction of a short vowel takes place despite the reduced final *-t*; for another objection, and the proper interpretation of the case-endings, see §187 and note 2, and Lex. s.v.

ably = *Artaxšaçā*), *Vašdāsaka*, *Vahyav·šdāpaya*, *Hadaxaya*.

§164. PERSONAL NAMES OF IRANIANS are of the usual IE types.

I. The typical IE name consisted of a compound of two stems; such names have mostly been interpreted in §160–§162. To these must be added the following, which are of uncertain interpretation: *Ka^mbūjiya-*, *Gaumāta-* (see Lex. s.vv.).

II. Compounds of which the prior part is an inseparable or a prepositional prefix are the following: ^h*U-vaxštra-*, *Vi-darna-*, *Vi-vāna-*, *Fra-varti-*, perhaps ^h*U-tāna-*. It is possible that some of these are only shortenings of longer compounds of which these were the prior part, and that they belong under III.

III. Hypocoristics or nicknames were formed in pIE by limiting the compound name to approximately its prior part, to which there might or might not be added a suffix. There are the following probable examples in the OP names: *Θuxra-*, *Bard-iya-*, *Vahau-ka-*, *Arša-ka-*, *Xšaθr-ita-*, *Frāda-*, *Martiya-*

IV. Still other names are appellatives indicating the qualities of the persons, like the reduplicated *Dā-darši-* 'Bold'. Possibly ^h*U-vaxštra-*, *Vi-darna-*, *Vi-vāna-* (given under II) also belong here. Or names may denote occupations, as perhaps in the adjectival derivative, possibly patronymic, *Mardun-iya-* 'Vintner's son'.

V. Uncertain names: *Cišpi-* (or *Ca^hišpi-*); *Kūru-*; *Dātuvahya-*; *Arxa-*, name of an Armenian, of unknown meaning, and probably belonging under III or IV.

§165. NAMES OF MONTHS in OP are adjectives, or substantives as adjectives, modifying the word 'month'; the phrase is always in the genitive.[1] All are compounds of two stems or of prefix + stem, and some end in an adjectival suffix.

With vriddhi in first part: *Θāigarci-* (etymology uncertain); perhaps in *Adu-kanaiša-* (etymology uncertain), *A-nāma-ka-*.

With vriddhi in both parts: *Bāga-yādi-*.

With vriddhi in second part: *Āçi-yād-iya-*, *Θūra-vāhara-*.

Perhaps with vriddhi in prefix: *Vi-yax-na-* (radical element uncertain).

---

[1] The form *māhyā* is more probably a contracted gen. *māhahyā, to stem *māha-*, than a loc. *māhyā* to stem *māh-*, with dependent substantive genitives of equivalence.

Without vriddhi in either part: *Garma-pada-*, and the restored *Varka-zana-* (but see Lex. s.v.).
For further details, see Lex. s.vv. and §161.

§166. NAMES OF PLACES are less likely to be of perspicuous etymology even than names of persons, since names of places often persist even when there has been a change of population and an attendant change of language.[1] The OP place-names include the following types: *dahyāuš* 'administrative province' and also 'district' of a province; 'city', generic word not given in OP; *vardanam* 'town'; *āvahanam* 'village', *didā* 'fortress'; *kaufa* 'mountain'; *rauta* 'river'. At the first introduction of less-known place names the generic word is regularly given; but it is given with names of provinces only when there is a list of all or several, and is omitted with some larger districts (*Karmāna*, *Varkāna*), with cities (*Pārsa*, if = 'Persepolis'; *Paišiyāuvādā* 'Pasargadae'; *Hagmatāna* 'Ecbatana'; *Arbairā* 'Arbela'; *Bābiruš* 'Babylon'), and with well-known rivers (*Ufrātuš* 'Euphrates'; *Tigrā* 'Tigris'). The place names may be geographically, and to a certain extent linguistically, grouped together as follows:[2]

I. Indo-Iranian provinces:

Pārsa 'Persis, Persia': including districts *Karmāna*, *Yautiyā*; cities *Paišiyāuvādā*, perhaps *Pārsa*; towns *Uvādaicaya*, *Kuganakā*, *Tāravā*, *Raxā*; mountains *Arakadriš*, *Parga*.

Māda 'Media': including districts *Asargarta* (given as administrative province in DPe 15), *Kapada*, *Nisāya*, *Ragā*; city *Hagmatāna*; towns *Kuduruš*, *Māruš*; fortress, *Sikayauvatiš*.

Parθava 'Parthia': including district *Varkāna* 'Hyrcania' and towns *Patigrabanā*, *Višpauzātiš*.

Harauvatiš 'Arachosia': including district *Gadutava*; fortresses *Aršādā*, *Kāpišakāniš*.

---

[1] Cf. the names of the states of the United States of America; about half of them are derived from aboriginal American languages, and the rest come directly or ultimately from English, German, Celtic, French, Spanish, Latin, Greek, Hebrew, and Indo-Iranian. For the OP place-names which can with certainty or with some probability be interpreted etymologically, see Lex. s vv. [2] This section attempts only to list and classify the nouns and ethnic adjectives used as geographical terms in the OP texts; a complete list of the provinces of the Persian Empire, as given in the OP texts, will be found in JNES 2 302–6, with discussion of the variations. The classification of *Yadā* DB 3 26, apparently the OP name for Anshan (see Lex. s.v. ²*Yadā-*), is somewhat uncertain.

Bāxtriš 'Bactria': including district *Marguš* 'Margiana'.

Ākaufaciyā 'Men of Akaufaka'; *Uvārazmīy* and *-miš* 'Chorasmia'; *Gadāra* 'Gandaritis'; *Θataguš* 'Sattagydia'; *Dahā* 'the Daae'; *Maka* or ethnic *Maciyā*; *Saka* or fem. *Sakā* 'Scythia' or *Sakā* 'the Scythians'; *Sug(u)da* 'Sogdiana'; *Haraiva* 'Aria'; *Hiduš* 'Sind'.

II. Elam:

Ū(v)ja 'Elam', including city *Çūšā*, village *Abirāduš*.

III. Semitic provinces:

Bābiruš 'Babylónia': including district *Dubāla*; city *Bābiruš* 'Babylon'; town *Zazāna*; rivers *Ufrātuš*, *Tigrā*.

Aθurā 'Assyria and Syria': including district *Izalā*; city *Arbairā*; mountain *Labanāna*.

Arabāya 'Arabia'.

IV. Armenia:

Armina or *Arminiya* 'Armenia': including district *Autiyāra*; village *Zūzahya*; fortresses *Uyamā*, *Tigrā*.

V. Provinces of Asia Minor and Southeastern Europe:

Katpatuka 'Cappadocia'; *Karkā* 'the Carians'; *Yauna* 'Ionia' or *Yaunā* 'the Ionians'; *Sparda* 'Sardis, Lydia'; *Skudra* 'Thrace and Macedonia'.

VI. Provinces of Africa:

Mudrāya 'Egypt' or *Mudrāyā* 'the Egyptians', including river *Pirāva* 'Nile'.

Kūša 'Ethiopia' or *Kūšiyā* 'the Ethiopians'.
Putāyā 'the Libyans'.

§167. PROVINCE NAMES AND ETHNICS. In certain instances the province name is merely the masculine ethnic, with ellipsis of a masculine noun for 'country'; once it is the feminine ethnic. But more frequently the ethnic is formed from the province name by the *-ya-* suffix; and the plural of the ethnic thus formed, as well as that of other ethnics, may be used as province name. Once the *-ya-* ethnic in the singular is used for the province as alternative to the suffixless form. In the accompanying table, the occurrence of the province name and the ethnic in identical form is indicated in the second column by x, and ethnics which in the singular are extant in full only in the late text A?P are indicated by a following *.

To these names may be added those of three large districts which were not governmental provinces: *Karmāna*, *Varkāna*, *Marguš* with ethnic *Mārgava*; ethnic *Pātišuvariš*, to an unknown place-name; *Haxāmanišiya*, patronymic family-name to *Haxāmaniš*; *Maguš*, denoting a member of the priestly clan of Media.

Of the province names used as ethnics, *Bābiruš* and *Ūvja* as ethnics are certainly errors. Of the ethnics in A?P, *Kūšāya* is probably miswritten for *Kūšiya*; *Gadāraya* for *Gadāriya*; *Θataguiya* for *Θataguviya*, or misread for *Θatagudaya*, a miswriting for *Θatagudiya*; *Hiduya* for *Hiduviya*.

Province	Same as Ethnic	Fem. as Province	Derivative Ethnic	Pl. Ethnic as Province	Masc. as Province
Aθurā			*Aθuriya*		
Arabāya	x*				
Armina			*Arminiya*		*Arminiya*
Asagarta			*Asagartiya*		
Ū(v)ja	x		*Ū(v)jiya*		
Uvārazm-īy -iš			*Uvārazm'ya**		
Katpatuka	x*				
			Karka	*Karkā*	
Kūša			*Kūšāya**	*Kūšiyā*	
Gadāra			*Gadāraya**		
Θataguš			*Θataguiya**		
				Dahā	
Parθava	x				
Pārsa	x				
			*Putāya**		*Putāyā*
Bāxtriš					

Province	Same as Ethnic	Fem. as Province	Derivative Ethnic	Pl Ethnic as Province	Masc. as Province
Bābiruš	x		Bābiruviya		
Maka			Maciya*	Maciyā	
Māda	x				
Mudrāya	x			Mudrāyā	
Yauna	x			Yaunā	
Saka	x		Sakā	Sakā	
Sug(u)da					
Skudra	x*				
Sparda			Spardiya		
Zraka	x*				
Haraiva					
Harauvatiš			Harauvatiya*		
Hiduš			Hiduya*		

CHAPTER V. DECLENSION OF NOUNS, ADJECTIVES, PRONOUNS

§168. DECLENSION IN OP. The OP noun, along with the pronoun and the adjective, shows approximately the expected assortment of forms. There are nouns and adjectives with stems ending in -a- -ā-, -i- -ī-, -u- -ū-, -āh- -ah- -iš-, -tār- -tar-, -an- -man- -van- -vin- -vant-, -t- -d- -θ- -s-. Some categories are but scantily represented, and in the discussion of each class all extant forms are listed, except where the examples are numerous.

All the cases found in Sanskrit and Avestan are found in OP, except the dative, which has been lost, its functions being assumed by the genitive form. The ablative has no distinctive form, but has been merged in the instrumental and the locative either by phonetic development or by analogy; except for one form, Bābirauš, which is identical with the genitive, as in Sanskrit. Similarly the accusative plural has become identical with the nominative, either by phonetic process or by analogy, except in the enclitic pronouns which have no nominative form.

Both singular and plural numbers are represented in OP, and there are a few dual forms.

§169. THE CASE-ENDINGS OF -o- STEMS IN pIE: these are added to the stem-vowel, which is either e or o, and when vowel is added to vowel a contraction results, giving either a long vowel or a diphthong.

I. The endings of the singular: Nom. -s and acc. -m are added to stem-vowel -o-, giving -os -om; and the voc. is the bare stem in -e: Lt. lupus lupum lupe, Gk. λύκος λύκον λύκε 'wolf'. The neuter has -m as ending for the nom. as well as for the acc.

Gen. ending -sio is found in Aryan and in Greek, added to stem-vowel -o-: *tosio, Skt. tásya, Gk. (Hom.) τοῖο, (classical) τοῦ; and with added -s in a few Latin words: eius, Skt. asyá; cuius, Skt. kásya, from *qᵘosio. This ending was original in pronouns only, and spread from pronouns to certain classes of nouns in some languages.

The inst. ended in -ē and -ō, evidently by contraction of the stem-vowel -e- and -o- with another vowel whose quality cannot be determined. The abl. had -ēd and -ōd, a similar contraction with an unidentifiable vowel plus a dental consonant, which may have been either t or d; sandhi processes make it impossible to determine its original nature.[1] The loc. ended in -i, added to either stem-vowel: cf. Gk. οἴκοι and οἴκει 'at home'.

II. The forms of the plural number: Nom. pl. ending -es, added to stem vowel -o-, gave -ōs, which remained in Aryan, Germanic (Gothic wulfōs 'wolves'), Oscan-Umbrian (but was replaced by -oi, with pronominal plural-sign -i, in Greek, Latin, Balto-Slavic). Acc. pl. ending -ns, added to -o-, gave -ons. Nom. -acc. nt. pl. in -ā was properly a fem. nom. sg. in -ā, with collective meaning. Gen. pl. ending -ōm, contracted with the

---

[1] For a theory of the origin of this ending, see Sturtevant, Lg. 8.1–10.

stem-vowel -o-, gave -ōm, as in Gk. λύκων, but in Aryan was remodeled after the gen. pl. of -n- stems. Inst. pl. ending -ais (-a- indeterminate for a e o!), contracting with stem-vowel -o-, gave -ōis, seén with shortening in Greek λύκοις, and with retained length in Skt. and Av.; but the pronominal -oibhis (stem-vowel -o- + pronominal pl. -i + inst. pl. -bhis), remodeling of masc. dat.-abl. -oibhios (Skt. *tébhyas*, demonstrative pronoun) after fem. inst. pl. -ābhis (Skt. *tā́bhiṣ*), is seen in OP. Loc. pl. ending -su, added to stem-vowel -o- + pron. pl. -i, is found in Aryan and in Slavic; but -oisu was remodeled to -oisi in Gk. (dat. pl. λύκοισι) after the loc. sg. ending -i.

III. The forms of the dual number: see §189.

§170. THE CASE-ENDINGS OF -o- STEMS IN ARYAN. A comparative table of the endings in pIE, pAr., Skt., Av., OP is here given, including the cases represented in the extant OP words; except that dual forms are in §189.

	pIE	pAr.	Skt.	Av.	OP
Sg. Nom.	-os	-aḥ[1]	-aḥ	-ō	-aʰ
Acc.	-om	-am	-am	-əm	-am
Inst.	-ē, -ō	-ā	-ena[2]	-ā -a[3]	-ā
Abl.	-ēd, -ōd	-ād	-āt[1]	-āṯ	-āᵗ
Gen.	-osi̯o	-asya	-asya	-ahyā -ahe[3]	-ahyā
Loc.	-ei, -oi	-ai	-e	{-ōi-, e[3] / -ay-a[3]}	{-aiy / -ay-ā}
Voc.	-e	-a	-a	-ā -a[3]	-ā
Pl. Nom.	-ōs	{-āḥ[1] / -āsaḥ[4]}	-āḥ / -āsaḥ	-ā -a[3] / -ā̊ṅhō	{-āʰ / -āhaʰ}
Acc.	-ons	-ān[5]	-ān	-ąs	-āʰ
Inst.	-āis	-āiš	-āiṣ	-āiš	-aibišⁱ[6]
Gen.	-ōm	-ānām[7]	-ānām	-ānąm	-ānām
Loc.	-oisu	-aišu	-eṣu	-aēšu	-aišuv-ā
Neuter					
Sg. Nom.-Acc.	-o-m	-am	-am	-əm	-am
Pl. Nom.-Acc.	-ā	-ā	-ā[8]	-ā -a[3]	-ā

[1] And other sandhi-products. [2] With different suffix. [3] Short-vowel final in LAv.; long vowels or diphthong in GAv. [4] Double ending, with added -as from nom. pl. of consonantal stems. [5] With analogical length; and -s retained in some sandhi combinations. [6] From -oibhis, cf. dat.-abl. pl. Skt. -ebhyaḥ, Av. -aēibyō from *-oibhios. [7] By influence of -n- stems. [8] Ved. -ā, but classical Skt. -āni after -n- stems.

§171. CASE-FORMS OF -o- STEMS IN OP:

Nom. Sg. *martiya, xšāyaθiya, kāra, baga, drauga, hamiçiya, anušiya*; man's name, *Kabūjiya*; place names and ethnics *Pārsa, Māda, Sugda Suguda, Saka, Sparda, Mudrāya, Ūja Ūvja, Yauna, Parθava, Armina, Arminiya, Asagarta, Gadāra, Mārgava, Ūvjiya*.

Acc. Sg. *martiyam, xšāyaθiyam, kāram, hamiçiyam; Kabūjiyam; Pārsam, Mādam, Sugdam, Mudrāyam, Ūvjam, Arminam, Asagartam, ufraštam.*

Inst. Sg. *kārā, Pārsā, Aurā*, probably *karšā*; nt. *artā, dātā, ariyā*; masc. or nt. *vašnā, pisā*.

Abl. Sg. *draugā; Kabujiyā, Pārsā, Sugudā, Spardā, Mudrāyā, Kūšā, Yaunā, Gadārā, Karmānā*; nt. *dušiyārā, vispā, gastā*.

Gen. Sg. *martiyahyā, xšāyaθiyahyā, kārahyā, Pārsahyā, visahyā*, probably *māhyā*; nt. *uškahyā, uvaipašiyahyā, jīvahyā, [ha]kartahyā*.

Loc. Sg. *Pārsaiy, Mādaiy, Mudrāyaiy, Ūjaiy Ūvjaiy, Parθavaiy, Arminiyaiy, Asagartaiy, Hagmatānaiy*; with added -ā, *duvarayā, dastayā, spāθmaidayā*, probably *karšayā, [da]rtanayā*; nt. *uzmayā*.

Voc. Sg. *martiyā, marīkā*.

Nom. Pl. *martiyā, xšāyaθiyā, hamiçiyā, anušiyā, takabarā, tigraxaudā, haumavargā, paruvā, Mādā, Sakā, Mudrāyā, Yaunā, Ūvjiyā*; with double ending, *aniyāha bagāha*.

Acc. Pl. *martiyā, xšāyaθiyā, hamiçiyā, Sakā, Ūvjiyā, ufrastā.*
Inst. Pl. *asabāraibiš, martiyaibiš, hamiçiyaibiš, bagaibiš, viθaibiš, kamnaibiš; Mādaibiš, Sakaibiš, Parθavaibiš, Mārgavaibiš, Ūvjiyaibiš*; nt. *ūvnaraibiš.*
Gen. Pl. *martiyānām, xšāyaθiyānām, bagānām.*
Loc. Pl. *Mādaišuv-ā.*
Nt. Nom. Sg. *xšaçam, dušiyāram, ardatam, daraniyam, aruvastam, dātam, θakatam, kartam, visam, kamnam*; acc. *xšaçam, stānam, daraniyam, aruvastam, kartam, visam, uvāipašiyam, uvaspam,* probably *cašam.*
Nt. Nom. Pl. *ūvnarā, θakatā, [d]ātā*; acc. *āyadanā, [uvaspā], uraθā.*

§172. The Development of the -*o*- Declension in OP.

Nom. Sg.: OP -*ă*, regular from pAr. -*aḥ*, pIE -*os*; the failure to write the final vowel long shows a final minimal consonant: -*aʰ*.
Acc. Sg.: OP -*am*, regular from pAr. -*am*, pIE -*om*.
Inst. Sg.: OP -*ā*, regular from pAr. -*ā*, pIE -*ē* or -*ō*.
Abl. Sg.: OP -*ā* for -*āt*, regular from pAr. -*āt*, pIE -*ēd* or -*ōd* (or -*t*).
Gen. Sg.: OP -*ahyā*, regular for pAr. -*asya*, pIE -*osi̯o*; OP -*ā* for -*ă* shows that no minimal consonant followed; for a few writings -*ahyă*, see §36.IV. For *māhyā* from **māhahyā,* see §131.
Loc. Sg.: OP -*aiy* in place-names, regular from pAr. -*ai*, pIE -*ei* or -*oi*; OP -*ayā* in common nouns, being -*ai* + postposition -*ā* (similar forms are found in Avestan.)[1]
Voc. Sg.: OP -*ā*, regular from pAr. -*ă*, pIE -*e*; with OP -*ā* because there is no final minimal consonant.
Nom. Pl.: OP -*ā* for -*āʰ*, regular from pAr. *āḥ*, pIE -*ōs*; also OP -*āha* for -*āhaʰ* in *aniyāha bagāha* 'other gods', cf. §10 and the similar formations Av. *ahurā̊ŋhō* 'Ahuras', Skt. *devā́sah* 'gods'.
Acc. Pl.: OP -*ā* for -*āʰ*, either regularly from pAr. -*āns* with reduced *n*, in some sandhi-positions; or the nom. pl. as acc., by analogy (§168).
Inst. Pl.: OP -*aibiš*, regular for pAr. -*aibhiš*.
Gen. Pl.: OP -*ānām*, regular for pAr. -*ānām*, with -*nām* from -*n*- stems §187); for writing -*ănām*, see §52.III.
Loc. Pl.: OP -*aišuvā*, regular from pAr. -*aišu*, pIE -*oisu*, + postposition -*ā*; -*šu-ā* should become -*švā*, but the OP writing does not distinguish between this value and -*šuvā*, in which the -*u*- is retained as a vowel by the influence of the original form and a glide consonant written between it and the following vowel.
Nt. Nom.-Acc. Sg.: OP -*am*, regular from pAr. -*am*, pIE -*om*.
Nt. Nom.-Acc. Pl.: OP -*ā*, regular from pAr. -*ā*, pIE -*ā*.

dātā DB 1.23, XPh 49, 52, when used with *pari-ay-* 'respect', is probably inst. rather than abl., because of the lack of prep. *hacā*; note that the text of DSe 37–9, as now restored, gives no support for the abl. in the other passages, despite my remarks JAOS 54.46, Lg. 13.303, JAOS 58.117. On inst. sg. *karšā*, loc. sg. *karšayā*, nt. acc. *cašam*, acc. pl. *ufrastā-diy*, see Lex. s.vv.

Artaxšaça- has the regular gen. -*çahyā*,[2] but nom. -*çā* and acc. -*çām* have been assimilated to *Xšayār-šā* -*šām* (§187), and gen. *Artaxšaçahyā* (A²Hc) may have been assimilated to the late gen. *Xšayāršāhyā* (§187; unless there is mere addition of a character, §53).

§173. The Case-Endings of -*ā*- Stems in pIE: only those relevant to extant OP forms will be discussed.

I. In the singular, nom. -*ā* is the strong grade of the stem-vowel, without special case-suffix. Acc. -*ām* is stem-vowel -*ā*- + case-suffix -*m*. From the evidence of non-Aryan languages, we should expect pIE to have inst. -*ā* (from -*ā*- + -*a*), abl.-gen. -*ās* (from -*ā*- + *es*), loc. -*āi* (from -*ā*- + -*i*);[1] but in Aryan we find dissyllabic terminations, inst. -*ăyā*, abl.-gen. -*āyās*, loc. -*āyā*. Either a pre-IE variant stem in -*ăyă*- here comes to light, though it does not appear outside these singular cases (and in the dative, lost in OP), or these cases are built upon a stem extracted from the loc. sg. -*āyā* (so in Iranian, but extended by -*m* in Skt.): for the loc. sg. should have been stem-vowel -*ā*- + ending -*i*, to which postposition -*ā* was added, making -*āyā*.

---

[1] The same phenomenon in Osc.-Umb.· **en* 'in' is attached to the loc ending as an integral part of the case-form, in Osc. *húrtín* 'in horto' from **-ei̯-en*, and in Umb. *arven* 'in arvo' from **-āi̯-en*.

[2] Unless this form also is a neologism (§57).

§173.[1] Although *ā* + *i* regularly contracted to *ăi* (§131), the loc of -*ā*- stems seems to have had -*āi* by the influence of -*ā*- in other cases; on Skt. inst. ending -*ăyā*, see Thumb-Hirt, Handbuch d. Skt. §259, §351.

To the extracted stem -āyă- it is simple to form inst. -āyā, gen.-abl. -āyās.

II. The plural has pIE nom. -ās from -ā- + -es; acc. -ās from -ā- + -ns, with pIE loss of n between long vowel and final s; gen. -ōm from -ā- + -ōm, replaced in pAr. by -ānām after -n- stems; loc. -āsu from -ā- + -su.

§174. THE CASE-ENDINGS OF -ā- STEMS IN ARYAN. The comparative table includes only cases represented in extant OP forms.

Sg.	pIE	pAr.	Skt.	Av.	OP
Nom.	-ā	-ā	-ā	-ā -a[1]	-ā
Acc.	-ām	-ām	-ām	-ąm	-ām
Inst.		-āyā[2]	-ayā	-ayă[1]	-āyā
Abl.		-āyās	-āyās	-āyāṱ[3]	-āyaʰ
Gen.		-āyās	-āyās	-ayå	-āyāʰ
Loc.	-āi	-āyā	-āyām	-aya	-āyā
Pl.					
Nom.	-ās	-ās	-ās	-å	-āʰ
Acc.	-ās	ās	ās	-å	-āʰ
Gen.	-ōm	-ānām	-ānām	-anąm	-ānām
Loc.	-āsu	-āsu	-āsu	-āhu -āhva[1]	-āʰuvā

[1] Avestan forms with short final -a belong to the LAv.; note that the indication of length in interior syllables of Avestan words is not reliable [2] Cf. §173n. [3] Remodeling of the gen ending in Late Avestan after the abl. -āṱ of -o- stems.

§175. CASE-FORMS OF -ā- STEMS IN OP:

Nom. Sg. taumā 'family', hainā, framānā, yauviyā, didā, θikā; Aθurā; adjectives kartā, gastā, hamiçiyā.

Acc. Sg. taumām, yauviyām, didām, θikam; Paišiyāuvādām, Sakām, adjective aθagainām.

Inst. Sg. framānāyā, aruvāyā, perhaps ha[natāyā].

Abl. Sg. Paišiyāuvādāyā, haināyā, taumāyā, Yadāyā.

Gen. Sg. taumāyā.

Loc. Sg. Arbairāyā, Aθurāyā, Çūšāyā; perhaps avastāyā, stūnāya (see §176); adj. vazrakāyā (unless gen. in some passages).

Nom. Pl. stūnā, hamiçiyā, kartā.

Acc Pl. [stūnā] (restored only).

Gen. Pl. paruzanānām, vispazanānām.

Loc. Pl. maškāʰuvā, aniyāʰuvā.

§176. THE DEVELOPMENT OF THE -ā- DECLENSION IN OP. Reference to the table of endings in §174 will show that OP faithfully represents the endings as they were in pAr., with a few slight modifications. The failure to write the minimal final consonants brings to a uniform writing -āyā the inst., abl., gen., loc. cases of the singular. It is impossible to determine whether OP shared the LAv. split of the Aryan abl.-gen. -āyās into gen. *-āyās, abl. *āyāt in imitation of the -o- stem abl. in -āt; in the absence of evidence we assume that OP abl. and gen. were identical, with -āyā from older -āyās. The OP loc. shared the general Aryan addition of -ā, but not the further Skt. addition of -m. The plural forms of OP also are quite regular, the gen. showing the Aryan remodeling after -n- stems, and the loc. the addition of -ā which occurs also in a few Avestan forms. There is the same ambiguity as to the phonetic value of -āʰuvā in this declension that there is in the -o- stems (§172).

The fact that the pAr. loc. sg. of -ā- stems has the added -ā which passes to the loc. sg. of common nouns and adjectives of other stem-classes, and to the loc. pl., in OP, and to a smaller extent in Avestan, makes it likely that the -ā- stems are the starting point for this remodeling of the ending.

The puzzling form stūnāya occurs only in the phrase apadānam stūnāya aθagainam 'palace stony ... column'; as it occurs only in texts of Darius II and later, it may be a miswriting with omission of the final a, and stand for stūnāyā, inst. or loc. of specification (cf. the use of inst. karšā and loc. karšayā with a numeral, Lg. 19.227–9): 'palace stony as to column(s)', stūnāya being singular in form but generic in meaning, and therefore to be taken as a collective.[1]

§177. THE CASE-ENDINGS OF -ĭ- AND -ī- STEMS IN pIE AND IN ARYAN: only those relevant to extant OP forms will be discussed.

I. The -ĭ- stems had pIE nom. sg. -i-s, acc. -i-m, gen. -ei-s or -oi-s (with strong grade of the stem-vowel); these are represented by Skt. agníṣ agním agnéṣ 'fire'. The loc. had the long diphthong, without case-suffix, -ēi; this became -ē in pIE, since long diphthongs in pIE regularly lost the semivowel when they were final: Skt. (Ved.) has agnā́.[1]

II. The -ī- stems had pIE nom. sg. -ī, acc. -ī-m,

---

[1] Hinz, ZDMG 95.250, takes as miswritten for stūnāyam, adj modifying apadānam: 'Saulenhalle'

§177.[1] Skt. agnáu is a new formation by influence of the -u- stem loc. śatrā́ śatráu 'enemy', where both forms were still used.

abl.-gen. -(i)i̯ēs or -(i)i̯ās,² inst. -(i)i̯ā,³ loc. -(i)i̯ē or -(i)i̯ā² (from the final long diphthong, as in -ī- stems). The nom. pl. was pIE -ī-es, giving -ii̯es. These are represented by Skt. devī́ devī́m devyā́s devyā́ devyā́-m 'goddess' (with -m attached to the loc., as in -ā- stems), pl. devyā̀s = devī́yas.

III. The -ī- stems were exclusively feminine, but the -ĭ- stems included both masculines and feminines; both in Skt. and in Av. the fem. -ĭ- stems optionally or regularly assumed the endings of -ī- stems in the inst., dat., abl.-gen., loc. singular. Occasionally, also, the fem. -ī- stems acquired a nom. sg. -s from the -ĭ- stems in Skt. and Av., giving nom. -īš.

§178. CASE-FORMS OF -ĭ- AND -ī- STEMS IN OP:
I. Masc. -ĭ- stems:
Nom. Sg.: skauθiš, pastiš, θarmiš, yāumainiš ayāu-(ma)iniš; the personal names Fravartiš, Dādaršiš, Cišpiš; the ethnic Pātišuvariš; perhaps the place-names Arakadriš, Kāpišakāniš, Viš-[pa]uz[ā]tiš.
Acc. Sg. skauθim, ušabārim, duvarθim, Fravartim, Dādaršim.
Gen. Sg. skauθaiš, Fravartaiš, Cišpaiš, Θāigarcaiš, Bāgayādaiš; also Cišpāiš, Cicixrāiš.
II. Fem. -ĭ- stems (some possibly -ī- stems):
Nom. Sg.: aršt[i]š, šiyātiš, ištiš, probably dipi[š].
Acc. Sg.: šiyātim, bājim, dipim; paθim (to a heteroclite stem).
Inst. Sg.: [nip]iš[tiyā].
Loc. Sg.: d[i]p[iy]ā.
III. Fem. -ī- stems:
Nom. Sg.: Uvārazmīy Uvārazmiš, Baxtriš; Harauvatiš (Skt. sárasvatī), Sika[ya]uvatiš; āpiš (in āpišim = āpiš-šim), BU 'earth' (ideogram only).
Acc. Sg.: Harauvatim, būmim, probably yau[datim].
Abl. Sg.: Harauvatiyā, Bāxtriyā, Uvārazmiyā.
Loc. Sg.: Harauvatiyā, Bāxtriyā, āpi[y]ā, būmiyā.
Nom. Pl.: aθagainiya.
IV: Not included here:
Inst. Pl.: abiš, arašaniš: see Lex. s.vv.

---

² Variation between -ii̯- and -i̯- by Sievers' Law (cf. Edgerton, Lg. 10.235-65); differentiation between pIE ē and pIE ā cannot be made because of lack of adequate non-Aryan cognates. ³ pAr. ā, cf. preceding note; probably pAr. -ā extended from -ŏ- stem instrumentals.

§179. THE DEVELOPMENT OF THE -ĭ- AND -ī- DECLENSIONS IN OP.¹

I. The -ĭ- stems and the -ī- stems fell together in OP into one declensional paradigm, having nom. sg. -iš, acc. -im, gen. -aiš, abl. -iyā^h (= Skt. -yās), loc. -iyā (= Skt. -yā-m), nom. pl. -iya^h. The only survival of separate declensional forms is nom. Uvārazmīy, with original -ī, replaced in later inscriptions by Uvārazmiš. There is the possibility that when nom. -ī of -ī- stems took the ending -s, the length of the vowel remained to distinguish the -ī- stems from the -ĭ- stems; and similarly the long vowel in acc. -īm may have remained. The OP system of writing leaves this ambiguous. But it is more likely that the new ending -īš and the old ending -īm became -iš and -im in imitation of the corresponding forms of -ĭ- stems.

II. It is true that in Aryan the abl. sg. and the gen. sg. of these stems have the same ending (so in all stems except -ŏ- stems!), and here we find gen. -aiš, abl. -iyā. But all the OP genitives are of masculine words, and all the locatives are of feminines; and as we noted in §177.III, feminine -ĭ- stems were likely to assume -ī- stem endings in certain oblique cases of the singular. It is possible then that the feminines may in OP have diverged in some case-forms from the pattern of the masculine -ĭ- stems, without in reality preserving a separate declensional type. Note that būmiyā seems to be loc. only; if the form occurred in a passage where the gen. were certainly required, this differentiation would seem to be established. Yet in -ŭ- stems we find both endings in masc. ablatives.

III. It is not always possible to determine whether the feminine common nouns are -ĭ- stems or -ī- stems; etymological comparison is necessary. The short vowel seems assured in aršti-, Skt. r̥ṣṭí- 'spear'; paθim, Skt. stem pathí- in some case-forms; but it is only a probability in šiyāti-, išti-, bāji-, dipi-. The long vowel seems assured in būmi- by Skt. Ved. nom. bhū́mī (once only; against 12 occurrences of the new formation bhū́miṣ), and is certain in nom. pl. aθagainiya, like Skt. pāpyā̀s to sg. fem. pāpī́ which is one fem. formation to pāpás 'evil'.

IV. The gen. -āiš in Cišpāiš and Cicixrāiš is only graphic for -aiš in words where the nom. and the gen. would be written alike: cᵃišᵃpᵃišᵃ = nom.

---

¹ Debrunner, IF 52.131-6; Kent, Lg. 19.221-4.

Cišpiš or gen. *Cišpaiš*; similarly -*rᵃiš*ᵃ = -*riš* or -*raiš*.

V. In forms ending in -*iyā*, the -*i*- is probably syllabic and not merely graphic; for *Harahvatyā would become *Harauvašiyā and not *Harauvatiyā*, and *dipyā would become *difiyā and not *dipiyā*.[2] In the others the long preceding syllable would cause Sievers' Law to operate, changing -*yā* to -*iyā*.

§180. The Case-Endings of -*ŭ*- Stems in pIE and in Aryan: again, only those relevant to extant OP forms will be discussed.

The -*ŭ*- stems had pIE nom. sg. -*u-s*, acc. -*u-m*, gen. -*eu-s* or -*ou-s* (with strong grade of the stem-vowel), seen in Skt. *śátruṣ śátrum śátroṣ* 'enemy', Av. *vaŋhuš vohūm vaŋhə̄uš* 'good'. The inst. sg. was the stem in -*ŭ*- + pAr. ending -*ā*; the -*ŭ*- remained vocalic if after a single consonant preceded by two consonants or by a single consonant after a long vowel or a diphthong, but became consonantal after a single consonant preceded by a short vowel. The loc. sg. ended in the strong grade or the lengthened grade of the stem vowel, -*eu* or -*ēu*, to which the postposition -*ā* was often added in Iranian: Skt. *śátrāu*, Av. *vaŋhāu*, also *aŋhava* to *aŋhuš* 'existence'. The nom.-acc. sg. nt. was the bare stem, and ended in -*u*: Skt. *mádhu* 'honey', GAv. *vohū* 'good' (all final vowels are long in GAv.). The gen. pl. was pIE -(*u*)*u̯ōm*, but became -*ū-nām* in pAr. in imitation of the -*n*- stems; Av. has both endings in *vaŋhvąm* and *vohunąm*.

§181. Case-Forms of -*ŭ*- Stems in OP:
Nom. Sg. Masc.: *maguš*, *piruš*, *sikabruš*, adj. *uvāmaršiyuš*; names of kings, *Dārayavaʰuš*, *Kūruš*; place-names, *Abirāduš*, *Kudᵘruš*, *θataguš*, *Bābiruš*, *Mā[ru]š*, *Marguš*, *Hinduš*.
Acc. Sg. Masc.: *magum*, *xraθum*, *gāθum*; *Dārayavaʰum*; *Bābirum*, *Margum*; *visadahyum*; perhaps [*agurum*].
Inst. Sg.: *Ufrātuvā*.
Gen. Sg. Masc.: *Kūrauš*; *Dārayavahauš*, with neologisms *Dārayavaušahyā Dārayavašahyā*.
Abl. Sg. Masc.: *Bābirauš Bābirauv*, *Hidauv*, *gāθavā*.
Loc. Sg. Masc.: *Bābirauv*, *Margauv*, *gāθavā*.

Gen. Pl. Masc.: *parūnām parūvnām*. Fem.: *parūnām*.
Nt. Nom. Sg.: *paruv*, *dāruv*.
Nt. Acc. Sg.: [*dār*]*uv*.

For forms of *tanūš*, *dahyāuš*, *uxšnauš*, *nāuš*, see §183.

§182. The Development of the -*ŭ*- Declension in OP. The development of the endings from pIE and pAr. are quite perspicuous for the most part, and call for but few remarks.

I. The neologisms *Dārayavaušahyā* and *Dārayavašahyā* are mere attempts to build up genitives on the nom. as a stem, at a time when the endings had worn down and were not distinguished in speech; §57.

II. The loc. in -*auv* represents the short diphthong (unlike the long diphthong in Skt.), without case-suffix; and that in -*avā* is the regular phonetic development of -*au* + -*ā*.

III. The abl. *Bābirauš* is the gen., for in Aryan the same form functioned as gen. and as abl., except in the -*ŏ*- stems; the other ablatives are locative forms (cf. the fusion of loc. and abl. forms and functions in Latin).

IV. The gen. pl. has the regular Aryan -*nām* from -*n*- stems; it is to be observed that the masc. form of the adjective functions also as fem.

V. The nom.-acc. nt. sg. inherits the old ending; OP nom. *paruv* is the exact equivalent of Av. *pouru*, Skt. *purú*, Gk. πολύ.

§183. The -*ū*- Stems and *u*-Diphthong Stems in OP.

I. The only -*ū*- stem in OP is *tanū*- 'body, self', which is shown by Skt. and Av. *tanū*- to have the long vowel; its forms in OP are nom. *tanūš*, acc. *tanūm*, unless indeed it has -*ŭš* -*ŭm* by assimilation to the -*ŭ*- stems.

II. OP fem. *dahyau*- 'land, province' has in most case-forms the diphthong and not the zero-grade -*u*-, a peculiarity which in general it shares with the Avestan cognate. The diphthong is lengthened as a mark of the nom. sg.: OP *dahyāuš* (but Av. *daiṅhuš*). This length is extended to the acc. sg. OP *dahyāvam* and *dahyāum* (of which the prior is phonetically correct[1] and the second is an-

---

[2] The tendency in OP is to level toward changed forms of the stem-consonant, not back to the original sound; cf. Lex.s.vv. *gāθu*- *xraθu*-, *arašan*-.

[1] In pIE, diphthong before nasal in the same syllable automatically became vowel + consonantal semivowel, after which the nasal became vocalic: thus -*ēum* > -*ēu̯m̥*, whence OP -*āvam*. But nom. -*ēus* remained and induced

alogical to the nom.;[2] Av. *daiṿhaom* graphic for -*ăvam*); but as second element of a compound we find -*dahyum* in *visadahyum* (or -*dahyaum*, as -*y^aum^a* is ambiguous), and in A³Pa 26 we have *DHy^aum^a*, which may be either *DHyaum* or *DHyum* (Av. *daḣyūm* is probably for -*yŭm*). OP loc. *dahyauvā* is *dahyauv* like *Bābirauv*, with added -*ā*; but the diphthong is here kept before the added vowel (unlike *gāθavā*). Nom. pl. *dahyāva* has the long diphthong extended from the nom. sg., and represents pAr. -*āvas* (so also Av. *daiṿhāvō*); this form was extended to serve as acc. pl. in OP (so also in Av.). OP gen. pl. *dahyūnām* and *dahyūvnām* is a regular gen. pl. of -*u*- stems in Aryan (Av. *daḣyunąm*). OP loc. pl. *dahyušuvā* is the -*u*- stem loc. pl. with ending -*su*, + the postposition -*ā*; whether phonetically -*ušuvā* or -*ušvā* depends on whether the *u* of -*su* was consonantized before the added vowel, or retained by analogy.[3]

III. Nom. sg. *u*[*xšna*]*uš* 'well satisfied' is formed with the case-suffix *s*, but no lengthening.

IV. Nom. pl. [*nāva*] corresponds to Skt. *nāv-as*, Gk. νῆ-ες, the regular nom. pl. of the diphthongal stem *nāu- (pIE **nāy̯-es*).

§184. THE CASE-ENDINGS OF CONSONANT-STEMS IN pIE AND IN ARYAN. Again only part of the cases have extant forms in OP.

Nom. Sg. Masc. and Fem.: formed by adding -*s*, or by lengthening the last vowel of the stem, rarely by both together. After a lengthened vowel a final liquid or nasal was lost in pIE.[1]

Acc. Sg. Masc. and Fem.: formed by adding -*m*, which here automatically became -*m̥*, since it stood after another consonant.

Nom.-Acc. Sg. Nt.: the bare stem, without suffix.

Gen. Sg.: pIE -*es* and -*os*,[2] Aryan -*as*.

Loc. Sg.: the bare stem, in the strong grade if having ablaut variation; or the same + case-ending -*i*.

Inst. Sg.: formed by adding (Aryan) -*ā*, from pIE -*ē* or -*ō*.

Inst. Pl.: formed by adding -*bhis*, Aryan -*bhiš*.

It is to be noted that in Aryan, when a word ended in two or more consonants, the final consonant or consonants fell off until only one was left; thus pIE nom. *nepōt-s 'grandson', Lt. *nepōs*, became pAr. *napāt, Skt. *nápāt*.

§185. THE -*s*- STEMS IN OP: of these there are several varieties.

I. The neuter formation with suffix -*os* in nom.-acc. sg., -*es*- in other forms: type Lt. *gen-us gen-er-is*, Gk. γέν-ος γέν-ε-ος, Skt. *ján-as ján-as-as*. OP has nom. *rautaʰ* 'river', Skt. *srótas*; nom.-acc. *raucaʰ* 'day', Av. *raocō* 'light', Skt. *rócas* 'light'; acc. *drayaʰ* 'sea' (and *draiyaʰ*, §48), Av. *zrayō*, Skt. *jráyas*; acc. *manaš-cā* (§105), Av. *manō*, Skt. *mánas*; acc. *zūraʰ* 'evil', Av. *zūrō*; acc. *miθaʰ* 'evil'. Inst. *manahā*, Skt. *mánasā*. Loc. *drayahy-ā* (with added -*ā*; also written *drayahiyā*, but whether the -*i*- is syllabic cannot be determined), Skt. *jráyasi*, cf. Av. *manahi-čā*. Inst. pl. *raucabiš*, probably for *raucaʰbiš, cf. Av. *manə̄bīš*, Skt. *mánobhis*: the -*h* from -*s* in certain sandhi positions here transferred to the medial position before the consonant of the case-suffix, and then voiced before the voiced consonant and lost with the same products as when final in the respective languages.

II. When a nt. -*es*-/-*os*- stem forms the second element of a compound, whether adjectival or a man's name, the nom. sg. has -*ēs*, the other cases have -*es*-: Gk. δυσμενής, Διογένης to μένος, γένος. This -*ēs* became Ar. -*ās* -*āh*, OP -*āʰ*: *Viⁿda-farnāʰ*, cf. Av. *xᵛarənō* 'royal splendor', pIE **su̯elnos*; *Aspa-canāʰ*, cf. Skt. *cánas* 'delight'.

III. Apparently there was also a nt. suffix -*əs*-, not varying within the paradigm nor in the corresponding masc. formation: type Skt. *kraviṣ* 'raw flesh', Gk. κρέας. OP nom.-acc. *hadiš* from *sed-əs, cf. Gk. ἔδος from *sed-os; acc. *abicariš* 'pastureland', see Lex. s.v. In names, *Haxā-maniš*, *Ardu-maniš*, perhaps *I-maniš*; late gen. *Haxāmaniš-ahyā* adds the gen. ending of -*o*- stems to the nom. as stem.[1]

OP acc. -*āum* (which indeed might have come down from pIE in the position before an initial vowel). An alternative development of a long diphthong before final *m* in pIE was the loss of the semivowel of the diphthong; there are no examples in OP. [2] Cf pIE nom. *nāus, acc **nāy̯m̥* 'ship': Skt. *náus*, *návam*; Gk. Hom. νηῦς νῆα, Att. ναῦς ναῦν. [3] For further speculations on the declension of *dahyāuš*, see Bv. Gr. §287.

§184.[1] The liquid or nasal was restored in the nom. in some IE branches, by the influence of the stem in the oblique cases thus Skt. *pitā́* 'father', but Gk πατήρ, Lt *pater*; Skt. *tákṣā* 'carpenter', but Gk. τέκτων. [2] -*es* as in Lt. *ped-is*, -*os* as in Gk. ποδ-ός.

---

[1] If we could accept *Haxāmanišahyā* at face-value, we could be quite sure that these three names are -*s*- stems and not -*i*- stems with nom. -*š*, as some have supposed;

IV. The remaining -s- stems of OP are *nāh-* 'nose', *tauvīyah-* 'stronger', *Aʰuramazdāh-* 'Ahuramazda', and possibly *māh-* 'month'.

OP acc. *nāh-am*, Skt. *nā́sam*, has the ending *-m̥* generalized in its antevocalic value, assisted by the *-am* of *-o-* stems. OP nom. sg. masc. *tauvīyāʰ* has the comparative suffix in the long-vowel form, pIE *-i̯ōs*, pAr. *-i̯ās*; Av. *spanyā̊* 'holier' has the same suffix and case-formation, while Skt. *sthávīyān* 'stronger' stands for *-yāns*, with an intrusive *-n-*[2] and loss of the final consonant of the cluster, but a stem-formation closer to that of OP *tauvīyā* (on *-auv-*, §48). OP *māhyā* probably does not belong here as loc. **māhi-* + *-ā*, cf. Skt. loc. *māsí*, but is rather gen. sg. **māhahyā* to *māha-*, Skt. *mā́sa-*, with reduction of *-āhah-* (§131).

OP nom. *Auramazdāʰ* ends in pIE *-dhḗs*, an *-s-* formation to a long-vowel root which in this formation shows no ablaut variation (cf. Lt. *flōs* *flōr-is* and other monosyllables); a nom. *-s* added to *-dhēs*, pAr. *-dhās-*, produces no change, since the *-ss* is shortened automatically to *-s*. Acc. *Auramazdām* instead of **-dāham* shows that the form was transferred to the *-ā-* stems.[3] Gen. *Auramazdāhaʰ* is regular for the stem in *-dāh-*, as is also the unique *Aurahya Mazdāhaʰ* declined in both parts,[4] gen. *Auramazdāhā̊ʰ* has *-āhā̊ʰ* by influence of gen. *-āyāʰ* of *-ā-* stems, since the nom. *-dā*, acc. *-dām* already agreed with the nom. *-ā*, acc. *-ām* of *-ā-* stems.[5] Gen. *Auramazdǎhā* is an error of writing which is to be classed with gen. pl. *xšāyaθiyǎnām* 'of kings', for *-ānām* (§52.III).

---

but *Haxāmanišahyā* stands in the much miswritten Ariaramnes inscription, and may replace a gen. in *-manaiš* as *Dārayavauš-ahyā* (in inscriptions of Artaxerxes I and II) replaces the old gen. *Dārayavahauš*. However, the derivative *Haxāmaniš-iya* 'Achaemenian' seems to justify us in regarding the *-š-* as belonging to the stem. [2] This *-n-* may come from the perf. ptc. nom. Skt. *vidvā́n*, pIE *-u̯ōs* as in Gk. *εἰδ(ϝ)ώς* 'knowing'; and in the perf. ptc of Skt it seems to have come from the *-nt-* of the pres. ptc. [3] Cf. similar phenomena in the declension of *Xšayāršan-*, §187. Pisani, Riv. Stud. Or. 19 81-2, argues that *Auramazdā* is by origin a root-noun in *-ā-*, with analogical gen. to avoid identity of nom. and gen , but this is very improbable [4] The divine name is always declined in both parts in the Avesta; in the *Gāthās* other words commonly intervene between its two parts, and in the Later Avesta *mazdå ahurō* is more frequent than *ahurō mazdå*. [5] This rather indicates that *-h* was lost in OP after *ā*, and remained only after *ǎ*; §40.

§186. THE *-r-* STEMS IN OP: these fall into two groups.

I. Agency nouns with suffixes pIE *-tor-* and *-ter-*, showing ablaut variation in the declension; the nom. sg. has the long vowel, which is commonly extended to some or all of the other case-forms: Lt. *dator*, gen. *datōr-is* (*ō* throughout); Gk. δώτωρ δώτορ-ος (*ō* only in nom. sg.), δοτήρ δοτῆρ-ος, δωτήρ δωτῆρος (*ē* throughout except in voc. sg. δῶτερ); Skt. *dātā́*, acc. *dātā́ram*, dat. *dātré*, loc. *dātári*, etc. OP has nom. sg. *janⁿtā* 'slayer', Av. *janta*, Skt. *hantā́*; *dauštā* 'friend'. OP acc. *framātāram* 'lord', with extension of the long vowel of the nom., and the antevocalic value of the acc. ending (§67.II).

II. Words of relationship had suffix *-ter-*, nom. *-tē* or restored *-tēr*, other cases *-ter-* or *-tr-*. OP has nom. *pitā* 'father', Skt. *pitā́*, Gk. πατήρ, Lt. *pater*; also in cpd. *hama-pitā* 'having the same father'. OP nom. *mātā* 'mother' in *hamātā* 'having the same mother', Skt. *mātā́*, Gk. (Dor.) μά̄τηρ, Lt. *māter*. OP nom. *brātā* 'brother', Skt. *bhrā́tā*, Gk. φρά̄τηρ 'clan-brother', Lt. *frāter*.[1] OP gen. *piçaʰ*, Gk. πατρός, Lt. *patris*, from **pətr-os* or *-es*, unlike Skt. *pitúṣ* from **pətr̥s*.

§187. THE *-n-* STEMS IN OP: these also fall into several groups.

Those with suffixes (Aryan) *-man- -van- -an-* (pIE vowel *-e-* or *-o-*) had nom. in *-mā -vā -ā*: OP *taumā* 'power', stem *tauman-*; *artāvā* 'blessed', GAv. *ašavā*, LAv. *ašava*, Skt. *r̥tā́vā*, cf. GAv. acc. *ašavanəm*; *asā* 'stone', cf. LAv. *asənga-* in cpds., OP *aθaⁿga-* 'stone'; *xšaçapāvā* 'kingdom-protecting, satrap', with stem *-pāvan-* as in Skt. (Ved.) *tanū-pāvan-* 'person-protecting'. Acc. with extension of the long vowel, in OP *asmānam* 'sky', cf. acc. Lith. *ãkmenį* 'stone' and Gk. ἄκμονα 'anvil' with *-mĕn-* and *-mŏn-* respectively. It is uncertain whether acc. *hᵃzānam* (for *hizānam*) is an *-an-* stem with the long vowel, or an *-āna-* stem; at any rate it is an extension of the stem seen in Av. *hizvā-* (see Lex. s.v. *hazāna-*). Neuters with suffix *-men-* have nom.-acc. in the zero-grade *-mn̥*;[1] acc. OP *nāmā*, Skt. *nā́ma*, Lt. *nōmen*, from **nōmn̥*.

---

[1] OP *hamapitā* and *hamātā* do not distinguish, and cannot distinguish, between the two vocalisms seen in Gk. ὁμοπάτηρ and ὁμοπάτωρ; but the *-ōr* forms are those proper in original compounds.

§187.[1] OP *cᵃšᵃmᵃ* is not to be read *cašma* as a neut. *-n-*

The stem *Xšayāršan-*[2] has the regular nom. *Xšayāršā*, but the other cases are remodeled to the type of *Auramazdā*, acc. *-dām*, gen. *-dāha* (§185.IV): acc. *Xšayāršām*, gen. *[Xšayār]šāha*, with late genitives *Xšayāršahyā* (§57) and *Xšayāršāhyā* (A²Hc), with the medial *-ā-* of the other cases. On forms of *Artaxšaça-*, see §172.

Of the other forms, OP *baršnā* is inst. sg. to stem *baršan-*, cf. Av. inst. *barəšna* to *barəzan-*, Skt. *rā́jñā* to *rājan-* 'king'. OP *nāma* is probably a suffixless loc. *nāmaⁿ*. Inst. pl. *taumaniš* and *arašaniš* are analogical for *-abiš*, since the paradigm would have been nom. *-anaʰ*, gen. *-anām*, inst. *-abiš* (from *-n̥-bhis*).[3]

OP nom. *manauviš* is probably for **manas-vī*, nom. to *-vin-* (cf. Skt. nom. *balī́* to stem *balin-* 'strong'), with added nom. *-s*.[4]

§188. THE STEMS IN STOPS, IN OP: these include stems ending in *t* (*napāt-* 'grandson'), *nt* (**tunvant-* 'strong'), *d* (*θard-* 'year', *pad-* 'foot', *rād-* 'cause'), *p* (*xšap-* 'night', *ap-* 'water' cf. *āpī-*) *k̂* (*viθ-* 'house', *vas-* 'will').

I. Nom. *napā* = *napāt*, Skt. *nápāt*, from pIE **nepōt-s* with Aryan loss of last consonant of the final cluster; or = *napāʰ* from a remade Iranian **napās* seen in Av. *napā̊*.

II. Nom. *tunuvā* = **tunvān* with pIE *-ōnt* (long vowel nom.) as in Gk. φέρων 'bearing', or the same + nom. *-s* as in Av. *hąs* 'being' from Iran. **hănt-s*, cf. Skt. nom. *sán* from **sant-s*, pIE **s-ent-s*. Acc. *tunuvatam* = **tunvantam*, with the regular acc. *-am* from *-m̥* (§67.II). Gen. *tunuvatahyā* = **tunvantahyă*, with transfer to *-o-* stem ending, and retention of the *-ant-* of the suffix as in Av. gsm. *fšuyantō* 'cattle-raising', despite Av. *hatō* = Skt. *sat-ás*, pIE gsm. **sn̥tés* (or **sn̥tós*) 'being' with strong grade in nsm. **sent-s*.

III. Acc. *θardam*, gen. *θarda*, gen. *xšapa*, loc. *rādiy*, *-padiy* in *ni-padiy*, *vasiy* (but cf. Lex. s.v.) have the regular pIE endings of their cases: acc. *-m̥*; gen. *-es* or *-os*; loc. *-i*, without added *-ā* because the forms function as preposition, phrasal adverb, adverb respectively.

---

stem, because of the final short vowel (§36.III), but is *cašam*, acc. nt. of an *-a-* stem. ² Bv Gr. §290 takes as stem *Xšayāršāh-* because of the gen. *-āha*, the second element being *arša-* 'just' made into an (Ar.) *-ās-* stem; the objection to this is that *-ās-* stems are hardly made upon *-ă-* stems. Cf. also §162 note ³ Lg. 15 175–6; for other interpretations of these two forms, see Lex. s vv. ⁴ Lg. 15 170.

IV. Acc. *viθam*, inst. *viθā*, loc. *viθiyā*, to stem *viθ-* from pIE **u̯ik̂-*, also have the regular endings: acc. *-m̥*, inst. *-ḗ* or *-ō*, loc. *-i*, here with added *-ā* because *viθiyā* is a true locative in use.

V. Inst. pl. *viθbiš* and *abiš* show the regular *-bhis* seen in Skt. *-bhiṣ*, Av. *-bīš*; *-θb-* as a cluster remains by the influence of the separate stem and ending (we expect *-db-* from *-k̂-bh-*), and the *-b-* of *abiš* is for *-bbh-* from *-p-bh-*.

§189. THE DUAL CASE-FORMS OF OP: nom. *ubā* 'both', *ušiy* 'two ears, understanding'; acc. *gaušā* 'two ears', *[uš]ī-cā*; inst. *dastaibiyā* 'with two hands', *pādaibiyā* 'with two feet', *ušībiya*, *ušīyā*, *gaušāyā*.[1] These are masculines, except *ušiy*, which is neuter.[2]

The nom.-acc. of *-o-* stems ended in pIE *-ō* or *-ōu*, seen in Skt. *ubhā́* *ubhā́u*, Lt. *am-bō*, OP *ubā*, *gaušā*. That of neuter *-i-* stems ended in *-ī*, seen in Skt. Ved. dual *trī* 'three', Lt. *trī-gintā* 'three tens', and this *-ī* was transferred in Aryan to consonant-stems, as in Skt. *mánas-ī*, dual to *mánas-* 'mind'; thus *ušiy* is the proper form whether the stem is *uš-* or *uši-*, a point which cannot be determined.

The inst. *dastaibiyā* and *pādaibiyā* have the stems *dasta-* and *pāda-*, with the pronominal plural element *-i*, plus the inst. ending *-bhi* + *-ā*, as in Av. dat. du. *aspaēibya* 'two horses' = **aspaibyā*: the dat., inst., loc. are identical in the dual, in Aryan languages. Skt. has in this form *áśvābhyām*, with *-bhyā* (as in Iranian) added to the dual in *-ā* as a stem, and a final *-m* attached, OP *ušībiya* is the same formation to *ušiy*, cf. Skt. *akṣíbhyām* to *akṣī́* 'two eyes'. OP *ušīyā* seems to be an inst. dual (it has the same use and meaning as *ušībiyā*) formed on the dual stem with the inst. sg. ending *-ā*; *gaušāyā* is a like formation to *gaušā*. The *ī* before the *-ā* in *ušīyā* is responsible for the glide *-y-*, which has spread to *gaušāyā* as a vowel-separator; the prior *ā* in *gaušāyā* indicates that the *-ī-* in *ušīyā* also is long.[3]

§190. ADJECTIVES IN OP have all their customary uses and forms. For those which are cardinal and ordinal numerals, see §204; for the semi-

---

[1] Nom *hamiçiyā* DB 2 93 is predicate to two singular masculine nouns, but is more probably plural than dual; cf. §259. [2] The form *karšā* does not belong here, nor probably *artā-cā brazmaniy* (if so normalized) nor *taumani-šaiy*, on these words see the Lexicon s vv [3] On these forms, cf. Kent. Lg. 19.225.

pronominal *aniya-, haruva-, hama-*, §203; for the demonstrative and determinative adjectives, which function also as pronouns, §199, §200, §202; for the relative, §198; for those which are participles, §239–244.

I. Adjectives are found in all classes of stems, and the history of their case-forms has been included with that of the substantives. The commonest type of adjectival stems ends in *-o-* for masc. and nt., with *-ā-* for the fem.: nom. pIE *-os -om -ā* = OP *-aʰ -am -ā* (§169–§176). The *-ĭ-* stems are *skauθ-iš -im -aiš, yāumainiš ayāu(ma)iniš, ušabārim*; the *-ī-* stems are acc. sg. *yau[datim]*, probably *yau[daⁿtim]*, to masc. *yaudant-*, and nom. pl. *aθagainiya* to masc. *aθagaina-* (§§177–9]. The *-ŭ-* stems are *paru-* (nt. *paruv*, gen. pl. *parūnām*), nom. sg. masc. *uvāmaršiyu-š* and *u[xšna]u-š*, acc. sg. masc. *visadahyu-m* (§§180–3). The consonantal stems are *artāvan-, manaʰuvin-, tauvīyah-, hamapitar-, hamātar-, tunuvaⁿt-*, all in nom. sg. masc.: *artāvā, manauviš, tauviyā, hamapitā, tunuvā* with acc. sg. *tunuvaⁿtam* and gen. sg. *tunuvaⁿtahyā* of *-o-* stem formation (§§184–8).

II. The oldest comparison of adjectives was by the suffixes *-i̯es-/-i̯os-* for the comparative, *-is-to-* for the superlative; both added to the root rather than to the stem of the adjective in the positive degree. There are these examples in OP:

Comp. nsm. *tauvīyā* with *-i̯ōs* (§48 for *-auv-*), to a positive **tau-ma-* 'strong'; cf. Skt. nsm. *sthávīyān* to positive *sthū-rá-*.

Comp. stem *vah-yas-* in *Vahyaz-dāta-* (for *z*, see §120), to positive *vaʰ-u-* 'good', Skt. *vásu-*, cf. Lex. s.v. *vaʰu-*.

Superl. nsm. *maθišta* 'greatest', asm. *maθištam* with *-isto-*; cf. Av. *masista-*, Gk. Dor. μάκιστος to μακρός.

Superl. asn. *duvaiš[ta]m* as adv. 'for a very long time', Skt. *dáviṣṭha-* 'farthest', superl. to OP Av. Skt. *dūra-* 'far'.

III. Secondary comparison, that is, comparison by suffixes attached to the stem of the adjective as seen in the positive degree, was made in Aryan by the use of *-tara-* and *-tama-*, cf. Gk. -τερος -τατος, Lt. *ex-terus* and *ex-timus*. The comparative is seen in OP *fratara-* and adv. *apataram*, the superlative in *fratama-*. Nt. comp. *fraθaram* has an alternative suffix with aspirated stop, seen in the Skt. superlative *prathamá-*. A simpler form of the comparative suffix is that in Aryan *-ra-* (pIE *-ro-*), seen in *apara-*, formed upon the local adverb OP *apa-*.

IV. Adjectives were used in OP not merely as attributive and predicate adjectives, but also as substantives: thus *skauθiš* 'lowly', as a masc. sg., means 'person of lowly station'. In certain caseforms they function as adverbs (§191).

§191. THE ADVERBS OF OP will be listed here, except the conjunctions (coordinating, §291; subordinating, §§293–9) and the prepositions and verbal prefixes, with the inseparable prefixes (§268–§271), which are elsewhere adequately discussed; further information may be sought in the Lexicon. These adverbs are by meaning local, temporal, modal, and serial, as in other languages; we group them here according to their formation:

I. Old Adverbs:

Negative: *naiy, mā* (§292).

Ending in *-i*: *apiy* (also enclitic), *upariy, -diy, patiy* (also enclitic).

II. Adverbs having special adverbial endings:

In modal (pAr.) **-thā*: *avaθā* (cf. conj. *yaθā*), [*paruv*]*iyaθā, an*[*iya*]*θā*.

In abl. (pIE) **-tos*: *amata, paruviyata, fravata*.

In loc. (pIE) **-ta*: *citā* (cf. conj. *yātā*).

In loc. (pIE) **-dhe*: *ada-, avadā, idā,* [*haruvadā*], *dūradā*.

In abl. (OP) *-ša*: *avadaša, dūradaša*, perhaps *avaθāša-*.

III. Case-forms as adverbs:

Acc. Nt.: *apataram, aparam, çitīyam, dargam, ragam, daršam, duvaištam, nūram, paranam, paruvam, duvitīyam, -ciy*, perhaps *hama* (DB 4.90); compounds *duvitā-paranam* (first part instr.), *fra-haravam* (first part adv.), *ha-karam* (first part insep. numeral), *hyāparam* (abl. *hyā + aparam*); cf. conj. *yad-iy*.

Inst.: *azdā, kā, ci*[*nā*]; dubious *avā* (see Lex. s.v.); cf. *duvitā-* above.

Abl.: probably *hyā* (cf. *hyāparam*, above).

Loc.: *ašnaiy, dūraiy, vasiy, -kaiy*; cf. conj. *yaniy*.

IV. Phrasal Adverbs, of prep. + acc. or loc., and of acc. or gen. + postpos.:

abiy-aparam (written *abᵃyapara*), *pati-padam, para-draya* (also as two words), *pasāva* (from **pasā ava*), *ni-padiy*.

ava-parā, avahya-rādiy: cf. conj. *yad-ā*.

§192. THE PRONOUNS OF OP are the following, which will be discussed in the order in which they are here listed:

(a) Personal pronouns: *adam* 'I', *tuvam* 'thou'.
(b) Enclitic pronouns of the third person: *ši-*, *di-*.
(c) Nom. pronoun of the third person: *hauv*.
(d) Survivals of the pIE relative *į̯o-*.
(e) The OP relative and article *hya hyā tya*.
(f) The demonstrative *iyam ima* and its suppletions.
(g) The demonstrative *ava-* 'that'.
(h) The interrogative-indefinite pIE *q̯ᵘo- *q̯ᵘi-*.
(i) Demonstrative *aita-* 'this'.
(j) Demonstrative *ama-* 'that', only in adv. *amata* 'from there'; see Lex. s.v.
(k) Reflexive *ʰuva-*, pronoun and possessive adjective of the third person, only in compounds; see Lex. s.v. *uva-*.
(l) Semi-pronominal adjectives: *aniya-* 'other', *haruva-* 'all', *hama-* 'one and the same'.

§193. THE FIRST PERSONAL PRONOUN.

I. Nom. sg. *adam*, Av. *azəm*, is pIE *eĝhom* or *eĝom*; it cannot be determined whether the Iranian forms agree with Skt. *ahám* in having *ĝh* by influence of the dat. *meĝhi* (Skt. *máhy-am*, Lt. *mihī*), or this extension of the aspirate was limited to Indic, and the Iranian preserved the unaspirated pIE *ĝ* and thus agreed with Lt. *ego*, Gk. ἐγώ.

II. Acc. sg. *mām* agrees with Skt. *mām*, in having the acc. ending *-m* of nouns added to the pIE *mē*, which was the accented form: enclitic acc. *-mā* is probably the same without the *-m*, since Skt. has *mā* as an enclitic (although OP *-mā*, Av. *mā* might be for pIE encl. *mĕ*, Gk. με, because OP writes final *ă* as long, and Av. writes all final vowels long in monosyllables).

III. Gen. sg. *manā*, before enclitics sometimes *mană-*, is for pAr. *mana*, Av. *mana*, cf. Skt. *máma* with consonantal assimilation: the case-suffix *-na*, which appears in a number of non-Indo-Iranian languages, is of uncertain origin, but possibly was transferred from the instrumental (OP *tyanā*; Skt. *kámena*, instr. to *káma-* 'desire'). Enclitic gen. *-maiy* (written *-ma* in A²Sa, §52.I) is for pIE *moi*, encl. gen.-dat. in GAv. *mōi*, Skt. *me*, Gk. dat. μοι.

IV. Encl. abl. *-ma* is for pIE *med*, Av. *maṭ*, Skt. *mat*, cf. accented pIE *mēd* in oLt. *mēd*, clLt. *mē*.

V. Nom. pl. *vayam* is pIE *u̯ei* + *-om* from other pronouns such as *adam*, *tuvam*; Skt. *vayám*, Av. *vaēm*, cf. Gothic *wei-s* with pluralizing *-s*.

VI. Gen. pl. *amāxam* corresponds to Av. *ahmākəm*, Skt. *asmā́kam*, nt. adj. in genitive function, from the stem seen in Skt. instr. *asmā́bhiṣ*, loc. *asmā́su*. The source of the aspiration which gives *-x-* in OP is unknown.

§194. THE SECOND PERSONAL PRONOUN.

I. Nom. sg. *tuvam* is the same as Skt. *tuvám*, from pIE *tū* + *-om* (spreading from 1st person *adam*, etc.): *tuva* without *-m*, §52.V.

II. Acc. Sg. θ*uvām* is the same as Skt. *tvā́m*, from pIE *tu̯ē* + acc. *-m* of nouns (cf. *mām* 'me').

III. Gen. encl. *-taiy* is the same as Skt. gen.-dat. *te*, pIE *toi*; *-tay*, §52.II.

§195. THE ENCLITIC PRONOUNS OF THE THIRD PERSON.

I. Acc. *-šim* is the acc. of pIE *sĭ-*, in the pAr. sandhi-form with *š* after final *-i* and *-u* (§117), Skt. *sīm* has the long vowel; Av. *hīm* has pAr. *h* which is regular initial antevocalic, but the long vowel is not significant because *ĭ* is in Av. often written long before final *-m*.[1] To *-šim*, the gen.-dat. *-šaiy* was formed by analogy to 1st person *-maiy*, 2d person *-taiy*. The abl. *-šaᵗ* was used only as a suffix to ablatival adverbs; in form it is analogical to 1st person *-maᵗ*, Av. *maṭ*, Skt. *mát*, and to 2d person Av. θ*waṭ*, Skt. *tvát*; but in DB 1.50 *-šim* functions as ablative. Pl. acc. *-šiš* (Av. *hīš*) and gen. *-šām* were formed by analogy, though *-šim* was used also to refer to a plural antecedent.

II. Acc. *-dim* (Av. *dīm*), not differentiated in function from *-šim*, seems to have originated by wrong division in such combinations as *pasāvad-im* (cf. DNa 33, where we divide it *pasāva-dim*), in which *-im* was acc. to *is*, Lt. *is* 'this, he'. Acc. pl. *-diš* (Av. *dīš*) is formed by analogy to *-šiš*, and is sometimes written as a separate word (DB 4.34, 35, 36); for a misread acc. pl. *daiy* (DB 5.11), see Lex. s.v. *daiy*.

III. *-šiš* and *-diš* are the only OP acc. pl. forms with endings distinctive of the case; all other OP acc. pl. forms are identical with the nom. pl., either by phonetic development or by analogy.

---

[1] The source of pIE *sĭ-* is not clear. Perhaps it is a conflux of pIE nsm. *so, nsf. *sā (Skt. *sá-s sā́*, Gk. ὁ ἡ) and pIE nsm. *i-s, nsf. *ī (Lt. nsm. *is*, Skt. nsf. *iyám* from *ī + -om), asm *i-m, asf *ī-m. In this way even the variation in vowel length is accounted for.

The form -*šiš*, upon which -*diš* was made by analogy, must be older than the coalescence of the two sets of forms, and have received its -*š* from pIE -*ns* of the acc. pl., reduced to -*s* in pIE after long vowels, as in Skt. acc. pl. *sénās* 'armies', *devı́ṣ* 'goddesses', *vadhū́ṣ* 'women', cf. GAv. encl. acc. pl. masc. *īš* to stem *i*-. We cannot be certain therefore that -*šiš* and -*diš* had a short rather than a long vowel. The reason for the preservation of these distinctive forms is that these stems had no regular nominative forms which could be transformed by analogy to accusative function.

§196. THE THIRD PERSONAL PRONOUN *hauv*, functioning also as an adjective, is from pIE *so + particle *u; see also Lex. s.v. This *so is the nsm. of the pIE demonstrative *so *sā *tod, seen in Av. *hō hā taṱ*, Skt. *sá-s sā́ tád*, Gk. ὁ ἡ τό. OP *hauv* serves both as nsm. (from *so-u) and as nsf. (from *sā-u) (§131); before an enclitic pronoun it is written either *hau*- or *hauv*- (§137). The form *hauvam* (DB 1.29) is *hauv* + -*am* from *adam*, *tvam*, etc., retaining the -*v* after the model of the separate *hauv*.

The same pIE demonstrative appears probably in the enclitic apm. -*tā* in *avaθāša-tā* (DB 4.72; see Lex. s.v. -*ta*-), and as the prior element in *hya hyā tya* (§198).

§197. THE pIE RELATIVE PRONOUN **i̯o*- survives in OP as the second element of *hya hyā tya* (§198); in the nom.-acc. nt. *yaciy* 'whatever' from **i̯od-qʷid*, and in the subordinating conjunctions *yātā*, *yaθā*, *yadā*, *yadiy*, *yaniy*, *yāvā*, the formation of which is given in the Lex. s.vv.

§198. THE OP RELATIVE AND ARTICLE *hya hyā tya* is for earlier *syas syā tyad, an amalgamation of the demonstrative *sa sā tad (pIE *so sā tod) with the relative **i̯as i̯ā i̯ad* (pIE **i̯os i̯ā i̯od*); its equivalent is not found in Avestan. The demonstrative *syá-s syā́ tyád* of Vedic Skt., though phonetically identical, differs in meaning and seems to be an -(*i*)*i̯os* extension of the old demonstrative, which has assumed the paradigmatic endings of the demonstrative itself (Lg. 20.1–6).

The forms extant in OP are the following:

		Masc.	Fem.	Neut.
Sg.	Nom.	*hya*	*hyā*	*tya*
	Acc.	*tyam*	*tyām*	*tya*
	Inst.			*tyanā*
Du.	Nom.	*tyā*		
Pl.	Nom.	*tyaiy tyai-*	*tyā tyaiy*	*tyā*
	Acc.	*tyaiy*	*tyā*	*tyā*
	Gen.		*tyaišām*	

The nom. sg. of the relative in pIE, as given above, is represented in the nom. sg. *hyaʰ hyā tyaᵈ*. Other forms follow the usual -*o*-/-*ā*- declension, except the following: inst. *tyanā* has the ending -*na* seen in Skt. *yéna*, Av. *kana* (to Av. *ka*- 'who?'); nom. pl. *tyaiy* has pronom. pl. -*i*, like Skt. *yé*, from pIE **i̯oi*, and this form, properly masc. nom., may function also as masc. acc. and as fem. nom. (alongside the regular fem. nom. *tyā*, Skt. *yā́s*); gen. pl. *tyaišām* has plural -*i* + pronominal gen. pl. -*sōm*, cf. Skt. *yéṣām*, and is used for the fem. as well as for the masc. (no extant masc. example).

While the stem with original initial *s* was originally limited to the nom. sg. masc. and fem., there is an occasional extension of the *s*- to other forms. In OP we have the absn. *hyā*, from pAr. **si̯ād*, as adverb in *hyā duvaištam* and in *hyāparam*.

§199. THE DEMONSTRATIVE PRONOUN 'THIS' was in OP a combination of two stems, each in two forms: *i*- and *ima*-, *a*- and *ahyā*-: their developments are described below. The extant forms are:

		Masc.	Fem.	Neut.
Sg.	Nom.	*iyam*	*iyam*	*ima*
	Acc.	*imam*	*imām*	*ima*
	Inst.	*anā*		
	Loc.		*ahyāyā*	
Pl.	Nom.	*imaiy*	*imā*	
	Acc.	*imaiy*	*imā*	*imā*
	Inst.			*imaibiš*
	Gen.	*imaišām*		

The stem *i- is that seen in Latin *is*, nt. *id*, pIE nsm. *is, nt. *id; the nsf. was presumably *ī, which, with the addition of (Ar.) -*am* from other pronouns, gives Skt. nsf. *iyám*, OP nsf. *iyam*, used also as masc. The asm. was pIE *im, which, with the same affix, is Skt. *imám*, OP *imam*, Av. *iməm*; from this a stem *ima*- was extracted, declined according to the pronominal endings: nt. *imad, OP *ima*, Av. *imaṱ*; npm. *imai, OP *imaiy*, Av. *ime*. Other forms from this stem are regular in case-formation, but in Skt. and Av. they are limited to the nom. and acc. cases; in OP the plural -*i* is kept before the case-ending in the inst. and gen.

From the gsm. **ahya* (Skt. *asyá*, GAv. *ahyā*, LAv. *ahe*), not found in extant OP, a stem *ahya*- was extracted in OP, to which a fem. stem *ahyā*- was formed, with a lsf. *ahyāyā*, sometimes also *ahiyāyā* (§27). The stem *a*-, on which **ahya* was formed, is pIE **e*-, seen in Lt. nt. **ed* in *ec-ce* 'lo'; on it also is formed the ism. OP *anā*, GAv. *anā*, with the inst. ending -*na* seen in *tyanā*.

§200. The Demonstrative Pronoun 'that' was in OP *ava*-, found also in Av. (Skt. only gen. du. *avóṣ*). The extant OP forms are:

		Masc	Fem	Neut.
Sg.	Nom.	*ava*		*ava avaš-ciy*
	Acc.	*avam*	*avām*	*ava avaš-cıy*
	Inst.			*avanā*
	Abl.	*avanā*		*avanā*
	Gen.	*avahyā*		
Pl.	Nom.	*avaiy*	*a[vā]*	*avā*
	Acc.	*avaiy*		
	Gen.	*avaišām*		

The nt. *ava* is for **avad*, with pron. -*d*; *avaš-ciy* is a sandhi-product (§105). Isn. *avanā* has inst. -*na*, like *tyanā* and *anā*. Abl. *avanā* is for **avasmād*, with the regular pronominal ending of the abl., as in Av. *ahmāṭ*, Skt. *asmāt*, to stem *a*-; whence OP **avaʰmād*, remade to *avanā* after inst. *avanā*. The remaining forms show no new peculiarities.

The adverbs from this stem are *avaθā*, *avadā*, *ava-parā*, *avahya-rādiy*, *pasāva* (from **pasā ava*).

§201. The Interrogative-Indefinite pIE **qᵘo-/*qᵘi*- occurs only sparingly in OP. Nsm. *kaš-ciy* 'anybody' is **qᵘo-s*, Skt. *kas*, Av. *kas*-, + encl. -*ciy*; asn. *čiš-ciy* 'anything' is **qᵘi-d*, Gk. τι, Lt. *quid*, + encl. -*ciy*: both with Median sandhi-development (§105). Enclitic -*ciy* is pIE **qᵘid*, Skt. *cid*, Av. -*čiṭ*, Lt. *quid*, etc. See also *aciy, yaciy, kā, -kaiy, citā, ci[nā], ciyăkara-* in the Lexicon.

§202. The Demonstrative *aita*- 'this' was perhaps the demonstrative pIE **e*- (§199) + deictic -*i* + demonstrative **to*- (§196). In OP we find nsn.-asn. *aita* (Av. *aētaṭ*, Skt. *etád*), apf. *aitā*.

§203. Semi-Pronominal Adjectives are those adjectives which to some extent are usable as pronouns, and therefore have assumed some of the special declensional forms of pronouns: such are, for example, Lt. *ūnus, alter*, etc., with gen. in -*ĩus*, dat. in -*ī*, like *is, quī, hīc*, etc.

I. OP *aniya*-, Av. *ainya*-, Skt. *anyá*- 'other (of two)'; forms:

		Masc.	Fem.	Neut.
Sg.	Nom.	*aniya*	*aniyā*	*aniya*
				aniyaš-ciy
	Acc.	*aniyam*	*aniyām*	
	Abl.	*aniyanā*		
Pl.	Nom.	*aniyai-ciy*	*aniyā*	
		aniyāha		
	Acc.		*aniyā*	
	Loc.		*aniyāuvā*	

Of these forms, nsn. *aniya* has -*d*, like Skt. *anyád*, Av. adv. *ainyaṭ* 'except'; *aniyaš-ciy* has the same sandhi-development which has been seen in *avaš-ciy, čiš-ciy*. Abl. *aniyanā* developed like abl. *avanā* (§200); cf. Skt. abl. *anyásmād*. Npm. *aniyai*- has the pronominal pl. -*i*; *aniyāha* has the double ending seen in *bagāha*, which it modifies (§10). Loc. *aniyāuvā* is equal to Skt. *anyásu*, with added postposition -*ā*; cf. *maškāuvā* (§§175-6).

II. OP *haruva*- 'all' (Av. *haurva*-, Skt. *sárva*-) has nsm. *haruva*; asn. -*haravam* in adv. *fraharavam* (with irregular writing of -*rv*-, §26); lsf. *haruva-hyāyā*, upon fem. stem *haruvahyā*- formed to gsm. **haruvahyă*, Skt. *sárvasya* (*haruvahyāya* is a defective writing not indicating the length of the vowel), cf. lsf. *ahyāyā* (§199).

III. OP *hama*- 'one and the same' (Av. *hama*-, Skt. *samá*-) has *hama* DB 4.92, either nsm. *hamaʰ* or asn. as adv. **hamaᵈ* with pron. nt. -*d* (in DB 4.90, asn. as adv., if correctly read); gsf. *hama-hyāyā*, formed on stem extracted from gsm. **hamahyă*, like lsf. *ahyāyā* and *haruvahyāyā*.

§204. The Numerals are scantily represented in OP, since they are commonly indicated by numerical signs (§43). There are the following written out in the cuneiform characters:

I. One: asm. *aivam*, Av. *aēva*-, Gk. Cypr. οἰϝος 'alone', from pIE **oiɥos*; probably demonstrative **o*- + deictic *i* + suffix -*ɥo*-, cf. with other suffixes Skt. *éka*- 'one' from pIE **oiqo*-, and Lt. *ūnus*, Gt. *áins*, from pIE **oino*-. pIE **sem* 'one' (Gk. nt. ἕν 'one', Lt. *sem-per* 'always') is seen in zero form **sm̥*- as first part of OP *ha-karam* 'once', cf. Skt *sa-kŕ̥t* 'once'; with this, the inseparable prefix

OP *ha- ham-* (see Lex. s.vv.), Skt. *sa- sam-*, is probably identical.

II. Two: nt. *duvitīyam* 'a second time' is the precise equivalent of Skt. *dvitīya-* 'second'; formed on **dṷi-* (as in Skt. *dviṣ* 'twice') + ordinal suffix *-to-* + a further suffix *-ii̯o-*. The simpler *dvita-* seems to appear in inst. sg. as the first part of *duvitā-paranam* 'former with a second', that is, 'one after another'. The stem *aniya-* 'one or other of two, other, rest of' is the same as Skt. *anyá-*; cf. Gt. *anþara-*, Eng. *other*, with the comparative suffix, see §190.III.

III. Three: nt. *çitīyam* 'a third time' and the conjectural asf. *ç[itām]* are related to the stem **tri-* 'three' in Av. *θritīm* (graphic for *-tīyam*) 'a second time' and to Gk. τρίτος 'third', as OP *duvitīyam* and *dvita-* are to the similar cognates (see II); Skt. *tṛtīya-* has the same suffix, but is based on a simpler form of the stem.

IV. Nine: nsm. *navama* 'ninth' is identical with Skt. *navamá-s*, and is formed from the ordinal pIE **neu̯ṇ*, Skt. *náva*, in imitation of **dekʹṃmos* to **dekʹṃ*, cf. Skt. *daśamá-s* to *dáśa*, Lt. *decimus* to *decem*. The *-ṇ* in 'nine' is seen in the Lt. ordinal *nōnus*, from **nou̯enos*.

V. Hundred: it is possible, but not certain, that the prior part of the province-name *θata-guš* is the stem of the pIE **kʹṃtó-m* '100', cf. Av. *satəm*, Skt. *śatám*, Lt. *centum*.

CHAPTER VI. STEMS AND FORMS OF VERBS

§205. THE VERB IN OLD PERSIAN shows the expected form-categories, though some of them are scantily represented:

Tense-Stems: present, aorist, perfect, with various formations.
Voices: active, middle, passive.
Moods: indicative, subjunctive, optative, injunctive, imperative.
Tenses: present, imperfect, aorist, perfect.
Persons: first, second, third.
Numbers: singular, dual, plural.
Infinitive: present.
Participles: present active, present middle, perfect passive, future passive.

§206. VERBAL PREFIXES.

(a) The following adverbs, occurring also in prepositional uses, are found as verbal prefixes in OP: *ā-, ati-, abi-, upa-, upari-, ni-, pati-, parā-*.

(b) The following, not found as prepositions in the extant remains of OP, are found as verbal prefixes: *apa-, ava-, ud-, nij-, fra-, vi-*.

(c) Double prefixes are perhaps found in two forms: *pati-ā-* in *patiyābaram* DB 1.68, *ava-ā-* in *avājaniyā* DB 1.51, 52; but there are some dubious features even about these, cf. JAOS 62.274-5.

§207. THE PRESENT-TENSE FORMATIONS which are found in OP include the following types, which are discussed in the following sections:

(a) Type of Skt. *ásti*.
(b) Type of Skt. *dádhāti*.
(c) Types of Skt. *kṛnóti, krīnā́ti, vénati*.
(d) Type of Latin *jungit*.
(e) Type of Skt. *pṛcchāti*.
(f) Types of Skt. *bhávati, rudáti*.
(g) Types of Skt. *náhyati, drúhyati*.
(h) Types of Skt. *pātáyati, patáyati*.
(i) Type with suffix *-i̯e-/-i̯o-*.
(j) Type of Skt. *namasyati* (denominative).

§208. THE PRESENT-TENSE SYSTEM OF TYPE SKT. *ásti*: the stem is the bare root, non-thematic, suffixless, without reduplication; the root has the strong grade in the singular indicative active and in the singular imperative active (except when the personal ending is pIE **-dhi*), and the zero grade in other forms unless paradigmatic leveling interferes:

pIE **ei-ti* 'he goes', OP *aitiy*, Skt. *éti*; **i-te* 'go ye', OP *-itā* in *paraitā*, Skt. *itá*; **i-dhi* 'go thou', OP *-idiy* in *parīdiy*, Skt. *ihí*; imf. **ēi̯-ṃ* 'I went', OP *-āyam* (for *-am*, §67.II) in *nij-āyam* [*up*]-*āyam*, Skt. *ā́yam*; imf. 3d sg. OP *āiš* (on *-š*, §228.III) and *atiy-āiš*; imf. 3d pl. with thematic vowel from 1st sg., OP *-āya*ⁿ in *apariy-āya*ⁿ, *-āiša*ⁿ (on *-ša*ⁿ, §232.III) in *patiy-āiša*ⁿ, mid. *āya*ⁿ*tā* from **ā-āya*ⁿ*tā*.

pIE **es-mi* 'I am', OP *aʰmiy*, Skt. *ásmi*; **es-ti* 'he is', OP *astiy*, Skt. *ásti*; **s-enti* 'they are', OP *ha*ⁿ*tiy*, Skt. *sánti*; pAr. **s-mas-i* 'we are', Skt. *smás-i*, OP *aʰmahy* (with full grade of root extended from the singular); imf. **ēs-ṃ* 'I was', in antevocalic development Skt. *ā́sam*, OP *āham*, whence with thematic vowel 3d sg. OP *āha*ᵗ,

STEMS AND FORMS OF VERBS

Av. aṇhaṭ, 3d pl. OP āhaⁿ, Skt. ásan, mid. OP āhaⁿtā (and āhaⁿta, §36.IV.c).

pIE *gʷhen-ti 'he smites', OP jaⁿtiy, Skt. hánti; *egʷhen-t 'he smote', OP ajaⁿ, Skt. áhan; 2d sg. imv. *gʷhn-dhi, OP jadiy, Skt. jahí; so also 2d pl. imv. *gʷhn-te, OP jatā, and 3d sg. imf. mid. *egʷhn-to, OP patiy-ajatā; imf. *egʷhen-m̥, OP ajanam, Skt. áhanam (with antevocalic development of m̥, §67.II), whence with thematic vowel 3d pl. OP -ajanaⁿ in avājanaⁿ and perhaps the restored subjunctive 3d pl. vi-janāⁿtiy.

pAr. *k(h)an- 'dig', in 3d pl. imf. OP viy-akaⁿ, 3d sg. imv. OP ni-kaⁿtuv.

pAr. *pā- 'protect', Skt. pā́ti 'he protects'; OP 2d sg. imv. pādiy, 3d sg. and pl. imv. pātuv pā́ⁿtuv.

pIr. *xšnau-ti, OP ā-xšnautiy 'he satisfies'; imv. *xšnu-dhi, OP ā-xšnudiy 'hear thou'.

pIE *gʷem- in opt. Skt. gam-yāt, OP ā-jamiyāᵗ (cf. §101).

pIE *bhu-i̯ēt to root *bheu-, in OP biyāᵗ, cf. Av. buyāṭ from *bhu-i̯ēt; on loss of -i̯-, §114.

§209. THE PRESENT-TENSE SYSTEM OF TYPE SKT. dádhāti: the stem is the root, non-thematic, suffixless, with reduplication; ablaut grades of the root the same as in the preceding class:

pIE *dhē- 'put, make'; imf. OP adadā, Skt. ádadhāt, Gk. ἐτίθη.

pIE *dō- 'give'; imv. OP dadātuv, Skt. dádātu, Gk. διδότω.

pIE *stā- 'put, (mid.) stand'; imf. mid. OP aʰištatā, Skt. átiṣṭhata, both probably shifted to thematic class (§213); Gk. ἵστατο.

pIE *dhī- 'think, see', in imv. Skt. dīdihí didīhí, OP dīdiy (with haplology, §129).

§210. THE PRESENT-TENSE SYSTEM OF TYPES SKT. kr̥ṇóti, krīṇā́ti, vénati: the stem is the root in the zero-grade (usually), with a suffix beginning with a nasal.

I. The suffix is -neu-, varying with -nu-:

pAr. *kr̥-nau- in OP kunautiy, Skt. kr̥ṇóti; imv. OP kunautuv, Skt. kr̥ṇótu; imf. OP akunavam (§226.II), akunauš (§228.III), Skt. ákr̥ṇavam ákr̥ṇot; with thematic vowel, OP 3d pl. act. akunavaⁿ, mid. akunavaⁿtā.

pAr. *dʰr̥š-nau- in OP adaršnauš, Skt. ádhr̥ṣṇot.

pAr. *ur̥-nau- in Skt. vr̥ṇóti; thematic in OP imf. mid. avarnavatā, imv. mid. varnavatām.

pAr. *tu-nau-/-nu- in pres. *tunauti, OP ptc. nsm. tunuv-ā, asm. -aⁿtam, gsm. -aⁿtahyā.

On danu[taiy] as alternative to danu[vatiy], see §216; on ā-xšnautiy and forms, see §208.

II. The suffix is -nā-, alternating with -nə-:

OP imf. adīnāᵗ 'he took away', cf. Av. zināiti 'he harms'; OP 1st sg. adīnam with -nə- as though thematic.

OP imf. adānāᵗ, Skt. ájānāt 'he knew', from *ĝn̥-nā-; unless from *ĝnō-nā- with full grade of the root and dissimilative loss of the prior n (§68).

III. The suffix is thematic -ne-/-no-:

pIE *u̯eid-ne-/-no- in OP vaināmiy 'I see', 3d sg. vainatiy, mid. vainataiy; Skt. vénāmi 'I desire', vénati, vénate.

§211. THE PRESENT-TENSE SYSTEM OF TYPE LATIN jungit: the stem is the root in zero grade, with an ablauting infix -ne-/-n-: Skt. yu-ná-k-ti 'he joins', pl. yu-ñ-j-ánti, to root *i̯eug-/*i̯ug-. In some languages the paradigm is leveled to the form of the plural, and the stem is made thematic; thus Latin jungit, jungunt. This is the situation in the Aryan root *mauth-, Skt. pres. muṇṭhate[1] 'he runs away', OP imf. amuⁿθaᵗ 'he fled', and probably in Ar. *paiś-, Skt. pres. piśáti, OP 3d sg. imf. apiθaᵗ (DSf 54).

The same formation is seen in Skt. vi-n-dáti 'finds'; the present participle OP viⁿdaᵗ- is seen as the prior element of Vidafarnā 'Intaphernes'.

§212. THE PRESENT-TENSE SYSTEM OF TYPE SKT. pr̥cchati: the stem has the thematic suffix -sk̑e-/-sk̑o-, the root being normally in a zero-grade; but some verbs have the full grade extended from other stems:

pIE *prek̑-, pres. *pr̥k̑-sk̑e-, OP parsāmiy 'I punish', Skt. pr̥cchā́mi 'I ask'; imf. OP aparsam, Skt. ápr̥ccham, imv. OP parsā, Skt. pr̥cchá.

pIE *i̯em- 'reach out', pres. *i̯m̥-sk̑e-, Skt. yácchati; imf. mid. OP āyasatā (to ā-yam-).

pIE *tres- in Skt. trásati; pres. *tr̥s-sk̑e-, OP tarsatiy 'he fears', pl. tarsaⁿtiy, imf. atarsaᵗ, pl. atarsaⁿ, inj. 1st sg. tarsam.

pIE *ĝnō-, pres. *ĝnō-sk̑e-, Lt. gnōscit 'he learns'; subj. OP xšnāsāhy xšnāsātiy, Lt. (fut. ind.) gnōscēs gnōscet.

pIE *r̥- in pres. *r̥-sk̑e-, Skt. r̥cchati; *re-sk̑e-, NPers. rasad, imf. OP arasam 'I went', 3d sg. -arasa in parārasaᵗ.

---

[1] Middle, with cerebral -ṇṭh- of post-classical development.

§213. THE PRESENT-TENSE SYSTEM OF TYPES SKT. *bhávati, rudáti*: the stem consists of the root ending in a thematic *-e-/-o-*; the root is regularly in the strong grade if accented, but in the zero-grade if the thematic vowel is accented:

pIE **bhere-*, Skt. *bhárati*; OP *baraⁿtiy* 'they bear', Skt. *bháranti*; imf. OP *abaram*, 3d sg. *abaraᵗ*, 3d pl. *abaraⁿ abarahaⁿ*, mid. *abaraⁿtā*; imv. 3d sg. *baratuv*; in cpds., 3d sg. pres. *ā-baratiy*, 2d sg. imv. *pari-barā*.

pIE **bheu̯e-*, Skt. *bhávati*, OP *bavatiy* 'he becomes'; 3d pl. *bavaⁿtiy*, imf. *abavam abavaᵗ abavaⁿ*.

pIE **pete-*, Skt. *pátati* 'he flies'; imf. mid. OP *ud-apatatā* 'he rose up, rebelled'.

pIE **i̯aǵe-*, Skt. *yájati* 'he worships'; mid. OP *yadataiy*, imf. 1st sg. *ayadaiy*, Skt. *áyaje*.

pIE **reǵhe-* (or **redhe-*, see Lex. s.v.), Skt. *rahati* 'he leaves'; inj. 2d sg. OP *ava-radaʰ*.

pIE **qi̯eu̯e-*, Skt. *cyávati* 'he moves'; imf. OP *ašiyavam* 'I set forth', *ašiyavaᵗ ašiyavaⁿ*.

pIE **k̂e(n)se-*, Skt. *śáṃsati* 'he praises', OP *θātiy* (§131) 'he says'; imf. OP *aθaham, aθahaᵗ*.

pIE **nei̯e-*, Skt. *náyati* 'leads'; OP imf. *-anayam* in *frānayam, anayaᵗ, anayaⁿ*, 3d sg. mid. *anayatā*.

pIE **mr̥de-*, Skt. *mr̥dáti* 'he crushes', OP *vi-mardatiy*, imf. *viyamardaᵗ* (cf. §44).

pIE **sr̥ǵe-*, Skt. *sr̥játi* 'he looses'; imf. OP *ava-har-[da]* (unaugmented).

pIE **sn̥ge-*, Skt. *sájati* 'he hangs', or **seu̯ge-* (Skt. accent is irregular for root in zero-grade); imp. OP *-ahajam* (or *-ahaⁿjam?*) in *frāhajam*.

Also, with strong-grade roots: OP *kana-* in imf. *avākanam*; *gauba-* in mid. *gaubataiy*, imf. *agaubatā*, pl. *agaubaⁿtā*; *taxša-* in mid. *haᵐtaxšataiy*, imf. *hamataxšaiy hamataxšatā hamataxšaⁿtā*; *yauda-* (Av. *yaozaiti*), in imf. *ayaudaᵗ ayaudaⁿ*, ptc. *yau[daⁿtim]*; apparently *vaja-* in *avajam*, *raxθa-* in imv. *raxθatuv*; perhaps *māva-* in 3d pl. imf. mid. *[am]āvatā*.

pAr. **kšai̯a-* in Skt. *kṣáyati* 'he possesses', OP imf. *patiy-axšayaiy* 'I ruled over', ptc. *xšayamna* 'ruling'; unless this is rather pIE **qᵖə-i̯e-* (§214) to **qᵖē-* seen in Gk. κέκτημαι 'I possess'.

pAr. **ǵīu̯a-*, OP *jīva-*, see §216.

§214. THE PRESENT-TENSE SYSTEM OF TYPES SKT. *náhyati, drúhyati*: there is a suffix *-i̯e-/-i̯o-* added to the root either in a strong grade or in a zero grade; this suffix may be identical with the passive suffix (§220), which is accented, and therefore this class may be merely passives which have assumed active (or middle) meanings, usually accompanied with a shift of the accent to the radical syllable. Those with strong-grade roots seems to be later formations, made from the roots by direct addition of the unaccented suffix.

pIE **dhreugh-*: pAr. **drughi̯a-* in Skt. *drúhyati* 'he deceives', OP imf. *adurujiyaᵗ*, pl. *adurujiyašaⁿ*.

pIE **men-*: pAr. **mani̯a-* in Skt. *mányate* 'he thinks', OP 1st sg. *maniyaiy*, imf. *amaniyaiy*.

pIE **mer-*: pAr. **mr̥i̯e-* or **mrii̯e-* in Skt. *mriyáte* (with accent of passive) 'he dies', OP imf. *amariyatā*.

pIE **ĝhu̯ā-* (vowel quality indeterminate) and **ĝhu̯ə-*: pAr. *žhu̯a-ya-* 'call' in Skt. *hváyati*, OP imf. *patiy-azbayam*.

pAr. **pā-* 'protect', and **pa-ya-* (from pIE **pə-*), in OP 1st sg. imf. *apayaiy*, 2d sg. imv. mid. *pati-payaʰuvā*.

pIE **gʷhedh-* in pAr. **ǵadhi̯a-*, Av. *jaiδyeiti*, OP *jadiyāmiy* 'I entreat'.

pAr. **as-* 'throw' in **asi̯a-*, Skt. *ásyati*, OP imf. mid. *[ā]h[yat]ā*.

pIE **stā-* in pAr. **stā-i̯a-*, OP imf. *-astāyam* in *niyaštāyam* 'I enjoined' (on *š* §117) and *avāstā yam* 'I restored', 3d sg. *niyaštāyaᵗ*.

pIE **mē-* 'measure' in pAr. **mā-i̯a-*, Skt. *māyate*: OP imf. mid. *-amāyatā* in *frāmāyatā* 'commanded'.

On OP *xšaya-*, see §213.

§215. THE PRESENT-TENSE SYSTEM OF TYPES SKT. *pātáyati, patáyati*: this is an original causative formation with the pIE suffix *-éi̯e-/-éi̯o-* attached to the root in the *o*-grade; in Aryan the suffix is *-ai̯a-* and the root has *-ă-* (also in the diphthongs *-ai-* and *-au-* before consonants) or *-ā-* (rarely, *-ī-* or *-ū-*).

pIE **dher-* 'hold firm': pAr. **dhārai̯a-* in Skt. *dhāráyati*; OP *dārayāmiy, dārayatiy*, pl. *dārayaⁿtiy*, imf. 3d sg. *adārayaᵗ*, mid. 1st sg. *ham-adārayaiy*, 3d sg. *adā[rayat]ā*.

pIE **k̂lei-* 'lean': pAr. **śrāi̯ai̯a-* in Skt. *śrāyáyati*; OP 1st sg. imf. *niy-açārayam*, with *-r-* after *dārayatiy*.

pIE **nek̂-* 'perish': pAr. **nāśai̯a-* in Skt. *nāśáyati*, OP *vi-nāθayatiy*, imf. 3d sg. *viy-anāθayaᵗ*, opt. 3d sg. *vi-nāθayaiš*.

pIE **sed-* 'sit': pAr. **sādai̯a-* 'seat' in Skt. *sādáyati*;

OP imf. *niyašādayam* 'I set down' (on -*š*-, §117).

pAr. *aiš-aịa- in Skt. *eṣayati*; OP imf. *frāišayam frāišayaᵗ*.

pAr. **ǵāu̯-aịa*- in Skt. *jāvayati*; OP imf. *abiyajāvayam* 'I promoted'.

pAr. **tāu̯-aịa*- in OP *tāvayati* 'has strength', imf. *atāvayam*.

pAr. *tar-aịa- 'cross', OP imf. *viy-atarayam* 'I put across', pl. *viy-atarayāmā*; cf. Skt. *tāráyati*.

pAr. *mān-aịa- 'remain', OP imf. *amānayaᵗ*.

pAr. **gau̯źh-aịa*- 'conceal', OP 2d sg. inj. *apagaudayaʰ*; cf. Skt. *gūháyati*.

pIr. *šadaịa- 'seem', Av. *sadayeiti*, OP 3d sg. inj. *θadayaᵗ*; cf. Skt. *chadáyati chandáyati*.

pIE **u̯ort-eịe*- 'cause to turn', Skt. *vartayati*; perhaps in OP [*va*]*rtaiyaiy* 'I appeal to' (for -*tayaiy*, §48).

pOP *ịas-aịa- derivative to pIr. *ịaša- (with pIE -*sḱe*-, OP imf. *āyasatā* 'took as his own'), *nīyasayaᵗ* 'set down' (for *niyayasayaᵗ, §23.I).

§216. The Present-Tense System with suffix -*u̯e*-/-*u̯o*-: this is found with certainty in OP only in inj. *staᵐba-vaʰ* 'revolt!', cf. NPers. *stamb*-. There are two other less certain examples:

OP *danu*[*vatiy*], Skt. *dhánvati*, stem pAr. *dhanva*-; unless we should restore OP *danu*[*taiy*], like Skt. *dhanuté*, stem pIE **dhn̥-nu*- (varying with -*neu*-, §210.I).[1]

OP imv. *jīvā* 'live!' from pIE **gʷī-u̯e*; OP 3d du. imf. *ajīvatam*; cf. Skt. *jī́vati* 'he lives': unless **gʷīu̯e*- is really a broken reduplication *gʷī-gʷe- to the root *gʷei- 'live', with dissimilative loss of the second *g*, cf. Lt. *vīvō* 'I live', *vīvos* 'living', Osc. npm. *bivus* 'living', but oEng. *cwĭcu* 'living', NEng. *quick*, Gm. *queck*, *erquicken*.

§217. The Present-Tense System of Denominative Verbs (type, Skt. *namas-yati* 'reveres', to *námas-* 'reverence') has the pIE suffix *-*ịe*-/-*ịo*- attached to the nominal stem; the suffix originally bore the accent:

OP *avah-ya*- in imf. *patiy-avahyaiy* 'I appealed for help', to stem in Av. *avah*- 'help'.

OP *garbā-ya*- in imf. *agarbāyam agarbāyaᵗ agarbāyaⁿ agarbāyatā*; to pAr. **gr̥bhā*-, cf. Skt. *gr̥bhā́yati*;

---

[1] But pAr. *dhanva- may be merely *dha-nu- made thematic, and therefore properly analyzable as **dha-nu-* + -*e*-, cf similar shifts from non-thematic to thematic in Greek verbs, such as δεικ-νύ-ε-τε 'you show' replacing δείκ-νυ-τε.

OP ptc. *ā-garbīta* has the final stem-vowel of the noun changed to *ī*, as in the next example.

OP *drauǰī-ya*- 'regard as a lie' in 2d sg. subj. [*drau*]*jīyāhy*, to *drauga*- 'the Lie', with change of the final stem vowel to *ī* before the suffix; cf. Whitney, Skt. Gram. §1059d.

§218. The Aorist-Tense Formations found in OP are few and scattering.

I. The Sigmatic Aorist is seen in *niy-apaišam* 'I inscribed' (or -*apišam*?)[1], to root *paiθ*-, pIE *peiḱ-; in mid. *adaršiy* 'I held', to root *dar*-, pIE *dher-; perhaps in pass. -*asahya* in *frāsah*[*ya*]. The aorist endings 3d sg. -*s-t*, pl. -*s-n̥t*, may also be responsible for the endings of *āiš* -*āišaⁿ* to root *ay*- (§208); *akunauš akunavaša* to *kar*-; *adurujiyaša* to *durujiya*-; *abaraha* to *bar*-.

II. The Strong or Suffixless Aorist, with strong grade of the root in the singular indicative active and zero grade in most other forms, is seen in OP *adāᵗ* 'he created', Skt. *ádhāt*, pIE *édhēt; OP *akutā* 'he made', *akumā* 'we made', *kušuvā* 'make thou', = Skt. *ákr̥ta*, **ákr̥ma*, **kr̥ṣva*. Possibly also there belong here the imv. *dīdiy*, if it is to be explained without haplology (§209), and the opt. *ā-jamiyā* (§208), which have been taken as presents; perhaps also the opt. 2d sg. *biyāʰ*, 3d sg. *biyāᵗ* (§223.I). On *amᵃxᵃmᵃtᵃa* if to be taken as (*h*)*am-axmatā*, see Lex. s.v. *amaxamatā*.

§219. The Perfect Tense is attested with certainty in OP only by a single form, the opt. *caxriyāᵗ*, from *qe-qr-ịēt, with regular reduplication and with zero grade of the root in the optative. There is a dubious restoration of a 3d sg. perf. indic. pass. [*c*]*āxr*[*iyatā*] or *caxr*[*iyatā*], DB 4.90, for KT's ..*axᵃrᵃ*.. .

§220. The Passive-Voice Present Stem of pIE was formed by the addition of the suffix pIE -*ịe*-/-*ịo*-, which is accented in Sanskrit; in OP the root regularly has the normal grade, with -*a*-: imf. 3d sg. and pl. *abariya abariyaⁿ*, to root *bar*-; *ayadiya ayadiyaⁿ*, to *yad*-; *akaniya*, to root *kan*- 'dig'; *aθahya* and *aθahiya*, to *θah*-; *avaniya*, to *van*-; *ajaniya*, to *jan*-; *akariya akariyaⁿta*, to *kar*-; pres. 1st pl. *θahyāmahy*, to *θah*-; opt. 3d sg. *kariyaiš* to *kar*-, *fraθiyaiš* to *fraθ*-, 3d pl. *yadiyaišaⁿ* to *yad*-.

---

[1] Though OP *nᵃiyᵃpᵃišᵐᵃ* permits either normalization, an *s*-aorist with strong ablaut-grade is to be expected rather than one with zero-grade

With the vocalism of the present-tense stem: *adāriya*, to *dar-*, pres. *dāraya-* (§215); and the uncertain [*ap*]*i*[*θ*]*i*[*ya*] (see Lex. s.v. *paiθ-*). Formed on the present-tense stem: 3d pl. *akunavaya*ⁿ*tā*, to *kar-*, pres. *kunav-a-* (§210.I); and the uncertain [*a*]*tīya*[*si*]*ya*, for *atiyayasiya (§215), to *yam-*, pres. *yasa-* (§212). Dubious forms on the sigmatic aorist stem, *frāsah*[*ya*] to root *sā-* (§218.I), and on the perfect stem, *caxr*[*iyatā*] or [*c*]*āxr*[*iyatā*], to *kar-*.

It is to be noted that with two exceptions active endings are used, the *-ya-* suffix being adequate to indicate the passive value.[1] The exceptions are *akunavayatā* and *caxr*[*iyatā*] or [*c*]*āxr*[*iyatā*].

§221. THE FINITE MOODS OF THE VERB IN OP: The indicative is formed directly upon the tense stem by the addition of the personal endings, as is also the imperative. The subjunctive and the optative have special mood-formations, and the injunctive differs from the indicative in lacking the augment; these three moods will therefore be considered separately. The indicative and the imperative will be considered only under the personal endings (§225–§237).

§222. THE SUBJUNCTIVE FORMATIONS: all subjunctives so far found in OP have primary personal endings (§225).

I. Non-thematic stems have subjunctives with the thematic vowel, long in the first person and short in the second and third persons: to *as-* 'be', Skt. *ásāni ásasi ásati*, OP *ahaniy āhy ahatiy*. In *ahăniy* the *ă*, if not an error in writing, is an extension from the other forms; *āhy* is for *ahahi (§131).

II. Thematic stems have subjunctives with the long thematic vowel throughout, 1st sg. and 1st and 3d pl. *ō*, other forms *ē*; 2d and 3d sg. and mid. as in Skt. *bhár-āsi -āti -āse -āte*: OP *xšnāsāhy*, *θāhy* (for *θahāhy), *apa-gaudayāhy*, [*drau*]*jīyāhy*, *pati-parsāhy*, *pari-barāhy* (and *-āhᵃ-diš*), *vaināhy*; *ni-rasātiy*, *xšnāsātiy*, *pati-parsātiy*, *bavātiy*, *vainātiy*; *maniyāhaiy* (for variant spellings, see Lex. s.v. ¹*man-*); *maniyātaiy*, *gaubātaiy*, *θadayātaiy*, *yadātaiy*, *vainātaiy*. 3d pl. act. as in Skt. *-ānti*: OP *vi-nāθayā*ⁿ*tiy* (restored form).

III. Certain non-thematic stems which in the indicative have in part been shifted to thematic stems, have subjunctives of the second type: *kar-*, pres. *kunav(a)-*: *kunavāhy*, mid. 1st sg. *kunavānaiy*, 3d sg. *kunavātaiy*.
var-, pres. *varnav(a)-*: *varnavātaiy*.
xšnav-, pres. *xšnav(a)-*: *ā-xšnavāhy*.
kan-, pres. *kan(a)-*: *vi-kanāhy* (and *-āhᵃ-diš*).
jan-, pres. *jan(a)-*: perhaps (restored) 3d pl. *vi-janā*ⁿ*tiy*, cf. Av. 3d sg. *janāiti*.

§223. THE OPTATIVE FORMATIONS: all optatives have in OP, as in other languages, secondary endings.

I. Non-thematic stems have optatives with pIE *-i̯ē-* in the sg. act., *-ī-* in other forms. The *-i̯ē-* suffix, which alone appears in extant OP, became *-ii̯ē-* after two consonants even in pIE; and in OP even *-i̯ē-* was of necessity written *-iyā-* after any consonant except *h* (§25). Examples: 2d sg. *b-iyā*ʰ; 3d sg. *b-iyā*ᵗ, *ā-jam-iyā*ᵗ, *avā-jan-iyā*ᵗ, perf. *caxriyā*ᵗ.

II. Thematic stems have optatives with *-ī-* (as zero-grade of *-i̯ē-*, cf. I) added to the thematic vowel pIE *-o-*, making pIE *-oi-*: cf. 2d and 3d sg. Gk. φέροις φέροι, Skt. *bháreṣ bháret*. Examples: 3d sg. *vi-nāθayaiš*, pass. *kariyaiš fraθiyaiš*, pass. pl. *yadiyaiša*ⁿ (for ending, §232.III); 2d sg. mid. with ending *-so*, *yadaiša*, cf. Gk. φέροιο.

§224. THE INJUNCTIVE FORMATIONS are merely secondary indicative forms lacking the augment; the following forms have been found in OP: 1st sg. *tarsam*; 2d sg. *stabava*ʰ *apa-gaudaya*ʰ *ava-rada*ʰ; 3d sg. *θadaya*ᵗ. See also §237.

§225. THE PERSONAL ENDINGS OF THE VERB, so far as they appear in extant OP forms, are listed in the table; they are given in the pAr. values, since the pIE values cannot in all instances be determined.

TABLE OF PERSONAL ENDINGS

		Active			Middle		
		Prim.	Sec.	Imv.	Prim.	Sec.	Imv.
Sg.	1	{-mi, -ni}	-m		{-i, -nai}	-i	
	2	-si	-s	{nil, -dhi}	-sai	-sa	-sya.
	3	-ti	-t	-tu	-tai	-to	-tām
Du.	3		-tam				
Pl.	1	-masi	-ma				
	2		-ta				
	3	-nti	-nt				-nta

---

[1] The same variation between active and middle endings in forms with the specifically passive stem-suffix is found in the Avesta (Reichelt, Aw. Elmb §615) and in Sanskrit (Whitney, Skt. Gram §774); but in both these languages the middle endings are more frequent than the active endings, in the *-ya-* passives.

The original quality of the pAr. *a* in some of these endings is seen in certain other languages, especially Greek: 2d pl. *-ta* is pIE *-te*; *-sai -tai* are pIE *-sai -tai*; *-sa*, 3d sg. *-ta*, *-tam*, *-nta* are pIE *-so -to -tom -nto*; *-masi* and *-ma* varied between *-e-* (as in Gk. Dor. *-μες*) and *-o-* (as in Lt. *-mus*); for the *-ă-* of *-nai*, *-sya*, *-tām* there is no evidence.

A number of variations from the pIE formations will be discussed in the following sections. The imperative endings are taken up collectively in §237.

It is to be noted that certain of these endings cannot be distinguished in the OP syllabary. The endings *-ti -tai -nti* are all written *-tᵃiyᵃ*, though normalized *-tiy -taiy -ⁿtiy* on the evidence of the context or of other forms of the same verb; *-ta* and *-nta* are both written *-tᵃa*, and normalized *-tā* and *-ⁿtā*; *-s -t -nt* are all unrepresented in the writing if preceded by *-ă-*, though, like the *n* in *-nti* and *-nta*, they may optionally be represented by raised letters in the normalization. The subjunctive endings *-ni* and *-nai* also are both written *-nᵃiyᵃ*, though normalized *-niy* and *-naiy*. Further, the Aryan change of both pIE *e* and pIE *o* to *a* makes it impossible to distinguish the quality of the thematic vowel by citation of Aryan forms merely; for this purpose, Greek cognates have been cited.

§226. The Personal Endings of the First Singular Active.

I. The primary ending *-mi* is attached directly to non-thematic stems, as in pIE **es-mi*, Skt. *ásmi*, Av. *ahmi*, OP *amiy*. The ending of thematic stems was the lengthening of the thematic vowel *o*, as in Lat. *ferō*, Gk. *φέρω*; but to this *-ō* there was added in Aryan the ending *-mi*, as in Skt. *bhárā-mi*, Av. *barāmi*, OP *pari-barāmiy*. Other OP examples: *parsāmiy*, Skt. *pṛcchámi*; *dārayāmiy*, Skt. *dhāráyāmi*; *vaināmiy*, *jadiyāmiy*.

The ending *-ni*, of unexplained origin, was similarly added to the 1st sg. subj. in *-ō*: pIE **es-ō* to *es-* 'be', Gk. Ion. *ἔω*, Lat. (fut. ind.) *erō*; but Skt. *ásā-ni*, OP *ahăniy* (with *ă* perhaps after the *ă* of other forms, as in 3d sg. *ahatiy*).

II. The secondary ending *-m* was attached directly to the thematic vowel *-o-*: pIE *ebhero-m* 'I bore', Skt. *ábharam*, Gk. *ἔφερον*, OP *abaram*; Skt. *ápṛcham*, OP *aparsam*. Other OP examples: *niyašādayam*, *frānayam*, *arasam*, etc. When attached to non-thematic stems, the *-m* became vocalic, and developed in pAr. to *-am*, a generalization of the antevocalic value, furthered by the identity with *-am* from thematic *-o-m*: pIE **ēs-m̥* 'I was', Skt. *ā́sam*, OP *āham*; Skt. *ákṛṇavam*, OP *akunavam*; OP *frājanam avājanam*, *viyakanam*, *avākanam*, *nij-āyam* [u]*pāyam upariy-ā*[ya]*m*, aor. *niyapaišam*. The suffix *-nā-* has become *-na-* in *adīnam*, in imitation of other first persons.

§227. The Personal Endings of the Second Singular Active.

I. The primary ending *-si* was attached directly to the present stem, whether thematic or non-thematic, but happens to occur in OP only in subjunctive forms: *pati-parsāhy* (on *-hy*, §37), Skt. *pṛcchási*; *pari-barāhy* and *-barāhᵃ-diš* (§136), *vikanāhy* and *-kanāhᵃ-diš*, *kunavāhy*, *xšnāsāhy*, *ā-xšnavāhy*, *vaināhy*, *apa-gaudayāhy*, [*drau*]*jīyāhy*; *θāhy* for **θahāhy* (§131); *āhy* for short-vowel subjunctive (§222.I) **ahahy* = Skt. *ásasi*.

II. The secondary ending *-s* is seen in Skt. *ábharas*, Gk. *ἔφερες*; in OP it happens to occur only in injunctive *ava-rada*, *apa-gaudaya*, *stabava*, and in opt. [*biy*]*ā*, in which it is not written because it is final after *ā* (§36).

§228. The Personal Endings of the Third Singular Active.

I. The primary ending is *-ti*, before which the thematic vowel is *-e-*: pIE **bheyeti*, Skt. *bhávati*, OP *bavatiy*; pIE **bhereti*, Skt. *bhárati*, OP *ā-baratiy*; OP *tarsatiy*, *dārayatiy*, etc.; *θātiy* for **θahatiy* after **θāhy* for **θahahy* (§131). Non-thematic: pIE **esti*, Skt. *ásti*, OP *astiy*; pIE **eiti*, Skt. *éti*, OP *aitiy*; Skt. *hánti*, OP *jaⁿtiy*; Skt. *kṛṇóti*, OP *kunautiy*; OP *ā-xšnautiy*. Subjunctives: Skt. *bhávāti*, OP *bavātiy*; Skt. *ásati*, OP *ahatiy*; etc. (§222).

II. The secondary ending is *-t*, which is not written in OP final after *ă* (§40); before *-t* the thematic vowel is *-e-*: pIE **ebheyet*, Skt. *ábhavat*, OP *abava*; pIE **ebheret*, Gk. *ἔφερε*, Skt. *ábharat*, OP *abara*; Skt. *ádruhyat*, OP *adurujiya*; Skt. *ádhārayat*, OP *adāraya*; *viyamarda*; unaugmented *ava-har*[*da*]; etc. Injunctive *θadaya*. Remodeled non-thematic, *āhaᵗ* 'was'. Passive, *abariya*, *adāriya*, etc. (§220). Non-thematic: *adānāᵗ* to *xšnā-*, *adadā* to *²dā-*, *adīnā* to *²dī-*, *viy-akaⁿ* to *kan-*, *avājaⁿ* to *ava-jan-*; in the last two, radical *n* as well as ending *t* is not represented in the OP orthography. Strong aorist: pIE **edhēt*, Skt. *ádhāt*, OP *adā*. Optatives: Skt. *gamyāt*, OP *ā-jamiyā*; OP *avājaniyā*, *biyā*, perf. *caxriyā*.

III. When *i* or *u* stands before the ending *t*, the OP form has a final *š*. Probably this is a transfer from the sigmatic aorist, where the terminations would be pIE -*is-m̥* -*is-s* -*is-t*, pAr. -*išam* -*iš* -*iš*; the identity of second and third personal forms gives an analogy to the 2d sg. imperfect in -*i-š* (no examples extant in OP), whence impf. 3d sg. in -*iš*.[1] After *u* the phenomena are the same.[2] The OP examples are *āiš* 'went', *atiy-āiš* 'went past', *akunauš* 'made' (Skt. *ákr̥ṇot*), *adaršnauš* 'dared' (Skt. *ádhr̥ṣṇot*); and the thematic optatives active *vināθayaiš*, passive *kariyaiš fraθiyaiš* (cf. for ending Gk. φέροι, Skt. *bháret*).

§229. THE PERSONAL ENDINGS OF THE THIRD DUAL ACTIVE. This occurs in OP only in *ajīvatam* '(the two) were living', with ending agreeing with the Greek primary ending in present φέρετον '(the two) are bearing', pIE -*tom*. In the corresponding imperfect, Gk. Dor. ἐφερέταν and Skt. *ábharatām* both have analogically lengthened vowels.

§230. THE PERSONAL ENDINGS OF THE FIRST PLURAL ACTIVE.

I. The primary ending was pIE -*mes*, as in Gk. Dor. φέρομες, or -*mos*, as in Latin *ferimus*; pAr. has -*mas* or, with added deictic -*i*, -*masi*. Both -*mas* and -*masi* occur in Skt., but only -*masi* in Iranian. Thus Skt. *smás* and *smási* 'we are', Av. *mahi*, OP *aʰmahy* (*a*- after sg. *aʰmiy*, *astiy*, as also in Gk. ἐσμέ-ν). The same ending stands in OP *θahyāmahy* 'we are called'.

II. The secondary ending was pIE -*me* or -*mo*, as in Gk. ἐφέρομε-ν, Skt. *ábharāma*; OP examples, imf. *viy-atarayāmā*, aor. *akumā*.

§231. THE PERSONAL ENDINGS OF THE SECOND PLURAL ACTIVE. The only OP forms are two injunctives as imperative: *paraitā* 'go ye forth' from *parā* + *itā*, cf. imv. Skt. *itá*, Gk. ἴτε, Lat. *īte* (with strong grade of root from singular); *jatā* 'smite ye', Skt. *hatá*. The ending is pIE secondary -*te*.

§232. THE PERSONAL ENDINGS OF THE THIRD PLURAL ACTIVE.

I. The primary ending was pIE -*nti*, which was attached to the thematic vowel -*o*-: pIE **bheronti*, Gk. Dor. φέροντι, Skt. *bháranti*, OP *baraⁿtiy*; Skt. *bhávanti*, OP *bavaⁿtiy*; Skt. *dhāráyanti*, OP *dārayaⁿtiy*; OP *tarsaⁿtiy*; (restored) subjunctives with -*ō*-, OP *vināθayāⁿtiy*, *vijanāⁿtiy* (cf. §222.III). When attached to an unaccented non-thematic stem, the -*nti* was of necessity accented, and took the form pIE -*énti*: pIE **s-énti* 'they are', Osc. *sent*, Gk. Dor. (enclitic) ἐντί, Skt. *sánti*, OP *haⁿtiy*. It is to be noted that the OP script does not permit the writing of the nasal in the ending (§111).

II. The secondary ending was pIE -*nt*, which lost the final *t* in pAr. unless sentence phonetics permitted its retention; for in pAr. only a single consonant could stand at the end of a word. In OP, also, the final *n* was not written (§112). Before this ending the thematic vowel was -*o*-: pIE **ebheront*, Gk. ἔφερον, Skt. *ábharan*, OP *abaraⁿ*, OP *abavaⁿ*, *anayaⁿ*, *ayaudaⁿ*, *ašiyavaⁿ*, *atarsaⁿ*, *agarbāyaⁿ*; passive *abariyaⁿ*, *ayadiyaⁿ*. Non-thematic stems would normally have pIE -*n̥t* after consonants, becoming pAr. -*at*; but this was commonly replaced by -*an(t)* after the -*am* of the 1st sg.: pIE **ēs-n̥t*, but Skt. *ā́san*, OP *āhaⁿ*; OP *apariyāyaⁿ*, *avājanaⁿ*.

III. The sigmatic aorist similarly remodeled its 3d pl. from -*sat* (< -*s-n̥t*) to -*san(t)*; thus in Gk., s-aorist ἔλῡσ-αν 'they loosed', whence strong aorist ἔδο-σαν 'they gave', and (late Greek) thematic ἐλάβο-σαν 'they took'. So also in OP, the -*san* spread to some verbs,[1] being regularly -*haⁿ* after *a* and -*šaⁿ* after *i*: *abarahaⁿ* alongside *abaraⁿ*, *patiyāišaⁿ*, opt. pass. *yadiyaišaⁿ*, and with extension of -*šaⁿ* to the position after *a*, *adurujiyašaⁿ*, *akunavašaⁿ* alongside *akunavaⁿ*.

§233. THE PERSONAL ENDINGS OF THE FIRST SINGULAR MIDDLE.

I. The perfect tense seems to have had an ending -*ai*, as in Skt. *tutudé*, Latin *tutudī*, with vowel quality determined by Faliscan PEPARAI 'peperi'; this looks like the perfect first active -*a*, seen in Gk. οἶδα, Skt. *véda*, + middle ending -*i* (see V, below).

II. Whatever the original ending in primary tenses, this was in Aryan replaced by -*ai*, identical with the ending in the perfect; probably this was facilitated by the change of the thematic vowel -*e*-/-*o*- to Aryan -*a*-, and the -*ai* of the 2d sg. -*sai*, 3d sg. -*tai*, as in Gk. (non-thematic) δίδο-σαι δίδο-

---

[1] A detailed discussion of this analogical process is given by Pisani, Riv. Stud Or 19.89–92. [2] While nothing stands in the way of assuming phonetic development of final *t* after *u* to *š* in OP, it is unlikely that this change occurred after *i*; for OP -*ciy* is from pIE **qʷid*, which is Skt. *cid*, Av. *čiṭ*, Lat *quid*. One must assume that the 3d sg -*š* after *u* is of the same origin as the same ending after *i*.

---

[1] This analogical extension is treated in detail by Pisani, Riv. Stud. Or. 19.92–3.

ται, (thematic) φέρῃ φέρεται. In OP we have pres. *maniyaiy* (= Skt. *mánye*), *patiy-avahyaiy*, and [*va*]*rtaiyaiy* (for *-tayaiy*, §48; = Skt. *vartaye*). The same *-ai* is found as primary ending of non-thematic stems in Avestan and Indic, but there are no OP examples.

III. This *-ai* was used in Aryan also as secondary ending in thematic imperfects, as in Skt. *ámanye*, OP *amaniyaiy*; OP *ayadaiy*, *apayaiy*, *ham-adārayaiy*, *ham-ataxšaiy*, *patiy-axšayaiy*.

IV. The present subjunctive middle *kunavānaiy* has the active *-ni* remodeled to *-nai* after the 2d sg. *-sai*, 3d sg. *-tai*; in this form *-ānai* is not found in Skt., which has only *-āi*, but in Av. both *-āi* and *-āne* (from *-ānai*) occur.

V. The ending *-i* seems to be original in non-thematic imperfects and aorists in Aryan; cf. Skt. *áneṣi* 'I led' to root *nī-*. There is one example in OP, the sigmatic aorist *adaršiy* 'I held' to root *dar-* (normalization *adaršaiy*, with *-aiy* like all other OP 1st sg. middles, is also possible).

§234. THE PERSONAL ENDINGS OF THE SECOND SINGULAR MIDDLE.

I. The primary ending was pIE *-sai*, seen in Gk. (non-thematic) δίδο-σαι, Skt. (thematic) *bhárase*. The only OP example is subj. *maniyāhaiy* (with varying orthographies, see Lex. s.v. ¹*man-*).

II. The secondary ending was pIE *-so*, seen in Gk. (non-thematic) ἐδίδο-σο, with which Avestan agrees (Skt. has a different ending, *-thās*). There is one OP example, opt. *yadaišā*; for formation and ending, cf. Gk. ἕποιο 'thou wouldst follow', Av. *haxšaēša* (written *hix-*).

§235. THE PERSONAL ENDINGS OF THE THIRD SINGULAR MIDDLE.

I. The primary ending was pIE *-tai*, as in Gk. φέρεται, Skt. *bhárate*; this is seen in OP *yadataiy* (= Skt. *yájate*), *gaubataiy*, *ha^m-taxšataiy*, *vainataiy*, *varnavataiy*, and in the subjunctives *yadātaiy*, *gaubātaiy*, etc. (§222).

II. The secondary ending was pIE *-to*, as in Gk. ἐφέρετο, Skt. *ábharata*; this is seen in OP *ud-apatatā* (Gk. ἐπέτετο, Skt. *ápatata*), *anayatā* (Skt. *ánayata*), *amariyatā*, *frāmāyatā*, *agarbāyatā*, *agaubatā*, *ham-ataxšatā*, *āyasatā*, [*ā*]*h*[*yat*]*ā*, *adā*[*rayat*]*ā*, [*am*]*āvatā*, passive *akunavayatā*, perhaps aor. (*h*)*amaxmatā* and perf. pass. *caxr*[*iyatā*] or [*c*]*āxr*[*iyatā*]; non-thematic remade to thematic, *avarnavatā* and *aʰištatā*; non-thematic aor. *akutā* (Skt. *ákr̥ta*) and imf. *patiy-ajatā* (Skt. *áhata*).

§236. THE PERSONAL ENDINGS OF THE THIRD PLURAL MIDDLE. The thematic vowel before the ending was *-o-*, as is shown by the Greek.

I. The primary ending was pIE *-ntai*, as in Gk. φέρονται, Skt. *bhárante*; but this is not attested in OP.

II. The secondary ending was pIE *-nto*, as in OP *abara^ntā*, Skt. *ábharanta*, Gk. ἐφέροντο; *agauba^ntā*, pass. *akariya^ntā*; non-thematic remade to thematic, *akunava^ntā* 'made', *āha^ntā* 'were', *āya^ntā* 'went'.

§237. THE PERSONAL ENDINGS OF THE IMPERATIVE. Apart from injunctive forms, there are imperatives with special endings, here discussed. The injunctives are those used in prohibitions with *mā*: 1st sg. *tarsam* (§226.II), 2d sg. *stabavaʰ apa-gaudayaʰ ava-radaʰ* (§227.II), 3d sg. *θadayaⁱ* (§228.II); and those used as regular imperatives: 2d pl. *paraitā jatā* (§231).

I. The second singular active of thematic stems is the stem without suffix: *jīvā*, Skt. *jíva*; *pari-barā*, Skt. *bhára*, Gk. φέρε; *parsā*, Skt. *pr̥cchá*, Lat. *posce*. That of non-thematic stems has an accented *-dhi*, attached to the zero grade of the root: pIE **i-dhi*, OP *-idiy* in *paraidiy* and *parīdiy*, Skt. *ihí*, Gk. ἴθι; pIE **gʷhn̥-dhi*, OP *jadiy*, Skt. *jahí*; OP *pādiy*, *dīdiy* (§129), *ā-xšnudiy*.

II. The third singular active and the third plural active have in Aryan the endings *-tu* and *-ntu*, possibly being injunctives in *-t* and *-nt* with the accretion of an emphatic particle *u* (familiar in Skt.): thematic *baratuv*, Skt. *bháratu*; *raxθatuv*; non-thematic *dadātuv*, Skt. *dádātu*; *kunautuv*, *pātuv*, *ni-ka^ntuv*; 3d pl. *pā^ntuv*.

III. The second singular middle had in Aryan an ending *-sva*: OP *pati-paya-ʰuvā*, cf. Skt. *bhárasva*; OP *ku-šuvā*, Skt. *kr̥-ṣvá*.

IV. The third singular middle had in Aryan an ending *-tām*, as in Skt. *bháratām*; the only OP example is *varnavatām*, a thematic form remade from a non-thematic stem.

§238. THE INFINITIVE occurs in OP only in the present active, with the suffix *-tanaiy*, the ancestor of the NPers. infinitive ending *-tan* or *-dan*: *cartanaiy* 'to do', to *kar-*; *ka^ntanaiy* 'to dig', to *kan-*, cf. NPers. *kandan*; *bartanaiy* 'to bear', to *bar-*; *nipaištanaiy* 'to engrave', to *ni-paiθ-*. The *c-* of *cartanaiy* is evidence for the *-e-* ablaut-grade in this formation (§98); NPers. *kardan* 'to do' has *k-* generalized from the rest of the paradigm. In form, the *-tanaiy* is dat. sg. of a *-tan-* stem (other forms of *-an-* stems[1] occur as infinitives in Indic and elsewhere, which makes it unlikely that *-tanaiy* is loc. sg. of a *-tana-* stem).

§239. The Participles found in OP include the present active with suffix *-nt-*; the present middle with suffix *-mno-*; the perfect passive with suffixes *-to-* and *-no-*; the future passive in *-eto-*, with meaning shifted to the past.

§240. The Present Active Participle has the suffix *-nt-*, before which the thematic vowel is *-o-*: nom. masc. pIE *-ōnt* or *-ont-s*, fem. *-ontī* or *-ontı̯ə*, nt. *-ont*; Gk. φέρ-ων -ουσα -ον; Skt. *bháran, bhárantī* or *bháratī, bhárat*. Where (Aryan) thematic forms have *-at-* rather than *-ant-*, it is by extension from non-thematic forms, where *-nt-* became *-ņt-* because of the preceding consonant; conversely, non-thematic forms might have (Aryan) *-ant-* by imitation of thematic forms or because the suffix, when accented, took the pIE value *-ent-* or *-ont-*. The OP examples are nsm. *tunuvā*, from *-ōnt*, probably with added *-s* in Iranian (§188.II), to present **tunau-ti*; asm. *tunuvⁿtam*; gsm. *tunuvⁿtahyā*, with thematic declension: the nom. *-s* and the *-ant-* of the stem agree with the Avestan formations. There is also an uncertain restored asf. *yau[daⁿtim]*, regularly formed to pres. **yaudati*.

The old neuter in pAr. *-at* survives in the first element of the compounds *Dārayaᵗ-vaʰu-* 'Darius'. *Viⁿdaᵗ-farnaʰ-* 'Intaphernes', *Vāyaᵗ-spāra-* (§162); and in the derivative *hašiya-* 'true', = Skt. *satyá-*, pIE **snt-i̯o-*, where (Skt.) *sát* is nt. ptc. to root *as-* 'be'.

§241. The Present Middle Participle has the suffix *-meno-*, which is seen in Gk. φερόμενος, but has a lengthened vowel in Skt.; as in *bhára-mānas*, or a zero grade, as in Av. *barəmna-*. The thematic vowel preceding *-meno-* is seen in Gk. to be *-o-*; but it is *-e-* in Gk. βέλε-μνον 'missile', which has the suffix in the form *-mno-*. The OP examples are *xšayamna* 'ruling', *jiyamnam* 'ending, end'.

§242. The Perfect Passive Participle in *-to-* may be formed to any verbal root, whether transitive or intransitive; when the root is intransitive in meaning, the participle is active in meaning, as in OP *para-itā* 'having gone forth', *marta* 'having died'.

I. The participial suffix *-to-* is accented, and the verbal root is therefore regularly in the zero grade: thus *para-itā*, Skt. *itá*, to *ay-* 'go'; *[p]ištā ni-pišta-*, Skt. *piṣṭá-*, to *paiθ-* 'adorn'; *xšnuta-* to *xšnav-*; *a-xšatā*, Skt. *kṣata-*, to *xšan-*; *ava-jata*, Skt. *hatá-*, to *jan-*; *karta*, Skt. *kṛtá-*, to *kar-*; *u-barta- parā-bartam*, Skt. *bhṛtá-*, to *bar-*; *marta-*, Skt. *mṛtá-*, to *mar-*; *arta-*, Skt. *ṛtá-*, to *ar-*; perhaps *parta[m]* to *par-*; *dītam*, cf. Av. *zyā-*; *hita-* in *An-ā-hitā*, of uncertain connections.

The cluster of a voiced aspirate stop + *t* in pIE resulted in pIE voiced cluster of non-aspirate + aspirate, the product of which remained in Indic, but which was replaced in Iranian by an analogical non-aspirate voiceless cluster:

pIE **dhreugh-*: ptc. **dhrugh-to-* > **dhrugdho-*, pAr. **drugdha-*, Skt. *drugdhá-*; but pIr. **druxta-*, GAv. *druxtō*, OP *duruxtam*.

pIE **bhendh-*: ptc. **bhṇdh-to-* > **bhṇdzdho-* (§58.D), Skt. *baddhá-*, but Av. *basta-*, OP *basta-*.

pIE **gendh-*: OP *gasta-* 'evil', cf. Skt. *gandhá-* 'smell'.

II. The *-to-* is sometimes attached to the strong grade of the root, as the result of leveling to the vocalism which stands in other verbal forms; in some instances the inconvenience of the consonantal clusters in the zero-grades was a factor.

pIE **dhē-*: **dhə-to-*, Skt. *hitá-*; but Av. *dāta-* 'right', OP *dātam* 'law'.

pAr. *pā-* 'protect': Skt. *pāta*, Av. *pāta-*, OP *pāta*.

pIE **mē-*: **mə-to-*, Skt. *mitá-*, Av. *mita-*; also Av. *māta-*, OP *ā-mātā, fra-mātam*.

OP *šiyāta* 'happy', Av. *šyāta-*, Lt. *quiētus*.

Skt. *khatá-* 'dug' to root *khan-*; but Av. *kanta-*, OP *kaⁿtam* 'excavation'.

pIE **prek̂-* 'ask': **pṛk̂-to-*, Skt. *pṛṣṭá-*, Av. *paršta-*; but OP *u-frašta- u-frasta-* 'well punished' (where the change of *p* to *f* shows that consonantal *r* immediately followed, §74.I).

pIE **nek̂-* 'perish': **nek̂-to-* with strong grade, Skt. *naṣṭá-*, Av. *našta-*, OP *vi-nastahyā*.

pIE **reĝ-* 'direct': **rēĝ-to-* with lengthening of the vowel (§93.n2), Latin *rēctus*, Av. *rāšta-*, OP *rāstam* 'straight, right'.

pIE **ghrebh-* 'seize': pAr. *gṛbhī-ta-* (on *-ī-*, §217), Skt. *gṛbhītá-*, OP *ā-garbīta-*.

Here belong, probably, also *garta-* in *Asagarta*

---

[1] Cf. Bv. Origines 105–6; Sturtevant, Lg. 20.206. The restored *[da]rtanayā* may belong to this type of formation, by transfer to the *-a-* stems, where it was felt as a loc. and took the postposition *-ā* like other locatives.

(see Lex. s.v.), *māta-* in *Gaumāta* (hardly the same as *māta-* in *āmātā*, above); *marta-* as base for *martiya-* (see Lex. s.v.).

§243. The Perfect Passive Participle in *-no-* is seen in Skt. *sanná-* 'seated' to *sad-*, Gk. ἁγνός 'holy' to ἅζομαι 'I revere', Latin *plēnus* 'full' to *plē-* 'fill', and in the Germanic participles such as Gm. *gesprochen*, Eng. *spoken*, etc. These formations also normally have the root in the zero grade, but show the same variation as do the *-to-* participles (§242). There are two examples in OP, both serving as the second element of personal names:

OP *ā-bigna-*, to an unidentified root, in *Bagābigna-*.
OP *ā-baušna-*, late form for **ābauxšna-*, to root *baug-* 'free', seen in Av. *pouru-baoxšna-*; in OP *Āθiyābaušna-* (see Lex. s.v.).

The same formation probably stands also in the adv. *ašnaiy* (see Lex. s.v.).

§244. The Future Passive Participle in *-eto-* is typified by Skt. *yajatá-*, Av. *yazata-* 'worthy of worship', to (Skt.) *yaj-* 'worship'; but the formation often comes to have virtually the force of a perfect passive in *-to-*: cf. Skt. *pacatá-*, but Gk. πεπτός, Lt. *coctus* 'cooked'. Cf. also Gk. ἄ-σχετος 'unchecked', to ἔχω 'I hold, have'. The OP examples happen to be from intransitives, and are therefore active in meaning: nsn. *θakatam*, npn. *θakatā* 'past', to root *θak-* 'pass'; and *-gmata-* 'gone' to *gam-* 'go', in npm. *ha^m-gmatā* 'assembled', nsf. *parā-gmatā* 'gone forth', perhaps nsf. [*ava-gmat*]*ā* 'gone down, fallen', cf. Av. γəmata- as well as the regular passive participle *gata-* (pIE **g^uṃ-to-*, also in Skt. *gatá-*, Gk. -βατος, Lt. *ventum*).

CHAPTER VII. SYNTAX AND STYLE

§245. The Syntax of OP has few features which differentiate it from that of other related languages; but from the paucity of the texts and the large amount of repetition in them the variety of constructions is very limited. As text and translation are both accessible in this volume, many examples are cited by reference and text, without translation; others are cited by reference only.

§246. The Syntax of the Noun in OP follows the expected lines, in the main. Its special features are the anacoluthic use of the nominative (§§312-4), the disappearance of the dative form and the assumption of the dative uses by the genitive form (§250), and a certain amount of syncretization of the locative, ablative, and instrumental cases (§254).

§247. The Nominative Case is found in OP in the following uses:

A. As subject of a finite verb expressed or implied: DB 1.1 *adam Dārayavauš*, 1.3f *θātiy Dārayavauš xšāyaθiya*.

B. As predicate to a nominative subject: DB 1.1 *adam Dārayavauš*, 1.7 *vayam Haxāmanišiyā θahyāmahy*, 2.27 *avaθāšām hamaranam kartam*.

C. As appositive to a nominative: DB 1.1 *adam Dārayavauš xšāyaθiya vazraka*.

D. By anticipation for another case, normally with a resumptive pronoun or adverb which defines the case-use; see §312, §314.

E. In late inscriptions, as a general form replacing a genitive (§313) or an accusative: A³Pa 5f *hya mām Artaxšaçā xšāyaθiya akunauš* 'who made me, Artaxerxes, king'.

§248. The Vocative Case is used in direct address: *martiyā* DNa 56.

§249. The Accusative Case is found in OP in the following uses:

A. As direct object of a transitive verb: DB 1.19 *manā bājim abaratā* 'they bore tribute to me'.

B. As direct object of a verbal noun: DB 4.55f *Auramazdā θuvām dauštā biyā* 'may Ahuramazda be a friend unto thee'.

C. As direct object anticipating the subject of an object clause: DB 1.52f. *mātyamām xšnāsātiy tya adam naiy Bardiya amiy* 'lest (the people) know me, that I am not Smerdis'.

D. As double object, one of the person and the other of the thing: DB 1.44f *aita xšaçam tya Gaumāta hya maguš adīnā Kabūjiyam* 'this kingship which Gaumata the Magian took away from Cambyses' or 'of which Gaumata deprived Cambyses'; so also 1.46f, 59, 65f, and its passive in 1.49f *hya avam Gaumātam tyam magum xšaçam dītam caxriyā* 'who might make that Gaumata the Median deprived of the kingship'. DB 4.65 *naiy škaurim* (= *skauθim*) *naiy tunuvatam zūra akunavam* 'neither to the weak nor to the powerful did I do wrong'. DPd 20-2 *aita adam yānam jadiyā-*

miy Auramazdām 'this I ask as a favor of Ahuramazda'. In the passive, the accusative of the thing remains unchanged: DNb 8f *tya skauθiš . . . miθa kariyaiš* 'that the weak should have wrong done to him'; also DNb 10f, and DB 1.49f (above).

E. As appositive to another accusative: DB 1.49f *Gaumātam tyam magum*; DPd 2f *hauv Dārayavaum xšāyaθiyam adadā* 'he created King Darius'.

F. As predicate to the direct object of a factitive verb: DNa 5f *hya Dārayavaum xšāyaθiyam akunauš* 'who made Darius king'; and of other verbs, cf. *yānam* in DPd 20-2 (quoted under D).

G. To express the goal; names of places are often used thus without a preposition (regularly with *fra-aiš-, ar-, ava-ar-, parā-ar-, šiyav-*), but names of persons always have the preposition: DB 3.82 *abiy avam Arxam ašiyava Bābirum*; exception DB 5.21f *ašiyavam abiy Sakām*, cf. DB 2.72, 3.73f (*šiyav-*), 2.72f (*fra-aiš-*), DB 5.23f (*ava-ar-*), DPe 24 (*ni-ar-*). With *ay-* 'go' places as well as persons take prepositions, cf. DB 1.91f, 3.73, DZc 11 for places, DB 1.93, 2.32f for persons.

H. With prepositions and postpositions, denoting not merely goal but sometimes other ideas, see §269.

I. With *kāma* 'desire', apparently a terminal accusative indicating that the desire has reached the person and is felt by him (JAOS 66.44-9): DB 4.35f *yaθā mām kāma* 'as was my desire', XPf 21f *Auramazdām avaθā kāma āha* 'thus was the desire unto Ahuramazda'.

J. To express duration of time, as in the adv. *dargam*: DB 4.56 *dargam jīvā* 'mayest thou live long'.

K. To express time when, as in the adverbs *paranam* and *paruvam* 'formerly', and with the postposition *patiy*: DB 1.20 *xšapavā raucapativā ava akunavayatā* 'either by night or by day, that was done'; DB 2.61f *Θūravāharahya māhya jiyamnam patiy avaθāšām hamaranam kartam* 'on the last of the month Thuravahara, then by them the battle was fought'.

L. To express specification: *nāmā* as in *Marguš nāmā dahyāuš* 'a province Margiana by name' (DB 3.11), if *nāmā* is really acc. nt. and not loc. with long-grade vowel (see Lex. s.v. *nāman-*).

§250. THE GENITIVE CASE appears in OP in the following uses:

A. Possessive,[1] as in DB 2.19f *manā badaka* 'my subject'; DB 4.82f *anušiyā manā* 'my followers', whence also with its opposite in DB 2.79f *hauvmaiy hamiçiya abava* 'he became rebellious toward me' (also DB 3.11, 4.12, instead of *hacāma* 'from me' and the like, DB 1.40, 2.6f, 3.27, 3.78, 3.81f); DB 1.4 *manā pitā*, 1.29f *Kabujiyahyā brātā*, and with other words of relationship. This is found also in the predicate: DB 3.9f *pasāva dahyāuš manā abava* 'afterwards the province became mine', cf. DB 5.19f, 35f, and DB 3.58f *avam kāram hya Dārayavahauš xšāyaθiyahyā gaubataiy* 'that army which calls itself King Darius's'.

B. Subjective, as in DB 1.11f *vašnā Auramazdāha* 'by the favor of Ahuramazda', DNa 56f *hyā Auramazdāhā framānā* 'Ahuramazda's command'; especially with passive participles, where it develops into the agent: DB 1.27 *tya manā kartam* 'which has been done by me', XPf 38 *tyamaiy piça kartam āha* 'which had been built by my father'. Alternative ways of expressing the agent are the genitive with postposition *rādiy* (see K), the ablative with *hacā* in *hacā-ma* (see §271 and Lex. s.v. *hacā*), and apparently by the accusative alone (A³Pa 22f *mām upā mām kartā* 'made by me in my time', A³Pa 26 *mām kartā* 'made by me'; both probably corrupt, but cf. the *mām kāma* idiom, §249.I).

C. Objective, as in DB 4.78f *Auramazdātaiy jatā biyā* 'may Ahuramazda be a smiter of thee' (unless this is a dative use); and especially with *xšāyaθiya* and *framātar-*, as in DB 1.1f *xšāyaθiya xšāyaθiyānām* 'king of kings' and DNa 7f *aivam parūvnām framātāram* 'one lord of many'. But only a plural genitive is used with *xšāyaθiya*; in the singular the locative is used (§251.A). The genitive with the verb 'to rule' probably belongs here: DNa 18f *adamšām patiyaxšayaiy* 'I ruled over them; DNb 15 *uvaipašiyahyā xšayamna* 'ruling over my own (impulses)'.

D. Partitive, expressing the whole: DB 1.37f

---

[1] The disappearance of dative forms in OP and the assumption of dative functions by the genitive form makes it impossible to differentiate possessive datives with the copula, from possessive genitives; thus in XPf 28f *Dārayavauš* (error for *-vahauš*) *puçā aniyaiciy āhatā* 'Of Darius other sons there were', the genitive may be either a true genitive of possession, or a possessive dative. When an orthotone genitive follows the word on which it depends, however, there may be a presumption in favor of the dative use; cf. §309.

Viyaxnahya māhyā XIV raucabiš θakatā āha '14 days of the month Viyakhna were past'; DB 1.49 *naiy amāxam taumāyā kaščiy* 'not anyone of our family', cf. *amāxam taumāyā* DB 1.28f depending directly on *Kabūjiyā*; DPd 1f *hya maθišta bagānām* 'the greatest of the gods'.

E. Expressing time within which: DB 4.4f *hamahyāyā θarda* 'in one and the same year'; from this use came the use of the genitive *xšapa*, DB 1.20, in a riming pair with acc. *rauca* and enclitic *patiy*, to indicate time when.

F. As appositive to a genitive, as in DB 3.58f *Dārayavahauš xšāyaθiyahyā*.

G. As dative of indirect object, in DB 1.12 *Auramazdā xšaçam manā frābara*, DB 1.31f *kārahyā naiy azdā abava* 'it was not known to the people', DB 1.75 *kārahyā avaθā aθaha*, DSa 5 *visahyā frašam θadayātaiy*.

H. As dative of reference, in DB 1.87 *aniyahyā asam frānayam* 'for the rest I brought horses', DNa 3f *hya šiyātim adā martiyahyā* 'who created happiness for man'; including the dative of possession, as in DB 4.56 *utātaiy taumā vasiy biyā* 'and to thee may there be family in abundance'.

I. As dative of goal, in DB 1.13 *imā dahyāva tyā manā patiyāiša* 'these are the provinces which came to me'.

J. With the idea of *hama-* 'like' in compounds: DB 1.30 *hamātā hamapitā Kabūjiyahyā* 'having the same mother and father as Cambyses'; the position of the genitive after the adjectives suggests that this is a dative use rather than a true genitive use (cf. §309).[2]

K. With prepositions, the mixed use with *-patiy* (see E); DB 3.32 *pasā manā* 'behind me'; with *anu-* 'according to', in DNb 16, 18; with following *rādiy*, to express agent, in DNb 9, 10f; with enclitic *-rādiy*, in *avahyarādiy* 'on account of this'.

§251. THE LOCATIVE CASE appears in OP in the following uses:

A. Expressing place where, without a preposition, as in DB 1.34f *pasāva drauga dahyauvā vasiy abava utā Pārsaiy utā Mādaiy utā aniyāuvā dahyušuvā* 'afterwards the Lie waxed great in the country, both in Persia and in Media and in the other provinces'; DB 2.75 *duvarayāmaiy basta adāriya* 'he was held bound at my palace en-

---

[2] Cf. Greek use of the dative with adjectives of which the prior element was ὁμο-; though in later times the genitive also was used with them.

trance'; DB 2.76 *pasāvašim Hagmatānaiy uzmayāpatiy akunavam* 'afterwards I put him on the stake (= impaled him) at Ecbatana'; DB 1.15 *tyaiy drayahyā* '(those) who (dwell) by the sea' (not 'islanders', since the term denotes the satrapy of which Dascylium was the capital, JNES 2.304). With 'king', singular nouns are in the locative, as in DB 1.2 *xšāyaθiya Pārsaiy* 'king in Persia', though plurals are in the genitive (§250.C), similarly DB 1.81 *xšaçam tya Bābirauv* 'the kingship in Babylon'. It is a substitute for the genitive in DB 2.23f *hya Mādaišuvā maθišta āha* 'who was chief among the Medes' (cf. §250.D).

B. Expressing place to which, with prep. *yātā* 'as far as', in DSf 32f *abara yātā Bābirauv* 'carried as far as Babylon', 34 *yātā Çūšāyā* 'as far as Susa'; perhaps also, because of the idea of motion which seems to be in the verbs, in *gāθavā avāstāyam* (DB 1.62f), *gāθavā niyašādayam* (DNa 36), *maškāuvā avākanam* (DB 1.86), *uzmayā-patiy* (DB 2.76, etc.).

C. Expressing specification: *nāma* 'as to name' (see Lex. s.v. for examples, and §312), and possibly *nāmā* (if long-vowel loc. and not acc.); probably Wc 1 *CXX karšayā* '120 (units) in weight', and D²Sa 1 (and A²Hb) *apadānam stūnāya* (if for *-āyā*) *aθagainam* 'palace made of stone as to its column(s)'.

D. Abnormal uses: The locative sometimes replaces the ablative with *hacā*, to denote place from which: *hacā Bābirauv* 'from Babylon' (DSf 33; but the abl. in *hacā Bābirauš* DB 2.64f), *hacā Hidauv* (DSf 44, DPh 7, DH 5f); and once even without the preposition: XPf 32-4 *yaθāmaiy pitā Dārayavauš gāθavā ašiyava* 'when my father Darius went from the throne (= died)'.

E. With prepositions: The locative is found with *yātā* (see B), *hacā* (see D), *ni-* in the adv. *nipadiy*, *-patiy* (see A, B). Further, all locative case-forms have the postposition *-ā*, except names of places in the singular and those which function as adverbs (such as *dūraiy*, *rādiy*, *ni-padiy*, etc.).

F. As appositive to a locative, as in DB 1.34f.

§252. THE INSTRUMENTAL CASE appears in OP in the following uses:

A. With *hadā*, to denote accompaniment either friendly or hostile: DB 2.21f *pasāva hauv Vidarna hadā kārā ašiyava* 'after that this Hydarnes with the army marched forth'; DB 2.23 *avadā hamaranam akunauš hadā Mādaibiš* 'there he made battle with the Medes'.

B. With *pari-ay-* 'to have respect for', to denote association: DB 1.23 *imā dahyāva tyanā manā dātā apariyāya* 'these provinces had respect for my law'.

C. Alone, to denote means: DB 1.11f *vašnā Auramazdāha adam xšāyaθiya amiy* 'by the favor of Ahuramazda I am king'.

D. Alone, to express specification: DNb 40f *yāumainiš amiy utā dastaibiyā utā pādaibiyā* 'trained am I both as to hands and as to feet'. So also with numerals: DB 2.56 *Anāmakahya māhyā XV raucabiš θakatā āha* 'of the month Anamaka, 15 by days were past'; Wa 1 *II karšā* '2 (units) by weight'; cf. Lg. 19.227-9.

E. With or without prepositions,[1] to denote place where or within which: DB 1.92 *vardanam anuv Ufrātuvā* 'a town beside the Euphrates', DB 3.26 *kāra Pārsa hya vᵘθāpatiy* 'the Persian army which (was) in the palace'; XPa 13f *vasiy aniyašciy naibam kartam anā Pārsā* 'much other good (construction) was built within this (city) Persepolis'.

F. With *hacā*, to denote place from which: DPh 5 (and DH 4) *hacā Sakaibiš* 'from the Scythians'; but perhaps the ablative form in the plural had been lost, and its functions been taken over by the instrumental form, for there is no distinctly ablative plural form recorded in OP.

G. Alone, to express cause: DB 1.86 *abiš nāviyā āha* 'on account of the waters there was navigability'; DSe 46f *didā ha[natāyā avagmat]ā* 'wall fallen down from lapse of time' (both examples doubtful, see Lex. s.vv.).

H. With *anuv*, to express accordance: DNb 24-6 *martiya tya kunautiy yadivā ābaratiy anuv taumanišaiy* 'what a man does or performs according to his natural powers'.

I. As a general case-form, added as the last of a series of accusatives: DB 1.64f *abicariš gaiθāmcā māniyamcā vᵘθbišcā*; XPh 50f and 53f *Auramazdām . . . artācā*. Apparently two locutions have been contaminated: 'Ahuramazda along with Arta' and 'Ahuramazda and Arta', giving 'Ahuramazda and along with Arta'. There is a similar but more extensive use of the instrumental as a general case-form in Avestan.[2]

J. With prepositions: *hadā* (see A); *anuv* (see E, H); *-patiy* (see E); *hacā* (see F).

§253. THE ABLATIVE CASE is found in OP in the following uses:

A. With *hacā*, to express the various 'from' ideas; listed §271.

B. With *yātā ā*, to express the goal in space: DPh 6 (and DH 5) *yātā ā Kūšā* 'as far as Ethiopia' DPh 7f (and DH 6) *yātā ā Spardā* 'as far as Sardis'; but cf. §270.II.

§254. SYNCRETISM OF THE CASES may have been a considerable factor in the forms and syntax of OP. With the reduction of final *-s -t* to a minimal sound, which perhaps was entirely lost after *ā* (though not lost after *-ă-*), the endings of certain cases, originally distinct, became identical. Thus in *-ā-* stems, a form ending in *-āyā* is gen., inst., loc., abl.; in *-ŏ-* stems, a form in *-ā* is both inst. and abl.; in *-ī-* stems, a form in *-iyā* is inst., loc., abl. (and possibly gen.; no example extant); while no such confusion is demonstrable in *-ĭ-* stems (no inst., loc., abl. forms extant), in consonant-stems (no abl. forms extant), in *-ŭ-* stems (no inst. or abl. forms extant; but see remarks below). So much for the singular; in the plural the nom. and acc. are always alike, the gen. is distinct, the inst. and loc. are different, the abl. form is entirely lacking.

It may be then that (except in enclitic pronouns: *-ma* in *hacāma*, *-ša* in *avadaša* etc.) the ablative as a distinct form was lacking in OP, since the original ablative forms had become identical with other case-forms, notably those of the instrumental and locative, and that therefore certain instrumental and locative forms, not by origin identical with the ablative, are used with *hacā* 'from' (§251.D, §252.F). This would explain also the regular use of the preposition with what we designate as the ablative, whereas other case

---

[1] Use of the instrumental without a preposition to denote place where or within which is not common, but is approached in various languages; for the whole IE field, cf Brugmann, Gdr.² 2 2. §480 (Der Instrumentalis als ortlicher und zeitlicher 'Prosecutivus',—der Raumerstreckung—der Zeiterstreckung); in Sanskrit, cf. Whitney, Skt. Gr.³ §281.d (Time passed through, or by the lapse of which anything is brought about); in Avestan, cf. Reichelt, Aw Elmb §448 (Prosekutivus zur Bezeichnung des Raums, mit dessen Zurucklegung eine Bewegung voranruckt).

[2] On this subject, Ed Schwyzer, Die sog. missbrauchlichen Instrumentale im Awesta, IF 47.214-71 (1929); but for such forms in the Gathas, also Maria W. Smith, Studies in the Syntax of the Gathas of Zarathushtra, esp. pages 19-35 (1929).

are used both with and without prepositions, and would also motivate the single exception in XPf 33, where the loc. *gāθavā* is used without *hacā*, but in an ablatival meaning. One form remains to be noted: DB 2.65 has *Bābirauš* as the old abl. form identical with the gen., as in Sanskrit; but a later inscription, DSf, has loc. *Bābirauv* with *hacā* in line 33, and *Hidauv* occurs with *hacā* in DSf 44, DPh 7, DH 5f, showing a shift in this declension. Late Avestan also departed from the old identity of gen. and abl. (outside the -ŏ- stems!), by creating new ablatives in -*t̰*; OP allowed a new amalgamation of the abl. with other cases to remain as normal.

§255. NUMBER has in OP its usual significance. The singular form has collective meaning in DB 1.87 *aniyahyā asam frānayam* 'for the rest I brought horse(s)'; in DB 5.24f *avadā hadā kārā pisā viyatarayam* 'there with the army I crossed by raft(s)'; and perhaps in D²Sa 1 and A²Hb *apadānam stūnāya aθagainam* 'palace stony as to column(s)' = 'palace with stone columns', if *stūnāya* is a miswriting for loc. *stūnāyā*. For *kāra* and *dahyāuš* as antecedents of plural masc. pronouns, see §258.III; for alternative singulars as antecedents of a plural pronoun, see §258.IV.

§256. GRAMMATICAL AGREEMENTS in OP follow the usual types found in IE languages, as to attributive adjectives, appositive nouns and adjectives, predicate nouns and adjectives, pronouns of the various kinds, and verbs with their subjects. A few peculiarities are listed in the following sections, with some instances of regular use.

§257. APPOSITIVES occur in the following cases; lack of examples in the other cases is accidental: nom. DB 1.1, 1.53, and almost everywhere; acc. DB 1.54, DPd 2, DNb 4f, etc.; gen. DB 3.59, DPd 9–11, XPc 14, etc.; loc. infrequent, DB 1.34f. More often the appositive, if more than a single word or if to an oblique case, is expressed by an anacoluthic nominative phrase, followed by a resumptive pronoun or adverb (§314a; §312). Partial appositives occur as in DB 1.34f *pasāva drauga dahyauvā vasiy abava utā Pārsaiy utā Mādaiy utā aniyāuvā dahyušuvā* 'afterward the Lie became great in the country, both in Persia and in Media and in other provinces'; also DB 1.40f, 1.48f, DSf 25f *θikā avaniya aniyā XL arašaniš baršnā aniyā XX arašaniš baršnā* 'the rubble was packed down, some 40 cubits in depth, another (part) 20 cubits in depth'. Appositive substantives do not necessarily agree in gender; thus DPd 6f *iyam dahyāuš Pārsa* 'this province Persia', where *dahyāuš* is feminine and *Pārsa* is masculine.

§258. AGREEMENTS OF PRONOUNS show the expected phenomena, and some special features which are here given.

I. The pronouns *hauv, ava-, -šim, -dim*, and their forms are often used to refer back to a preceding phrase or relative clause; a preceding phrase is usually in the nominative, as in DB 2.30f *kāra hya hamiçiya manā naiy gaubataiy avam jadiy* 'the rebel army which does not call itself mine—that do thou smite', but sometimes in its own proper case, as in DB 2.84 *kāram hamiçiyam hya manā naiy gaubātaiy avam jatā* 'the rebel army which may not call itself mine—that do ye smite'.

II. The enclitics -*šim* and -*dim* and their forms may have antecedents of any gender, and the singular forms may refer to antecedents of any number; for details, see Lex. s.vv. -*ša-* and -*di-*.

III. Plural pronouns are often used where the antecedent is 'men' implied in a preceding *kāra* 'people, army' or *dahyāuš* 'province' or the like: thus DB 1.65 -*diš* goes back to 64 *kārahyā*; DB 2.19–21 -*šām* in two occurrences and the two plural imperatives go back to *kāram*; DB 3.11f *akunavaⁿtā* is plural by the meaning of *dahyāuš*, as are *agarbāyaⁿ* 3.48 and *agarbāyaⁿ* 3.49 by reference to *kāra* 3.45. DNa 36f -*šām* refers back to -*šim* 36, denoting 'men' (cf. II, above) implied from *būmim* 32. DB 4.5f -*šim* has the meaning 'foe(s)' by reference to *hamaranā* 'battles' (see JAOS 35.344–50, 41.74–5).

IV. Other features: In DSe 32–7 the fem. pl. *dahyāva* motivates the masc. *aniya aniyam*. In DB 4.68f the masc. pl. *avaiy* refers back to masc. sg. *martiya* to which are attached two alternative relative clauses connected by -*vā* 'or'. In XPh 30f *atar aitā dahyāva tyaiy upariy nipištā* 'within these provinces which are inscribed above', the masc. relative *tyaiy* refers to fem. *dahyāva* though *dahyāva* has the fem. attribute *aitā*. DB 1.65 *tyā* and DSs 6 [-*diš*] are neuter plurals with multiple antecedents of different genders.

§259. AGREEMENT OF PREDICATES is of the normal types. But an adjective in the singular neuter may be used as predicate to any subject:[1] DB 2.18f *kāra Pārsa utā Māda hya upā mām āha hauv kamnam āha* 'the Persian and Median army which was with me—this was a small thing'; so also DB 1.47 *uvāipašiyam* (referring to *Pārsam utā Mādam utā aniyā dahyāva*), DNa 39 *ciyākaram āha avā dahyāva*, DNb 6f *avākaram amiy*, DNb 27f *avākaram-ca-maiy ušiy utā framānā*, DNb 50f *ciyākaram amiy ciyākaram-ca-maiy ūvnarā*. A neuter subject may have a masculine substantive as predicate: DNb 11f *tya rāstam ava mām kāma* 'what is right, that is my desire'.

In DB 2.92f *Parθava utā Varkāna hamiçiyā abavan hacāma Fravartaiš agaubantā* 'Parthia and Hyrcania became rebellious from me, they called themselves Fravartis's', the plural verbs indicate that the predicate adjective *hamiçiyā* is plural rather than dual, although it is predicate to two singular nouns.

In DB 1.8 *hacā paruviyata hyā amāxam taumā xšāyaθiyā āha*, the probability is that *xšāyaθiyā* is nom. pl. 'kings', in which case *āha* is plural, agreeing with its predicate; but if *xšāyaθiyā* is taken as nom. sg. adj. 'royal', *āha* is singular, agreeing with its subject *taumā* 'family'.

§260. The Pronouns of OP, including those which have also adjectival use, are the following:

I. The personal pronouns *adam* 'I' and *tuvam* 'thou' have no peculiarities of syntax; the genitive forms are used in all uses and not replaced by possessive adjectives (unlike the use of Latin *meus* and *tuus* to replace the possessive genitive, and sometimes other genitive uses). The only use of *tuvam* and its forms is, from the nature of the texts, to refer to a hypothetical second person of general character.

II. The enclitic pronouns of the third person, *-šim* and *-dim* and their forms, show no variation of form for gender; cf. Lex. s.vv. For forms of *-dim* written as separate words, see Lex. s.v. *-di-*, and §133.

III. Certain other pronouns may be grouped together as Demonstratives, though they seem to combine demonstrative and determinative meanings that cannot be definitely separated from each other, these are all used both as pronouns and as adjectives:

hauv (§263), much like Latin *is*.

ava- (§264), equivalent to Latin *ille*.

iyam and its suppletions (§265), like Latin *hic* and *is*.

aita- (§266), like Latin *hic*.

All these are used as resumptive pronouns, referring to something already mentioned which is frequently without grammatical construction (§314, §312), as well as in more usual ways. The adverbs *avadā* and *avaθā* are also used as resumptives.

The adverb *amata* 'from there' indicates a stem *ama-* 'that', found in OP in the adverb only.

IV. The relative pronoun of OP is *hya hyā tya* (§261), used also as definite article (cf. §262) and (rarely) as pronoun of the third person.

V. The interrogative-indefinite pronoun, pIE *q^uo- q^ui-*, has a few remnants in OP; see §201.

VI. The pIE relative *$i̯o$-* also has a few remnants in OP; see §197.

§261. The Relative Demonstrative of OP is *hya hyā tya*, in form and in functions combining Skt. demonstrative *sa-s sā tad* and relative *ya-s yā yad* (cf. Gk. ὁ ἡ τό, ὅς ἥ ὅ). In OP the use as relative occurs much more commonly than the use as article or demonstrative pronoun. Scrutiny of the examples makes it probable that the original dominant use was that of the relative; that in attributive clauses modifying a nominative the omission of the copula led to an understanding as an appositive marked by the article; that this use was extended to accusative antecedents, and rarely to substantives in other cases; that the appositive shifted to a mere attribute and was occasionally placed before the modified substantive, that the article was ultimately preposed to an adjective in a generic sense.[1]

I. The relative use is clear where the clause has a finite verb, as in DB 1.51, or a participle without the copula as the passive equivalent of an active actually found: DB 4.1f *tya manā kartam* 'what (was) done by me' = DB 4.3f *tya adam akunavam* 'what I did', also when the relative differs in case from its antecedent: XPf 22f *Dārayavaum hya manā pitā*, cf. DSf 57f, DSf 42, DPh 5f.

---

[1] Cf the predicate neuter to a masc. or fem. subject sometimes used in Latin· Verg Ecl. 3 80 *triste lupus stabulīs*, Aen. 4 569f *varium et mūtābile semper fēmina*. Similarly in Greek· Xen. Anab 2 3.15 (τὰ τραγήματα) ἦν καὶ παρὰ πότον ἡδὺ μέν, κεφαλαλγές δέ, 3 2.22 εἰ τοὺς ... ποταμοὺς ἄπορον νομίζετε εἶναι.

[1] Lg 20 1–10 (1944), with details of the argument leading to the views summarized in this section.

II. From the originally relative type *Gaumāta hya maguš* (DB 1.44, etc.) without the copula, there came the accusative type *Gaumātam tyam magum* (DB 1.49f, etc.), where the articular use is assured.

III. This pronoun as article is used after a noun to introduce modifiers: an appositive substantive alone (DB 1.44, 1.50) or with preceding genitive (XPf 30, DB 1.39); a common adjective (DB 2.25f, DPe 3f, DSf 30f, 37), two successive common adjectives (DSf 11f), an ethnic (DBk 2, DB 1.79, 2.21); a superlative with following genitive of the whole (DSf 9); a possessive genitive of a personal name (DB 1.89) or of a pronoun (DB 2.35, 1.69); a locative substantive (DB 1.81 *xšaçam tya Bābirauv*) or an instrumental with enclitic postposition (DB 3.26 *kāra Pārsa hya vᵢθāpatiy*).

IV. This pronoun as article occasionally precedes its noun to attach to it an adjective or a genitive; there are these examples: DB 1.8 and DBa 12f *hyā amāxam taumā*; DB 1.23 *tyanā manā dātā*, cf. DNa 21; DB 3.32 *hya aniya kāra Pārsa*; DB 4.87f *tyām imaišām martiyānām taumām*; DB 5.12 *tyamšām maθištam*; DNa 56f *hyā Auramazdāhā framānā*; DSf 12f *hya manā pitā Vištāspa*.[2]

V. This pronoun as generic article has two occurrences in DSe 39f *hya tauvīyā tyam skauθim*; elsewhere generic force is given by use of *martiya-* 'man', as in DNb 12 *martiyam draujanam*, or is unmarked, as with *skauθiš* DNb 8f, *tunuvā* DNb 10.

VI. In two passages *tya-* is demonstrative: DB 3.73 *nipadiy tyaiy* 'close after them', where the text is certain, and DSf 14 *tyā* 'these two', which rests upon only slight traces of the characters.[3]

§262. THE ARTICLES IN OP.

I. The definite article, properly speaking, is lacking in OP, despite the uses given in the preceding section (cf. Lg. 20.6–8); for *hya hyā tya* as article function only to attach modifiers to another substantive, or to indicate generic value. Thus we find *kāra Pārsa utā Māda hya upā mām āha hauv kamnam āha* 'the Persian and Median army which was with me, this was a small thing' (DB 2.18f); *adam Dārayavauš xšāyaθiya vazraka* 'I (am) Darius the Great King' (DB 1.1). It is noticeable that Xenophon uses βασιλεύς without the article in reference to the Persian king (Anab. 1.7.1, 2, etc.).

II. The indefinite article is entirely lacking in OP, except in the phrase *I martiya* 'one man', used in introducing a new personage, where the numerical sign has virtually the value of the indefinite article (DB 1.36, 74, 77, etc.).

III. The generic article is discussed in §261.V.

§263. THE DEMONSTRATIVE *hauv* (once *hauvam*, DB 1.29) is either a pronoun referring to a previously mentioned substantive, or an adjective immediately followed by its substantive, which is then sometimes explained by a relative clause (DB 1.92; 2.66; 3.35, 54, 70).

§264. THE DEMONSTRATIVE *ava-* 'that' is similarly either pronoun or adjective; it commonly refers to something already mentioned, but sometimes has a forward reference, as in *naimā ava kāma tya tunuvā skauθaiš rādiy miθa kariyaiš* 'that is not my desire, that the mighty should have wrong done to him by the weak' (DNb 10f; also DB 3.58, 5.2f, DNa 39, DNb 20, 53, 55, 57, DSa 4, DSe 34, XPh 49, 51f). It has also the meaning 'yonder' as applied to the sky: *Auramazdā hya imām būmim adā hya avam asmānam adā* 'Ahuramazda, who created this earth, who created yonder sky' (DNa 1–3, etc.).

§265. THE DEMONSTRATIVE NSM.-NSF. *iyam* 'this', with its suppletions (§199), is likewise either pronoun or adjective, mainly of the following types: *iyam Pārsa* 'this is the Persian' (DN I), *hya imam tacaram akunauš* 'who built this palace' (DPa 5f), *xšāyaθiya ahyāyā būmiyā vazrakāyā* 'king in this great earth' (DNa 11f). It is a pronoun with rather distant reference in *tya imaiy kāram adurujivaša* 'so that these deceived the people' (DB 4.34f), where *imaiy* refers to the rebel pretenders listed in DB 4.7–30.

§266. THE DEMONSTRATIVE *aita-* 'this' more often refers to the preceding, but also sometimes to the following (DB 1.44, DNa 48, XPh 43, perhaps XSc 4°), when it may be repeated by *aita-* or *ava-*.

§267. THE PRONOUNS IN RELATIVE CLAUSES show some interesting syntactic features.

I. Except for *aita tya* 'this which' (DNa 48, XPh 43), the relative never has a preceding pronominal antecedent of general character; cf. DB 1.27 *ima tya manā kartam* 'this (is that) which

---

[2] DPe 22 *hyā* is not nom. sg fem article before its noun, but an ablatival adverb; see Lex. s.v. [3] Lg. 20 3 for another possibility.

was done by me'. But there may be a general substantive antecedent, as in DB 1.21 *martiya hya agriya āha avam* 'a man who was excellent, him ...'

II. A general antecedent may be incorporated within the clause, as in DB 1.57f *utā tyaišaiy fratamā martiyā anušiyā āhatā*[1] 'and those men who were his foremost followers'; but more commonly the antecedent precedes the relative, as in DB 2.77 *utā martiyā tyaišaiy fratamā anušiyā āhatā*.

III. A descriptive adjective is likewise incorporated within the clause, in DB 2.30f (and 2.50f) *kāra hya hamiçiya manā naiy gaubataiy* 'the hostile army which does not call itself mine'; but such adjectives usually stand outside, as in DB 2.84 *kāram hamiçiyam hya manā naiy gaubātaiy*, cf. also DB 2.21, 3.86.

IV. The antecedent of a relative pronoun is commonly repeated after the clause by a resumptive pronoun in its immediate context, such as DB 1.21 *avam* (see above, I), DB 4.75f *tya kunavāhy ava-taiy Auramazdā ucāram kunautuv* 'what thou shalt do, that may Ahuramazda make successful for thee'.[2] In one passage the resumptive pronoun is repeated: DNb 16f *martiya hya hataxšataiy anu-dim [ha]kartahyā avaθā-dim paribarāmiy* 'the man who cooperates, him according to his cooperative service, him thus do I reward'.

V. In one passage a relative which is the object of two verbs is repeated by *-diš* as object of the second verb: DNb 45–7 *ūvnarā tyā Auramazdā upariy mām niyasaya utā-diš atāvayam bartanaiy* 'the skills which Ahuramazda bestowed upon me and I had the strength to bear THEM'.[3]

VI. The relative as subject is omitted before *ayauda* in XPh 31.

§268. THE PREPOSITIONS AND POSTPOSITIONS found in the OP texts, with certain others found only as prefixes to verbs and nouns, are given in the following list, with a summary of their uess:

ā, prep. w. adv.; postp. to loc.; pref. to verbs and nouns.
aⁿtar, prep. w. acc.
ati-, pref. w. verbs.
aθiy, prep. w. acc.
anuv, prep. w. instr. and gen.
apa-, pref. w. verbs and nouns.
abiy, prep. w. acc.; pref. w. verbs and nouns.
ava-, pref. w. verbs.
ud-, pref. w. verbs and nouns.
upā, prep. w. acc.; pref. w. verbs and nouns.
upariy, prep. w. acc.; pref. w. verbs.
tara, prep. w. acc.
ni-, prep. w. loc. in phrasal adv.; pref. w. verbs.
nij-, pref. w. verbs.
nipadiy, prep. w. acc.
patiy, prep. w. acc.; postp. w. acc., inst., loc.; pref. w. verbs and nouns.
patiš, prep. w. acc.
para, prep. w. acc.; perhaps prefix in nouns.
parā, postp. w. acc.; prefix w. verbs.
pariy, prep. w. acc.; pref. w. verbs; used as root of derivative noun.
pasā, prep. w. acc. and gen.
fra-, pref. w. verbs and nouns, and in phrasal adverb.
yātā, prep. w. loc.
yātā ā, prep. w. abl.
rādiy, postp. w. gen.
vi-, pref. w. verbs and nouns.
hacā, prep. w. abl., loc., instr., adv.
hadā, prep. w. instr.

The inseparable prefixes are the following:
a- an-, the common negative prefix.
u- (= *ʰu-*) 'well'.
duš- 'ill'.
ha- ham-, equal in meaning to Gk. σύν and Lt. *com-* as prefixes.

The uses as prepositions (and postpositions) will be discussed in the following sections; other uses are adequately described in the Lexicon.

§269. PREPOSITIONS WITH THE ACCUSATIVE are the following; for *patiy* and *pasā*, used also with other cases, see §271:

aⁿtar 'inside', of place where.
aθiy 'to', of goal.
abiy 'to', of arrival at a goal, either person or

---

[1] Bv. TPS 1945 61n suggests that the engraver accidentally omitted *martiyā* before *tyaišaiy*, and then inserted it after *fratamā* when he noticed the omission.
[2] Cf. the similar usage in Latin. Caesar, BG 1.12 *quae pars cīvitātis Helvētiae īnsignem calamitātem populō Rōmānō intulerat, ea prīnceps poenās solvit* [3] The same use occurs also in Latin Cic ad Fam. 12.23.2 *legiōnibus ... quās sibi conciliāre pecūniā cōgitābat eāsque ad urbem addūcere*

place; except in 'I was near to . . .' (DB 2.12), 'I made additions to . . .' (XPg 10).

upā 'under', always of a person, in figurative uses: 'was under me, under my command, with me' (DB 2.18, 3.30); 'under Artaxerxes, in the time of A.' (A²Sa 4); 'made under me, in my time (A³Pa 23).

upariy 'over', with slight idea of motion, shading down to 'according to' (DB 4.64); once placed as second word after its object (DNb 49, variant of 46).

tara 'through', with motion.

nipadiy 'close after', see §270.IV.

patiš 'against', governing a person as goal.

para 'beyond', of place where.

parā 'along', of motion; enclitic postposition.

pariy 'about = concerning = against', of a person.

§270. PREPOSITIONS WITH OTHER CASES are the following:

I. With the instrumental; see also *anuv*, *patiy*, *hacā*, §271.

hadā 'with', of accompaniment; of hostile association (as in DB 2.23).

II. With the ablative; see also *hacā*, §271:

yātā ā 'unto, as far as', of limit in place; see also *ā* and *yātā*, IV.

III. With the genitive; see also *anuv*, *patiy*, *pasā*, §271:

rādiy 'on account of', enclitic postposition in *avahyarādiy* 'on account of this'; also orthotone postposition, indicating the agent (DNb 9, 10f).

IV. With the locative; see also *patiy*, *hacā*, §271:

ā, enclitic postposition attached to the locative singular of all common nouns and adjectives except in phrasal adverbs, and to all locatives plural; also preposition with phrasal adverb *pasāva* to denote limit in time (DSe 48); see also *yātā ā*, II.

ni- 'down', only in phrasal adverb *nipadiy* 'down on the footstep, on the track of, close after', itself functioning as a preposition governing the accusative *tyaiy* (DB 3.73; for form, see §198).

yātā 'unto', of goal in place; see also *yātā ā*, II.

§271. PREPOSITIONS WITH TWO OR MORE CASES are the following; see also *ā*, *yātā*, §270.IV, and *yātā ā*, §270.II:

anuv 'along', of motion past, with instrumental; 'according to', with instrumental (DNb 25) and genitive (DNb 16, 18).

patiy with accusative, 'against' (DNb 22), 'on' in phrasal adverb *patipadam* (DB 1.62); as orthotone postposition with accusative, 'on', expressing time when (DB 2.62); as enclitic postposition, local 'in, at' with instrumental in *v̥θāpatiy* (DB 2.16°, 3.26), 'on' with locative in *uzmayāpatiy* (DB 2.76, 91; 3.52, 92), temporal 'during' with genitive and accusative in *xšapa-vā raucapati-vā* (DB 1.20), with accusative in [*pa*]*tiy a*[*vā*]*mcᵃ ç*[*itām*] *θardam* (DB 5.2f).

pasā 'after', with accusative of time in *pasā tanūm* 'after himself' and in the phrasal adverb *pasāva* 'after that'; with genitive of place in *pasā manā* 'after, behind me' (DB 3.32).

hacā 'from', with ablative of noun or pronoun, or ablatival adverb; occasionally with nouns of locative or instrumental form (once with an anacoluthic nominative phrase, DZc 9, and once with an accusative enclitic pronoun as invariable, which it follows, DB 1.50). It governs place-names as the starting-point from which there is motion or action (DB 3.80) or extension (DPh 5, 7) or separation (XPh 16); names of persons of whom fear is felt, from whom commands proceed (= agent), from whom rebellion takes place, from whom something is taken away (DB 1.61), adverbs of time as starting-point; names of persons and things and abstracts from which protection is to be given (DPd 16f, etc.).

§272. THE VOICES OF THE VERB in OP include forms of the active, the middle, and the passive; but the meanings are not in all instances typical of the voice-forms.

§273. THE ACTIVE FORMS have the usual meanings of the active voice, but they are sometimes replaced, without difference of meaning, by middle forms (§274.b).

§274. THE MIDDLE FORMS have usually the proper meanings of the middle voice, but sometimes the meanings of the other voices.

(a) The middle meaning is clear in such examples as the following: DB 1.41f *xšaçam hauv agarbāyatā* 'he seized the kingship for himself'; DB 1.47 *uvaipašiyam akutā* 'he made (the provinces) his own possession'; DB 1.55 *patiyāvahyaiy* 'I asked aid for myself'; DB 1.93 *hya Nabuku̯dracara agaubatā* 'who called himself Nebuchadrezzar'; DB 4.38 *patipayauvā* 'protect thyself'.

(b) In some passages the middle is used with purely active meaning, as in *akunavantā* DSf 48 'they wrought', but act. *akunavašan* DSf 51, 53; *manā bājim atarantā* DB 1.19 'they bore tribute to me', but act. *abaran* DPe 9f, *abarahan* DNa 19f, XPh 17, in the same phrase; *azdā kušuvā* DNb 50 'do thou make known'; mid. *āhantā* 'they were', but also act. *āhan*.[1] Perhaps the ambiguity of *abara* for sg. *abarat* and pl. *abaran*, *akuunava* for *akunavat* and *akunavan*, etc., led to the use of the middle form as distinctive for the plural; however, this does not account for some examples, such as the imv. *kušuvā*.

(c) Some verbs are found only in the middle voice, though the middle meaning is no longer evident: such are *maniyaiy* 'I think', *yadataiy* 'he worships', *amariyatā* 'he died', and their forms. That these may originally have represented middle voice ideas, is indicated by the fact that Latin *arbitror, veneror, morior*, representing the same ideas (though only the last is etymologically cognate with the OP correspondent), are all deponents, as are indeed the etymological or semantic equivalents in various other languages.

(d) The following middle forms have passive meaning: ind. *vainataiy* 'is seen, is seen to be, seems' DNb 2, XPa 16, and subj. *vainātaiy* DNb 35; *anayatā* 'was led' DB 1.82, 2.73, 5.26°; probably *kunavātaiy* DNb 56, and the restored forms [ā]h[yat]ā 'was thrown' DB 1.95 and *adā*-[*rayat*]ā DB 4.90f. This use of the middle is found in Avestan (Reichelt, Aw. Elmb. §614); and the middle forms are the basis of the passive forms of Greek and Latin.

§275. THE PASSIVE FORMS forms fall into two groups, those with the passive suffix *-ya-* (§220), which are always passive in meaning, and those which are composed of the past participle with or without the verb 'to be'—usually omitted; the combinations in which it is expressed are listed in §276. That the participle without the auxiliary is a true indicative passive is shown by the equivalence of DB 4.1f *tya manā kartam* 'what (was) done by me' and DB 4.3f *tya adam akunavam*

---

[1] Bv. TPS 1945.61–3 seeks to show that active *āha* always denotes existence, but middle *āhatā* is always used in an expression of possession, with a genitive-dative. His argument is not quite convincing, especially for DB 4.81; and no motivation for the specialization seems to exist.

'what I did'. When the verb is intransitive, the past participle has active meaning, as in DB 2.32, 38, 43, 52, 57f, 3.65 *hamiçiyā hagmatā paraitā* 'the rebels assembled (and) came out'; DNa 43–5 *Pārsahyā martiyahyā dūraiy arštiš paragmatā* 'the spear of a Persian man has gone afar'.

§276. THE VERB 'TO BE' WITH PASSIVE PARTICIPLE is usually omitted; it is expressed only in the following examples:

I. True passives of action are perhaps to be seen in the following:

DB 1.61f *xšaçam tya hacā amāxam taumāyā parābartam āha*.

DB 4.46f *aniyašciy vasiy astiy kartam*.

DB 4.51f *avaišām ava(θ)ā naiy astiy kartam*.

XPf 38 *tyamaiy piça kartam āha*.

II. The predicate participle is clearly adjectival in the following:

DB 1.37f *Viyaxnahya māhyā XIV raucabiš θakatā āha* (so also in 17 other dates).

DB 3.7f *Garmapadahya māhyā I rauca θakatam āha*.

DPe 22 *yadiy kāra Pārsa pāta ahatiy*.

DNb 26 *xšnuta amiy*, cf. the adj. in the parallel clause *uxšnauš amiy*, in line 27.

XPh 47 *šiyāta ahaniy*, cf. adj. in 48 *artāvā ahaniy*, and the similar pair in 55f, *šiyāta bavatiy . . . artāvā bavatiy*, the prior of which seems in meaning nearer to a true present passive of action than any of the other phrases.

III. The verb *bav-* 'become' may fairly be considered here, cf. the German true passive with *werden* 'become', while Gm. *sein* 'be' forms only a passive of state, in which the participle is merely an adjective. With predicate participles OP *bav*- appears only in XPh 55, just cited; in DSf 25 *yaθā katam abava* the participle has become substantival and is subject.

IV. Four heavily restored passages, DSe 31f, DSf 56f, DNb 54f, DNb 56, give no additional evidence of value.

§277. THE INDICATIVE MOOD has in OP the usual uses to denote present and past time in independent clauses. In dependent clauses, it is used in the following:

(a) In relative clauses descriptive or restrictive, occasionally in clauses of general significance, in both of which types it may vary with the subjunctive (§301.a, b).

(b) In substantive clauses: object clauses of

fact, direct and indirect quotations of fact, direct and indirect questions (§302.a, d, e).

(c) In temporal clauses introduced by 'when', 'after', 'while', 'as long as', 'until', in past time (§304.a, b, d, e, f), and by 'whenever', 'until' in present time as generalizations (§304.c, f).

(d) In modal, local, causal, and consecutive clauses in present or past time; in consecutive clauses with present result depending on present or imperfect in the main clause (§305).

§278. THE SUBJUNCTIVE MOOD has a number of uses in OP, including those of future time, of volitions, and of wishes. These may be divided into uses in independent clauses, uses in relative clauses, uses in other subordinate clauses.

I. In independent clauses:
(a) Future uses: mere futurity in apodosis of future condition, *nirasātiy* DPe 24: future of determination almost equal to command, *xšnāsātiy* DNa 42.
(b) Volitional uses: affirmative commands *bavātiy* DNa 43, 45f, *vaināṭaiy* DNb 35; negative commands with *mā* or *mātya*, *draujīyāhy* DB 4.43, *vikanāhy* DB 4.71, *kunavātaiy* DNb 56, *bavātiy* DNb 59. Negative wishes possibly in (restored) *vijanātiy*, *vināθayātiy* A²Sa 5, A²Ha 7 (though optative or injunctive or imperative forms are equally possible in these passages).
(c) Uses in future possible wishes: *ahaniy* XPh 47, 48, *ahatiy* DB 4.39f, *θadayātaiy* DSa 5, DSj 6.

II. In relative clauses:
(a) In a relative clause of general future meaning, depending upon an expression of command or prayer: *āhy* DB 4.37, 68, 87, DSt 10°; *ahatiy* DB 4.38, 68, 68f; *kunavāhy* DB 4.75, 79; *patiparsāhy* DB 4.42; *patiparsātiy* DB 4.48; *vaināhy* DB 4.70; *vainātiy* DSj 5°.
(b) In a relative clause equivalent to a present general condition, with the conclusion in the present indicative: *yadātaiy* DB 5.19, 5.34f.
(c) In a defining relative clause, not differing from one with the present indicative, the main clause being a command: *gaubātaiy* DB 2.84, 3.86; cf. ind. *gaubataiy* DB 2.21, 31, 51, 3.15, 59 in the same meaning.

III. In other subordinate clauses:
(a) In future conditions with *yadiy* 'if', the negative is *naiy*, and the main clause is a command or a prayer, once a future statement (DPe 22): *apagaudayāhy* DB 4.55; *θāhy* DB 4.55, 58; *vaināhy* DB 4.73, 77; *vikanāhy* DB 4.73; *vikanāhᵒ-diš* DB 4.77; *patibarāhᵒ-diš* DB 4.74; *patibarāhy* DB 4.78; *maniyāhaiy* DB 4.39, DPe 20, DNa 38, XPh 47; *ahatiy* DPe 22.
(b) In temporal clauses of future time, with *yāvā* 'as long as'; the main clause has an imv. or a subjunctive in future meaning: *āhy* DB 4.72; *ahatiy* DB 4.74°, 78, 5.19, 35°.
(c) In alternative general clauses, the first introduced by *yaθā* 'when' and the second by *yadi-vā* 'or if'; the main clause omits the copula: *vaināhy* ... *āxšnavāhy* DNb 29f.
(d) In negative clauses of purpose, introduced by *mātya*, with an implication of fear: *xšnāsātiy* DB 1.52, depending on a potential optative; *θadayātaiy* ... *varnavātaiy* ... *maniyātaiy* DB 4.49f, depending upon a timeless present.
(e) In a volition, object of a verb of mental action, without conjunction: *tya amanayaiy kunavānaiy* DSl 3f 'what I thought I will do'.

§279. THE OPTATIVE MOOD has a variety of uses in OP, fairly parallel to those of the subjunctive except that the uses as a future are lacking; they are as follows:

I. In independent clauses:
(a) Commands: *yadaišā* XPh 50; negative with *mā*, *biyā* DB 4.69, *yadiyaišaⁿ* XPh 39.
(b) Prayers: *biyā* DB 4.56, 56, 58, 74f, 75, 78f; negative with *mā*, *biyā* DB 4.59, 79°, *ājamiyā* DPd 19.

II. In a relative clause of characteristic, with potential meaning: *caxriyā* DB 1.50.

III. In other subordinate clauses:
(a) In optative clauses explanatory of *kāma* 'desire', introduced by *tya* 'that': *kariyaiš* DNb 9, 11; *vināθayaiš* DNb 20; *fraθiyaiš* DNb 21 (without *tya*).
(b) Potential in an object clause to a verb of fearing in a secondary tense; no introductory conjunction: *avājaniyā* DB 1.51, 52.[1]

---

[1] Or perhaps potential as principal verbs of informal indirect discourse; but not principal verbs denoting repeated action in the past, as taken by Bv. TPS 1945.50–1 (cf. opt. in this use in Avestan; Reichelt, Aw. Elmb. §638).

(c) Potential in a future less vivid condition with *yadiy* 'if': *vināθayaiš* DNb 21 (conclusion *fraθiyaiš*, see IIIa).

§280. THE IMPERATIVE MOOD has in OP the meanings of command and prayer.

I. Commands, addressed to men; very common, cf. *parsā* DB 4.38, 69, *jadiy* DB 2.31 etc., *kušuvā* DNb 50. In *jīvā* DB 4.56, 75, the command approaches a wish in value; in *mā ... raxθatuv* DNb 60, the negative command seems to become a threat. In *varnavatām* DB 4.42, 53, the man addressed is not subject, but object.

II. Prayers, addressed to Ahuramazda with or without other gods; frequent, with *pātuv pāⁿtuv*, *dadātuv, baratuv, kunautuv, nikaⁿtuv*.

§281. THE INJUNCTIVE MOOD, which is a secondary indicative form lacking the augment, has in OP only the use in a negative prohibition, with *mā*: in the first person, *tarsam* DPe 21; in the second person, *apagaudaya* DB 4.54, *avarada* and *stabava* DNa 60; in the third person, *θadaya* DNa 58, DNb 53.

§282. THE INFINITIVE occurs in OP in two uses:

(a) as direct object of verbs meaning 'order', 'dare', 'be able': *niyastāyam ... katanaiy* DZc 9 'I ordered to dig'; *niyaštāyam ... nipaištanaiy* XV 23f 'I ordered to inscribe', cf. the restorations in DSn 1 and DSf 19f (subject of passive *framātam*); *kašciy naiy adaršnauš cišciy θastanaiy* DB 1.53f 'no one dared say anything'; *utādiš atāvayam bartanaiy* DNb 46f 'and I had the strength to develop them'.

(b) to express purpose, with verbs of motion: only in the phrase *hamaranam cartanaiy* 'to make battle' (DB 1.93f, and 10 other occurrences), depending upon *āiš* 'he went', *paraitā* (pl. ptc.) 'they went forth', *fraišaya* 'he sent forth'.

§283. THE PARTICIPLES in OP have no peculiarities of syntax. The following are examples of their uses: as attributive adjective, *axšatā* DPe 23; as appositive adjective, *marta* XPh 48; predicate adjective to a nom., *xšnuta* DNb 26, *xšayamna* DNb 15, *θakatā* DB 1.38; predicate adjective to an accusative, *dītam* DB 1.50, *duruxtam* DB 4.44f; predicate nominative without the copula, serving as finite verb, *paraitā* DB 2.32f; substantivized by gender, masc. *tunuvā* DNb 10, neut. *katam* DSf 25, *gastā* DNa 52, *rāstam* DNb 11, *vinastahyā* DNb 18, *jiyamnam* DB 2.62.

§284. THE TENSES in OP are the present, the imperfect, the strong aorist, the sigmatic aorist, in the indicative; the present, in the subjunctive, the optative, and the imperative. There are also one perfect optative, one strong aorist imperative (and possibly a second), and one heavily restored perfect indicative.

§285. THE PRESENT TENSE OF THE INDICATIVE is used to denote a real present, as in DB 1.3f *θātiy Dārayavauš xšāyaθiya* 'Saith Darius the King', 1.12 *adam xšāyaθiya amiy* 'I am king'; also to denote that which is true without respect to time, as DZc 10 *draya tya hacā Pārsā aitiy* 'the sea which extends from Persia', XPh 51 *martiya ... 56 bavatiy*.

With an adverbial expression the present may, as in other languages, indicate time begun in the past and extending into the present, and the imperfect similarly may express time begun in a remoter past and extending into a nearer past; the best examples are in DB 1.7f *hacā paruviyata āmātā amahy hacā paruviyata hya amāxam taumā xšāyaθiyā āha* 'from long ago we are (= have been) noble, from long ago our family was (= had been) royal (or kings)', and 9–11 *VIII manā taumāyā tyaiy paruvam xšāyaθiyā āha adam navama IX duvitāparanam xšāyaθiyā amahy* '8 of my family (there were) who were (= had been) kings; I (am) the ninth; 9 in succession we are (= have been) kings'.

In XPh 30 *astiy* 'there is' seems to have been used illogically for *āha* 'there was'. The present *kunautiy* in DSs is an historical present, of timeless connotation, for the usual aorist *adā* 'created'.

§286. THE IMPERFECT AND AORIST TENSES OF THE INDICATIVE are in OP used to express action in past time, whether in progress or definitely terminated or habitual and repeated. The two tenses are seen in the variations of the same phrase: aorist in DB 1.90 *avaθā hamaranam akumā* 'then we made battle', and imperfect in DB 2.23 *avadā hamaranam akunauš* 'there he made battle', both denoting terminated action. So also the imperfect *adadā* 'created' is used in the phrases at the beginning of DPd, DNb, DSe, precisely as the aorist *adā* is used in DNa, DSf, and other inscriptions of Darius and Xerxes. Action in progress appears in the main clause of DB 2.62f *Vaumisa citā mām amānaya Arminiyaiy yātā adam arasam Mādam* 'Vaumisa waited for me so long, until I reached Media'. There seems to be no difference of aspect between *arasam* in this clause and its compound in DB 2.65 *yaθā Mādam parārasam* 'when I reached Media'. Habitual repeated action is seen in DB 1.23f *yaθāšām hacāma aθahya avaθā akunavayatā* 'as was said to them by me, thus 'twas done'. For action begun in a remoter past and extending into a nearer past, see examples in §285.

§287. TENSE ASPECT was not a living phenomenon of OP. The difference between imperfective (in progress, habitual, repeated) and perfective (definitely terminated) may be detected by examination of the meaning of the passages, but does not correspond to any difference of form in the verbs, as is seen from examples in §286, cf. §288.

§288. THE PERFECT TENSE is virtually lacking in OP. The one certain form, *caxriyā* DB 1.50, is an optative, and the passive indicative in DB 4.90 is an uncertain conjecture; in neither instance can any reason be seen for a perfect in the normal meaning of resultant state. The meaning which in English is normally expressed by the perfect tense seems to be present in all the instances where the participle is accompanied by the present copula: *astiy kartam* 'has been done' DB 4.46, 51; *kartam astiy* DNb 56; restored uncertain text, DNb 54f. Where the copula *āha* 'was' is expressed, the meaning seems to be that of the pluperfect: DB 1.62 *parābartam āha* 'had been taken away'; XPf 38 *kartam āha* 'had been made'. But it is doubtful if such distinctions would have been felt by the speaker of OP, since all past ideas seem to have been merged into one set of forms, including imperfects, aorists, and perfects, and a passive periphrastic of the past participle with or without the copula (usually without it, §§275–6).

§289. THE FUTURE is in OP expressed by forms of the subjunctive, the optative, and the imperative. The only future statement in a main clause is in DPe 24, where the subjunctive *nirasātiy* means 'will come down'. Elsewhere the future ideas in main clauses are commands and prayers, and in subordinate clauses are expressive of time relative to that of the verb on which they depend.

In some of these subordinate clauses the mood expresses a subordinated volition or wish or potentiality.

The aorist imperative *kušuva* 'do thou make' (DNb 50) is clearly imperfective in meaning; the repeated phrases 'go, smite' (DB 2.20f *paraitā . . . jatā*; etc.) are presents and are as clearly perfective.

§290. COORDINATION AND SUBORDINATION. Not infrequently the OP texts express by coordinate clauses ideas which are logically subordinate; the result is a series of short sentences, syntactically simple, independent of each other grammatically, but logically and semantically connected. Thus, for example, DB 4.46–8 *vašnā Auramazdāha apimaiy aniyašciy vasiy astiy kartam ava ahyāyā dipiyā naiy nipištam avahyarādiy naiy nipištam mātya . . .* 'by the favor of Ahuramazda indeed, much other (work) was done by me; that (work) is not inscribed in this inscription; for the following reason it is not inscribed, lest . . .'; this could have been expressed in one complex sentence somewhat as follows: 'much other work was done by me, which has not been inscribed in this inscription for the following reason, lest . . .'. Another excellent example is found in XPf 20–25 *utā Vištāspa utā Aršāma ubā ajīvatam aciy Auramazdām avaθā kāma āha Dārayavaum hya manā pitā avam xšāyaθiyam akunauš ahyāyā būmiyā* 'Hystaspes and Arsames both were living, then—unto Ahuramazda thus was the desire—Darius who (was) my father, him he made king in this land'; in the parallel passage DSf 13–5, *yadiy* 'when' is used instead of *aciy* 'then', and instead of *Auramazdām avaθā kāma āha* (found also XPf 29f, DSf 15f), we find in DNa 37f (and elsewhere) *yaθā mām kāma āha* 'as unto me was the desire'. In dating sentences we regularly have expressions of the type seen in DB 1.42f *Garmapadahya māhyā IX raucabiš θakatā āha avaθā xšaçam agarbāyatā* 'of the month Garmapada, 9 days had passed—then he seized the kingship'; only in DB 1.38 the date is followed by a subordinated clause, *yadiy udapatatā* 'when he rose up in rebellion'. The same phenomenon is probably present where conjunctions are omitted as introductory to subordinate clauses, such as the absence of *tya* in DNb 20 and 50 (cf. DNa 39).

§291. THE COORDINATING CONJUNCTIONS are *utā* 'and', and the enclitics *-cā* 'and' and *-vā* 'or'.

I. *utā* and *-cā* connect either single words or entire clauses; if used also with the first word or clause of a series, the meaning is 'both ... and'. In a series of three single words there is no asyndeton, except that in A²Sa 4f, A²Ha 5f, the 'and' is omitted between the first and second words. Principal clauses may or may not be connected by an 'and' (both uses in DB 1.76f), and similarly with two subordinate clauses (DSf 28f and DNb 36) and with the two parts of one subordinate clause (both uses in DB 4.73f). A series *-cā ... -cā utā ...* occurs DB 1.66f.

II. No special word for 'but' occurs in the OP inscriptions. However, *utā* functions to counteract a preceding negative, like Lt. *et* (DB 4.73). Note that *naiy* 'not' is not 'and not', like Lt. *neque*, though this would often be a suitable meaning (as in DB 4.73); for in many passages (as in DB 1.71) it is merely the negative to a verb, even to a verb already introduced by *utā* 'and' (DB 4.78). Yet when repeated, *naiy* is best translated 'neither ... nor', with words and with clauses.

III. *-vā* is attached to the second of a pair of words or of subordinate clauses; in DB 1.20 it is attached to both words of a pair. In DNb 25 and 29 *yadivā* 'or if' merely brings in an alternative verb in a relative clause introduced by *tya* '(that) which' or by *yaθā* 'when'.

IV. Other adverbs which show the relations between main clauses are essentially adverbs which may be used with reference outside the clause. Note that *aciy* 'then' in XPf 21 is a substitute for *yadiy* 'when' in DSf 14.

§292. THE NEGATIVE ADVERBS in OP are *naiy* and *mā*.

(a) The adverb *naiy* is used with the indicative; with the subjunctive in future relative clauses, DB 2.84, 3.86, and in future conditional clauses, DB 4.55, 4.58, 4.73, 4.78; with the optative in the conclusion of a future less vivid condition, DNb 21; with the subjunctive in a negative clause of purpose, to negative the introductory *mātya*, DB 4.49.

(b) The adverb *mā* is used with subjunctive, optative, injunctive, and imperative, in negative wishes and commands. In DPd 18-20, after *mā* and the optative, three subjects are given, each preceded by an additional *mā* intensifying the negative. The compound negative *mātya* is used with the subjunctive in principal clauses to express a negative command, DB 4.43, 4.71, and in subordinate clauses to express a negative purpose, DB 1.52, 4.48f (see a).

§293. THE SUBORDINATING CONJUNCTIONS OF OP are derivatives of the pIE relative stem, in the forms *yātā*, *yaθā*, *yadātya* (also miswritten *yadāyā*), *yadiy*, *yaniy*, *yāvā*; *tya*, from the OP relative stem; and *mā*, in the form *mātya*. Except *mā*, which is treated in §292.b, these will be treated in the following sections.

Subordination is achieved also by the use of the relative *hya-/tya-* (§261); and of the interrogative *ciyǎkaram* 'how great, how much, how many', introducing a direct or an indirect question with the indicative.

Perhaps there should be included here also *aciy* 'then' (§291.IV); and *hakaram* 'once' (DNb 34f), used with the subjunctive as the equivalent of a future general condition ('once let there be seen ...' = 'if at any time there shall have been seen').

§294. THE CONJUNCTION *yātā* has the meanings 'until' (twice with correlative *citā* 'so long'), 'while', 'as long as', 'when' (with correlative *adakaiy* 'then'). It usually refers to past time, and takes the imperfect indicative; once (DNb 23) it is in a general statement, expressed in the present tense. In two passages (DB 1.25 and 1.69) the 'until' has become virtually the equivalent of 'so that'.

§295. THE CONJUNCTION *yaθā* has the meanings 'as' (marked by the correlative *avaθā*, once miswritten *avā*; sometimes no correlative with *yaθā mām kāma āha*); 'when', shading into 'after' (which is marked by the correlative *pasāva* 'after that'); 'that', introducing an object clause (DB 4.44); 'so that', introducing a result clause;[1] 'because' (marked by correlative *avahyarādiy* 'on account of this', DB 4.63). In all these the time is past, and the verb is in the imperfect indicative; except that the time is present and the verb is in the present indicative, in DSe 35, 39, and the time is future and the verb is in the present subjunctive, in DNb 28f. In DNb 39 the present indicative of general timeless statement is used in two conditional clauses compared by *yaθā* ('as' = 'as well as').

---

[1] So in DB 1.70, DSe 35, 39; *yaθā* never introduces a hypothetical proposition or a purpose Cf. Bv. TPS 1945.54-6.

§296. The Conjunction *yadātya* (XPh 35f; miswritten *yadāyā* XPh 39) 'where' and *yaniy* (XV 22) 'where' are used with the imperfect indicative; in XPh 39 there is a following correlative *avadā* 'there'.

§297. The Conjunction *yadiy* 'if, when' has several uses. In the meaning 'if', it most often takes the present subjunctive as the protasis of a future condition; the apodosis has the affirmative imperative or optative, the negative injunctive or optative, or the present subjunctive (DPe 22) as a future indicative. In DNb 20f *yadiy* introduces a future less vivid condition, with present optative in both parts. In DNb 25 and 29 *yadi-vā* 'or if' repeats *tya* '(that) which' in introducing an alternative verb; in 29 the verb is in the subjunctive with the main verb omitted, and in 25 both verbs are in the present indicative. In general conditions the 'if' easily passes into 'whenever', as in the two instances in DNb 38f, where the present indicative is used in both parts in a timeless general condition; and 'whenever' passes into 'when', used of past facts with the imperfect indicative, DB 1.38 and DSf 14.

§298. The Conjunction *yāvā* 'as long as' refers to the future in all its occurrences, and takes the present subjunctive; the verb in the clause on which it depends is also in the subjunctive, with future meaning.

§299. The Conjunction *tya* 'that' is used to introduce clauses of fact, of volition, of directly and indirectly quoted statement and question, of result; it has the present or imperfect indicative except in clauses of volition, which have the optative (DNb 8, 10, 19). For the compound *mātya*, see §292.b; for *yadātya*, §296; the phrase *yaθā tya* 'when that' (XPh 29) has the imperfect indicative precisely like *yaθā* 'when'.

§300. Subordinate Clauses in OP fall into the usual types: relative clauses, introduced by a relative pronoun (§301); substantival clauses of various types (§302); adverbial clauses, including conditional (§303), temporal (§304), and miscellaneous (modal, causal, consecutive, final, local; §305). In addition, logical subordination is often expressed by coordination, with or without an adverb indicating the logical relations (§290).

Two or more subordinate clauses which are coordinate with one another have the following arrangements:

(a) Additive: the clauses may be connected by *utā* 'and', with repetition of the introductory word, as at DSf 28f; or the single clause may contain three coordinate verbs and their adjuncts, the first two asyndetic, but *utā* between the second and third (DB 4.73f, 4.77f.)

(b) Alternative: the alternative to a general relative clause is introduced by the relative with the enclitic *-vā* (DB 4.68f) when the relative is in the nominative case, but it is introduced by *yadi-vā* 'or if' (DNb 25) when the relative is in the accusative; the alternative to a general temporal clause introduced by *yaθā* 'when' is introduced by *yadi-vā* 'or if' (DNb 29).

(c) Comparative: a general condition introduced by *yadiy* 'if' (= 'whenever') is compared with a preceding clause of the same kind by an intervening *yaθā* 'as well as' (DNb 39).

§301. Relative Clauses in OP are of various kinds.

(a) Most relative clauses are descriptive or restrictive, with the verb in the present or imperfect or aorist indicative; with a predicate nominative, participial or otherwise, or a predicate phrase (as in DH 4f, DB 1.15), the copula *astiy* or *ha^{n}tiy* or *āha* may be omitted. In DB 2.84, 3.86, the present subjunctive is without apparent reason substituted for the present indicative in a restrictive clause of special (= not general) application.

(b) Relative clauses of general significance (= timeless) may have the present indicative (DNb 22–6, XPh 51–6) or the present subjunctive (DB 5.19, 5.34f), with the present indicative in the main clause; the sentence is virtually a present general condition.

(c) Relative clauses of general future meaning, depending upon an expression of command or prayer, have the verb in the subjunctive (§278.IIa).

(d) A relative clause of characteristic, with a general negative antecedent, has the optative in a potential sense (DB 1.50); the main clause contains an imperfect indicative.

§302. Substantive Clauses in OP are of several kinds.

(a) Objects clauses of fact: *tya* 'that' with imf. ind., three clauses, objects of a following *akunauš* 'made, did', DSf 28f; *yaθā* 'how', = 'that', with imf. ind., as object of preceding *Auramazdāha vartaiyaiy* 'I appeal to Ahuramazda', DB 4.44f.

(b) Object clause with potential optative, depending upon *atarsa* 'feared', without conjunction, DB 1.51, 1.52.

(c) Substantive clause of wish, nominative as subject to *kāma* (*astiy*) 'is the desire' or appositive of *ava* in *ava kāma* 'that (is) the desire'; with optative introduced by *tya* 'that', DNb 8, 10, 19; without *tya* DNb 21.

(d) Clauses of directly quoted statement as object or subject, normally without introductory conjunction: quotations of fact, with past participle or imf. ind., depending on *xšnāsāhy* and *azdā bavātiy*, DNa 42–7; of volition, expressed by the subjunctive, depending upon *amaniyaiy*, DSl 3f; of wish, with the subjunctive or injunctive, depending upon *maniyāhaiy*, DB 4.39, DPe 20f, XPh 47; of negative command, with *mā* and the opt., depending upon *patiyazbayam*, XPh 38f; of direct question, with the imf. ind., introduced by *ciyākaram* 'how many' which is preceded by a superfluous *tya* 'that', and depending on *maniyāhaiy*, DNa 38f.

(e) Clauses of indirectly quoted statement as subject or object, normally introduced by *tya* 'that': with past ptc. as verb, as subject of *naiy azdā abava*, DB 1.32; with pres. ind. as verb, as object of *xšnāsātiy*, DB 1.52f; with pres. ind. as verb and no *tya*, indirect question introduced by *ciyākaram* 'how great' (and two other coordinate clauses without verbs) as object of *kušuvā* in *azdā kušuvā* 'do thou make known', DNb 50–2.

§303. CONDITIONAL CLAUSES occur as follows in OP:

(a) Future conditions occur only addressed to an idealized hearer in the second person; the protasis has the subjunctive in the second person, and the apodosis has a command or a prayer or a future statement; see §278.IIIa. General relative clauses with the subjunctive are often a virtual substitute for this form of the condition; see §278.IIb.

(b) A future less vivid condition, with optative in both parts, is found in DNb 20f, where it functions as appositive to *ava* in *naipatimā ava kāma* 'that again is not my desire'. The protasis has *yadiy*.

(c) For *yadi-vā* 'or if' as correlative to *tya* 'that', see §297.

§304. TEMPORAL CLAUSES in OP are of considerable variety.

(a) Introduced by 'when': to express past time, the temporal clause has imf. ind., and the main clause has the imf. ind. or a ptc. with *āha*; introduced by *yadiy*, DB 1.38, DSf 14; by *yātā*, DB 4.81; by *yaθā*, DB 1.31, 91°, 2.22, 65, 3.34, DNb 28f, DSi 3, XPf 24, 32, 36; by *yaθā tya*, XPh 29. To express future time, the temporal clause has the subjunctive, and the main clause has an expression of prayer or command. Introduced by *yaθā* DNb 28f, subjunctive in a general statement with omitted copula in main clause.

(b) Introduced by 'after', expressed by *yaθā* preceded or followed by *pasāva*; the temporal clause has the imf. ind., and the main clause has the imf. ind. or the past ptc. without the copula: DB 1.27, 33, 72, 73, 2.32, 52, 3.3, 4.5, 5.3, 23, DNa 31f, DSf 25, XSc 3.

(c) Introduced by *yadiy* 'whenever', with pres. ind.; the main clause also has the pres. ind.: DNb 38, 39.

(d) Introduced by *yātā* 'while', with imf. ind. in both parts of the sentence: DB 2.6, 3.77.

(e) Introduced by 'as long as', with *yātā* and the imf. ind. to denote past time, the main clause having *astiy kartam*, DB 4.51; with *yāvā* and the subjunctive to denote future time, the main clause also having the imperative in a prohibition, DB 4.71, or the subjunctive in a condition, DB 4.74, 78, or in a general relative clause, DB 5.19, 35.

(f) Introduced by *yātā* 'until', with pres. ind. in both parts of the sentence in a timeless generalization, DNb 23f, and the imf. ind. in both parts to denote past time, DB 1.25, 54, 69, 2.28, 48, 63, DNa 51, DSf 24, XPh 45f.

§305. MISCELLANEOUS ADVERBIAL CLAUSES of the following types are found in OP:

(a) Modal, introduced by *yaθā* 'as', with the imperfect ind. or an omitted *āha* 'was'; the main clause has the imf. ind.: DB 1.23, 63, 67, 69, 4.35, 5.17, 29, 33, DNa 37, DSj 3, DZc 11, 12. Exception, DB 4.51f *naiy astiy kartam yaθā manā kartam* 'has not been done as (has) been done by me', with past ptc. and copula.

(b) Local, introduced by 'where', with imf. ind. in both parts of the sentence: with *yaniy* XV 22, *yadātya* XPh 35f, *yadāya* XPh 39.

(c) Causal, introduced by 'because': *yaθā* DB

4.63, with imf. ind. in both parts of sentence; *tya* DNb 33, with pres. ind. in both parts.

(d) Consecutive, introduced by *yaθā* 'so that', with imf. ind. in both parts DB 1.70, with pres. ind. in both parts DSe 38–41, with pres. ind. depending on an imf. ind. DSe 34–7; introduced by *tya* 'so that', with imf. ind. in both parts DB 4.34, with pres. ind. in both parts DNb 7.

(e) Volitive in a negative clause of purpose introduced by *mātya* 'lest': with subj. depending on potential opt. DB 1.52, with subj. depending on past ptc. with omitted *astiy* DB 4.48f.

§306. The Position of Adjectives.

I. Attributive adjectives precede their nouns if they are demonstrative, numerical, quantitative, or month-names. Exceptions: DB 1.40 *kāra haruva* 'the people entire', and DB 1.79f *kāra hya Bābiruviya haruva* 'the Babylonian people entire' (*hya* with *Bābiruviya* only), where *haruva-* 'all' (elsewhere preceding its noun) may perhaps be an appositive; XPf 28f *Dārayavauš* (error for *-vahauš*) *puçā aniyaiciy āhatā* 'of Darius there were other sons', where the unusual position may be for emphasis.

II. Descriptive adjectives, if attributive, follow their nouns. Exceptions, (a) in a fixed phrase, DNb 23f *uradanām hadugām* 'the Ordinance of Good Regulations'; (b) with a preceding demonstrative, as in DPe 8f *hadā anā Pārsā kārā* 'with this Persian army', DPe 21 *imam Pārsam kāram* (but also DPe 22 *kāra Pārsa*, etc.); (c) for emphasis, in DNa 46 *Pārsa martiya*, DNa 43f *Pārsahyā martiyahyā*.

III. Attributive adjectives preceded by articular *hya* follow the same principles; *hya* is required if *ava-* precedes the noun, as in *avam kāram tyam hamiçiyam* 'that rebellious army' (DB 2.35, etc.). The only instance which precedes is DB 3.32 *hya aniya kāra Pārsa* 'the rest of the Persian army'.

IV. Adjectives as predicates and as appositives have the same position as nouns in the same uses (§307, §308).

§307. The Position of Predicate Nouns and Adjectives. A predicate noun or adjective stands between the subject and the verb, unless the subject follows the verb; in this instance the order is predicate, verb, subject. Exceptions: DB 4.46f *aniyašciy vasiy astiy kartam* 'much other (work) was done'; DB 4.51f *avaθā* (miswritten *avā*) *naiy astiy kartam* 'thus it was not done'. In DNb both positions are found, for stylistic reasons: 34 *hamaranakara amiy ušhamaranakara* 'as battle-fighter I am a good battle-fighter', 41f *asabāra uvāsabāra amiy* 'as horseman a good horseman am I', 42f *θanuvaniya uθanuvaniya amiy* 'as bowman a good bowman am I', 44 *āršṭika amiy uvāršṭika* 'as spearman I am a good spearman'.

§308. The Position of Appositives. Appositives, whether nouns or adjectives, usually follow[1] that to which they are appositive; but the position is otherwise free. Appositives to a subject implied in the verbal ending may stand in any place; cf. DNb 41–5. Chiasmus sometimes is the result of stylistic considerations: XPh 47f *šiyāta ahaniy jīva utā marta artāvā ahaniy* 'happy may I be while living, and when dead blessed may I be'; DSf 12f *hya manā pitā Vištāspa utā Aršāma hya manā niyāka* 'my father Hystaspes and Arsames my grandfather', in which the appositive precedes in one instance.

An appositive is usually attached to its noun by an articular *hya* (§261.III), if the fact thus expressed is considered to be known by the hearer or reader.

§309. The Position of the Genitive. A genitive used as a genitive (not in a dative use), and depending upon a noun or adjective, precedes that noun or adjective, unless the genitive is attached to its noun by the article, in which instance it follows: DB 1.4 *manā pitā* 'my father', but DB 2.27 *kāra hya manā* 'my army'. The exception is only seeming in DB 1.9f *VIII manā taumāyā tyaiy paruvam xšāyaθiyā āha* 'eight (there were) of our family, who were kings before'; for *amāxam taumāyā* is an appositive, equal to '(members) of our family', cf. DB 1.28 *Kabūjiya nāma Kurauš puça amāxam taumāyā* 'Cambyses by name, a son of Cyrus, (a member) of our family'.

Other exceptions belong exclusively to governmental and religious formulas: *xšāyaθiya xšāyaθiyānām* 'kings of kings', *xšāyaθiya dahyūnām* 'king of countries', *hya maθišta bagānām* 'the greatest of gods', *vašnā Auramazdāha* 'by the will of Ahuramazda'. It is possible that the postposition of the genitive in these phrases is a Median usage.

Enclitic genitive pronouns are somewhat freer

---

[1] In the phrase *asā dāruv* (DSf 41; see Lex. s.v. *dāru-*) it is uncertain which word is appositive to the other; is it 'stone that is wood', or 'wood that is stone'?

in their position; for while they normally preceded the noun which they modify, we find also DNb 25f *anuv taumanišaiy* 'according to his powers', and the restored DB 5.27 [*maθ*]*išta*[*šām :*] *S*[*ku*]*xa : nāma* 'the chief of them, Skunkha by name', where the *-šām* has no earlier word to which it may be attached, and space does not permit [*hyašām : maθ*]*išta* [*:*] *S*[*ku*]*xa : nāma*. Cf. also §311.I end.

§310. THE WORD-ORDER IN THE SENTENCE in OP is quite free, but the normal order is subject—object—verb: DB 1.85 *kāra hya Naditabairahyā Tigrām adāraya* 'the army of Nidintu-Bel held the Tigris'. There are the following types of exceptions:

I. The verb may come before the subject, for emphasis, as in *θātiy Dārayavauš xšāyaθiya* 'Saith Darius the King'; to give substantive force to the verb 'to be', as in DB 1.48 *naiy āha martiya* 'there was not a man', and XPh 30 *astiy*; in direct and indirect questions, DNa 39, cf. DNb 50-2.

II. The object may precede the subject, for emphasis, as in DB 1.41f *xšaçam hauv agarbāyatā* 'the sovereignty he seized', and when the object is a resumptive pronoun and the subject is a pronoun, as in DB 1.62 *ava adam patipadam akunavam* 'that (sovereignty) I put back on its base'.

III. When there are two or more subjects or objects, the second and later subjects or objects commonly follow the verb, as in DB 4.60f, 1.57f, DSf 57f.

IV. When a verb takes two accusatives, one denoting a person and the other a thing, the order is variable; with *dī-* 'take away from', DB 1.46 (both objects follow; cf. passive in DB. 1.50, where both nouns precede); DPd 20-2 *aita adam yānam jadiyāmiy Auramazdām* 'this as a boon I beg of Ahuramazda', DNa 53f *aita adam Auramazdām jadiyāmiy*.

V. A predicate to the object of a factitive verb usually follows the object, as in DSf 3f *hya Dārayavaum XŠyam akunauš* 'who made Darius king'; but occasionally precedes, as in DSf 16f *ha*[*r*]*uvahyāy*[*ā BUy*]*ā mar*[*tiyam*] *mām avar*[*navatā*] 'chose me as his man in all the earth'.

VI. The indirect object may stand before or after the direct object, or after the verb: DB 1.12 *Auramazdā xšaçam manā frābara* 'Ahuramazda conferred the sovereignty upon me'; DB 1.19 *manā bājim abaratā* '(the provinces) bore tribute to me'; DZc 3f *hya Dārayavahauš XŠyā xšaçam frābara* 'who conferred the sovereignty upon King Darius'; DNa 4 *hya šiyātim adā martiyahyā* 'who created happiness for man' (and so elsewhere; but DNb 2f *hya adadā šiyātim martiyahyā* has the verb before the direct object).

VII. Other adjuncts of the sentence are free in position, standing either at the beginning or between the subject and the verb or at the end: resp. DB 1.8 *hacā paruviyata*, 1.45 *hacā paruviyata*, 1.82 *Ūvjam* and *abiy mām*. The phrase *vašnā Auramazdāha* 'by the favor of Ahuramazda' stands first in its clause in 63 of its 77 occurrences. Resumptive pronouns (*hauv* and forms of *ava-*) and adverbs (*avadā, avaθā*) stand first after a nominative phrase; *pasāva* 'afterward' leads off its clause in 77 of its 82 occurrences, standing last in DB 1.27, 4.5, 5.3, XSc 3, before *yaθā* 'when', while in DSe 48 the text is uncertain. Other adjuncts are variable in position; thus the goal may precede or follow the verb: DB 2.3 *pasāva adam Bābirum ašiyavam* 'afterward I set forth to Babylon', DB 2.30 *avam adam frāišayam Arminam* 'him I sent forth to Armenia'.

VIII. Subordinate clauses may stand either before or after the main clause; the order of the elements in them is the same as the order in main clauses, though the verb is more likely to stand in final position. Occasionally a word belonging to the clause stands before the relative or conjunction which introduces it: DB 4.37 *tuvam kā xšāyaθiya hya aparam āhy* 'thou who shalt be king hereafter', 4.67f, 4.87, cf. especially DNb 21f, 24f. In one phrase an adjective belonging to the antecedent is incorporated within the relative clause: DB 2.31, 2.51 *kāra hya hamiçiya manā naiy gaubataiy* 'the rebel army which does not call itself mine', cf. DB 2.84 *kāram hamiçiyam hya manā naiy gaubātaiy*.

§311. THE POSITION OF ENCLITIC WORDS. The enclitics of OP may be divided into four groups: (1) pronominal forms *-maiy -mā -ma, -taiy, -šaiy -šim -šām -šiš, -dim -diš*; (2) adv. *patiy*, conj. *tya*; (3) conjj. *-cā, -vā*, advv. *apiy -ciy -diy*; (4) postpositions (see §133 for others in fixed combinations; §134–§139 for phonetic phenomena).

Some enclitic words are occasionally written as separate words; thus *diš* DB 4.34, 35, 36, *taiy* DNb 58 (*mā taiy*, but *mā-taiy* DNb 52, 55), *tya* in *yaθā tya* XPh 29 despite *yadā-tya* XPh 35f and *mā-tya* DB 1.52, 4.43, 48, 71, *patiy* in *ima pati-maiy* DNb 32f despite *nai-pati-mā* DNb 20. Regular orthotone *mām* is written with the preceding in *mā-tya-mām* DB 1.52. On adv. *patiy*, see II; on *apiy*, see III; on the postpositions, see IV.

I. The enclitic pronouns are attached to the first word of their sentence or clause or phrase, even though this be *utā* 'and': DB 1.25 *Auramazdā-maiy upastām frābara* 'Ahuramazda bore me aid'; DPh 8 *tya-maiy Auramazdā frābara* '(the kingdom) which Ahuramazda conferred upon me'; DPh 9f *mām Auramazdā pātuv utā-maiy viθam* 'me may Ahuramazda protect, and my royal house'. But the phrase *vašnā Auramazdāha* does not count in fixing the position of an enclitic: DB 1.13f *vašnā Auramazdāha adam-šām xšāyaθiya āham* 'by the favor of Ahuramazda I was king of them'; except in two partly restored passages, see under III. An enclitic in a dependent clause is sometimes attached to *utā* preceding a conjunction or relative: DB 4.73f *utā-taiy yāvā taumā ahatiy* 'and as long as strength shall be unto thee'; XPa 15 *uta-maiy tya pitā akunauš* 'and what my father built', but also XPa 19f *utā tya-maiy piça kartam* 'and what was built by my father'; DNb 28f *yaθā-maiy tya kartam vaināhy* 'when thou shalt see what was built by me'. An attributive enclitic genitive normally precedes the word which it modifies (cf. §309); but the meaning sometimes governs the position, as in A²Sa 3 *apanᵃyāka-ma* 'my grandfather's grandfather', A²Sa 4 [*nᵃyā*]*kama* (for -*am-ma*, §138.I) 'my grandfather', both with -*mᵃ* for -*mᵃiyᵃ* = -*maiy* (§52.I). The abl. -*ma* is found only in *hacā-ma* 'from me', standing anywhere in its clause. These formulations are violated in three heavily restored passages, but the available space and the other versions favor these restorations: DSf 20 [*ava ucāramaiy* (= -*am-maiy*) *akunauš*] 'that he made successful for me'; DSf 23 [*hacā-ci*]*y dūradaša* [*arjanam-šaiy abariya*] 'from afar its ornamentation was brought'; DNb 54f *tya parta*[*m-taiy as*]*tiy* 'what is communicated to thee' (this restoration is highly conjectural).

II. The adverb *patiy*, when enclitic, was attached to the first word of its clause (for DNb 32f, see V), but also in an equal number of passages is orthotone and leads its clause. The conjunction *tya*, when enclitic, stands immediately after a conjunction which leads its clause (*mā-tya*, *yadā-tya*, *yaθā tya*).

III. The conjunctions -*cā* and -*vā* are attached to the word which they introduce, which of necessity is the first word in the word-group concerned; *apiy*, either directly attached or as separate word, emphasizes the preceding *dūraiy* 'far off', which never begins a clause (for a restored instance, see Lex. s. v.), -*ciy* is attached to the word which it emphasizes, wherever it stands; the rather doubtful -*diy* also is attached to the word which it emphasizes, which stands first in DB 4.69 and second in A²Sd 3.

IV. The postpositions are *upariy* (§269; only once postposed, as separate word); *parā*, only in *ava-parā*; *rādiy*, in *avahya-rādiy* and separately; *patiy*, as enclitic postposition, as separate postposition, and also as preposition; -*ā*, as formative of the locative case; *hacā* once (DB 1.50), separately, governing a preceding enclitic. Position in the clause varies.

V. When two enclitics stand in succession, they are attached to the first word of the sentence or clause, and the pronominal enclitic stands last. There are the following occurrences:

DNb 20 *nai-pati-mā*; with separation, DNb 32f *ima pati-maiy*.

DNb 27f *avākaram-ca-maiy*; DNb 51, 51f *ciyā-karam-ca-maiy*.

DB 1.52 *mā-tya-mām*, where the regular orthotone acc. *mām* is used as an enclitic instead of the unaccented form -*ma*.

§312. THE NAMING PHRASES. It is a feature of OP style, that at the first mention of a person (other than of the ruling king) or of a place (other than of a governmental province) the name of that person or place should be followed by *nāma* or *nāmā*; there are a few exceptions, as in DSf 12f, where the names of Arsames and Hystaspes lack *nāma*, and in DB 3.11 and 5.4, where the province-names *Marguš* and *Ūvja* are accompanied by *nāmā*. These phrases are always[1] in the nominative case, whether or not that is their function in the sentence; they are usually followed by a resumptive pronoun or adverb. The form *nāma* is used unless there is a following generic term of feminine gender (*dahyāuš*, *didā*), when *nāmā* is

---

[1] The only exception is A²Hc 14f *Vištāspahyā nāma puça* 'son of Hystaspes by name', where *nāma* modifies the genitive and is not followed by a generic word, the cast of the sentence eliminates the possibility of a resumptive pronoun.

used as though itself also a feminine; for case formation, see Lex. s.v. *nāman-*. Typical examples:

DB 2.29f *Dādarśiš nāma Arminiya manā badaka avam frāišayam Arminam* 'Dadarshi by name, an Armenian, my subject—him I sent forth to Armenia.'

DB 1.58f *Sikayauvatiš nāmā didā Nisāya nāma dahyāuš Mādaiy avadašim avājanam* 'a fortress by name Sikayauvati, a district by name Nisaya, in Media—there I smote him.'

These phrases are perhaps based on similar phrasings in Aramaic, which suggest this manner of expression, if indeed they are not caused merely by the difficulty of expressing clearly by case endings such a statement as that just cited, with an accumulation of locatives the relation of which to each other might be obscure: 'in the fortress Sikayauvati in the district Nisaya in Media' (the same difficulty was met in expressing genealogical lines with a string of genitives; note the substitutes in DB 1.4–6 and A²Sa).

I. With names of persons, 41 occurrences (9 in a list, DB 4.8–29, and 6 in another list, DB 4.83–6). The resumptive is *hauv, hauvam* (DB 1.29), *avam, abiy avam* (DB 3.56f). In some passages the phrase has *āha* 'was' and makes a complete sentence (DB 1.30, 36; 4.8; XPf 18, 19); in three of these (DB 1.30; XPf 18, 19) the continuation precludes reference by resumptive pronoun. There is also no resumptive in Sa, where the name-phrase is the entire inscription, nor in the corrupt A³Pa 19f, where *nāma* is used twice with genitives (one a nominative form in genitive function) Further, the *nāma*-subject in DB 2.8f and 3.22 is not repeated by a pronoun before the verb, because a *nāma*-phrase of place intervenes, which has its own resumptive *avadā* in each passage. The six helpers of Darius (DB 4.83–6) are not followed by resumptives, because they stand in a list appositive to a preceding substantive, and are not further mentioned. Typical phrasings are those of DB 2.29f (quoted above) and of 1.77f *I martiya Bābiruviya Naditabaira nāma Ainairahyā puça hauv udapatatā Bābirauv* 'One man, a Babylonian, Nidintu-Bel by name, son of Ainaira—he rose up in Babylon.' A preceding *I martiya*, as in this passage, is the only generic term used for persons. The most interesting example is DB 3.12–4, where the nominative *nāma*-phrase stands after the verb and functions as direct object, without resumptive: *pasāva adam frāišayam Dādarśiš nāma Pārsa manā badaka Bāxtriyā xšaçapāvā abiy avam* 'Afterward I sent forth a Persian by name Dadarshi, my subject, satrap in Bactria, against him (= Frada).'

II. With names of places, 32 occurrences. The common sequence is typified by DB 2.39 *Tigra nāma didā Arm'niyaiy avadā hamaranam akunava* 'A stronghold by name Tigra, in Armenia—there they made battle.' A more elaborate phrase is in DB 1.58f, quoted above. After the place name and *nāma* or *nāmā* follows a generic name, then commonly but not always a locative stating the governmental province in which the place is located (replaced in DB 1.92 by *anuv Ufrātuvā* 'beside the Euphrates'), and then a resumptive adverb. The generic names are *dahyāuš* 'district, province', *didā* 'fortress, stronghold', *vardanam* 'town', *āvahanam* 'village', *kaufa* 'mountain', *rauta* 'river'. The resumptive adverbs are *avadā* 'there', *hacā avadaša* 'from there' (DB 1.37, 3.79; DSf 47), *hacā avanā* 'from that (mountain)' (DSf 31), *avaparā* 'along there' (DB 2.72). The aberrant example is DZc 9 *hacā Pirāva nāma rauta* 'from a river by name Nile', where the nominative phrase functions as an ablative depending on *hacā*.

§313. THE ARTAXERXES GENEALOGIES take a form not found in earlier inscriptions; type, 'A son of B son of C son of D, an Achaemenian'. Since 'Achaemenian' applies to 'A', it is clear that the intervening phrases are dependent phrases (not independent sentences, as they are sometimes translated). This makes a difficulty in OP, for a succession of genitives from 'B' to 'D' would hardly be intelligible; therefore the appositive *puça* 'son' is always in the nominative, as are other embarrassing appositives (cf. §257, §312).

I. Inscriptions A¹I, A²Sa, A²Sc, A²Ha, A²Hc have genealogies of the type found in A²Sa 1–3: *Artaxšaçā...Dārayavaušahyā XŠhyā puça Dārayavaušahyā Artaxšaçahyā XŠhyā puça Artaxšaçahyā Xšayārcahyā XŠhyā puça Xšayārcahyā Dārayavaušahyā XŠhyā puça D[āra]yavaušahyā V'štāspahyā puça Haxamān°šiya.*[1] In this the first phrase of parentage is grammatically correct; in the second, the gen. *Dārayavaušahyā* is repeated as a basis for clarity, and the appositive *puça* is in the nom. (see above), with proper depending

---

[1] The neologisms in the passage are treated in §57.

genitives; further phrases are of the type of the second. At the end, 'Achaemenian' is appositive to the initial 'Artaxerxes'. We may imitate this scheme in English, as follows: 'Artaxerxes, ... son of Darius the King, of Darius (who was) son of Artaxerxes the King, of Artaxerxes (who was) son of Xerxes the King, of Xerxes (who was) son of Darius the King, of Darius (who was) son of Hystaspes, an Achaemenian.'[2]

II. The inscriptions A²Sb, A²Sd, A²Hb, AsH, A³Pa have a different scheme, in which the nominative of the royal name replaces the genitive. Only A³Pa is truly cogent, for the others have only these slightly varying versions of 'son of Darius the King': A²Sb *Dārayavauš XŠyā puça*, A²Sd *Dārayavauš XŠāhyā puça*, A²Hb *Dārayavauš XŠ puçā*; and 'son of Ariaramnes the King', in AsH *Ariyāramna xšāyaθiyahyā puça*. But A³Pa has a full lineage from Artaxerxes III back to Arsames, and uses the nominative for all royal names except for Hystaspes, also replacing the genitive of 'king' by nom. *xšāyaθiya*, like *XŠ* in A²Hb. Apparently OP had by this time become virtually a dead language employed only in writing ceremonial official records, its spoken form having suffered a wearing down of the endings (seen very clearly in Pahlavi). With the loss of the genitive ending it was natural to employ the nominative as a general case, as it had already been thus used in appositions. The gen. *V¹štāspahyā* probably persisted because in the earlier inscriptions available to the scribes of Artaxerxes I and later the name of Hystaspes occurred much more frequently in the genitive than in the nominative, and the scribes therefore used the familiar form in the inscriptions which they composed.

Another use of the nominative as genitive is seen in A²Sa 4 [*vašnā : AM : Ana*]*hᵃta* [*: u*]*tā : [Mᶦ]θra* 'by the favor of Ahuramazda, Anaitis, and Mithras' (so also in A²Ha, restored), where the occurrence of the same forms as nominatives in lines 4f sets a model; though the position of the gaps makes it possible to restore the genitive endings in A²Sa, their insertion would make the line unduly long.

§314. ANACOLUTHON is the use of a grammatical element in a form which does not find its justification in the remainder of the sentence. This occurs in OP in connection with *nāma*-phrases (§312) with genealogies (§313), with relative clauses, and occasionally elsewhere.

(a) A relative clause may have a preceding general antecedent in the nominative,[1] and a following resumptive pronoun in the logical case: DB 1.21f *martiya hya agriya āha avam ubartam abaram*, where the nom. *martiya* is resumed and set in proper syntactical relation by the acc. *avam*; DNa 48–50 *aita tya kartam ava visam vašnā Auramazdāha akunavam*, where acc. *ava* repeats the presumably nom. *aita*;[2] DNb 16f *martiya hya hataxšataiy anu-dim* [*ha*]*kartahyā avaθā-dim paribarāmiy*, where nom. *martiya* is resumed by acc. *-dim* (expressed twice).

(b) In AmH the misuse of cases seems to rest upon *iyam dahyāuš Pārsā* (for *Pārsa*, §53) 'this country Persia' in line 5, after which the resumptive *avām* is lacking in 6 as object of *frābara* in 7. From *iyam dahyāuš Pārsā* comes the nominative for locative in line 2, *xšāyaθiya Pārsā* 'king in Persia', and in lines 8f *xšāyaθiya iyam dahyāuš* 'king in this country'.

(c) A relative and its antecedent are both omitted in XPh 30–2 *astiy atar aita dahyāva tyaiy upariy nipištā ayaudā* 'there is (= 'was', §285) among these provinces which (are) inscribed above (one which) was in turmoil'.

§315. FEATURES OF OP STYLE. While OP had no developed literary style, and probably many of its fashions of expression are taken over direct from Aramaic, lingua franca of the ancient Orient, still there are some peculiarities which may be listed as stylistic: the use of the naming phrases (§312), anacoluthon and its phenomena of resumptive pronouns and adverbs (§314), asyndeton between main clauses and between coordinate parts of subordinate clauses (§290, §291), certain types of omissions (§§275–6), chiasmus (§317), riming phrases (§318), the use of the neuter singular as predicate to a masculine (§259), the repetition of *mā* with successive subjects in a pro-

---

[2] Cf. J. R. Ware, TAPA 55 56–7; a different view on the syntax of these genealogies is expressed by E. H. Sturtevant, JAOS 48.66–73.

[1] More commonly without the preceding antecedent, as in DB 4.50f *tyaiy paruvā xšāyaθiyā yātā āha avaišām avā* (= *avaθā*, §52.VI) *naiy astiy kartam* 'who (were) the former kings, as long as they were, by them thus has not been done ...'. [2] But in XPh 43–5 *aita tya adam akunavam visam vašnā Auramazdāha akunavam* I take *aita* as acc., since a resumptive *ava* is lacking.

hibition (§292.b), abnormal position of adjectives (§306), variation in order of predicate noun and the copula (§307).

§316. STYLISTIC OMISSIONS occur in OP, especially of the copula when there is a predicate adjective or phrase; cf. §275, §276. Examples: DB 1.5f *Cišpāiš pitā* (sc. *āha*) *Haxāmaniš*; 1.9 *VIII manā taumāyā* (sc. *āhaⁿ*) *tyaiy* ...; 1.10 *adam* (sc. *amiy*) *navama*; 1.13 *imā* (sc. *haⁿtiy*) *dahyāva tyaiy* ...; 1.15 *tyaiy drayahyā* (sc. *haⁿtiy*; or possibly *dārayaⁿtiy*, cf. XPh 23f); 1.27 *ima* (sc. *astiy*) *tya manā kartam* (sc. *astiy*).

The pronoun 'that' is omitted before an immediately following relative, as in DB 1.27 *ima tya manā kartam* 'this (is that) which (was) done by me'.

Another type of stylistic omission is found when a clause is repeated, and one or more words of the prior clause are not repeated in the second, but are to be understood from the prior clause. Thus DNb 35-7 *yaciy vaināmiy hamiçiyam yaciy naiy vaināmiy* (sc. *hamiçiyam*) 'whatever I see (to be) rebellious, whatever I see (to be) not (rebellious)'; and similarly in DNb 38-40.

§317. CHIASMUS, or change of order in corresponding pairs so as to give the sequence a-b—b-a, suits the shift in emphasis which attends the repetition; it occurs several times in the OP texts. DSf 12f *hya manā pitā Vištāspa utā Aršāma hya manā [ni]yāka* 'my father Hystaspes and Arsames my grandfather'. DSf 36f *tya ida akariya* comes at the end of its sentence, 38 *hya idā karta* comes immediately after the subject, 40 *hya idā karta* comes at the end of its sentence. XPh 47f *šiyāta ahaniy jīva utā marta artāvā ahaniy* 'happy may I be while living, and when dead blessed may I be'; but there is no such variation in the order when the ideas are repeated in 54-6. On DNb 34, 41-4, see §307.

§318. RIMING PHRASES are sometimes used in OP for the expression of semantic coordinates, even though the coordinate words are of different grammatical forms; but we must not assume that the OP vowels gave as precise rimes in pronunciation as they do in writing. The following examples may be cited:

DB 1.20 *xšapa-vā rauca-pati-vā* 'by either night or day', in which *xšapa-* is gen. and *rauca-* is acc.

DPe 13f *tyaiy uškahyā utā tyaiy drayahyā* 'those which are of the mainland and those which are beside the sea', where a gen. in **-ahyă* is paired with a loc. in **-ahi + -ā*.

DB 4.56 (and 4.75) *utātaiy taumā vasiy biyā utā dargam jīva* 'and may family be unto thee in abundance, and do thou live long', where opt. *biyāⁱ* rimes with imv. **jīvă*.

DNa 44f *parāgmatā*, nom. sg. fem. of the past participle, and 47 *patiyajatā*, 3d sg. imf. ind. mid., occur at the ends of successive corresponding sentences.

INDEX OF PASSAGES CITED IN CHAPTER VII

AmH   314b
   2: 314b
   5: 314b
   6: 314b
   7: 314b
   8f: 314b
AsH 3f: 313.II
DB I 1: 247A, B, C; 257; 262.I
   1f: 250C
   2: 251A
   3f: 247A; 285
   4: 250A; 309
   4-6: 312
   5f: 316
   7: 247B
   7f: 285
   8: 259; 261.IV; 310.VII
   9: 316

   9f: 309
   9-11: 285
   10: 316
   11f: 250B; 252C
   12: 250G; 285; 310.VI
   13: 250.I; 316
   13f: 311.I
   15: 251A; 301a; 316
   19: 249A; 274b; 310.VI
   20: 249K; 250E; 271; 291.III; 318
   21: 267.I, IV
   21f: 314a
   23: 252B; 261.IV; 305a
   23f: 286
   25: 294; 304f; 311.I
   27: 250B; 267.I; 304b; 310.VII; 316 bis
   28: 309
   28f: 250D

INDEX OF PASSAGES CITED FOR SYNTAX

29: 263; 312.I
29f: 250A
30: 250J; 312.I bis
31: 304a
31f: 250G
32: 302e
33: 304b
34f: 251A, F; 257 bis
36: 262.II; 312.I
37: 312.II
37f: 250D; 276.II
38: 283; 290; 297; 304a
39: 261.III
40: 250A; 306.I
40f: 257
41f: 274a; 310.II
42f: 290
44: 261.II, III; 266
44f: 249D
45: 310.VII
46: 310.IV
46f: 249D
47: 259; 274a
48: 310.I
48f: 257
49: 250D
49f: 249D bis; 249E; 261.II
50: 261.III; 271; 279.II; 283; 288; 301d; 310.IV; 311.IV
51: 261.I; 279.IIIb; 302b
52: 278.IIId; 279.IIIb; 292b; 302b; 305e; 311 bis; 311.V
52f: 249C; 302e
53: 257
53f: 282a
54: 257; 304f
55: 274a
57f: 267.II; 310.III
58f: 312; 312.II
59: 249D
61: 271
61f: 276.I
62: 271; 288; 310.II
62f: 251B
63: 305a
64: 258.III
64f: 252.I
65: 258.III, IV
65f: 249D
66f: 291.I

67: 305a
69: 261.III; 294; 304f; 305a
70: 295.n1; 305d
71: 291.II
72: 304b
73: 304b
74: 262.II
75: 250G
76f: 291.I
77: 262.II
77f: 312.I
79: 261.III
79f: 306.I
81: 251A; 261.III
82: 274d; 310.VII
85: 310
86: 251B; 252G
87: 250H; 255
89: 261.III
90: 286
91: 304a
91f: 249G
92: 252E; 263; 312.II
93: 249G; 274a
93f: 282b
95: 274d
DB II 3: 310.VII
6: 304d
6f: 250A
8f: 312.I
12: 269
16: 271
18: 269
18f: 259; 262.I
19f: 250A
19-21: 258.III
20f: 289
21: 261.III; 267.III; 278.IIc
21f: 252A
22: 304a
23: 252A; 270.I; 286
23f: 251A
25f: 261.III
27: 247B; 309
28: 304f
29f: 312; 312.I
30: 310.VII
30f: 258.I; 267.III
31: 278.IIc; 280.I; 310.VIII
32: 275; 304b

32f: 249G; 283
35: 261.III; 306.III
38: 275
39: 312.II
43: 275
48: 304f
50f: 267.III
51: 278.IIc; 310.VIII
52: 275; 304b
56: 252D
57f: 275
61f: 249K
62: 271; 283
62f: 286
63: 304f
64f: 251D
65: 254; 286; 304a
66: 263
72: 249G; 312.II
72f: 249G
73: 274d
75: 251A
76: 251A, B; 271
77: 267.II
79f: 250A
84: 258.I; 267.III; 278.IIc; 292a; 301a; 310.VIII
91: 271
92f: 259
DB III 3: 304b
7f: 276.II
9f: 250A
11: 249L; 250A; 312
11f: 258.III
12-4: 312.I
15: 278.IIc
22: 312.I
26: 252E; 261.III; 271
27: 250A
30: 269
32: 250K; 261.IV; 271; 306.III
34: 304a
35: 263
45: 258.III
48: 258.III
49: 258.III
52: 271
54: 263
56f: 312.I
58: 264

58f: 250A, F
59: 257, 278.IIc
65: 275
70: 263
73: 249G; 261.VI; 270.IV
73f: 249G
77: 304d
78: 250A
80: 271; 312.II
81f: 250A
82: 249G
86: 267.III; 278.IIc; 292a; 301a
92: 271
DB IV 1f: 261.I; 275
3f: 261.I; 275
4f: 250E
5: 304b; 310.VII
5f: 258.III
7-30: 265
8: 312.I
8-29: 312.I
12: 250A
34: 305d; 311
34f: 265
35: 305a; 311
35f: 249.I
36: 311
37: 278.IIa; 310.VIII
38: 274a; 278.IIa; 280.I
39: 278.IIIa; 302d
39f: 278.Ic
42: 278.IIa; 280.I
43: 278.Ib; 292b; 311
44: 295
44f: 283; 302a
46: 288
46f: 276.I; 307
46-8: 290
48: 278.IIa; 305e; 311
48f: 292b
49: 292a
49f: 278.IIId
50f: 314.n1
51: 288; 304e
51f: 276.I; 305a; 307
53: 280.I
54: 278.Ib; 281
55: 278.IIIa bis; 292a
55f: 249B

INDEX OF PASSAGES CITED FOR SYNTAX

56: 249J; 250H; 279.Ib bis; 280.I; 318
58: 278.IIIa; 279.Ib; 292a
59: 279.Ib
60f: 310.III
63: 295; 305c
64: 269
65: 249D
67f: 310.VIII
68: 278.IIa bis
68f: 258.IV; 278.IIa; 300b
69: 279.Ia; 280.I; 311.III
70: 278.IIa
71: 278.Ib; 292b; 304e; 311
72: 278.IIIb
73: 278.IIIa bis; 291.II bis; 292a
73f: 291.I; 300a; 311.I
74: 278.IIIa; 278.IIIb; 279.Ib; 304e
74f: 279.Ib
75: 278.IIa; 280.I; 318
75f: 267.IV
77: 278.IIIa bis
77f: 300a
78: 278.IIIa; 278.IIIb; 291.II; 292a; 304e
78f: 250C; 279.Ib
79: 278.IIa; 279.Ib
81: 274.n1; 304a
82f: 250A
83–6: 312.I bis
87: 278.IIa; 310.VIII
87f: 261.IV
90: 288
90f: 274d
DB V 2f: 264; 271
3: 304b; 310.VII
4: 312
12: 261.IV
17: 305a
19: 278.IIb, IIIb; 301b; 304e
19f: 250A
21f: 249G
23: 304b
23f: 249G
24f: 255
26: 274d
27: 309
29: 305a
33: 305a
34f: 278.IIb, 301b
35: 278.IIIb; 304e
35f: 250A

DBa 12f: 261.IV
DB k 2: 261.III
DPa 5f: 265
DPd: 286
1f: 250D
2: 257
2f: 249E
6f: 257
9–11: 257
16f: 271
18–20: 292b
19: 279.Ib
20–2: 249D, F; 310.IV
DPe 3f: 261.III
8f: 306.IIb
9f: 274b
13f: 318
20: 278.IIIa
20f: 302d
21: 281; 306.IIb
22: 261.n2; 276.II; 278.IIIa bis; 297; 306.IIb
23: 283
24: 249G; 278.Ia; 289
DPh 5: 252F
5f: 261.I; 271
6: 253B
7: 251D; 254; 271
7f: 253B
8: 311.I
9f: 311.I
DNa: 286
1–3: 264
3f: 250H
4: 310.VI
5f: 249F
7f: 250C
11f: 265
18f: 250C
19f: 274b
21: 261.IV
31f: 304b
32: 258.III
36: 251B; 258.III
36f: 258.III
37: 305a
37f: 290
38: 278.IIIa
38f: 302d
39: 259, 264; 290; 310.I
42: 278.Ia

42–7: 302d
43: 278.Ib
43f: 306.IIc
43–5: 275
44f: 318
45f: 278.Ib
46: 306.IIc
47: 318
48: 266; 267.I
48–50: 314a
51: 304f
52: 283
53f: 310.IV
56: 248
56f: 250B; 261.IV
58: 281
60: 281
DNb: 286
  2: 274d
  2f: 310.VI
  4f: 257
  6f: 259
  7: 305d
  8: 299; 302c
  8f: 249D; 261.V
  9: 250K; 270.III; 279.IIIa
  10: 261.V; 283; 299; 302c
  10f: 249D; 250K; 264; 270.III
  11: 279.IIIa; 283
  11f: 259
  12: 261.V
  15: 250C; 283
  16: 250K; 271
  16f: 267.IV; 314a
  18: 250K; 271; 283
  19: 299; 302c
  20: 264; 279.IIIa; 290; 311; 311.V
  20f: 297; 303b
  21: 279.IIIa, c; 292a; 302c
  21f: 310.VIII
  22: 271
22–6: 301b
  23: 294
  23f: 304f; 306.IIa
  24f: 310.VIII
24–6: 252H
  25: 271; 291.III; 297 bis; 300b
  25f: 309
  26: 276.II; 283
  27: 276.II

  27f: 259; 311.V
  28f: 295; 304a bis; 311.I
  29: 291.III; 297 bis; 300b
  29f: 278.IIIc
  32f: 311; 311.II, V
  33: 305c
  34: 307; 317
  34f: 293
  35: 274d; 278.Ib
35–7: 316
  36: 291.I
  38: 304c
  38f: 297
38–40: 316
  39: 295; 300c; 304c
  40f: 252D
  41f: 307
41–5: 308; 317
  42f: 307
  44: 307
45–7: 267.V
  46: 269
  46f: 282a
  49: 269
  50: 274b; 280.I; 289; 290
  50f: 259
50–2: 302e; 310.I
  51: 311.V
  51f: 311.V
  52: 311
  53: 264; 281
  54f: 276.IV; 288; 311.I
  55: 264; 311
  56: 274d; 276.IV; 278.Ib; 288
  57: 264
  58: 311
  59: 278.Ib
  60: 280.I
DN I: 265
DSa 4: 264
  5: 250G; 278.Ic
DSe: 286
  31f: 276.IV
  32–7: 258.IV
  34: 264
  34–7: 305d
  35: 295, n1
  38–41: 305d
  39: 295, n1
  39f: 261.V

INDEX OF PASSAGES CITED FOR SYNTAX

    46f: 252G
    48: 270.IV; 310.VII
DSf: 286
  3f: 310.V
  9: 261.III
  11f: 261.III
  12f: 261.IV; 308; 312; 317
  13–5: 290
  14: 261.VI; 291.IV; 297; 304a
  15f: 290
  16f: 310.V
  19f: 282a
  20: 311.I
  23: 311.I
  24: 304f
  25: 276.III; 283; 304b
  25f: 257
  28f: 291.I; 300a; 302a
  30f: 261.III
  31: 312.II
  32f: 251B
  33: 251D; 254
  34: 251B
  36f: 317
  37: 261.III
  38: 317
  40: 317
  41: 308.n1
  42: 261.I
  44: 251D; 254
  47: 312.II
  48: 274b
  51: 274b
  53: 274b
  56f: 276.IV
  57f: 261.I; 310.III
DSi 3: 304a
DSj 3: 305a
  5: 278.IIa
  6: 278.Ic
DSl 3f: 278.IIIe; 302d
DSn 1: 282a
  DSs: 285
  6: 258.IV
DSt 10: 278.IIa
DZc 3f: 310.VI
  9: 271; 282a; 312.II
  10: 285
  11: 249G; 305a

  12: 305a
DH 4: 252F
  4f: 301a
  5: 253B
  5f: 251D; 254
  6: 253B
XPa 13f: 252E
  15: 311.I
  16: 274d
  19f: 311.I
XPc 14: 257
XPf 18: 312.I bis
  19: 312.I bis
  20–5: 290
  21: 291.IV
  21f: 249.I
  22f: 261.I
  25: 304a
  28f: 250.n1; 306.I
  29f: 290
  30: 261.III
  32: 304a
  32–4: 251D
  33: 254
  36: 304a
  38: 250B; 276.I; 288
XPg 10: 269
XPh 16: 271
  17: 274b
  23f: 316
  29: 299; 304a; 311
  30: 285, 310.I
  30f: 258.IV
  30–2: 314c
  31: 267.VI
  35f: 296; 305b; 311
  38f: 302d
  39: 279.Ia; 296 bis; 305b
  43: 266; 267.I
  43–5: 314.n2
  45f: 304f
  47: 276.II; 278.Ic; 278.IIIa; 302d
  47f: 308; 317
  48: 276.II; 278.Ic; 283
  49: 264
  50: 279.Ia
  50f: 252.I
  51f: 264
  51–6: 285; 301b
  53f: 252.I

54–6: 317
55: 276.III
55f: 276.II
XSc 3: 304b; 310.VII
  4: 266
XV 22: 296; 305b
  23f: 282a
A¹I: 313.I
D²Sa 1: 251C; 255
A²Sa: 312; 313.I, II
  1–3: 313.I
  3: 311.I
  4: 269; 311.I; 313.II
  4f: 291.I; 313.II
  5: 278.Ib
A²Sb: 313.II bis
A²Sc: 313.I

A²Sd: 313.II bis
  3: 311.III
A²Ha: 313.I, II
  5f: 291.I
  7: 278.Ib
A²Hb: 251C; 255; 313.II ter
A²Hc: 313.I
  14f: 312.n1
A³Pa: 313.II ter
  5f: 247E
  19f: 312.I
  22f: 250B
  23: 269
  26: 250B
Wa 1: 252D
Wc 1: 251C
  Sa: 312.I

PART II. THE TEXTS

This part contains first a summary description of the inscriptions, with their special bibliography; certain inscriptions extant in Elamite or in Akkadian or in both, but not in OP, are listed in the bibliography, but only to explain a gap in the alphabetic labeling of the OP inscriptions.

Then follow the OP texts, each attended by notes of critical and exegetical nature, if needed, and by translation.

DESCRIPTION AND BIBLIOGRAPHY OF THE INSCRIPTIONS

Bibliographical items of 1906 and earlier are given only for special reasons, but may be traced in Wb. KIA and elsewhere.

AmH = ARIARAMNES, HAMADAN: A slightly incomplete OP text in 10 lines, on a gold tablet; there is no evidence that the lost part of the tablet held Elam. and Akk. versions. Hz. AMI 2.117–27 (1930), 4.132–9 (1932), 8.17–35 (1938), ApI 1–2 No. 1 (1938); Hz. Die Goldtafel des Āriyāramna, in Berliner Museen, Berichte aus den preussischen Kunstsammlungen 52.3.52–5, with plate (1931); HHSchaeder, SbPAW 1931.635–45, 1935.494–8; WBrandenstein, WZKM 39.13–9 (1932); Bv. Gr. §3 (1931); RGKent, JAOS 56.215 (1936); Sen, OPI 176–7 (1941); Sidney Smith, Isaiah Chapters XL–LV 122–3 (1944); RGKent, JAOS 66.206–12 (1946). See also §18, with note 2.

AsH = ARSAMES, HAMADAN: OP only, 14 lines, on a gold tablet in three pieces, complete except for lower right corner; about 9 x 13 cm.; found at Hamadan; see §18, with note 2. Sidney Smith, Isaiah Chapters XL–LV 122 (1944); RGKent, JAOS 66.209–12 (1946); AUPope, The Illustrated London News, July 17 1948, pp. 58–9. On exhibition at the Musée Cernuschi (Paris), in the summer of 1948, where it was No. 54 of the Catalogue Illustré (no date).

CMa = CYRUS, MURGHAB a: 5 or more copies of a trilingual inscription, OP two lines, Elam. and Akk. one line each, on columns and pillars of the palace. Wb. ZDMG 48.653–65 (1894), KIA xxviii–xxix, lxvii–lxix, 126–7 (1911); Hz. Klio 8.60 (1906); Jn. Persia Past and Present 281–2 (1908); Tm. Lex. 55–6 (1908); Sen, OPI 1 (1941); RGKent, JAOS 66.209 (1946).

CMb = CYRUS, MURGHAB b: A number of small fragments of a trilingual inscription, OP at least 6 lines, Elam. and Akk. 4 lines each, which stood above the royal figure in the doorways of the palace. Hz. ApI 2–4 No. 3 and Plate 2 (1938); Sen, OPI 239 (1941); RGKent, JAOS 66.209 (1946).

CMc = CYRUS, MURGHAB c: A trilingual inscription, each version in one line, on the folds of the king's garments in three doorways of the palace; the OP text now entirely destroyed. Hz. AMI 1.14–6 (1929); ApI 2 No. 2 and Plate 1 fig. 2 (1938); RGKent, JAOS 66.209 (1946).

DB = DARIUS, BEHISTAN: The inscription of Behistan, trilingual, is inscribed on the face of a gorge in the cliff rising on the left-hand side of the main caravan route from Baghdad to Teheran, about 65 miles before reaching Hamadan. Here, at the height of about 225 feet (obliquely 322 feet) above the road, the last 100 feet being steep and difficult rock-climbing—the final portion being in part cut smooth by Darius's orders, to prevent access by vandals—sculptures and accompanying inscriptions are engraved in the natural rock. The panel of the sculptures contains at the left the standing figure of Darius, with two attendants behind him; his right foot is firmly planted on the prostrate figure of Gaumata. Beyond Gaumata stand in line the captive rebels, 9 in number, with hands tied behind their backs and a rope around their necks linking them together. Above, there is a figure of the God Ahuramazda. The inscriptions in OP, Elam., and Akk. occupy the free parts of the panel and its lower margin, as well as the spaces below, to right, to left, and diagonally below to the left. These have suffered both from erosion by water torrents and by limestone incrustations deposited by water in and over the engraved characters. Further damage was suffered by the sculptures in both World Wars, when soldiers marching past on the highway below used the figures as targets for potshots.

Behistan is a much used but not recorded spelling which is intermediate between the OP *bagastāna*—'Place of the God', for which Greek has βαγίστανον (Diodorus 2.13), and the *Behistūn* of the medieval Arabic Geographers, the Modern Persian *Bīsitūn* or *Bīsutūn* (or even *Bīstūn*, without the anaptyctic vowel; understood by popular etymology as 'without columns'). The inscription was first reached and copied by Lieutenant (afterward Major General Sir) Henry C. Rawlinson in 1836-47; again in 1903, by Professor A. V. Williams Jackson of Columbia University, who was able to make only a partial examination, but did make the first photographs taken from the narrow ledge below the inscriptions; by L. W. King and R. C. Thompson of the British Museum in 1904; and finally by Professor George G. Cameron of the University of Michigan in 1948, who made a thorough examination of the entire inscription, including the Elamite text to the right of the sculptured panel, which had previously been pronounced completely illegible.

The Great Inscription: the OP text is in 5 columns, beneath the panel of sculptures; containing 96, 98, 92, 92, 36 lines respectively. Column 5 is at the right and is a later addition. The Elam. text is in two copies; one copy, in 4 columns totaling 323 lines, stands to the right of the sculptures, the final addition to which has cut into the first column (this is the supposedly illegible inscription, formerly dubbed 'supplementary texts', now for the first time read by Cameron). The second Elamite copy is in 3 columns, to the left of the OP text; containing 81, 85, 94 lines respectively, the equivalent of the first 4 OP columns, to the end of §69. A short column of 10 lines, in the upper left of the sculptured panel, is the Elam. equivalent of OP §70. The Akk. text is in a single column, running past an obtuse-angled corner so as to cover two faces of the rock to the left of the sculptured panel, and translates OP §1-§69; it contains 112 lines (lines 1-35 on front face only, lines 36-112 on the two faces of the rock).

The 11 small inscriptions have to do with Darius and his captive foes; they are placed as close as space permits, to the person whom they label. Insc. a has to do with Darius; the OP version has 18 lines, the Elam. 10, there is no Akk. Inscriptions b-j are all trilingual; the OP texts run from 6 to 12 lines each, the Elam. 2 to 8, the Akk. 3 to 4. Insc. k, in OP and Elam., was like OP Column 5 added later, and has 2 lines in each language.

A dolerite block from Babylon contains part of a duplicate copy of the Akkadian version, corresponding to lines 55-8 and 69-72.

Fragments have also been found of an Aramaic version, on papyrus documents from Elephantine.

Rawlinson, JRAS vols. 10-11 (1846, 1849); vol. 12, i-civ (1851). Jn. JAOS 24.77-95 (1903) = Persia Past and Present 186-212 (1906). KT, The Sculptures and Inscriptions of Darius the Great on the Rock of Behistûn in Persia (London, 1907). Tm., The Behistan Inscription of King Darius (Vanderbilt Univ. Studies I, Nashville, 1908). Wb. and WBang, Die Altpersischen Keilinschriften in Umschrift und Übersetzung, fasc. 1 pp. 4-5, 12-33 (Leipzig 1893), fasc. 2 pp. x-xvi (Leipzig 1908). Tm., Ancient Persian Lexicon and Texts 2-36 (Nashville 1908). A. Hoffmann-Kutschke, Die altp. Keilinschriften d. Grosskönigs Dārajawausch d. Ersten am Berge Bagistān, bei Behistun (Stuttgart, Kohlhammer 1908 and 1909). Wb. Die Keilinschriften der Achämeniden xi-xiv, 8-79 (Leipzig 1911). FMEPereira, Iscrição de Dario o Grande, Rei da Persia, no Rochedo de Bisutun (Coimbra 1913). Shapurji Kavasji Hodivala, Cuneiform Inscriptions transcribed into Sanskrit and Avestan: Behistan Inscriptions, in JCOI 19.58-158 (1931). FWKonig, Relief und Inschrift des Konigs Dareios I am Felsen von Bagistan (Leiden 1938). Sen, OPI 2-88 (1941). GGCameron, Life May 23 1949 pp. 149-52, National Geographic Magazine (shortly to appear), Journal of Cuneiform Studies (shortly to appear).

On Column 5 only: WHinz, ZDMG 93.364-75 (1939); Wb. ZfA 46.52-82 (1940); WHinz, ZDMG 96.331-43 (1942); Kent, JNES 2.105-14 (1943), 3.233-4 (1944); WEilers, JNES 7.106-10 (1948).

On the Aramaic version: ESachau, Aramäische Papyrus und Ostraka aus einer jüdischen Militär-Kolonie zu Elephantine, 187-205 and Plates 52 and 64-6 (Leipzig 1911); ECowley, Aramaic Papyri of the Fifth Century B.C., pages 248-71 (Oxford 1923).

DPa = DARIUS, PERSEPOLIS A: Trilingual, six

lines each, several times on doorposts of the inner room of the palace, above figures of Darius and his attendants. Tm. Lex. 35-6 (1908); Wb. KIA xvi, 80-1 (1911); Sen, OPI 89 (1941).

DPb = DARIUS, PERSEPOLIS B: OP only, in one line, on the garment of Darius; now in the Cabinet des Médailles of the Bibliothèque Nationale, Paris. Tm. Lex. 35-6 (1908); Wb. KIA xvi, 80-1; Sen, OPI 89 (1941).

DPc = DARIUS, PERSEPOLIS C: Trilingual, one line only, repeated 18 times on the window cornice of the same room of Darius's palace. Tm. Lex. 35-6 (1908); Wb. KIA xvi, 80-1 (1911); Hz. ApI 22-3 No. 9; Sen, OPI 89-90 (1941).

DPd = DARIUS, PERSEPOLIS D: OP only, 24 lines, on the south retaining wall of the palace. Tm. Lex. 36-8 (1908); Wb. KIA xvi, 80-3 (1911); Sen, OPI 90-2 (1941).

DPe = DARIUS, PERSEPOLIS E: OP only, 24 lines, on the south retaining wall of the palace. Tm. Lex. 37-8 (1908); Wb. KIA xvi, 82-3 (1911); Sen, OPI 92-5 (1941).

DPf and **g** = DARIUS, PERSEPOLIS F and G: Elam. and Akk. respectively, 24 lines each, without OP text. Wb. KIA xvi, 82-7 (1911).

DPh = DARIUS, PERSEPOLIS H: Trilingual, on two gold and two silver plates; now in Teheran. OP 10 lines, Elam. 7, Akk. 8; same text as DH. New York Times, Feb. 9, 1936, 2d news section, page 8; Univ. of Chicago Mag. 28.4.23-5, Feb. 1936; Hz. ApI 18-9 No. 6 and Plate 6 (1938).

DPi = DARIUS, PERSEPOLIS I: Trilingual, one line each, on doorknob of artificial lapis lazuli. Hz. ApI 23 No. 10 and Plate 7 (1938); EFSchmidt, The Treasury of Persepolis 62-3 (1939); Sen, OPI 252 (1941).

DN = DARIUS, NAQŠ-I-RUSTAM: Some miles north of Persepolis, on the south face of a steep ridge known as Ḥusain Kūh or 'Mountain of Husain', there are four gigantic niches, cut in the shape of Greek crosses, and serving as entrances to the tombs lying in the rock behind them. The second from the east is the tomb of Darius I, and bears inscriptions.

The entire niche is about 73 feet high; the crossbeam is 20 feet high and 36 feet wide, and is divided by columns into five panels, thus giving the appearance of the front of a Persian palace. The central panel contains the doorway to the tomb behind. The upper part of the cross is occupied by a throne platform, supported by 30 throne-bearers in two lines; Darius stands on a basis of three steps, facing right toward an altar, while beyond the altar there floats in the air the figure of Ahuramazda. At the extreme left of the field are three attendants of Darius, arranged vertically one above the other, the lowest one being on a level with the lower line of throne-bearers.

The inscription Naqš-i-Rustam **a** is inscribed behind the figure of Darius; first OP in 60 lines, then a second column of Elam. in 48 lines, finally, outside the niche on the adjacent rock the Akk. in 36 lines. Inscription **b** stands on the two sides of the door in the center of the crossbeam: OP in the panel to its left, in 60 lines; Elam., 43 lines, in the panel to the right, with an Aramaic version in 25 lines at the bottom; in the last panel to the right, the Akk. version in 39 lines, with the space of one line vacant between lines 31 and 32. Inscription **c**, trilingual, 2 lines for each language, is attached to Darius's spear-bearer, the topmost figure of the three at the left margin behind the king: **d**, trilingual, the OP filling 2 of the 5 lines of text, is attached to his bow-bearer, standing beneath the spear-bearer. Inscriptions I to XXX, trilingual, attach to the throne-bearers, but not all of them are legible.

Tm. Lex. 43-8 (1908); Wb. Grab, in AbkSGW 29.1.1-54 and 8 Plates (1911); Wb. KIA xvii-xx, 86-99 (1911); Tm. The Grave of King Darius at Naksh-i-Rustam, in Madrassa Jubilee Volume 168-72 (1914); Hz. ZDMG 80.244 (1926; on Aramaic version), AMI 3.8 (1931), ApI 4.13 No. 4 and Plates 3-5 (1938; some fragments of a second copy of DNb, found at Persepolis, on Plate 5); Kent, Lg. 15.160-77 (1939); Sen, OPI 96-107, 240-51 (1941); Kent, JNES 4.39-52, 232-3 (1945); Bv. TPS 1945.39-50 (1946); GGCameron, Persepolis Treasury Tablets 29 (1948; on Aramaic version); Hinz, Orientalia [Rome] 1950 No. 4 (shortly to appear).

DSa = DARIUS, SUSA A: OP only, on two broken clay tablets, in 5 lines; one copy in the Louvre, Paris. Tm. Lex. 47-8 (1908); Wb. KIA xx, 98-9 (1911); Scheil 21.52 No. 11 (1929); Bv. BSLP 30.1.63-4 (1930); Kent, JAOS 51.217-8

(1931), 58.326 (1938); Brd. WZKM 39.19–21 (1932); Sen, OPI 116, 131 m (1941); Hinz, ZDMG 95.222–5 (1941).

DSb = DARIUS, SUSA B: Two clay tablets, one complete and the other badly mutilated, with an OP inscription in 11 lines. One tablet is in the Louvre, Paris. Tm. Lex. 47–8 (1908); Wb. KIA xx, 98–9 (1911); Scheil 21.48–9 No. 8 (1929); Kent, JAOS 51.216 (1931); Brd. WZKM 39.22–3 (1932); Sen, OPI 117, 127 e, 129 j (1941); Hinz, ZDMG 95.225–6 (1941); Kent, JAOS 67.31, 152 (1947).

DSc = DARIUS, SUSA C: Trilingual, each version in one line, on the base of a column; two copies, of which one is in the Louvre, Paris. Wb. KIA xx, 98–9 (1911); Scheil 21.35–6 No. 2 (1929); Kent, JAOS 51.212 (1931); Brd. WZKM 39.23–4 (1932); Sen, OPI 127 d (1941); Hinz, ZDMG 95.226 (1941).

DSd = DARIUS, SUSA D: Parts of 2 OP copies and of 2 Elam. copies, on columns. Wb. KIA xx, 98–9 (1911); Scheil 21.38–9 No. 4 (1929); Kent, JAOS 51.213 (1931); Brd. WZKM 39.24–5 (1932); Sen, OPI 127 f (1941); Hinz, ZDMG 95.226–7 (1941).

DSe = DARIUS, SUSA E: On Restoration of Order in the Empire; 10 OP fragments, representing several copies; 3 Elam. fragments; one nearly complete Akk. copy and two partial Akk. copies, all on tablets. Our text is arranged according to an OP copy having 52 lines. CBezold, ZfA 25.393–4 (1911); Wb. AbkSGW 29.1.36–8 (1911), KIA xx, xxix, 99–101, 130 inc. b (1911); Scheil 21.61–4 No. 15 (1929); Kent, JAOS 51.221–2 (1931); Brd. WZKM 39.25–7 (1932); Scheil 24.116–25 (1933); Kent, JAOS 54.40–50 (1934); Wb. ZDMG 91.80–6 (1937), ZfA 44.150–69 (1938); Kent, JAOS (58.112–21, 324 (1938); Hz. API 19–21 No. 7 (1938); Sen, OPI 132–4 q (1941); Hinz, ZDMG 95.227–33 (1941).

DSf = DARIUS, SUSA F: On the Building of the Palace; trilingual, with fragments of many copies on clay and marble tablets, and on the glazed tiles of the frieze of the great hall. Our text is arranged according to the best preserved copy, a much broken baked clay tablet, with 58 lines: 27 on the front face, 3 on the lower edge, 27 on the reverse, 1 on the top edge. Scheil 21.3–34 No. 1 and 53–6 No. 12 (1929); Konig, Burgbau, in MVAG 35.1.1–76 and 16 plates (1930); R.Bleichsteiner, WZKM 37.93–104 (1930); Hz. AMI 3.29–124 (1931); Wb. AfOF 7.39–44 (1931); Kent, JAOS 51.193–212, 218–20 (1931); Brd. WZKM 39.28–39 (1932); Schaeder, Arch. Anz., Beibl. z. Jb. d. DAI 47.269–74 (1932); Kent, JAOS 53.1–23 (1933); Scheil 24.105–15 (1933); Kent, JAOS 54.34–40 (1934); Hz. ApI 13–7 No. 5 (1938); Sen, OPI 118–27, 132 n2 (1941); VIAbayev, Iranskie Yazyki 1.127–33 (Izd. Ak. Nauk, Iranica vol. 3; Moscow-Leningrad, 1945); Hinz, JNES 9.1–7 (1950).

DSg = DARIUS, SUSA G: Parts of 2 OP and 3 Akk. copies, on columns; every copy in 3 lines. Scheil 21.40–1 No. 5 (1929); Kent, JAOS 51.213–4 (1931); Brd. WZKM 39.39–40 (1932); Sen, OPI 127–8 g (1941); Hinz, ZDMG 95.236–8 (1941).

DSh = DARIUS, SUSA H: A two-line fragment, Scheil 21.41 infra; recognized by Kent as identical with D²Sa, q.v.

DSi = DARIUS, SUSA I: Bilingual, OP in 4 lines, Elam. in 6 lines, on a column. Scheil 21.42–3 No. 6 (1929); Kent, JAOS 51.214 (1931); Brd. WZKM 39.43–4 (1932); Sen, OPI 128 h (1941); Hinz, ZDMG 95.238–9 (1941).

DSj = DARIUS, SUSA J: Trilingual, OP in 6 lines, Elam. and Akk. each in 5 lines, on a column. Scheil 21.44–7 No. 7 (1929); Kent, JAOS 51.214–6 (1931); Wb. AfOF 7.45 (1931); Brd. WZKM 39.44–52 (1932); Hz. ApI 21–2 No. 8 (1938); Sen, OPI 128–9 i (1941); Hinz, ZDMG 95.239–42 (1941).

DSk = DARIUS, SUSA K: OP only, in 5 lines, stamped on a baked clay brick. Scheil 21.50 No. 9 (1929); Kent, JAOS 51.216–7 (1931); Brd. WZKM 39.53 (1932); Sen, OPI 130 (1941); Hinz, ZDMG 95.242 (1941).

DSl = DARIUS, SUSA L: OP only, in 5 lines, stamped on a baked clay brick. Scheil 21.51 No. 10 (1929); Bv. BSLP 30.1.64–5 (1930); Kent, JAOS 51.217 (1931); Brd. WZKM 39.54–5 (1932); Sen, OPI 130–1 (1941); Hinz, ZDMG 95.242–3 (1941).

DSm = DARIUS, SUSA M: Trilingual, on enameled bricks forming a frieze in one of the halls; one line only to the brick, and the fragments very limited in quantity. Scheil 21.53–6 No. 12 (1929); Brd. WZKM 39.55–8 (1932); Sen, OPI 131 n 1 (1941).

DSn = DARIUS, SUSA N: Trilingual, small fragments of an inscription on the garment of a statue; OP in 2 lines. Scheil 21.57–8 No. 13 and Plate 13 (1929); Kent, JAOS 51.220–1 (1931); Brd. WZKM 39.58–9 (1932); Sen, OPI 132 o (1941); Hinz, ZDMG 95.243–4 m (1941).

DSo = DARIUS, SUSA O: Bilingual, on a marble plaque; OP in 4 lines, Akk. in 5 lines. Scheil 21.59–60 No. 14 (1929); Kent, JAOS 51.221 (1931); Brd. WZKM 39.59–60 (1932); Sen, OPI 132 p (1941); Hinz, ZDMG 95.255–7 D²Sd (1941).

DSp = DARIUS, SUSA P: OP fragment in 3 lines, on a marble plaque. Scheil 21.65 No. 16 A (1929); Kent, JAOS 51.222–3 (1931); Brd. WZKM 39.61–2 (1932); Sen, OPI 135 ra (1941); Hinz, ZDMG 95.244 n (1941).

DSq = DARIUS, SUSA Q: Two fragments of OP in 2 lines, on a marble plaque. Scheil 21.65 No. 16 B (1929); Kent, JAOS 51.223 (1923); Brd. WZKM 39.63 (1932); Sen, OPI 135 rb (1941); Hinz, ZDMG 95.245 o (1941).

DSr = DARIUS, SUSA R: OP only in 4 lines, on a marble plaque. Scheil 21.66 No. 16 C; recognized by Wb. ZDMG 91.643–8 as being part of a copy of A²Sd, q.v.

DSs = DARIUS, SUSA S: OP only, in 7 lines, on a marble plaque. Scheil 21.66 No. 16 D (1929); Kent, JAOS 51.223–4 (1931); Brd. WZKM 39.65–6 (1932); Sen, OPI 135–6 rd (1941); Hinz, ZDMG 95.245–8 p (1941).

DSt = DARIUS, SUSA T: OP only, in 10 lines, of which 2 lines are entirely lost; on the two sides of a marble plaque. Scheil 21.67 No. 16 E (1929); Kent, JAOS 51.224 (1931); Brd. WZKM 39.66–8 (1932); Sen, OPI 136 re (1941); Hinz, ZDMG 95.248–9 q (1941).

DSu, v, w, x = DARIUS, SUSA U, V, W, X: In Elamite (u and x) or in Akkadian (v and w). Scheil 21.68–76 Nos. 17–21 (1929); Brd. WZKM 39.68–74 (1932). But DSx (Scheil Nos. 20–1) is in reality part of two Elam. copies of DSe; Wb. ZDMG 91.80–6 (1937); Kent, JAOS 58.112, 118–21 (1938).

DSy = DARIUS, SUSA Y: On the base of a column; trilingual, the OP in 3 lines. Here printed from a carbon rubbing courteously furnished by Director André Godard, of the Archaeological Museum of Teheran. A fragmentary copy (OP and Akk.) is correctly restored by Scheil 21.37 No. 3 (1929), cf. Kent, JAOS 51.213 (1931); it was wrongly identified with DSb by Brd. WZKM 39.12 (1932). Kent, JAOS 67.30–2 (1947).

DZa, b, c = DARIUS, SUEZ A, B, C: On a granite stele, not far from the 33d kilometer-stone from Suez, slightly to the west of the modern canal. Insc. a is the name of Darius in a cartouche; two copies. Insc. b is trilingual: OP 6 lines, Elam. 4 lines, Akk. 3 lines. Insc. c records Darius's opening of a canal from the Red Sea to the Nile: OP 12 lines, and below it the Elamite, of which 7 lines are preserved in part, while the Akk., presumably standing below the Elam., is entirely lost. On the reverse of the stele is a longer inscription in hieroglyphic Egyptian, presumably recording in fuller form the opening of the canal.

Tm. Lex 49–52 (1908); Wb. KIA xxi–xxii, 102–5 (1911); Sen, OPI 108–11 (1941); Kent, JNES 1.415–21 (1942). On a small fragment of a duplicate copy: Scheil, BIFAO 30.292–7 (1930); Brd. WZKM 39.76 (1932); Sen, OPI 111 (1941).

DE = DARIUS, ELVEND: Trilingual, each version in 20 lines, in a niche cut in the face of Mt. Elvend, one hour's riding time southwest of Hamadan; probably cut not in Darius's time, but simultaneously with XE, by orders of Xerxes, cf. HHSchaeder, SbPAW 1931.644, and AVWJackson, Persia Past and Present 172 (1906). Tm. Lex. 51–3 (1908); Wb. KIA xx, 100–3 (1911); Sen, OPI 113 (1941).

DH = DARIUS, HAMADAN: Trilingual, in duplicate on a gold and a silver plate; now in Teheran. OP 8 lines, Elam. 7 lines, Akk. 8 lines. The two copies vary slightly in the line-division; our text follows the gold plate. The text is repeated in DPh. JMUnwalla, Jame Jamshed, Sept. 30, 1926; Hz. DLZ 47.2105–8 (Oct. 16, 1926); SSmith, JRAS 1926.433–6; CDBuck, Lg. 3.1–5 (1927); LHGray, JRAS 1927.97–101; JMUnwalla, JCOI 10.1–3 (1927); Wb. ZfA 37.291–4 (1927); ESchwentner, ZII 6.171–3 (1928); Hz. Memoirs of the Archaeological Survey of India

No. 34, 7 + iii pp. (1928); LDBarnett, JRAS 1930.452; Kent, JAOS 51.229-31 (1931); Brd. WZKM 39.74-6 (1932); Hz. ApI 18-9 No. 6 and Plate 6 (1938); Sen, OPI 114-5 (1941).

XPa = XERXES, PERSEPOLIS A: Trilingual, each version in 20 lines, in 4 copies designated aa, ab, ac, ad, differing only slightly in line division, engraved on the inner walls of the great doorway; our text follows aa. Tm. Lex. 38-40 (1908); Wb. KIA xxiii, 106-9 (1911); Sen, OPI 138-40 (1941).

XPb = XERXES, PERSEPOLIS B: OP only, in 30 lines, on the north side of the colonnaded hall of Xerxes; also trilingual on the east side of the same, OP 30 lines, Elam. 18, Akk. 19. Tm. Lex. 39-40 (1908); Wb. KIA xxiii-xxiv, 108-11 (1911); Hz. ApI 24-6 No. 13 and Plate 9 (1938); Sen, OPI 140-1 (1941).

XPc = XERXES, PERSEPOLIS C: Trilingual, in triplicate; copy ca on the standing west pillar of the portico of Darius's palace, OP 15 lines, Elam. 14 lines, Akk. 13 lines; copy cb on the south boundary wall of the terrace on which the palace stands, each version in 25 lines; copy cc on the fallen east pillar of the portico, number of lines as in ca, but line-divisions slightly different. Tm. Lex. 40-2 (1908); Wb. KIA xxiv, 110-3 (1911); Sen, OPI 141-2 (1941); on copy cc, data by courtesy of E. F. Schmidt.

XPd = XERXES, PERSEPOLIS D: Trilingual, in quadruplicate; two identical copies da, on the pillars at the northeast and the northwest corners of the hall of Xerxes' palace, OP 19 lines, Elam. 12 lines, Akk. 11 lines; two identical copies db, on the walls beside the steps at the east and the west of the front terrace, OP 28 lines (with slight differences in line-divisions), Elam. 23 lines, Akk. 22 lines. Tm. Lex. 41-2 (1908); Wb. KIA xxiv-xxv, 112-5 (1911); Sen, OPI 142-3 (1941).

XPe = XERXES, PERSEPOLIS E: Trilingual, in duplicate (see below), each version 4 lines, with slightly differing line-divisions in OP; ea on a post of the north door, above the sculptured figure of the king; eb on a post of the east door, also above the king's figure. There are also numerous other copies of this inscription inside and outside the doors and windows, frequently in one-line and two-line arrangements (Cameron's data). Tm. Lex. 41-2 (1908); Wb. KIA xxv, 114-5 (1911); Sen, OPI 143 (1941).

XPf = XERXES, PERSEPOLIS F: The Accession of Xerxes, bilingual, OP 48 lines, Akk. 38 lines; a limestone tablet simulating a clay tablet, found under the wall at the southeast corner of the southeast palace, now shown to be the harem of Darius and Xerxes. Hz. AMI 4.117-32 (1932), Oriental Inst. Series, Stud. in Ancient Or. Civilization No. 5 (Chicago, 1932); Bv. BSLP 33.2.144-56 (1932); Wb. ZfA 41.318-21 (1933); Kent, Lg. 9.35-46 (1933); Schaeder, SbPAW 1935.496-506; JCTavadia, JCOI 27.137-8 (1935); Hz. AMI 8.35-46 (1937), ApI 35-8 No. 15 and Plates 13-4 (1938); Sen, OPI 143-6 (1941).

XPg = XERXES, PERSEPOLIS G: An ornamental plaque in colored enameled bricks, intended to be placed on the wall of the palace, and found in fragmentary condition; 2 copies of the OP, in 14 lines, a number of fragments of the Akk. version, and a very few of the Elamite. Ill. London News, April 8, 1933 (colored illustration on page 488); Bv. BSLP 34.1.32-4 (1933); Kent, Lg. 9.229-31 (1933); Hz. ApI 38-41 No. 16 and Plate 15 (1938); Sen, OPI 147 (1941).

XPh = XERXES, PERSEPOLIS H: The Daiva Inscription: Trilingual, on stone tablets, found in the building on the southeast corner of the terrace; 2 OP copies, one complete in 60 lines, the other stopping in the middle of line 51; 1 Elam. copy in 50 lines, 1 Akk. copy in 50 lines. New York Times, Feb. 9, 1936; Univ. of Chicago Mag. 28.4.23-5 (Feb. 1936); EFSchmidt, Ill. London News, Feb. 22, 1936, page 328; Kent, JAOS 56.212-5 (1936); AfOF 11.91 (1936); Hz. AMI 8.56-77 (1936), RHRel. 113.21-41 (Jan.-Feb. 1936); HHartmann, OLZ 40.145-60 (1937); Kent, Lg. 13.292-305 (1937); Hz. ApI 27-35 No. 14 and Plates 10-3 (1938); Wb. Symbolae Koschaker 189-98 (1938; on the Elamite version); ILevy, Revue historique 185.105-22 (1939); EFSchmidt, The Treasury of Persepolis 12-5 (1939); Sen, OPI 148-56 (1941); VIAbayev, Iranskie Yazyki 1.134-40 (Izd. Ak. Nauk, Iranica vol. 3; Moscow-Leningrad, 1945).

XPi = XERXES, PERSEPOLIS I: on a doorknob (or similar object) of artificial lapis lazuli, from the harem building; OP and Elamite, each in 1 line. Hz. ApI 23-4 No. 11 and Plate 7 (1938); Sen, OPI 254 (1941).

XPj = Xerxes, Persepolis j: Trilingual, each version in one long line, on the bases of at least five columns; found in small fragments. Cameron reports finding many fragments other than those which Hz. records. Hz. ApI 41-2 No. 17 (1938); Sen, OPI 254 (1941).

XPk = Xerxes, Persepolis k: OP and Elam., each in one line, on the garment of the king's figure in the eastern part of the middle door of the tacara. Hz. ApI 42 No. 18 (1938); Sen, OPI 255 (1941).

XSa = Xerxes, Susa a: Trilingual, each version in 2 lines, on the base of a column; now in the Louvre, Paris. Tm. Lex. 1 (1908); Wb. KIA xxv, 114-5 (1911). A second copy is given by Scheil 21.81 No. 23 (1929); Kent, JAOS 51.225 (1931); Brd. WZKM 39.79 (1932); Sen, OPI 160 a, b (1941).

XSb = Xerxes, Susa b: Akk., on column base. Scheil 21.82-3 (1929); Brd. WZKM 39.79-80 (1932).

XSc = Xerxes, Susa c: OP only, in 5 lines, on a fragmentary marble tablet. Scheil 21.86 No. 26 (1929); Kent, JAOS 51.226 (1931); Brd. WZKM 30.80-1 (1932); Sen, OPI 160 c (1941).

XE = Xerxes, Elvend: To the right of Darius's inscription; trilingual, each version in 20 lines. Tm. Lex. 52-4 (1908); Wb. KIA xxv, 116-7 (1911); Sen, OPI 157 (1941).

XV = Xerxes, Van: Trilingual, each version in 27 lines, in a rectangular niche high on the precipitous rocky wall of the castle. Tm. Lex. 53-4 (1908); Wb. KIA xxv-xxvi, 116-9 (1911); Sen, OPI 158-9 (1941).

XH = Xerxes, Hamadan: OP only, in one line, on a fragment of a silver pitcher. Hz. AMI 2.115-6 (1930); Brd. WZKM 39.83 (1932); Hz. ApI 43 No. 19 (1938); Sen, OPI 161 (1941).

A¹Pa = Artaxerxes I, Persepolis a: OP and Akk. The OP is a small fragment of 11 lines with a left edge, on a marble block found in the court before the south front of the palace; Hz. ApI 44-5 No. 21 (1938); Sen, OPI 256 (1941). The Akk. is a fragment of 14 lines with a left edge; Wb. KIA xxvi, 121 (1908); Hz. ApI 43-4 No. 20 and Plate 15 (1938). The two are combined and the OP reconstructed by Kent, JNES 4.228-32 (1945); cf. also Cameron, Persepolis Treasury Tablets 16-7 (1948). The complete OP inscription had 24 lines, the complete Akk. had 18 lines. A second Akk. inscription, relevant to the same matters, is undamaged: Hz. ApI 45-6 No. 22 and Plate 16 (1938).

A¹I = Artaxerxes I, incerto loco: OP only, in one line, identical inscription on four silver dishes. Hz. AMI 7.1-8 and 4 Plates (1935); Schaeder, SbPAW 1935.489-96; Hz. AMI 8.6-17, 46-51 (1937); Bv. JAs. 228.233-4 (1936); Kent, JAOS 56.215 (1936), 58.327 (1938); Hz. ApI 46 No. 23 (1938); Sen, OPI 178 (1941).

D²Sa = Darius II, Susa a: OP only, in 3 lines on the base of a column; a fragmentary Akk. inscription of different content stands on the same column. Scheil 21.82-3 No. 24 (1929); Kent, JAOS 51.227-8 (1931); Brd. WZKM 39.83-5 (1932); Sen, OPI 162 b (1941); Hinz, ZDMG 95.249-51 (1941). Another fragmentary inscription, named Dar. Susa h by Brd., was published separately by Scheil 21.41 infra (1929), Kent JAOS 51.226-7 (1931), Brd. WZKM 39.40-2 (1932), Sen OPI 162 a (1941), but is now recognized by Kent, JNES 1.421-3 (1942), as part of another copy of this inscription; given as D²Sc by Hinz, ZDMG 95.253-5 (1941).

D²Sb = Darius II, Susa b: Bilingual, OP 4 lines, Akk. 5 and 6 lines, two copies of each on the base of a column. Scheil 21.84-5 No. 25 (1929); Kent, JAOS 51.225 (1931); Brd. WZKM 39.85-8 (1932); Sen, OPI 163 (1941); Hinz, ZDMG 95.251-2 (1941).

A²Sa = Artaxerxes II, Susa a: Trilingual, each version in 5 lines, on the bases of 4 columns. Tm. Lex. 47-50 (1908); Wb. KIA xxvii, 122-5 (1911); Scheil 21.94-5 No. 29 (1929), giving two fragments of another Akk. copy in 7 lines; Brd. WZKM 39.88-9 (1932); Sen, OPI 166-7 (1941).

A²Sb = Artaxerxes II, Susa b: Trilingual, each version in one line, on the base of a column; now in the Louvre, Paris. Tm. Lex. 49-50 (1908); Wb. KIA xxvii, 124-5 (1911); Sen, OPI 167 (1941).

A²Sc = Artaxerxes II, Susa c: OP only, in 7 lines, on a stone tablet now in the Louvre, Paris.

Tm. Lex. 49–50 (1908); Wb. KIA xxvii, 124–5 (1911); Sen, OPI 167 (1941).

A²Sd = ARTAXERXES II, SUSA D: Trilingual, each version in 4 lines, on the base of a column; further fragments of two more OP copies, two more Akk. copies, and one more Elamite copy were later published. Scheil 21.91–3 No. 28 (1929); Kent, JAOS 51.228–9 (1931); Brd. WZKM 39.89–92 (1932); Scheil 24.126–8 (1933); Kent, JAOS 54.50–2 (1934); Sen, OPI 168 (1941). Wb. ZDMG 91.643–51 (1937) recognized the identity of his Frag. inc. a (KIA xxix, 130 [1911]; Mordtmann, ZDMG 14.555–6 [1860]; Sen, OPI 175 c [1941]) with Scheil's No. 16 C (21.66; Kent, JAOS 51.223 [1931]; Brd. WZKM 39.63–4 [1932]; Sen, OPI 175 b [1941]), and that this belonged to A²Sd. Copy **da** is that published by Scheil 21.91–3; **db** and **dc** those published by Scheil 24.128; **dd** the fragment recognized by Wb. Our copy has the line-division of da.

A²Ha = ARTAXERXES II, HAMADAN A: Trilingual, OP 7 lines, Elam. and Akk. 5 lines each, on a fragment of a column base; reported to be in private possession in England. Tm. Lex. 54–5 (1908); Wb. KIA xxviii, 126–7 (1911); Sen, OPI 164–5 (1941).

A²Hb = ARTAXERXES II, HAMADAN B: OP only, in one long line on the base of a column. Hz. Altorient. Stud. B. Meissner gewidmet = Mitteil. d. altorient. Ges. 4.85–6 (1928); Kent, JAOS 51.231–2 (1931); Brd. WZKM 39.92–4 (1932); Hz. ApI 50 No. 25 (1938); Sen, OPI 165 (1941).

A²Hc = ARTAXERXES II, HAMADAN C: OP only, in 20 lines on a gold tablet, about 13 x 13 cm.; found at Hamadan; see §18 n2. AUPope, The Illustrated London News, July 17 1948, pp. 58–9. On exhibition at the Musée Cernuschi (Paris), in the summer of 1948, where it was No. 53 of the Catalogue Illustré (no date).

A?P = ARTAXERXES II OR III, PERSEPOLIS: Trilingual, labeling the throne-bearers of the south tomb. Davis, JRAS 1932.373–7 and Plates 2–3; Hz. ApI 46–50 No. 24 (1938); Sen, OPI 172–3 (1941).

A³Pa, b, c, d = ARTAXERXES III, PERSEPOLIS A, B, C, D: OP only, 4 copies with identical text but differing line-division; a, c, d on the north wall of the terrace of the palace of Artaxerxes, originally 26 lines each; b, in 35 lines, beside the stairway on the west side of the palace of Darius. Tm. Lex. 42–4 (1908); Wb. KIA xxix, 128–9 (1911); Photographs of Casts of Persian Sculptures of the Achaemenid Period, mostly from Persepolis, London, British Museum, 1932 (Plate 6 shows this inscription very legibly); Sen, OPI 170–1 (1941). The portion of copy c which was missing when Stolze took his photographs was found by the University of Chicago Expedition in 1939 (Cameron's data). Our text has the line division of copy a.

Wa = DARIUS, WEIGHT A: Trilingual, OP 8 lines, Elam. 7 lines, Akk. 5 lines, on a blunted pyramid of dark green diorite, 5.1 cm. high, 4.4 cm. long, 4.1 cm. wide; weighing 166.724 grams. It is now in the British Museum, London. Tm. Lex. 56–7 (1908); Wb. KIA xxii, 104–5 (1911); Sen, OPI 137 (1941).

Wb = DARIUS, WEIGHT B: Trilingual, OP 9 lines, Elam. 6 lines, Akk. 4 lines, on a blunted pyramid of dark green diorite (height 10.5 cm., base 10.9 by 10.7 cm.), weighing 2222.425 grams; found in a tomb a day's journey from Kerman, and often called Darius Kerman; now in the Asiatic Museum, Leningrad. Jn. JAOS 27.193–4 and 3 plates (1906), reprinted in Persia Past and Present 184 and 3 plates (1906); Tm. Lex. 51–2 (1908); Scheil, Rec. de Trav. 31.137 (1909); Wb. Bull. de l'Acad. Imp. des Sci. de St. Pet. 1910.481 ff; Wb. KIA xxii–xxiii, lxxiv–lxxv, 104–5 (1911); Sen, OPI 112 (1941).

Wc = DARIUS, WEIGHT C: Trilingual, OP 10 lines, Elam. 7 lines, Akk. 4 lines, on a blunted pyramid of grayish-green diorite weighing 9.950 kg. (original weight slightly greater, since some chips have been broken from the base), found in the southern part of the Treasury at Persepolis. Hz. ApI 24 No. 12 and Plate 8 (1938); Schmidt, Treasury of Persepolis 62–3 including plate (1939); Sen, OPI 253 (1941).

Wd = DARIUS, WEIGHT D: OP 10 lines, Elam. 6 lines (the last continuing around the right face), Akk. 5 lines (on the right face; damaged), on a blunted pyramid of grayish-green diorite weighing 4.930 kg. (original weight slightly greater, since some damage has been suffered); found 1936 in the Treasury at Persepolis. Publication here by special permission of E. F. Schmidt.

SDa = DARIUS, SEAL A: Trilingual, each version in one line, on a crystal cylinder, now in the British Museum. Tm. Lex. 55–6 (1908); Wb. KIA xxiii, 106–7 (1911); HFrankfort, Cylinder Seals Pl. xxxvii d (1939); Sen, OPI 137 (1941).

SDb, SXa, SXb, SXc = DARIUS, SEAL B, trilingual, each version in one line; XERXES, SEAL A, B, C, OP only, in two lines (second line of c illegible); several copies of each. Seal impressions (not seals) on tablets found in the Persepolis Treasury by The University of Chicago Expedition. EFSchmidt, The Treasury of Persepolis 39 (1939); GGCameron, Persepolis Treasury Tablets 55–8 (1948).

Sa = SEAL A: OP in 7 lines, now in the British Museum. Tm. Lex. 55–6 (1908); Wb. xxx, 130–1 (1911); Sen, OPI 174 (1941).

Sb = SEAL B: OP in 3 lines, the second illegible; in the British Museum. Tm. Lex. 56–7 (1908); Wb. KIA xxx, 130–1 (1911); Sen, OPI 174 (1941).

Sc, Sd = SEAL C and SEAL D: OP only, on oval gems with Sasanian heads, the characters being in front of and behind the heads; present location of these seals unknown. Tm. Lex. 56–7 (1908); Wb. xxx, 130–1 (1911); Sen, OPI 174 (1941).

Se = SEAL E: OP only, in 3 lines; in the Musée des Armures, Brussels. Tm. Lex. 56–7 (1908); Wb. KIA xxx, 130–1 (1911); Sen, OPI 174 (1941).

Sf = SEAL F: OP only, in 4 lines, of which the fourth is lost and all of the third except parts of the first two characters; in a cartouche on an Egyptian roll-seal. H. H. von der Osten, Ancient Oriental Seals in the Collection of Mr. Edward T. Newhall no. 453, pages 66 and 166, and plate 31 (Univ. of Chicago, Oriental Institute Publ., vol. 22; 1934); A. Goetze, Berytus 8.100 (1944).

XVs = XERXES, VASES: Of alabaster, bearing the king's name in OP, Elam., Akk., and Egyptian hieroglyphics. Vase **a**, in the Cabinet des Médailles of the Bibliothèque Nationale, Paris; Vase **b**, from Halicarnassus, in the British Museum; Vase **c**, in the University Museum, Philadelphia; some fragments found by Loftus at Susa are in the British Museum, and other fragments found by Dieulafoy in 1854–5 at Susa, and some found by the expedition of de Morgan, are at the Louvre. Tm. Lex. 56–8 (1908); Wb. KIA xxvi, 118–9 (1911); Sen, OPI 161 (1941).

AVs = ARTAXERXES, VASES: In four languages, like those of Xerxes, which is why they are assigned to Xerxes's son rather than to a later Artaxerxes. Vase **a**, of gray porphyry, in the Treasury of St. Mark's, Venice; Vase **b**, in the University Museum, Philadelphia; Vase **c**, in the Imperial Museums, Berlin; some fragments also were found at Susa by the expedition of de Morgan. Tm. Lex. 56–8 (1908); Wb. KIA xxvii, 120–1 (1911); Sen, OPI 169 (1941). Vase **d**, acquired in 1910 at Aleppo by Noel Giron, who published it in Rev. d'Ass. 18.143–5 (1921).

SPURIOUS INSCRIPTIONS:

Spur. a: From Tarku. Wb. Gdr. IP 2.62 §25 (1895).

Spur. b, c, d, e: Four baked clay tablets secured by Chantre near Caesarea; OP only. Tablets b, c, d contain on the recto more or less badly written copies of DPa, and on the verso copies of XPe. Tablet e has on the recto 3 lines of the same, then a mixture of OP signs and similar but meaningless signs on the balance of the recto and all of the verso. The tablets are now in the Musée Asiatique de Paris (Musée Guimet). Ménant, Comptes-Rendus de l'Ac. d. Inscr., 4th series, 23.126–41 (1895); Wb. Gdr. IP 2.62 §25 (1895).

Spur. f: OP only, on a glazed tile inscribed on both sides, bought by Sayce at Saqqara. Sayce, AfOF 8.225 (1933); Wb. ZDMG 91.87 (1937); Kent, JAOS 56.215–6 (1936), 58.327–9 (1938); Sen, OPI 179 (1941).

Spur. g: OP only, in 14 lines interrupted by figures in hollow relief, on a red brick tablet in a small private museum in Philadelphia. Dyen, JAOS 56.91–3 (1936); Eilers, ZDMG 91.407–20 (1937); Kent, JAOS 58.327 (1938); Sen, OPI 180 (1941).

Spur. h, a jesting composition in OP by Weissbach, ZDMG 91.644; listed here only because it was misunderstood by Sen to be a genuine OP text (his Frag. a on page 175).

THE TEXTS WITH NOTES AND TRANSLATION

AmH = Ariaramnes, Hamadan.

1 Ariyāramna : xšāyaθiya : vazraka : xšāyaθ
2 iya : xšāyaθiyānām : xšāyaθiya : Pārsā
3 : Cišpaiš : xšāyaθiyahyā : puça : Haxāmanišah
4 yā : napā : θātiy : Ariyāramna : xšāyaθiya
5 : iyam : dahyāuš : Pārsā : tya : adam : dārayā
6 miy : hya : uvaspā : umartiyā : manā : baga
7 : vazraka : Auramazdā : frāba*ra* : vašnā : Au
8 ramazdāha : adam : xšāyaθiya : iyam : da
9 hyāuš : amiy : θātiy : Ariyāramna
10 : xšāyaθiya : Auramazdā : manā : upastā
11 *m : baratuv*

Translation of AmH:
§1. 1–4. Ariaramnes, the Great King, King of Kings, King in Persia, son of Teispes the King, grandson of Achaemenes.
§2. 4–9. Saith Ariaramnes the King: This country Persia which I hold, which is possessed of good horses, of good men, upon me the Great God Ahuramazda bestowed (it). By the favor of Ahuramazda I am king in this country.
§3. 9–11. Saith Ariaramnes the King: May Ahuramazda bear me aid.

AsH = Arsames, Hamadan.

1 Aršāma : xšāyaθiya : vazraka : x
2 šāyaθiya : xšāyaθiyānām : x
3 šāyaθiya : Pārsa : Ariyāramna : xš
4 āyaθiyahyā : puça : Haxāmanišiya
5 : θātiy : Aršāma : xšāyaθiya : Au
6 ramazdā : baga : vazraka : hya : maθiš
7 ta : bagānām : mām : xšāyaθiya
8 m : akunauš : hauv : dahyāum : P
9 ārsam : manā : frābara : tya : ukāram
10 : uvaspam : vašnā : Auramazdāha : im
11 ām : dahyāum : dārayāmiy : mām :
12 Auramazdā : pātuv : utāmaiy : v
13 iθam : utā : imām : dahyāum : *tya :*
14 adam : dārayāmiy : hauv : pāt*uv*

Translation of AsH:
§1. 1–4. Arsames, the Great King, King of Kings, King (in) Persia, son (of) Ariaramnes the King, an Achaemenian.
§2. 5–14. Saith Arsames the King: Ahuramazda, great god, the greatest of gods, made me king. He bestowed on me the land Persia, with good people, with good horses. By the favor of Ahuramazda I hold this land. Me may Ahuramazda protect, and my royal house, and this land which I hold, may he protect.

CMa = Cyrus, Murghab (Pasargadae) a.

1 adam : Kūruš : xšāya
2 θiya : Haxāmanišiya

Translation of CMa: I am Cyrus the King, an Achaemenian.

CMb = Cyrus, Murghab b.

1 *Kūruš : xšāyaθiya : vazraka : Kabūjiya*
2 *hyā : xšāyaθiyahyā : puça : Haxāmanišiya :*
3 *θātiy : yaθā .*
4 . *akutā*

Note to CMb· The other versions show that the inscription mentioned the sculptured figure in the doorway below, with a prayer to Ahuramazda for protection; but further reconstruction is as yet impossible. Not all the fragments given in Herzfeld's Plate belong to the same inscription; one such fragment contains clearly the word *v]iθi[yā* 'in the palace'.

Translation of CMb: Cyrus the Great King, son of Cambyses the King, an Achaemenian. He says: When   made

CMc = Cyrus, Murghab c.

Kūruš : xšāyaθiya : vazraka : Haxāmanišiya

Translation of CMc: Cyrus the Great King, an Achaemenian.

DB = Darius, Behistan.

Text of DB, Column I:

1 : adam : Dārayavauš : xšāyaθiya : vazraka : xšāyaθiya : xšāyaθiy
2 ānām : xšāyaθiya : Pārsaiy : xšāyaθiya : dah*yū*nām : V¹št
3' āspahyā : puça : Aršāmahyā : napā : Haxāmaniš*iya*   θātiy :
4 Dārayavauš : xšāyaθiya : manā : pitā : V¹štāspa : V¹štāspa*hyā : pitā* : Arš
5 āma : Aršāmahyā : pitā : Ariyāramna : Ariyāramnahyā : pit*ā : Cišpiš* : Cišp
6 āiš : pitā : Haxāmaniš   : θātiy : Dārayavauš : xšāya*θiya : a*vahyarā

DB I — TEXTS WITH NOTES AND TRANSLATION

7 diy : vayam : Haxāmanišiyā : θahyāmahy : hacā : paruv*iyata* : *ā*mātā : ama
8 hy : hacā : paruviyata : hyā : amāxam : taumā : xšāyaθ*iyā* : *ā*ha : θ
9 ātiy : Dārayavauš : xšāyaθiya : VIII : manā : taumāyā : *tyaiy* : *p*aruvam
10 : xšāyaθiyā : āha : adam : navama : IX : duvitāparanam : *vayam* : xšāyaθi
11 yā : amahy : θātiy : Dārayavauš : xšāyaθiya : va*šnā* : Auramazd
12 āha : adam : xšāyaθiya : amiy : Auramazdā : xšaçam : manā : *f*rābara : θ
13 ātiy : Dārayavauš : xšāyaθiya : imā : dahyāva : tyā : manā : patiyāiša : vašn
14 ā : Auramazdāha : *a*damšām : xšāyaθiya : āham : Pārsa : Ūvja : *B*ābiruš : A
15 θurā : Arabāya : Mudrāya : tyaiy : drayahyā : Sparda : Yauna : *Māda* : Armina : Kat
16 patuka : Parθava : Zraka : Haraiva : Uvārazmīy : Bāxtriš : *Su*guda : Gadāra : Sa
17 ka : Θataguš : Ha*r*auvatiš : Maka : fraharavam : dahyāva : XXIII : θātiy : Dāra
18 yavauš : xšāyaθiya : imā : dahyāva : tyā : manā : pati*y*āi*š*a : vašnā : Au
19 ramazdāha : ma*n*ā : badakā : āhatā : manā : bājim : abaratā : *ty*ašām : hacāma
20 : aθahya : xšapavā : raucapativā : ava : akunavayatā : θātiy : *D*ārayava
21 uš : xšāyaθiya : atar : imā : dahyāva : martiya : hya : agriya : āha : avam : u
22 bartam : abaram : hya : arika : āha : avam : ufrastam : aparsam : vašnā : Auramazdā
23 ha : imā : dahyāva : tyanā : manā : dātā : apariyāya : yaθāšām : hacāma : aθah
24 ya : avaθā : akunavayatā : θātiy : Dārayavauš : xšāyaθiya : Auramazdā
25 ma*iy* : ima : xšaçam : frābara : Auramazdāmaiy : upastām : abara : yātā : ima : xšaçam :
26 ha*m*adārayai*y* : vašnā : Auramazdāha : ima : xšaçam : dārayāmiy : θā
27 tiy : Dārayavauš : xšāyaθiya : ima : tya : manā : kartam : pasāva : yaθā : xš
28 āyaθiya : abavam : Kabūjiya : nāma : Kūrauš : puça : amāxam : taumāy
29 ā : hauvam : idā : xšāyaθiya : āha : avahyā : Kabūjiyahyā : brā
30 tā : *Bardi*ya : nāma : āha : hamātā : hamapitā : Kabūjiyahyā : pasāva : Ka
31 b*ū*jiya : avam : Bardiyam : avāja : yaθā : Kabūjiya : Bardiyam : avāja : kārahy
32 ā : naiy : azdā : abava : tya : Bardiya : avajata : pasāva : Kabūjiya : Mudrāyam
33 : a*š*iyava : yaθā : Kabūjiya : Mudrāyam : ašiyava : pasāva : kāra : arika : abava
34 : *pasāva* : drauga : dahyauvā : vasiy : abava : utā : Pārsaiy : utā : Mādaiy : ut
35 ā : *a*niyāuvā : dahyušuvā : θātiy : Dārayavauš : xšāyaθiya : pa
36 *sāva* : I martiya : maguš : āha : Gaumāta : nāma : hauv : udapatatā : hacā : Paiši
37 *y*āuvādāyā : Arakadriš : nāma : kaufa : hacā : avadaša : Viyaxnahya : māh
38 *y*ā : XIV : raucabiš : θakatā : āha : yadiy : udapatatā : hauv : kārahyā : avaθā
39 : *a*durujiya : adam : Bardiya : amiy : hya : Kūrauš : puça : Kabūjiyahyā : br
40 *ā*tā : pasāva : kāra : haruva : hamiçiya : abava : hacā : Kabūjiyā : abiy : avam :
41 a*š*iyava : utā : Pārsa : utā : Māda : utā : aniyā : dahyāva : xšaçam : hauv
42 : agarbāyatā : Garmapadahya : māhyā : IX : raucabiš : θakatā : āha : avaθā : xša
43 çam : agarbāyatā : pasāva : Kabūjiya : uvāmaršiyuš : amariyatā : θātiy
44 : Dārayavauš : xšāyaθiya : aita : xšaçam : tya : Gaumāta : hya : maguš : adīn
45 ā : Kabūjiyam : aita : xšaçam : hacā : paruviyata : amāxam : taumāyā : ā
46 ha : pasāva : Gaumāta : hya : maguš : adīnā : Kabūjiyam : utā : Pārsam : utā
47 : Mādam : utā : aniyā : dahyāva : hauv : āyasatā : uvāipašiyam : akutā : hau
48 v : xšāyaθiya : abava : θātiy : Dārayavauš : xšāyaθiya : naiy : āha : martiya :
49 naiy : Pārsa : naiy : Māda : naiy : amāxam : taumāyā : kašciy : hya : avam : Gau
50 mātam : tyam : magum : xšaçam : dītam : caxriyā : kārašim : hacā : daršam : a
51 tarsa : kāram : vasiy : avājaniyā : hya : paranam : Bardiyam : adānā : avahyar
52 ādiy : kāram : avājaniyā : mātyamām : xšnāsātiy : tya : adam : naiy : Bard
53 iya : amiy : hya : Kūrauš : puça : kašciy : naiy : adaršnauš : cišciy : θastana
54 iy : pariy : Gaumātam : tyam : magum : yātā : adam : arasam : pasāva : adam : Aura
55 maz(d)ām : patiyāvahyaiy : Auramazdāmaiy : upastām : abara : Bāgayādaiš :
56 māhyā : X : raucabiš : θakatā : āha : avaθā : adam : hadā : kamnaibiš : martiyaibi

118 OLD PERSIAN DB I

57 š : avam : Gaumātam : tyam : magum : avājanam : utā : tyaišaiy : fratamā : mar
58 tiyā : anušiyā : āhatā : Sika*y*auvatiš : nāma : dıdā : Nısāya : nā
59 mā : dahyāuš : Mādaiy : avadašim : avājanam : xšaçamšim : adam : adīnam : va
60 šnā : Auramazdāha : adam : xšāyaθiya : abavam : Auramazdā : xšaçam : manā : fr
61 ābara : θātiy : Dārayavauš : xšāyaθiya : xšaçam : tya : hacā : amāxam : ta
62 umāyā : parābartam : āha : ava : adam : patipadam : akunavam : adamšim : gāθa
63 vā : avāstāyam : yaθā : paruvamciy : avaθā : adam : akunavam : āyadan
64 ā : tyā : Gaumāta : hya : maguš : viyaka : adam : niyaçārayam : kārahyā : abi
65 carıš : gaiθāmcā : māniyamcā : v¹θbišcā : tyādiš : Gaumāta : h*y*a :
66 maguš : adīnā : adam : kāram : gāθavā : avāstāyam : Pārsamcā : Mādam*c*
67 ā : utā : aniyā : dahyāva : yaθā : paruvamciy : avaθā : adam : tya : parāba*rta*
68 m : patiyābaram : vašnā : Auramazdāha : ima : adam : akunavam : adam : hamataxš*aiy* :
69 yātā : v¹θam : tyām : amāxam : gāθavā : avāstāyam : yaθā : *paruvamciy* :
70 avaθā : adam : hamataxšaiy : vašnā : Auramazdāha : yaθā : Gaumāta : hya : magu
71 š : v¹θam : tyām : amāxam : naiy : parābara : θātiy : Dārayavauš : xšāyaθ
72 iya : ima : tya : adam : akunavam : pasāva : yaθā : xšāyaθiya : abavam : θātiy
73 : Dārayavauš : xšāyaθiya : yaθā : adam : Gaumātam : tyam : magum : avājanam : pa
74 sāva : I martiya : Āçina : nāma : Upadarmahyā : puça : hauv : udapata*tā* : *Ūvjai*
75 y : kārahyā : avaθā : aθaha : adam : Ūvjaiy : xšāyaθiya : amiy : pas*āva* : *Ūv*
76 jiyā : hamiçiyā : abava : abiy : avam : Āçinam : ašiyava : hauv : x*šāyaθiya*
77 : abava : Ūvjaiy : utā : I martiya : Bābiruviya : Naditabaira : nāma : Aina*ira*hy
78 ā : puça : hauv : udapatatā : Bābirauv : kāram : avaθā : adurujiya : adam : Nab
79 ukᵘdracara : amiy : hya : Nabunaitahyā : puça : pasāva : kāra : hya : Bābiruviya
80 : haruva : abiy : avam : Naditabairam : ašiyava : Bābiruš : hamiçiya : abava : x
81 šaçam : tya : Bābirauv : hauv : agarbāyatā : θātiy : Dārayavauš : xšāya
82 θiya : pasāva : adam : frāišayam : Ūvjam : hauv : Āçina : basta : anayatā : a*biy* : *m*ā
83 m : adamšim : avājanam : θātiy : Dārayavauš : xšāyaθiya : pasāva : adam : Bā
84 birum : ašiyavam : abiy : avam : Naditabairam : hya : Nabukᵘdracara : aga*uba*tā
85 : kāra : hya : Naditabairahyā : Tigrām : adāraya : avadā : aištatā : utā :
86 abiš : nāviyā : āha : pasāva : adam : kāram : maškāuvā : avākanam : aniyam : uša
87 bārim : akunavam : aniyahyā : asam : frānayam : Aura*maz*dāmaiy : upas*tā*m
88 : abara : vašnā : Auramazdāha : Tigrām : vıyatarayāmā : *avadā* : avam : kāram :
89 tyam : Naditabairahyā : adam : ajanam : vasiy : Āçiyādiya*hya* : māhyā : XXVI : rau
90 cabiš : θakatā : āha : ava*θā* : hamaranam : akumā : θātiy : Dārayavauš : x
91 šāyaθiya : pasāva : a*dam* : Bābirum : ašiyavam : a*θ*iy : Bābiru*m* : *yaθā* : *naiy* : *up*
92 āyam : Zāzāna : nāma : vardanam : anuv : Ufrātuvā : avadā : *hauv* : *N*adita
93 baira : hya : Nabukᵘdracara : agaubatā · āiš : hadā : kārā : patiš : *mām* : *hamaranam* :
94 cartanaiy : pasāva : hama*ranam* : akumā : Auramazdāmaiy : upastām : abara : *vašnā* : *Aurama*
95 zdāha : kāram : tyam : Naditabairahyā : adam : ajanam : vasiy : aniya : āpiyā : āhyatā : ā
96 pišım : parābara : Anāmakahya : māhyā : II : raucabiš : θakatā : āha : avaθā : hama*ranam* : a*kum*ā

NOTES TO DB I

Our text of DB is based essentially on KT's examination and edition, supplemented by the examinations of the original by Jackson and Cameron The notes include the additional characters and words recorded as visible by Rl , and by WB from Wb 's reading of Rl.'s squeezes In the text are embodied Cameroñ's readings, so far as they are available through his kindness; Cameron removed the limestone incrustations that had covered many of the engraved characters, and succeeded in establishing the original text of a number of passages that had previously been in part unreadable and had been wrongly restored (so especially 1 21, 2 33, 74, 89, 3 26; 4 44, 46, 54, 65, 85, 89), as well as numerous single letters elsewhere For these readings due credit is given in the notes attached to the passages Citation of KT's reading in the notes, without comment, means that KT's reading corrects a previous text based on an incorrect reading by Rl or WB Accepted restorations which fill the gaps are credited to their authors, except where they are of an obvious nature; but erroneous readings and discarded emendations are for the most part omitted Mere differences of normalization have been disregarded where they do not imply a difference of interpretation; and for ease of comparison, all readings which are not presented character by character are given in the normalization employed in this volume

⁵ *Ariyāram-* KT, both occurrences, not *-rām-*, with Rl ⁷ *[a]mᵃtᵃa* KT, cf *a[mᵃ]tᵃa* DBa 11 KT, not *ādātā* with Andreas and Husing KZ 38 255 ⁹*VIII · manā : taumāyā:* cf. Hist App I ¹⁰ *duvitāparanam,* see Lex ¹⁴ On list of provinces, see Kent, JNES 2 302-6 ¹⁵ *Yauna* Bv. Gr. §348, not *yᵃunᵃ[a] = Yaun[ā],* with KT, cf Rl 's *Yau[na]* ¹⁶ [*Sug*]*uda* KT ¹⁷ *fᵃrᵃhᵃrᵃvᵃmᵃ* Rl , KT, instead of the expected *fᵃrᵃhᵃrᵘuvᵃmᵃ* ²¹ *agᵃrᵃ[++]* KT, cf Rl 's *agᵃtᵃ,* *agᵃrᵃiyᵃ* Cameron; see Lex s v. *agriya-.* ²³ *tyanā : manā · dātā* of Rl and KT is correct; not dittography for *tyā : manā,* cf the idiom in XPh 49 and 51-2 ²³ *apariyāya,* from *pari- + ay-,* for wrong interpretations, see Lex ²⁴⁻⁵ *Auramazdā | m[aiy .] ima* KT. ²⁶ *ha[ma]dārayai[y]* KT ²⁹*hauvam* KT ³²*avajata* Rl , KT; not to be emended to *avājata,* with Gray, Bthl ³⁶ On Gaumāta-Bardiya, see Hist App II. ³⁷ On the OP calendar, see Hist App IV.

⁵¹ *avājaniyā,* cf. Kent, JAOS 62 274 ⁵⁵ *mᵃzᵃamᵃ* KT, with omission of the *dᵃ* ⁵⁵ *patiyāvahyaiy* Jn , KT ⁵⁸ *Sika-[ya]uvatiš* KT ⁶⁴⁻⁵ *abᵃicᵃrᵃiṧᵃ* Rl , WB, Jn , KT ⁶⁵ *viθᵃbᵃ-iṧᵃcᵃ* Jn , KT, for Rl 's *viθᵃibᵃiṧᵃ[cᵃ]a;* cf Lex for lit. on various normalizations and interpretations ⁶⁶ Bv MSLP 23 182-3 finds an haplography and would read *adinā : adam [: patiyābaram · adam] : kāram* ⁷⁴ *Upadar-mahyā* Rl , Wb KIA; *Upadaraⁿmahyā* Opp Mèd , Husing, KT, Tm., *Uⁿpadaraⁿmahyā* HK

⁸⁵ *āistatā* WB, KT, *aistatā* Rl., Tm , Wb ⁸⁶⁻⁷ *ušabārim* Jn , KT; *uš[tra]bārim* Bthl AiW 421; cf §79 ⁸⁷ *asam* Jn , KT. ⁸⁷ *frānayam* KT. ⁸⁸ *viyatarayāmā* acc to KT's cuneiform text; *viyatarayāma* WB ⁸⁸ [*a*]*vadā · avam · kāram* KT. ⁹⁰ *akumā,* with final *a* legible acc to Rl , WB, Jn ; but not acc to KT ⁹¹ *aθiy* Rl , KT ⁹¹⁻² [*u*]*pāyam* KT, recording that part of the *pᵃ* is visible; this eliminates Foy's [*abiy*]*āyam* ⁹² *Ufratuvā* KT. ⁹⁵ [+]*hᵃ*[+++]*a* Rl ; [*a*]*ha[rat]ā* Opp. 169, Gray AJP 21.22; [*a*]*haⁿ[jat]ā* WB; [*a*]*ha[dat]ā* Bthl. AF 1.61; [*aharat*]*ā* KT, [*a*]*h[yat]ā* Kern ZDMG 23 269, Foy KZ 37.554, Bthl. AiW 279, Wb KIA.

Rl has the following correct readings, in which he records as visible certain characters, here indicated by roman type, which were not visible to KT ¹*xšāyaθiya* [: *xšāya*]*θiy-,* ² *dahy[ūnām;* ⁴ *Vištāspahyā;* ⁶ *xšāyaθ[iya;* ¹⁴ *adamšām;* ¹⁷ *Harauvatiš;* ¹⁹ *manā;* ²⁰ *Dārayava-;* ²² [*vašn*]*ā,* ²⁴ *avaθā;* ³⁰ *Bardiya,* ³¹ *būji*]*ya avam,* ³⁴ *pasā*]*va,* ⁶⁵ *hya;* ⁶⁹ *par[u]va[m]c[iy;* ⁸² *Āçi[na;* ⁸⁴ *agau[batā;* ⁸⁷ *Auramazdāmaiy,* ⁹⁰ *avaθā;* ⁹¹ *Bābirum . ya[θā;* ⁹³ *m[ām;* ⁹⁴ *hamaranam;* ⁹⁵ *āpiyā*

WB, from Wb 's reading of Rl.'s squeezes, add the following, also in roman, which were not visible to KT, nor to Rl ³³ *aši*]*yava,* ⁶⁶ *Mādamc-,* ⁸² *abiy . mā-.*

TRANSLATION OF DB I:

§1. 1.1–3. I am Darius the Great King, King of Kings, King in Persia, King of countries, son of Hystaspes, grandson of Arsames, an Achaemenian.

§2. 1.3–6. Saith Darius the King: My father was Hystaspes; Hystaspes' father was Arsames; Arsames' father was Ariaramnes; Ariaramnes' father was Teispes; Teispes' father was Achaemenes.

§3. 1.6–8. Saith Darius the King: For this reason we are called Achaemenians. From long ago we have been noble. From long ago our family had been kings.

§4. 1.8–11. Saith Darius the King: VIII of our family (there are) who were kings afore; I am the ninth; IX in succession we have been kings.

§5. 1.11–2. Saith Darius the King: By the favor of Ahuramazda I am King; Ahuramazda bestowed the kingdom upon me.

§6. 1.12–7. Saith Darius the King: These are the countries which came unto me; by the favor of Ahuramazda I was king of them: Persia, Elam, Babylonia, Assyria, Arabia, Egypt, (those) who are beside the sea, Sardis, Ionia, Media, Armenia, Cappadocia, Parthia, Drangiana, Aria, Chorasmia, Bactria, Sogdiana, Gandara, Scythia, Sattagydia, Arachosia, Maka: in all, XXIII provinces.

§7. 1.17–20. Saith Darius the King: These are the countries which came unto me; by the favor of Ahuramazda they were my subjects; they bore tribute to me; what was said unto them by me either by night or by day, that was done.

§8. 1.20–4. Saith Darius the King: Within these countries, the man who was excellent, him I rewarded well; (him) who was evil, him I punished well; by the favor of Ahuramazda these countries showed respect toward my law; as was said to them by me, thus was it done.

§9. 1.24–6. Saith Darius the King: Ahuramazda bestowed the kingdom upon me; Ahuramazda bore me aid until I got possession of this kingdom; by the favor of Ahuramazda I hold this kingdom.

§10. 1.26–35. Saith Darius the King: This is what was done by me after that I became king. A son of Cyrus, Cambyses by name, of our family—he was king here. Of that Cambyses there was a brother, Smerdis by name, having the same mother and the same father as Cambyses. Afterwards, Cambyses slew that Smerdis. When Cambyses slew Smerdis, it did not become known to the people that Smerdis had been slain. Afterwards, Cambyses went to Egypt. When Cambyses had gone off to Egypt, after that the people became evil. After that the Lie waxed great in the country, both in Persia and in Media and in the other provinces.

§11. 1.35–43. Saith Darius the King: Afterwards, there was one man, a Magian, Gaumata by name; he rose up from Paishiyauvada. A mountain by name Arakadri—from there XIV days of the month Viyakhna were past when he rose up. He lied to the people thus: "I am Smerdis, the son of Cyrus, brother of Cambyses." After that, all the people became rebellious from Cambyses, (and) went over to him, both Persia and Media and the other provinces. He seized the kingdom; of the month Garmapada IX days were past, then he seized the kingdom. After that, Cambyses died by his own hand.

§12. 1.43–8. Saith Darius the King: This kingdom which Gaumata the Magian took away from Cambyses, this kingdom from long ago had belonged to our family. After that, Gaumata the Magian took (it) from Cambyses; he took to himself both Persia and Media and the other provinces, he made (them) his own possession, he became king.

§13. 1.48–61. Saith Darius the King: There was not a man, neither a Persian nor a Mede nor anyone of our family, who might make that Gaumata the Magian deprived of the kingdom. The people feared him greatly, (thinking that) he would slay in numbers the people who previously had known Smerdis; for this reason he would slay the people, "lest they know me, that I am not Smerdis the son of Cyrus." Not anyone dared say anything about Gaumata the Magian, until I came. After that I besought help of Ahuramazda; Ahuramazda bore me aid; of the month Bagayadi X days were past, then I with a few men slew that Gaumata the Magian, and those who were his foremost followers. A fortress by name Sikayauvati, a district by name Nisaya, in Media—there I slew him. I took the kingdom from him. By the favor of Ahuramazda I became king; Ahuramazda bestowed the kingdom upon me.

§14. 1.61–71. Saith Darius the King: The kingdom which had been taken away from our family, that I put in its place; I reestablished it on its foundation. As before, so I made the sanctuaries which Gaumata the Magian destroyed. I restored to the people the pastures and the herds, the household property and the houses which Gaumata the Magian took away from them. I reestablished the people on its foundation, both Persia and Media and the other provinces. As before, so I brought back what had been taken away. By the favor of Ahuramazda this I did: I strove until I reestablished our royal house on its foundation as (it was) before. So I strove, by the favor of Ahuramazda, so that Gaumata the Magian did not remove our royal house.

§15. 1.71–2. Saith Darius the King: This is what I did after that I became king.

§16. 1.72–81. Saith Darius the King: When I had slain Gaumata the Magian, afterwards one man, by name Açina, son of Upadarma—he rose up in Elam. To the people thus he said: "I am king in Elam." Afterwards the Elamites became rebellious, (and) went over to that Açina; he became king in Elam. And one man, a Babylonian, by name Nidintu-Bel, son of Ainaira—he rose up in Babylon; thus he deceived the people: "I am Nebuchadrezzar the son of Nabonidus." Afterwards the Babylonian people all went over to that Nidintu-Bel; Babylonia became rebellious; he seized the kingdom in Babylon.

§17. 1.81–3. Saith Darius the King: After that I sent (a message) to Elam. This Açina was led to me bound; I slew him.

§18. 1.83–90. Saith Darius the King: After that I went off to Babylon, against that Nidintu-Bel who called himself Nebuchadrezzar. The army of Nidintu-Bel held the Tigris; there it took its stand, and on account of the waters (the Tigris) was unfordable. Thereupon (some of) my army I supported on (inflated) skins, others I made camel-borne, for others I brought horses. Ahuramazda bore me aid; by the favor of Ahuramazda we got across the Tigris. There I smote that army of Nidintu-Bel exceedingly; of the month Açiyadiya XXVI days were past, then we fought the battle.

§19. 1.90–6. Saith Darius the King: After that I went off to Babylon. When I had not arrived at Babylon, a town by name Zazana, beside the Euphrates—there this Nidintu-Bel who called himself Nebuchadrezzar came with an army against me, to deliver battle. Thereupon we joined battle; Ahuramazda bore me aid; by the favor of Ahuramazda I smote that army of Nidintu-Bel exceedingly. The rest was thrown into the water, (and) the water carried it away. Of the month Anamaka II days were past, then we fought the battle.

DB II — TEXTS WITH NOTES AND TRANSLATION — 121

TEXT OF DB, COLUMN II:

1 : θātiy : Dārayavauš : xšāyaθiya : *pasāva* : Naditabaira : ha
2 dā : kamnaibiš : asabāraibiš : a*muθa* : *Bābi*rum : ašiya
3 va : pasāva : adam : Bābirum : ašiyavam : *vašnā* : *Auramazdā*ha : utā : Bā
4 birum : agarbāyam : utā : avam : Naditaba*iram* : *agarbāya*m : pasāva : ava
5 m : Naditabairam : adam : Bābirauv : avāja*nam* : *θātiy* : *Dārayavauš* : x
6 šāyaθiya : yātā : adam : Bābirauv : āha*m* : *imā* : *dahyāva* : tyā : hacāma : ha
7 miçiyā : abava : Pārsa : Ūvja : Māda : Aθurā : *Mudrāya* : *Par*θava : Marguš : Θa
8 taguš : Saka : θātiy : Dārayavauš : xšāyaθiya : *I marti*ya : Martiya : nā
9 ma : Cicixrāiš : puça : Kuganakā : nā*ma*. *vardanam* : *Pārsaiy* : avadā : adāraya :
10 hauv : udapatatā : Ūvjaiy : kārahyā : ava*θā* : *aθaha* : *adam* : Imaniš : amiy : Ū
11 vjaiy : xšāyaθiya : θātiy : Dārayavauš : *xšāyaθıya* : adakaiy : adam : ašna
12 iy : āham : abiy : Ūvjam : pasāva : hacā*ma* : *atarsa* : *Ūvji*yā : avam : Marti
13 yam : agarbāya : hyašām : maθišta : āha : *utāšim* : *avājana* : θātiy : D
14 ārayavauš : xšāyaθiya : I martiya : Fravartiš : *nāma* : *Māda* : hauv : udapatat
15 ā : Mādaiy : kārahyā : avaθā : aθaha : *adam* : *Xšaθrita* : *am*iy : Uvaxštrah
16 yā : taumāyā : pasāva : kāra : Māda : hya : *v*ᵊ*θāpatıy* : *hauv* : hacāma : hamiçiya : a
17 bava : abiy : avam : Fravartim : ašiyava : hauv : *xšāyaθiya* : abava : Mādaiy
18 θātiy : Dārayavauš : xšāyaθiya : kāra : Pārsa : u*tā* : *Māda* : hya : upā : mām : ā
19 ha : hauv : kamnam : āha : pasāva : adam : kāram : frāišay*am* : *Vidarna* : nāma : Pārsa : man
20 ā : badaka : avamšām : maθištam : akunavam : avaθāšā*m* : *aθaha*m : paraitā : avam : k
21 āram : tyam : Mādam : jatā : hya : manā : naiy : gaubataiy : pasāva : hauv : Vidarna : ha
22 dā : kārā : ašiyava : yaθā : Mādam : parārasa : Māru*š* : nāma : vardanam : Mā
23 daiy : avadā : hamaranam : akunauš : hadā : Māda*ibıš* : hya : Mādaišuvā
24 : maθišta : āha : hauv : adakaiy : naiy : avadā : āha : Auramazdāmaiy : u
25 pastām : abara : vašnā : Auramazdāha : kāra : *hya* : *manā* : avam : kāram : t
26 yam : hamiçiyam : aja : vasiy : Anāmakahya : māh*yā* : XXVII : raucabiš : θakat
27 ā : āha : avaθāšām : hamaranam : kartam : pasāva : hauv : *kāra* : hya : manā : Kapada : nām
28 ā : dahyāuš : Mādaiy : avadā : mām : amānaiya : yātā : adam : arasam : Māda
29 m : θātiy : Dārayavauš : xšāyaθiya : Dādaršiš : nāma : Arminiya : man
30 ā : badaka : avam : adam : frāišayam : Arminam : avaθāš*aiy* : *aθaha*m : paraidiy : kā
31 ra : hya : hamiçiya : manā : naiy : gaubataiy : avam : *jadiy* : pasāva : Dādarši
32 š : ašiyava : yaθā : Arminam : parārasa : pasāva : *hamiçıyā* : hagmatā : parai
33 tā : patiš : Dādaršim : hamaranam : cartanaiy : Zūzahya : nāma : āvahanam : A
34 rmᵊniyaiy : avadā : hamaranam : akunava : Auramazdāmaiy : upastām : a
35 bara : vašnā : Auramazdāha : kāra : hya : manā : avam · *k*āram : tyam : hamiçiyam :
36 aja : vasiy : Θūravāharahya : māh*yā* : *VIII* : *raucabiš* : θakatā : āha : avaθ
37 āšām : hamaranam : kartam : θātiy : Dārayavauš : *xšāyaθiya* : patiy : duv
38 itīyam : hamiçiyā : hagmatā : paraitā : *patiš* : *Dādarši*m : hamaranam : carta
39 naiy : Tigra : nāmā : didā : Armᵊniyaiy : avadā : hamaranam : akunava : A
40 uramazdāmaiy : upastām : abara : vašnā : Aura*mazdā*ha : kāra : hya : manā : a
41 vam : kāram : tyam : hamiçiyam : aja : vasi*y* · Θūravāharahya : māhyā : XVIII
42 : raucabiš : θakatā : āha : avaθāšām : hamaranam : ka*rtam* : θātiy : Dāraya
43 vauš : xšāyaθiya : patiy : çitīyam : ha*miçıyā* : hagmatā : paraitā : pat
44 iš : Dādaršim : hamaranam : cartanaiy : Uyamā : nā*ma* : didā : Armᶦniyaiy : a
45 vadā : hamaranam : akunava : Auramazdāmaiy : upastām : abara : vašnā : Aurama
46 zdāha : kāra : hya : manā : avam : kāram : tyam : hamiçiyam : aja : vasiy : Θāigarca
47 iš : māhyā : IX : raucabiš : θakatā : āha : avaθāšām : hamaranam : kartam : pasāva
48 : Dādaršiš : citā : mām : amānaya : Armᵊniyaiy : yātā : adam : arasam : Mā

49 dam   : θātiy : Dārayavauš : xšāyaθiya : *pasāva* : Vaumisa : nāma : Pārsa : manā : ba
50 daka : avam : adam : frāišayam : Arminam : avaθāšaiy : aθaham : paraidiy : kāra :
51 hya : hamiçiya : manā : naiy : gaubataiy : avam : jadiy : pasāva : Vaumisa : a
52 šiyava : yaθā : Arminam : parārasa : pasāva : hamiçi*y*ā : hagmatā : paraitā : pa
53 tiš : Vaumisam : hamaranam : cartanaiy : Izalā : nāmā : dahyāuš : Aθurāy
54 ā : avadā : hamaranam : akunava : Auramazdā*m*aiy : upastām : abara : vašnā : Au
55 ramazdāha : kāra : hya : manā : avam : kāram : *tyam* : hamiçiyam : aja : vasiy :
56 Anāmakahya : māhyā : XV : raucabiš : θakatā : āha : avaθāšām : hamaranam :
57 kartam   : θātiy : Dārayavauš : xšāyaθiya : patiy : duvitīyam : ham
58 içiyā : hagmatā : paraitā : patiš : Vaumisam : hamaranam : cartanaiy : Au
59 tiyāra : nāmā : dahyāuš : Arminiyaiy : avadā : hamaranam : akunava :
60 Auramazdāmaiy : upastām : abara : vašnā : Auramazdāha : kāra : hya : ma
61 nā : avam : kāram : tyam : hamiçiyam : aja : vasiy : Θūravāharahya : māh
62 yā : jiyamnam : patiy : avaθāšām : hamaranam : kartam : pasāva : Vaumisa
63 : citā : mām : amānaya : Arminiyā*iy* : yātā : adam : arasam : Mādam
64 : θātiy : Dārayavauš : xšāyaθiya : pasāva : adam : nijāyam : hacā :
65 Bābirauš : ašiyavam : Mādam : yaθā : Mādam : parārasam : Kud^uruš : nāma :
66 vardanam : Mādaiy : avadā : hauv : Fravartiš : hya : Mādaiy : xšāyaθiya : a
67 gaubatā : āiš : had*ā* : kārā : patiš : mām : hamaranam : cartanaiy : pasāva : hamarana
68 m : akumā : Auramazdāmaiy : upastām : abara : vašnā : Auramazdāha : kāram
69 : tyam : Fravartaiš : adam : ajanam : vasiy : Aduka*naiš*ahya : māhyā : XXV : ra
70 ucabiš : θakatā : āha : avaθā : hamaranam : akumā   : θātiy : Dārayavauš : x
71 šāyaθiya : pasāva : hauv : Fravartiš : hadā : kamnaibiš : asabāraibiš : amuθa : Ra
72 gā : nāmā : dahyāuš : Mādaiy : avaparā : ašiyava : pasāva : adam : kāram : f
73 rāišayam : nipadiy : Fravartiš : āgarbī*ta* : anayatā : abiy : mām : ada
74 mšai*y* : utā : nāham : utā : gaušā : utā : h^azānam : frājanam : utāša
75 iy : I cašam : avajam : duvarayāmaiy : basta : adāriya : haruvašim : k
76 āra : avaina : pasāvašim : Hagmatānaiy : uzmayāpatiy : akunavam
77 : utā : ma*r*tıyā : tyaišaiy : fratamā : anušiyā : āhatā : avaiy : Ha
78 gmatā*naiy* : *atar* : didām : frāhajam   : θātiy : Dārayavauš : xš
79 āyaθiya : I ma*r*tiya : Ciçataxma : nāma : Asagartiya : hauvmaiy : hamiçiya :
80 abava : kārahyā : avaθā : aθaha : adam : xšāyaθiya : amiy : Asagarta
81 iy : Uvaxštrah*yā* : taumāyā : pasāva : adam : kāram : Pārsam : ut
82 ā : Mādam : frāišayam : Taxmaspāda : nāma : Māda : manā : badaka : avam
83 šām : maθištam : akunavam : *ava*θāšām : aθaham : paraitā : k
84 āram : hamiçiyam : hya : manā : naiy : gaubātaiy : avam : jatā : pas
85 āva : Taxmaspāda : hadā : kārā : *a*šiyava : hamaranam : akunauš : had
86 ā : Ciçataxmā : Auramazdāmaiy : upastām : abara : vašnā : Auramaz
87 dāha : kāra : hya : manā : avam : kāram : tyam : hamiçiyam : aja : utā : C
88 içataxmam : agarbāya : anaya : abiy : mām : pasāvašaiy : adam : utā : n
89 āham : utā : gaušā : frājanam : utāšaiy : I cašam : avajam : duvarayā
90 maiy : basta : adāriya : haruvašim : kāra : *avaina* : pasāvašim : Arbairāyā :
91 uzmayāpati*y* : akunavam   : θātiy : Dārayavauš : xšāyaθiya : ima : tya : ma
92 nā : kartam : Mādaiy   : θātiy : Dārayavauš : xšāyaθiya : Parθava : utā : Var
93 kāna : *hamiçiyā* : abava : hac*āma* : Fravar*taiš* : *agaubatā* : V¹štāspa : manā : pitā : ha
94 uv : Par*θ*avaiy : āha : avam : kāra : avahar*da* : *hamiçiya* : abava : pasāva : V¹štāspa :
95 *a*š*ı*yava : hadā : *k*ārā : hyašaiy : anuši*ya* : āha : Viš*p*auzātiš : nāma : varda
96 *nam* : Parθavaiy : avadā : hamaranam : *akunauš* : hadā : Parθavaibiš : A*uramazdā*maiy
97 : upastām : abara : vašnā : A*uramazdāha* : V¹štāspa : avam : kāra*m* : *tyam* : hamiçiya
98 m : *aja* : *vasiy* : V*iy*axnahya : māhyā : *XXII* : *raucabiš* : θakatā : āha : avaθāšām : hamaranam :
                                                                                                                        kartam

Notes to DB II: ² *asabāraıbıš*, form established by *asabāra* DNb 41-5   ² *a*[*muθa*] Husing, Wb , for *a*[*bıy*] Rl , *ab*[*ıy*] KT. ⁷ [*Mudrāya*] Wb., KT, after the Elam ²⁴ *avadā : āha* legible, acc to Cameron ²⁵ [*ma*]*nā* KT. ²⁶ *XXVII* KT ²⁸ *amᵃanᵃıyᵃ* KT ³³ *zᵃuzᵃhᵃyᵃ* legible, acc to Cameron ³³⁻⁴ *arᵃmᵢnᵃıyᵃıyᵃ* KT; so also in 39, 44 ⁴⁴ *uyᵃmᵃa* legible, acc to Cameron.

⁵³ *ızᵃlᵃa* legible, acc to Cameron, eliminating various conjectures ⁶² *jıyamnam*, for KT's *jıyamanam*. ⁶⁹ *Adukanaıš* WB; *Aduka*[*nı*]*šahya* KT ⁷² *avaparā* KT. ⁷³ *nıpadıy* KT ⁷³ *āgarbī*[*ta*] Bthl WZKM 22 65, for KT's *agarbı*[*ta*]; immediately followed by *anayatā*, without intervening *utā*, acc. to KT ⁷⁴ *hᵃzᵃanᵃmᵃ* legible, acc to Cameron, eliminating the conjectures ⁷⁵ [*I caša*]*m*, after 2 89, q v. ⁷⁶ *pasāvašım* KT ⁷⁶ For 'impaled' rather than 'crucified', cf. Wb. KIA 39n

⁸⁴ *kāram : hamıçıyam* KT, without Rl 's *tyam* between the words. ⁸⁹ *I cᵃšᵃmᵃ* legible, acc to Cameron, settling old disputes; [*u*]*cšam* KT, +*cašma* Jn , *ucašma* Wb , *ucašam* Kent Lg. 19.225-6; *cašma* Bv TPS 1945 53-4, after Jn. IF 25 182-3 (cf. conj. of Spiegel, Altp. Keilinsch. 21n, 218), whence *cašam* Kent; see Lex s v. *caša*- ⁹²⁻⁹⁸ Except as noted, the supplements are those of WB and KT. ⁹³ Rl records *hya* as visible before *manā pıtā*; but KT omit without comment. ⁹⁴ *avahar*[+] KT, *avahar*[*ta*] Wb. ZDMG 61.726, *avahar*[*ja*] Tm VS 1 22, Lex 16, corrected to *avahar*[*da*] Tm CS 21. ⁹⁵ *Vıs*[*pa*]*uz*[*ā*]*tıš* KT; *Vısp*]*āvaušatıš* Rl ; *Vıspauzatıš* WB. ⁹⁶ *akunava* WB, *a*]*kunau*[*š* KT.

Rl has the following correct readings, in which he records as visible certain characters, here indicated by roman type, which were not visible to KT. ⁴ *Nadıtabaı*[*ram*]; ⁵ *θāti*]y . *Dārayavauš*; ⁶ *āham · *ı[*mā*, ⁷ *A*θ*urā*; ⁸ *xšāya*[*θıya*; ⁹ *nāma · var*[*danam*]; ¹⁰ *avaθā*; ¹¹ *Dārayavauš* : *xšāya*[*θıya*; ¹² *hacāma*; ²⁵ *hya*; ³⁶ *māhyā : VI* ra[*ucabıš* (*VI* is corrected to *VIII* by Rl on page 218); ³⁸ *paraıtā* : *pat*[*ıš*; ³⁹ *Armaniyaiy* (Rl. misread the third character); ⁴¹ *vasiy*; ⁴³ *ham*[*ıçıya*; ⁸¹ *Uvax*[*štra*]*hyā*; ⁹¹ *uzmayāpat*]*ıy*.

WB, from Wb 's reading of Rl 's squeezes, add the following, also in roman, which were not visible to KT, nor to Rl : ¹¹ *xšāyaθ*[*ıya*]; ¹⁴ *Frava*[*rtıš*]; ⁶³ *Armınıya*ı[*y*; ⁹⁰ *ava*[*ına*; ⁹³ *Fravartaıš* [·] *agaubatā*, ⁹⁵ *anušıya*; ⁹⁶ nam.

TRANSLATION OF DB II:

§20. 2.1–5. Saith Darius the King: After that, Nidintu-Bel with a few horsemen fled; he went off to Babylon. Thereupon I went to Babylon. By the favor of Ahuramazda both I seized Babylon and I took that Nidintu-Bel prisoner. After that, I slew that Nidintu-Bel at Babylon.

§21. 2.5–8. Saith Darius the King: While I was in Babylon, these are the provinces which became rebellious from me: Persia, Elam, Media, Assyria, Egypt, Parthia, Margiana, Sattagydia, Scythia.

§22. 2.8–11. Saith Darius the King: One man, by name Martıya, son of Cincikhri—a town by name Kuganaka, in Persia—there he abode. He rose up in Elam; to the people thus he said, "I am Imanish, king in Elam."

§23. 2.11–3. Saith Darius the King: At that time I was near unto Elam. Thereupon the Elamites were afraid of me; they seized that Martiya who was their chief, and slew him.

§24. 2.13–7. Saith Darius the King: One man, by name Phraortes, a Median—he rose up in Media. To the people thus he said, "I am Khshathrita, of the family of Cyaxares." Thereafter the Median army which (was) in the palace, became rebellious from me, (and) went over to that Phraortes. He became king in Media.

§25. 2.18–29. Saith Darius the King: The Persian and Median army which was with me, this was a small (force). Thereupon I sent forth an army. A Persian by name Hydarnes, my subject—him I made chief of them; thus I said to them: "Go forth, smite that Median army which does not call itself mine!" Thereupon this Hydarnes with the army marched off. When he arrived in Media, a town by name Maru, in Media—there he joined battle with the Medes. He who was chief among the Medes, he at that time was not there. Ahuramazda bore me aid; by the favor of Ahuramazda my army smote that rebellious army exceedingly. Of the month Anamaka XXVII days were past, then the battle was fought by them. Thereafter this army of mine, a district by name Kampanda, in Media— there it waited for me until I arrived in Media.

§26. 2.29–37. Saith Darius the King: An Armenian by name Dadarshi, my subject—him I sent forth to Armenia. Thus I said to him: "Go forth, that rebellious army which does not call itself mine, that do thou smite!" Thereupon Dadarshi marched off. When he arrived in Armenia, thereafter the rebels assembled (and) came out against Dadarshi to join battle. A place by name Zuzahya, in Armenia—there they joined battle. Ahuramazda bore me aid; by the favor of Ahuramazda my army smote that rebellious army exceedingly; of the month Thuravahara VIII days were past, then the battle was fought by them.

§27. 2.37–42. Saith Darius the King: Again a second time the rebels assembled (and) came out against Dadarshi to join battle. A stronghold by name Tigra, in Armenia—there they joined battle. Ahuramazda bore me aid; by the favor of Ahuramazda my army smote that rebellious army exceedingly; of the month Thuravahara XVIII days were past, then the battle was fought by them.

§28. 2.42–9. Saith Darius the King: Again a third time the rebels assembled (and) came out against Dadarshi to join battle. A fortress by name Uyama, in Armenia—there they joined battle. Ahuramazda bore me aid; by the favor of Ahuramazda my army smote that rebellious army exceedingly; of the month Thaigarci IX days were past, then the battle was fought by them. Thereafter Dadarshi waited for me until I arrived in Media.

§29. 2.49–57. Saith Darius the King: Thereafter a Persian by name Vaumisa, my subject—him I sent forth to Armenia. Thus I said to him: "Go forth; the rebellious army which does not call itself mine—that do thou smite!" Thereupon Vaumisa marched off. When he arrived in Armenia, then the rebels assembled (and) came out against Vaumisa to join battle. A district by name Izala, in Assyria—there they joined battle. Ahuramazda bore me aid; by the favor of Ahuramazda my army smote that rebellious army exceedingly; of the month Anamaka XV days were past, then the battle was fought by them.

§30. 2.57–63. Saith Darius the King: Again a second time the rebels assembled (and) came out against Vaumisa to join battle. A district by name Autiyara, in Armenia—there they joined battle. Ahuramazda bore me aid; by the favor of Ahuramazda my army smote that rebellious army exceedingly; on the last day of the month Thuravahara—then the battle was fought by them. After that, Vaumisa waited for me in Armenia until I arrived in Media.

§31. 2.64–70. Saith Darius the King: Thereafter I went away from Babylon (and) arrived in Media. When I arrived in Media, a town by name Kunduru, in Media—there this Phraortes who called himself king in Media came with an army against me to join battle. Thereafter we joined battle. Ahuramazda bore me aid; by the favor of Ahuramazda that army of Phraortes I smote exceedingly; of the month Adukanaisha XXV days were past, then we fought the battle.

§32. 2.70–8. Saith Darius the King: Thereafter this Phraortes with a few horsemen fled; a district by name Raga, in Media—along there he went off. Thereafter I sent an army in pursuit; Phraortes, seized, was led to me. I cut off his nose and ears and tongue, and put out one eye; he was kept bound at my palace entrance, all the people saw him. Afterward I impaled him at Ecbatana; and the men who were his foremost followers, those at Ecbatana within the fortress I (flayed and) hung out (their hides, stuffed with straw).

§33. 2.78–91. Saith Darius the King: One man by name Ciçantakhma, a Sagartian—he became rebellious to me; thus he said to the people, "I am king in Sagartia, of the family of Cyaxares." Thereupon I sent off a Persian and Median army; a Mede by name Takhmaspada, my subject—him I made chief of them. Thus I said to them: "Go forth; the hostile army which shall not call itself mine, that do ye smite!" Thereupon Takhmaspada with the army went off; he joined battle with Ciçantakhma. Ahuramazda bore me aid; by the favor of Ahuramazda my army smote that rebellious army and took Ciçantakhma prisoner, (and) led him to me. Afterwards I cut off his ears and nose and tongue, and put out one eye; he he was kept bound at my palace entrance, all the people saw him. Afterwards I impaled him at ' Arbela.

§34. 2.91–2. Saith Darius the King: This is what was done by me in Media.

§35. 2.92–8. Saith Darius the King: Parthia and Hyrcania became rebellious from me, called themselves (adherents) of Phraortes. Hystaspes my father—he was in Parthia; him the people abandoned, became rebellious. Thereupon Hystaspes went forth with the army which was faithful to him. A town by name Vishpauzati, in Parthia— there he joined battle with the Parthians. Ahuramazda bore me aid; by the favor of Ahuramazda Hystaspes smote that rebellious army exceedingly; of the month Viyakhna XXII days were past— then the battle was fought by them.

TEXT OF DB, COLUMN III:

1 : θātiy : Dārayavauš : xšāyaθiya : pasāva : adam : kāra
2 m : Pārsam : frāišayam : abiy : V¹štāspam : hacā : Ragā
3 yā : yaθā : hauv : kāra : parārasa : abiy : V¹štāspam

DB III   TEXTS WITH NOTES AND TRANSLATION   125

4 : pasāva : Vᵢštāspa : āyasatā : avam : kāram : ašiyava : Patigraba
5 nā : nāma : vardanam : Parθavaiy : avadā : hamaranam : akunauš : hadā :
6 hamiçiyaibiš : Auramazdāmaiy : upastām : abara : vašnā : Auramaz
7 dāha : Vᵢštāspa : avam : kāram : tyam : hamiçiyam : aja : vasiy : Ga
8 rmapadahya : māhyā : I : rauca : θakatam : āha : avaθāšām : hamaranam : ka
9 rtam   : θātiy : Dārayavauš : xšāyaθiya : pasāva : dahyāuš : ma
10 nā : abava : ima : tya : manā : kartam : Parθavaiy   : θātiy : Dārayavau
11 š : xšāyaθiya : Marguš : nāmā : dahyāuš : hauvmaiy : hamiçiyā : abava
12 : I martiya : Frāda : nāma : Mārgava : avam : maθištam : akunavatā : pasā
13 va : adam : frāišayam : Dādaršiš : nāma : Pārsa : manā : badaka : Bāxtriy
14 ā : xšaçapāvā : abiy : avam : avaθāšaiy : aθaham : paraidiy : ava
15 m : kāram : jadiy : hya : manā : naiy : gaubataiy : pasāva : Dādaršiš : hadā : k
16 ārā : ašiyava : hamaranam : akunauš : hadā : Mārgavaibiš : Auramazd
17 āmaiy : upastām : abara : vašnā : Auramazdāha : kāra : hya : manā : avam : kāram
18 : tyam : hamiçiyam : aja : vasiy : Āçiyādiyahya : māhyā : XXIII : raucabi
19 š : θakatā : āha : avaθāšām : hamaranam : kartam   : θātiy : Dārayavau
20 š : xšāyaθiya : pasāva : dahyāuš : manā : abava : ima : tya : ma
21 nā : kartam : Bāxtriyā   : θātiy : Dārayavauš : xšāya
22 θiya : I martiya : Vahyazdāta : nāma : Tāravā : nāma : vardanam
23 : Yautiyā : nāmā : dahyāuš : Pārsaiy : avadā : adāraya : ha
24 uv : duvitīyam : udapatatā : Pārsaiy : kārahyā : avaθā
25 : aθaha : adam : Bardiya : amiy : hya : Kūrauš : puça : pasāva
26 : kāra : Pārsa : hya : vᵢθāpatiy : hacā : Yadāyā : frataram : ha
27 uv : hacāma : hamiçiya : abava : abiy : avam : Vahyazdāta
28 m : ašiyava : hauv : xšāyaθiya : abava : Pārsaiy   : θā
29 tiy : Dārayavauš : xšāyaθiya : pasāva : adam : kāram : Pārsa
30 m : utā : Mādam : frāišayam : hya : upā : mām : āha : Artavard
31 iya : nāma : Pārsa : manā : badaka : avamšām : maθištam : aku
32 navam : hya : aniya : kāra : Pārsa : pasā : manā : ašiyava : Mā
33 dam : pasāva : Artavardiya : hadā : kārā : ašiyava : Pārsam
34 : yaθā : Pārsam : parārasa : Raxā : nāma : vardanam : Pārsaiy : a
35 vadā : hauv : Vahyazdāta : hya : Bardiya : agaubatā : āiš :
36 hadā : kārā : patiš : Artavardiyam : hamaranam : cartanaiy : pas
37 āva : hamaranam : akunava : Auramazdāmaiy : upastām : abara : va
38 šnā : Auramazdāha : kāra : hya : manā : avam : kāram : tyam : Vahya
39 zdātahya : aja : vasiy : Θūravāharahya : māhyā : XII : raucabiš : θaka
40 tā : āha : avaθāšām : hamaranam : kartam   : θātiy : Dārayavauš : xšāyaθi
41 ya : pasāva : hauv : Vahyazdāta : hadā : kamnaibiš : asabāraibiš : a
42 muθa : ašiyava : Paišiyāuvādām : hacā : avadaša : kāram : āyasa
43 tā : hyāparam : āiš : patiš : Artavardiyam : hamaranam : cartana
44 iy : Parga : nāma : kaufa : avadā : hamaranam : akunava : Auramazdāma
45 iy : upastām : abara : vašnā : Auramazdāha : kāra : hya : manā : ava
46 m : kāram : tyam : Vahyazdātahya : aja : vasiy : Garmapadahya : māh
47 yā : V : raucabiš : θakatā : āha : avaθāšām : hamaranam : kartam : utā : ava
48 m : Vahyazdātam : agarbāya : utā : martiyā : tyaišaiy : fratam
49 ā : anušiyā : āhata : agarbāya   : θātiy : Dārayavauš : xš
50 āyaθiya : pasāva : adam : avam : Vahyazdātam : utā : martiyā :
51 tyaišaiy : fratamā : anušiyā : āhata : Uvādaicaya : nāma : var
52 danam : Pārsaiy : avadašiš : uzmayāpatiy : akunavam   : θā
53 tiy : Dārayavauš : xšāyaθiya : ima : tya : manā : kartam : Pārsaiy   :

54 θātiy : Dārayavauš : xšāyaθiya : hauv : Vahyazdāta : hya : Bardiya
55 : agaubatā : hauv : kāram : frāišaya : Harauvatim : Vivāna :
56 nāma : Pārsa : manā : badaka : Harauvatiyā : xšaçapāvā : abiy : ava
57 m : utāšām : I martiyam : maθištam : akunauš : avaθāšām : a
58 θaha : paraitā : Vivānam : jatā : utā : avam : kāram : hya : Dāraya
59 vahauš : xšāyaθiyahyā : gaubataiy : pasāva : hauv : kāra : ašiya
60 va : tyam : Vahyazdāta : frāišaya : abiy : Vivānam : hamaranam : cartanaiy : K
61 āpišakāniš : nāmā : didā : avadā : hamaranam : akunava : Auramazdāmai
62 y : upastām : abara : vašnā : Auramazdāha : kāra : hya : manā : avam : kāram : tya
63 m : hamiçiyam : aja : vasiy : Anāmakahya : māhyā : XIII : raucabiš : θakatā : āha : a
64 vaθāšām : hamaranam : kartam   : θātiy : Dārayavauš : xšāyaθiya : patiy : h
65 yāparam : hamiçiyā : hagmatā : paraitā : patiš : Vivānam : hamaranam : cartana
66 iy : Gadutava : nāmā : dahyāuš : avadā : hamaranam : akunava : Auramazdāma
67 iy : upastām : abara : vašnā : Auramazdāha : kāra : hya : manā : avam : kāram : t
68 yam : hamiçiyam : aja : vasiy : Viyaxnahya : māhyā : VII : raucabiš : θakatā :
69 āha : avaθāšām : hamaranam : kartam   θātiy : Dārayavauš : xšāyaθiya :
70 pasāva : hauv : mart*iya* : hya : avahyā : kārahyā : maθi*šta* : *āha* : tyam : Va
71 hyazdāta : frāišaya : abiy : Vivānam : hauv : am*uθa* : *hadā* : kamnaib
72 iš : asabāraibiš : ašiyava : Aršādā : nāmā : didā : *H*arauvatiyā : a
73 vaparā : atiyāiš : pasāva : Vivāna : hadā : kārā : nipadiy : tyaiy : ašiya
74 va : avadāšim : agarbāya : u*ta* : martiyā : tyaišaiy : fratamā : anušiyā :
75 āhatā : avāja   θātiy : Dārayavauš : xšāyaθiya : pasāva : dahyāuš : ma
76 nā : abava : ima : tya : manā : kartam : Harauvatiyā   θātiy : Dārayavauš : xšā
77 yaθiya : yātā : adam : Pārsai*y* : u(t)ā : Mādaiy : āham : patiy : duvitīyam :
78 Bābiruviyā : hamiçiyā : abava : hacāma : I martiya : Arxa : nāma : *Ar*mini
79 ya : Halditahya : puça : hauv : udapatatā : Bābirauv : Dubāla : nāmā : *dahyā*
80 uš : hacā : avadaša : hauv : *k*ārahyā : avaθā : adurujiya : adam : Nabukud
81 racara : amiy : hya : Nabunaitahya : puça : pasāva : kāra : Bābiruviya : hacāma : ha
82 miçiya : abava : abiy : avam : Arxam : ašiyava : Bābirum : hauv : agarbāyat
83 ā : hauv : xšāyaθiya : abava : Bābirauv   : θātiy : Dā*rayavauš* : *x*šāyaθi
84 ya : pasāva : adam : kāram : frāišayam : Bābirum : Vidafar*nā* : nāma : Pārsa : manā
85 : badaka : avamšām : maθištam : akunavam : avaθāšām : aθaham : para*itā* : *ava*m : kāram
86 : Bābiruvi*yam* : jatā : hya : manā : naiy : *ga*ubātaiy : pasāva : *Vi*da*far*nā : hadā : kār
87 ā : ašiyava : Bābirum : Auramazdāmaiy : upastām : *a*bara : vašnā : Auramaz
88 dāha : Vida*far*nā : Bābiruviyā : aja : utā : *bastā* : *anaya* : Varkazanahya : māhyā : XXII : ra
89 ucabiš : θakatā : āha : avaθā : avam : Arxam : hya : Nabukudracara : a
90 gaubatā : utā : martiyā : tyaišaiy : fratamā : anušiyā : āhatā : agarbāya : pa
91 sāva : niyaštāyam : *hauv* : Arxa : utā : martiyā : tyaišaiy : fratamā : an
92 ušiyā : āhatā : Bābirauv : uzmayāpatiy : akariyatā

NOTES TO DB III. [8]θakatam KT. [11]hamiçiyā KT. [14]paraidiy KT [16]Mārgavaibiš KT [18]Açiyādiyahya KT. [26]yadāyā Rl., KT, Cameron; not yaudādā nor yutiyā with Foy, nor Ma^ndāyā with Hz ApI 244-9; but see Lex s v. ²yadā- [26]frataram Cameron, confirmed by the Elamite ir-pi, this does away with the frātarta of Rl. and KT. [47]V KT [49]āhata Rl , KT; so also in 51; cf §36 IVc. [53-4]Rl lost a line here by haplography; corrected by KT. [55]agaubatā is engraved ag^aur^at^a, KT [66]g^ad^ut^av^a Rl , KT, Wb KIA; perhaps to be read g^ad^um^av^a, with Justi ZDMG 51 240, HK, Tm , because of Elam gan-du-ma-+, but see Wb KIA 144 [67] abara is engraved ar^ar^a, KT. [71] maθ[išta Rl.; am[uθa KT. [73] nipadiyam iy Rl ; nipadiy : tyaiy WB; nipadi[y :] t[ya]iy KT [77] utā is engraved ua, KT.

[80] [k]ārahyā KT [81] Nabunaitahya KT; cf §36 IVb. [84] v^id^af^ar^[n^a KT, cf 86 and 88; v^id^af^ar^a Rl [84] Pā[rsa] KT, cf 4 83; Māda Rl [86] Rl 's tyam at the beginning of the line is not there, acc to KT. [86] Bābiruvi[ya]m KT. [86] [ga]ubātaiy KT; gaub&taiy Rl [87] Rl.'s abiy between ašiyava and Bābirum is not on the Rock, acc to KT. [88] v^id^a[f^ar^]n^a KT, v^id^a[f^ar^]a Rl [88]Bābiruvi[y]ā : aja KT; Bābirum agarbāya Rl , WB [88] [agarbāya] WBn, HK, [basta : anaya] or [anaya : abiy . mām] Tm. VS [88] r nahya WB, WBn; Margazānahyā HK; [Ma]r[gaja]nahya

Wb KIA, stating that the first character could be also v^a, the third k^a or c^a, the fourth c^a or z^a; [Varkazanahya] Kent (all after the Elamite and the traces of OP characters in Rl's squeezes) [88] XXII KT

[90-2] As read and restored by KT (who followed WB's restorations), except as noted in the following [90] The t^a before and after the first gap were visible to Cameron, though not to KT. [90] tyaıšaı[y : fratamā :] anušıyā [: āhatā : agarbāya] Wb, after the traces seen by KT; tyaıšaı[y now confirmed by Cameron, who found the rest illegible [90-1] [pasāva : nıyaš]tāyam Wb after traces seen by KT; $t^a ay^a m^a$ still legible, acc to Cameron [92] asarıyatā KT, ākarıyatām WB; akarıya^{n}tā Bthl., WBn

Rl has the following correct readings, in which he records as legible certain characters, here indicated by roman type, which were not visible to KT. [73] nıpadiy; [74] utā, [78] Armını-; [79] dahyā-; [83] Dārayavauš . xšāyaθı-; [85] paraıtā avam; [87] upastam; [87] abara; [89] θakatā

TRANSLATION OF DB III:

§36. 3.1–9. Saith Darius the King: After that I sent forth a Persian army to Hystaspes, from Raga. When this army came to Hystaspes, thereupon Hystaspes took that army (and) marched out. A town by name Patigrabana, in Parthia—there he joined battle with the rebels. Ahuramazda bore me aid; by the favor of Ahuramazda Hystaspes smote that rebellious army exceedingly; of the month Garmapada I day was past—then the battle was fought by them.

§37. 3.9–10. Saith Darius the King: After that the province became mine. This is what was done by me in Parthia.

§38. 3.10–9. Saith Darius the King: A province by name Margiana—it became rebellious to me. One man by name Frada, a Margian—him they made chief. Thereupon I sent forth against him a Persian by name Dadarshi, my subject, satrap in Bactria. Thus I said to him: "Go forth, smite that army which does not call itself mine!" After that, Dadarshi marched out with the army; he joined battle with the Margians. Ahuramazda bore me aid; by the favor of Ahuramazda my army smote that rebellious army exceedingly; of the month Açiyadiya XXIII days were past—then the battle was fought by them.

§39. 3.19–21. Saith Darius the King: After that the province became mine. This is what was done by me in Bactria.

§40. 3.21–8. Saith Darius the King: One man by name Vahyazdata—a town by name Tarava, a district by name Yautiya, in Persia—there he abode. He made the second uprising in Persia. To the people thus he said: "I am Smerdis, the son of Cyrus." Thereupon the Persian army which (was) in the palace, (having come) from Anshan previously—it became rebellious from me, went over to that Vahyazdata. He became king in Persia.

§41. 3.28–40. Saith Darius the King: Thereupon I sent forth the Persian and Median army which was by me. A Persian by name Artavardiya, my subject—him I made chief of them. The rest of the Persian army went forth behind me to Media. Thereupon Artavardiya with his army went forth to Persia. When he arrived in Persia, a town by name Rakha, in Persia—there this Vahyazdata who called himself Smerdis came with his army against Artavardiya, to join battle. Thereupon they joined battle. Ahuramazda bore me aid; by the favor of Ahuramazda my army smote that army of Vahyazdata exceedingly; of the month Thuravahara XII days were past—then the battle was fought by them.

§42. 3.40–9. Saith Darius the King: After that, Vahyazdata with a few horsemen fled; he went off to Paishiyauvada. From there he got an army; later he came against Artavardiya to join battle. A mountain by name Parga—there they joined battle. Ahuramazda bore me aid; by the favor of Ahuramazda my army smote that army of Vahyazdata exceedingly; of the month Garmapada V days were past—then the battle was fought by them, and that Vahyazdata they took prisoner, and those who were his foremost followers they captured.

§43. 3.49–52. Saith Darius the King: After that I that Vahyazdata and those who were his foremost followers—a town by name Uvadaicaya, in Persia—there them I impaled.

§44. 3.52–3. Saith Darius the King: This is what was done by me in Persia.

§45. 3.54–64. Saith the King: This Vahyazdata who called himself Smerdis had sent an army to Arachosia—a Persian by name Vivana, my subject, satrap in Arachosia—against him; and he had made one man their chief. Thus he said to them: "Go forth; smite Vivana and that army which calls itself King Darius's!" Thereupon this army marched off, which Vahyazdata had sent forth against Vivana to join battle. A fortress by name Kapishakani—there they joined battle. Ahuramazda bore me aid; by the favor of Ahuramazda my army smote that rebellious army exceedingly; of the month Anamaka XIII days were past—then the battle was fought by them.

§46. 3.64.-9. Saith Darius the King: Again later the rebels assembled (and) came out against Vivana to join battle. A district by name Gandutava—there they joined battle. Ahuramazda bore me aid; by the favor of Ahuramazda my army smote that rebellious army exceedingly; of the month Viyakhna VII days were past—then the battle was fought by them.

§47. 3.69–75. Saith Darius the King: After that, this man who was the chief of that army which Vahyazdata had sent forth against Vivana —he fled with a few horsemen (and) got away. A fortress by name Arshada, in Arachosia—past that he went. Afterwards Vivana with his army went off in pursuit of them; there he took him prisoner and the men who were his foremost followers, (and) slew (them).

§48. 75–6. Saith Darius the King: After that the province became mine. This is what was done by me in Arachosia.

§49. 3.76–83. Saith Darius the King: While I was in Persia and Media, again a second time the Babylonians became rebellious from me. One man by name Arkha, an Armenian, son of Haldita— he rose up in Babylon. A district by name Dubala —from there he thus lied to the people: "I am Nebuchadrezzar the son of Nabonidus." Thereupon the Babylonian people became rebellious from me, (and) went over to that Arkha. He seized Babylon; he became king in Babylon.

§50. 3.83–92. Saith Darius the King: Thereupon I sent forth an army to Babylon. A Persian by name Intaphernes, my subject—him I made chief of them. Thus I said to them: "Go forth; that Babylonian army smite, which shall not call itself mine!" Thereupon Intaphernes with the army marched off to Babylon. Ahuramazda bore me aid; by the favor of Ahuramazda Intaphernes smote the Babylonians and led them in bonds; of the month Varkazana XXII days were past— then that Arkha who called himself Nebuchadrezzar and the men who were his foremost followers he took prisoner. Afterwards I issued an order: this Arkha and the men who were his foremost followers were impaled at Babylon.

TEXT OF DB, COLUMN IV:

1 : θātiy : Dārayavauš : xšāyaθiya : ima : t
2 ya : manā : kartam : Bābirauv : θātiy : D
3 ārayavauš : xšāyaθiya : ima : tya : adam : akuna
4 vam : vašnā : Auramazdāha : hamahyāyā : θar
5 da : pasāva : yaθā : xšāyaθiya : abavam : XIX : hamaran
6 ā : akunavam : vašnā : Auramazdāha : adamšim : a
7 janam : utā : IX : xšāyaθiyā : agarbāyam : I Gaumāta :
8 nāma : maguš : āha : hauv : adurujiya : avaθā : aθaha : adam :
9 Bardiya : amiy : hya : Kūrauš : puça : hauv : Pārsam : ha
10 miçiyam : akunauš : I Āçina : nāma : Ūvjiya : hauv : adu
11 rujiya : avaθā : aθaha : adam : xšāyaθiya : amiy : Ūvjaiy
12 : hauv : Ūvjam : hamiçiyam : akunauš : manā : I Naditabaira : n
13 āma : Bābiruviya : hauv : adurujiya : avaθā : aθaha :
14 adam : Nabukudracara : amiy : hya : Nabunaitahya : puça :
15 hauv : Bābirum : hamiçiyam : akunauš : I Martiya : nā
16 ma : Pārsa : hauv : adurujiya : avaθā : aθaha : adam : Imani
17 š : amiy : Ūvjaiy : xšāyaθiya : hauv : Ūvjam : hamiçiya
18 m : akunauš : I Fravartiš : nāma : Māda : hauv : adurujiya
19 : avaθā : aθaha : adam : Xšaθrita : amiy : Uvaxštrahya : taumāy
20 ā : hauv : Mādam : hamiçiyam : akunauš : I Çiçataxma : nāma : Asa
21 gartiya : hauv : adurujiya : avaθā : aθaha : adam : xšāyaθ
22 iya : amiy : Asagartaiy : Uvaxštrahya : taumāyā : hauv
23 : Asagartam : hamiçiyam : akunauš : I Frāda : nāma :
24 Mārgava : hauv : adurujiya : avaθā : aθaha : adam :

25 xšāyaθiya : amiy : Margauv : hauv : Margum : hamiçi
26 yam : akunauš : I Vahyazdāta : nāma : Pārsa : hauv : a
27 durujiya : avaθā : aθaha : adam : Bardiya : amiy : hya : Kū
28 rauš : puça : hauv : Pārsam : hamiçiyam : akunauš : I Ar
29 xa : nāma : Arminiya : hauv : adurujiya : avaθā : aθaha : adam : Nab
30 ukudracara : amiy : hya : Nabunaitahya : puça : hauv : Bābirum : ham
31 içiyam : akunauš   : θātiy : Dārayavauš : xšāyaθiya : imaiy :
32 IX : xšāyaθiyā : adam : agarbāyam : atar : imā : hamaranā
33 : θātiy : Dārayavauš : xšāyaθiya : dahyāva : imā : tyā : hamiçiy
34 ā : abava : drauga : diš : hamiçiyā : akunauš : tya : imaiy : kāram : adur
35 ujiyaša : pasāva : diš : Auramazdā : manā : dastayā : akunauš : yaθā : mām : k
36 āma : avaθā : diš : akunavam   : θātiy : Dārayavauš : xšāyaθi
37 ya : tuvam : kā : xšāyaθiya : hya : aparam : āhy : hacā : drauga : daršam :
38 patipayauvā : martiya : hya : draujana : ahatiy : avam : ufraštam : parsā : ya
39 diy : avaθā : maniyāhaiy : dahyāušmaiy : duruvā : ahati
40 y   : θātiy : Dārayavauš : xsāyaθiya : ima : tya : adam : akunavam :
41 vašnā : Auramazdāha : hamahyāyā : θarda : akunavam : tuvam : kā : hya
42 : aparam : imām : dipim : patiparsāhy : tya : manā : kartam : varnavatām
43 : θuvām : mātya : draujīyāhy   : θātiy : Dārayavauš : xšā
44 yaθiya : Auramazdāha : ragam : vartaiyaiy : yaθā : ima : hašiyam : naiy : duru
45 xtam : adam : akunavam : hamahyāyā : θarda   : θātiy : Dārayavauš : xšāya
46 θiya : vašnā : Auramazdāha : utāmaiy : aniyašciy : vasiy : astiy : karta
47 m : ava : ahyāyā : dipiyā : naiy : nipištam : avahyarādiy : naiy : n
48 ipištam : mātya : hya : aparam : imām : dipim : patiparsātiy : avah
49 yā : paruv : θadayātaiy : tya : manā : kartam : naišim : ima : varnavātaiy : d
50 uruxtam : maniyātaiy   : θātiy : Dārayavauš : xšāyaθiya : tyaiy
51 : paruvā : xšāyaθiyā : yātā : āha : avaišām : avā : naiy : astiy : kar
52 tam : yaθā : manā : vašnā : Auramazdāha : hamahyāyā : θarda : kartam   : θā
53 tiy : Dārayavauš : xšāyaθiya : nūram : θuvām : varnavatām : tya : man
54 ā : kartam : avaθā : kārahyā : rādiy : mā : apagaudaya : yadiy : imām :
55 hadugām : naiy : apagaudayāhy : kārahyā : θāhy : Auramazdā : θuvām :
56 dauštā : biyā : utātaiy : taumā : vasiy : biyā : utā : dargam : jīvā
57 : θātiy : Dārayavauš : xšāyaθiya : yadiy : imām : hadugām : apagaudayā
58 hy : naiy : θāhy : kārahyā : Auramazdātay : jatā : biyā : utātaiy : taum
59 ā : mā : biyā   : θātiy : Dārayavauš : xšāyaθiya : ima : tya : adam : akunavam :
60 hamahyāya : θarda : vašnā : Auramazdāha : akunavam : Auramazdāmaiy : upas
61 tām : abara : utā : aniyāha : bagāha : tyaiy : hatiy   : θātiy : Dārayavau
62 š : xšāyaθiya : avahyarādiy : Auramazdā : upastām : abara : utā : ani
63 yāha : bagāha : tyaiy : hatiy : yaθā : naiy : arika : āham : naiy : draujana : āham : na
64 iy : zūrakara : āham : naiy : adam : naimaiy : taumā : upariy : arštām : upariy
65 āyam : naiy : škaurim : naiy : tunuvatam : zūra : akunavam : martiya : hya : hamata
66 xšatā : manā : v¹θiyā : avam : ubartam : abaram : hya : viyanāθaya : avam : ufrasta
67 m : aparsam   : θātiy : Dārayavauš : xšāyaθiya : tuvam : kā : xšāyaθiya :
68 hya : aparam : āhy : martiya : hya : draujana : ahatiy : hyavā : zūrakara : ahat
69 iy : avaiy : mā : dauštā : biyā : ufraštādiy : parsā   : θātiy : Dāra
70 yavauš : xšāyaθiya : tuvam : kā : hya : aparam : imām : dipim : vaināhy : ty
71 ām : adam : niyapaišam : imaivā : patikarā : mātya : vikanāhy : yāvā : u
72 tava : āhy : avaθāšatā : paribarā   : θātiy : Dārayavauš : xšāyaθiya : ya
73 diy : imām : dipim : vaināhy : imaivā : patikarā : naiydiš : vikanāhy : utā
74 taiy : yāvā : taumā : ahatiy : paribarāhªdiš : Auramazdā : θuvām : dauštā : biy

75 ā : utātaiy : tau*mā* : vasiy : bi*y*ā : utā : dargam : jīvā : utā : tya : kunavāhy
76 : avataiy : Auramazdā : ucāram : kunautuv   θātiy : Dārayavauš : xšā
77 yaθiya : yadiy : imām : dipim : imaivā : patikarā : vaināhy : vikanāh[a]diš : ut
78 ātaiy : yāvā : tau*mā* : ahati*y* : *nai*ydiš : paribarāhy : Auramazdātaiy : jatā : b
79 iyā : utātaiy : tau*mā* : *mā* : bi*y*ā : utā : tya : kunavāhy : avataiy : Auramazd
80 ā : nikatuv   θātiy : Dā*r*ayavauš : xšāyaθiya : imaiy : martiyā : tyaiy
81 : adakaiy : avadā : āhatā : yātā : adam : Gaumātam : tyam : magum : avājanam :
82 hya : Bardiya : aga*u*batā : adakaiy · imaiy : martiyā : hamataxšatā : anušiyā : man
83 ā : Vidafarnā : nā*ma* : Vāyaspārahyā : puça : Pārsa : Utāna : nā*ma* : Θuxrahyā
84 : puça : Pārsa : G*au*baruva : nāma : Marduniyahyā · puça : Pārsa : V*i*darna : nāma : Ba
85 *gā*bignahyā : puça : Pārsa : Ba*gā*buxša : nāma : Dāt*u*vahyahyā : puça : Pārsa :
86 Ar*du*maniš : nāma : Vahau*ka*hyā : puça : Pārsa   θātiy : Dārayavauš : xšāyaθ
87 iya : tuvam : *kā* : xšāyaθiya : hya : aparam : āhy : tyām : imaišām : martiyā*nā*
88 m : taumām : ubartām : par*i*barā   θātiy : Dārayavauš : xšāyaθiya : vašnā : *A*u
89 *r*amazdāha : i(mā)m : dipim : ani*y*aθā : adam : akunavam : patišam : ariyā : āha : utā : avast
90 āyā : cāxri*y*atā : patišam : iya : *d*ipiš : hama : āθahavaja : *n*ipištiyā : adā
91 *ray*atā : utā : apiθiya : utā : atīyas*i*ya : paišiyā : mā*m* : pasāva : i(ya)m : d
92 ipiš : *h*acāma : amāvatā : *har*uvadā : atar : dahyā*v*a : *kā*ra : hama : amaxmatā

NOTES TO DB IV. [4] *Aura[mazd]āha* WBn, for Rl's *Au[ramazdā ā]ha*, KT's *Aura[mazdāha :] āha* [5] Correctly read by WB from Rl's squeezes (against Rl's wrong readings), as well as by KT [6-7] *adamšim* KT is correct (confirmed by Cameron, who notes a space between *š*[a] and the following *i*), see §258 III and Lex s v. *ša-*; the suggestion has been made that the clauses have been shifted in order, the original being *adam : IX : xšāyaθiyā : agarbāyam : utāšim · ajanam*, but uncompounded *jan-* means only 'defeat (the foe)', not 'put (individuals) to death' (JAOS 35 349-50) [9] *amiy* Rl, KT; with blank unengraved space on each side of the *a*, acc. to KT [12] *[ma]nā [. I* KT; *manā : [I* Cameron [26] A blank space of one character at the beginning of the line, KT.
[36] A blank space of one character between the divider and the following *di[š*, KT [36] *[akunavam]* WB, KT; but KT state that the traces of the last letter are possibly those of *š*[a], which leads to a restored *akunauš* (so also Rl), of which *Auramazdā* would have to be the implied subject (cf Oppert's restoration, IdA 150) It is more probable that the phrase is here as in DB 5 17, 29, 33, and that *akunavam* is correct [37] *ah*[a]*y*[a] Rl, KT; first correctly normalized *āhy* by Tm VS 1 30 So also 4 68, 72, 87 [38] *ufraštam* KT [39] *man[iyāhy]* Opp IdA, etc , KT, *man[iyāhay]* Tm after DPe 20, *man[iyāhaiy]* Kent, since there is no reason to assume here the defective writing of DPe
[43]]*iy*[a]*ah*[a]*y*[a] Rl ; *[duruj]iyāhy* Spiegel, KT; *[duruxtam : man]iyāhy* WB, *[duru]jiyāhy* WBn, *[drau]jiyāhy* Bthl AiW 769, after Rl JRAS 12 vi, who states that *u* and *j*[1] are still to be read [44] *Auramaz[dā] Rl , Auramazd-[iya]taiyiya* WB, from Rl's squeezes, *Auramazd[ā]rtaiyiya* with room for 4 or 5 characters in the gap, KT, various restorations and interpretations, Bthl WZKM 22 69, Tm VS 1.30, Lex 122 (with lit), HK 1 28, 1 61 (with lit), 2.26, Wb KIA 62-3n, Kent JAOS 63 67-8; all supplanted now by Cameron's reading, *aur*[a]*m*[a]*z*[a]*d*[a]*ah*[a]*d*[u]*g*[a]*m*[a] *: [v*[a]*]r*[a]*taiy*[a]*iy*[a] (part of *v*[a] legible), which must be reinterpreted to *Auramazdāha : ragam : vartaiyaiy* (gen-dat. of goal, §250 I; and see Lex s vv. *raga-, vart-*). [46] *tya]maiy* Rl ; *api]maiy* WB, *ap]imaiy* KT; *ut]āmaiy* Bthl AiW 83, Gray AJP 30.457; *utāmaiy* (all characters visible) Cameron [49] θā[Rl., θada[yātiy WB; θā[dutiy, with traces of the third character still visible, KT, θa[n]da[yātaiy HK 1 28; θada[yā]h Bthl. AiW 1559; θadayā legible, Cameron. The second character was *d*[a] rather than KT's *a*, Jn , and KT's traces of the third character fit *y*[a] as well as they do *d*[u] Elsewhere (except in DNa 58) forms of this verb are all middle, and as the subjunctive always has primary endings in OP (§222), the restoration is θadayā[taiy], the necessary space being the same as for KT's restoration
[51] *avā* Rl, KT; reading assured, but apparently an omission in the engraving (*av*[a]*a* for *av*[a]θ[a]*a*), Mt. Gr. 59. [52] *kartam* KT. [53] No gap between *xšāyaθiya* and *nūram*, Jn , KT. [54] *sā[ ]d*[a]*[ ]ādiy* with vertical hasta at end of last gap, KT; *kā[rahyā . θ]ā[hy : avahya]rādiy* Tm. (after Rl.'s *[avah]yarādiy*), but this is too long; Cameron's *kārahya [:] rādiy*, with *rā* of *rādiy* slightly doubtful, is to be accepted, though Cameron finds in Elam 3 74 'to the people tell (it)' for this phrase.
[55] *hadugām* WB, KT, for Rl 's incorrect *dipim*
[64] *arštām* Foy KZ 35 45 (conj), Jn , KT, for Rl.'s incorrect *abištām* [64-5] Definitive reading by Cameron, *upariy | ā[ya]m [ ] naiy : šakaurim : naiy : t[u]nuvatam*, confirming *upariy[āyam]* of WB, HK, Wb. KIA; *šakaurim* WB, Jn , *šakauri[m]* KT, Tm , Wb. KIA (read rather *škaurim*, see Lex s v. *skauθi-*); *[naiy]* Spiegel; *uvata* Rl , *]nuvatam* Jn , *t[u]nuvatam* KT. [65] *zuku* Rl , *zūra* Rl. later [65] *hya* WB (from Rl's squeezes), Jn.; omitted by KT. [66] *v*[a]θ[a]*ib*[a] Rl ; *v[i]θiyā* WB, Jn.; *v*[a]θi[yā KT [66] *viyanā[sa]ya* WB, KT, HK, Tm , Wb. KIA; correctly *viyanā[θa]ya* Foy KZ 35 46 [66] *avam : ufrasta-* WB; wrongly *ava : ufrasta-* KT. [68] *[zū]rakara : ++ :* KT, with possibly traces of two characters in the gap; but Cameron finds *[zū]rakara : ahat-* with only a gap for one

character, perhaps miswritten and erased, after the divider ⁶⁹ *dauštā* WB, KT. ⁶⁹ *ā* KT, *b₁y]ā* WBn, HK, Tm ⁶⁹ *atifraštādıy* Rl.; *ahıfraštādıy* WB, Jn.; *ufraštādıy* KT
⁷¹ *vısanāhy* Rl, KT; *vıkanāhy* WB, Jn, Cameron; similarly 4 73, 4 77. ⁷¹⁻² *dᵃ-* | *tᵃsᵃ* with *dᵃ* and *sᵃ* uncertain, KT; *utava* HK, Cameron is dubious about *utava*, and notes that 71 ends with a divider and *dᵃ*, which if combined make *u*, but if so there is no divider (i e, haplography of two angle-signs). ⁷² *avaθāšta* KT; *avaθāšatā* Kent JAOS 62.272-3, see Lex s v ⁷² *parı[ba]rā* KT, cf 4 74 ⁷²⁻³ *y-* | *[āv]ā* Rl; *ya-* | *dıy* WB; *ya-* | *[dıy]* KT ⁷³⁻⁴ *utā-* | *taıy* KT ⁷⁴ *parıbarāhᵃdıš* KT ⁷⁶ *[ava]taıy · aparam* Rl; *avataıy* WB, Jn, KT (there is no *aparam*) ⁷⁶ +++*m* with traces of the lost characters, KT, *ucāram* after DSl 5, Bv. BSLP 30 1 65-6 ⁷⁵ *dᵃnᵃutᵘuvᵃ* Rl; *kunautuv* WB, KT ⁷⁷⁻⁸ *ut-* | *ātaıy* KT. ⁷⁸ *parıbarāhy* KT
⁸⁰⁻⁶ On the Helpers of Darius, see Hist. App. III
⁸³ *Utāna : nāma* WB, *U]tā[na · n]āma*, though the middle gap is hardly adequate for two characters and a divider, KT, perhaps the divider was not engraved because it followed an identical stroke as final part of *nᵃ* ⁸⁶ *Dāduhyahyā* WB; *[Dādu]hyahyā* KT; *[Dātu]hyahyā* WBn; *[Dātu]hyahyā* or *[Daduva]hyahyā* Wb KIA; *Dāt-[u]vahyahyā* Cameron, with *tᵘ* not absolutely certain and *vᵃ* damaged but sure ⁸⁷⁻⁸ *tyām : ımaıšām · martıyā : u* | ++ : *ımām : : ā+ : par[ıbar]ā* KT; *martıyānā* | *m : taumām : [ubart]ām* WBn, agreeing with traces noted by KT and slightly emending some other characters.
⁸⁹⁻⁹² See JAOS 63 266-9, where a complete restoration is attempted; also Wb KIA 70-2 and Konig, Klotho 4 42-9. Except as noted here, the restorations in the text are mine, though depending in some points upon Wb and Konig. In 89, Cameron reads *ımᵃ · dıpı+anᵃ++vᵃmᵃ* and thence through *utā*, Kent emends, to fit Cameron's translation The OP lacks the Elam clause 'which formerly (was) not' ⁸⁹⁻⁹⁰ *avast[ā]ya[m]* KT; *avast[ā]y[ā]* Konig ⁹² *k]āra* Wb

Rl has the following correct readings, here indicated by roman type, which were not visible to KT ¹ *Dā]rayava-[uš*, ³ *xšā[yaθıya*; ¹² *ham[ıçıyam*; ¹² *manā : I Nadıtabaıra*, ²² *Asagar[taıy*, ²⁴ *adu]rujıya*; ³¹ *θā]tıy*; ³⁷ *hya*, ⁴¹ *ha]-mahyāyā*; ⁶³ *arıka*; ⁷³ *dıpım*; ⁷⁵ *taumā*; ⁸⁰ *Dārayavauš*; ⁸² *agaubatā*; ⁸² *ada[ka]ıy*; ⁸³ *nāma* (prior occurrence); ⁸³ *Pārsa*; ⁸³ *Θux]rahyā*; ⁸⁴ *Gau[baruva*

WB, from Wb.'s reading of Rl.'s squeezes, add the following, also in roman, which were not visible to KT, nor to Rl. ¹¹ *aθaha adam*; ³⁸ *draujana*; ⁵⁵ *apagaudayāhy*, ⁷¹ *nıyapaıšam . ımawı*; ⁷⁴ *ahatıy*, ⁷⁸ *taumā · ahatıy naıydıš*; ⁸¹ *āhatā*; ⁸³ *Vāyaspārahyā*; ⁸⁴ *puça · Pārsa Gaubaruva*; ⁸⁴ *puça : Pārsa : Vıdarna*; ⁸⁵ *gābıgnahyā · puça*, ⁸⁵ *Bagabuxša*; ⁸⁶ *Ardumanıš nāma . Vahaukahyā puça*; ⁸⁷ *kā : xšāyaθıya*.

TRANSLATION OF DB IV:

§51. 4.1-2. Saith Darius the King: This is what was done by me in Babylon.

§52. 4.2-31. Saith Darius the King: This is what I did by the favor of Ahuramazda in one and the same year after that I became king. XIX battles I fought; by the favor of Ahuramazda I smote them and took prisoner IX kings. One was Gaumata by name, a Magian; he lied; thus he said: "I am Smerdis, the son of Cyrus;" he made Persia rebellious. One, Açina by name, an Elamite; he lied; thus he said: "I am king in Elam;" he made Elam rebellious. One, Nidintu-Bel by name, a Babylonian; he lied; thus he said: "I am Nebuchadrezzar, the son of Nabonidus;" he made Babylon rebellious. One, Martiya by name, a Persian; he lied; thus he said: "I am Imanish, king in Elam;" he made Elam rebellious. One, Phraortes by name, a Mede; he lied; thus he said: "I am Khshathrita, of the family of Cyaxares;" he made Media rebellious. One, Ciçantakhma by name, a Sagartian; he lied; thus he said: "I am king in Sagartia, of the family of Cyaxares;" he made Sagartia rebellious. One, Frada by name, a Margian; he lied; thus he said: "I am king in Margiana," he made Margiana rebellious. One, Vahyazdata by name, a Persian; he lied; thus he said: "I am Smerdis, the son of Cyrus," he made Persia rebellious. One, Arkha by name, an Armenian; he lied; thus he said: "I am Nebuchadrezzar, the son of Nabonidus;" he made Babylon rebellious.

§53. 4.31-2. Saith Darius the King: These IX kings I took prisoner within these battles.

§54. 4.33-6. Saith Darius the King: These are the provinces which became rebellious. The Lie made them rebellious, so that these (men) deceived the people. Afterwards Ahuramazda put them into my hand; as was my desire, so I did unto them.

§55. 4.36-40. Saith Darius the King: Thou who shalt be king hereafter, protect thyself vigorously from the Lie; the man who shall be a Lie-follower, him do thou punish well, if thus thou shalt think, "May my country be secure!"

§56. 4.40-3. Saith Darius the King: This is what I did; by the favor of Ahuramazda, in one and the same year I did (it). Thou who shalt hereafter read this inscription, let that which has been done by me convince thee; do not thou consider it false.

§57. 4.43-5. Saith Darius the King: I turn myself quickly to Ahuramazda, that this (is) true, not false, (which) I did in one and the same year.

§58. 4.45-50. Saith Darius the King: By the

favor of Ahuramazda and of me much else was done; that has not been inscribed in this inscription; for this reason it has not been inscribed, lest whoso shall hereafter read this inscription, to him what has been done by me seem excessive, (and) it not convince him, (but) he think it false.

§59. 4.50–2. Saith Darius the King: Those who were the former kings, as long as they lived, by them was not done thus as by the favor of Ahuramazda was done by me in one and the same year.

§60. 4.52–6. Saith Darius the King: Now let that which has been done by me convince thee; thus for the people's sake do not conceal it: if this record thou shalt not conceal, (but) tell it to the people, may Ahuramazda be a friend unto thee, and may family be unto thee in abundance, and may thou live long!

§61. 4.57–9. Saith Darius the King: If this record thou shalt conceal, (and) not tell it to the people, may Ahuramazda be a smiter unto thee, and may family not be to thee!

§62. 4.59–61. Saith Darius the King: This which I did, in one and the same year by the favor of Ahuramazda I did; Ahuramazda bore me aid, and the other gods who are.

§63. 4.61–7. Saith Darius the King: For this reason Ahuramazda bore aid, and the other gods who are, because I was not hostile, I was not a Lie-follower, I was not a doer of wrong—neither I nor my family. According to righteousness I conducted myself. Neither to the weak nor to the powerful did I do wrong. The man who cooperated with my house, him I rewarded well, whoso did injury, him I punished well.

§64. 4.67–9. Saith Darius the King: Thou who shalt be king hereafter, the man who shall be a Lie-follower or who shall be a doer of wrong—unto them do thou not be a friend, (but) punish them well.

§65. 4.69–72. Saith Darius the King: Thou who shalt hereafter behold this inscription which I have inscribed, or these sculptures, do thou not destroy them, (but) thence onward protect them, as long as thou shalt be in good strength!

§66. 4.72–6. Saith Darius the King: If thou shalt behold this inscription or these sculptures, (and) shalt not destroy them and shalt protect them as long as unto thee there is strength, may Ahuramazda be a friend unto thee, and may family be unto thee in abundance, and may thou live long, and what thou shalt do, that may Ahuramazda make successful for thee!

§67. 4.76–80. Saith Darius the King: If thou shalt behold this inscription or these sculptures, (and) shalt destroy them and shalt not protect them as long as unto thee there is strength, may Ahuramazda be a smiter unto thee, and may family not be unto thee, and what thou shalt do, that for thee may Ahuramazda utterly destroy!

§68. 4.80–6. Saith Darius the King: These are the men who were there at the time when I slew Gaumata the Magian who called himself Smerdis; at that time these men cooperated as my followers: Intaphernes by name, son of Vayaspara, a Persian; Otanes by name, son of Thukhra, a Persian; Gobryas by name, son of Mardonius, a Persian; Hydarnes by name, son of Bagabigna, a Persian; Megabyzus by name, son of Datuvahya, a Persian; Ardumanish by name, son of Vahauka, a Persian.

§69. 4.86–8. Saith Darius the King: Thou who shalt be king hereafter, protect well the family of these men.

§70. 4.88–92. Saith Darius the King: By the favor of Ahuramazda this inscription in other ways I made. In addition, it was in Aryan, and has been made on leather. In addition, this inscription as a whole has been confirmed by the impression of a seal. And it was written, and the written document was read off to me. Afterwards this inscription was sent by me everywhere among the provinces; the people universally were pleased.

TEXT OF DB, COLUMN V:

1 : θātiy : Dārayavauš : xšāyaθiya :
2 ima : tya : adam : akunavam : patiy : avā
3 mcᵃ : çitām : θardam : pasāva : yaθā : xšāya
4 θiya : abavam : Ūvja : nāmā : dahyāuš : hau
5 v : hamiçiyā : abava : I martiya : Atamaita : nāma : Ū
6 vjiya : avam : maθištam : akunavatā : pasāva : ada
7 m : kāram : frāišayam : Ūvjam : I martiya : Gaubaruva :

DB V TEXTS WITH NOTES AND TRANSLATION

8 nāma : Pārsa : manā : badaka : avaṃšām : maθištam : aku
9 navam : pasāva : hauv : Gaubaruva : hadā : kārā : ašiyava :
10 Ūvjam : hamaranam : akunauš : hadā : Ūvjiyaibiš : pas
11 āva : Gaubaruva : Ūvjiyā : aja : utā : viya : marda :
12 utā : tyamšām : maθištam : agarbāya : anaya : abi
13 y : mām : utāšım : adam : avājanam : pasāva : dahyā
14 uš : manā : abava   : θātiy : Dārayavauš : xšāyaθi
15 ya : avaiy : Ūvjiyā : arıkā : āha : utāšām : Aurama
16 zdā : naiy : ayadiya : Auramazdām : ayadaiy : vašnā : A
17 uramazdāha : yaθā : mām : kāma : avaθādiš : akunavam
18 : θātiy : Dārayavauš : xšāyaθiya : hya : Auramazdā
19 m : yadātaiy : yāvā : taumā : ahatiy : utā : jīvah
20 yā : utā : martahyā : šiyātiš   : θātiy : Dārayavauš : xš
21 āyaθiya : pasāva : hadā : kārā : adam : ašiyavam : abiy : Sak
22 ām : abiy : Sakā : tyaiy : xaudām : tigrām : barat[a]
23 y : pasāva : yaθā : adam : ašnaiy : abiy : draya : a
24 vārasam : avadā : hadā : kārā : pisā : viyatara
25 yam : pasāva : adam : Sakā : vasiy : ajanam : aniyam : aga
26 rbāyam : hauv : basta : anayatā : abiy : mām : ut
27 āšım : avājanam : maθištašām : Skuxa : nāma : avam : aga
28 rbāya : utā : anaya : abiy : mām : avadā : aniyam : maθ
29 ištam : akunavam : yaθā : mām : kāma : āha : pasāva : da
30 hyāuš : manā : abava   : θātiy : Dārayavauš : xšāya
31 θiya : avaiy : Sakā : arıkā : āha : utā : naiy : Auramazd
32 āšām : ayadiya : Auramazdām : ayadaiy : vašnā : Aurama
33 zdāha : yaθā : mām : kāma : avaθādiš : akunavam   : θāt
34 iy : Dārayavauš : xšāyaθiya : hya : Auramazdām : yadāta
35 iy : yāvā : taumā : ahatiy : utā : jīvahyā : utā
36 : martahyā : šiyātiš

NOTES TO DB V: The text is badly weathered or entirely destroyed at many points. A full critical discussion is given in JNES 2 105-14, 3 233; cf. also Wb ZfA 46 52-82, Hinz ZDMG 96 331-43. The following gives only the advances upon KT's text as read and restored in their edition:

[2] pa]tıy Wb. [2-3] a[vā]mc[a] Hinz. [3] ç[ıtam Kent (after Wb). [5]]m[a]m[a]ıt[a] KT, U]mamaıta later editors; A]tamaita Husing; A]mamaıta Hinz, after Wb. [7] [I] Rl [11] [Ūvjıyā] WBn; aja Foy (not av]āja) [11] utā : daıy : marda Rl., KT, corrected to utā : viyamarda, with wrongly inserted divider, by Wb. ZfA 46.55; see also §44 and note 3, and Lex s v mard- [12] [tyamšām] WBn. [15] a[vaıy Kent, for Hınz's a[vā [15] [hamıçıyā : āha] Hinz; [arıkā] Hınz later. [16] [naıy : ayadiya] Hinz; A[uramazdām] Wb KIA. [19] ya[dātaıy Tm VS [20] [utā Foy; artah]yā [. bavatıy Hinz, after Oppert's translation; martah]yā Wb , [šiyātış] Kent JNES 7 107 n5

[21] hadā : kār]ā : Sa[kām KT; hadā · kār]ā : Sa[kā Hinz; pasāva : had]ā : k[ārā Kent. [22] [abıy · Sakā Kent, for Hinz's [abiy : avā (quoting Wb. for avā) [22] tyaıy : xaudā]m Oppert [23] pa[sāva · yaθā : adam : ašna]ıy Hinz (quoting Wb for pasāva : yaθā). [23-4] avā[rasam : avad]ā : ha[dā : kār]ā Hinz [25] Sak[ıyā · av]ājanam KT; Sak[ā : av]ājanam Tm. Lex ; pasāva : adam ·] Sak[ā : vasıy] ajanam Hinz [26] [hauv] Kent apud Hinz. [27] maθ]ištā-[mšām Hinz; maθ]ıšta[šām Kent [27] S[ku]xa KT (in their errata), after Oppert's translation. [28] utā : āna]ya [: abiy : mām Hınz (quoting Wb); a]naya Kent. [29] ya[θā : mām : k]āma WBn, after Oppert's translation. [31] avā :] Sa[k]ā [: hamıçıyā : āha : u]tā Hinz; [avaıy] Kent; [arıkā] Hinz later. [32] ā [: ayad]ı[ya Hinz; ā[šām : aya]dı[ya Kent; A]ura[mazdām : a]yadaıy Tm. Lex. [34] hya] Foy, after Oppert's translation. [35] : utā : yāvā :] ta[umā WBn, [yāvā : tau]m[ā HK; [ahatıy] Foy, u]tā Rl. [36] [artahyā : bavatıy] Hinz; m[artahyā Wb.; šıyātıš] Kent JNES 7.107 n5.

Wb. ZfA 46 53-82 makes and adopts the following emendations which are not discussed in my article, and which I do not accept [21] hadā : kār]ā : S[ugdam; [25] [aniyam] for [vasiy], [26] [aniya] for [hauv], [26-7] utāš[ış for utāš[ım; [27] hya]š[ām : maθišta, which violates the recorded length of the gaps

Eilers JNES 7 106-10 proposes, after yadātaıy in 19 and 34f, the following text (composite of the legible characters and traces in the two passages), after XPh 53-5. [: šı]yāt[ış · a]hatiy : utā : jīvahyā : utā : ma[rtahyā : artam, with avahyā after šiyātiš if space permits, and artāvastam as an alternative for artam.

Rl has the following correct readings, in which he

records as legible certain characters, here indicated by roman type, which were not visible to KT: ¹ *Dā]rayavau-[š*; ² *akunava[m*, ⁴ *nā[ma*, ⁵ *ha[miçiy]ā*, ⁶ *vjiya*; ⁶ *maθ]-ištam a[kunava*; ⁷ *mart]iya* ; ⁸ *P[ārsa*; ⁸ *a[vamšām*; ⁹ *Ga]ubar[uva*, ¹⁰ *ak]unau[š*, ¹⁷ *uramaz[dā]ha*; ²¹ *āyaθ[iya*, ²⁶ *· abiy*, ²⁷ *Sk]uxa*; ³⁵ *utā* (prior occurrence).

TRANSLATION OF DB V:

§71. 5.1–14. Saith Darius the King: This is what I did in that third year after that I became king. A province by name Elam—this became rebellious. One man by name Atamaita, an Elamite—him they made chief. Thereupon I sent forth an army to Elam. One man by name Gobryas, a Persian, my subject—him I made chief of them. After that this Gobryas with an army marched off to Elam; he joined battle with the Elamites. Thereupon Gobryas smote and crushed the Elamites, and captured the chief of them; he was led to me, and I killed him. After that the province became mine.

§72. 5.14–7. Saith Darius the King: Those Elamites were faithless and by them Ahuramazda was not worshipped. I worshipped Ahuramazda; by the favor of Ahuramazda, as was my desire, thus I did unto them.

§73. 5.18–20. Saith Darius the King: Whoso shall worship Ahuramazda as long as (his) strength shall be, of him both living and dead (there is) happiness.

§74. 5.20–30. Saith Darius the King: Afterwards with an army I went off to Scythia, against the Scythians who wear the pointed cap. Afterwards, when I arrived near unto the sea, there with the army I crossed by raft(s). Afterwards, I smote the Scythians exceedingly; another (leader) I took captive, this one was led bound to me, and I slew him. The chief of them, by name Skunkha—him they seized and led to me. Then I made another (their) chief, as was my desire. After that, the province became mine.

§75. 5.30–3. Saith Darius the King: Those Scythians ... (= DB 5.15–7).

§75. 5.33–6. ... (= DB 5.18–20).

TEXT OF DB, MINOR INSCRIPTIONS:

DBA:

1 : adam : Dārayavauš : xšāyaθiya : vazraka : xšāya
2 θiya : xšāyaθiyānām : xšāyaθiya : Pārsaiy : xš
3 āyaθiya : dahyūnām : V¹štāspahyā : puça :

4 Aršāmahyā : napā : Haxāmanišiya : θātiy : Dāra
5 yavauš : xšāyaθiya : manā : pitā : V¹štāspa : V¹
6 štāspahyā : pitā : Aršāma : Aršāmahyā : pi
7 tā : Ariyāramna : Ariyāramnahyā : pitā :
8 Cišpiš : Cispaiš : pitā : Haxāmaniš :
9 θātiy : Dārayavauš : xšāyaθiya : avahya
10 rādiy : vayam : Haxāmanišiya : θahyā
11 mahy : hacā : paruviyata : āmātā
12 : amahy : hacā : paruviyata : hyā : amā
13 xam : taumā : xšāyaθiyā : āha : θā
14 tiy : Dārayavauš : xšāyaθiya : VIII : ma
15 nā : taumāyā : tyaiy : paruva
16 m̐ : xšāyaθiya : āha : adam : na
17 vama : IX : duvitāparanam : vayam : x
18 šāyaθiya : amahy :

DBB
1 : iyam : Gaumā
2 ta : hya : maguš : a
3 durujiya :
4 avaθā : aθaha : adam : Ba
5 rdiya : amiy : hya : K
6 ūrauš : puça : adam : xš
7 āyaθiya : amiy :

DBc
1 : iyam : Āç
2 ina : adu
3 rujiya :
4 avaθā
5 : aθaha : a
6 dam : x
7 šāyaθ
8 iya : am
9 iy : Ū
10 vjaiy :

DBD
1 : iyam : Naditabaira :
2 adurujiya : ava
3 θā : aθaha : adam : Nab
4 ukudracara : ami
5 y : hya : Nabunaita
6 hya : puça : adam : x
7 šāyaθiya : amiy : B
8 ābirauv :

DBE
1 : iyam : Fra
2 vartiš :
3 aduru
4 jiya : ava
5 θā : aθaha : adam :
6 Xšaθrita : amiy
7 : Uvaxštrahya
8 : taumāyā : adam
9 : xšāyaθiya : amiy
10 : Mā
11 daiy :

DBF
1 : iyam : Martiya : a
2 durujiya : a
3 vaθā : aθaha : a
4 dam : Imaniš : am
5 iy : Ūvjaiy : x
6 šāyaθi
7 ya :

TEXTS WITH NOTES AND TRANSLATION 135

DBg

1 : iyam : Ciça
2 taxma : ad
3 urujiya
4 : avaθā : a
5 θaha : adam :
6 xšāyaθi
7 ya : ami
8 y : Asaga
9 rtaiy : Uva
10 xštrahya
11 : taumāy
12 ā

DBh

1 : iyam : Vahya
2 zdāta : adu
3 rujiya : ava
4 θā : aθaha : ada
5 m : Bardiya : a
6 miy : hya : K
7 ūrauš : puça
8 : adam : xšā
9 yaθiya : amiy

DBi

1 : iyam : Arxa
2 : aduruj
3 iya : avaθā :
4 aθaha : adam :
5 Nabuku(d)ra
6 cara : amiy :
7 hya : Nabuna
8 itahya : pu
9 ça : adam : xšā
10 yaθiya : amiy
11 : Bāb^{a}rauv :

DBj

1 : iyam : Frāda :
2 aduruji
3 ya : avaθā : aθaha
4 : adam : xšāyaθ
5 iya : amiy : Marga
6 uv :

DBk

1 : iyam : Sku
2 xa : hya : Saka

NOTES TO DB, MINOR INSCRIPTIONS:
DBa Despite KT, the divider is at the end of 7 and not at the beginning of 8 (Cameron)

DBg This has 12 lines (so WB 5, after Rl's squeezes; confirmed by Cameron) and not 11 (as in KT and a number of other editions, which omit line 7)

DBi. $^{5-6}$ n^{a}b^{a}uk^{u}ur^{a}c^{a}r^a on the Rock, d^a is omitted.
^{11} b^{a}ab^{a}r^{a}uv^a, with omission of the i which should follow the second b^a

TRANSLATION OF DB, MINOR INSCRIPTIONS:
DBa: §1. 1–4.   (= DB 1.1–3).
    §2. 4–8.   (= DB 1.3–6).
    §3. 9–13. (= DB 1.6–8).
    §4. 13–8. (= DB 1.8–11).
DBb: This is Gaumata the Magian.   (= DB 4.8–9); I am king.
DBc: This is Açina.   (= DB 4.10–1).
DBd: This is Nidintu-Bel.   (= DB 4.13–4); I am king in Babylon.
DBe: This is Phraortes.   (= DB 4.18–20); I am king in Media.
DBf: This is Martiya.   (= DB 4.16–7).
DBg: This is Ciçantakhma.   (= DB 4.21–2).
DBh: This is Vahyazdata.   (= DB 4.26–8); I am king.
DBi: This is Arkha.   (= DB 4.29–30); I am king in Babylon.
DBj: This is Frada.   (= DB 4.24–5).
DBk: This is Skunkha the Scythian.

DPa = DARIUS, PERSEPOLIS A.

1 Dārayavauš : xšāyaθiya :
2 vazraka : xšāyaθiya : xšā
3 yaθiyānām : xšāyaθiya :
4 dahyūnām : Vištāspahy
5 ā : puça : Haxāmanišiya : h
6 ya : imam : tacaram : akunauš

TRANSLATION OF DPa: Darius the Great King, King of Kings, King of countries, son of Hystaspes, an Achaemenian, who built this palace.

DPb = DARIUS, PERSEPOLIS B:

Dārayavauš : XŠ : vazraka : Vištāspahyā : puça : Haxāmanišiya

TRANSLATION OF DPb: Darius the Great King, son of Hystaspes, an Achaemenian.

DPc = DARIUS, PERSEPOLIS C.

ardastāna : aθagaina : Dārayavahauš : XŠhyā : viθiyā : karta

TRANSLATION OF DPc: Stone window-frame, made in the house of King Darius.

DPd = DARIUS, PERSEPOLIS D.

1 Auramazdā : vazraka : hya : maθišta : bag
2 ānām : hauv : Dārayavaum : xšāyaθi
3 yam : adadā : haušaiy : xšaçam : frāba
4 ra : vašnā : Auramazdāha : Dārayavau
5 š : xšāyaθiya : θātiy : Dārayavauš :
6 xšāyaθiya : iyam : dahyāuš : Pār
7 sa : tyām : manā : Auramazdā : frāba
8 ra : hyā : naibā : uvaspā : umarti
9 yā : vašnā : Auramazdāha : manac
10 ā : Dārayavahauš : xšāyaθiyahy
11 ā : hacā : aniyanā : naiy : tarsat
12 iy : θātiy : Dārayavauš : xšāya
13 θiya : manā : Auramazdā : upastām :
14 baratuv : hadā : viθaibiš : bagai
15 biš : utā : imām : dahyāum : Aura
16 mazdā : pātuv : hacā : haināy
17 ā : hacā : dušiyāıā : hacā : dıa
18 ugā : abiy : imām : dahyāum : mā

19 : ājamiyā : mā : hainā : mā : duš
20 iyāram : mā : drauga : aita : adam :
21 yānam : jadiyāmiy : Auramazd
22 ām : hadā : viθaibiš : bagaibiš : a
23 *itamaiy* : *yānam* : *A*uramazdā : dadāt
24 u*v* : *hadā* : *vi*θ*ai*biš : bagaibiš :

NOTES TO DPd: [17] *dušiyārā* Jn (not *d*ᵘ*aš*ᵃ-). [18] *abiy* Stolze (not *an*ᵃ*ıy*ᵃ). [19-20] *dušıyāram* Jn. (not *d*ᵘ*aš*ᵃ-) [20] *i yᵃarᵃmᵃ* : *m*ᵃ*a* with divider and all characters visible, and a gap between *i* and *y*ᵃ, acc to Cameron [21] *yᵃan*ᵃ *m*ᵃ, with separation caused by a defect in the stone (so Stolze's photograph) [23] The insertion of *yānam* is required for the filling of the gap, in which some slight traces of the characters are still visible; so Cameron, from photo.

TRANSLATION OF DPd:

§1. 1-5. Great Ahuramazda, the greatest of gods—he created Darius the King, he bestowed on him the kingdom; by the favor of Ahuramazda Darius is King.

§2. 5-12. Saith Darius the King: This country Persia which Ahuramazda bestowed upon me, good, possessed of good horses, possessed of good men—by the favor of Ahuramazda and of me, Darius the King, does not feel fear of (any) other.

§3. 12-24. Saith Darius the King: May Ahuramazda bear me aid, with the gods of the royal house; and may Ahuramazda protect this country from a (hostile) army, from famine, from the Lie! Upon this country may there not come an army, nor famine, nor the Lie; this I pray as a boon from Ahuramazda together with the gods of the royal house. This boon may Ahuramazda together with the gods of the royal house give to me!

DPe = DARIUS, PERSEPOLIS E.

1 adam : Dārayavauš : xšāyaθiya : vaz
2 raka : xšāyaθiya : xšāyaθiyānā
3 m : xšāyaθya : dahyūnām : tyai
4 šām : parūnām : Vištāspahyā :
5 puça : Haxāmanišiya : θātiy : Dāra
6 yavauš : xšāyaθiya : vašnā : Aurama
7 zdāhā : imā : dahyāva : tyā : adam
8 : adaršiy : hadā : anā : Pārsā : kā
9 rā : tyā : hacāma : atarsa : manā : bāj
10 im : abara : Ūvja : Māda : Bābiru
11 š : Arabāya : Aθurā : Mudrāy
12 ā : Armina : Katpatuka : Sparda : Ya
13 unā : tyaiy : uškahyā : utā : tya
14 iy : drayahyā : utā : dahyāva : t
15 yā : para : draya : Asagarta : Parθava : Zra
16 ka : Haraiva : Bāxtriš : Sugᵘda : Uv
17 ārazmīy : Θataguš : Harauvatiš : H
18 iduš : Gadāra : Sakā : Maka : θātiy
19 : Dārayavauš : xšāyaθiya : yadiy
20 : avaθā : maniyāhay : hacā : aniya
21 nā : mā : *ta*rsam : imam : Pārsam : kāram : pādi
22 y : yadiy : kāra : Pārsa : pāta : ahatiy : hyā :
23 duvai*štam* : šiyātiš : axšatā : hauvci
24 y : Aurā : nirasātiy : abiy : imām : viθam

NOTES TO DPe: [8] *hadā* not 'by means of', as previously taken, but 'along with, in addition to', as shown by Bv. TPS 1945 51-3, which is its normal meaning [15] *pᵃrᵃu* + *yᵃ*, with a vertical hasta in the mutilated character, followed by a gap, according to the earliest editors; restored as *paruvaıy* by Rl ; misread *pᵃrᵃu ıyᵃ* with a blank unengraved space in the gap, by Jn ; correctly read *pᵃrᵃ · dᵃrᵃ yᵃ = para · draya* by Cameron, JNES 2.307-8, with a wide space between the *rᵃ* and the *yᵃ*. [20] *manıyāhay* for *-haıy* [22] A divider is visible between *pāta* and *ahatıy*, acc. to Jn. and to Stolze's photographs.

TRANSLATION OF DPe:

§1. 1-5. I am Darius the Great King, King of Kings, King of many countries, son of Hystaspes, an Achaemenian.

§2. 5-18. Saith Darius the King: By the favor of Ahuramazda these are the countries which I got into my possession along with this Persian folk, which felt fear of me (and) bore me tribute: Elam, Media, Babylonia, Arabia, Assyria, Egypt, Armenia, Cappadocia, Sardis, Ionians who are of the mainland and (those) who are by the sea, and countries which are across the sea; Sagartia, Parthia, Drangiana, Aria, Bactria, Sogdiana, Chorasmia, Sattagydia, Arachosia, Sind, Gandara, Scythians, Maka.

§3. 18-24. Saith Darius the King: If thus thou shalt think, "May I not feel fear of (any) other," protect this Persian people; if the Persian people shall be protected, thereafter for the longest while happiness unbroken—this will by Ahura come down upon this royal house.

DPh = DARIUS, PERSEPOLIS H.

1 Dārayavauš : XŠ : vazraka : XŠ : XŠyanām : XŠ
2 : dahyūvnām : Vištāspahyā : puça
3 : Haxāmanišiya : θātiy : Dārayavau
4 š : XŠ : ima : xšaçam : tya : adam : dāray
5 āmiy : hacā : Sakaibiš : tyaiy : para
6 : Sugdam : amata : yātā : ā : Kūšā :
7 hacā : Hidauv : amata : yātā : ā : Spa

8 rdā : tyamaiy : Auramazdā : frābara
9 : hya : maθišta : bagānām : mām : Au
10 ramazdā : pātuv : utāmaiy : viθam

TRANSLATION OF DPh:

§1. 1–3. Darius the Great King, King of Kings, King of countries, son of Hystaspes, an Achaemenian.

§2. 3–10. Saith Darius the King: This is the kingdom which I hold, from the Scythians who are beyond Sogdiana, thence unto Ethiopia; from Sind, thence unto Sardis—which Ahuramazda the greatest of the gods bestowed upon me. Me may Ahuramazda protect, and my royal house.

DPi = DARIUS, PERSEPOLIS I.

mayūxa : kāsakaina : Dārayavahauš : XŠhyā : viθiyā : karta

TRANSLATION OF DPi: Door-knob of precious stone, made in the house of Darius the King.

THE INSCRIPTIONS OF NAQŠ-I-RUSTAM.

DNa = DARIUS, NAQŠ-I-RUSTAM A.

1 baga : vazraka : Auramazdā : hya : im
2 ām : būmim : adā : hya : avam : asm
3 ānam : adā : hya : martiyam : adā : h
4 ya : šiyātim : adā : martiyahyā
5 : hya : Dārayavaum : xšāyaθiyam : ak
6 unauš : aivam : parūvnām : xšāyaθ
7 iyam : aivam : parūvnām : framātā
8 ram : adam : Dārayavauš : xšāyaθiya : va
9 zraka : xšāyaθiya : xšāyaθiyānām
10 : xšāyaθiya : dahyūnām : vispazanā
11 nām : xšāyaθiya : ahyāyā : būmi
12 yā : vazrakāyā : dūraiapiy : Vištās
13 pahyā : puça : Haxāmanišiya : Pārsa : P
14 ārsahyā : puça : Ariya : Ariya : ci
15 ça : θātiy : Dārayavauš : xšāya
16 θiya : vašnā : Auramazdāhā : imā :
17 dahyāva : tyā : adam : agarbāya*m* :
18 apataram : haca : Pārsā : adam šā*m*
19 patiyaxšayaiy : manā : bājim : aba*ra*
20 ha : tyašām : hacāma : aθahya : ava : a
21 kunava : dātam : tya : manā : avadiš :
22 adāraiya : Māda : Ūvja : Parθava : Hara*i*
23 va : Bāxtriš : Suguda : Uvāraz*m*
24 iš : Zraka : Harauvatiš : Θataguš : Ga
25 dāra : Hiduš : Sakā : haumavargā : Sa
26 kā : tigraxaudā : Bābiruš : A
27 θurā : Arabāya : Mudrāya : Arm*ina*

28 : Katpatuka : Sparda : Yauna : Sakā : tyai*y* : *pa*
29 radraya : Skudra : Yaunā : takabarā : Put*āy*
30 ā : Kūšiyā : Maciyā : Karkā : θātiy : D
31 ārayavauš : xšāyaθiya : Auramazdā : *ya*θ
32 ā : avaina : imām : būmim : yau*datim* :
33 pasāvadim : manā : frābara : mām : *xšā*
34 yaθiyam : akunauš : adam : xšā*ya*θiya
35 : amiy : vašnā : Auramazdāha : a
36 damšim : gāθavā : niyašādayam : *tya* šā
37 m : adam : aθaham : ava : akunava : ya*θā* : mām:
38 kāma : āha : yadipatiy : mani*yāhaiy : t*
39 ya : ciyakaram : *āha* : avā : dahyāva
40 : tyā : Dārayava*u*š : xšāyaθiya
41 : adāraya : patikarā : dīdiy : tyai*y* : g
42 āθum : baratiy : a*vadā* : xšnāsāhy :
43 adataiy : azdā : bavā*tiy* : Pārsahyā :
44 martiyahyā : dūraiy : arštiš : pa
45 rāgmatā : adataiy : azdā : bavāti
46 y : Pārsa : martiya : dūrayapiy : *hacā* : Pā
47 rsa : partaram : patiyajatā : θātiy : Dā
48 rayavauš : xšāyaθiya : aita : *tya* : karta
49 m : ava : visam : vašnā : Auramazdāha : ak
50 unavam : Auramazdā(ma)iy : upastām : aba
51 ra : yātā : kartam : akuna*vam* : *mām* : A
52 uramazdā : pātuv : hacā : ga*stā* : utāma
53 iy : viθam : utā : imām : dahyāum : aita : ada
54 m : Auramazdām : jadiyāmiy : aitama
55 iy : Auramazdā : dadātuv :
56 martiyā : hyā : Auramazdāh
57 ā : framānā : hauvtaiy : gas
58 tā : mā : θadaya : paθim :
59 tyām : rāstām : mā
60 : avarada : mā : stabava

NOTES TO DNa· The text of DNa now rests upon the photographs of F. Stolze (Persepolis Berlin, 1882) and of A Sevruguin (accessible in Wb Grab, Plates 2–3) The following readings, which either replace older wrong readings or confirm older doubted readings, are assured by the photographs; the restorations agree with the length of the gaps: ⁷⁻⁸ *framātā-* | *ram*; ¹² *dūraiapiy*; ¹⁹ *patiyaxšayaiy*; ¹⁹⁻²⁰ *aba[ra]-* | *ha*; ²² *adāraiya* (for normalization, cf §48), ²⁵ *haumavargā*; ³⁷ *akunava*; ³⁸ *yadipatiy : maniy[āhaiy : t]-* | *ya* (for *-haiy*, cf note on DB 4 39); ³⁹ *[āha]* Wb ; ⁴¹ no space for *[manā]* before *gāθum*, ⁴² *a[va]dā*; ⁴⁴ *dūraiy*; ⁴⁶ *dūrayapiy*; ⁵⁰ *Auramazdā(ma)iy*, with omission of *mᵃ*; ⁵² *ga[stā]*, see Lex s v (not *sᵃrᵃ+*).

Other textual notes: ²⁸⁻⁹ *[pa]-* | *radraya*, after other occurrences, see Lex s v ; not *[ta]-* | *radraya*. ²⁹⁻³⁰ *Put-[ā]yā*, after other occurrences, see Lex. s v ; not *Put[i]yā*. ³² *yau[datim]* Bthl., see Lex s v *yaud-*, hardly *yau[dinim]*, with Wb [60] *stabava* (as Rl JRAS 10 310 hád it), see Lex s v , not *starava* nor *stakava*

TRANSLATION OF DNa:

§1. 1–8. A great god is Ahuramazda, who created this earth, who created yonder sky, who created man, who created happiness for man, who made Darius king, one king of many, one lord of many.

§2. 8–15. I am Darius the Great King, King of Kings, King of countries containing all kinds of men, King in this great earth far and wide, son of Hystaspes, an Achaemenian, a Persian, son of a Persian, an Aryan, having Aryan lineage.

§3. 15–30. Saith Darius the King: By the favor of Ahuramazda these are the countries which I seized outside of Persia; I ruled over them; they bore tribute to me; what was said to them by me, that they did; my law—that held them firm; Media, Elam, Parthia, Aria, Bactria, Sogdiana, Chorasmia, Drangiana, Arachosia, Sattagydia, Gandara, Sind, Amyrgian Scythians, Scythians with pointed caps, Babylonia, Assyria, Arabia, Egypt, Armenia, Cappadocia, Sardis, Ionia, Scythians who are across the sea, Skudra, petasos-wearing Ionians, Libyans, Ethiopians, men of Maka, Carians.

§4. 30–47. Saith Darius the King: Ahuramazda, when he saw this earth in commotion, thereafter bestowed it upon me, made me king; I am king. By the favor of Ahuramazda I put it down in its place; what I said to them, that they did, as was my desire. If now thou shalt think that "How many are the countries which King Darius held?" look at the sculptures (of those) who bear the throne, then shalt thou know, then shall it become known to thee: the spear of a Persian man has gone forth far; then shall it become known to thee: a Persian man has delivered battle far indeed from Persia.

§5. 47–55. Saith Darius the King: This which has been done, all that by the will of Ahuramazda I did. Ahuramazda bore me aid, until I did the work. Me may Ahuramazda protect from harm, and my royal house, and this land: this I pray of Ahuramazda, this may Ahuramazda give to me!

§6. 56–60. O man, that which is the command of Ahuramazda, let this not seem repugnant to thee; do not leave the right path; do not rise in rebellion!

DNb = DARIUS, NAQŠ-I-RUSTAM B.

1 baga : vazraka : Auramazdā : hya : adadā : i
2 ma : frašam : tya : vainataiy : hya : adadā : ši
3 yātim : martiyahyā : hya : xraθum : ut
4 ā : aruvastam : upariy : Dārayavaum : xšā
5 yaθiyam : nīyasaya : θātiy : Dārayavauš : xšāya
6 °θiya : vašnā : Auramazdāhā : avākaram : a
7 miy : tya : rāstam : dauštā : amiy : miθa : na
8 iy : dauštā : amiy : naimā : kāma : tya : skauθ
9 iš : tunuvatahyā : rā°diy : miθa : kariyaiš
10 : naimā : ava : kāma : tya : tunuvā : skauθaiš : r
11 ādiy : miθa : kariyaiš : tya : rāstam : ava : mām :
12 kāma : martiyam : draujanam : naiy : dauštā : am
13 iy : naiy : manauviš : amiy : tyāmaiy : dartana
14 yā : bavatiy : daršam : dārayāmiy : manahā :
15 uvaipašiyahyā : daršam : xšayamna : amiy :
16 martiya : hya : hataxšataiy : anudim : hakarta°
17 hyā : avaθādim : paribarāmiy : hya : v°
18 ināθayatiy : anudim : vinastahyā : avaθ
19 ā : parsāmiy : naimā : kāma : tya : mar°tiya
20 : vināθayaiš : naipatimā : ava : kāma : yadi
21 y : vināθayaiš : naiy : fraθiyaiš : martiya :
22 tya : pat°iy : martiyam : θātiy : ava : mām :
23 naiy : varnavataiy : yātā : uradanām : hadu
24 gām : āxšnautiy : martiya : tya : kunau
25 tiy : yad°ivā : ābaratiy : anuv : tauman

26 išaiy : xšnuta : °° amiy : utā : mām : vas
27 iy : kāma : utā : uxšnauš : amiy : avākaram
28 camaiy : °ušīy : utā : framānā : yaθāmai
29 y : tya : kartam : vaināhy : yadivā : āxšnav-
30 āhy : utā : viθ°i°yā : °° uta : spāθma
31 i°da°yā : aitamai°y ° : °°° aruvastam :
32 upariy : manašcā : °° ušīcā : ima : patimai
33 y : aruvastam : t°ya°maiy : tanūš : tāvaya
34 ti°y : hamaranakara : am°iy : ušhamaranakara : hakara
35 mci°y : ušīyā : gāθa°vā : vaināṭaiy : yaciy :
36 vaināmiy : hamiçiya°m : yaciy : naiy : vainā
37 miy : utā : ušībiyā : utā : framānāyā
38 : a°dakaiy : fratara : maniyaiy : aruvāyā : ya
39 di°y : vaināmiy : hamiçiyam : yaθā : yadiy :
40 nai°y : vaināmiy : yāumainiš : amiy : u
41 tā ° : dastaibiyā : utā : pādaibiyā : asaba
42 ra : ° uvāsabāra : amiy : θanuvaniya : uθa
43 n°uvaniya : amiy : utā : pastiš : utā
44 : asabāra : ārštika : amiy : uvārštika :
45 utā : pastiš : utā : asabāra : utā : ūvnarā
46 : tyā : Auramazdā : upariy : mām : nīyasaya : utā
47 diš : atāvayam : bartanaiy : vašnā : Auramazdāh
48 ā : tyamaiy : kartam : imaibiš : ūvnaraibiš : aku
49 navam : tyā : mām : Auramazdā : upariy : nīyasaya
50 : marī°kā : daršam : azdā : kušuvā : ciyākaram
51 : amiy : ciyākaramcamaiy : ūvnarā : ciyākara
52 mcamaiy : pariyanam : māṭaiy : duruxtam :
53 θadaya ° : tyaṭaiy : gaušāyā : xšnutam : avaš
54 ciy : ° āxšnudiy : tya : partamṭaiy : asti
55 y : marī°kā : māṭaiy : avašciy : duruxta
56 m : kuna°vāṭaiy : tya : manā : kartam : astiy
57 : avašciy : dīdiy : yaciy : nipištam : mā :
58 ṭaiy : dātā : +++++ : mā : +++++++ātiy
59 ā : ayāu(ma)iniš : bavātiy : marīkā : xšāyaθiya
60 : mā : raxθatuv : +++++++++++++++ina :

NOTES TO DNb: Our text of DNb is that given in JNES 4.39–52, based upon the photographs of Schmidt taken in 1938, supplemented by Hz.'s chart and transliteration, ApI 4–6. The intercalated ° °° °°° in our text marks blank spaces adequate for one, two, three characters respectively, where the rock was too rough to permit engraving

A different interpretation of 34–40, with other textual restorations, by I Gershevitch, TPS 1948.66–8, does not convince me Certain alterations of the OP text and of the interpretation, esp. in 52–60, by W Hinz, on the basis of the Elam version, cannot be evaluated until his article is in print.

[14] *bavatiy* on the Rock; *bauvatiy* in fragmentary 2d copy (Hz ApI Plate 5). [19] *mar°tiya* Schmidt photo; last character not *mᵃ*, despite Hz. [22] *pat°iy* Kent, *par[sa]iy* 'in court' Hz ApI 273 [31] The gap is inadequate for Hz.'s restored *dīdiy*; and the Schmidt photo shows a divider in the middle of the space [38] *anᵘuvᵃaθᵃa*, with dubious *nᵘ*, Wb KIA 94, from Sevrugin's photo; *afᵃuvᵃayᵃa* Hz, which he emends to *arᵘuvᵃaθᵃa*; *afᵃuvᵃayᵃa*, with *fᵃ* to be emended to *rᵘ*, and *yᵃ* rather than *θᵃ*, Kent from Schmidt photo.

[49] The divider is not at the end of 49, but at the beginning of 50 Between the two lines there is the vacant space of one line, to indicate the break in the subject-matter. [51, 51⁻²] *cᵃiyᵃakᵃrᵃmᵃmᵃcᵃiyᵃ* in both places, Hz, confirmed by Schmidt photo, with metathesis for *mᵃcᵃmᵃ*, and to be normalized *ciyākaramcamaiy*. [52] *[durux]tam* Bv., after DB 4 44f, 49f. [53] *[xšnutam]* Kent; the space is inadequate for Bv.'s *āxšnūtam*. [55⁻⁶] *[durux]tam* Kent, after Bv's restoration in 52. [56⁻60] The remaining restorations, quite dubious, are largely my own [59] The *mᵃ* of *ayāumainiš* was omitted on the Rock

For my variations from Hz.'s text, see Lg. 15 166–74, JNES 4.39–52.

TRANSLATION OF DNb:

§7. 1–5. A great god is Ahuramazda, who created this excellent work which is seen, who created happiness for man, who bestowed wisdom and activity upon Darius the King.

§8a. 5–11. Saith Darius the King: By the favor of Ahuramazda I am of such a sort that I am a friend to right, I am not a friend to wrong. It is not my desire that the weak man should have wrong done to him by the mighty; nor is that my desire, that the mighty man should have wrong done to him by the weak.

§8b. 11–5. What is right, that is my desire. I am not a friend to the man who is a Lie-follower. I am not hot-tempered. What things develop in my anger, I hold firmly under control by my thinking power. I am firmly ruling over my own (impulses).

§8c. 16–21. The man who cooperates, him according to his cooperative action, him thus do I reward. Who does harm, him according to the damage thus I punish. It is not my desire that a man should do harm; nor indeed is that my desire, if he should do harm, he should not be punished.

§8d. 21–4. What a man says against a man, that does not convince me, until he satisfies the Ordinance of Good Regulations.

§8e. 24–7. What a man does or performs (for me) according to his (natural) powers, (therewith) I am satisfied, and my pleasure is abundant, and I am well satisfied.

§8f. 27–31. Of such a sort is my understanding and my command: when what has been done by me thou shalt see or hear of, both in the palace and in the war-camp, this is my activity over and above my thinking power and my understanding.

§8g. 31–40. This indeed is my activity: inasmuch as my body has the strength, as battle-fighter I am a good battle fighter. Once let there be seen with understanding in the place (of battle), what I see (to be) rebellious, what I see (to be) not (rebellious); both with understanding and with command then am I first to think with action, when I see a rebel as well as when I see a not-(rebel).

§8h. 40–45. Trained am I both with hands and with feet. As a horseman I am a good horseman. As a bowman I am a good bowman both afoot and on horseback. As a spearman I am a good spearman both afoot and on horseback.

§8i. 45–9. And the (physical) skillfulnesses which Ahuramazda has bestowed upon me and I have had the strength to use them—by the favor of Ahuramazda what has been done by me, I have done with these skillfulnesses which Ahuramazda has bestowed upon me.

§9a. 50–5. O menial, vigorously make thou known of what sort I am, and of what sort my skillfulnesses, and of what sort my superiority. Let not that seem false to thee, which has been heard by thy ears. That do thou hear, which is communicated to thee.

§9b. 55–60. O menial, let that not be made (to seem) false to thee, which has been done by me. That do thou behold, which [has been inscribed]. Let not the laws [be disobeyed] by thee. Let not [anyone] be untrained [in obedience]. [O menial], let not the king (feel himself obliged to) inflict punishment (?) [for wrong-doing (?) on the dwellers (in the land) (?)].

TEXT OF DN, MINOR INSCRIPTIONS:

DNc 1 Gaubaruva : Pātišuvariš : Dāra
2 yavahauš : xšāyaθiyahyā : arštibara

DNd 1 Aspacanā : vaçabara : Dārayavahauš : xš
2 āyaθiyahyā : isuvām : dārayatiy

DN I iyam : Pārsa
II iyam : *Māda*
III iyam : Ūvja
IV iyam : Parθava
XV iyam : Sakā : tigraxa*udā*
XVI *iyam : Bābiruš*
XVII iyam : Aθuriya
XXIX iyam : Maciyā

NOTES TO DN, MINOR INSCRIPTIONS DNc ²arštibara, engraved š*ᵃ*r*ᵃ*s*ᵃ*t*ᵃ*ɩb*ᵃ*r*ᵃ*; the original draft was miswritten ar*ᵃ*s*ᵃ*t*ᵃ*ɩb*ᵃ*r*ᵃ*, and the š*ᵃ*, intended to replace the s*ᵃ*, was by error inserted in the place of the a (But the first engraved character is read by Cameron from photographs not as š*ᵃ*, but as h*ᵃ*; for a miswritten h*ᵃ* I can offer no explanation).

DNd· Aspathines has a heavy bow, or a bowcase, slung over his left shoulder, and holds a battle-ax in his hand, cf JNES 4 233.

TRANSLATION OF DN, MINOR INSCRIPTIONS:

DNc: Gobryas, a Patischorian, spear-bearer of Darius the King.

DNd: Aspathines, bowbearer, holds the battle-ax of Darius the King.

DN I: This is the Persian.

DN II: This is the Mede.

DN III: This is the Elamite.
DN IV: This is the Parthian.
DN XV: This is the Scythian with pointed cap.
DN XVI: This is the Babylonian.
DN XVII: This is the Assyrian.
DN XXIX: This is the man of Maka.

DSa = Darius, Susa a.

1 adam : Dārayavauš : XŠ : vazraka : XŠ
 XŠyān
2 ām : XŠ DHnām : V¹štāspahyā : puça : Ha
3 xāmaniš^aya : θātiy : Dārayavauš : XŠ
4 : vašnā : AMha : adam : ava : akunavam :
 tya :
5 akunavam : visahyā : frašam : θadayātaiy

Note to DSa ⁵ frašam : θadayātaiy, Hz. ApI 156-8, for the previously accepted frašta : θadayāmaiy; but Hinz, ZDMG 95 223-5, supports a[dam : visa]hyā : frašta : θadayāmaiy.

Translation of DSa:
1. 1-3. I am . (= DPa 1-5).
§2. 3-5. Saith Darius the King: By the favor of Ahuramazda I have done that which I have done; to every one may it seem excellent.

DSb = Darius, Susa b.

1 adam : Dārayavau
2 š : xšāyaθiya
3 : vazraka : xšāya
4 θiya : xšāyaθi
5 yānām : xšāya
6 θiya : dahyūnā
7 m : xšāyaθiya :
8 haruvahyāya :
9 būmiyā : V¹št
10 āspahyā : puça
11 : Haxāmanišiya

Translation of DSb: I am (= DPa 1-4), King in all the earth, (= DPe 4-5).

DSc = Darius, Susa c.

adam : Dārayavauš XŠ : vazraka XŠ XŠyānām : Vištāspahyā : puça

Translation of DSc: I am ...(= DPa 1-3, 4-5).

DSd = Darius, Susa d.

1 adam Dārayavauš XŠ vazraka XŠ XŠyānām
 XŠ DHnām XŠ
2 ahyāyā BUyā Vištāspahyā : puça :
 Haxāmanišiya θā
3 tiy Dārayavauš XŠ vašnā AMha imam :
 dacaram akunavam

Translation of DSd:
§1. 1-2. I am ... (= DPa 1-4), King in this earth, ... (= DPe 4-5).
§2. 2-3. Saith Darius the King: By the favor of Ahuramazda I built this palace.

DSe = Darius, Susa e.

1 baga : vazraka : Auramazdā : hya : ima
2 m : būmim : adadā : hya : avam : as
3 mānam : adadā : hya : martiyam : ad
4 adā : hya : šiyātim : adadā : mart
5 iyahyā : hya : Dārayavaum : XŠm : ak
6 unauš : aivam : parūvnām : XŠm : a
7 ivam : parūvnām : framātāram : a
8 dam : Dārayavauš : XŠ : vazraka : XŠ : XŠy
9 ānām : XŠ : dahyūnām : vispazanā
10 nām : XŠ : ahyāyā : būmiyā : vaz
11 rakāyā : dūraiy : apiy : V¹štās
12 pahyā : puça : Haxāmanišiya : Pār
13 sa : Pārsahyā : puça : Ariya : Ari
14 ya : ciça : θātiy : Dārayavauš : XŠ :
15 vašnā : Auramazdāha : imā : dahy
16 āva : tyā : adam : agarbāyam : apata
17 ram : hacā : Pārsā : adamšām : pat
18 iyaxšayaiy : manā : bājim : abara :
19 tyašām : hacāma : aθahya : ava : aku
20 nava : dātam : tya : manā : avadiš : a
21 dāraya : Māda : Ūja : Parθava : Haraiva :
22 Bāxtriš : Suguda : Uvārazmiš
23 : Zraka : Harauvatiš : θataguš : Maci
24 yā : Gadāra : Hiduš : Sakā : haumava
25 rgā : Sakā : tigraxaudā : Bābir
26 uš : Aθurā : Arabāya : Mudrāya :
27 Armina : Katpatuka : Sparda : Yaun
28 ā : tyaiy : drayahyā : utā : tyai
29 y : paradraya : Skudra : Putāyā :
30 Kūšiyā : Karkā : θātiy : Dāra
31 yavauš : XŠ : vasiy : tya : duškarta
32 m : āha : ava : naibam : akunavam : da
33 hyāva : ayauda : aniya : aniyam :
34 aja : ava : adam : akunavam : vašnā
35 : Auramazdāha : yaθā : aniya : a
36 niyam : naiy : jatiy : cinā : gā
37 θavā : kašciy : astiy : dātam :
38 tya : manā : hacā : avanā : tarsati
39 y : yaθā : hya : tauvīyā : tyam : s
40 kauθim : naiy : jatiy : naiy : vi
41 mardatiy : θātiy : Dārayavauš :

42 XŠ : vašnā : Auramazdāhā : dastaka
43 rtam : vasiy : tya : paruvam : naiy
44 : gāθavā : kartam : ava : adam : gāθa
45 vā : akunavam : ++++ : nāma : varda
46 nam : didā : ha*natāyā* : avagmat
47 ā : paruvam : akartā : hacā : ava
48 daša : ā : pasā*va* : didām : aniy
49 ām : a*kunavam* : θātiy : Dārayavau
50 š : XŠ : mām : AM : pātuv : hadā : ba
51 gaibiš : utamaiy : viθam : u
52 tā : tyamaiy : *ni*pištam

NOTES TO DSe: For the restoration of this text, see the references in the bibliography.

21-30 The list of provinces is restored by retranslation from the Akk. version; whether both *Putāyā* and *Kūšiyā* stood in 29-30 depends upon whether the gap at the end of line 21 of the Akk. is adequate to hold both names. 36 ci[nā] Kent, JAOS 58 116-7; ci[tā] Sen 134 45-9 The restorations are quite uncertain; but cf. Hinz, ZDMG 95 229-32.

TRANSLATION OF DSe:
§1. 1-7.   . (= DNa 1-8).
§2. 7-14.   (= DNa 8-15).

§3. 14-30.   (= DNa 15-24), men of Maka, (= DNa 24-8), Ionians, (those) who are by the sea and (those) who are across the sea, Skudra, Libyans, Ethiopians, Carians.

§4. 30-41. Saith Darius the King: Much which was ill-done, that I made good. Provinces were in commotion; one man was smiting the other. The following I brought about by the favor of Ahuramazda, that the one does not smite the other at all, each one is in his place. My law—of that they feel fear, so that the stronger does not smite nor destroy the weak.

§5. 41-9. Saith Darius the King: By the favor of Ahuramazda, much handiwork which previously had been put out of its place, that I put in its place. A town by name   , (its) wall fallen from age, before this unrepaired—I built another wall (to serve) from that time into the future.

§6. 49-52. Saith Darius the King: Me may Ahuramazda together with the gods protect, and my royal house, and what has been inscribed by me.

DSf = DARIUS, SUSA F.

1 baga : vazraka : Auramazdā : hya : imām : būmim : a
2 dā : hya : avam : asmānam : adā : hya : martiyam : adā
3 : hya : šiyātim : adā : martiyahyā : hya : Dāra
4 yavaum : XŠyam : akunauš : aivam : parūnām : XŠ
5 yam : aivam : parūnām : framātāram : adam : Dāra
6 yavauš : XŠ : vazraka : XŠ : XŠyānām : XŠ : DHnām : XŠ
7 : ahyāyā : BUyā : Vištāspahyā : puça : Haxāma
8 nišiya : θātiy : Dārayavauš : XŠ : Auramazdā :
9 hya : maθišta : bagānām : hauv : mām : adā : ha
10 u*v* : mām : XŠyam : akunauš : haumaiy : ima : xša
11 çam : frābara : tya : vazrakam : tya : uvaspam : uma
12 rtiyam : vašnā : Auramazdāha : hya : manā : pitā
13 : Vištāspa : utā : Aršāma : hya : manā : niyāka :
14 tyā : ubā : ajīvatam : yadiy : Auramazdā : mā
15 m : XŠyam : akunauš : ahyāyā : BUyā : Auramazd
16 ām : avaθā : kāma : āha : haruvahyāyā : BUyā : mar
17 tiyam : mām : avarnavatā : mām : XŠyam : akunauš :
18 haruvahāyā : BUyā : adam : Auramazdām : ayadaiy :
19 Auramazdāmaiy : upastām : abara : tyamaiy : fram
20 ātam : cartanaiy : ava : ucāramaiy : akunauš : t
21 ya : adam : akunavam : visam : vašnā : Auramazdāha :
22 akunavam : ima : hadiš : tya : Çūšāyā : akunavam :
23 hacāciy : dūradaša : arjanamšaiy : abariya : frava
24 ta : BU : akaniya : yātā : aθagam : BUyā : avārasam :
25 yaθā : katam : abava : pasāva : θikā : avaniya : aniyā :
26 XL : arašaniš : baršnā : aniyā : XX : arašaniš : barš

TEXTS WITH NOTES AND TRANSLATION

27 nā : upariy : avām : θikām : hadiš : frāsah*y*a
28 : utā : tya : BU : akaniya : fravata : utā : tya : θikā :
29 avaniya : utā : tya : ištiš : ajaniya : kāra : hya : Bā
30 *b*iruviya : hauv : akunauš : θarmiš : hya : nau
31 caina : hauv : Labanāna : nāma : kaufa : hacā : avanā : aba
32 *r*iya : kāra : hya : Aθuriya : haudim : abara : yātā :
33 Bābirauv : hacā : *B*ābirauv : Karkā : utā : Yau
34 n*ā* : *a*bara : yātā : *Ç*ū*š*āyā : yakā : hacā : Gadārā
35 : *a*bariya : utā : *h*acā : Karmānā : daraniyam : hacā
36 : S*p*ardā : utā : hacā : Bāxtriyā : abariya : tya
37 : *i*dā : akariya : kāsaka : hya : kapautaka : utā : sikab
38 ruš : hya : idā : karta : hauv : hacā : Sugudā : aba
39 riya : kāsaka : hya : axšaina : hauv : hacā : Uvāraz
40 miyā : abariya : hya : idā : karta : ardatam : utā : a
41 sā : dāruv : hacā : Mudrāyā : abariya : ar
42 janam : tyanā : didā : *p*ištā : ava : hacā : Yaun
43 ā : *a*bariya : piruš : *h*ya : idā : karta : hacā : Kūš
44 ā : utā : hacā : Hidauv : utā : hacā : Harauvat
45 iyā : abariya : stūnā : aθagainiya : tyā : id
46 ā : kartā : Abirāduš : nāma : āvahanam : Ūjaiy
47 : hacā : avadaša : abariya : martiyā : karnuvakā : t
48 *y*aiy : aθagam : akunavatā : avaiy : Yaunā : utā
49 : S*p*ardi*y*ā : *m*arti*y*ā : dāraniyakarā : tyaiy : daran
50 *i*yam : *a*kunavaša : avaiy : Mādā : utā : Mudrāy
51 ā : martiyā : *t*ya*iy* : *d*āruv : akunavaša : avaiy :
52 S*p*ardi*y*ā : utā : *M*udrāyā : marti*y*ā : tyaiy
53 : *a*gurum : *a*kunavaša : avaiy : Bābiruviy
54 ā : martiy*ā* : *t*ya*iy* : didām : apiθa : avaiy : *M*ād
55 ā : utā : Mudrāyā : θāt*i*y : Dārayava*u*š : X*Š* :
56 Çūšāyā : paruv : frašam : *f*ramātam : par*uv* : fraša
57 *m* : *ā*ha : mām : *A*uramazdā : pātuv : *u*tā : V
58 *i*štāspam : hya : manā : pitā : utama*i*y : DHum

NOTES TO DSf. The line-division is that of Scheil's tablet a, completed with the evidence of numerous fragments of other copies and that of the Elamite and Akkadian versions All copies had the same text, except as stated in the note to line 55, there is no basis for the variations given by Brd , WZKM 39 30-9

[14] *tyā* Konig, Burgbau 29; *imā* Hz. AMI 3.34; but the traces are very faint and indecisive, cf. Kent, JAOS 53 8 [20] Retranslation of Elam version by Hinz, JNES 9 1-7, because of Elam. *ú-ṣa-ra-um-mi*, transliteration of OP *ucāramaiy* = *ucāram-maiy*, the Akk. version is here, as often, quite different. [21] The Akk does not warrant *ava* with *visam*; in this phrase, *ava* always precedes, but the OP has no gap at that point. [27] *frāsah[ya]* (passive) is probably better than my *frāsaha[m]* (active), JAOS 53.13 [41] *dāruva* Scheil 21.18, etc , is a better reading than *sāruva*, Hz. ApI 299; but normalize *dāruv*, with Duchesne-Guillemin (*d*ᵃ certain, according to Duchesne-Guillemin, who inspected the original tablet at the Louvre in 1948); for meaning and normalization, see Lex. s v *dāruv* [42] [*p*]*ištā* Bv. BSLP 30 1.62-3; [*d*]*ištā* Hz. AMI 3 37. [51] [*dār*]*uv* Hinz, rather than [*išmal*]*uv*; see Lex. s.vv.

[53] 'Babylonians' here seems to denote 'Ionians resident in Babylonia', cf. Konig, Burgbau 25; confirmed by the reading of Akk frag. Y line 9 of obverse (Akk. 21 = OP 30), given by Scheil 24.107. [55] Between the text of 55 and that of 56, Scheil's fragment θ indicates the presence of *vašnā Auramazdāha* (JAOS 51 196), but there is no space for it in tablet a There is also no room for *aita tya*, inserted here by Hz. AMI 3 38, 3.77. [57] [*āha*] Brd. WZKM 39 36, probably better than *abava*, Kent, JAOS 52.22-3.

TRANSLATION OF DSf:
§1. 1–5.   (= DNa 1–8).
§2. 5–8.   (= DSd 1–2).
§3a. 8–12. Saith Darius the King: Ahuramazda, the greatest of the gods—he created me; he made me king; he bestowed upon me this kingdom,

great, possessed of good horses, possessed of good men.

§3b. 12-5. By the favor of Ahuramazda my father Hystaspes and Arsames my grandfather— these both were living when Ahuramazda made me king in this earth.

§3c. 15-8. Unto Ahuramazda thus was the desire: he chose me as (his) man in all the earth; he made me king in all the earth.

§3d. 18-22. I worshipped Ahuramazda. Ahuramazda bore me aid. What was by me commanded to do, that he made successful for me. What I did, all by the favor of Ahuramazda I did.

§3e. 22-7. This palace which I built at Susa, from afar its ornamentation was brought. Downward the earth was dug, until I reached rock in the earth. When the excavation had been made, then rubble was packed down, some 40 cubits in depth, another (part) 20 cubits in depth. On that rubble the palace was constructed.

§3f. 28-30. And that the earth was dug downward, and that the rubble was packed down, and that the sun-dried brick was molded, the Babylonian people—it did (these tasks).

§3g. 30-5. The cedar timber, this—a mountain by name Lebanon—from there was brought. The Assyrian people, it brought it to Babylon; from Babylon the Carians and the Ionians brought it to Susa. The *yakā*-timber was brought from Gandara and from Carmania.

§3h. 35-40. The gold was brought from Sardis and from Bactria, which here was wrought. The precious stone lapis-lazuli and carnelian which was wrought here, this was brought from Sogdiana. The precious stone turquois, this was brought from Chorasmia, which was wrought here.

§3i. 40-5. The silver and the ebony were brought from Egypt. The ornamentation with which the wall was adorned, that from Ionia was brought. The ivory which was wrought here, was brought from Ethiopia and from Sind and from Arachosia.

§3j. 45-9. The stone columns which were here wrought, a village by name Abiradu, in Elam— from there were brought. The stone-cutters who wrought the stone, those were Ionians and Sardians.

§3k. 49-55. The goldsmiths who wrought the gold, those were Medes and Egyptians. The men who wrought the wood, those were Sardians and Egyptians. The men who wrought the baked brick, those were Babylonians. The men who adorned the wall, those were Medes and Egyptians.

§4. 55-8. Saith Darius the King: At Susa a very excellent (work) was ordered, a very excellent (work) was (brought to completion). Me may Ahuramazda protect, and Hystaspes my father, and my country.

DSg = DARIUS, SUSA G.

1 adam : *Dārayavauš* XŠ *vazraka* XŠ XŠ*yānām* XŠ DH*nām* XŠ *ah*
2 *yāyā* BU*yā* : Vi*štāspahyā puça Haxāmanišiya* θ*āt*
3 *iy* : *Dārayavauš* XŠ *viθiyā imā stūnā adam akunavam*

NOTE TO DSg: ³[*viθiyā imā stūnā*] Brd., for which Hinz, ZDMG 95.238, prefers [*imam apadānam*].

TRANSLATION OF DSg:
§1. 1-2.   (= DSd 1-2).
§2. 2-3. Saith Darius the King: In (my) house I made these columns.

DSi = DARIUS, SUSA I.

1 ada*m* : *Dārayavauš* XŠ : *vazraka* : XŠ XŠ*yānām* : XŠ DH*nām* : XŠ *a*
2 h*yāyā* BU*yā* : Vi*štāspahyā* : *puça* : Haxāmanišiya : θ
3 *ātiy* : *Dārayavauš* XŠ : *ya*θ*ā* : AM : *mām* : XŠ*yam* : *akunauš* :
4 a*hyāyā* BU*yā* : *vašnā* : A*Mha* : *visam* : *naibam* : *akunavam*

NOTE TO DSi. ⁴ For restoration, cf. XPg 4, XV 20; but the Akk. does not warrant Brd's *visam tya naibam*, WZKM 39.43; cf. XPh 43.

TRANSLATION OF DSi:
§1. 1-2.   (= DSd 1-2).
§2. 2-4. Saith Darius the King: After Ahuramazda made me king in this earth, by the favor of Ahuramazda everything (that) I did (was) good.

DSj = DARIUS, SUSA J.

1 *adam* : *Dārayavauš* XŠ : *vazraka* XŠ XŠ*yānām* : XŠ *ahyāyā* BU*yā* : Vi*štāspahyā* :
2 *puça* : Haxāmanišiya : θ*ātiy* : *Dārayavauš* XŠ : *ima* : *tya* : *adam* : *akunavam* :
3 *paruv*iya θ*ā* : *naiy* : *akunavam* : *ya*θ*ā* : A*Mhā* : *framānā* : *āha* : *ava*θ*ā* : *akunava*

4 m : mām : AM : dauštā : āha : tya : akunavam : avamaiy : visam : ucāram : āha : θā
5 tiy : Dārayavauš XŠ : vašnā AMhā : hya : ima : hadiš : vainātiy : tya : manā : ka
6 rtam : visahyā : frašam : θadayātaiy : mām : AM : pātuv : utamaiy : DHum

NOTES TO DSj · ³ [paruv]iyaθā naiy 'nicht in einem einzigen Anhieb' Brd.; [aparuv]iyaθā naiy 'wie nie zuvor' Hz. ApI 103; [++++]iyaθā naiy 'nicht planlos' Hinz, ZDMG 95 240-1. ⁶ frašam θadayā[taiy] Hz, as in DSa 5, q v; frašta θadayā[maiy] Scheil, supported by Hinz, ZDMG 95 224.

TRANSLATION OF DSj:
§1. 1-2. . . (= DSd 1-2, with an omission).
§2. 2-4. Saith Darius the King: That which I did, I did not do at first attempt. As was Ahuramazda's command, so I did. Unto me Ahuramazda was a friend; what I did, all that was successful for me.
§3. 4-6. Saith Darius the King: By the favor of Ahuramazda, to every one who shall see this palace which has been built by me, may it seem excellent. Me may Ahuramazda protect, and my country.

DSk = DARIUS, SUSA K.

1 adam : Dārayavauš : XŠ : vazraka : XŠ : XŠy
2 ānām : XŠ : DHnām : V¹štāspahyā :
3 puça : Haxāmanišiya : θātiy : Dā
4 rayavauš : XŠ : manā : AM : AMha : adam :
            AMm :
5 ayadaiy : AMmaiy : upastām : baratuv

TRANSLATION OF DSk:
§1. 1-3. I am (= DPa 1-5).
§2. 3-5. Saith Darius the King: Ahuramazda is mine, I am Ahuramazda's. I worshipped Ahuramazda; may Ahuramazda bear me aid.

DSl = DARIUS, SUSA L.

1 θātiy : Dārayavauš : x
2 šāyaθiya : vašnā : Aura
3 mazdāha : tya : amaniyai
4 y : kunavānaiy : avamai
5 y : visam : ucāram : āha :

TRANSLATION OF DSl: Saith Darius the King: By the favor of Ahuramazda, what I thought I will do, all that was successful for me.

DSm = DARIUS, SUSA M.

1 adam : Dārayavauš : XŠ : vazraka : XŠ : XŠyānam :
2 XŠ : DHnām : Vištāspahyā : puça : Haxāmanišiya :
3 θātiy : Dārayavauš : XŠ : AMmaiy : xšaçam : frābara :
4 tya : vazrakam : tya : umartiyam : mām : xšāyaθiyam :
5 ahyāyā : būmiyā : akunauš : vašnā : AMhā : imā : dah
6 yāva : tyaišām : adam : xšāyaθiya : abavam : Pārsa :
7 Ūja : Bābiruš : Aθurā : Arabāya : Mudrāya : Sparda :
8 Yauna : Māda : Armina : Katpatuka : Parθava : Zraka :
9 Haraiva : Uvārazmiš : Bāxtriš : Suguda : Gadāra :
10 θataguš : Harauvatiš : Hiduš : Skudra : Yaunā : taka
11 barā :

NOTE TO DSm · The reconstructed text of Brd. WZKM 39 55-8 is here given, despite inconsistencies in the use of the ideograms

TRANSLATION OF DSm:
§1. 1-2. I am (= DPa 1-5).
§2. 3-11. Saith Darius the King: Ahuramazda bestowed upon me the kingdom, great, possessed of good men; he made me king in this earth. By the favor of Ahuramazda these are the countries of which I became king: Persia, Elam, Babylonia, Assyria, Arabia, Egypt, Sardis, Ionia, Media, Armenia, Cappadocia, Parthia, Drangiana, Aria, Chorasmia, Bactria, Sogdiana, Gandara, Sattagydia, Arachosia, Sind, Skudra, petasos-wearing Ionians,

DSn = DARIUS, SUSA N.

1 imam : patikaram : Dārayavauš : XŠ :
        niyaštāya : cartanaiy : +++
2 . +++na : Dārayavaum : XŠyam : AM :
        pātuv : utā : tya : kartam

TRANSLATION OF DSn: This sculpture Darius the King commanded to make; Darius the

King may Ahuramazda protect, and what was made (by him).

DSo = Darius, Susa o.

1 +++++ +++++ +++++ našᵃ
2 tam : akunavam : θātiy : Dā
3 rayavauš : XŠ : vašnā : AMha : Çūš
4 āyā : idā : frašam : akunavam

NOTE TO DSo· Hinz, ZDMG 95.255-7, restores in part as an inscription of Darius II (D²Sd).

TRANSLATION OF DSo: I made. Saith Darius the King: By the favor of Ahuramazda, I constructed here at Susa an excellent (building).

DSp = Darius, Susa p.

1 Auramazdā : vazraka : hya : maθišta : bagānām : hauv : Dā
2 rayavaum : XŠyam : adā : haušaiy : xšaçam : frābara : tya : nai
3 bam : tya : uraθaram : uvaspam : umartiyam : ....

NOTES TO DSp: ³ [u]raθaram Brd. WZKM 39 61-2; [f]raθaram Bv. BSLP 33 2 151 The complete version given above is Brd's; Hinz, ZDMG 95 244 proposes the following
1 [baga : vazraka : Auramazd]ā [: hya : maθišta · bagān
2 ām · hya : Dārayavaum :] XŠya[m : akunauš : θāti
3 y · Dārayavauš XŠ : ima : f]raθaram [adam : akunavam]

TRANSLATION OF DSp: Great Ahuramazda, the greatest of the gods—he created Darius the King, he bestowed upon him the kingdom, good, possessed of good charioteers, of good horses, of good men

DSq = Darius, Susa q.

1   a
2   : Dārayavauš : XŠ :   : cašam :
3   : adānā :   .   nasᵃtā .
4   . m : mā : ka   : mā : yā

TRANSLATION OF DSq: Darius the King eye   he knew   let not   let not

DSs = Darius, Susa s.

1 baga : vazraka : Auramazdā : hya : frašam : ah
2 yāyā : būmiyā : kunautiy : hya : mart
3 iyam : ahyāyā : būmiyā : kunau
4 tiy : hya : šiyātim : kunautiy :
5 martiyahyā : hya : uvaspā : uraθācā :
6 kunautiy : manā : haudiš : frābara : mām : Au
7 ramazdā : pātuv : utā : tyamaiy : kartam :

NOTE TO DSs Hinz, ZDMG 95.245-8, restores one more line at the beginning, and has a different wording in line 6, as follows·
0 baga : vazraka : Auramazdā : hya : maθišta · bag
1 ānām : hya : Dārayavaum : xšāyaθiyam :] ah

6 [kunautiy : hyamaiy : upastām : aba]ra : mām : Au

TRANSLATION OF DSs: A great god is Ahuramazda, who makes excellence in this earth, who makes man in this earth, who makes happiness for man, who makes good horses and good chariots. On me he bestowed them. Me may Ahuramazda protect and what has been built by me.

DSt = Darius, Susa t.

1 baga : vazraka : Auramazdā : hya : ima
2 m : būmim : adā : hya : avam : as
3 mānam : adā : hya : martiyam : a
4 dā : hya : šiyātim : adā : mart
5 iyahyā : hya : Dārayavaum : xš
6 āyaθiyam : akunauš : θāti
7 y : Dārayavauš : XŠ : mām : Auramaz
8 dā : pātuv : hadā : bagaibiš
9 : utamaiy : viθam : utā : θuv
10 ām : kā : XŠ : hya : aparam : āhy

TRANSLATION OF DSt:
§1. 1-6.   (= DNa 1-6).
§2. 6-10. . . (= DSe 49-51) and thee, whoever shalt be king hereafter.

DSy = Darius, Susa y.

1 adam : Dārayavauš XŠ : vazraka XŠ XŠyānām
2 XŠ DHyūnām XŠ : ahyāyā BUyā : Vi
3 štāspahyā : puça : Haxāmanišiya

NOTE TO DSy. Text read from a carbon rubbing, which assures the omission of the word-dividers; but the space in the lost part of line 3 requires its presence The defective copy has slightly different line division.

TRANSLATION OF DSy: (= DSd 1-2).

DZ = Darius, Suez inscriptions.

NOTE TO DZ· Our text of the Suez inscriptions is based on the original publications of Ménant and Daressy in Recueil de Travaux, vols. 9 and 11, with comparison of Oppert, Le Peuple et la Langue des Mèdes 217-8; cf. JNES 1.415-21.

DZa = Darius, Suez a.

1 Dā   2 raya   3 va   4 uš

TRANSLATION OF DZa: Darius.

DZb = Darius, Suez b.

1 Dārayavauš : XŠ : vazraka
2 : XŠ : XŠyānām : XŠ : dahy

3 ūnām : XŠ : ahyāyā :
4 būmiyā : vazrakāyā :
5 Vištāspahyā : pu

6 ça : Haxāmanišiya

TRANSLATION OF DZb: (= DNa 8–12, lacking two words).

DZc = DARIUS, SUEZ C.

1 baga : vazraka : Auramazdā : hya : avam : asmānam : adā : hya : imām : būm
2 im : adā : hya : martiyam : adā : hya : šiyātim : adā : martiyahy
3 ā : hya : Dārayavaum : XŠyam : akunauš : hya : Dārayavahauš : XŠyā : xsaça
4 m : frābara : tya : vazrakam : tya : uwaspam : umartiyam : adam : Dārayavauš :
5 XŠ : vazraka : XŠ : XŠyānām : XŠ : dahyūnām : vispazanānām : XŠ : ahyāy
6 ā : būmiyā : vazrakāyā : dūraiy : apiy : Vištāspahyā : puça : Ha
7 xāmanišiya : θātiy : Dārayavauš : XŠ : adam : Pārsa : amiy : hacā : Pā
8 rsa : Mudrāyam : agarbāyam : adam : niyaštāyam : imām : yauviyā
9 m : katanaiy : hacā : Pirāva : nāma : rauta : tya : Mudrāyaiy : danuvatiy : ab
10 iy : draya : tya : hacā : Pārsā : aitiy : pasāva : iyam : yauviyā : akaniya :
11 avaθā : yaθā : adam : niyaštāyam : utā : nāva : āyatā : hacā : Mudrā
12 yā : tara : imām : yauviyām : abiy : Pārsam : avaθā : yaθā : mām : kāma : āha

NOTES TO DZc. The Fragment has ⁹⁻¹⁰ a]biy [: draya and ¹⁰⁻¹ akani]ya : a[vaθā

TRANSLATION OF DZc:
§1. 1–4. . (= DNa 1–6, with one change of order); who upon Darius the King   (= DSf 11–2).
§2. 4–7.   (=DNa 8–13).
§3. 7–12. Saith Darius the King: I am a Persian; from Persia I seized Egypt; I gave order to dig this canal from a river by name Nile which flows in Egypt, to the sea which goes from Persia. Afterward this canal was dug thus as I had ordered, and ships went from Egypt through this canal to Persia thus as was my desire.

DE = DARIUS, ELVEND.

1 baga : vazraka : Auramazdā
2 : hya : imām : būmim :
3 adā : hya : avam : asmā
4 nam : adā : hya : martiya
5 m : adā : hya : šiyāti
6 m : adā : martiyahyā :
7 hya : Dārayavaum : xšāya
8 θiyam : akunauš : aiva
9 m : parūnām : xšāyaθ
10 iyam : aivam : parūnām
11 : framātāram : adam :
12 Dārayavauš : xšāyaθi
13 ya : vazraka : xšāyaθiya :
14 xšāyaθiyānām : xš
15 āyaθiya : dahyūnām : pa
16 ruzanānām : xšāyaθ
17 iya : ahyāyā : būmiy
18 ā : vazrakāyā : dūraiy
19 : apiy : Vištāspahy
20 ā : puça : Haxāmanišiya

TRANSLATION OF DE:
§1. 1–11.   (= DNa 1–8).
§2. 11–20.   (= DNa 8–10), containing many men,   (= DNa 11–3).

DH = DARIUS, HAMADAN.

1 Dārayavauš : XŠ : vazraka : XŠ : XŠyanām : XŠ : dahy
2 ūvnām : Vištāspahyā : puça : Haxāmanišiya :
3 θātiy : Dārayavauš : XŠ : ima : xšaçam : tya : ada
4 m : dārayāmiy : hacā : Sakaibiš : tyaiy : pa
5 ra : Sugdam : amata : yātā : ā : Kūšā : hacā : Hida
6 uv : amata : yātā : ā : Spardā : tyamaiy : Aurama
7 zdā : frābara : hya : maθišta : bagānām : m
8 ām : Auramazdā : pātuv : utāmaiy : viθam

NOTE TO DH Our text follows the line-divisions of the copy on the gold plate.

TRANSLATION OF DH:
§1. 1–2.   (= DPh 1–3).
§2. 3–8.   (=DPh 3–10).

XPa = XERXES, PERSEPOLIS A.

1 baga : vazraka : Auramazdā : hya : imām : būmim : a
2 dā : hya : avam : asmānam : adā : hya : martiyam :

3 adā : hya : šiyātim : adā : martiyahyā : hya
4 : Xšayāršām : xšāyaθiyam : akunauš : aivam :
5 parūnām : xšāyaθiyam : aivam : parūnām : fram
6 ātāram : adam : Xšayāršā : xšāyaθiya : vazraka :
7 xšāyaθiya : xšāyaθiyānām : xšāyaθiya : dahy
8 ūnām : paruv : zanānām : xšāyaθiya : ahyāy
9 ā : būmiyā : vazrakāyā : dūraiy : apiy : Dā
10 rayavahauš : xšāyaθiyahyā : puça : Hāxāmaniš
11 iya : θātiy : Xšayāršā : xšāyaθiya : vašnā :
12 Auramazdāhā : imam : duvarθim : visadahyum
13 : adam : akunavam : vasiy : aniyašciy : naibam
14 : kartam : anā : Pārsā : tya : adam : akunavam :
15 utamaiy : tya : pitā : akunauš : tyapatiy : ka
16 rtam : vainataiy : naibam : ava : visam : vašnā : A
17 uramazdāhā : akumā : θātiy : Xšayāršā :
18 xšāyaθiya : mām : Auramazdā : pātuv : utamai
19 y : xšaçam : utā : tya : manā : kartam : utā : tyamai
20 y : piça : kartam : avašciy : Auramazdā : pātuv

NOTE TO XPa: [11-2] *Hāxāmanišiya*, incorrect engraving for *Hāxā-*.

TRANSLATION OF XPa:

§1. 1–6.   (= DNa 1–4), who made Darius king, one king of many, one lord of many.

§2. 6–11. I am Xerxes,   (= DE 12–9), son of King Darius, an Achaemenian.

§3. 11–7. Saith Xerxes the King: By the favor of Ahuramazda, this Colonnade of All Lands I built. Much other good (construction) was built within this (city) Persepolis, which I built and which my father built. Whatever good construction is seen, all that by the favor of Ahuramazda we built.

§4. 17–20. Saith Xerxes the King: Me may Ahuramazda protect, and my kingdom, and what was built by me, and what was built by my father, that also may Ahuramazda protect.

XPb = XERXES, PERSEPOLIS B.

1 baga : vazraka : Auramazdā
2 : hya : imām : būmim :
3 adā : hya : avam : asmā
4 nam : adā : hya : martiya
5 m : adā : hya : šiyāti
6 m : adā : martiyahyā :
7 hya : Xšayāršām : xšā
8 yaθiyam : akunauš : ai
9 vam : parūnām : xšāyaθ
10 iyam : aivam : parūnām
11 : framātāram : adam : X

12 šayāršā : xšāyaθiya :
13 vazraka : xšāyaθiya : xš
14 āyaθiyānām : xšāyaθ
15 iya : dahyūnām : paruv
16 zanānām : xšāyaθiya :
17 ahiyāyā : būmiyā :
18 vazrakāyā : dūraiy :
19 piy : Dārayavahauš : axš
20 āyaθiyahyā : puça : Hax
21 āmanišiya : θātiy : X
22 šayāršā : xšāyaθiya :
23 vazraka : tya : manā : karta
24 m : idā : utā : tyamaiy
25 : apataram : kartam : ava : v
26 isam : vašnā : Auramazdā
27 ha : akunavam : mām : Aura
28 mazdā : pātuv : hadā : ba
29 gaibiš : utāmaiy : xšaça
30 m : utā : tyamaiy : kartam

NOTE TO XPb: Our text has the line-divisions of the second copy, as seen in Hz. ApI, Tafel IX.

TRANSLATION OF XPb:

§1. 1–11.   (= XPa 1–6).

§2. 11–21.   (= XPa 6–11).

§3. 21–30. Saith Xerxes the Great King: What has been built by me here, and what has been built by me at a distance (from here), all that by the favor of Ahuramazda I built. Me may Ahuramazda together with the gods protect, and my kingdom, and what has been built by me.

TEXTS WITH NOTES AND TRANSLATION   149

XPc = Xerxes, Persepolis c.

1 baga : vazraka : Auramazdā : hya : imām : būmim :
2 adā : hya : avam : asmānam : adā : hya : marti
3 yam : adā : hya : šiyātim : adā : martiyahyā
4 : hya : Xšayāršām : XŠm : akunauš : aivam : pa
5 rūnām : XŠm : aivam : parūnām : framātāram
6 : adam : Xšayāršā : XŠ : vazraka : XŠ : XŠānām : XŠ :
7 dahyūnām : paruv : zanānām : XŠ : ahyāyā : b
8 ūmiyā : vazrakāyā : dūraiy : apiy : Dārayava
9 hauš : XŠhyā : puça : Haxāmanišiya : θātiy : X
10 šayāršā : XŠ : vazraka : vašnā : Aurahya Mazdāha : i
11 ma : hadiš : Dārayavauš : XŠ : akunauš : hya : manā :
12 pitā : mām : Auramazdā : pātuv : hadā : baga
13 ibiš : utā : tyamaiy : kartam : utā : tyamaiy :
14 piça : Dārayavahauš : XŠhyā : kartam : avašciy
15 : Auramazdā : pātuv : hadā : bagaibiš

NOTE TO XPc. The divider is lacking between *Aurahya* and *Mazdāha* (ca 10, cb 17, cc 11), acc. to Cameron's examination of the photographs

TRANSLATION OF XPc:
§1. 1–5. .   (= XPa 1–6).
§2. 6–9.   (= XPa 6–11).
§3. 9–15. Saith Xerxes the Great King: By the favor of Ahuramazda this palace Darius the King built, who was my father. Me may Ahuramazda together with the gods protect, and what was built by me, and what was built by my father Darius the King, that also may Ahuramazda together with the gods protect.

XPd = Xerxes, Persepolis d.

1 baga : vazraka : Auramazdā : hya : i
2 mām : būmim : adā : hya : avam
3 : asmānam : adā : hya : martiya
4 m : adā : hya : šiyātim : adā : mar
5 tiyahyā : hya : Xšayāršām : x
6 šāyaθiyam : akunauš : aivam : par
7 ūnām : xšāyaθiyam : aivam : parū
8 nām : framātāram : adam : Xšayārš
9 ā : xšāyaθiya : vazraka : xšāyaθiya :
10 xšāyaθiyānām : xšāyaθiya : dahy
11 ūnām : paruvzanānām : xšāyaθiya
12 : ahiyāyā : būmiyā : vazrakāyā
13 : dūraiy : apiy : Dārayavahauš : xš
14 āyaθiyahyā : puça : Haxāmanišiya :
15 θātiy : Xšayāršā : xšāyaθiya : va
16 zraka : vašnā : Auramazdāha : ima : had
17 iš : adam : akunavam : mām : Auramaz
18 dā : pātuv : hadā : bagaibiš : utama
19 iy : xšaçam : utā : tyamaiy : kartam

NOTE TO XPd: Copy db on the eastern stairway has a distinct divider at the end, after *kartam*; db on the western stairway has room for a divider at the end, but the stone is damaged and no divider can be seen (Cameron's data).

TRANSLATION OF XPd:
§1. 1–8.   (= XPa 1–6).
§2. 8–14.   (= XPa 6–11).
§3. 15–9. Saith Xerxes the Great King: By the favor of Ahuramazda this palace I built.   . (= XPb 27–30).

XPe = Xerxes, Persepolis e.

1 Xšayāršā : xšāyaθiya : vazra
2 ka : xšāyaθiya : xšāyaθiyā
3 nām : Dārayavahauš : xšāyaθ
4 iyahyā : puça : Haxāmanišiya :

TRANSLATION OF XPe: . (= XPa 6–7, 9–11).

XPf = Xerxes, Persepolis f.

1 baga : vazraka : Auramazdā : hya : imā
2 m : būmim : adā : hya : avam : asm
3 ānam : adā : hya : martiyam : adā :
4 hya : šiyātim : adā : martiyahy
5 ā : hya : Xšayāršām : xšāyaθiyam
6 : akunauš : aivam : parūnām : xš
7 āyaθiyam : aivam : parūnām : fram
8 ātāram : adam : Xšayāršā : xšā
9 yaθiya : vazraka : xšāyaθiya : xšā
10 yaθiyānām : xšāyaθiya : dahyū
11 nām : paruv : zanānām : xšāyaθ
12 iya : ahyāyā : būmiyā : vazrak
13 āyā : dūraiy : apiy : Dārayavaha
14 uš : xšāyaθiyahyā : puça : Haxā

150   OLD PERSIAN

15 manišiya : θātiy : Xšayāršā :
16 xšāyaθıya : manā : pitā : Dāraya
17 vauš : Dārayavahauš : pitā : Vıš
18 tāspa : nāma : āha : Vištāspahy
19 ā : pitā : Aršāma : nāma : āha : u
20 tā : Vıštāspa : utā : Aršāma :
21 ubā : ajīvatam : aciy : Auramaz
22 dām : avaθā : kāma : āha : Dārayava
23 um : hya : manā : pıtā : avam : xš
24 āyaθiyam : akunauš : ahyāyā :
25 būmiyā : yaθā : Dārayavahauš : xš
26 āyaθiya : abava : vasiy : tya : fraθara
27 m : akunauš : θātiy : Xšayāršā
28 : xšāyaθiya : Dārayavauš : puçā :
29 aniyaiciy : āhatā : Auramazdām
30 : avaθa : kāma : āha : Dārayavauš : hya
31 : manā : pitā : pasā : tanūm : mām
32 : maθištam : akunauš : yaθāmaiy
33 : pitā : Dārayavauš : gāθavā : a
34 šiyava : vašnā : Auramazdahā : ada
35 m : xšāyaθiya : abavam : piça : gā
36 θavā : yaθā : adam : xšāyaθiya : a
37 bavam : vasiy : tya : fraθaram : aku
38 navam : tyamaiy : piça : kartam : āha
39 : ava : adam : apayaiy : utā : ani
40 ya : kartam : abījāvayam : tyapati
41 y : adam : akunavam : utamaiy : tya
42 : pıtā : akunauš : ava : visam :
43 vašnā : Auramazdahā : akumā : θ
44 ātiy : Xšayāršā : xšāyaθiya :
45 mām : Auramazdā : pātuv : utama
46 iy : xšaçam : utā : tya : manā : kar
47 tam : utā : tyamaiy : piça : kartam
48 : avašciy : Auramazdā : pātuv

NOTES TO XPf ²⁵ Dārayavahauš, for nom. -vauš; in the original draft, the hᵃ had been omitted ın the gen in lıne 28, and when the error was noted the correction was made in the wrong occurrence of the word. ²⁸ On the accessıon of Xerxes, see Hist App V.

TRANSLATION OF XPf:
§1. 1–8.   (=XPa 1–6).
§2. 8–15. (= XPa 6–11).
§3. 15–27. Saith Xerxes the King: My father was Darıus; Darius's father was Hystaspes by name; Hystaspes's father was Arsames by name. Both Hystaspes and Arsames were both living, at that time—thus unto Ahuramazda was the desire —Darius, who was my father, him he made king in this earth When Darius became king, he built much excellent (construction).

§4. 27–43. Saith Xerxes the King: Other sons of Darius there were, (but)—thus unto Ahuramazda was the desire—Darius my father made me the greatest after himself. When my father Darius went away from the throne, by the will of Ahuramazda I became king on my father's throne. When I became king, I built much excellent (construction). What had been built by my father, that I protected, and other building I added. What moreover I built, and what my father built, all that by the favor of Ahuramazda we built.
§5. 43–48.   (= XPa 17–20).

XPg = XERXES, PERSEPOLIS G.

1 θātiy : Xšayāršā :
2 xšāyaθiya : vazraka : vaš
3 nā : Auramazdāha : vasi
4 y : tya : naibam : akunau
5 š : utā : frāmāyatā :
6 Dārayavauš : xšāyaθiya
7 : hya : manā : pitā : vaš
8 nāpiy : Auramazdāha
9 : adam : abiyajāvayam
10 : abiy : ava : kartam :
11 utā : frataram : akuna
12 vam : mām : Auramazdā
13 : pātuv : hadā : bagai
14 biš : utamaiy : xšaçam

NOTE TO XPg: ⁷⁻⁸ vašnā[pı]y Bv. BSLP 34.1.32-4, which I now regard as better than my own vašnā[ci]y or vašnā[dı]y, Lg. 9.230.

TRANSLATION OF XPg: Saith Xerxes the Great King: By the favor of Ahuramazda, King Darius my father built and ordered (to be built) much good (construction). By the favor also of Ahuramazda I added to that construction and built further (buildıngs).   (= XPb 27–30).

XPh = XERXES, PERSEPOLIS H.

1 baga : vazraka : Auramazdā : hya : imām : būm
2 im : adā : hya : avam : asmānam : adā : hya
3 : martiyam : adā : hya : šiyātim : adā :
4 martiyahyā : hya : Xšayāršām : xšāyaθi
5 yam : akunauš : aivam : parūnām : xšāyaθ
6 iyam : aivam : parūnām : framātāram : ada
7 m : Xšayāršā : xšāyaθiya : vazraka : xšāya
8 θiya : xšāyaθiyānām : xšāyaθiya : dahy
9 ūnām : paruv : zanānām : xšāyaθiya : ah
10 yāyā : būmiyā : vazrakāyā : dūraiy : a

PLATE III

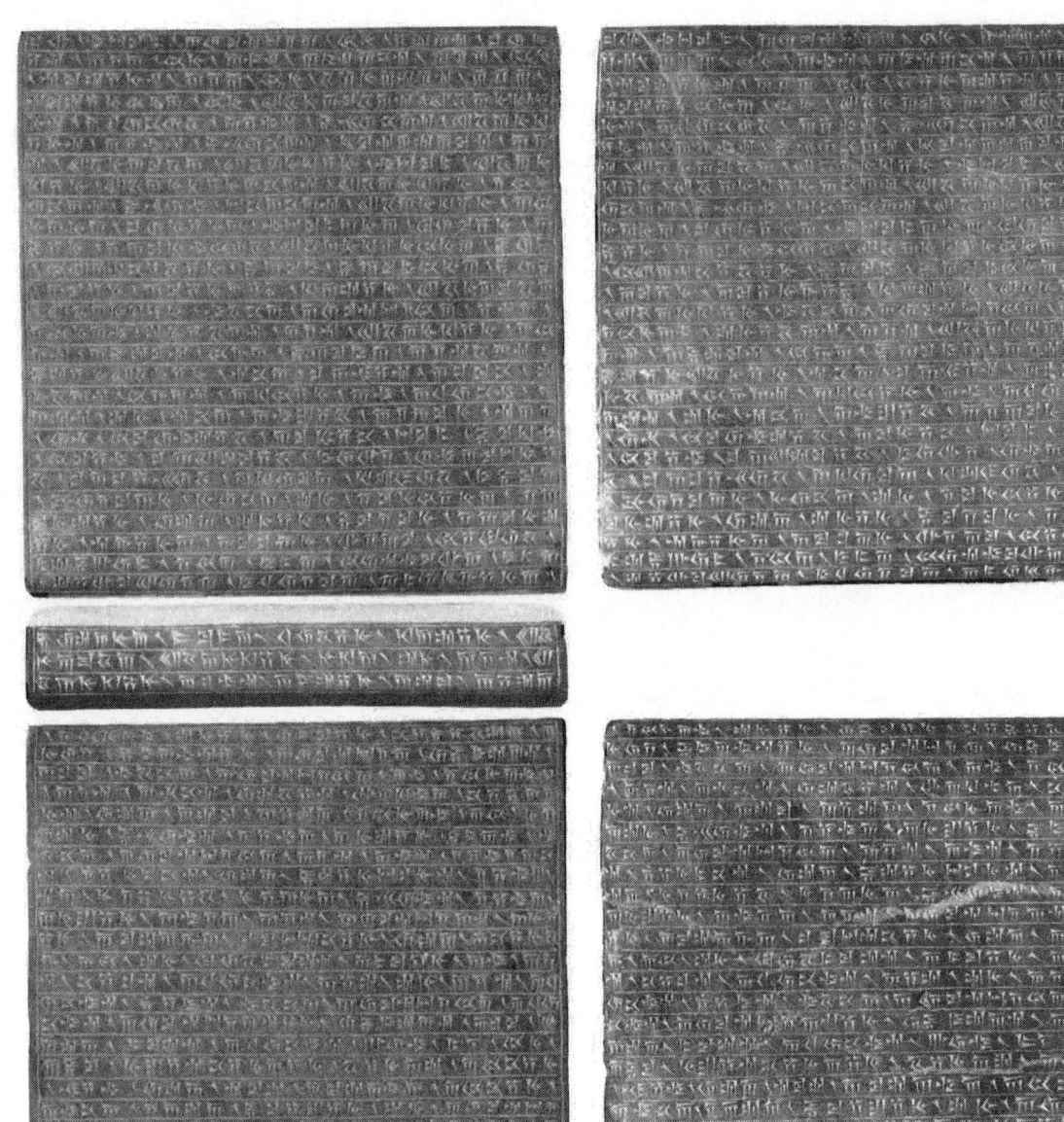

copy a   copy b

THE DAIVA INSCRIPTION OF XERXES

Reproduced by courtesy of the Oriental Institute of the University of Chicago

11 piy : Dārayavahauš : xšāyaθiyahyā : puça
12 : Haxāmanišiya : Pārsa : Pārsahyā : puça
13 : Ariya : Ariyaciça : θātiy : Xšayāršā
14 : xšāyaθiya : vašnā : Auramazdahā : imā :
15 dahyāva : tyaišām : adam : xšāyaθiya : āh
16 ām : apataram : hacā : Pārsa : adamšām :
17 patiyaxšayaiy : manā : bājim : abaraha : t
18 yašām : hacāma : aθahiya : ava : akunava : d
19 ātam : tya : manā : avadiš : adāraya : Māda
20 : Ūja : Harauvatiš : Armina : Zraka : Parθava
21 : Haraiva : Bāxtriš : Sugda : Uvārazmi
22 š : Bābiruš : Aθurā : Θataguš : Sparda
23 : Mudrāya : Yaunā : tya : drayahiyā : dā
24 rayatiy : utā : tyaiy : paradraya : dārayat
25 iy : Maciyā : Arabāya : Gadāra : Hiduš :
26 Katpatuka : Dahā : Sakā : haumavargā : Sakā
27 : tigraxaudā : Skudrā : Ākaufaciyā :
28 Putāyā : Karkā : Kūšiya : θātiy : Xša
29 yāršā : xšāyaθiya : yaθā : tya : adam : x
30 šāyaθiya : abavam : astiy : atar : aitā
31 : dahyāva : tyaiy : upariy : nipištā : a
32 yauda : pasāvamaiy : Auramazdā : upastām :
33 abara : vašnā : Auramazdahā : ava :
                                              dahyāvam
34 : adam : ajanam : utašim : gāθavā : nīšāda
35 yam : utā : atar : aitā : dahyāva : āha : yad
36 ātya : paruvam : daivā : ayadiya : pasāva : va
37 šnā : Auramazdahā : adam : avam : daivadāna
38 m : viyakanam : utā : patiyazbayam : daivā :
39 mā : yadiyaiša : yadāyā : paruvam : daivā :
40 ayadiya : avadā : adam : Auramazdām : ayada
41 iy : artācā : brazmaniya : utā : aniyaš
42 cᵃ : āha : tya : duškartam : akariya : ava : ada
43 m : naibam : akunavam : aita : tya : adam : ak
44 unavam : visam : vašnā : Auramazdahā : aku
45 navam : Auramazdāmaiy : upastām : abara : y
46 ātā : kartam : akunavam : tuva : kā : hya :
47 apara : yadimaniyāiy : šiyāta : ahaniy
48 : jīva : utā : marta : artāvā : ahaniy :
49 avanā : dātā : parīdiy : tya : Auramazd
50 ā : niyaštāya : Auramazdām : yadaišā : a
51 rtācā : brazmaniya : martiya : hya : avan
52 ā : dātā : pariyaitᵃ : tya : Auramazdā : n
53 īštāya : utā : Auramazdām : yadataiy : a
54 rtācā : brazmaniya : hauv : utā : jīva :
55 šiyāta : bavatiy : utā : marta : artāvā
56 : bavatiy : θātiy : Xšayāršā : xšāyaθ
57 iya : mām : Auramazdā : pātuv : hacā : ga
58 stā : *u*tamaiy : viθam : utā : imām : dah

59 yāvam : aita : adam : Auramazdām : jadiy
60 āmiy : aitamaiy : Auramazdā : dadātuv

Notes to XPh [17] The *hᵃ* of *abaraha* has become *nᵃ* by failure to engrave the prior angle. [23] *tᵃyᵃ* for *tᵃyᵃiyᵃ* = *tyaiy*. [31] The *pᵃ* of *upariy* lacks the two small verticals in copy a [37] The *daivadāna-* of copy a is *daivadāva-* in copy b; the engraver was misled by the *vᵃ* ending the previous line (Hz. AMI 8 62) [39] *yᵃdᵃiyᵃišᵃ* for *yᵃdᵃiyᵃišᵃ* = *yadiyaiša* [41] For the normalization *brazmaniya* here and in 51 and 54, see Lex s v [41–2] *aniyašcᵃ* for *-cᵃiyᵃ* = *-ciy* [46] The *mᵃ* of *-maiy* lacks the small middle vertical in copy b [46] The *a* of *kā*, in both copies, has the horizontal over a single vertical only [47] *apara* is perhaps an error for *aparam*, which elsewhere stands in this idiom [51] Copy b ends midway in this line, with the left-hand part lacking; the engraver was accustomed to Aramaic writing, which went from right to left, Hz AMI 8 62. [52] *pariyaitᵃ* = *-tᵃiyᵃ* = *-tiy*. [58] In the prior *utā* the space for the first character is left blank; probably the character in the model copy was illegible to the engraver.

Translation of XPh:

§1. 1–6.   (= XPa 1–6).
§2. 6–13. (=XPa 6–11, DNa 13–5).

§3. 13–28. Saith Xerxes the King: By the favor of Ahuramazda these are the countries of which I was king (= DNa 18–22); Media, Elam, Arachosia, Armenia, Drangiana, Parthia, Aria, Bactria, Sogdiana, Chorasmia, Babylonia, Assyria, Sattagydia, Sardis, Egypt, Ionians, those who dwell by the sea and those who dwell across the sea, men of Maka, Arabia, Gandara, Sind, Cappadocia, Dahae, Amyrgian Scythians, Pointed-Cap Scythians, Skudra, men of Akaufaka, Libyans, Carians, Ethiopians.

§4a. 28–35. Saith Xerxes the King: When that I became king, there is among these countries which are inscribed above (one which) was in commotion. Afterwards Ahuramazda bore me aid; by the favor of Ahuramazda I smote that country and put it down in its place.

§4b. 35–41. And among these countries there was (a place) where previously false gods were worshipped. Afterwards, by the favor of Ahuramazda, I destroyed that sanctuary of the demons, and I made proclamation, "The demons shall not be worshipped!" Where previously the demons were worshipped, there I worshipped Ahuramazda and Arta reverent(ly).

§4c. 41–6. And there was other (business) that had been done ill; that I made good. That which I did, all I did by the favor of Ahuramazda.

Ahuramazda bore me aid, until I completed the work.

§4d. 46–56. Thou who (shalt be) hereafter, if thou shalt think, "Happy may I be when living, and when dead may I be blessed," have respect for that law which Ahuramazda has established; worship Ahuramazda and Arta reverent(ly). The man who has respect for that law which Ahuramazda has established, and worships Ahuramazda and Arta reverent(ly), he both becomes happy while living, and becomes blessed when dead.

§5. 56–60. Saith Xerxes the King: (= DNa 51–5).

XPi = Xerxes, Persepolis i.

*may*ūxa : kāsakaina : Xšayāršāha : XŠhyā : viθiyā : karta

TRANSLATION OF XPi: .   (= DPi) of Xerxes.

XPj = Xerxes, Persepolis j.

adam : Xšayāršā : XŠ : vazraka : XŠ : XŠyānām : XŠ : DHyūnām : XŠ : ahyāyā : būmi*y*ā : Dārayavahauš : XŠyahyā : puça : Haxāmanišiya : θātiy : Xšayāršā : XŠ : imam : tacaram : adam : akunavam

XSc = Xerxes, Susa c.

1 adam : Xšayāršā : xšāyaθiya : vazraka : xšāyaθiya : xšāyaθiyānām : xšāya
2 θiya : dahyūnām : Dārayavahauš : xšāyaθiyahyā : puça : Haxāmanišiya : θāt
3 iy : Xšayāršā : xšāyaθiya : ima : hadiš : akunām : pasāva : yaθā : adam : xšāya
4 θiya : abavam : aita : adam : yānam : jadiyāmiy : Auramazdām : mām : Au
5 ramazdā : pātuv : hadā : bagaibiš : utamaiy : xšaçam : utā : tyamaiy : kartam

TRANSLATION OF XSc:
§1. 1–2.   (= XPa 6–8, 9–11).
§2. 2–5. Saith Xerxes the King: This palace I built after that I became king. This I ask as a boon from Ahuramazda: (= XPb 27–30).

XE = Xerxes, Elvend.

1 baga : vazraka : Auramazdā :
2 hya : maθišta : bagānām :
3 hya : imām : būmim : ad
4 ā : hya : avam : asmānam :
5 adā : hya : martiyam : ad
6 ā : hya : šiyātim : adā
7 : martiyahyā : hya : Xša
8 yāršām : xšāyaθiyam :
9 akunauš : aivam : parūn
10 ām : xšāyaθiyam : aivam
11 : parūnām : framātāram

NOTE TO XPj. The additional fragments found by Cameron fill most of the gaps left by Herzfeld's fragments, and give also the readings *ahiyāyā* and *XŠyahıyā* for some of the copies.

TRANSLATION OF XPj:
§1. 1–3.   (= XPa 6–11, with two omissions).
§2. 3–4. Saith Xerxes the King: This palace I built.

XPk = Xerxes, Persepolis k.

Xšayāršā : Dārayavahauš : XŠhyā : puça : Haxāmanišiya

TRANSLATION OF XPk: Xerxes, son of King Darius, an Achaemenian.

XSa = Xerxes, Susa a.

1 θātiy : Xšayāršā : xšāyaθiya : vašnā :
                Auramazdāha : ima :
2 hadiš : Dārayavauš : xšāyaθiya : akunauš :
                hya : manā : pitā

NOTES TO XSa· This is the line-division of Scheil's copy; the other copy divides before *ima*. Scheil's hand-drawn copy has *ak*^u*un*^a*uu*^š*a*, against Wb's normal *ak*^u*un*^a*u*š^a.

TRANSLATION OF XSa: ...   (= XPc 9–12, with slight omissions).

12 : adam : Xšayāršā : xšā
13 yaθiya : vazraka : xšāyaθi
14 ya : xšāyaθiyānām : xš
15 āyaθiya : dahyūnām : par
16 uzanānām : xšāyaθiya :
17 ahiyāyā : būmiyā : va
18 zrakāyā : dūraiy : apiy
19 : Dārayavahauš : xšāyaθiya
20 hyā : puça : Haxāmanišiya

TRANSLATION OF XE:
§1. 1–11.   (= XPa 1–6).
§2. 12–20. ..   (= XPa 6–11).

XV = Xerxes, Van.

1 baga : vazraka : Auramazdā : hya : maθi
2 šta : bagānām : hya : imām : būm
3 im : adā : hya : avam : asmānam :
4 adā : hya : martiyam : adā : hya :

5 šiyātim : adā : martiyahyā :
6 hya : Xšayāršām : xšāyaθiyam
7 : akunauš : aivam : parūnām : x
8 šāyaθiyam : aivam : parūnām :
9 framātāram : adam : Xšayāršā :
10 xšāyaθiya : vazraka : xšāyaθiya :
11 xšāyaθiyānām : xšāyaθiya : da
12 hyūnām : paruv : zanānām : xš
13 āyaθiya : ahyāyā : būmiyā : va
14 zrakāyā : dūraiy : apiy : Dāraya
15 vahauš : xšāyaθiyahyā : puça : Ha
16 xāmanišiya : θātiy : Xšayāršā
17 : xšāyaθiya : Dārayavauš : xšāya
18 θiya : hya : manā : pitā : hauv : va
19 šnā : Auramazdāha : vasiy : tya :
20 naibam : akunauš : utā : ima : st
21 ānam : hauv : niyaštāya : katanaiy
22 : yaniy : dipim : naiy : nipišt
23 ām : akunauš : pasāva : adam : ni
24 yaštāyam : imām : dipim : nipa
25 ištanaiy : mām : Auramazdā : pā
26 tuv : hadā : bagaibiš : utāmai
27 y : xšaçam : utā : tyamaiy : kartam

NOTE TO XV· The entire line 25 is clearly legible in the photograph reproduced by Lehmann, SbPAW 1900 1.628 Taf. 2.

TRANSLATION OF XV:

§1. 1–9. A great god is Ahuramazda, the greatest of gods, . (= XPa 1–6).

§2. 9–16. (= XPa 6–11).

§3. 16–27. Saith Xerxes the King: King Darius, who was my father—he by the favor of Ahuramazda built much good (construction), and this niche he gave orders to dig out, where he did not cause an inscription (to be) engraved. Afterwards I gave order to engrave this inscription. (= XPb 27–30).

XH = XERXES, HAMADAN.

Xšayāršaha : XŠhyā : viθiyā : kartam

NOTES TO XH. Probably the word for 'pitcher' has been lost at the beginning, as the inscription is engraved on a pitcher. *XŠhyā* acc. to Hz ApI 43, probably correct rather than the exceptional writing *XŠyā* given in Hz. AMI 2.115.

TRANSLATION OF XH: (Pitcher) made in the house of Xerxes the King.

A¹Pa = ARTAXERXES I, PERSEPOLIS A.

1 *baga : vazraka : Auramazdā : hya :*
2 *imām : būmim : adā : hya : ava*
3 *m : asmānam : adā : hya : marti*
4 *yam : adā : hya : šiyātim : ad*
5 *ā : martiyahyā : hya : Artaxšaç*
6 *ām : xšāyaθiyam : akunauš : a*
7 *ivam : parūnām : xšāyaθiyam :*
8 *aivam : parūnām : framātāram*
9 *: adam : Artaxšaçā : xšāyaθiya*
10 *: vazraka : xšāyaθiya : xšāyaθi*
11 *yānām : xšāyaθiya · dahyūnā*
12 *m : paruzanānām : xšāyaθiya :*
13 *ahyāyā : būmiyā : vazrak*
14 *āyā : dūraiy : apiy : Xšay*
15 *āršahyā : xšāyaθiyahyā : pu*
16 *ça : Dārayavahauš : napā : Haxāmanišiya*
17 *: θātiy : Artaxšaçā : xšā*
18 *yaθiya : vazraka · vašnā : Au*
19 *ramazdahā : ima : hadiš : Xšaya*
20 *ršā : xšāyaθiya : hya : manā : pi*
21 *tā : frataram : pasāva : adam : aku*
22 navam *: mām : Auramazdā : pāt*
23 *uv : hadā : bagaibiš : utamaiy :*
24 *xšaçam : utā : tyamaiy : kartam*

NOTE TO A¹Pa: For reconstruction, see JNES 4.228-32.

TRANSLATION OF A¹Pa:

§1. 1–8. (= DNa 1–4), who made Artaxerxes king, one king of many, one lord of many.

§2. 9–16. I am Artaxerxes, (= DE 12–9), son of Xerxes the King, grandson of Darius, an Achaemenian.

§3. 17–24. Saith Artaxerxes the Great King: By the favor of Ahuramazda, this palace Xerxes the King, my father, previously (began to build), afterwards I built (to completion). (= XPb 27–30).

A¹I = ARTAXERXES I, INCERTO LOCO.

Artaxšaçā : XŠ : vazraka : XŠ : XŠyānām : XŠ : DHyūnām : Xšayāršahyā : XŠhyā : puça : Xšayāršahyā : Dārayavaušahyā : XŠhyā : puça : Haxāmanišiya : hya : imam : bātugara : siyamam : viθiyā : karta

NOTE ON A¹I: For syntax of last clause, cf. the idiom in DPi, XPi, XH

TRANSLATION OF A¹I: Artaxerxes the Great King, King of Kings, King of Countries, son of Xerxes the King, of Xerxes (who was) son of Darius the King; in whose royal house this silver saucer was made.

D²Sa = Darius II, Susa a.

1 imam : apadānam : stūnāya : aθagainam :
2 Dārayavauš : XŠ : vazraka : akunauš : Dāraya
3 vaum : XŠm : AM pātuv : hadā : BGibiš

Translation of D²Sa: This palace, of stone in its column(s), Darius the Great King built; Darius the King may Ahuramazda together with the gods protect.

D²Sb = Darius II, Susa b.

1 adam : Dārayavauš : XŠ : vazraka : XŠ .
    XŠyānām : XŠ : DHyūnām XŠ : a
2 hyāyā : BUyā : Artaxšaçahyā : XŠhyā : puça :
    Haxāmanišiya :
3 θātiy : Dārayavauš : XŠ : ima : hadiš :
    Artaxšaçā : paranam : akunauš :
4 hya : manā : pitā : ima : hadiš : pasāva :
    vašnā : AMha : adam : akunavam

Notes to D²Sb Brd WZKM 39.85-7, after the Akk., restored ³ [apara]m 'upper part' = 'part at the top of the slope', and ⁴ [adaram] 'lower part' = 'part lower on the hill'; but Hinz, ZDMG 91 251-2, restores [parana]m and [pasāva], in temporal sense, which is preferable. ³akunaš in copy b.

Translation of D²Sb:

§1. 1-2. (= DNa 8-12, with one omission), son of Artaxerxes the King, an Achaemenian.

§2. 3-4. Saith Darius the King: This palace Artaxerxes previously built, who was my father; this palace, by the favor of Ahuramazda, I afterwards built (to completion).

A²Sa = Artaxerxes II, Susa a.

1 θātiy : Artaxšaçā : XŠ : vazraka : XŠ :
  XŠyānām : XŠ : DHyūnām : XŠ : ahyāyā :
  BUyā : Dārayavaušahyā : XŠhyā : puça : D
2 ārayavaušahyā : Artaxšaçāhyā : XŠhyā :
  puça : Artaxšaçahyā : Xšayārcahyā : XŠhyā :
  puça : Xšayārcahyā : Dāra
3 yavaušahyā : XŠhyā : puça : Dārayavaušahyā
  : V¹štāspahyā : puça : Haxamānᵃšiya : imam :
  apadāna : Dārayavauš : apanᵃyākama : ak
4 unaš : abᵃyapara : upā : Artaxšaçām :
  nᵃyākama : + + + + : vašnā : AM : Anahᵃta
  : utā : M¹θra : imam : apadāna : adam : akunām
  : AM : A
5 nahᵃta : utā : M¹θra : mām : pātuv : hacā :
  vispā . gastā . utā : imam : tya : akunām : mā :
  vijanātiy : mā : vināθayātiy

Note to A²Sa. Lines 4-5 are restored after the OP text of A²Ha and the Akk. version of A²Sa.

Translation of A²Sa: Saith Artaxerxes the Great King, King of Kings, King of Countries, King in this earth, son of Darius the King, of Darius (who was) son of Artaxerxes the King, of Artaxerxes (who was) son of Xerxes the King, of Xerxes (who was) son of Darius the King, of Darius (who was) son of Hystaspes, an Achaemenian: This palace Darius my great-great-grandfather built; later under Artaxerxes my grandfather it was burned; by the favor of Ahuramazda, Anaitis, and Mithras, this palace I built. May Ahuramazda, Anaitis, and Mithras protect me from all evil, and that which I have built may they not shatter nor harm.

A²Sb = Artaxerxes II, Susa b.

adam : Artaxšaçā : XŠ : vazraka : XŠ XŠyānā :
XŠ : Dārayavauš : XŠhyā : puça

Note to A²Sb. The XŠ after XŠyānā is a dittographic insertion, to which nothing corresponds in the other two versions.

Translation of A²Sb: (= A²Sa 1, with omissions).

A²Sc = Artaxerxes II, Susa c.

0 Dārayavaušahyā : XŠhyā : puça :
0 Dārayavaušahyā : V¹štāspahyā : puça
1 : Haxāmanišiya : θātiy : Artaxšaçā :
2 xšāyaθiya : vazraka : xšāyaθiya : x
3 šāyaθiyanām : xšāyaθiya : dahyūn
4 ām : xšāyaθiya : ahyāyā : būmiyā : i
5 mām : hadiš : utā : imam : usta
6 canām : tya : aθagainām : ta + + + + +
7   : Auramazdā :
8

Note to A²Sc The first two lines are restored to include the fragment mentioned by Wb. KIA 125n.; but this fragment has the ideogram for 'king', and the other part has the word written in full. Cf. note on DSm.

Translation of A²Sc:

§1. 0-1.   (= A²Sa 2-3).

§2. 1-7.   (= A²Sa 1): This palace and this stone staircase   Ahuramazda ..

A²Sd = Artaxerxes II, Susa d (copies da, db, dc).

1 adam : Artaxšaçā : XŠ : vazraka : XŠ :
  XŠyānām : XŠ : DHyūnām : XŠ : ahyāyā :
2 BUyā : Dārayavauš : XŠāhyā : puça :
  Haxāmanišiya : θātiy : Artaxšaçā : XŠ :

TEXTS WITH NOTES AND TRANSLATION 155

3 vašnā : AMhā : imām : hadiš : tya : j¹vadiy :
paradayadām : adam : akunavām : AM :
Anah

4 ita : utā : M¹tra : mām : pātuv : hacā : vispā
: gastā : utamaiy : kartam

NOTES TO A²Sd: Text according to the line-divisions of copy da. ¹ a[da; ahyāyā db; ahyā dc ² Haxāmanišiya db; Haxāmanišᵃya da, dc. ³ aku[da; akunavām db; akuvanašāša dc. ⁴ hacā da; lost in db; hašā dc. ⁴ vispā da, dc; v¹āspā db. ⁴ gāstā da, db; gastā dc. ⁴ uta[da; utamaiy db; utamay dc.

TRANSLATION OF A²Sd:
§1. 1-2.   (= A²Sa 1), an Achaemenian.
§2. 2-4. Saith Artaxerxes the King: By the favor of Ahuramazda this is the palace which I built in my lifetime as a pleasant retreat. May Ahuramazda, Anaitis, and Mithras protect me from all evil, and my building.

A²Ha = ARTAXERXES II, HAMADAN A.

1 θātiy : Artaxšaçā : XŠ : vazraka : XŠ :
XŠyānām : XŠ : DHyūnām : XŠ : ah

2 yāyā : BUyā : Dārayavašahyā : XŠhyā :
puça : Dārayavašahyā : Artaxšaθra

3 hyā : XŠhyā : puça : Artaxšaθrahyā :
Xšayāršahyā : XŠhyā : puça : Xšayār

4 šahyā : Dārayavašahyā : XŠhyā : puça :
Dārayavašahyā : V¹štāspahyā : puça

5 : Haxāmanišiya : imam : apadāna : vašnā :
AM : Anahᵃta : utā : M¹tra : adam : akun

6 ām : AM : Anahᵃta : utā : M¹tra : mām :
pātuv : hacā : vispā : gastā : ut

7 ā : imam : tya : akunā : mā : vijanātiy : mā :
vināθayātiy

NOTES TO A²Ha: ²,³ Artaxšaθrahyā, acc. to Tm Lex. 54, and not -çahyā. ⁶ [hacā : gastā] WB; [utamaiy · xšaçam] Tm., [hacā : vispā : gastā] Kent, after A²Sd ⁷ akunā for akunām, and mā with following lost verb, as in A²Sa; but akunā : mā emended to akunaumā Tm. PAPA 36.xxxii, Lex. 81, and to akunavam Bthl. AiW 444

TRANSLATION OF A²Ha:
§1. 1-5. .   (= A²Sa 1-3).
§2. 5-7. .   (= A²Sa 4-5).

A²Hb = ARTAXERXES II, HAMADAN B.

apadānam : stūnāya : aθagainam : Artaxšaçā :
XŠ : vazraka : akunauš : hya : Dārayavauš :
XŠ : puçā : Haxāmanišiya : Mitra : mām :
pātuv

NOTE TO A²Hb· Probably the demonstrative imam stood before apadānam at the beginning, and other phrases of the protective prayer may have stood at the end.

TRANSLATION OF A²Hb: This palace, of stone in its column(s), Artaxerxes the Great King built, the son of Darius the King, an Achaemenian. May Mithras protect me

A²Hc = ARTAXERXES II, HAMADAN C.

1 baga : vazraka : Auramazdā : hya : maθišta :
2 bagānām : hya : imām : būmım : adā :
3 hya : avam : asmānam : adā : hya : martiya
4 m : adā : hya : šiyātim : adā : martiyahy
5 ā : hya : Artaxšaçām : XŠm : akunauš : ai
6 vam : parūnām : XŠm : aivam : parūnām :
7 framātāram : θātiy : Artaxšaçā : XŠ : va
8 zraka : XŠ : XŠyānām : XŠ : DHyūnām : XŠ
9 : ahyāyā : BUyā : adam : Dārayavaušahy
10 ā : XŠhyā : puça : Dārayavaušahyā : Artax
11 šaçāhyā : XŠhyā : puça : Artaxšaçāhy
12 ā : Xšayāršāhyā : XŠhyā : puça : Xšay
13 āršahyā : Dārayavaušahyā : XŠhyā : p
14 uça : Dārayavaušahyā : Vištāspahyā : nā
15 ma : puça : Haxāmanišiya : θātiy : Artaxša
16 çā : XŠ : vašnā : Auramazdāhā : adam : XŠ
 : a
17 hyāyā : BUyā : vazrakāyā : dūraiy : a
18 piy : amiy : Auramazdā : xšaçam : manā :
frāba
19 ra : mām : Auramazdā : pātuv : utā : xšaça
20 m : tyamaiy : frābara : utāmaiy : viθam

TRANSLATION OF A²Hc:
§1. 1-7. A great god is Ahuramazda, the greatest of gods,   (= A¹Pa 1-8).
§2. 7-15. .   (= A²Sa 1): I (am)   (= A²Sa 1-2), son of Hystaspes by name, an Achaemenian.
§3. 15-20. Saith Artaxerxes the King: By the favor of Ahuramazda I am king in this great earth far and wide; Ahuramazda bestowed the kingdom upon me. Me may Ahuramazda protect, and the kingdom which he bestowed upon me, and my royal house.

A?P = ARTAXERXES II OR III, PERSEPOLIS.

1 iyam : Parsa :
2 iyam : Māda :
3 iyam : Ūvja :
4 iyam : Parθava :
8 *iyam : Uvārazm¹ya*
9 iyam : Zrakā
10 iyam : Harauvatiya

11 iyam : Θataguiya
12 iyam : Gadāraya :
13 iyam : Hiduya
14 iyam : Sakā : haumavargā :
15 iyam : Sakā : tigraxaudā :
16 iyam : Bābiruš :
17 iyam : Aθuriya
18 iyam : Arabāya
19 iyam : Mudrāya
20 iyam : Arminiya
21 iyam : Katpatuka :
22 imay : Spardiya
23 iyam : Yaunā :
24 iyam : Sakā : paradraiya :
25 iyam : Skudra :
26 iyam : Yauna : takabarā :
27 iyam : Putāya :
28 iyam : Kūšāya
29 iyam : Maciya
30 iyam : Karka :

NOTES TO A?P: [11] Θataguiya Smith, Hz.; if correct, for Θataguviya; or a wrong writing for Θatagudaya or Θatagudiya, cf. Gk. Σατταγύδαι [14] There is an extra vertical hasta between the gᵃ and the a in haumavargā. [22] imᵃyᵃ, miswritten for iyᵃmᵃ.

TRANSLATION OF A?P:
1. This is the Persian. 2. This is the Mede. 3. This is the Elamite. 4. This is the Parthian. [5–7. This is the Arian, the Bactrian, the Sogdian.] 8. This is the Chorasmian. 9. This is the Drangian. 10. This is the Arachosian.
11. This is the Sattagydian. 12. This is the Gandarian. 13. This is the man of Sind. 14. This is the Amyrgian Scythian. 15. This is the Pointed-Cap Scythian. 16. This is the Babylonian. 17. This is the Assyrian. 18. This is the Arab. 19. This is the Egyptian. 20. This is the Armenian.
21. This is the Cappadocian. 22. This is the Sardian. 23. This is the Ionian. 24. This is the Scythian across the sea. 25. This is the Skudrian. 26. This is the Petasos-Wearing Ionian. 27. This is the Libyan. 28. This is the Ethiopian. 29. This is the man of Maka. 30. This is the Carian.

A³Pa = ARTAXERXES III, PERSEPOLIS a, b, c, d.

1 baga : vazraka : Auramazdā : hya :
2 imām : būmām : adā : hya : a
3 vam : asmānām : adā : hya : marti
4 yam : adā : hya : šāyatām : adā : mart
5 ihyā : hya : mām : Artaxšaçā : xšāya
6 θiya : akunauš : aivam : parūvnām :
7 xšāyaθiyam : aivam : parūvnām
8 : framatāram : θātiy : Artaxsaçā :
9 xšāyaθiya : vazraka : xšāyaθiya
10 : xšāyaθiyanām : xšāyaθiya :
11 DHyūnām : xšāyaθiya : ahyāyā : BUyā : ada
12 m : Artaxšaçā : xšāya
13 θiya : puça : Artaxšaçā : Darayavau
14 š : xšāyaθiya : puça : Dārayavauš : A
15 rtaxšaçā : xšāyaθiya : puça : Artaxša
16 çā : Xšayāršā : xšāyaθiya : puça : X
17 šayāršā : Dārayavauš : xšāyaθ
18 iya : puça : Dārayavauš : Vˡštāspa
19 hyā : nāma : puça : Vˡštāspahyā :
20 Aršāma : nāma : puça : Haxāmaniši
21 ya : θātiy : Artaxšaçā : xšāyaθi
22 ya : imam : ustašanām : aθaganām : mā
23 m : upā : mām : kartā : θātiy : Arta
24 xšaçā : xšāyaθiya : mām : Auramazdā :
25 utā : Mˡθra : baga : pātuv : utā : imā
26 m : DHyaum : utā : tya : mām : kartā :

NOTES TO A³Pa: The text is arranged according to the line-divisions of copy a, with faithful representation of all orthographic errors; all four copies have identical orthography, though the line-divisions vary somewhat. [12] The translation of lines 12–20 is intended to show the anacoluthic use of the nominative forms; the passage is obviously intended to convey the same ideas as A²Sa 1–3 [23] For upā mām 'in my time' (here emphatic only, as it is otiose), cf A²Sa 4 [u]pā Arta[xšaçām] 'in the time of Artaxerxes'.

TRANSLATION OF A³Pa:
§1. 1–8.   (= DNa 1–4), who made me, Artaxerxes, king,   (= DNa 6–8).
§2. 8–21.   (= A²Sa 1): I am the son (of) Artaxerxes the King, (of) Artaxerxes (who was) the son (of) Darius the King, (of) Darius (who was) the son (of) Artaxerxes the King, (of) Artaxerxes (who was) the son (of) Xerxes the King, (of) Xerxes (who was) the son (of) Darius the King, (of) Darius (who was) the son of Hystaspes by name, of Hystaspes (who was) the son (of) Arsames by name, an Achaemenian.
§3. 21–3. Saith Artaxerxes the King: This stone staircase was built by me in my time.
§4. 23–6. Saith Artaxerxes the King: Me may Ahuramazda and the god Mithras protect, and this country, and what was built by me.

INSCRIPTIONS ON WEIGHTS.

Wa = DARIUS, WEIGHT A.

1 II karšā
2 adam : Dāra

TEXTS WITH NOTES AND TRANSLATION

3 yavauš : xš
4 āyaθiya : va
5 zraka : Viš
6 tāspahyā
7 : puça : Hax
8 āmanišiya

TRANSLATION OF Wa: II (units) by weight.
(= Wb 1-2, 7-9):

Wb = DARIUS, WEIGHT B.

1 adam : Dārayavauš : x
2 šāyaθiya : vazraka : x
3 šāyaθiya : xšāyaθ
4 iyānām : xšāyaθ
5 iya : dahyūnām : xš
6 āyaθiya : ahyāyā
7 : būmiyā : Vištā
8 spahyā : puça : Haxā
9 manišiya

TRANSLATION OF Wb: (= DSf 5-8).

Wc = DARIUS, WEIGHT C.

1 CXX karšayā
2 adam : Dārayavauš : x
3 šāyaθiya : vazraka : x
4 šāyaθiya : xšāyaθ
5 iyānām : xšāyaθ
6 iya : dahyūnām : x
7 šāyaθiya : ahyāy
8 ā : būmiyā : Višt
9 āspahyā : puça : Hax
10 āmanišiya

TRANSLATION OF Wc: CXX (units) in weight.
(= Wb 1-9).

Wd = DARIUS, WEIGHT D.

1 LX karšayā
2 adam : Dārayavauš :
3 xšāyaθiya : vazraka :
4 xšāyaθiya : xšāyaθ
5 iyānām : xšāyaθ
6 iya : dahyūnām : xš
7 āyaθiya : ahyāyā
8 : būmiyā : Vištā
9 spahyā : puça : Hax
10 āmanišiya

TRANSLATION OF Wd: LX (units) in weight.
(= Wb 1-9).

INSCRIPTIONS ON SEALS

SDa = DARIUS, SEAL A: adam : Darayavauš XŠ
SDb = DARIUS, SEAL B: adam : Dārayavauš
SXa = XERXES, SEAL A: 1 Xšayāršā
 2 : XŠ : vazraka
SXb = XERXES, SEAL B: 1 adam : Xšay
 2 āršā : XŠ
SXc = XERXES, SEAL C: 1 *adam* : Xšayāršā : XŠ
 2 .
Sa = SEAL A: 1 Aršа   5 yāba
 2 ka : n   6 ušna
 3 āma :   7 hyā :
 4 Āθi   8 *puça*
Sb = SEAL B: 1 Hadaxaya
 2
 3 θadaθa :
Sc = SEAL C: Vašdāsaka
Sd = SEAL D: Vahyav¹šdāpaya
Se = SEAL E: 1 ma : Xa 2 ršа 3 dašyā
Sf = SEAL F: 1 upā 2 Arta 3 xšaç 4 *ām*

NOTES. Se: For Justi's reading *Xišyāršā*, see Lex.
s.v. *Xaršadašyā*. Sf: There is no word-divider after *upā*.

TRANSLATION OF THE SEALS:
SDa: I (am) Darius the King.
SDb: I (am) Darius.
SXa: Xerxes the Great King.
SXb-c: I (am) Xerxes the King.
Sa: Arshaka by name, son of Athiyabaushna.
Sb-e: ???
Sf: Under Artaxerxes.

VASE INSCRIPTIONS.

XVs = XERXES, VASE:
 Xšayāršā : XŠ : vazraka
AVsa = ARTAXERXES, VASE A:
 : Ardaxcašca : XŠ : vazraka
AVsb-d = ARTAXERXES, VASES B, C, D:
 Artaxšaçā : xšāyaθiya

TRANSLATION:
XVs: Xerxes the Great King.
AVsa: Artaxerxes the Great King.
AVsb-d: Artaxerxes the King.

OLD PERSIAN

HISTORICAL APPENDIX

I. THE ACHAEMENIAN DYNASTY

Darius and the other Persian Kings who have left us cuneiform inscriptions composed in Old Persian, all belonged to the Achaemenian line, so called because they were descended from Achaemenes. Full information may be found in PW 1.200–204 s.v. Achaimenidai, and under the names of the individual persons; a complete genealogical table is given by PW facing 1.192. A table of the most important Achaemenians is given here; the names of the kings are in large and small capitals, with the dates of their reigns, and an asterisk marks those Achaemenians who are named in the Old Persian inscriptions.

Darius, in Behistan §4, and again in Behistan

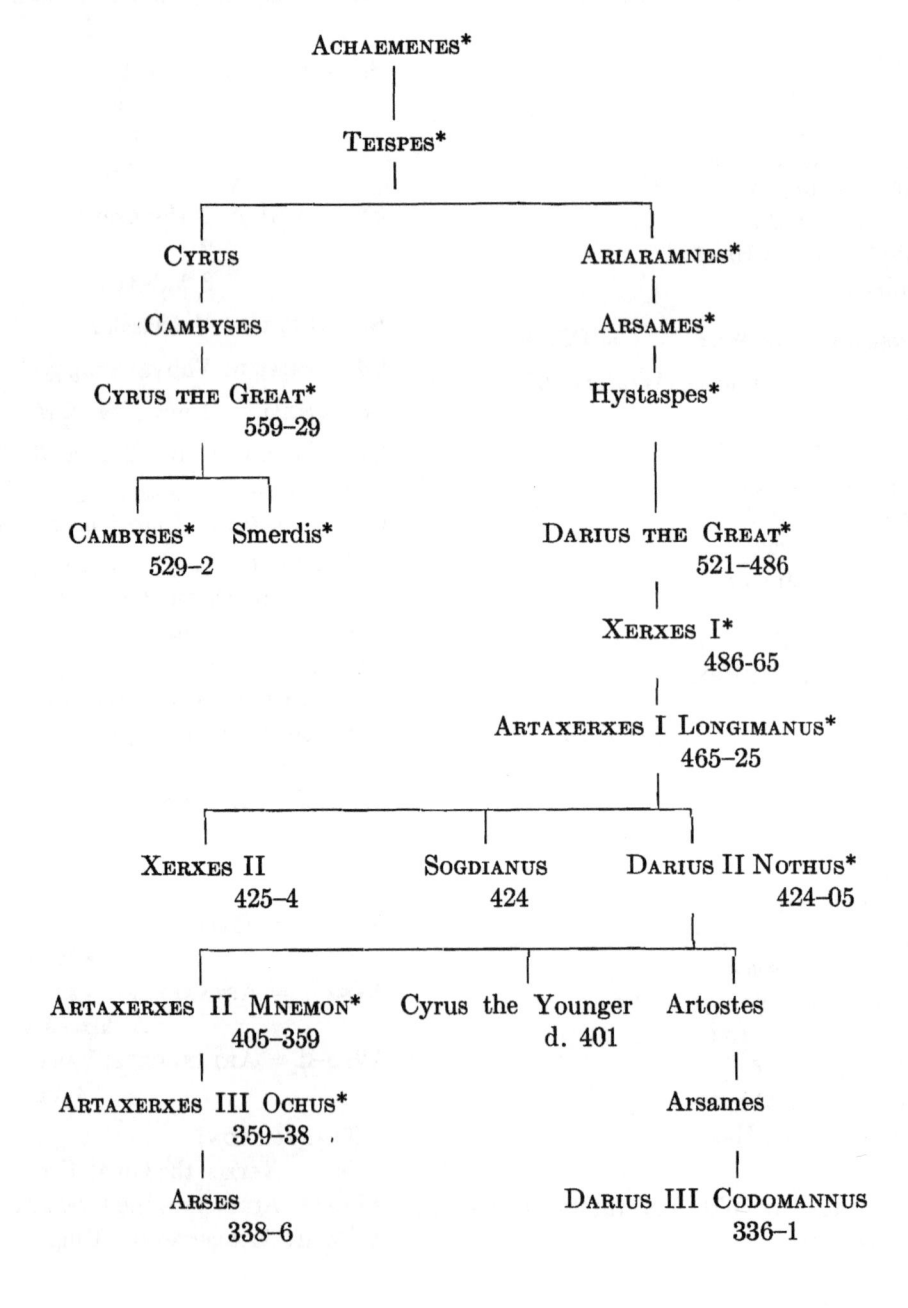

```
                          ACHAEMENES*
                              |
                           TEISPES*
                              |
              ┌───────────────┴───────────────┐
            CYRUS                         ARIARAMNES*
              |                                |
           CAMBYSES                         ARSAMES*
              |                                |
        CYRUS THE GREAT*                    Hystaspes*
           559–29                              |
              |                                |
       ┌──────┴──────┐                         |
     CAMBYSES*   Smerdis*                 DARIUS THE GREAT*
      529–2                                 521–486
                                               |
                                             XERXES I*
                                             486-65
                                               |
                                    ARTAXERXES I LONGIMANUS*
                                             465–25
                                               |
              ┌────────────────────┬───────────┘
          XERXES II            SOGDIANUS     DARIUS II NOTHUS*
           425–4                  424             424–05
                                                   |
              ┌────────────────────┬───────────────┘
     ARTAXERXES II MNEMON*   Cyrus the Younger    Artostes
          405–359                 d. 401             |
              |                                      |
     ARTAXERXES III OCHUS*                        Arsames
          359–38                                     |
              |                                      |
            ARSES                          DARIUS III CODOMANNUS
           338–6                                  336–1
```

a, states that there had been eight kings in their family before him, and that he was the ninth in order. We must count them thus: 1 Achaemenes, 2 Teispes, 3 Cyrus, 4 Cambyses, 5 Cyrus the Great, 6 Cambyses, 7 Ariaramnes, 8 Arsames, 9 Darius. The last three belong to the younger line of Ariaramnes, while Nos. 3 to 6 belong to the line of Teispes' older son. Hystaspes father of Darius is not included in the count, because he nowhere receives the title of King, even when mentioned as father of Darius—whereas the other kings all give to their fathers the title King in statements of parentage.

Herodotus 7.11, however, gives Darius' line thus: Achaemenes, Teispes, Cambyses, Cyrus, Teispes, Ariaramnes, Arsames, Hystaspes, Darius: in which Darius is the ninth. But Darius surely knew his own genealogy better than did Herodotus. Herodotus either has a dittographic error made in copying from a list covering both branches, or erroneously looked upon Cambyses and Cyrus as ancestors of Darius and inserted Teispes the second time to make the list agree with the known fact that the father of Ariaramnes was named Teispes.

There are other accounts also, different in important respects. Thus Nicolaus Damascenus, who is supposed to have used the Persica of Ctesias, states that Cyrus the Great was not an Achaemenian by birth, but a person of lowly origin who gained favor with Cambyses and eventually rebelled against him and overthrew him; see C. J. Ogden's translation of Nicolaus' account, in Dastur Hosang Memorial Volume 465–81 (Bombay 1918).

All the accounts, literary and inscriptional, are presented and evaluated by Weissbach in PW, Suppl.-Bd. 4.1132–44, s.v. Kyros. His conclusions are as follows: Of the sons of Teispes, Ariaramnes was king in Persis (then called *Parsua*) and Cyrus I was king in the city (or district?) Anshan, lying between Persis and Elam, or possibly farther north, between Persis and Media. On coming to the throne of Anshan, Cyrus II found Arsames ruling in *Parsua*, and shortly deposed him, himself becoming now king in *Parsua*, later called *Pārsa*. Arsames, however, was not put to death, but (as the OP inscriptions tell us) lived on until after his grandson Darius got the throne of the Persian Empire. Thus Hystaspes never was king, and is not counted among the nine Achaemenian kings. Cyrus II thereafter conquered Media and added it to his dominions, and then extended his conquests in all directions. But he did belong by ancestry to the Achaemenian line; one can hardly brand him as a rank outsider.

Possibly Ctesias' story, as repeated by Nicolaus Damascenus, originated in the line of Darius as a means of discrediting the line of Cyrus and of justifying Darius in his seizure of the imperial power. The particular occasion might well be the unsuccessful revolt of Cyrus the Younger against his brother Artaxerxes II, whom Ctesias served as personal physician. Cf. JAOS 66.211 (1946).

II. Smerdis and Gaumata

According to Behistan §10–§13, Cambyses son of Cyrus killed his full-brother Smerdis, with such secrecy that his death was not known to the people; he then invaded Egypt. While he was on this expedition, rebellions developed in Persia and in Media and elsewhere. Notably a Magian named Gaumata headed the rebels, claiming to be Smerdis son of Cyrus, and he gained the kingship in all the rebellious territory. Cambyses, still in Egypt, committed suicide.

Gaumata started his rebellion in XII 14 of 523/2, and received the adherence of the Empire on IV 9 of 522/1. But Darius, a distant cousin of Cambyses, knowing that Gaumata was not the real Smerdis, with the aid of a few men fought with and slew Gaumata and his chief followers, on VII 10 of the same year, at Sikayauvati, a fortress in Nisaya, a district of Media. Thereafter Darius became King.

Herodotus tells the same story at much greater length, in Book 3, chapters 1–38, 61–88. Cambyses invaded Egypt (chap. 1), and the reasons for the invasion and the course of the campaign are given (1–26). At Memphis he inflicted a fatal wound on the sacred bull which was worshipped as the God Apis (27–9), and thereupon lost his reason. Jealous of his brother Smerdis's prowess with the great bow which had come from the Ichthyophagi, he sent Smerdis back to Persia, and then, after a dream which betokened that Smerdis would supplant him, he sent his henchman Prexaspes to murder him secretly, which he did (30–8), esp. 30).

The Magus Patizeithes had been left by Cambyses as managing steward of his palace at Susa, and he was one of the few who knew of the death of Smerdis. He had himself a brother who greatly resembled Smerdis in appearance, and, says Herodotus, this brother's name was also Smerdis. Patizeithes put his brother Smerdis on the throne, under the pretense that he was Smerdis son of Cyrus and brother of Cambyses. The false Smerdis, by not admitting to his presence any one who had known the true Smerdis, successfully concealed his true identity for some time (61-2). But the news reached Cambyses in Egypt, and he knew the truth, because Prexaspes assured him that he had slain the real Smerdis. Resolved to fight the usurper, he leaped upon his horse to lead his army back to Susa, but as he did so he accidentally struck the point of his sword into his thigh, and from the wound he died (63-6). Thus the false Smerdis ruled for some months; but a Persian nobleman, Otanes son of Pharnaspes, suspecting his identity, managed by a ruse to prove it to himself (67-9), and secured the help of five other trusted noblemen, to whom there was added Darius, who had come to Susa from his father Hystaspes, governor of Persia (70; see App. III). Darius insisted on immediate action against the two Magi (71-3). Helped by the confusion following the public confession of Prexaspes that he had murdered the true Smerdis, and by his suicide, the seven men burst into the presence of the two Magi and slew them (74-9). They then agreed upon a method of selecting one of their number to hold the throne, and Darius, aided by the trickery of his groom Oebares, was the winner (80-8).

The two accounts, it will be seen, agree in the main features, but differ considerably in the details. Herodotus' story has clearly entered into the field of historical romance. See also PW 3A.710-2, s.v. Smerdis.

III. The Helpers of Darius

The names of the six Persian noblemen who cooperated with Darius in slaying Gaumata the false Smerdis, are given in Behistan §68 and in Herodotus 3.70; there is agreement in the names of the first five:

Behistan	Herodotus
Vindafarnā son of *Vāyaspāra*	Intaphernes
Utāna son of *Θuxra*	Otanes son of Pharnaspes
Gaubaruva son of *Marduniya*	Gobryas
Vidarna son of *Bagābigna*	Hydarnes
Bagabuxša son of *Dātuvahya*	Megabyzus
Ardumaniš son of *Vahauka*	Aspathines

Herodotus, it will be seen, differs from the Behistan account in the name of the father of Utāna-Otanes; but he gives (7.82) Mardonius, the general in the third invasion of Greece, as son of Gobryas, which indicates agreement as to the name of Gobryas's father. But Megabyzus son of Zopyrus (7.82) may or may not be the Behistan Bagabuxša son of Datuvahya, or his grandson. Herodotus does, in fact, mention all six of the helpers of Darius in passages outside 3.68-88, in passages which may be found in any Index Nominum Propriorum to the text of Herodotus.

The Behistan inscription mentions *Vidarna* again in §25, as defeating one of Phraortes' armies in Media; *Vindafarnā* in §50, as defeating the rebels at Babylon; *Gaubaruva* in §71, as crushing the last revolt of the Elamites.

IV. The Persian Calendar and Behistan I-IV

In Behistan 4.4, Darius states that the 19 battles recorded by him in the first three columns of the inscription, with the attendant capture of 9 usurpers, took place *hamahyāyā θarda* 'in one and the same year'. For eighteen of the battles dates are given in the Persian calendar, with translation into the Elamite and the Akkadian. The difficulty has been to arrange these dates within one year, beginning with the killing of Gaumata, the false Smerdis; for the order of the months in the Persian calendar, and in the other calendars, was by no means certain. Now, however, with evidence from additional Akkadian and Elamite tablets which have no Old Persian version, Arno Poebel has succeeded in reconstructing the lists of months, as follows:[1]

---

[1] AJSLL 55.139-42. The Persian calendar has been the subject of many studies, but Poebel's studies have supplanted them all. ALSLL 55.130-65, 285-314, 56.121-45. Cf also Hinz, ZDMG 96.326-31.

Old Persian	Elamite	Akkadian	Equivalent
1 *Adukanaiša*	*Ḫadukannaš*	*Nīsabbu*	Mch.-Apr.
2 *Θūravāhara*	*Turmar*	*Aiiāru*	Apr.-May
3 *Θāigarciš*	*Sākurriṣiš*	*Simannu*	May-June
4 *Garmapada*	*Karmabadaš*	*Du'ūzu*	June-July
5	*Turnabaṣiš*	*Ābu*	July-Aug.
6	*Qarbaši(ia)š*	*Ulūlu*	Aug.-Spt.
7 *Bāgayādiš*	*Bagiiātiš*	*Tašrītu*	Spt.-Oct.
8 *Varkazana	*Marqašanaš*	*Araḫsamna*	Oct.-Nov.
9 *Āçiyādiya*	*Ḫaššiiāti(ia)š*	*Kislīmu*	Nov.-Dec.
10 *Anāmaka*	*Ḫanāmakaš*	*Ṭebētu*	Dec.-Jan.
11	*Sami(ia)maš*	*Šabāṭu*	Jan.-Feb.
12 *Viyaxna*	*Mi(ia)kannaš*	*Addāru*	Feb.-Mch.

The narrative of the revolts, however, is not given in temporal sequence in Columns I-III, but rather in a geographical order conditioned by the order in which the rebellious provinces are named in §22: Persia, Elam, Media, Assyria, Egypt, Parthia, Margiana, Sattagydia, Scythia. If we should reduce the story to a more easily intelligible pattern, it would be as follows:

After Cambyses, son of Cyrus the Great, secretly slew his full-brother Smerdis and went on the expedition to conquer Egypt, uprisings against his rule took place in Persia and in Media and elsewhere (§10). Notably a Magian named Gaumata led the revolt, claiming to be Smerdis, whose death was known to but few; he started his revolt on XII 14 of 523/2, and received the adherence of the entire Empire, becoming King on IV 9 of 522/1.[2] Cambyses died by his own hand, either intentionally or accidentally, in Egypt soon after hearing of Gaumata's revolt (§11).

Three months later Darius and his associates killed Gaumata and his chief followers at Sikayauvati in Media, on VII 10 of 522/1. Thereby Darius became King, but at the very outset his rule was contested by Açina in Elam, and by Nidintu-Bel (claiming to be Nebuchadrezzar son of Nabonidus) in Babylon, who were recognized as King each in his locality. But Açina did not last long; Darius, after organizing the government in Media and Persia, gathered an army of Medes and Persians and marched toward Babylon, passing near Elam. As he passed he sent orders to the Elamites, and in terror they seized Açina and brought him in fetters to Darius, who slew him (§17).

Darius with his army went on toward Babylon against Nidintu-Bel (§18), and in his absence from Media and Persia several rebellions started (§21)—some perhaps started earlier, but news of them did not reach Darius before he had set out against Nidintu-Bel: (a) that of Vahyazdata in Persia, with the adherence of Sattagydia and perhaps of a faction in Arachosia (§45); (b) that of Martiya in Elam; (c) that of Phraortes in Media, with the adherence of Armenia (§26), of Assyria, and of Parthia, including Hyrcania (§35); (d) that of Frada in Margiana; (e) that of Egypt; (f) that of Skunkha in Scythia (§21).

Darius came upon Nidintu-Bel and his army at the Tigris, forced the crossing, and defeated him in IX 26 (§18), and though Nidintu-Bel rallied his forces and took the offensive, again defeated him at Zazana on the Euphrates, X 2 (§19); he pursued him and his few remaining horsemen to Babylon, took that city and Nidintu-Bel with it, and put the rebel to death (§20).

Meanwhile events were progressing elsewhere. Against Frada, who had made himself ruler of Margiana, Darius had sent Dadarshi, a Persian officer who was governor of the neighboring province of Bactria, with his local forces, and Dadarshi won a decisive victory on IX 23 (§38), restoring Darius's rule in Margiana (§39).

Phraortes, claiming to be Khshathrita, of the family of Cyaxares, had made himself king of a great part of the Empire (§24). Darius's first step was to send Vaumisa, a Persian officer, against the rebels in Armenia; he must have sent Vaumisa early in the Babylonian campaign, for Vaumisa, on the way north, was met by the rebels at Izala in Assyria, on X 15. What forces Vaumisa had at his disposal is not stated, but no mention is made of sending troops with him; presumably he gathered up loyal troops on the way. By this battle Vaumisa

---

[2] The months will be indicated by Roman numerals.

drove the rebels back into Armenia, where he fought a second battle with them some months later (§30; see below).

Although the force of Medes and Persians which Darius had with him in Babylonia was small, he had been obliged, at an early date, probably not much after the battle at the Tigris, to send Hydarnes, a Persian officer, with a strong force against Phraortes in Media. Hydarnes met an army of Phraortes (but not Phraortes himself) in battle at Maru in Media, and fought a battle on X 27; but it seems to have been indecisive, for thereafter Hydarnes waited for the arrival of Darius and his army from Babylonia (§25).

Parthia and the neighboring district of Hyrcania had both gone over to Phraortes, but Darius's father Hystaspes was in command of the army in Parthia, and the army remained loyal. In a battle at Vishpauzati, on XII 22, Hystaspes fought the rebels, but the victory was not decisive.

After the death of Nidintu-Bel at Babylon, Darius set forth for Media against Phraortes (§31). His march took him near Elam, where a Persian named Martiya had set himself up as King under the name of Imanish. At the approach of Darius the Elamites were terrified, and seized Martiya and killed him (§22–§23).[3] Darius now sent a force of Persians and Medes under Artavardiya, a Persian officer, against Vahyazdata, who had made himself King in Persia; he himself, with the rest of the Persian force, went on into Media (§41) and at Kunduru was attacked by Phraortes himself and his army, on I 25, 521/0 (§31). Phraortes' army was routed; he himself escaped with a few horsemen, but was overtaken and captured at Raga, and mutilated and put to death with torture at Ecbatana (§32). From Raga Darius sent a force of Persians to reinforce Hystaspes in Parthia (§36).

Hereupon a Sagartian named Ciçantakhma, perhaps commander of local forces that had adhered to Phraortes, declared himself King in Sagartia, a district of northern Media; he claimed to be of the family of Cyaxares. Darius sent a force of Medes and Persians under Takhmaspada, a Median officer, who defeated and captured Ciçantakhma, bringing him to Darius. Darius mutilated him and put him to death with torture, at Arbela (§33). Thus ended rebellion in Media (§34); but there was still a strong rebel force in Armenia, against which Darius sent an Armenian officer named Dadarshi. Dadarshi, thrice attacked by the rebels, defeated them successively at Zuzaya on II 8 (§26), at Tigra on II 18 (§27), and at Uyama on III 9, whereafter he waited for Darius to come and make final governmental dispositions (§28). This third battle by Dadarshi was only nine days after Vaumisa in a second engagement beat off the other force of Armenian rebels in the district of Autiyara, on II 30; after which he also awaited Darius's arrival (§30). There was no further fighting in Armenia.

Hystaspes, reinforced in Parthia by the Persians whom Darius had sent to him from Raga, sought out the rebel army and crushed it at Patigrabana, on IV 1 (§36). This restored Darius's rule in Parthia.

While Darius was in Babylon, one Vahyazdata, a Persian, claiming to be Smerdis son of Cyrus, had revolted and made himself King of Persia (§40). Apparently confident in his own position, he had sent a force east to Arachosia,[4] against the Persian governor Vivana, who had remained loyal to Darius; but Vivana beat off the rebels at Kapishakani, on X 13 (§45). The rebels again attacked at Gandutava on XII 7, and here were decisively defeated (§46); their commander and a few horsemen escaped, but were overtaken and captured at Arshada by Vivana, who put them to death (§47).

Vahyazdata in Persia had a few months of undisturbed rule, but this was ended by the approach of Artavardiya, sent by Darius on his way to Media, with a force of Persians and Medes. Vahyazdata attacked Artavardiya at Rakha on II 12 (§41), and again near Mt. Parga on IV 5. In the second battle Vahyazdata and his chief followers were taken prisoner (§42); they were handed over to Darius at the Persian town of

---

[3] Poebel, AJSLL 55.154, sets the undated killing of Martiya after the death of Phraortes, because in the sculptured line of captives on the Behistan Rock the order is Gaumata, Açina, Nidintu-Bel, Phraortes, Martiya, Ciçantakhma, Vahyazdata, Arkha, Frada. I reject this interpretation of the series of sculptures, since it would oblige us to set the death of Frada at the very end of the series, dating his defeat not IX 23, 522/1, but IX 23, 521/0, and thus extending the series of events from 13 months 12 days to 14 months 13 days

[4] I regard the revolt in Sattagydia (§22) as to be included under the events in Arachosia (§45–§47).

Uvadaicaya, and Darius executed them with torture (§43). Darius was now back in Persia, which had been restored to his rule (§44), as well as the other rebellious territories except Egypt and Scythia. It was not quite nine months since he had slain the usurper Gaumata.

But while Darius was putting down the rebellions in Media and in Persia, an Armenian named Arkha, claiming to be Nebuchadrezzar son of Nabonidus, had established himself as King in Babylon (§49). Against him Darius sent a Persian officer named Intaphernes with an army, and Intaphernes routed Arkha and his forces on VIII 22, capturing and executing at Babylon both Arkha and his chief officers (§50).

This is the latest event related in the first three columns of the Behistan inscription, 13 months and 12 days after the death of Gaumata; the time does not seriously exceed the one year which Darius boastfully mentions in Column IV.

Column V gives an account of a third rebellion in Elam, under Atamaita; against him Gobryas was sent with an army by Darius, and he defeated and captured him, bringing him to Darius, who put him to death (§71). The date of this rebellion seems to be in the third year of Darius' reign, 520/19,[5] though the Behistan text is here badly mutilated. After this rebellion in Elam Darius went to Scythia and defeated and captured Skunkha (§74). The reconquest of Egypt, though not mentioned in the Behistan inscription, must have followed in the same or the next year.[6]

V. The Accession of Xerxes.

In XPf, Xerxes gives us an account of his succession to the throne: Darius had a number of sons, but—as was Ahuramazda's desire—he made Xerxes (presumably not his eldest son, though this is not stated in the inscription) the 'greatest after himself;' and when Darius 'went from the throne,' Xerxes—as was Ahuramazda's desire—became king on the throne of his father.

The account given by Herodotus 7.1–4 agrees with this, but gives more details: After Darius received the news that his forces had been defeated at Marathon and somewhat later that Egypt had risen in rebellion, he started preparations for one campaign against the Athenians and another against the Egyptians. At this time there was a dispute between Artobazanes, eldest son of Darius by his first wife, a daughter of Gobryas, and Xerxes, eldest son of Darius by Atossa, daughter of Cyrus the Great, whom Darius had married after his accession to the throne, as to which should have the succession. On the advice of Damaratus, exiled king of Sparta, Xerxes went to his father and pressed his claim on the ground that he was the oldest son of Darius the King, while Artobazanes was only the oldest son of Darius the private individual. Darius approved the claim, though perhaps the argument was not really needed (Atossa as daughter of Cyrus must have had great influence with Darius, and Xerxes was probably the ablest of Darius's sons), and named Xerxes to succeed him. Before he had finished the preparations for the campaigns, Darius died; whereupon Xerxes ascended to his father's throne.

---

[5] Kent, JNES 2 109–10 ; cf. R. A Parker, AJSLL 58 373–7.
[6] Parker, l.c.

PART III. LEXICON

This Lexicon includes a concordance to the words in the inscriptions, as well as materials for etymological comparison.

The alphabetic order is ă ĭ ŭ k x g c j t θ ç d n p f b m y r l v s š z h, while final y and v are disregarded (thus naıy has the alphabetic place of nai, and precedes naıba-). Raised letters inserted to show sounds omitted in the OP system of writing also have no effect on the alphabetic order.

References to Part I (the Grammar) are marked by §; they include all mentions of the word or form which add to the information given in the Lexicon, but are not in all instances complete listings. The Chapter on Syntax is only sparingly referred to in this Lexicon, since the citations in that Chapter are mostly for passages rather than for words; there is an Index of Passages at the end of the Chapter.

ā adv. as prefix and prep. 'to': Av. Skt. *ā*, prep. with acc. and abl., 'to, as far as' (also with other uses and meanings); pIE **ā* if = Lt. *ā* 'from' (Sturtevant, Lg. 15.145–54), or **ō* if = Gk. ώ- in ώ-κεανός '(lying round about), ocean'.

(1) Prefix with verbs *ay-, xšnav-, gam-, grab-, jan-, bar-, mā-, yam-*; in verbal nouns *āyadana-, āvahana-*, and in the second parts of compounds *Āθıyābaušna-, Ariyāramna-, Bagābigna-*, also in *Ākaufaciya-*.

(2) Postposition attached to loc. sg. and pl. (§270.IV) and in conj. *yadā*.

(3) Prep. with abl.: *yātā ā* 'as far as', DPh 6, 7; DH 5, 6.

(4) Prep. with adv.: DSe 48.

¹ *a-* neg. prefix before consonants (§67, §67.I, §132.I; *an-* antevocalic, q.v.): Av. Skt. *a-*, Gk. *a-*, Lt. *in-*, Gmc. *un-*, pIE **ņ-*. See *akarta-, axšaina-, axšata-, Anāmaka-, ayaumani-*.

² *a-* demonst. 'this': Av. *a-* as in GAv. gsm. *ahē*, Skt. *a-* as in gsm. *asyá*, Gk. lsn. εἰ 'if', Lt. nsn. **ed* in *ecce* 'lo'; pIE **e-*. See also *aciy, ada-*. Decl., §199.

anā ism. DPe 8 (not to Av. Skt. *ana-*, cf. Mt. MSLP 19.49–52); XPa 14 (with Wb. KIA 109, Mt. Gr. §326; translated by Akk. *a-ga-'*, Elam. *hi* 'this', which refutes interpretation of Bv. Gr. §368, §388, as prep. w. inst. 'throughout', Av. *ana* with acc. 'along, on', Gk. ἀνά 'along'). *ahyāyā* lsf. DB 4.47; DNa 11; DSd 2°; DSe 10; DSf 7, 15; DSg lf; DSi lf, 4; DSj 1°; DSm 5°; DSs lf, 3°; DSy 2; DZb 3; DZc 5f; DE 17; XPa 8f; XPc 7; XPf 12, 24; XPh 9f; XPj; XV 13; A¹Pa 13; D²Sb lf; A²Sa 1; A²Sc 4; A²Sdb 1 (*ahyā* dc, §52.VI); A²Ha lf; A²Hc 9, 16f; A³Pa 11; Wb 6, Wc 7f; Wd 7. *ahiyāyā* (§27) XPb 17; XPd 12, XPjv; XE 17.

aita- demonst. 'this' (§260.III, §266): Av. *aēta-*, Skt. *etá*, PAr. **aita-*. *aita* nsn. (§202) DB 1.44, 45; DNa 48. *aita-maiy* DNb 31. *aita* asn. DPd 20; DNa 53; XPh 43, 59; XSc 4°. *aita-maiy* DPd 22f; DNa 54f; XPh 60. *aitā* apf. XPh 30, 35.

Ainaira- sb. 'Ainaira', a Babylonian, father of Nidintu-Bel: Elam. *ha-a-na-a-ra*, Akk. *a-ni-ri-'*. *Aina[ira]hyā* gsm. DB 1.77f.

aiva- adj. 'one' (§150; §204.I): Av. *aēva-* 'one', Gk. Hom. οἶος, Cypr. οἰϝος 'alone', pIE **oiuos*. *aıvam* asm. DNa 6, 7; DSe 6°, 6f; DSf 4, 5; DE 8f, 10; XPa 4, 5; XPb 8f, 10; XPc 4, 5; XPd 6, 7; XPf 6, 7; XPh 5, 6; XE 9, 10; XV 7, 8; A¹Pa 6f°, 8°; A²Hc 5f, 6; A³Pa 6, 7.

aiš- vb. 'hasten', caus. *aišaya-* 'send': Av. *aēš-*, caus. *aēšaya-*, Skt. *iṣ-*, caus. *eṣayati* (§117).

fra + aiš- caus. 'send forth': Av. *fraēš-*, Skt. *preṣ-*. *frāišayam* 1st sg. imf. (§24, §72, §131, §215) DB 1.82; 2.19, 30, 50, 72f, 82; 3.2, 13, 30, 84; 5.7. *frāišaya* imf. DB 3.55, 60, 71.

Autiyāra- sb. 'Autiyara', a district in Armenia: Elam. *ha-u-ti-ia-ru-iš*, Akk. *ú-ti-ia-a-ri*. *Autiyāra* nsm. DB 2.58f.

Aura- (i.e. *Aʰura-*) sb. 'Lord, God': Av. *ahura-*, Skt. *ásura-* 'demon', pIE **esuro-* (§148.I). *Aurahya Mazdāha* gsm. (§36.IVb, §44) XPc 10. *Aurā* ism. DPe 24 (otherwise Bv. BSLP 30 1.70–3, Gr. §179, §389; 'downward', isn. of *aura-*, zero-grade of *avara-*, comparative of ²*ava-*, cf. LAv. *aora* 'down'). Elsewhere always in cpd. *Auramazdāh-*.

Auramazdāh- sb. 'Wise Lord, Ahuramazda', supreme deity of the Zoroastrian religion: Av. nsm. *ahurō mazdå*, Phl. *ōhrmazd*, NPers. *hormızd*; Elam. *u-ra-mas-da*, Akk. *ú-ra-ma-az-da ú-ri-mi-*

iz-da-' a-ḫu-ru-ma-az-da-' etc., Gk. Ὀρομάσδης; in Av., always two words, usually separated in the Gathas and often in reverse order (Kent, Or. Stud. Hon. Pavry 200–8), but in OP always one word except XPc 10 (§44; for *Aurā*] alone, see under *Aura-*). Cpd. of **ahura-* (see *Aura-*) + **ma(n)dzdhā-* with *s*-suffix (another view by Pisani, cf. §185.n3); this is cpd. of pIE **menth-* (or is the full grade pIE **math-*?) seen in Gk. ἔμαθον 'I learned', + pIE **dhē-* 'put', see *²dā-* (Pisani, Riv. Stud. Or. 81–2, takes prior element as **mn̥s-*, zero-grade to pAr. *manas-*, after Wackernagel-Debrunner, Altind. Gram. 3.282–3); for formation, cf. Skt. *śrad-dhā-* 'trust', Lt. *crēdit*. §70, §156.I, §160.II; decl., §185.IV.

Auramazdā nsm. AmH 7, 10; AsH 5f, 12; DB 1.12, 60; 4.35, 55, 62, 74, 76, 79f; 5.15f; DPd 1, 7, 13, 15f, 23; DPh 8, 9f; DNa 1, 31, 51f, 55; DNb 1, 46, 49; DSe 1; DSf 1, 8, 14, 57; DSp 1; DSs 1°, 6f; DSt 1°, 7f; DZc 1; DE 1; DH 6f, 8; XPa 1, 18, 20; XPb 1, 27f; XPc 1, 12, 15; XPd 1, 17f; XPf 1, 45, 48; XPg 12; XPh 1, 32, 49f, 52, 57, 60; XSc 4f°; XE 1; XV 1, 25; A¹Pa 1°, 22°; A²Sc 7; A²Hc 1, 18, 19; A³Pa 1, 24. *Auramazdā-maiy* DB 1.24f, 25, 55, 87, 94; 2.24, 34, 39f, 45, 54, 60, 68, 86, 96; 3.6, 16f, 37, 44f, 61f, 66f, 87; 4.60; DNa 50 *-dāiy*, with omission of *mᵃ* (§52.VI); DSf 19; XPh 45. *Auramazdā-taiy* DB 4.78. *Auramazdā-tay* (§52.II) DB 4.58. *Auramazdā-[šām]* DB 5.31f.

Auramazdām asm. DB 1.54f (*Auramazām*, §52.VI); 5.16, 18f, 32, 34; DPd 21f; DNa 54; DSf 15f, 18; XPf 21f, 29; XPh 40, 50, 53, 59; XSc 4.

Auramazdāha gsm. AmH 7f; AsH 10; DB 1.11f, 14, 18f, 22f, 26, 60, 68, 70, 88, 94f; 2.3, 25, 35, 40, 45f, 54f, 60, 68, 86f, 97; 3.6f, 17, 38, 45, 62, 67, 87f; 4.4, 6, 41, 44, 46, 52, 60, 88f; 5.16f, 32f; DSf 12, 21°; DSfv 55f°; DSl 2f; XPb 26f; XPd 16; XPg 3, 8; XSa 1; XV 19. *Auramazdāha* DPd 4, 9; DPe 6f; DNa 16, 35, 49, 56f; DNb 6, 47f; DSe 15, 35, 42; XPa 12, 16f; A²Hc 16. *Auramazdahā* (§52.III; §131; §185.IV) XPf 34, 43; XPh 14, 33, 37, 44; A¹Pa 18f.

AM nsm. (§42) DSe 50°; DSi 3°; DSj 4, 6°; DSk 4; DSn 2°; D²Sa 3; A²Sa 4° (as gen., §313.II), 4; A²Sd 3; A²Ha 5° (as gen.), 6. *AMmaiy* DSk 5; DSm 3°. *AMm* asm. DSk 4. *AMha* gsm. DSa 4; ligature (§42) DSk 4. *AMhā* DSj 3°, 5; A²Sd 3. *AMha* or *AMhā* DSd 3°; DSi 4°; DSm 5°; DSo 3°; D²Sb 4°.

Ākaufaciya- adj. sb. 'man of Akaufaka'; pl. a province of the Persian Empire: Akk. *a-ku-pi-i-iš*. Deriv. of **Ākaufaka-* 'Kohistan', prefix *ā* + *kaufa-* 'mountain' + adj. suffix (§113, §144.III; cf. Hz. AMI 8.72; Kent, Lg. 13.298–9). *Ākaufaciyā* npm. XPh 27.

akarta- adj. 'not made, not built, unrepaired'; neg. *a-* + ptc. of *kar-* 'make'. [*akartā*] nsf. DSe 47 (conj. of Kent, JAOS 54.43).

axšaina- adj., with *kāsaka-*, 'turquois' (so Bleichsteiner, WZKM 37.103–4, and König, Burgbau 63–4, but considered dubious by Hinz, ZDMG 95.235–6; hardly 'gray amber', with Hz. AMI 3.65–7, ApI 232; not 'hematite', with Scheil 21.29–30): Av. *axšaēna-* 'dark-colored', borrowed in Gk. Πόντος Ἄξεινος 'Black Sea' ('in-hospitable', by Gk. popular etymology, and euphemistically changed to Εὔξεινος), from neg. *a-* + *xšaina-*, cf. Av. *xšaēta-* 'shining' (§102, §147.I). *axšaina* nsm. DSf 39.

axšata- adj. 'unhurt, undisturbed': neg. *a-* + ptc. of *xšan-* (§102, §242.I), Skt. *kṣaṇóti* 'injures', Gk. κτείνει 'kills' (otherwise Foy KZ 35.49, Hz. ApI 70–1). *axšatā* nsf. DPe 23.

aguru- sb. 'baked brick' (§153.I). [*agurum*] asm. DSf 53, supplied by König, Burgbau 52, after *a-gur-ru* of the Akk. text, cf. NPers. *āgūr* in the same meaning. *a[g]ura[vā]* lsm. DB 4.89 (restored by Kent, JAOS 62.267, after König, Klotho 4.45); but read *ariyā āha* with Cameron.

agriya- adj. 'topmost, excellent, loyal': Av. *aγrya-* 'first in quality, etc.', Skt. *agriyá- agryá-* 'foremost, principal, etc.', deriv. (§144.IV) to Av. *aγra* 'der erste, oberste; (nt.) Anfang, Spitze', Skt. *ágra-* 'foremost, prominent, best; (nt.) tip, summit, best part' (§148.I). *agriya* nsm. DB 1.21, as read by Cameron, replacing KT's *agᵃrᵃ* + + (and the restorations thereof: *āgar[tā]* Wb. ZDMG 61.725, Tm. Vdt. Stud. 1.9, cf. Bthl. WZKM 22.72; *āgrаⁿ[θa]* Jn. Indian Stud. Lanman 255–7; *āgr[mata]* König, RuID 65; *āgr[mā]* Hz. ApI 59–62).

aciy adv. 'then, at that time' (§291.IV): Av. *aṯčiṯ* 'and indeed', Lt. *ecquid* (interrog.) 'anything', pIE **ed-qᵘid*, see *²a-* 'this' and particle *-ciy* (§105, §130; Bv. BSLP 33.2.152–3; Hz. AMI 4.125–6, 8.41, ApI 55–6; Wb. ZfA 41.319). XPf 21.

Atamaita- sb. 'Atamaita', an Elamite rebel: Elam. *Atameta* (§54.I, §76.V; Hüsing ap. Prašek,

GMP 2.73.n3; König, RuID 78; not *Umamaita* after the *Ummaıma* of Oppert, Mèdes 158, based on Rawlinson's +*imªimª*, later altered by KT's +*mªmªitª*). [*A*]*tamaıta* nsm DB 5.5.

ātar- sb. 'fire': Av. *ātar*- *āθr*-, NPers. *āδar*; in *Āçıyādıya*- and perhaps in *Āçına*- (§152.I).

atar (i.e. *aⁿtar*), prep. with acc, 'within, among': Av. *antarə*, Skt. *antar*, Lt. *ınter*, pIE *enter (§31). DB 1.21; 2.78; 4.32, 92; XPh 30, 35.

atı-, prefix, 'beyond, across': Av. *aiti*, Skt. *áti*, Gk. ἔτι 'yet, longer', Lt. *et* 'and', pIE *eti; with *ay*-, *yam*-. Cf. also *aθiy*.

aθaga- (i.e. *aθaⁿga*-) sb. 'stone': Av. *asənga*-, NPers. *sang*, cf. OP *asan*-, *asman*- (§87, §151, §155.I); see also *aθagaına*-. *aθagam* asm. DSf 24, 48.

aθagaina- (i.e. *aθaⁿgaina*-) adj. 'of stone': deriv. of *aθaga*- (§147.III), perhaps with vriddhi (§126; *āθagaina*- ?). *aθagaina* nsm. DPc. *aθagainam* asm. D²Sa 1; A²Hb. *aθagaināṁ* asf. A²Sc 6, *aθaganāṁ* asf. (§52.VI) for nsf. (§56.V) A³Pa 22. *aθagainiya* npf. (§152.II, §179.III, §190.I; JAOS 53.20; wrongly König, Burgbau 68; not *aθagaınīy* nsf. to sg. collective *stūnā*, as taken by Hz. AMI 3.68) DSf 45.

āθahavaja, word of unknown meaning, DB 4.90 (reading of KT); hardly, with Morgenstierne, Acta Or. 1.252, *āθaⁿha-vaja* 'word, speech of proclamation', cf. Skt. *āśqsā*- 'hope, expectation', + *vacas*- 'word'. Perhaps *āθaha*- (§143.I; with Morgenstierne) + root-noun *vaj*- (§142) 'proclamation-strengthener, seal', gsm. (JAOS 62.268; not abl. as instr., with König, Klotho 4.44–5).

aθiy prep. with acc. 'to': DB 1.91. Apparently doublet to *atiy* (Bv. Gr. §102), possibly by contamination of *aθį antevocalic and *atı* anteconsonantal, in sandhi (§80; Mt. Gr. §103).

Āθiyābaušna- sb. 'Athiyabaushna', father of Arsaces (§163.III): cpd. of (Av.) *āθi*- 'destruction, misfortune' + pass. ptc. of *ā-baug*- 'to free' (§243) with late -*šn*- from -*xšn*- (Bv. BSLP 29.2.104, cf. Av. *pouru-baoxšna*- 'bringing abundant rescue', Bthl. AiW 901): 'Freed from misfortune' (§160.Id; not active 'bringing freedom from misfortune', as taken by Bthl. Aiw 322–3; otherwise Hz. ApI 191–2: *haθiya*- 'truth', with late loss of *h*-, + deriv. of *ā-baud*- 'be fragrant', cf. Av. *baoδi*- 'fragrance', therefore 'having the fragrance of the truth'). *Āθiyābaušnahyā* gsm. Sa 4–7.

Aθurā sb. 'Assyria (and Syria)', a province of the Persian Empire (§6, §166.III): Elam. *aš-šú-ra*, Akk. *áš-šur*, Gk. Ἀσσυρία, but Aram. *aθur*. *Aθurā* nsf. DB 1.14f; 2.7; DPe 11; DNa 26f; DSe 26°; DSm 7°; XPh 22. *Aθurāyā* lsf. (§136) DB 2.53f.

Aθuriya- adj. 'Assyrian': deriv. to preceding (§144.III), perhaps with vriddhi in first syllable (§126; *Āθuriya*- ?). *Aθuriya* nsm. DN xvii; DSf 32; A?P 17.

Āçina- sb. 'Açina', an Elamite rebel: Elam. *ha-iš-ši-na*, Akk. *a-ši-na*. Either borrowed from Elam. (Foy, KZ 37.498); or shortened from an IE name beginning with OP *āç*- = Av. *ātar*- *āθr*- 'fire' (§147.II, §152.I), cf. *ātərə-dāta*- 'Fire-given or Fire-created' and other names (Vd. 18.52; Justi, INB 50; Bthl. AiW 324). *Āçina* nsm. DB. 1.74, 82, 4.10; DBc 1f. *Āçinam* asm. DB 1.76.

Āçiyādiya- adj. 'Açiyadiya', the ninth month, Nov.–Dec.: Elam. *ḫaššiyatiyaš*, Akk. *kislīmu*. Cpd. of *ātar*- 'fire' + deriv. of *yad*- 'worship' (§126; §152.I): 'Fire-Worship Month'. *Āçiyādıyahya* gsm. DB 1.89; 3.18.

ada- adv. 'then': GAv. *adā*, LAv. *aδa*, Skt. *ádha* 'therefore' cf. Gk. πρόσ-θε (and -θεν) 'in front of': pIE *e-dhe, to root in ²*a*- (§76.III; §191.II); see also *adakaiy*. *ada-taıy* DNa 43, 45.

adakaiy adv. 'then': OP *ada*- + -*kaıy*, Gk. adv. ποι 'somewhere', pIE *qʷoi, lsn. to int.-indef. stem (§135). DB 2.11, 24; 4.81, 82; DNb 38.

adam pron. 'I': Av. *azəm*, Skt. *ahám*, pIE *eĝhom (§109), cf. pIE *eĝō in Gk. ἐγώ, Lt. *ego* (§193.I). *adam* nsm. AmH 5, 8; AsH 14, CMa 1; DB 1.1, 10, 12, 39, 52, 54 bis, 56, 59, 60, 62, 63, 64, 66, 67, 68 bis, 70, 72, 73, 75, 78, 82, 83, 86, 89, 91, 95; 2.3, 5, 6, 10°, 11, 15°, 19, 28, 30, 48, 50, 63, 64, 69, 72, 80, 81, 88, 3.1, 13, 25, 29, 50, 77, 80, 84; 4.3, 8, 11°, 14, 16, 19, 21, 24, 27, 29, 32, 40, 45, 59, 64, 71, 81, 89; 5.2, 6f, 13, 21°, 23°, 25°; DBa 1, 16; DBb 4, 6; DBc 5f; DBd 3, 6; DBe 5, 8; DBf 3f, DBg 5; DBh 4f, 8; DBi 4, 9; DBj 4; DPd 20; DPe 1, 7; DPh 4; DNa 8, 17, 34, 37, 53f; DSa 1, 4; DSb 1; DSc; DSd 1°; DSe 7f, 16°, 34, 44°; DSf 5, 18°, 21°; DSg 1, 3°; DSi 1, DSj 1°, 2°, DSk 1, 4, DSm 1°, 6°; DSy 1; DZc 4, 7, 8, 11;

DE 11; DH 3f; XPa 6, 13, 14; XPb 11; XPc 6; XPd 8, 17; XPf 8, 34f, 36, 39, 41, XPg 9, XPh 6f, 15, 29, 34, 37, 40, 42f, 43, 59, XPj bis, XSc 1°, 3°, 4°; XE 12; XV 9, 23; A¹Pa 9°, 21°; D²Sb 1°, 4°; A²Sa 4; A²Sb; A²Sd 1, 3; A²Ha 5°; A²Hc 9, 16; A³Pa 11f; Wa 2; Wb 1; Wc 2; Wd 2; SDa; SDb; SXb 1; SXc 1. *adam-šaiy* DB 2.73f. *adam-šim* (§39) DB 1.62, 83, 4.6; DNa 35f. *adam-šām* DB 1.14; DNa 18; DSe 17 *adam-[šām]*; XPh 16.

mām asm. (Av. *mąm*, Skt. *mām*, pIE **mē* + acc. *-m*; §193.II) AsH 7, 11; DB 1.52 (*mātya-mām*, §133), 82f, 93°; 2.18, 28, 48, 63, 67, 73, 88; 3.30; 4.35, 91; 5.13, 17, 26, 28°, 29°, 33; DPh 9; DNa 33, 37, 51; DNb 11, 22, 26, 46, 49, DSe 50°; DSf 9, 10, 14f, 17 bis, 57; DSi 3°; DSj 4, 6°; DSm 4°; DSs 6; DSt 7°; DZc 12; DH 7f; XPa 18; XPb 27; XPc 12, XPd 17; XPf 31, 45; XPg 12; XPh 57; XSc 4°; XV 25, A¹Pa 22°; A²Sa 5°; A²Sd 4; A²Ha 6; A²Hb°; A²Hc 19; A³Pa 5, 23, 24; 22f, 26 (§56.V, for *manā* ?).

-mā asm. encl. (Av. *mā*, Skt. *mā*, pIE **mē*, §193.II; cf. encl. **me* in Gk. με): *nai-mā* DNb 8 (*na[imā]*), 10, 19; *nai-pati-mā* DNb 20.

manā gsm. (Av. *mana*, Skt. *máma*, pAr. **mana*, cf. Lith. *màno*; §193.III) AmH 6, 10; AsH 9; DB 1.4, 9, 12, 13, 18, 19 bis, 23, 27, 60; 2.19f, 21, 25, 27, 29f, 31, 35, 40, 46, 49, 51, 55, 60f, 82, 84, 87, 91f, 93; 3.9f, 10, 13, 15, 17, 20, 20f, 31, 32, 38, 45, 53, 56, 62, 67, 75f, 76, 84, 86; 4 2, 12, 35, 42, 49, 52, 53f, 66, 82f; 5.8, 14°, 30; DBa 5, 14f; DPd 7, 13; DPe 9; DNa 19, 21, 33; DNb 56°; DSe 18°, 20°, 38; DSf 12, 13, 58; DSj 5°; DSk 4; DSs 6°; XPa 19; XPb 23; XPc 11; XPf 16, 23, 31, 46; XPg 7; XPh 17, 19; XSa 2; XV 18; A¹Pa 20°, D²Sb 4°; A²Hc 18. *mana-cā* (§135) DPd 9f.

-maiy gsm. (gen.-dat. GAv. *mōi*, LAv. *mē*, Skt. *me*, Gk. dat. μοι, pIE **moi*) enclitic to *aita* (nsn., asn.), *Auramazdā*, *AM*; *ava* (nsn); *avākaram*, *avākaramca-*; *ucāram*; *utā*, *uta-*; *tya* (nsn., asn.); *dahyāus*; *duvarayā*; *nai-*; *pati-*; *pasāva*; *yaθā*; *hauv*, *hau-*: AsH 12; DB 1.25 bis, 55, 87, 94; 2.24, 34, 40, 45, 54, 60, 68, 75, 79, 86, 90, 96, 3.6, 11, 17, 37, 44f, 61f, 66f, 87; 4 39, 46, 60, 64; DPd 23°; DPh 8, 10, DNa 50 (*mᵃ* omitted, §52.VI), 52f, 54f; DNb 13, 28, 28f, 31, 32f, 33, 48, 51, 52; DSe 51°, 52°, DSf 10, 19°, 20°, 58, DSj 4°, 6°; DSk 5; DSl 4f; DSm 3°, DSs 7°; DSt 9°; DH 6, 8; XPa 15, 18f, 19f, XPb 24, 29, 30, XPc 13 bis, XPd 18f, 19; XPf 32, 38, 41, 45f, 47; XPg 14; XPh 32, 45, 58, 60; XSc 5° bis; XV 26f°, 27°; A¹Pa 23°, 24°; A²Sdb 4 (*-may* dc, §52.VI); A²Hc 20 bis.

-ma gsm. for *-maiy* (§193.III); *apanᵃyāka-ma* A²Sa 3; [*nᵃyā*]*kama* for *nᵃyākam-ma* (§130) A²Sa 4. Not *kamna-ma* DB 2.19, as taken by Tolman.

-ma absm. encl. (Av. *mat̰*, Skt. *mat*, pIE **med*, §193.IV; orthotone pIE **mēd* in oLt. *mēd*, clLt. *mē*); only in *hacā-ma* DB 1.19, 23; 2.6, 12°, 16, 93; 3.27, 78, 81; 4.92, DPe 9; DNa 20; DSe 19°; XPh 18 Not *duvitīya-ma* DB 3.24 (with Bthl.); not *apara-ma* DB 4.37, 68, 87 (with Bthl.), nor DSt 10°.

vayam npm. (Av. *vaēm*, Skt. *vayám*, pIE **yei* + pAr. *-am*, cf. Gt. *wei-s*; §193.V) DB 1.7, 10°; DBa 10, 17.

amāxam gpm. (Av. *ahmākəm*, Skt. *asmā́kam*; §118.II, §193.VI) DB 1.8, 28, 45, 49, 61, 69, 71; DBa 12f.

Adukanaiša- adj. 'Adukanaisha', first month, March–April: Elam. *ha-du-kan-na-iš*, Akk. *nīsannu*: *-naiša-* on the evidence of the Elam., acc. to MB Gr. §96, rather than *-niša-* (§117). Cpd. of *adu-* '?' + *kan-* 'dig', possibly with vriddhi (§126; *Ādu-* ?): 'Irrigation-Canal-Cleaning Month', referring to the cleaning of the underground conduits for irrigation water, regularly done in the spring (cf. Bthl. AiW 61). *Aduka[nai]šahya* gsm. DB 2.69.

an- neg. prefix before vowels, cf. ¹*a-* before consonants: Av. Skt. *an-*, Gk. ἀν-, Lt. *in-*, Gt. *un-*, pIE **n̥-* (§67.I); in *Anāhatā-*.

anā ism. to ²*a-* (q.v.), DPe 8 (not to Av. Skt. *ana-*); XPa 14 (not prep.).

Anāmaka- adj. 'Anamaka', tenth month, Dec.–Jan.: Elam. *hanāmakaš*, Akk. *ṭebētu*. Cpd. of neg. *a-* + *nāma-* 'name' (see *nāman-*) + adj. suffix *-ka-* (§146.II), possibly with vriddhi (§126; *Ānāmaka-* ?): 'Month of the Nameless (= Highest) God'. *Anāmakahya* gsm. DB 1.96; 2.26, 56; 3.63.

Anāhitā- sb. 'Anahita, Anaitis', a goddess: Elam. *a-na-ḫi-ud-da*, Akk. *a-na-aḫ-i-tu-'*, Gk. Ἀναῖτις; Av. *anāhitā-*. Cpd. of neg. *an-* + ptc. pass. *āhita-* 'spotted, defiled', of uncertain connections (§67.I, §118.V, §242.I): 'The Spotless'. The OP writings, being late, fail to show length of *ā* in either position. *Anahita* (§27, §52.III) nsf. A²Sd 3f; *Anahᵃta* A²Sa 4 (as gen., §313.II), 4f; A²Ha 5° (as gen.), 6.

aniya- adj. 'the one or the other (of two), other (of any number), rest of' (JNES 3.233-4; not 'enemy', cf. Kent, JAOS 35.345.n6 and Bv. TPS 1945.56-9): Av. *ainya-*, Skt. *anyá-*, pIE **anio-*, cf. **alio-* in Gk. ἄλλος, Lt. *alius*, and **antero-* in Gt. *anþara-*, Gm. *ander*, NEng. *other* (§39, §144.II, §204.II; decl., §203). *aniya* nsm. DB 1.95; 3.32; DSe 33°, 35. *aniyam* asm. DB 1.86; 5.25, 28; DSe 33, 35f. *aniyahyā* gsm. DB 1.87. *aniyanā* absm. DPd 11; DPe 20f. *aniyai-ciy* npm. XPf 29. *aniyāha* npm. (§10, §172) DB 4.61, 62f. *aniyā* nsf. DSf 25, 26 (not with Bv. Gr. §334, inst. as adv. 'on one side ... on the other'). *aniyām* asf. DSe 48f. *aniyā* npf. DB 1.41. *aniyā* apf. DB 1.47, 67. *aniyāuvā* lpf. (§72) DB 1.35. *aniya* asn. XPf 39f. *aniyaš-ciy* nsn. (§9.VI, §105) DB 4.46; XPa 13; XPh 41f (written *aniyašcᵃ*, §52.I).

an[iya]θā adv. 'in other ways' (§191.II); Cameron's interpretation for his reading *anᵃ + + vᵃmᵃ*, DB 4.89.

anuv (i.e. *anu*) prep. 'along, according to': Av. *anu* with acc., loc., 'toward, along', Skt. *ánu* with acc. 'after, along'; see also *anušiya-*. (1) With inst., DB 1.92; DNb 25 (cf. Lg. 15.176). (2) With gen., DNb 16, 18 (§137, §267.IV; *anu-dim* + gen.).

anušiya- adj. as sb. 'follower, ally': from *anu-* (see *anuv*) + adj. suffix *-ija-* (§80, §144.VI). *anušiya* nsm. DB 2.95. *anušiyā* npm. DB 1.58; 2.77; 3.49, 51, 74, 90, 91f; 4.82.

apa- prefix (§206b) 'away': Av. Skt. *apa*, Gk. ἀπό, Lt. *ab*, Gt. *af*, Gm. *ab*, NEng. *of, off*, pIE **apo*. Used with vb. *gaud-* and in sbb. *apadāna-*, *apaniyāka-*; with suffix in *apatara-*, *apara-*.

apataram adv. 'farther off, far off'; nsn. of *apatara-*, which is *apa-* + comp. *-tara-* (§32, §190.III), cf. Gk. adv. ἀπωτέρω. DNa 18; DSe 16f; XPb 25; XPh 16.

apadāna- sb. 'palace': from *apa-* + *dāna-* (§147.I) to root *²dā-*, cf. Skt. *apadhā́-* 'concealment', Gk. ἀποθήκη 'storehouse'. For development in later Iranian, with *āpa-* by secondary lengthening (but not OP *appa-*, cf. §130), see Henning, Trans. Philol. Soc. 1944.110n. *apadānam* asm. D²Sa1; A²Hb. *apadāna* (§52.V) A²Sa 3, 4; A²Ha 5.

apaniyāka- sb. 'great-great-grandfather': from *apa-* + *niyāka-* 'grandfather', cf. Lt. *ab-avos* 'great-great-grandfather'. *apanᵃyāka-ma* (§22, §52.I) nsm. A²Sa 3.

apara- adj. 'later, after': Av. Skt. *apara-*, from *apa-* + comp. *-ra-* (§32, §190.III). *apara* nsm. XPh 47. *aparam* asn. as adv. DB 4.37, 42, 48, 68, 70, 87; DSt 10° (not *apara-ma*, nsm. with encl. abl., DB 4.37, 68, 87—and DSt 10°—as Bthl. AiW 77 suggests, following Akk. *ša be-la-a ar-ki-a* 'who shall rule after me').

āpi- sb. 'water': Av. *āp-*, NPers. *āb*, Skt. pl. nom. *ā́pas*, acc. *apás*, pIE **ắp-*, with or without *ī*-extension, which seems to have become *ī* in OP (§122). *āpišim* (= *āpiš-šim*; §41, §130) nsf. DB 1.95f. *āpiyā* lsf. DB 1.95. *abiš* (Skt. *adbhíṣ*, and dat.-abl. Skt. *adbhyás*, Av. *aiwyō*, both from **ap-bh-*; §75.IV, §130, §188.V, JAOS 62.269-70; see also s.v. *abiš*) ipf. DB 1.86.

apiy adv. 'thereto, very': Av. *aipi*, Skt. *ápi*, Gk. prep. ἐπί 'on', pIE **epi* (§44, §191.I). In OP, normally enclitic, but sometimes written separately; often with *dūraiy* 'afar' (§136): *dūrai-apiy* 'far and wide' DNa 12; *dūray-apiy* DNa 46; *dūraiy apiy* as two words, DSe 11, DZc 6, DE 19, XPa 9, XPb 18f, XPc 8, XPd 13, XPf 13, XPh 10f, XE 18, XV 14, A¹Pa 14°, A²Hc 17f. Probably *vašnā[pi]y* XPg 7f (Bv. BSLP 34.1.32-4) with crasis, rather than *vašnā-[ci]y* or *vašnā-[di]y* (Lg. 9.230); KT's *[ap]i-maiy* is eliminated by Cameron's reading of *utāmaiy* as completely visible, DB 4.46 (cf. note ad loc.).

afuvāyā, error of writing for *aruvāyā* (§55.II); see *aruvā-*.

abiy prep. and prefix 'to, against, in addition to': GAv. *aibī*, LAv. *aiwi*, Skt. *abhí*; conflux of pIE **m̥bhi*, oHG *umbi* 'round about', and pIE **obhi*, oCS *obĭ* 'beside, by'.

(1) Prep. with acc., DB 1.40, 76, 80, 82, 84; 2.12, 17, 73, 88; 3.2, 3, 14, 27, 56, 60, 71, 82; 5.12f, 21, 22°, 23, 26, 28°; DPd 18; DPe 24; DZc 9f, 12; XPg 10.

(2) Prefix with verb *jav-*, and first element in *abicariš*, *abyapara*, perhaps in *Abirāduš*, but probably not the base of *abiš*.

abicariš DB 1.64f, word of uncertain form and meaning, probably asn. of *s*-stem (§185.III), to *abi-* + root *car-* 'move, go' (Av. *caraiti*, Skt. *cárati*, Lt. *colit* 'tills'; §107), giving, in association with the following *gaiθām* 'living personal property', a meaning 'pasture lands', cf. NPers. *carīdan* 'to pasture' (Spiegel, KT, Bthl. AiW 89). Cf. also Tm. Lex. 64–5; Gray, JAOS 33.281–3; Hüsing, KZ 48.155–6; Hz. ApI 51–4.

abiyaparam adv. 'later, afterward', from *abiy* + *aparam* (§191.IV). *ab*ᵃ*yapara* (§22, §52.V) A²Sa 4.

Abirādu- sb. 'Abiradu', a village in Elam: first part perhaps *abi-*. *Abirāduš* nsm. DSf 46.

abiš DB 1.86, probably not adv. 'thereby', *abi-* + adverbial *-s*, but ipf. of *āpi-* 'water' (q.v.): not an error for *āpiš* nsf. 'water' as proposed by König, RuID 70–1.

abyapara see *abiyaparam*.

-am, enclitic particle extracted by wrong division from pAr. **aźham* 'I', perhaps even in pIE times, and therefore **-om* from **eĝ(h)om*; seen in OP *tuvam* (cf. *adam* 'I'), *iyam*, *imam*, *patišam*, cf. Skt. *tuvám iyám imám* etc.

ama- sb. 'offensive power', see *Aršāma-*.

amaxamatā, DB 4.92, read by KT, and apparently corresponding to Elam. 'were pleased (at the inscription)' (cf. Wb. KIA 72n, quoting variant interpretations): possibly for *ham-axmatā*, aor. mid. of *ham-* + *kam-* 'like, love' (OP *kāma-* 'wish', Skt. vb. *kam-* 'love'), formed like Gk. ἔσχετο to root **seĝh-*, ἕπτετο to root **pet-* (JAOS 62.269; §55.II, §103.II).

amata adv. 'thence': demonst. stem *ama-*, found (though rarely) in Skt., + adv. *-tos*, as in Skt. *tátas* 'thence', Gk. ἐκτός 'outside', Lt. *caelitus* 'from the sky': Buck, Lg. 3.4–5; Jn. quoted by Gray, JRAS 1927.101: cf. Kent, JAOS 51.231. Hardly, with Gray, JRAS 1927.99–100, and Hz. ApI 65–6, the same as Skt. abl. *asmāt* remade to **asmatas*, with *-tos* ending. DPh 6, 7; DH 5, 6.

amuθa, see *mauθ-*.

ay- vb. 'go': Av. *ay-* (pres. *aēiti*), Skt. *i-* (pres. *éti*), Gk. εἶσι, Lt. *it*: conj., §208. Cf. also *yauviyā-*. *aitiy* (§69) DZc 10. *āiš* imf. (§72, §228.III) DB 1.93; 2.67; 3.35, 43.

ā + *ay-* 'come': *āya*ⁿ*tā* 3d pl. imf. mid. (§131, §208) DZc 11.

ati- + *ay-* 'go beyond, go along': *atiyāiš* imf. (§72, §122, §228.III) DB 3.73.

upa- + *ay-* 'go to, arrive at': [*u*]*pāyam* 1st sg. imf. (§122, §131, §226.II) DB 1.91f.

upari- + *ay-* 'behave, conduct one's self': *upariyā*[*ya*]*m* 1st sg. imf. (§122, §226.II) DB 4.64f.

nij- + *ay-* 'go forth': *nijāyam* 1st sg. imf. (§120, §208, §226.II) DB 2.64.

pati- + *ay-* 'come to, come into the possession of': *patiyāiša*ⁿ 3d pl. imf. (§140.III, §208, §232.-III) DB 1.13, 18.

parā + *ay-* 'go forth, proceed': *paraidiy* 2d sg. imv. (§122, §131, §237.I) DB 2.30, 50; 3.14. *paraitā* 2d pl. imv. (§131, §208, §231, §237) DB 2.20, 83; 3.58, 85. *paraitā* npm. past ptc. (§122, §242, §242.I) DB 2.32f, 38, 43, 52, 58; 3.65.

pari- + *ay-* 'go around before, respect', with inst.: *pariyaitiy* XPh 52 (written *-ait*ᵃ, §52.I; wrongly interpreted by Hz. AMI 8 66f, ApI 219). *parīdiy* 2d sg. imv. (§122, §131, §208, §237.I) XPh 49 (also wrongly interpreted by Hz. ibid.). *apariyāya*ⁿ 3d pl. imf (with double augment, §208) DB 1.23 (not *āpariyāya*, for **ahapa-*, to Skt. *saparyáti* 'worships', despite Bthl. Stud. 2.67, AiW 1765: not to be emended to *upariyāya*, as done by WBn xi, Wb. KIA 12); see JAOS 35.331–6, Lg. 13.303.

ayāumani- adj. 'untrained': neg. *a-* (§67.I) + *yāumani-*. *ayāu*(*ma*)*iniš* nsm. DNb 59 (§52 VI; with epenthesis of *-i-*, §127, as in Avestan).

āyadana- sb. 'sanctuary': deriv. (§147.I) of prefix *ā* + vb. *yad-* 'worship'. *āyadanā* apn. DB 1.63f.

ar- vb. 'move, go or come toward': Av. *ar-*, Skt. *r̥-*, Lt. *oritur* 'rises'; pres. inchoative (§97), OP *rasa-*, NPers. *rasað*, Skt. *r̥ccháti*, pIE **r̥sḱe-* (and **re-sḱe-*, §32). See also *arta-*, *hamarana-*. *arasam* 1st sg. imf. (§212) DB 1.54; 2.28, 48, 63.

ava- + *ar-* 'go down to, arrive at': *avā*[*rasam*] 1st sg. imf. (§131) DB 5.23f; [*a*]*vārasam* DSf 24.

parā + *ar-* 'come to, arrive at', with acc. of place and *abiy* + acc. of person: *parārasam* 1st sg. imf. (§131) DB 2.65. *parārasa* imf. DB 2.22, 32, 52; 3.3, 34.

ni- + *ar-* 'come down, descend', with *abiy* and acc. of place: *nirasātiy* subj. (§140.I; §289) DPe 24.

Arakadri- sb. 'Arakadri', a mountain in Persia (§32): Elam. *ha-rak-qa-tar-ri-iš*, Akk. *a-ra-ka-ad-ri-'*; a possible etymology, Foy, KZ 35.62. *Arakadriš* nsm. DB 1.37.

Arabāya- sb. 'Arabia', a province of the

Persian Empire (§32, §75.V, §166.III), also 'Arab', ethnic to same: Elam. *ḫar-ba-ya*, Akk. *a-ra-bi*, Gk. Ἀραβία. (1) 'Arabia': *Arabāya* nsm. DB 1.15; DPe 11; DNa 27; DSe 26°; DSm 7°; XPh 25 (2) 'Arab': *Arabāya* nsm. A?P 18.

arašan- sb. 'cubit' (§32, §82, §155.II): Av. nom. dual *arəθnā̊*, to Iran. stem *aratan- araθn-*, cf. Skt. *aratnı́-*; Lg. 15.176–7 (borrowed from Iran. into General Slavic as *aršın* 'ell', Wb. AfOF 7.41, against Berneker, Slav. etym. Wrtb. 31, who thinks it borrowed from Turkish); cf. also Bv. Orig. 105. *arašaniš* ipm. (§187) DSf 26 bis (not nom. sg , with Bv. Gr. §308, §318: not acc. pl.).

arika- adj. 'evil, faithless': deriv. (§146.II) of **asra-*, GAv. *aŋra-*, LAv. *aŋra-* 'hostile, enemy', to pAr. root **ans-*, seen in Av. *ąsta-* 'hate, enmity'; cf. also Av. (nom.) *aŋrō mainyuš* 'evil spirit, Ahriman' (Bthl. AiW 189); not to Skt. *ari-* 'enemy' (MB Gr. §273), nor to Skt. *alīkā́-* (Wackernagel, KZ 59.28–9). *arika* nsm. DB 1.22, 33; 4.63. *arīkā* npm. DB 5.15°, 31°.

Ariya- adj. 'Aryan' (perhaps *Āriya-*, §126): Av. *airya-*, Skt. *ā́rya-* 'noble', cf. NPers. *ērān* 'Iran, Persia', Irish *Eire* 'Ireland', to pIE root **er-*, OP *ar-* (§35.I, §144.I). See also *Ariyaciça-*, *Ariyāramna-*. *Ariya* nsm. DNa 14; DSe 13; XPh 13. *ariyā* isn. as sb. 'in Aryan (language)' DB 4.89.

Ariyaciça- adj. 'of Aryan lineage' (§161.IIa): *Ariya-* + *ciça-*. *Ariyaçica* nsm. XPh 13; *Ariya ciça* (written as two words, §44) DNa 14f, DSe 13f.

Ariyāramna- sb. 'Ariaramnes', great-grandfather of Darius: Elam. *ḫar-ri-ya-ra-um-na*, Akk. *ar-ya-ra-am-na-'*, Gk. Ἀριαράμνης. From *ariya-* + pass. ptc. of *ā-ram-* (§131; Av. Skt. *ram-* 'to be at peace, to pacify'): 'Having the Aryans at peace' (§161.IIc). Hardly *Ariyā* pl. + *ramna-* (Foy, KZ 35.9), or *Ariya-* + *aramna-* pres. ptc. mid. to *ar-* (Hz. ApI 237). *Ariyāramna* nsm. AmH 1, 4, 9; DB 1.5; DBa 7; as gsm. AsH 3 (§313.II). *Ariyāramnahyā* gsm. DB 1.5; DBa 7.

aruva- sb. 'action' (JNES 4.44, 52; §35.II, §150; so also Bv. TPS 1945.42–3): fem. to adj. *aruva-*, Av. *aurva-* 'schnell, tapfer' (Bthl. AiW 200), doublet to Av. *aurvant-* (q.v., under *aruvasta-*). *aruvāyā* lsf. DNb 38 (inscribed *afuvāyā*, §55.II; not *anuvāθā* with Wb. Grab 28, KIA 94; not to be emended with Hz. ApI 293–6 to *aruvāθā* 'love', cf. Av. *urvaθa-* 'amicus, befreundet', Bthl. AiW 1537; *āfuvāyā* acc. nt. pl. 'measures to be taken', from **āpy-āya-*, acc. to Pisani, Riv. Stud. Or. 19.82–5, to root **ăp-* 'get', cf. Av. *āfənte* 'they obtain', Bthl. AiW 70 and 72, note 1 to *ap-*).

aruvasta- sb. 'activity' (JNES 4.50–2, 232), 'physical prowess' (Bv. TPS 1945.40–1): *-ta-* abstract (§145) to *arvant-* 'moving', Av. *aurvant-* 'schnell, tapfer, Held' (Bthl. AiW 200), Skt. *arvant-* 'running, hasting, horse', from Ar. *ar-* 'move' + suffix *-vant-* (§35.II, §85, §126, §157), cf. Lt. *orior* 'arise'; cf. Akk. translation *lu*it-ba-ru-tum* 'activity', to *abāru* 'be strong' (Schaeder, OLZ 43.289–93). See also *aruvā-*. Not with Hz. RHRel. 113.29–31, ApI 80–6, 'Gut-sein', to Av. *urvaθa-* 'amicus', with *it-ba-ru-tum* as 'companionship' to *ibru* 'friend' (cf. JNES 4.51); no valid evidence for meaning in Arm. loanword *arwest* 'wonders', cited by Nyberg, Rel. 351, from St. John 4.48. *aruvastam* nsn. DNb 31, 33; asn. DNb 4.

Arxa- sb. 'Arkha', an Armenian rebel (§31, §164.V): Elam. *ḫa-rak-qa*, Akk. *a-ra-ḫu*. *Arxa* nsm. DB 3.78, 91°; 4.28f; DBi 1. *Arxam* asm. DB 3.82, 89.

arjana- sb. 'ornamentation', as shown by Akk. *si-ım-ma-nu-u* 'decoration' (§34, §126, §147.I): for meaning, see JAOS 51.208, 53.13, 53.19, Schaeder, Arch. Anz. 47.272–4, against Hz.'s 'limestone' (AMI 3.52–3) and 'building material' (ApI 88–93). Cf. Av. pres. *arəja-* 'be worth', Skt. *árhati*, and Ars. Phl. *aržān*, NPers. *arzān*, Av. *arəjah-* 'worth, value', Skt. *argha-*. *arjanam* nsn. DSf 41f; *arjanam-šaiy* DSf 23°.

arta- sb. 'Law, Justice', an archangel attending Ahuramazda: ptc. to *ar-* as sb., Av. *aša-* and *arəta-*, Skt. *r̥tá-* 'cosmic order', Lt. *ortus* 'risen, originated', pIE **r̥to-* (§30, §66, §242.I). See also *Artaxšaça-*, *artāvan-*, *Artavardiya-*. *artā-cā* isn. (§252.I, Lg. 21.223–9) XPh 41, 50f, 53f (not with Hartmann, OLZ 40.145–60; nor with Nyberg, Rel. 367, 478; Bailey ap. Nyberg, Rel. 478; Henning, TPS 1944.108; hardly, with Sen 155, *artācā brazmaniy* apn. 'and the divine fulfillments'; nor with Pisani, Riv. Stud. Or. 19.85–8, as elliptic dual 'Arta and Brazman', the *-cā* connecting with the preceding *Auramazdām*, and Brazman being the OP for the Av. *vohū manō* 'Good Thought').

Artaxšaça- sb. 'Artaxerxes' (I, son of Xerxes; II, son of Darius II; III, son of Artaxerxes II): Elam. *ir-tak-ša-aš-ša*, Akk. *ar-tak-šat-su*, Gk. ᾽Αρταξέρξης (§29.n2, §30). From *arta-* 'justice' + *xšaça-* 'kingdom', 'Having a kingdom of justice' (hardly, with Nyberg, Rel. 352, 'whose *xšaça-* derives from *arta-*'); imitation of *Xšayāršā*, acc. *-ām*, explains the long vowel of the ultima in the nom. and acc. (§78, §161.Ib; decl. §172, §187). *Artaxšaçā* nsm. A¹Pa 9°, 17°; A¹I; D²Sb 3°; A²Sa 1; A²Sb; A²Sc 1°; A²Sd 1, 2; A²Ha 1; A²Hb; A²Hc 7, 15f; A³Pa 5 (as acc., §247E), 8, 12 (as gen., §313.II), 13 (as gen.), 14f (as gen.), 15f (as gen.), 21, 23f; AVsb-d. *Ardaxcašca* (§49; or *-šda*) AVsa. *Artaxšaçām* asm. A¹PA 5f°; A²Sa 4; A²Hc 5; Sf 2–4. *Artaxšaçahyā* gsm. D²Sb 2°; *Artaxšaθrahyā* (Tm. Lex. 54) A²Ha 2f, 3; *Artaxšaçāhyā* (§53) A²Sa 2 bis; A²Hc 10f, (as nom., §313.I) 11f.

artāvan- adj. 'righteous, blessed', denoting the blissful state of the true religionists after death: identical with Av. *ašavan-* 'characterized by Arta or Asha, righteous', Skt. *r̥tā́van-* 'true to sacred law' (cf. Hz. ApI 289–93); from *r̥ta-*, OP *arta-*, with lengthened final vowel, + adj. suffix *-van-* (§30, §155.IV). *artāvā* nsm. (§124.5, §187) XPh 48, 55.

Artavardiya- sb. 'Artavardiya', one of Darius's generals: Elam. *ir-du-mar-ti-ịa*, Akk. *ar-ta-mar-zi-ịa*. From *arta-* + *vard-* 'to work' + adj. suffix (§30, §31, §144.IV, §160.Ia): 'Doer of Justice' (not from *vard-* 'to increase', Skt. *vardh-*, because of *-z-* in Akk. and in Aram. *'rtvrzy*, as Bv. BSLP 31.2.66–7 shows). *Artavardiya* nsm. DB 3.30f, 33. *Artavardiyam* asm. DB 3.36, 43.

Ardaxcašca (or *-šda*), probably miswritten for *Artaxšaçā*, q.v.

ardata- sb. 'silver': Av. *ərəzata-*, Skt. *rajatá-*, cf. Gk. ἄργυρος, Lt. *argentum* (§30, §88, §145); Yezdi *ālī* 'silver' has Iran. *ar-*, not *r̥-* (Bv. BSLP 30.1.60, Origines 12). See also *ardastāna-*. *ardatam* nsn. DSf 40.

ardastāna- sb. 'window-frame, window cornice': *arda-* 'light' as in OP *ardata-* 'silver', Skt. *rajatá-* 'white', *r̥jrá-* 'red', Gk. ἀργός 'shining' + *stāna-* 'place' (§31, §160.Ib; Foy, KZ 35.48; hardly as with Bthl. AiW 193, or Hz. ApI 74–6); 'light-place'. *ardastāna* nsm. DPc.

Ardumaniš- sb. 'Ardumanish', ally of Darius against Gaumata: Akk. *a-ar-dı-ma-ni-iš*. From *ardu-* 'upright', GAv. *ərəzu-*, Skt. *r̥jú-* + *maniš-*, see *manah-* 'mind' (§34, §63.II, §124.4, §156.IV, §161.IIa, §185.III): 'Upright-minded' (hardly *Ardimaniš-* 'dessen *manah-* glühend ist', as taken by Nyberg, Rel. 352). *Ar[duma]n[iš]* nsm. DB 4.86.

Arbaırā- sb. 'Arbela', a city in Assyria: Elam. *ḫar-be-ra*, Akk. *ar-ba-'-il*, Gk. ῎Αρβηλα (§31, §107, §166, §166.III). *Arbairāyā* lsf. DB 2.90.

Armına- sb. 'Armenia', a province of the Persian Empire (§31, §106): see also under *Armınıya-*. *Armına* nsm. DB 1.15; DPe 12; DNa 27; DSe 27°; DSm 8°; XPh 20. *Armınam* asm. DB 2.30, 32, 50, 52.

Armınıya- (1) adj. 'Armenian', (2) sb. (Armenia', a province of the Persian Empire: Elam. *ḫar-mi-nu-ịa*, Akk. *u-ra-aš-ṭu*, Gk. ᾽Αρμενία. Adj. to *Armına-* (§144.III).

(1) *Armınıya* nsm. DB 2.29; 3.78f, 4.29; A?P 20.

(2) *Armınıyaiy* lsm. DB 2.59, 63; *Arm'nıyaiy* DB 2.33f, 39, 44, 48 (§22; Lg. 19.233n).

Aršaka- sb. 'Arsaces': Gk. ᾽Αρσάκης. Deriv. of *arša-*, see *aršan-*; §30, §146.II, §163.III, §164.III. *Aršaka* nsm. Sa 1f.

Aršādā- sb. 'Arshada', a fortress in Arachosia: Elam. *ir-ša-da* (§30). *Aršādā* nsf. DB 3.72.

aršan- and *arša-* (§155.I) sb. 'male, hero, bull': Av. *aršan-*, Skt. *r̥ṣa-bhá-* 'bull', Gk. ἄρσην 'male'; in *Aršaka-*, *Aršāma-*, *Xšayāršan-*, perhaps in *Aršādā-*.

Aršāma- sb. 'Arsames': Elam. *ir-ša-um-ma*, Gk. ᾽Αρσάμης (§29, §29.n2, §30). From *arša-* + (OP Av. Skt.) *ama-* 'offensive power' (Benveniste-Renou, Vr̥tra et Vr̥θragna 11): 'Having the might of a hero' (§161.Ib). *Aršāma* nsm. AsH 1, 5; DB 1.4f; DBa 6; DSf 13; XPf 19, 20; A³Pa 20 (as gen.; §313.II). *Aršāmahyā* gsm. DB 1.3, 5; DBa 4, 6.

arštā- sb. 'rectitude' (§30; §93): haplologic for **aršta-tā-* (§129), abstract to *aršta-* 'upright' (§145), pIE **r̥ĝ-ta-*, with zero-grade to root **reĝ-* (§122; Mt. Gr. §123, §125), cf. Av. *arštāt-* 'goddess of rectitude', OP *ardu-* in *Ardumaniš-*, *rāsta-*; or merely fem. **r̥ĝ-tā-* as abstract (Bv. Gr. §123, §125). *arštām* asf. DB 4.64.

aršti- sb. 'spear' (§30): Av. *aršti-*, Skt. *ṛṣṭí-*, pIE *ṛs-ti-* (§152.III, §179.III), to root in Skt. *árṣati ṛṣáti* 'rush, push'. See also *ārštika-, arštibara-*. *aršt[i]š* nsf. DNa 44.

āršlika- sb. 'spearman': from *aršti-* 'spear' with vriddhi (as in *uvārštika-*, §126), + suffix *-ka-* (§146.II). *āršlika* nsm. DNb 44.

arštibara- sb. 'spear-bearer': *aršti-* 'spear' + *bara-* 'bearer' (§122, §143.V, §160.Ia). *arštibara* nsm. DNc 2 (written *šᵃrᵃsᵃtᵃibᵃrᵃ*, §51; the original draft seems to have had *arᵃsᵃtᵃibᵃrᵃ*; on proofreading, the *šᵃ* which was to have replaced the *sᵃ* was wrongly substituted for the *a*, and this falsely corrected orthography was inscribed on the rock).

¹*ava-* demonst. adj. and pron. 'that' (§260.III, §264): Av. *ava-*, Skt. gen. du. *avóṣ*, oCS *ovŭ*; see also *avā, avaθā, avadā, avaparā, avahyarādiy, pasāva*. Decl., §200.
avam asm. DB 1.21, 22, 31, 40, 49, 57, 76, 80, 84, 88; 2.4, 4f, 12, 17, 20, 25, 30, 31, 35, 40f, 46, 50, 51, 55, 61, 84, 87, 94, 97; 3.4, 7, 12, 14, 14f, 17, 27, 38, 45f, 47f, 50, 56f, 58, 62, 67, 82, 85, 89; 4.38, 66 bis; 5.6°, 27; DNa 2; DSe 2; DSf 2°; DSt 2°; DZc 1; DE 3; XPa 2; XPb 3; XPc 2; XPd 2; XPf 2, 23; XPh 2, 37; XE 4; XV 3; A¹Pa 2f°; A²Hc 3; A³Pa 2f. *avamšām* DB 2.20, 82f; 3.31, 85; 5.8°. *auahyā* gsm. DB 1.29; 3.70; 4.48f. *avanā* absm. DSf 31. *avaiy* npm. DB 5.15, 31°; DSf 48, 50°, 51, 53, 54. *avaiy* apm. DB 2.77; 4.69. *avaišām* gpm. DB 4.51.
avām asf. DSf 27; *a[vā]m-cᵃ* (= *-ciy*, §52.I) DB 5.2f; *ava* as asf. (§56.V) XPh 33. [*a*]*vā* npf. DNa 39.
ava nsn. DB 1.20, 4.47; DNb 10, 11, 20, 22; DSf 42. *ava-maiy* DSj 4; DSl 4f. *ava-diš* DNa 21; DSe 20°; XPh 19. *avaš-ciy* (§9.VI, §105) DNb 55. *ava* asn. DB 1.62; DNa 20, 37, 49; DSa 4; DSe 19°, 32°, 34, 44°; DSf 20°; XPa 16; XPb 25; XPf 39, 42; XPg 10; XPh 18, 42. *ava-taiy* DB 4.76, 79. *avaš-ciy* DNb 53f, 57; XPa 20; XPc 14; XPf 48. *avanā* absm. DSe 38. *avanā* isn. XPh 49, 51f.

²*ava-* prefix 'away, down': GAv. *avā*, LAv. *ava*, Skt. *áva*; with verbs *ar-*, ²*kan-*, *gam-*, *jan-*, *ā-jan-*, ¹*rad-*, *stā-*, *hard-*. Cf. JAOS 62.274–5.

avā adv. 'thus', correlative to *yaθā*: perhaps isn. of ¹*ava-*, but more probably error for *avaθā* (§52.VI), by omission of one character, as taken by MB Gr. §59; see also *avākara-*. DB 4.51.

avākanam, see ²*kan-*.

avākara- adj. 'of such sort': *avā* 'thus' + *kara-* 'doer' (§160.Ia; wrongly Hz. ApI 101–3, who takes *-kara-* in *avākara-* and *ciyākara-* not from *kar-* 'do', but as *kara-* 'time', as in *hakaram*, q.v.). *avākaram* nsn. (§259) DNb 6; *avākaram-ca-maiy* (§109, §133, §135) DNb 27f.

avajam, see *vaj-*.

avaθā adv. 'thus, then': LAv *avaθa*: ¹*ava-* + adv. suffix *-θā* (§191.II), cf. Skt. *tá-thā*. Often with preceding or following correlative *yaθā*; see also *avaθāšᵃtā*.
(1) 'thus: DB 1.24, 38, 63, 67, 70, 75, 78; 2.10, 15, 80; 3.24, 80; 4.8, 11, 13, 16, 19, 21, 24, 27, 29, 36, 39, 54; DBb 4; DBc 4; DBd 2f; DBe 4f; DBf 2f; DBg 4; DBh 3f; DBi 3; DBj 3; DPe 20; DNb 18f; DSf 16; DSj 3°; DZc 11, 12; XPf 22, 30 (written *avaθa*, §52.III). *avaθā-dim* DNb 17. *avaθā-diš* DB 5.17, 33. *avaθā-šaiy* DB 2.30, 50; 3.14. *avaθā-šām* DB 2.20, 83; 3.57, 85.
(2) 'then': DB 1.42, 56, 90, 96; 2.70; 3.89. *avaθā-šām* DB 2.27, 36f, 42, 47, 56, 62, 98; 3.8, 19, 40, 47, 63f, 69.

avaθāšᵃtā DB 4.72, uncertain word read by KT; perhaps *avaθāša-tā*, from *avaθā* with abl. *-ša* (§191.II; as in *avadaša*) + encl. apm. *-tā* (§133), 'thenceforward them(= the sculptures).' So Kent, JAOS 62.272–3, after Tolman's emendation *avaθā : tā* 'thus them'; cf. HK's *avaθā štā* 'thus stand (as I stand over the rebels)', and Sen's *avaθāštā* adj. apm. 'thus standing'.

avadā (i.e. *avadă*) adv. 'there, then': LAv. *avaδa*; from ¹*ava-* + suffix seen in OP *idā* (§191.II). Usually resumptive of an immediately preceding place-phrase, which is thus made locàtive (so always in DB except 1.85, 88; 2.24; 3.74; 4.81; 5.24, 28). See also *avadaša*.
(1) 'there': DB 1.85, 88, 92; 2.9, 23, 24, 28, 34, 39, 44f, 54, 59, 66, 96; 3.5, 23, 34f, 44, 61, 66; 4.81; 5.24, 28; XPh 40. *avada-šim* (§135) DB 1.59; *avadā-šim* DB 3.74; *avada-šiš* DB 3.52.
(2) 'then ': DNa 42.

avadaša adv. 'from there, from then': *avadă* + abl. *-ša* (§191.II; Bthl. AiW 170, with lit.; against his view, Bv. Gr. §325), always after *hacā*. (1) 'from there': DB 1.37; 3.42, 80; DSf 47. (2) 'from then': DSe 47f.

LEXICON 173

avaparā phrasal adv. 'along there': *ava* asn. + postpos. *parā* (§191.IV). DB 2.72; 3.72f.

avastā- sb. 'leather' (König, Klotho 4.45-6): etymology uncertain (§145). *avast[ā]y[ā]* lsf. DB 4.89f (JAOS 62.267); hardly *avast[ā]ya[m]* as read and restored by KT, which could be only an unaugmented imf. of *ava-* + *stā-*. Probably not a reference to the Avesta, as suggested by Wb. ZDMG 61.730.

āvahana- sb. 'village' (§166): deriv. (§147.I) of *ā* + *vah-* 'dwell', Av. *vah-*, Skt. *vas-*, Gm. *Wesen* 'being'. *āvahanam* DB 2.33; DSf 46.

avahar[da] DB 2.94, see *hard-*.

avahya- denom. vb. (§217) 'ask for help': Av. *avahya-*, Skt. *avasya-* in dsm. pres. ptc. *avasyaté* (RV 1.116.23), to Av. *avah-* 'aid', Skt. *ávas-* (Jn. JAOS 27.190, MB Gr. §209, Bv. Gr. §193).

pati- + *avahya-* 'ask for help': *patiyāvahyaiy* (§140.III) 1st sg. imf. mid. DB 1.55.

avahyarādiy phrasal adv. (§191.IV) 'for this reason': *avahyă* (§135) gsn. of ¹*ava-*, + *rādiy* 'on account of', q.v. For phrasing, cf. Gk. τούτου ἕνεκα, τούνεκα, Lt. *huius reī causā*; JAOS 35.322-9. DB 1.6f, 51f; 4.47, 62; DBa 9f.

asa- sb. 'horse' (§90, §143.III): Med. *aspa-*, Av. *aspa-*, Skt. *áśva-*, Lt. *equos*, pIE **eḱu̯os*. See also *Asagarta-*, *asabāra-*, *aspa-*. *asam* asm. (collective, §255) DB 1.87.

Asagarta- sb. 'Sagartia', a northwestern province of the Persian Empire (§29.n2, §31): Elam. adj. *aš-ša-kar-ti-i̯a*, Akk. adj. *sa-ga-ar-ta-a-a*, Gk. Σαγαρτία. Probably *asan-* 'stone' (with Med. *s* < pIE *ḱ*; §9.I, §87) + **garta-* 'cave' (Skt. *gárta-*), 'Land of Stone-Cave Dwellers' (§161.Ib, §166.I; Bthl. AiW 207, zAiW 119-20); hardly *asa-* 'horse' (with OP *s* < pIE *ḱu̯*, §90) + **garta-* 'wagon' (Skt. *gárta-*), 'Land of Horse-drawn Wagons'. See also *Asagartiya-*. *Asagarta* nsm. DPe 15. *Asagartam* asm. DB 4.23. *Asagartaiy* lsm. DB 2.80f; 4.22; DBg 8f.

Asagartiya- adj. 'Sagartian': adj. to preceding (§144.III, §159). *Asagartiya* nsm. DB 2.79; 4.20f.

asan- sb. 'stone': pIE **aḱen-* (§9.V, §87, §155.I), cf. *asman-*. See also *Asagarta-*. *asā* (§124.5, §187) nsm. DSf 40f; but see also under *dāru-*.

asabāra- sb. 'horseman': NPers. *suvār*, cf. also Tedesco, ZII 2.40-1; *asa-* 'horse' (§126) + *bāra-* 'carried by, rider' (§122, §143.V, §159, §160.Ic). See also *uvāsabāra-*. *asabāra* nsm. DNb 41f, 44, 45. *asabāraibiš* ipm. DB 2.2, 71; 3.41, 72.

aspa- sb. 'horse', Median for OP *asa-* (§90), q.v.; in *Aspacanah-*, *uvaspa-*, *Vištāspa-*.

Aspacanah- sb. 'Aspathines', bow-bearer of Darius: Elam. *aš-ba-za-na*, Akk. *as-pa-[si-na]*, Gk. Ἀσπαθίνης; *aspa-* 'horse' (§9.II, §9.n2, §90) + *canah-* 'desire', Av. *-činah-*, Skt. *cánas-*; 'Lover of Horses' (§161.Ia, §163.Ib). *Aspacanā* nsm. (156.II, §185.II) DNd 1.

asman- sb. 'sky': Av. *asman-*, Skt. *áśman-*, Gk. ἄκμων 'anvil', Lith. *akmuõ* 'stone', pIE **aḱmen-/mon-* (§95, §155.III); for variant meanings, cf. Reichelt, IF 32.23-57; for Iranian ideas of its creation, cf. Bailey, Zoroastrian Problems 120-48. Not *āsman-*, despite NPers. *āsmān*, which has length of later origin (Debrunner, IF 52.153, against Bv. Gr. §175). See also *asan-*, *aθaga-*. *asmānam* asm. (§67.II, §124.6, §187) DNa 2f; DSe 2f; DSf 2; DSt 2f; DZc 1; DE 3f; XPa 2; XPb 3f; XPc 2; XPd 3; XPf 2f; XPh 2; XE 4; XV 3; A¹Pa 3°; A²Hc 3. *asmānām* (§53) A³Pa 3.

ašnaiy adv. 'near', lsn. of *ašna-* 'near' (Hz. ApI 98-9), Av. *ăsna-* 'near', in loc. *āsnaē-ca*, *asne* 'near', abl. *asnāṯ* 'from near'; from pAr. root ending in *ś* or *ź* (pIE *ḱ* or *ĝ*: Skt. *aśnóti* 'attains' and *ájati* 'drives' hardly suit); not **ā-zd-na-*, ptc. to *ā* + ²*had-* 'herangehen' (Bthl. AiW 1755; but ²*had-*, which always has prefix *ā*, is only a semantic variation of ¹*had-* 'sit'), cf. Skt. *ásanna-* as adj. 'near' (Bthl. AiW 220). Possibly from pIE **anĝh-* 'choke, throttle', cf. Lt. *angō*, Gk. ἄγχω, sb. Lt. *angor*, Av. *ązah-*, Skt. *áhas-*: **anĝh-* + ptc. *-no-* (§96, §147.I, §191.III, §243); for semantics, cf. Gk. ἄγχι adv. 'near' (JAOS 62.276-7). Not 'on the march', to pAr. root **aź-*, Skt. *ájati*, Lt. *agit* (Bthl. AiW 264); nor 'in friendship' on the basis of the Elam. *kanna enni git* (WB; KT); nor 'at peace', cf. Av. *āxštiš* 'peace', *āxšta-* 'peaceful' (Bv. BSLP 31.2.67-9). Elam. *kan-* recurs as the translation of *dauštā* 'friend', but this meaning eliminates only 'on the march', since 'friendship', 'peace', and 'nearness' are related ideas. *ašnaiy* DB 2.11f; [*ašna*]*iy* DB 5.23.

azdā adv. 'known': GAv. *azdā* 'thus', Phl. *azd*,

Skt. *addhā́* 'surely', from pAr. **adzdhā* (§85); cf. MB Gr. §118. DB 1.32; DNa 43, 45; DNb 50.

¹*ah-* vb. 'be': Av. *ah-* Skt. *as-*, Gk. ἐστί, Lt. *est*, Gt. *ist*, pIE **es-*. See also *hašiya-*, *Āθiyābaušna-*. Conj., §208.

amiy 1st sg., Av. *ahmi*, Skt. *ásmi*, Gk. Lesb. ἔμμι, Att. εἰμί, NEng. *am* (§118.II, §226.I): AmH 9; DB 1.12, 39, 53, 75, 79; 2.10, 15, 80; 3.25, 81; 4.9, 11, 14°, 17, 19, 22, 25, 27, 30; DBb 5, 7; DBc 8f; DBd 4f, 7; DBe 6, 9; DBf 4f; DBg 7f; DBh 5f, 9; DBi 6, 10; DBj 5; DNa 35; DNb 6f, 7, 8, 12f, 13, 15, 26, 27, 34, 40, 42, 43, 44, 51; DZc 7; A²Hc 18.

astiy, Av. *asti*, NPers. *ast*, Skt. *ásti* (§116, §228.I): DB 4.46, 51; DNb 54f, 56; DSe 37; XPh 30.

aʰmahy, Av. *mahi*, Skt. *smás-i*, Gk. Dor. εἰμές (§118.II, §230.I): DB 1.7f, 11; DBa 12, 18.

haⁿtiy 3d pl., Av. *hənti*, Skt. *sánti*, Gk. Dor. ἐντί, Osc. *sent* (§39, §122, §232.I): DB 4.61, 63°.

āham 1st sg. imf., Skt. *ā́ham*, Gk. Hom. ἦα (§67.II, §122, §226.II): DB 1.14; 2.6, 12; 3.77; 4.63 bis, 64. *āhām* XPh 15f (§53, §131; hardly with Hz. AMI 8.65, ApI 63–4).

āha imf. **ēset* (§228.II), but Av. *ās* from **ēst*: DB 1.21, 22, 29, 30, 36, 45f; 48, 62, 86, 89; 2.13, 18f, 19, 24 bis, 94, 95; 3.8, 30, 70; 4.8; 5.29; DNa 38; DSe 32°; DSf 16, 57°; DSj 3°, 4, 4°; DSl 5; DZc 12°; XPf 18, 19, 22, 30, 38; XPh 35, 42.

āhaⁿ 3d pl. imf., Skt. *ā́san* (§232.II; §274.n1): DB 1.8 (§259), 10, 38, 42, 56, 90, 96; 2.27, 36, 42, 47, 56, 70, 98; 3.19, 40, 47, 63, 69, 89; 4.51; 5.15°, 31°; DBa 13, 16; DNa 39°.

āhaⁿtā 3d pl. imf. mid. (§236.II, §274.n1) DB 1.19, 58; 2.77; 3.75, 90°, 92; 4.81; XPf 29. *āhaⁿta* (§36.IVc) DB 3.49, 51.

ahaniy 1st sg. subj., Skt. *ásāni* (§226.I): XPh 47, 48 (-*ă*- extended from rest of tense, acc. to Ogden ap. Kent, JAOS 58.325; §52.III, §131, §222.I).

āhy 2d sg. subj., Skt. *ásasi* (§131, §227.I): DB 4.37, 68, 72, 87; DSt 10°.

ahatiy subj., GAv. *aṇhaitī*, Skt. *ásati* (§222.I): DB 4.38, 39f, 68, 68f, 74°, 78; 5.19, 35°; DPe 22.

²*ah-* vb. 'throw': Av. ²*ah-*, Skt. *as-*, pres. *ásyati*. [*ā*]*h*[*yat*]*ā* imf. mid. as pass. (§214, §274d) DB 1.95 (restoration of Kern, ZDMG 23.239).

idā (i.e. *idă*) adv. 'here': GAv. *idā*, LAv *iδa* Skt. *ihá*, Gk. adv. ending -θε, pIE **i-dhe* (§76.III, §191.II), formed on pronominal root seen in OP *iyam*, Skt. *ayám iyám idám*, Lt. *is ea id*. DB 1.29; DSf 37, 38, 40, 43, 45f; DSo 4°; XPb 24.

ima- demonst. adj. and pron. 'this': Av. *ima-*, Skt. *ima-*; stem extracted from Ar. **im-am* = acc. **i-m* + encl. *-am* (q.v.; wrongly Mt. MSLP 19.49–52). Decl., §199.

imam asm. DPa 6; DPe 21; DSd 3; DSn 1°; XPa 12; XPj; A¹I (as nsm., §56.V); D²Sa 1°; A²Sa 3, 4°, 5° (as asn., §56.V); A²Ha 5, 7 (as asn.); A³Pa 22 (as nsf., §56.V). *imaiy* npm. DB 4.34, 80, 82. *imaiy* apm. DB 4.31; *imai-vā* (§136) DB 4.71, 73, 77. *imaišām* gpm. DB 4.87.

imām asf. AsH 10f, 13; DB 4.42, 48, 54, 57, 70, 73, 77, 89 (*imᵃ* Cameron; for *imām*, §52.VI); DPd 15, 18; DPe 24; DNa 1f, 32, 53; DSe 1f; DSf 1; DSt 1; DZc 1, 8, 12; DE 2; XPa 1; XPb 2; XPc 1; XPd 1f; XPf 1f; XPh 1, 58; XE 3; XV 2, 24; A¹Pa 2°; A²Sc 4f (as asn., §56.V), 5; A²Sd 3 (as nsn., §56.V); A²Hc 2; A³Pa 2, 25f. *imā* npf. DB 1.13, 18, 23; 2.6°; 4.33; DPe 7; DNa 16; DSe 15; DSm 5°; XPh 14. *imā* apf. DB 1.21; DSg 3°.

ima nsn. DB 1.27, 72; 2.91; 3.10, 20, 53, 76; 4.1, 3, 40, 49, 59; 5.2; DPh 4; DNb 32; DSf 22; DH 3. *ima* asn. DB 1.25 bis, 26, 68; 4.44; DNb 1f; DSf 10; DSj 2°, 5°; XPc 10f; XPd 16; XSa 1; XSc 3°; XV 20; A¹Pa 19°; D²Sb 3°, 4°. *imā* apn. DB 4.32. *imaibiš* ipn. DNb 48.

Imaniš- sb. 'Imanish', name assumed by the Elamite rebel Martiya (§163.V): Elam. *um-man-nu-iš*, Akk. *im-ma-ni-e-šu*. *Imaniš* nsm. (§185.III) DB 2.10; 4.16f; DBf 4.

iyam demonst. adj. and pron. 'this' (§11, §260.III, §265): from **ī* nsf. (perhaps also from **i* suffixless nsm.) + pronominal *-am* (q.v.). Decl., §199. See also *idā*, *ima-*. *iyam* pron. nsm. DBb 1; DBc 1; DBd 1; DBe 1; Dbf 1; DBg 1; DBh 1; DBi 1; DBj 1; DBk 1; DN i–iv, xv, xvi°, xvii, xxix; A?P 1–4, 8°, 9–21, 22 (written *imᵃyᵃ*, §51), 23–8, 29°, 30. *iyam* adj. nsf. AmH 5, 8 (as lsf., §56.V); DPd 6; DZc 10; *iya* (§52.V) DB 4.90; *i(ya)m* DB 4.91 (written *imᵃ*, §52.VI).

isuvā- sb. 'battle-ax' (Junge, Klio 33.22–3; Kent, JNES 4.233): etymology unknown (stem-formation §143.IV). Not 'bowcase', for *išuvā-*, to Av. *išu-* 'arrow', Skt. *íṣu-* (cf. for variant views Wb. Grab 41–3). *isuvām* asf. DNd 2.

LEXICON

iš- vb., see *aiš*-.

išti- sb. 'sun-dried brick' (§152.III, §179.III): Av. *ištya*-, NPers. *xišt*, Skt. *iṣṭakā*-, Medieval Skt. *iṣṭikā*- (König, Burgbau 51–2; Wb. AfOF 7.41; Hz. AMI 3.57–8; W. N. Brown, Lg. 8.13). *ištiš* nsf. DSf 29.

[*išmal*]*uv* or [*ismar*]*uv* asn., of uncertain meaning, possibly '(gold) inlay' (Cameron, Persepolis Treasury Tablets 129–30), DSf 51; supplied by Hz. AMI 3.74–5, as a borrowing from Elam. *is-ma-lu* (*ᵛⁱˢma-lu* 'wood' Hinz, Orientalia 1950, shortly to appear), or from the lost Akk. original of both; cf JAOS 53.21, 56.220. But read rather [*dār*]*uv* with Hinz, see Lex. s.v.

Izalā- sb. 'Izala', a district in Assyria (§6, §107): Elam. *iṣ-ṣi-la*. *I*[*zal*]*ā* nsf. DB 2.53, as restored by Wb ZDMG 61.726 (*Izarā* Tm. Lex. 74), after the Elam.; but Cameron found all the characters visible: *iz*ᵃ*l*ᵃ*a*.

ʰ*u*- insep. prefix 'good, well' (*uv*- before vowels): Av. *hu*-, Skt. *su*-, Gk. ὑ-γιής 'having good life, healthy', pIE **su*- (§140.IV): in *uxšnav*-, *ukāra*-, *ucāra*-, *Utāna*-, *utava*-, *uθanuvaniya*-, *ufrašta-ufrasta*-, *ubarta*-, *umartiya*-, *uraθa*-, *uradana*-, *Uvaxštra*-, *Uvārazmi*-, *uvārštika*-, *uvāsabāra*-, *uvaspa*-, *ūvnara*-, *ushamaranakara*-.

ukāra- adj. 'having good people or army': from *u*- 'good' + *kāra*- 'people, army'. *ukāram* asn. for asf. AsH 9 (§52.III).

uxšnav- adj. 'well satisfied' (§142): from *u*- 'good' + *xšnav*- 'satisfy' ('wohlgeneigt', Hz. ApI 199–200; *uxšnuš* 'well-informed', Sen 233). *u*[*xšna*]*uš* nsm. (§183.III, §190.I) DNb 27.

ucāra- adj. 'well done, successful', as sb. nt. 'good deed': from *u*- + *cāra*-, to root *kar*- 'do' (§99, §122, §123.3), cf. LAv. *čārā*- 'Hilfsmittel', NPers. *čāra* (Bv. BSLP 30.1.65–6, Gr. §292; cf. Bthl. AiW 584); but Wb. AfOF 7.39–40, Hz. ApI 193–8, take from Ar. *car*- 'move' (Av. *čaraiti*, Skt. *cárati*; but Skt. has only *sucārā* as a woman's name!). *ucāram* nsn. DSj 4°; DSl 5. *ucāram* asn. DB 4.76; *ucāramaiy* DSf 20° (= *ucāram-maiy*, §138.I).

ucašma, incorrect reading for *c*ᵃ*š*ᵐ*m*ᵃ = *cašam*; see *caša*-.

ʰ*Ūja*- ʰ*Ūvja* (§23.II) sb. 'Elam, Susiana', a province of the Persian Empire (§166.II); also as ethnic, 'Elamite, Susian': Elam. *hal-tam-ti*, Akk. *e-lam-mat*, cf. MPers. *Hu̇ž* (*Ūja* distinct from *Ūvja*, wrongly König, Burgbau 9–11, and Hz. AMI 3.69–73). See also *Ūjiya*-. (1) 'Elam': *Ūja* nsm. DSe 21°, DSm 7°; XPh 20. *Ūvja* DB 1.14, 2.7, 5.4; DPe 10; DNa 22. *Ūvjam* asm. DB 1.82; 2.12; 4.12, 17; 5.7, 10. *Ūjaiy* lsm. DSf 46. *Ūvjaiy* DB 1.74f, 75, 77; 2.10, 10f; 4.11, 17; DBc 9f; DBf 5. (2) 'Elamite': *Ūvja* nsm. DN iii; A?P 3.

ʰ*Ūjiya*- ʰ*Ūvjiya*- (§144.III) adj. 'Elamite, Susian': deriv. of preceding. *Ūvjiya* nsm. DB 4.10, 5.5f. *Ūvjiyā* npm. DB 1.75f, 2.12, 5.15. *Uvjıyā* apm. DB 5.11°. *Ūvjiyaibiš* ipm. DB 5.10.

utā (for *ută*, §36.I) conj. 'and' (§291.I–II): Av. *uta*, Skt. *utá*, Gk. Hom. ἠ-ὑτε 'like', pIE **ute* (hardly both -*ă* and -*ā* in Aryan, despite Mt. MSLP 19.57–8, MB Gr. §151). Correlative with preceding -*cā*, DB 1.66f (cf. Gk. τὲ καί); *utā* ... *utā* 'both ... and' DB 1.34f, 41, 46f; 2.74, 88f; 5.19f, 35; DNb 30, 37, 40f, 43, 45; XPf 19f; XPh 54f.

utā AsH 13; DB 1.34 bis, 34f, 41 ter, 46 bis, 47, 57, 67, 77, 85; 2.3, 4, 18, 74 ter, 77, 81f, 87, 88, 89, 92; 3.30, 47, 48, 50, 58, 74, 77 (written *uā*, §52.VI), 88, 90, 91; 4.7, 56, 61, 62, 75 bis, 79, 89, 91 bis; 5.11, 12, 19, 20°, 28°, 31, 35 bis; DPd 15; DPe 13, 14; DNa 53; DNb 3f, 26, 27, 28, 30 bis, 37 bis, 40f, 41, 43 bis, 45 ter; DSe 28°, 51f; DSf 13, 28 bis, 29, 33, 35, 36, 37, 40, 44 bis, 48, 50, 52, 55, 57; DSn 2°; DSs 7°; DSt 9; DZc 11; XPa 19 bis; XPb 24, 30; XPc 13 bis; XPd 19; XPf 19f, 20, 39, 46, 47; XPg 5, 11; XPh 24, 35, 38, 41, 48, 53, 54, 55, 58; XSc 5°; XV 20, 27°; A¹Pa 24°; A²Sa 4, 5, 5°; A²Sc 5; A²Sd 4; A²Ha 5°, 6, 6f; A²Hc 19; A³Pa 25 bis, 26.

utā-maiy AsH 12; DB 4.46 (visible to Cameron; cf. note ad loc.); DPh 10; DNa 52f; DH 8; XPb 29; XV 26f°; A²Hc 20. *utā-taiy* DB 4.56, 58, 73f, 75, 77f, 79. *utā-šaiy* DB 2.74f, 89. *utā-šim* DB 2.13°; 5.13, 26f. *utā-šām* DB 3.57; 5.15. *utā-diš* DNb 46f.

uta-maiy (§135) DSe 51°; DSf 58; DSj 6°; DSt 9°; XPa 15, 18f; XPd 18f; XPf 41, 45f; XPg 14; XPh 58 (space for *u* left blank; Lg. 13.303); XSc 5°; A¹Pa 23°; A²Sd 4. *uta-šim* (§135) XPh 34. (In restorations there is almost always uncertainty between *utā*- and *ută*-.)

Utāna- sb. 'Otanes', ally of Darius against Gaumata: Elam. *ḫu-ud-da-na*, Akk. *ú-mi-it-ta-na*-',

Gk. 'Οτάνης; perhaps u- 'good' + tāna- to root tan- 'stretch, extend' (§164.II), Av. Skt. tan-, Gk. τείνει, Lt. tendit, cf. Skt. tána-m 'offspring': 'Having good posterity'. [U]tā[na] nsm. DB 4.83.

utava- adj. 'strong, in health': *u-* 'good' + deriv. of *tav-* 'be strong' (§122). *utava* nsm. DB 4.71f (emendation of HK, ApKI 1.63, 2.29, for KT's d*ªtªsª*, with first and third characters very faint; §54.I).

uθanuvaniya- sb. 'good bowman': *u-* 'good' + *θanuvaniya-* 'bowman'. *uθanuvaniya* nsm. DNb 42f.

ud prep. and prefix 'up', becoming Iran. *us-uz-* before dentals (§85): Av. *us- uz-*, Skt. *ud*, pIE **ud* (and **ūd* in NEng. *out*, NHG *aus*): *ud* with verbal root *pat-*, *us-* in *ustašanā-*, *u(z)-* in *uzma-* (§84).

upā (i.e. *upă*, cf. §140.I) prep. and prefix 'toward': Av. *upa*, Skt. *úpa*, Gk. ὑπό, Lt. *s-ub* 'under', pIE **upo*.

(1) Prep. with acc., 'under, with, in the time of' (hardly 'belonging to', as taken by Hz. ApI 353): DB 2.18, 3.30; A²Sa 4; A³Pa 23; Sf.

(2) Prefix, 'under', in *Upadarma-*; 'toward', with verb *ay-*; 'beside', in *upastā-*.

Upadarma- sb. 'Upadarma', father of *Āçina*: Elam. *uk-ba-[tar]-ra-an-ma*. From *upa + darma-* (root *dar-*), Skt. *dhárma-* 'right conduct' (§163.V): 'He who is under (= behaves himself according to) right conduct' (so Bthl. AiW 390, with lit.; hardly *Upadaraⁿma-*, after the Elam.; hardly as taken b Hz. ApI 190). *Upadarmahyā* gsm. DB 1.74.

upariy adv., prep., prefix, 'above': Av. *upairi*, Skt. *upári*, Gk. ὑπέρ, Lt. *s-uper*, Gt. *ufar*, pIE **uperi* (§191.I).

(1) Adv. 'above', XPh 31.

(2) Prep. with acc., 'over, over and above, upon, according to': DB 4.64; DNb 4, 32, 46, 49; DSf 27.

(3) Prefix, 'over', with verb *ay-*.

upastā- sb. 'help, aid': *upa-* + verbal root *stā-* (§140.I, §142), cf. Gm. *Bei-stand* for meaning. *upastām* asf. AmH 10f; DB 1.25, 55, 87, 94; 2.24f, 34, 40, 45, 54, 60, 68, 86, 97°; 3.6, 17, 37, 45, 62, 67, 87; 4.60f, 62; DPd 13; DNa 50; DSf 19°; DSk 5; XPh 32, 45.

Ufrātu- sb. 'Euphrates', river of Babylonia: Elam. *ú-ıp-ra-tu-ıš*, Akk. *purattu*, Gk. Εὐφράτης (§75.V, §76.V, §166, §166.III). Etymology uncertain, probably a popular etymologizing in OP of a local non-Iranian name, cf. Bthl. AiW 1830; Fick, BB 24.310; Justi, IFA 17.116; Tm. Lex. 77. *Ufrātuvā* ism. DB 1.92 (not gen., as taken by Hz. ApI 71–2).

ufrašta- ufrasta- adj. 'well punished': *u-* 'well' + ptc. *frašta-* or *frasta-* (§93) 'questioned, investigated' to root *fraθ-*: pIE **su-preḱto-* (§33, §75.II, §242.II). *ufrastam* asm. DB 1.22, 4.66f; *ufraštam* DB 4.38. *ufraštā-diy* apm. DB 4.69 (JAOS 35.351-2, cf. Bv. Gr. §345; not loc. *ufrastā* + prep. *adiy*, as taken by Bthl. IF 12.110, AiW 60–1, Mt. Gr. §318).

uba- adj. 'both': GAv. *uba-*, Skt. dual *ubhá́(u)*, pIE **ubhō(u)*, cf. Gk. ἄμ-φω, Lt. *am-bō* (§143.III). *ubā* ndm. (§189) DSf 14; XPf 21.

ubarta- adj. 'well-borne, lifted, esteemed': *u-* well' + *barta-* 'borne', ptc. to *bar-* 'bear', pIE **su-bhr̥to-* (§30, §122, §242.I). *ubartam* asm. DB 1.21f; 4.66. *ubartām* asf. DB 4.88. On meaning, cf. Altheim, ZII 3.33–5: hardly as taken by Kónig, RuID 69.

[U]mamaita, see *Atamaita-*.

umartiya- adj. 'containing good men': *u-* 'good' + *martiya-* 'man'. *umartiyā* nsf. AmH 6; DPd 8f. *umartiyam* asn. DSf 11f; DSm 4°; DSp 3°; DZc 4.

Uyamā- sb. 'Uyama', a fortress in Armenia: Elam. *ú-i-ja̱-ma*, Aram. *huyaw* (Cowley, AP 251 line 4, 257). *Uyamā* nsf. DB 2.44 (all characters visible to Cameron).

uraθa- adj. 'having good chariots'; Skt. *suratha-* as man's name: *u-* 'good' + *raθa-* 'wagon', Av. *raθa-*, Skt. *rátha-*, Lt. *rota* 'wheel' (§143.III). See also *uraθara-*. *uraθā-cā* apn. as sb. 'good chariots' DSs 5.

uraθara- adj. 'having good charioteers': deriv. of *uraθa-* (§148.I). [*u*]*raθaram* asn. DSp 3 (Bv. BSLP 33.2.151 and Hz. AMI 4.126 restore [*f*]*raθaram*).

uradana- adj. 'of good regulation': *u-* 'good' + deriv. of ²*rad-* 'direct' (§122, §147.I): see Hz. ApI 206–7 (but he is wrong in drawing in also Lt. *lēx* 'law'). *uradanām* asf. DNb 23.

ʰuva- refl. pron. 'self' and poss. adj. 'own' (§118.IV): Av. *xᵛa-*, Skt. *sva-*, Gk. ἕ and ὅς, Lt. *sē* and *suos*, pIE **sṷe* and **sṷos* (§143.III); in *uvādā-*, *uvaipašiya-*, *uvāmaršiyu-*.

uvaipašiya- adj. 'belonging to self' (wrongly 'wayward', Sen 246), nt. as sb. 'own possession': Av. *xᵛaēpaiθya-* 'own'; OP *uvai-*, nom. of *uva-*, as in Skt. *svay-ám* 'self' (MB Gr. §293), + pAr. **patįa-*, formed on pIE **poti-*, Av. *paitiš* 'master, husband', Skt. *pati-*, Gk. πόσις 'husband', Lt. *potis* 'able', Lith. *pàts* 'self': pIE **sṷoi-potįo-* (§53, §143.-II, §152.III, §161.IIb). *uvaipašiyahyā* gsn. DNb 15.

uvāipašiya-, same as preceding, with vriddhi in initial syllable (§126; MB Gr. §298); but *uvāi-* may be an error for *uvai-*, or *uvai-* for *uvāi-* (§53). *uvāipašiyam* asn. DB 1.47.

ʰUvaxštra- sb. 'Cyaxares', former King of Media: Elam. *ma-ak-iš-tar-ra*, Akk. *ú-ma-ku-iš-tar*, Gk. Κυαξάρης. From *u-* 'good' + *vaxštra-* 'growth' (§9.II, §79, §148.III), to *vaxš-*, Av. *vaxš-*, Skt. *vakṣ-*, Gm. *wachsen*, NEng. *wax* (§102): 'Having good growth' (§164.II, IV). So Bthl. AiW 1836; but Hz. ApI 209 interprets 'having good oversight', to Av. *aiwy-axštrāi* (dat.) 'oversight' (otherwise Husing, OLZ 2.139–40). *Uvaxštrahyā* gsm. DB 2.15f, 81. *Uvaxštrahya* (§36.IVb) DB 4.19, 22; DBe 7; DBg 9f.

Uvaja- Uvajıya-, read *Ūvja- Ūvjiya-*: see *Ūja- Ūjiya-*.

uvādā- sb. 'abode', vriddhi-form to Skt. *svadhā́-* 'innate character', from *sva-* 'own' + *dhā-* 'make' (§142; OP *uva-* + *²dā-*); in *Paιšiyāuvādā-*, q.v.

Uvādaicaya- sb. 'Uvadaicaya', a town in Persia (§159): Elam. *ma-te-ṣi-iš*. *Uvādaιcaya* nsm. DB 3.51.

uvāmaršiyu- adj. '(having self-death =) dying by one's own hand', either by intent or by accident: *uva-* 'own', with vriddhi, + **mr̥tįu-* 'death', Av. *mərəθyu-*, Skt. *mr̥tyú-*, to *mar-* 'die' (§30, §80, §113, §122, §126, §152.III, §153.I, §161.IIa); used of Cambyses, who, acc. to Herod. 3.64–6, died from the after-effects of an accidentally self-inflicted wound. This interpretation is strongly supported by the Akk. and (although the exact Elam. text is somewhat in doubt) the Elam. renderings. So KT 9; Tm. Lex. 78; Wb. KIA 17 with note; Hz. BSOS 8.589–97 and ApI 216–9, W. Hinz, Altpers. Wortschatz 141. Not to be taken with W. Schulze, SbPAW 1912.685–703, 1918.331-2, as 'by a natural death', citing semantic parallels in other languages; who is followed by MB Gr. §144, §286, §298 (Bv. takes *uvā-* as instr. and not vriddhied), and by H. H. Schaeder, Nachrichten d. Ak. d. Wiss. in Gottingen, phıl.-hist. Kl. 1946-7.24–36. *uvāmaršiyuš* nsm. DB 1.43.

Uvārazmī- sb. 'Chorasmia', a province of the Persian Empire: Elam. *ma-ra-iš-mi-iš*, Akk. *ḫu-ma-ri-ız-ma-'*, Gk. Χωρασμίη, Av. asf. *xᵛāιrιzəm*. From *u-* 'good' + *vāra-* '?' (§126, §143.III), + *zmī-* (§95, §120, §152.II) to *zam-* 'land'. See also *Uvārazmıya-*. *Uvārazmīy* nsf. (§179.I; Lg. 19.223) DB 1.16, DPe 16f; *Uvārazmiš* DNa 23f, DSe 22°, DSm 9°, XPh 21f. *Uvārazmıyā* absf. DSf 39f.

Uvārazmıya- adj. 'Chorasmian': deriv. to preceding (§144.III). [*Uvāra*]*zmᵛya* (§22) nsm. A?P 8.

uvārštıka- sb. 'good spearman': *u-* 'good' + *ārštıka-* 'spearman' (§126). *uvārštıka* nsm. DNb 44.

uvāsabāra- sb. 'good horseman': *u-* 'good' + *asabāra-* 'horseman', with vriddhi (§126). *uvāsabara* nsm. DNb 42.

uvaspa- adj. 'having good horses': *u-* 'good' (§118.IV, §140.IV) + *aspa-* 'horse' (§9.III). *uvaspā* nsf. AmH 6; DPd 8. *uvaspam* asn. DSf 11; DSp 3°; DZc 4°, for asf. AsH 10 (§52.III). *uvaspā* apn. as sb. 'good horses' DSs 5°.

Ūvja- Ūvjiya-, see *Ūja- Ūjiya-*: cf. Wb. AfOF 7.43, Schaeder SbPAW 1931.636.n3.

ūvnara- sb. 'skill, accomplishment': adj. formation to pAr. **su-* 'good' + **nar-* 'man' (§142, §143.II, V), = 'having the good quality of a man', Av. *hunara-* 'ability, skill', Skt. *sūnára-* 'glad, joyous, merry', with vriddhi of the first vowel in OP and Skt. to show the derivative nature (§23.II, §126: Lg. 15.173, JNES 4.51–2: cf. Hz. RHRel. 113.30, ApI 200–6, who accepts this meanıng but seeks another etymology, as does also Pisanı, Riv. Stud. Or. 19.93–4). *ūvnarā* npn. DNb 45, 51. *ūvnaraιbıš* ipn. DNb 48.

ustašanā- (*ustašnā-* Bv. Gr. §294) sb. 'staircase': *us-* (see *ud-*, §84, §85) + *tašanā-* (§102), deriv. (§147.I) to root *taš-* 'cut, fashion' (see under *taxš-*), pIE **ud-tek̂penā-*.   *ustašanām* asf. A³Pa 22 (as nom., §56.V). [*usta*]*canām* (§49b) A²Sc 5f.

ušabāri- adj. 'camel-borne': *uša-* 'camel' (§79, §130), Av. *uštra-* (MB Gr. §109; cf. Justi, GGA 1882.488), + *bāri-* 'borne by' (§122¦, §126, §152.I, §160.Ic), to root *bar-* 'bear'. Cf. Jn. Indo-Iranian Studies Sanjana 18–20. *ušabārim* DB 1.86f.

uši- sb. dual 'two ears, hearing, understanding' (cf. JNES 4.232; Hz. RHRel. 113.30, ApI 342–4): LAv. dual *uši*, cf. Gk. *οὖς*, Lt. *auris*, Gt. *ausō*.   *ušīy* ndn. (§189) DNb 28. [*uš*]*ī-cā* adn. (§136) DNb 32. *ušībiyā* idn. (§189) DNb 37; *ušīyā* idn. (with sg. ending, §189; Lg. 19.224–5) DNb 35.

uška- adj. 'dry'; nt. as sb., 'land, mainland': Av. *huška-* 'dry', NPers. *xušk*, Skt. *śúṣka-*, *śúṣyati* 'dries', Lith. *saũsa-s* 'dry', NEng. *sere*, *sear* (§146.I). *uškahyā* gsn. DPe 13.

ušhamaranakara- sb. 'good warrior': *u-* 'good' + *hamaranakara-* 'warrior' (§140.VI). *ušhamaranakara* nsm. DNb 34.

uzma- adj. as sb. 'that which is up from the earth, stake': from *ud-* 'up' + *zma-* to *zam-* 'earth' (§84, §95, §120, §130, §142, §143.II, VI): otherwise Wackernagel, KZ 61.208; Lommel, OLZ 37.180.n2, König, RuID 72. *uzmayā-patiy* lsn. DB 2.76, 91; 3.52, 92.

ka- interrog.-indef. pron. 'who': Av. Skt. *ka-*, Gk. πο-, Lt. *quo-*, NEng. *wha-t*, pIE **qᵘo-* (§201). See also *kā*, *-kaiy*, *ci-* (§132.2). With encl. *-ciy*, 'any': *kaš-ciy* (§9.VI, §99, §105) nsm. DB 1.49, 53; DSe 37.

kā, generalizing particle after 2d pers. pron.: probably isn. of *ka-* (§191.III; Kern ap. Caland, z. Syntax der Pron. im Av. 47; Kieckers, Etymol. Miszellen 1934.135; otherwise Gray, JAOS 23.60). DB 4.37, 41, 67°, 70, 87°; DSt 10°; XPh 46.

-kaiy, emphatic encl. particle, in *ada-kaiy* (q.v.): probably lsn. to *ka-* (§191.III), cf. Gk. ποι 'somewhither' (Bv. Gr. §336 takes as **kaᵈ-ιᵈ*, cf. *naiy* from **na-iᵈ*).

kaufa- sb. 'mountain': Av. *kaofa-*, Phl. *kōf*, NPers. *kōh* (§75.II, §166). See also *Ākaufaciya-*. *kaufa* nsm. DB 1.37; 3.44; DSf 31.

kaⁿta- ptc. as sb. (§276.III) 'excavation': pAr. **kṇta-*, to ¹*kan-*, with restored *n* (§242.II) as in *Samar-kand*, wherein *-kand* has been transferred from the ditch to the wall alongside it (König, Burgbau 32n; Hz. AMI 3.54–5, ApI 224). *katam* nsn. DSf 25.

Katpatuka- sb. 'Cappadocia', a province of the Persian Empire; also, as adj., 'Cappadocian': Elam. *qa-at-ba-du-qa*, Akk. *ka-at-pa-tuk-ka*, Gk. Καππαδοκία (§83.III).

(1) 'Cappadocia': *Katpatuka* nsm. DB 1.15f; DPe 12; DNa 28; DSe 27°; DSm 8°; XPh 26.

(2) 'Cappadocian': *Katpatuka* nsm. A?P 21.

¹*kan-* vb. 'dig': Av. *kan-*, Skt. *khan-* (§100). See also *Adukanaiša-*, *kata-*. *kaⁿtanaiy* (§238; NPers. *kandan*) inf. DZc 9; XV 21. *akaniya* imf. pass. (§113, §220) DSf 24, 28 (25, 29 read *avaniya*: see under *van-*); DZc 10°.

ni- + *kan-* 'destroy, obliterate': *nikaⁿtuv* imv. (§208, §237.II) DB 4.80.

vi- + *kan-* 'dig apart, destroy': *viyakanam* 1st sg. imf. XPh 38. *viyakaⁿ* imf. (§208, §228.II) DB 1.64. *vikanāhy* 2d sg. subj. (§27) DB 4.71, 73; *vikanāhᵃ-diš* (§27, §54.II, §136) DB 4.77.

²*kan-* vb. of uncertain connections, probably 'throw, place': cf. NPers. *awgandan* 'heap up' from *ava-kan-* (Bv. Gr. §184; Morgenstierne, Acta Or. 1.249; Hz. ApI 225).

ava- + *kan-* 'put down on, place on': *avākanam* 1st sg. imf. (§213, §226.II) DB 1.86.

Kaᵐpaⁿda- (§111) sb. 'Kampanda', a district in Media (cf. Konig, RuID 71): Elam. *qa-um-pan-taš*, Akk. *ḫa-am-ba-nu*. *Kapada* nsm. DB 2.27.

kapautaka- adj. 'blue', in *kāsaka hya kapautaka* 'lapis lazuli': deriv. (§146.II) of stem in Phl. *kapōt*, NPers. *kabōd* 'gray-blue', Skt. *kapóta-* 'pigeon, pigeon-color, gray' (Scheil 21.29; Bv. BSLP 30.1.61; König, Burgbau 62; Bleichsteiner, WZKM 37.94–101; Wb. AfOF 7.42, cf. PW 10.1887 s.v. *kapauta*; Hz. AMI 3.64–5). *kapautaka* nsm. DSf 37.

Kāpišakāni- sb. 'Kapishakani', a fortress in Arachosia (§117, §126): Elam. *qa-ap-pi-iš-ša-qa-nu-iš*. *Kāpišakāniš* ns. DB 3.60f.

Kaᵐbūjiya- sb. 'Cambyses', (1) father of Cyrus the Great; (2) son of Cyrus the Great, king of Persia before Darius: Elam. *kan-bu-ṣi-ia*, Akk.

kam-bu-zi-i̯a, Gk. Καμβύσης (§111, §144.IV): etymology disputed (cf. Bthl. AiW 437; Charpentier, ZII 2.140–52). *Kabūjiya* nsm. DB 1.28, 30f, 31, 32, 33, 43. *Kabūjiyam* asm. DB 1.45, 46. *Kabūjiyahyā* gsm. CMb 1f; DB 1.29, 30, 39. *Kabūjiyā* absm. DB 1.40.

kam- vb. 'like', see *amaxamatā*, if for (*h*)-*amaxmatā*. See also *kāma-*, and possibly *canah-*.

kāma- sb. 'wish, desire': Av. Skt. *kāma-* (§126, §143.I, V, VI). See also *kam-*. For syntax of dependent acc., §249.I, JAOS 66.44–9. *kāma* nsm. DB 4.35f; 5.17°, 29, 33°; DNa 38; DNb 8, 10, 12, 19, 20, 27; DSf 16; DZc 12°; XPf 22, 30.

kamna- adj. 'small, few': Av. *kamna-*, NPers. *kam* (§147.II). *kamnam* nsn. (as pred. sb. §259) DB 2.19. *kamnaibiš* ipm. DB 1.56; 2.2, 71; 3.41, 71f.

kar- vb. 'do, make, build': Av. *kar-*, pres. *kərənaoiti*, Skt. *kr̥-*, pres. *kr̥ṇóti karóti* (§99, §122, §132.2, §132.3). See also *akarta-*, *ucāra-*, *kara-*, *dastakarta-*, *duškarta-*, *hakarta-*.

kunautiy (§66.I, §70, §99, §210.I) DNb 24f; DSs 2°, 3f, 4, 6°.

akunavam (§66.I) 1st sg. imf. DB 1.62, 63, 68, 72, 87; 2.20, 76, 83, 91; 3.31f, 52, 85; 4.3f, 6, 36°, 40, 41, 45, 59, 60, 65, 89; 5.2, 8f, 17, 29, 33; DNa 49f, 51; DNb 48f; DSa 4, 5; DSd 3°; DSe 32, 34, 45, 49; DSf 21, 22 bis; DSg 3°; DSi 4°; DSj 2°, 3, 3f°, 4, DSo 2°, 4; XPa 13, 14; XPb 27; XPd 17; XPf 37f, 41; XPg 11f; XPh 43, 43f, 44f, 46; XPj; A¹Pa 21f; D²Sb 4. *akunavām* (§53, §55.I) A²Sdb 3; *akuvanašāša* (§55.I) A²Sdc 3. [*akun*]*ām* (§55.I) XSc 3; A²Ha 5f; [*akunām*] A²Sa 4, 5; *akunā* (§55.I) A²Ha 7.

akunauš imf. (§84, §218.I, §228.III) AsH 8; DB 2.23, 85, 96; 3.5, 16, 57; 4.10, 12, 15, 18, 20, 23, 26, 28, 31, 34, 35; 5.10; DPa 6; DNa 5f, 34; DSe 5f; DSf 4, 10, 15, 17, 20°, 30; DSi 3°; DSm 5°; DSt 6°; DZc 3; DE 8; XPa 4, 15; XPb 8; XPc 4, 11; XPd 6; XPf 6, 24, 27, 32, 42; XPg 4f; XPh 5; XSaa 2 (-*nauuš* in ab, §53); XE 9; XV 7, 20, 23; A¹Pa 6°; D²Sa 2; D²Sb 3; A²Hb; A²Hc 5; A³Pa 6. *akunaš* (§55.I) D²Sbb 3; A²Sa 3f.

akunavan 3d pl. imf. DB 2.34, 39, 45, 54, 59; 3.37, 44, 61, 66; DNa 20f, 37; DSe 19f°; XPh 18. *akunavaša* (§232.III) DSf 50°, 51, 53.

akumā 1st pl. aor. (§218.II, §230.II) DB 1.90, 94, 96; 2.68, 70; XPa 17; XPf 43.

akunavantā 3d pl. imf. mid. (§210.I, §236.II) DB 3.12; 5.6; DSf 48 (Hz. ApI 229–30 takes as from *ā* + *kart-* 'cut'; but see Kent, Lg. 18.81–2).

akutā aor. mid. (§66.I, §218.II, §235.II) CMb 4; DB 1.47.

akunavayatā imf. pass. (§220, §235.II) DB 1.20, 24.

akariya imf. pass. (§35.I, §99, §220) DSf 37; XPh 42.

akariyantā 3d pl. imf. pass. (§35.I, §66.II, §220, §236.II) DB 3.92.

[*c*]*āxr*[*iyatā*] or *caxr*[*iyatā*] perf. pass. (§219, §220) DB 4.90 (Kent, JAOS 62.267–8, for KT's ... *axᵃrᵃ* ..., after Konig, Klotho 4.46).

kunavāhy 2d sg. subj. (§222.III) DB 4.75, 79.

kunavānaiy 1st sg. subj. mid. (§66.I, §222.III, §233.IV) DSl 4 (Bv. BSLP 30.1.65; not act. *-niy*, with Wb. AfOF 7.39).

kunavātaiy subj. mid. (§222.III) DNb 56.

caxriyā perf. opt. (§99, §103.I, §122, §219, §223.I, §228.II) DB 1.50.

kariyaiš opt. pass. (§35.I, §220, §223.II, §228.-III) DNb 9, 11 (not desiderative future, as taken by Hz. ApI 228).

kunautuv imv. (§210.I, §237.II) DB 4.76.

kušuvā 2d sg. aor. imv. mid. (§218.II, §237.III) DNb 50.

cartanaiy inf. (§31, §99, §122, §238) DB 1.94; 2.33, 38f, 44, 53, 58, 67; 3.36, 43f, 60, 65f; DSf 20°; DSn 1°.

karta nsm. past ptc. pass. (Av. *kərəta-*, NPers. *kard*, Skt. *kr̥tá-*; §30, §66, §122, §242.I) DPc; DPi; DSf 38, 40, 43; XPi°; A¹I.

[*kartā*] nsf. A³Pa 23. *kartā* npf. (§119) DSf 46.

kartam nsn. DB 1.27; 2.27, 37, 42, 47, 57, 62, 92, 98; 3.8f, 10, 19, 21, 40, 47, 53, 64, 69, 76; 4.2, 42, 46f, 49, 51f, 52, 54; DNa 48f; DNb 29, 48, 56°; DSe 44; DSj 5f°; DSn 2; DSs 7; XPa 14, 15f, 19, 20; XPb 23f, 25, 30; XPc 13, 14; XPd 19; XPf 38, 46f, 47; XSc 5°; XV 27°; XH; A¹Pa 24°. *kartā* (for nsn., §56.V) A³Pa 26. *kartam* asn. DNa 51; XPf 40, XPg 10; XPh 46; A²Sd 4.

kara- sb. 'doer, maker', as 2d element of cpd.: deriv. of *kar-* (§32, §143.I); found in *avākara-*, *ciyākara-*, *dāraniyakara-*, *zūrakara-*, *hakara-*, *hamaranakara-*, and with passive meaning, 'thing made', in *patikara-* (cf. Bv. Gr. §289).

kāra- sb. 'people, army': Lith. *kāras* 'war', dialectal 'army', Gt. *harjis* 'army', NGm. *Heer* (§143.III); cf. Konig, RuID 66. See also *ukāra-*.

kāra nsm. DB 1.33, 40, 79, 85; 2.16, 18, 25, 27, 30f, 35, 40, 46, 50, 55, 60, 75f, 87, 90, 94; 3.3, 17, 26, 32, 38, 45, 59, 62, 67, 81; 4.92; DPe 22; DSf 29, 32. *kāra-šim* DB 1.50. *kāram* asm. DB 1.51, 52, 66, 78, 86, 88, 95; 2.19, 20f, 25, 35, 41, 46, 55, 61, 68, 72, 81, 83f, 87, 97; 3.1f, 4, 7, 15, 17, 29, 38, 42, 46, 55, 58, 62, 67, 84, 85; 4.34; 5.7; DPe 21. *kārahyā* gsm. DB 1.31f, 38, 64, 75; 2.10, 15, 80; 3.24, 70, 80; 4.54, 55, 58. *kārā* ism. DB 1.93; 2.22, 67, 85, 95; 3.15f, 33, 36, 73, 86f; 5.9, 21, 24; DPe 8f.

Karka- adj. 'Carian'; pl., also a province of the Persian Empire: Elam. *kur-qa-ap*, Akk. *kar-sa*, Gk. Κᾶρες, Καρικοί (§31, §106); cf. Eilers, OLZ 38.201-13, with lit. *Karka* nsm. A?P 30. *Karkā* npm. DNa 30; DSe 30°; DSf 33; XPh 28.

karnuvaka- sb. 'stonemason': from root *kart-* 'cut', Av. pres. *kərənv-*, Skt. *kr̥t-*, pIE **qert-*, + suffix *-aka-* (§30, §146.I), cf. JAOS 51.210. There are also forms of this root without *-t-* (JAOS 53.20), such as Gk. κείρω (cf. Boisacq, Dict. étym. de la langue grecque, s.v.). See also Bv. BSLP 30.1.66; Hz. AMI 3.73; Konig, Burgbau 69-70; Wb. AfOF 7.43. *karnuvakā* npm. DSf 47.

Karmāna- sb. 'Carmania', a district of Southern Iran (§166.I): NPers. Kirmān, Gk. Καρμανία. *Karmānā* absm. DSf 35.

karša- sb. 'weight, (unit by) weight' (like Lt. *pondō*, Lg. 19.227-9), = 83.33 gr. or slightly less than 3 oz. avoirdupois (Gray, JAOS 20.55; Schmidt, Treasury of Persepolis 62): Skt. *karṣa-* 'pull, unit by weight' (§29.n2, §30, §143.I, VI). The OP *karša-* was one-sixth of the Babylonian *mana* 'mina' (weight; not unit of value). Elam. transcribes *kur-ša-um*, = *kr̥šam*, which may mark the word as neuter, since Elam. transcriptions commonly represent the nom. sg. of the foreign word; but the other evidence is rather for the masc. *karšā* ism. (§252D; Lg. 19.227-9; not ndm.) Wa 1. *karšayā* lsm. (§251C; Lg. 19.227-9; not npm.) Wc 1; Wd 1.

kāsaka- sb. 'semi-precious stone'; Elam. *qa-si-qa* causes Konig and Wb. to write *kās'ka*, but this is not warranted by the OP writing. Deriv. of Iran. root **kas-* (§9.V, §87, §126, §146.II), = Skt. *kaś-* 'be visible, appear, shine' (so Kónig, Burgbau 61, not to Skt. *kācá-* 'crystal, quartz', despite Bv. BSLP 30.1.61); for meaning, cf. NEng. brilliant. Cf. also Scheil 21.29; Wb. AfOF 7.42; Hz. AMI 3.65, ApI 230-3; Bv. Gr. §273. See also *kāsakaina-*. *kāsaka* nsm. DSf 37, 39.

kāsakaina- adj. 'of semi-precious stone', namely, of lapis lazuli: adj. to preceding (§147.-III). *kāsakaina* nsm. DPi; XP1.

Kuganakā- sb. 'Kuganaka', a town in Persia: Elam. *ku-ug-gan-na-qa-an*, Akk. *ku-gu-na-ak-ka*. *Kuganakā* nsf. DB 2.9.

Kunduru- sb. 'Kunduru', a town in Media: Elam. *ku-un-tar-ru-iš*, Akk. *ku-un-du-ur*. *Kuduruš* (§22) nsm. DB 2.65.

Kūru- sb. 'Cyrus', founder of the Persian Empire: Elam. *ku-raš*, Akk. *ku-ra-aš*, Gk. Κῦρος (§164.V). *Kūruš* nsm. CMa 1; CMb 1; CMc°. *Kūrauš* gsm. DB 1.28, 39, 53; 3.25; 4.9, 27f; DBb 5f; DBh 6f.

Kūša- sb. 'Ethiopia', a province of the Persian Empire: Elam. *ku-ša-a-i̯a*, Akk. *ku-ú-šu*, Heb. *kūš*. See also *Kūšiya-*. *Kūšā-* absm. DPh 6; DSf 43f; DH 5.

Kūšiya- adj. 'Ethiopian'; pl., a province of the Persian Empire: adj. to preceding (§144.III). *Kūšāya* (sic!) nsm. A?P 28. *Kūšiyā* npm. DNa 30; DSe 30°; XPh 28 (written *Kūšiya*, §51; cf. Lg. 13.298).

xaudā- sb. 'hat, cap' (§100, §143.IV): Av. χαοδα-, Oss. *xoda*, NPers. *xoδ*, Arm. (borrowed) *xoir* 'headband' (cf. Duchesne-Guillemin, BSOS 9.865, for further connections). See also *tigraxaudā-*. [*xaudā*]*m* asf. DB 5.22.

Xaršādašyā (or *Xaršaišyā*), word of doubtful meaning, Se; apparently gsm. of owner's name. Justi, INB 173, reads lines 1-3-2, and gets *Xišyāršā*, approximately the Akk. form of the name of Xerxes (§163.VII); against this, see Wb. KIA 131.

xraθu- sb. 'wisdom', meaning given by Akk. equivalent *ṭēmē ḫissatum* 'word or message of wisdom': Av. *xratav- xraθw-* 'geistiges Wollen und Konnen' (Bthl. AiW 535), Skt *krátu-* 'power', Gk. κρατύς 'strong' (§33, §81, §103.I, §153.III, §179.-n2); cf. Hz. RHRel. 113.27-9, ApI 235-7. *xraθum* asm. DNb 3.

Xšaθrita- sb. 'Khshathrita', name assumed by the Median rebel Phraortes (§9.II, §78): Elam.

LEXICON 181

ša-at-tar-rı-da, Akk. ḫa-ša-at-ri-it-ti; shortening of compound name (§145, §164.III) such as *Xšaθradāra- (found in Phl., cf. Justi, INB 176). Xšaθrita nsm. DB 2.15°; 4.19; DBe 6.

    xšaça- sb. 'kingship, kingdom': Av. xšaθra-, NPers. šahr 'city', Skt. kṣatrá-, pIE *qpetro-, deriv. of root in OP xšay- (§78, §148.III). See also Artaxšaça-, Xšaθrita-, xšaçapāvan-.   xšaçam nsm. DB 1.44, 45; DPh 4; DH 3. xšaçam asn. DB 1.12, 25 bis, 26, 41, 42f, 50, 60, 61, 80f; DPd 3; DSf 10f; DSm 3°; DSp 2°; DZc 3f; XPa 19; XPb 29f; XPd 19; XPf 46; XPg 14; XSc 5; XV 27°; A¹Pa 24°; A²Hc 18, 19f. xšaçam-šım DB 1.59.

    xšaçapāvan- sb. 'satrap': Gk. σατράπης; xšaça- + root pā- 'protect' + suffix -van- (§155.IV, §160.Ia). xšaçapāvā nsm. (§124.5, §187) DB 3.14, 56.

    xšan- vb., see axšata-.

    xšap- sb. 'night': Av. xšap-, NPers. šab, Skt. kṣap- (§102, §142). xšapa-vā gsf. DB 1.20 (for case, §188.III, cf. Skt. gen kṣapas . . . usras 'night and day', RV 6.52.15, 7.15.8; gen. riming with acc. rauca in phrase, §318, rather than acc. xšapam remade to xšapa to rime with rauca).

    xšay- vb. 'rule': Av. xšā(y)-, Skt. kṣáyatı 'possesses', Gk. κτάομαι 'I acquire', κτῆμα 'piece of property', pIE *qþei- (§102). See also xšaça-, xšāyaθiya-, Xšayāršan-. xšayamna nsm. ptc. mid. (§213, §241) DNb 15.

    upari + xšay- 'rule over': upariya[xšayaiy] 1st sg. imf. mid. DB 4.64f. (Tm. Lex. 85) is an erroneous restoration for upariyā[ya]m as read by Cameron (already conjectured by Wb. KIA 66, ZDMG 61.729).

    patı- + xšay- 'have lordship over': patiyaxšayaiy 1st sg. imf. mid. (§213, §233.III) DNa 19; DSe 17f; XPh 17.

    xšāyaθiya- sb. 'king'; possibly in original adj. use, 'royal', DB 1.8 (Bthl. AiW 553): pAr. *kšāıatıa- (Med. -θy-, Bv. Gr. §147, Hz. AMI 3.97; not orig. -θiıa-, as Mt. Gr. §147 had it), to root ın OP xšay- (§9.III, §80, §126, §144.VI).

    xšāyaθiya nsm. AmH 1, 1f, 2, 4, 8, 10; AsH 1, 1f, 2f, 5; CMa 1f; CMb 1°; CMc°; DB 1.1 bis, 2 bis, 4, 6, 9, 11, 12, 13, 14, 18, 21, 24, 27, 27f, 29, 35, 44, 48 bis, 60, 61, 71f, 72, 73, 75, 76, 81f, 83, 90f; 2.1, 5f, 8, 11, 11°, 14, 17°, 18, 29, 37, 43, 49, 57, 64, 66, 70f, 78f, 80, 91, 92; 3.1, 9, 11, 20, 21f, 28, 29, 40f, 49f, 53, 54, 64, 69, 75, 76f, 83, 83f; 4.1, 3, 5, 11, 17, 21f, 25, 31, 33, 36f, 37, 40, 43f, 45f, 50, 53, 57, 59, 62, 67 bis, 70, 72, 76f, 80, 86f, 87, 88; 5.1, 3f, 14f, 18, 20f, 30f, 34; DBa 1, 1f, 2, 2f, 5, 9, 14; DBb 6f; DBc 6f; DBd 6f; DBe 9; DBf 5f; DBg 6f; DBh 8f; DBi 9f; DBj 4f; DPa 1, 2, 3; DPd 5, 6, 12f; DPe 1, 2, 3, 6, 19; DNa 8, 9, 10, 11, 15f, 31, 34, 40, 48; DNb 5f, 59; DSb 2, 3f, 5f, 7; DSl 1f, DSm 6°; DE 12f, 13, 14f, 16f; XPa 6, 7 bis, 8, 11, 18; XPb 12, 13, 14f, 16, 22; XPd 9 bis, 10, 11, 15; XPe 1, 2; XPf 8f, 9, 10, 11f, 16, 25f, 28, 35, 36, 44; XPg 2, 6; XPh 7, 7f, 8, 9, 14, 15, 29, 29f, 56f; XSa 1, 2; XSc 1°, 1, 1f°, 3°, 3f°; XE 12f, 13f, 14f, 16; XV 10 bis, 11, 12f, 17, 17f; A¹Pa 9°, 10°, 11°, 12°, 17f, 20; A²Sc 2, 2°, 3, 4; A³Pa 5f (§247E), 9 bis, 10, 11, 21f, 24; Wa 3f; Wb 1f, 2f, 4f, 5f; Wc 2f, 3f, 5f, 6f; Wd 3, 4, 5f, 6f; AVsb-d.

    xšāyaθiyam asm. AsH 7f; DPd 2f; DNa 5, 6f, 33f; DNb 4f; DSm 4; DSt 5f°; DE 7f, 9f; XPa 4, 5; XPb 7f, 9f; XPd 5f, 7; XPf 5, 6f, 23f; XPh 4f, 5f; XE 8, 10; XV 6, 7f; A¹Pa 6°, 7°; A³Pa 7.

    xšāyaθiyahyā gsm. AmH 3; AsH 3f; CMb 2; DB 3.59; DPd 10f; DNc 2; DNd 1f; XPa 10; XPb 19f; XPd 13f; XPe 3f; XPf 14; XPh 11; XSc 2; XE 19f; XV 15; A¹Pa 15°. xšāyaθiya as gsm. (§313.II) A³Pa 12f, 14, 15, 16, 17f.

    xšāyaθıyā npm. DB 1.8 (or nsf. adj. ?), 10, 10f; 4.51; DBa 13, 16, 17f.

    xšāyaθıyā apm. DB 4.7, 32.

    xšāyaθiyānām gpm. AmH 2; AsH 2; DB 1.1f; DBa 2; DPa 2f; DPe 2f; DNa 9; DSb 4f; DE 14; XPa 7; XPb 13f; XPd 10; XPe 2f; XPf 9f; XPh 8; XSc 1; XE 14; XV 11; A¹Pa 10f°; Wb 3f; Wc 4f; Wd 4f. xšāyaθiyanām (§52.III) A²Sc 2f; A³Pa 10. On the title 'king of kings', see von Wesendonk, Or. Stud. Pavry 488–90.

    XŠ nsm. (§42) DPb; DPh 1 ter, 4; DSa 1 bis, 2, 3; DSc bis; DSd 1 bis, 1° bis, 3°; DSe 8°, 8, 9°, 10°, 14°, 31°, 42, 50°; DSf 6 quater, 8, 55°; DSg 1° quater, 3°; DSi 1, 1° ter, 3; DSj 1 bis, 1°, 2°, 5; DSk 1 bis, 2, 4; DSm 1° bis, 2°, 3°; DSn 1°; DSo 3°; DSt 7°, 10°; DSy 1 bis, 2 bis; DZb 1, 2 bis, 3°; DZc 5 ter, 5°, 7; DH 1 ter, 3; XPc 6 ter, 7, 10, 11; XPj quinquies; A¹Ì ter; D²Sa 2°; D²Sb 1° ter, 1, 3°; A²Sa 1 quater; A²Sb ter; A²Sd 1 quater, 2; A²Ha 1 bis, 1° bis; A²Hb; A²Hc 7, 8 ter, 16 bis; SDa; SXa 2; SXb 2; SXc 1; XVs; AVsa.

    XŠm asm. DSe 5, 6; XPc 4, 5; D²Sa 3; A²Hc 5, 6. XŠyam DSf 4, 4f, 10, 15, 17; DSi 3°; DSn 2; DSp 2; DZc 3.

Xšyā gsm. DZc 3; A²Hc 10, 11, 12, 13. *XŠhyā* DPc; DPi; XPc 9, 14; XPi°; XPk; XH; A¹I bis; D²Sb 2°; A²Sa 1, 2 bis, 3; A²Sb; A²Sc 0; A²Ha 2, 3, 3°, 4. *XŠāhyā* (§53) A²Sd 2. *XŠyahyā* XPj; *XŠyahiyā* (§27) XPjv. *XŠ* as gsm. (§313.II) A²Hb.

XŠānām gpm. XPc 6. *XŠyānām* DSa 1f; DSc; DSd 1; DSe 8f; DSf 6; DSg 1°; DSi 1°; DSj 1; DSk 1f; DSm 1°; DSy 1; DZb 2, DZc 5; XPj; A¹I; D²Sb 1°; A²Sa 1; A²Sd 1; A²Ha 1°, A²Hc 8. *XŠyanām* (§52.III) DPh 1; DH 1. *XŠyānā* (§52.V) A²Sb.

Xšayāršan- sb. 'Xerxes': Elam. *ik-še-ir-iš-ša*, Akk. *ḫi-ši-'-ar-ša*, Gk. Ξέρξης: from *xšaya-* 'king', Av. *xšaya-*, to root *xšay-*, + *aršan-* 'male' (§131): 'Hero among Kings', cf. Skt. *rāja-ṛṣabha-* (Bthl. AiW 550; but Hz. AMI 1.121n, Bv. Gr. §290, take second part to be *arša-* 'just', on which cf. §162.n1, §187.n2; cf. also Hz. AMI 7.82-137, esp. 135-6, on which see Henning, BSOS 10.502-3). Decl., §187.

Xšayāršā nsm. XPa 6, 11, 17; XPb 11f, 21f; XPc 6, 9f; XPd 8f, 15; XPe 1; XPf 8, 15, 27, 44; XPg 1; XPh 7, 13, 28f, 56; XPj bis; XPk; XSa 1; XSc 1°, 3°; XE 12; XV 9, 16; A¹Pa 19f; A³Pa 16, 16f (both as gen., §313.II); SXa 1; SXb 1f; SXc 1; XVs.

Xšayāršām asm. XPa 4; XPb 7; XPc 4; XPd 5; XPf 5, XPh 4; XE 7f; XV 6.

Xšaya[ršāha] gsm. XPi; [*Xšayar*]*šāha* XH. *Xšayāršahyā* (§57) A¹Pa 14f; A¹I bis; A²Ha 3, 3f. *Xšayārcahyā* (§49b) A²Sa 2 bis. *Xšayāršāhyā* A²Hc 12, (as nom., §313.I) 12f. *Xaršadašyā*, q.v.

xšnā- vb. 'learn, come to know, know': Av. *xšnā-*, Skt. *jñā-*, Gk. γιγνώσκω, Lt. *gnōscō*, NEng. *know*, pIE *ĝnō-* (§96, §110, §212). See also *xšnav-*, *dan-*. *adānā* imf. (NPers. *dānam*, §68, §210) DB 1.51; DSq 3. *xšnāsāhy* 2d sg. subj. (§212, §227.I) DNa 42. *xšnāsātiy* subj. (§62, §97, §110, §122) DB 1.52.

xšnav- vb. 'hear, satisfy' (§96): cf. Av. *xšnav-* 'Genüge haben an', adj. *xšnav-* 'Genüge leistend', ptc. *xšnūta-*, sb. *xšnūtay-* 'Zufriedenstellung' (Bthl. AiW 557-60); apparently an extension of root *xšnā-* 'learn' (cf. pIE *dō-* and *doy̯-* 'give'), with semantic development 'learn, hear of, hear', and 'hear, hearken to, satisfy' (Lg. 15.171; cf. also Bv. TPS 1945.47-50). Hz. ApI 238-40 gives an impossible equation with Skt. *śru-* 'hear' (pIE *ḱlu-*); Sen 247, 251, has wrong meanings. Pisani, Acme 1.319-20, gives another etymology. See also *uxšnav-*.

xšnuta- past ptc. pass. (§71, §242.I), cf. *uxšnav-*: *xšnuta* nsm. 'satisfied' DNb 26. [*xšnutam*] nsn. 'heard' DNb 53.

ā + *xšnav-*: *āxšnautiy* (§71, §122, §208) 'satisfy' DNb 24. *āxšnavāhy* 2d sg. subj. (§227.I) 'satisfy' DNb 29f. *āxšnudiy* 2d sg. imv. (§208, §237.I) 'hear' DNb 54.

gaiθā- sb. '(living) personal property, cattle': Av. *gaēθā-* 'individual living being, pl. world; household, property', Phl. *gēhān* 'world' (from gen. pl.), to root pIE *gʷei-* seen in OP *jīv-* (§69, §101, §151). For varying interpretations, see Tm. Lex. 85, with lit. *gaiθām-cā* (§39) asf. DB 1.65.

gaud- vb. 'conceal': Av. *gaoz-*, Skt. *gūhati* (§88).

apa- + *gaud-* 'conceal, hide away': *apagaudayāhy* 2d sg. subj. (§227.I) DB 4.55, 57f. *apagaudaya* 2d sg. inj. (§215, §224, §227.II, §237) DB 4.54.

gaub- vb. 'say', mid. 'call one's self' (§213): Sas. Phl. *gōwēt* 'he says', NPers. *gōyaδ*, inf. *guftan*: perhaps a *-bh-* extension of pIE root *ĝheu-* seen with *-s-* extension in *gauša-* (q.v.; Bv. BSLP 31.2.70). *gaubataiy* mid. (§235.I) DB 2.21, 31, 51; 3.15, 59. *agaubatā* imf. mid. DB 1.84, 93; 2.66f; 3.35, 55 (written *agauratā*, §54.II), 89f; 4.82. *agaubaⁿtā* 3d pl. imf. mid. (§236.II) DB 2.93. *gaubātaiy* subj. mid. (§235.I) DB 2.84; 3.86.

Gaubaruva- sb. 'Gobryas', ally of Darius against Gaumata: Elam. *kam-bar-ma*, Akk. *gu-ba-ru-'*, Gk. Γωβρύης; from *gav-* 'cattle' + **baruva-*, cf. Skt. *bharu-* 'lord', to vb. *bar-* (§35.II, §101, §122, §142, §143.II, §150, §153.I, §160.Ib): 'Cattle-Possessor' (Justi, IFA 17.111; otherwise Foy, ZDMG 54.360). *Gaubaruva* nsm. DB 4.84; 5.7, 9, 11; DNc 1.

Gaumāta- sb. 'Gaumata', Median pretender who took the name Smerdis (§164.I): Elam. *kam-ma-ad-da*, Akk. *gu-ma-a-tú*; from *gav-* 'cattle' + ptc. *māta-* of unknown meaning (§242.II). *Gaumāta* nsm. DB 1.36, 44, 46, 64, 65, 70; 4.7; DBb 1f. *Gaumātam* asm. DB 1.49f, 54, 57, 73; 4.81.

gauša- sb. 'ear': Av. *gaoša-*, NPers. *gōš*, Skt. *ghóṣa-* 'noise'; Iran. root **gauš-* 'hear', pIE **gheus-* (§70, §101, §143.I). *gaušā* adm. (§189) DB 2.74,

89. *gaušāyā* idm. (§189; with sg. ending, Lg. 19.225) DNb 53.

gāθu- sb. 'place, throne, place of battle' (JNES 4.49–50): Av. *gātav- gāθw-*, NPers. *gāh*, Skt. *gātu-*, to pAr. root *gam-*, pIE *$g^u em$-* 'come' (§68, §81, §153.III, §179.n2). *gāθum* asm. DNa 41f. *gāθavā* lsm. (§137, §182.II) DB 1.62f, 66, 69; DNa 36; DNb 35 (JNES 4.49–50); DSe 36f, 44, 44f; XPf 33 (as abl., §182.III, though without *hacā*: Lg. 9.41–6; Bv. BSLP 33.2.148–50; Wb. ZfA 41.319–20; Schaeder, SbPAW 1935.503; Hz. AMI 4.130–2, 8.45, ApI 177–80), 35f; XPh 34.

gad- vb., see *jad-*.

Ga^n dāra- sb. 'Gandara, Gandaritis', a province of the Persian Empire: Elam. *gan-da-ra*, Akk. *gan-da-ri*. See also *Gadāraya-*. *Gadāra* nsm. DB 1.16; DPe 1.18; DNa 24f; DSe 24°; DSm 9°; XPh 25. *Gadārā* absm. DSf 34.

Ga^n dāraya- adj. 'Gandarian': adj. to preceding (§144.III, §167). *Gadāraya* nsm. A?P 12.

Ga^n dutava- sb. 'Gandutava', a district in Arachosia: Elam. *gan-du-ma-*+. Cf. Tm. Lex. 86. *Gadutava* nsm. DB 3.66.

gan- vb., see *jan-*.

ġand- vb., see *gasta-*.

gam- vb. 'come': Av. *gam-*, Skt. *gam-*, Gk. βαίνω, Lt. *veniō*, Gt. *qiman*, pIE *$g^u em$-* (§101, §244). See also *gāθu-*.

ā + gam- 'come': *ājamiyā* opt. (Skt. *gamyāt*; §67.I, §101, §122, §132.2, §218.II, §223.I, §228.II) DPd 19.

ava- + gam- 'go down, fall down': [*avagmat*]*ā* nsf. past ptc. (§244) DSe 46f (conj. of Kent, cf. JAOS 54.46).

parā + gam- 'go forth': *parāgmatā* nsf. past ptc. (§101, §103.IV, §122, §132.2, §244) DNa 44f.

ham- + gam- 'come together, assemble': *ha^m gmatā* npm. past ptc. (§101, §103.IV, §132.2, §140.V, §244) DB 2.32, 38, 43, 52, 58; 3.65. See also *Hagmatāna-*.

gay- vb., see *jīv-*.

gara- 'devouring', see *bātugara-*.

garta- sb., either 'cave' or 'wagon', see *Asagarta-*.

Garmapada- adj. 'Garmapada', the fourth month, June–July: Elam. *karmabadaš*, Akk. *du-'ūzu*. From *garma-* 'heat', Av. *garəma-*, Skt. *gharmá-*, Lt. *formus* 'hot', NEng. *warm*, pIE *$g^u hormo$-*, cf. Gk. θερμός (with analogical -*e*-), + *pada-* 'step, station' (§29, §31, §149.I, §161.Ib, §165): 'Heat-Station Month'. *Garmapadahya* gsm. DB 1.42; 3.7f, 46.

gav- sb. 'cow, cattle' (§101): Av. *gāuš*, Skt. *gā́uṣ*, Gk. βοῦς, NEng. *cow*, pIE nom. *$g^u ōus$*: in *Gaubaruva-*, *Gaumāta-*, perhaps in Θαταγυ-.

gasta- adj. 'repugnant, evil'; nt. as sb., 'evil, harm': past ptc. (§85, §242.I) of vb. **gant- *gandh-* 'smell', Av. *ganti-* 'evil odor' (AiW 493), *duž-ganti-* 'evil-smelling' (AiW 757), Skt. *gandhá-* 'odor' (Bv. Gr. §179); for meaning, cf. Lt. *odor* 'smell', *ōdī* '(I have smelled), I hate', *odium* 'dislike, hatred'. Nt abstract to same root, **gant-tāt-*, nom. *gastāt*, abl. shortened by haplology, as taken by Hz. AMI 8.68, ApI 173–7. *gastā* nsf. DNa 57f. *gastā* absn. DNa 52, XPh 57f; A²Sa 5°; A²Sdc 4 (*gāstā* da, db; §53); A²Ha 6°.

gud- vb., see *gaud-*.

gub- vb., see *gaub-*.

grab- vb. 'seize (as possession), seize (as prisoner)', pres. *garbāya-* (§30, §217): Av. *grab-*, pres. *gə̄urvāya-*, Skt. *grabh-*, pres. *gr̥bhāyati*, NEng. *grab*, pIE **ghrebh-*. See also *Patigrabanā-*. *agarbāyam* 1st sg. imf. DB 2.4 bis; 4.7, 32; 5.25f; DNa 17; DSe 16; DZc 8. *agarbāya* imf. DB 2.88; 3.74, 90°; 5.12. *agarbāya^n* 3d pl. imf. (§232.II) DB 2.13; 3.48, 49; 5.27f. *agarbāyatā* imf. mid. (§235.II) DB 1.42, 43, 81; 3.82f. When meaning 'seize as prisoner' (DB 2.4 second occurrence, 13, 88; 3.48, 49, 74, 90; 4.7, 32; 5.12, 25f, 27f) perhaps not *agarb-* but *āgarb-*, from *ā + grab-* (see below).

ā + grab- 'seize (as prisoner)': *āgarbīta* nsm. past ptc. pass. (§30, §217, §242.II) DB 2 73. For uncertain examples, see under *grab-* (uncompounded).

-cā (i.e. -*că*) encl. conj. 'and': GAv. -*čā*, LAv. -*ča*, Skt. *ca*, Gk. τε, Lt. -*que*, pIE **$q^u e$*. -*cā* ... -*cā* 'both ... and' DB 1.65, DNb 32, -*cā* ... -*cā* *utā* 'both ... and ... and' DB 1.66–7. -*cā* DB 1.65 ter, 66, 66f; DPd 9f; DNb 32 bis; XPh 41, 51, 54. -*ca-maiy* DNb 28, 51, 52 (§51).

+++ *canām*, see *ustašanā-*.

canah- sb. 'desire', see *Aspacanah-*; cf. also *kam-*.

car- vb. 'move', see *abicariš*; cf. also under *ucāra-*.

cāra- (§126), see *ucāra-*.

caša- sb. 'eye': to root in Skt. *cakṣ-* 'see, speak', derivatives *cákṣas- cakṣu- cakṣus- cakṣan-*, and Av. *čašman-*, Phl. NPers. *čašm* 'eye'; initial *u-* of *ucašma* is an error (Bv. TPS 1945.53–4, quoting Jn. IF 25.182). The stem is *caša-*, not *cašman-* (Kent, Lg. 19.225–6), since the nom.-acc. of nt. *casman-* would be *cašmā* and not *cašma*. Cf. §102, §143.I, §187.n1. Attempts to explain the erroneous *u-* of *ucašma*, Wb. ZDMG 61.726; Wackernagel, KZ 61.205–8. *cašam* asn. DB 2.75, 89 (Cameron found *I cᵃšᵃmᵃ* legible in 89, but only the final *mᵃ* in 75); *caša[m]* (case and form uncertain) DSq 2.

ci- interrog.-indef. pron. 'what, any'; collateral stem (§201) to OP *ka-*. See also *-ciy*, *citā*, *cinā*, *ciyăkara-*. *ciš-ciy* asn. 'anything' (§9.VI, §105, §132.2, §201) DB 1.53, Lt. *quicquid*, pIE *qᵘid-qᵘid*: reduplicated form with Med. sandhi; see OP *-ciy* for exact cognates.

-ciy encl. particle, emphasizing or generalizing, nsn. or asn. of *ci-*: Av. *-čit̰*, Skt. *cid*, Gk. τι, Lt. *quid*, pIE *qᵘid* (§40, §84, §113, §191.III, §201, §228.n1). In the following combinations: *aciy* (q.v.) XPf 21. *aniyaš-ciy* nsn. DB 4.46; XPa 13; *aniyaš-cᵃ* (§52.I) XPh 41f; *aniyai-ciy* npm. XPf 29. *avaš-ciy* nsn. DNb 55; asn. DNb 53f, 57; XPa 20; XPc 14; XPf 48. *a[vā]m-cᵃ* (§52.I) DB 5.2f. *kaš-ciy* nsm. DB 1.49, 53; DSe 37. *ciš-ciy* asn. DB 1.53. *paruvam-ciy* DB 1.63, 67, 69. *yaciy* (q.v.) DNb 35, 36, 57. *hauv-ciy* DPe 23f. *hakaram-ciy* DNb 34f. *[hacā-ci]y* DSf 23. *vašnā-[ci]y* XPg 7f, less likely than *vašnā[pi]y*, see under *apiy*.

Cⁱⁿcixri- sb. 'Cincikhri', father of Martiya (§163.V): Elam. *ṣi-in-ṣa-ak-ri-iš*, Akk. *ši-in-ša-aḫ-ri-iš*. *Cicixrāiš* gsm. (§179.IV) DB 2.9.

citā adv. 'so long', correlative with *yātā* 'until': from *ci-* + suffix seen in Gk. ἔπει-τα 'then' (§191.II; wrongly König, RuID 72, and Sen 40). DB 2.48, 63.

ciça- sb. 'seed, lineage': Av. *čiθra-*, NPers. *čihr* 'origin' (§78, §148.III). In *Arıyaciça-*, *Ciçataxma-*.

Ciçaⁿtaxma- sb. 'Ciçantakhma', a Sagartian rebel: Elam. *ṣi-iš-ša-an-tak-ma*, Akk. *ši-it-ra-an-taḫ-ma*, Gk. Τριτανταίχμης. From *ciça-* (§9.n1) + *taxma-* 'brave' (§9.II): 'Brave-by-Lineage' (§160.-Ie); the *-xm-* is Median (§163.II; Jacobsohn, KZ 54.261; Bv. BSLP 31 2.79). For the nasal ending the prior element, see §159.n1. *Ciçataxma* nsm. DB 2.79; 4.20; DBg 1f. *Ciçataxmam* asm. DB 2.87f. *Ciçataxmā* ism. DB 2.86.

ci[nā] emphasizing adv. after neg., 'at all': Av. *cinā̆* 'also, likewise'; perhaps isn. of *ci-*, cf. JAOS 58.116–7, 324, and Harl, KZ 63.2 (not *ci[tā]*, with Sen 134). DSe 36.

ciyăkara- (§53) adj. 'how great'; nt. as sb., 'how great a thing': *ciya(n)t-*, cf. Skt. *kíyat* nsn. 'how much, how many', + *kara-* to root *kar-* 'make' (§160.Ia; Bthl. AiW 597; hardly to *kara-* 'time', cf. *hakaram*, as taken by MB Gr §293, Hz. ApI 101–3). *ciyakaram* nsn. (§259) DNa 39; *ciyākaram* DNb 50; *ciyākaram-ca-maiy* (written *-rᵃmᵃmᵃcᵃiyᵃ*; §41, §51, §133, §138.I; Lg. 15.173, against Hz. ApI 240) DNb 51, 51f.

Cišpi- (so Schaeder, SbPAW 1931.641.n4; *Caʰišpi-* acc. to Justi, INB 152, on the evidence of certain spellings in Greek) sb. 'Teispes', King of Elam about 610 B.C., ancestor of Cyrus and Darius: Elam. *ṣi-iš-pi-iš*, Akk. *ši-iš-pi-iš*, Gk. Τεἴσπης (§117, §124.3, §164.V). *Cišpiš* nsm. (§24, §179.IV) DB 1.5°; DBa 8. *Cišpāiš* gsm. (§24, §179.IV) DB 1.5f; *Cišpaiš* (§24, §179.IV) AmH 3; DBa 8.

jaⁿtar- sb. 'smiter, slayer': Av. *jantar-*, Skt. *hantár-*; pIE *gᵘhen-tor-*, agent noun to OP root *jan-* (§154.II). *jatā* nsm. (§186.I) DB 4.58, 78.

jad- vb. 'pray, ask', with acc. of person and acc. of thing: Av. *jad-* (*gad-*, Bthl. AiW 487), pres. *jaidya-* (§214), Gk. aor. inf. mid. θέσσασθαι, pIE *gᵘhedh-*. *jadıyāmiy* 1st sg. (§226.I) DPd 21; DNa 54; XPh 59f; XSc 4.

jan- vb. 'strike; smite, defeat (enemy in battle); mould (brick)': Av. *jan-* (*gan-*, Bthl. AiW 490), Skt. *han-*, Gk. θείνει 'strikes', φόνος 'murder', Lt. *dē-fendit* 'wards off', pIE *gᵘhen-* (§101, §110, §208); see also *jatar-*.

jaⁿtiy (Skt. *hánti*; §208, §228.I) DSe 36, 40. *ajanam* 1st sg. imf. (§110, §122, §208) DB 1.89, 95; 2.69; 4.6f; 5 25; XPh 34. *ajaⁿ* imf. (§101, §208) DB 2.26, 36, 41, 46, 55, 61, 87, 98°; 3.7, 18, 39, 46, 63, 68, 88; 5.11; DSe 34. *ajanıya* imf. pass.

(§220) DSf 29. *jadiy* (Skt. *jahí*; §101, §122, §208, §237.I) 2d sg. imv. DB 2.31, 51; 3.15. *jatā* 2d pl. imv. (§208, §231) DB 2.21, 84; 3.58, 86.

ava- + *jan-* and *ava-* + *ā* + *jan-* 'smite down, slay' (apparently *ava-* in *avajata*, *ava-ā-* in *avājaniyā*, others ambiguous; cf. §206c, JAOS 62.274): *avājanam* 1st sg. imf. (§226.II) DB 1.57, 59, 73, 83; 2.5; 4.81; 5.13, 27°. *avāja*ⁿ imf. (§228.II) DB 1.31 bis; 3.75. *avājana*ⁿ 3d pl. imf. (§208, §232.-II) DB 2.13. *avājaniyā* opt. (§206c, §223.I, §228.II) DB 1.51, 52 (§53, JAOS 62.274; hardly with Foy, KZ 35.34). *avajata* nsm. past ptc. pass. (§122, §242.I) DB 1.32 (error for *avājata*, acc. to Gray AJP 21.13, Bthl. AiW 491).

pati- + *jan-* 'fight against': *patiyajatā* imf. mid. (§140.III, §208, §235.II) DNa 47.

fra- + *jan-* 'cut off': *frājanam* 1st sg. imf. (§226.II) DB 2.74, 89.

vi- + *jan-* 'shatter': *vijanā*ⁿ*tiy* 3d pl. subj. (§208, §222.III, §232.I) A²Sa 5°, A²Ha 7° (conj. Kent).

jav- vb. 'press forward': Skt. *jū-* 'press forward, impel quickly, excite, promote', pres. *jávate* 'hastens', caus. *jāvayati*. Cf. Bv. BSLP 33.2.152; Hz. AMI 4.127, 8.37-8, 65-6, ApI 366-7; Wb. ZfA 41.320; Bailey, BSOS 7.292-4; Schaeder SbPAW 1935.502; Kent, Lg. 9.43, 231.

abi- + *jav-* caus. 'promote, increase, add to': *abiyajāvayam* 1st sg. imf. (§215) XPg 9; *abījāvayam* (§23.I, §140.III) XPf 40.

jiyamna- ptc. as adj. 'growing old', nt. as sb. 'end' (§109, §241): Av. *jyamna-*, ptc. to root *jyā-* 'grow weak', Skt. *jināti* 'grows old'. *jiyamnam* asn. DB 2.62.

jiv- vb. 'live': Av. *jivaiti* (*gay-*, Bthl. AiW 502), Skt. *jívati*, Lt. *vīvit*, pIE *$g^u\bar{\iota}ueti$ (§216); see also *gaiθā-*, *jīva-*. *ajīvatam* 3d du. imf. (§229) DSf 14; XPf 21. *jīvā* 2d sg. imv. (§237.I) DB 4.56, 75.

jīva- adj. 'living': Av. *jva-*, Skt. *jīvá-*, Lt. *vīvos*, pIE *$g^u\bar{\iota}uo-$, cf. *g^uiuo- in Gk. βίος 'life', *g^uig^uo- in OEng. *cwicu* 'living', NEng. *quick* (§101, §114, §150). See also *jīv-*. *jīva* nsm. XPh 48, 54. *jiva-diy* A²Sd 3 (dubious §22, §55.II; cf. JAOS 51.229, Scheil 21.93, Wb. AfOF 7.45). *jīvahyā* gsm. DB 5.19f, 35.

jū- vb., see *jav-*.

-ta- encl. demonst. pron. 'this, it': Av. Skt. *ta-*, cf. OP *tya-*. Only *-tā* apm., referring to *patikarā*, in *avaθāša-tā* DB 4.72 (§133, §196; JAOS 62.272-3).

taumā- sb. 'family' (§149.I): Av. *taoxman-*, NPers. *tuxm*, Skt. *tokά-m* 'offspring', *tókman-tokma-s* 'young blade of barley'; *-xm-* became OP *-hm-* (§103.II, §118.II), but remained in Med. (Bv. BSLP 31.2.76-9, Gr. §133; wrongly Mt. Gr. §75, Kent JAOS 35.329-31). *taumā* nsf. DB 1.8; 4.56, 58f, 64, 75, 79; DBa 13. *taumām* asf. DB 4.88. *taumāyā* gsf. (§119) DB 1.9, 28f, 45, 49; 2.16, 81; 4.19f, 22; DBa 15; DBe 8; DBg 11f. *taumāyā* absf. DB 1.61f.

tauman- sb. 'power, strength': deriv. of root *tav-* 'be strong', with suffix *-man-* as in Skt. *nắma* 'name', Lt. *nōmen* (§122, §155.III). For separation from *taumā-* 'family', see Tm. Lex. 91, and Kent, JAOS 35.329-31. See also *tauvīyah-*. *taumā* nsn. (§187) DB 4.74, 78; 5.19°, 35. *taumanišaiy* (= *taumaniš-šaiy*; §41, §130, §138.I, §187) ipn. DNb 25f (Lg. 15.171-2, 176; not gen. sg. with Hz. ApI 327; hardly loc. sg. with Sen 247; possibly acc. du., 'two powers [of mind and of body]', with Pisani, Riv. Stud. Or. 19.88-9).

tauvīyah- adj. 'stronger': comp. to *tauma-*, adj. to *tauman-* 'power'; for formation (§48, §122, §156.III, §190.I-II), cf. Skt. *sthūrá-* 'strong' and comp. *sthávīyas-*, Av. *stūra-* and comp. *staoyah-*, *taxma-* 'brave' and comp. *tąsyah-*: JAOS 58.324. *tauvīyā* nsm. (§185.IV) DSe 39 (not to pres. ptc. *tavya-nt-*, as taken by Hz. ApI 328).

takabara- adj. 'wearing the petasos' (§76.V, §160.Ia), as proved by Akk. 'who bear shields on their heads' (Andreas, Verh. d. 13. Internat. Orientalisten-Kong. 1902, 96-7; Wb. AbkSGW 29.1.33; other views by Foy KZ 35.63, 37.545-6, Bthl. AiW 626, Tm. Lex. 91, PAPA 44.liii-lv). *takabarā* npm. DNa 29; DSm 10f°; A?P 26 (for nsm., §56.III).

taxma- adj. 'brave' (§9.II, §103.II, §149.I; with Med. *-xm-*, Bv. Gr. §133): Av. *taxma-*, NPers. *tahm*; in *Ciçataxma-*, *Taxmaspāda-*.

Taxmaspāda- sb. 'Takhmaspada', one of Darius's generals: Elam. *tak-mas-ba-da*; *taxma-* 'brave' + *spāda-* 'army' (§9.II, §103.II, §116, §161.IIa, §163.II). *Taxmaspāda* nsm. DB 2.82, 85.

taxš- vb. 'be active': contamination of pIr. *taš-, Av. *taš-* 'cut, form', Skt. *takṣ-* 'form by cutting', Gk. τέκτων 'builder', Lt. *texit* 'braids, weaves', pIE *tekþ-, and pAr. *tṷakš-, Av. θwaxš- '(mid.) be busy', Skt. *twakṣ-* 'create, work', pIE *tṷeqþ-. Cf. also Hz. ApI 322–4, and *ustašanā-*.

ham- + *taxš-* 'work with, cooperate with, effect': *ha^mtaxšataiy* mid. (§140.V, §213, §235.I) DNb 16. *hamataxšaiy* 1st sg. imf. mid. (§213, §233.III) DB 1.68, 70. *hamataxšatā* imf. mid. (§235.II) DB 4.65f. *hamataxša^ntā* 3d pl. imf. mid. DB 4.82.

tacara- sb. 'palace': NPers. *tazar*, Elam. *da-iš-ṣa-ra-um*, Akk. *bıt* (§76.V, §148.I). Cf. Gray, AJP 53.67; Hz. Klio 8.51, AMI 2.77; Hinz, ZDMG 95.227. *tacaram* asm. DPa 6; XPj. *dacaram* (§49a) DSd 3.

tanū- sb. 'body, self' (§153.II): Av. *tanū-*, Skt. *tanú-*; cf. Debrunner, IF 52.136. Decl., §183.I. *tanūš* nsf. DNb 33. *tanūm* asf. XPf 31.

tar- vb. 'cross over': Av. *tar-*, Skt. *tárati*, caus. *tāráyatı*, Lt. *trāns* ptc. as prep. 'across', cf. NEng. *through*. See also *tara*.

vı- + *tar-* 'go across', caus. 'put across': *viyatarayam* 1st sg. imf. (§215) DB 5.24f. *viyatarayāmā* 1st pl. imf. (§230.II) DB 1.88.

tara prep. with acc. 'through': Av. *tarō*, NPers. *tar*, Skt. *tirás*; formed on root *tar-* (q.v.) similarly to *para* (q.v.). *ta[ra]* DZc 12.

Tāravā- sb. 'Tarava', a town in Persia; Elam. +-*ra-ú-ma*, Akk. *ta-ar-ma-'. Tāravā* nsf. DB 3.22.

tarsa- pres. stem. of vb. 'fear', with *hacā* + abl.: Av. *tərəsaiti*, NPers. *tarsaδ*, pIE *tr̥s-ske-ti (§31, §97, §212), cf. pIE *tres- in Skt. *trásatı*, Gk. τρέει, also *trem-*-*trep- in Lt. *tremit* 'trembles (with fear)', *trepidus* 'agitated (with fear)'. *tarsatıy* (§228.I) DPd 11f. *tarsa^ntiy* 3d pl. (§232.I) DSe 38f. *atarsa* imf. DB 1.50f. *atarsa^n* 3d pl. imf. (§232.II) DB 2.12°; DPe 9. *tarsam* 1st sg. inj. (§224, §237) DPe 21.

tav- vb. 'be strong': Av. *tav-*, Skt. *tu-*, cf. Gk. ταῦρος 'bull', Lt. *taurus*. See also *utava-, tauman-, tauvīyah-, tunuvat-* (but cf. Hz. ApI 328–33). *tāvayatı* (§122, §123.2, §215) DNb 33f. *atāvayam* 1st sg. imf. (§215) DNb 47.

taš- vb., see under *taxš-*; in *ustašanā-*.

¹*Tıgra-* sb. 'Tigra', a fortress in Armenia: Elam. *tı-ıg-ra* (§103.IV). *Tigra* nsf. DB 2.39.

²*tıgra-* adj. 'pointed' (§103.IV, §148.I): Av. *tiγrı-* 'arrow', Skt. *tigmá-* 'pointed', cf. with strong grade Av. *bıtaēγa-* 'two-edged', Skt. *téjate* 'is sharp'. See also *tıgraxaudā-*. *tigrām* asf. DB 5.22.

Tıgrā- sb. 'Tigris' (§76 V, §103.IV, §107, §166): Elam. *ti-ıg-ra*, Akk. *dı-iq-lat*, Gk. Τίγρις. *Tıgrām* asf. DB 1.85, 88.

tıgraxauda- adj. 'wearing the pointed cap' (§161.IIa), as is shown in the sculpture of Skunkha the Scythian at Behistan (cf. also Hdt. 7.64): ²*tıgra-* 'pointed' + *xaudā-* 'cap' (§159). *tıgraxaudā* npm. DNa 26, DSe 25°, XPh 27; for nsm. (§56.III) DN xv, A?P 15.

tunuva^nt- adj. 'powerful': ptc. (§240) to *tunautıy*, pres. to *tav-* (§122; JAOS 15.170; otherwise Hz. ApI 329–32). Decl., §190.I, §240. *tunuvā* nsm. (§210.I) DNb 10. *tunuva^ntam* (§39) DB 4.65. *tunuva^ntahyā* gsm. DNb 9.

tuvam pron. 'thou': GAv. *tvə̄m*, LAv. *tūm*, Skt. *tuvám*, pIE *tuṷom; cf. Skt. *tvám*, Gk. Dor. τύ, Lt. *tū*, Gt. *þū* (§76.I, §137). Decl., §194. *tuvam* nsm. DB 4.37, 41, 67, 70, 87; *tuva* (§52.V; not *tūv* = pIE *tū, as taken by Hz. ApI 329) X̱Ph 46. *θuvām* asm. (Skt. *tvā́m*; §81, §114, §132.3) DB 4.43, 53, 55, 74; DSt 9f. *taiy* gsm. (Skt. *te*, Gk. adv. τοι) DNb 58 (§133). -*taıy* encl. gsm. in the following: *Auramazdā-tay* (§52.II) DB 4.58; *Auramazdā-taıy* DB 4.78; *ada-taiy* DNa 43, 45; *ava-taıy* DB 4.76, 79; *utā-taıy* DB 4.56, 58, 73f, 75, 77f, 79; *tya-taıy* DNb 53; *parta[m-taıy]* DNb 54; *mā-taıy* DNb 52, 55 (cf. *mā : taıy* 58); *hauv-taıy* DNa 57.

¹*tya-* rel. pron., def. art., demonst. pron.; cf. similar stem in Skt. (Ved.) demonst. *tya-*; recent (Iran. or OP) contamination (§261; Lg. 20.1–8) of demonst. *ta-*, Av. Skt. *ta-*, Gk. τo-, pIE *to- (cf. Lt. *is-tud*, NEng. *tha-t*) with rel. stem *ya-*, Av. Skt. *ya-*, Gk. ὅ-ς, pIE *i̯o- (rather than extension of stem *ta-* by suffix -(ı)i̯a-, as taken by MB Gr. §331), and written *t^ay^a*- rather than *t^aiy^a*- because of the similar orthography of nsm. *hya*, nsf. *hyā* (not because unaccented, as taken by MB Gr. §331); *t*- unchanged before *i̯* by influence of the *ta*- from which the word is derived (Foy, KZ 35.4n; Bthl. Gdr. IP §416a.n1). Decl., §198; uses, §261, §262. See also ²*tya* conj., *hya*.

(1) Rel. 'who, which': *tyam* asm. DB 3.60, 70. *tyaıy* npm. DB 1.9, 15; 4.50, 61, 63, 80; 5.22; DBa 15; DPe 13, 13f; DPh 5; DNa 28, 41; DSe 28°,

LEXICON 187

28f°; DSf 47f, 49, 51°, 52, 54°; DH 4; XPh 24. *tyai-šaiy* (§136) DB 1.57; 2.77, 3 48, 51, 74, 90, 91. *tya* as npm. (§52.I) XPh 23.

tyām asf. DB 4.70f; DPd 7. *tya* as asf. (§56.V) AmH 5; AsH 13°. *tyā* npf. DB 1.13, 18; 2.6; 4.33; DPe 9, 14f; DSf 45. *tyaiy* as npf. (§258.IV) XPh 31. *tyā* apf. DPe 7; DNa 17, 40; DSe 16. *tyaišām* gpf DSm 6°; XPh 15.

tya nsn (§40) DB 1.27, 61, 67; 2 91; 3.10, 20, 53, 76; 4.1f, 42, 49°, 53; DNa 48; DNb 2, 11, 29, 54, 56, DSe 31, 43; DSf 36; DSj 5°; DSn 2°; DZc 9, 10; XPa 19; XPb 23; XPf 26, 37, 46; XPg 4; XPh 42; XV 19; A³Pa 26. *tya-šām* DB 1.19; DNa 20; DSe 19°; XPh 17f. *tya-maiy* DNb 48; DSe 52°; DSf 19°; DSs 7°; XPa 19f; XPb 24, 30; XPc 13 bis; XPd 19; XPf 38, 47; XSc 5°; XV 27°; A¹Pa 24°; A²Hc 20. *tya-taiy* DNb 53. *tya-patiy* XPa 15. *tya* asn. DB 1.44, 72; 4.3, 40, 59, 75, 79; 5.2; DPh 4; DNb 22, 24; DSa 4; DSf 20f, 22°; DSj 2°, 4; DSl 3; DH 3; XPa 14, 15; XPf 41; XPh 43, 49, 52; A²Sa 5°; A²Sd 3; A²Ha 7. [*tya*]-*šām* DNa 36f. *tya-maiy* DPh 8; DH 6. *tya-patiy* XPf 40f. *tyanā* isn. DSf 42 *tyā* npn. in *tyā-maiy* DNb 13. *tyā* apn. DB 1.64; DNb 46, 49. *tyā-diš* DB 1.65.

(2) Def. art., 'the': *tyam* asm. DB 1.50, 54, 57, 73, 89, 95; 2.21, 25f, 35, 41, 46, 55, 61, 69, 87, 97°; 3.7, 18, 38, 46, 62f, 67f; 4.81; DSe 39. *tyam-šām* DB 5.12°.

tyām asf. DB 1.69, 71; 4.87; DNa 59. *tya* as asf. (§56.V) AsH 9, A²Sc 6. *tyaišām* gpf. DPe 3f.

tya nsn. DNa 21; DSe 20°, 38; XPh 19. *tya* asn. DB 1.81; DSf 11 bis; DSm 4° bis; DSp 2°, 3°; DZc 4 bis. *tyanā* isn. DB 1.23.

(3) Demonst. pron., 'this': *tyā* ndm. DSf 14. *tyaiy* apm. DB 3.73.

²*tya* conj. 'that', nt. sg. of preceding; cf. similar uses of Gk. ὅτι, Lt. *quod*, NEng. *that*, NGm. *dass*. In various uses (§299):

(1) 'that', introducing clause of fact as object, DSf 28 bis, 29.

(2) 'that', introducing clause of volition, with opt., DNb 8, 10, 19.

(3) 'that', introducing indirect or direct quotation, DB 1.32, 52; DNa 38f.

(4) 'because', introducing causal clause, DNb 33 (*tya-maiy*).

(5) 'so that', introducing result clause, DB 4.34, DNb 7.

(6) *mā-tya* 'in order that ... not, lest, not', DB 4.43, 48, 71, and in *mā-tya-mām* DB 1.52.

(7) *yadā-tya* 'where' XPh 35f, cf. *yadāyā* 'where' XPh 39.

(8) *yaθā tya* 'when' XPh 29.

Θāigarci- adj. 'Thaigarci', third month, May–June: Elam. *sākurrisiš*, Akk. *simannu* (§30, §72, §87, §126, §152.I, §165); an etymology as 'Garlic-Collecting Month', involving normalization Θāigraci-, is given by Justi, ZDMG 51.243 (cf. Bthl. AiW 786). Θāigarcaiš gsm. DB 2.46f.

θakata- ptc. adj. 'completed': Av. *sak-* '(of time) pass', pIE *ḱeq-*; fut. ptc. pass. (§244) like Av. *yazata-* 'worthy of worship' (Bv. BSLP 30.1.68–70), passing into past meaning, like Skt. *pacatá-* 'cooked', Gk. ἀρι-δείκ-ετος 'much pointed out, famous' (Schwyzer, Griech. Gram. 501–2); rather than pres. act. ptc. θakaⁿt- made thematic (cf. Bthl. WZKM 22.79–80). θakatam nsn. DB 3.8. θakatā npn. DB 1.38, 42, 56, 90, 96; 2.26f, 36, 42, 47, 56, 70, 98; 3.19, 39f, 47, 63, 68, 89.

Θatagu- sb. 'Sattagydia', a province of the Persian Empire: Elam. *sa-ad-da-ku-iš*, Akk. *sa-at-ta-gu-ú*, Gk. Σατταγυδία (§67, §87, §122, §153.I, §161.IIa, §204.V). From θata- 'hundred', Av. *sata-*, Skt. *śatám*, Gk. ἑ-κατόν, Lt. *centum*, NEng. *hundred*, pIE *ḱmto-m*, + *gav-* 'cattle': 'having hundreds of cattle' (hardly '[Land of] Seven Streams', with Hz. AMI 1.99n, 3.100–2, 8.73, König RuID 63). See also Θataguiya-. Θataguš nsm. DB 1.17; 2.7f; DPe 17; DNa 24; DSe 23°; DSm 10°; XPh 22.

Θataguiya- adj. 'Sattagydian': adj. to preceding (§144.III, §167). Θataguiya nsm. A?P 11; for *-guuiya*, unless *-gudaya* is to be read (§54.I, §167), cf. Gk. Σατταγύδαι, in which case the etymology given under Θatagu- must be revised.

θaⁿd- vb. 'seem': Av. *sand-*, Skt. *chand-* (§87, §215). θadayātaiy subj. mid. (§222.II) DB 4.49; DSa 5; DSj 6 (for text, see under *fraša-*; cf. §54.I). θadaya inj. (§224, §228.II, §237) DNa 58; DNb 53.

θadaθa, word of uncertain meaning, Sb 3.

θanuvaniya- sb. 'bowman': deriv. (§144.IV) of stem in Av. θanvar/n- 'bow', cf. Skt. *dhanvan-* 'bow' (§83.II, §114, §155.IV) and Hz. ApI 339. See also *uθanuvaniya-*. θanuvaniya nsm. DNb 42.

θard- sb. 'year': Av. sarəd- 'year', NPers. sāl, Skt. śarád- 'autumn' (§31, §87, §142). For the chronology of the rebellions against Darius, see Hist. App. IV. θardam asf. DB 5.3. θarda gsf. DB 4.4f, 41, 45, 52, 60.

θarmi- sb. 'timber' (§6, §29, §34, §152.IV): no probable etymology, despite König, Burgbau 52–4; Hz. AMI 3.58; Gray, AJP 53.67–8. θarmiš DSf 30.

θah- vb. 'declare, say': Av. saȟ-, pres. saṿha-, Skt. śáṣsati, Lt. cēnset, pIE *ḱens- (§87); perhaps lacking the nasal in the OP present (§108.n1; MB Gr. §134, cf. Wackernagel, IF 45.321–7; dubious theories on the pronunciation, Hz. AMI 3.83–6).

θātiy (§131, §213, §228.I; JAOS 35.332–4) AmH 4, 9; AsH 5; CMb 3; DB 1.3, 6, 8f, 11, 12f, 17, 20, 24, 26f, 35, 43, 48, 61, 71, 72, 81, 83, 90; 2.1, 5°, 8, 11, 13, 18, 29, 37, 42, 49, 57, 64, 70, 78, 91, 92; 3.1, 9, 10, 19, 21, 28f, 40, 49, 52f, 54, 64, 69, 75, 76, 83; 4.1, 2, 31, 33, 36, 40, 43, 45, 50, 52f, 57, 59, 61, 67, 69, 72, 76, 80, 86, 88; 5.1, 14, 18, 20, 30, 33f; DBa 4, 9, 13f; DPd 5, 12; DPe 5, 18; DPh 3; DNa 15, 30, 47; DNb 5, 22; DSa 3; DSd 2f°; DSe 14, 30°, 41, 49°; DSf 8, 55; DSg 2f; DSi 2f; DSj 2, 4f°; DSk 3; DSl 1; DSm 3; DSo 2°; DSt 6f; DZc 7; DH 3; XPa 11, 17; XPb 21; XPc 9; XPd 15; XPf 15, 27, 43f; XPg 1; XPh 13, 28, 56; XPj; XSa 1; XSc 2f°; XV 16; A¹Pa 17; D²Sb 3°; A²Sa 1; A²Sc 1°; A²Sd 2; A²Ha 1; A²Hc 7, 15; A³Pa 8, 21, 23. aθaham 1st sg. imf. (§131, §132.2–3, §213) DB 2.20, 30, 50, 83; 3.14. 85; DNa 37. aθaha imf. DB 1.75; 2.10°, 15, 80; 3.25, 57f; 4.8, 11, 13, 16, 19, 21, 24, 27°, 29; DBb 4; DBc 5; DBd 3; DBe 5; DBf 3; DBg 4f; DBh 4; DBi 4; DBj 3. θahyā- mahy 1st pl. pass. (§220, §230.I) DB 1.7; DBa 10f. aθahya imf. pass. (§220) DB 1.20, 23f; DNa 20; DSe 19°; aθahiya (§27) XPh 18. θāhy 2d sg. subj. (§131, §222.II, §227.I) DB 4.55, 58. θastanaiy inf. (§132.2–3) DB 1.53f.

θikā- sb. 'gravel, rubble, broken stone' (wrongly König, Burgbau 50, cf. Kent, JAOS 53.14): probably pIE *ḱiǵā- (§87, §143.IV), cf. Skt. sikatā- 'sand, gravel' (with Prakrit s for Skt. ś, or borrowed from an Iranian dialect, Bv. BSLP 30.1.60–1), and perhaps OP Sikayauvatiš (with Med. s-), fem. to *śikayas-vant- (cf. Bv. BSLP 30.1.61; Hz. AMI 3 55–6; Kent, JAOS 51.203). θikā nsf. DSf 25, 28. θikām asf. DSf 27.

Θuxra- sb. 'Thukhra', father of Otanes (§163.Ib, §164.III): Elam. du-uk-kur-ra, Akk. su-uḫ-ra-'. Perhaps same as Av. suxra- 'red', NPers. surx, Skt. śukrá- 'bright' (§87, §103.I, §148.I; cf. Foy, KZ 35.20). Θuxrah[y]ā gsm. DB 4.83.

Θūravāhara- adj. 'Thuravahara', second month, April–May: Elam. turmar, Akk. aịịāru. Cpd. of θūra- 'vigorous', Av. sūra-, Skt. śúra-, Gk. κύριος 'valid', pIE *ḱūro- (§87), + vāhara- 'spring time', Skt. vāsará- 'bright', NPers. bahār 'spring', Lith. vāsara 'summer' (§118.I, §126, §143.II, §148.I, §154.I; cf. Bv. Origines 16): '(Month) of Strong Spring' (§161.IIa, §165). Θūravāharahya gsm. DB 2.36, 41, 61; 3.39.

çay- vb. 'lean': Av. sray-, Skt. śri-, Gk. κλίνει, Lt. in-clīnat, NEng. lean, pIE *ḱlei- (§94).

ni- + çay-, causative (§123, §215) 'restore'; form influenced by dāraya- in Av. and OP (Ware, JAOS 44.285–7): niyaçārayam 1st sg. imf. DB 1.64.

çita- adj. 'third': Gk. τρίτος, pIE *tritos (§204.- III). See also çitīya-. ç[itām] asf. DB 5.3 (JNES 2.109–10).

çitīya- adj. 'third': Av. θritya-, Sks. tr̥tīya-, Lt. tertius, pIE *tritiịo- (§78, §144.II, §204.III); see also çita-. çitīyam asn. as adv. DB 2.43.

Çūśā- sb. 'Susa', a capital city of Darius, in Elam: Elam. šu-ša-an, Akk. šu-ša-an, Gk. Σοῦσα (§78, §117). Çūšāyā lsf. DSf 22, 34, 56; DSo 3f.

¹dā- vb. 'give': Av. Skt. dā-, Gk. δίδωμι, Lt. dat 'gives', dōnum 'gift', pIE *dō- (§62, §76.III). dadātuv imv. (§209, §237.II) DPd 23f; DNa 55; XPh 60.

²dā- vb. 'put, make, create': Av. dā-, Skt. dhā-, Gk. τίθημι, Lt. fēcit 'made', NEng. do, deed, pIE *dhē-. See also uvadā-, dāta-, dāna-. adadā imf. (§209, §228.II) DPd 3; DNb 1, 2; DSe 2°, 3°, 3f, 4. adā aor. (§62, §76.III, §122, §218.II, §228.II) DNa 2, 3 bis, 4; DSf 1f°, 2 bis, 3, 9; DSp 2°; DSt 2°, 3, 3f°, 4°; DZc 1, 2 ter; DE 3, 4, 5, 6; XPa 1f, 2, 3 bis; XPb 3, 4, 5, 6; XPc 2 bis, 3 bis; XPd 2, 3, 4 bis; XPf 2, 3 bis, 4; XPh 2 bis, 3 bis; XE 3f, 5, 5f, 6; XV 3, 4 bis, 5; A¹Pa 2°, 3°, 4°, 4f°; A²Hc 2, 3, 4 bis; A³Pa 2, 3, 4 bis.

daiy, see -di-.

daiva- sb. '(false) divinity, demon' (cf. Hz. RHRel. 113.32–7, AMI 8.74–5, ApI 126–30): Av.

daēva-, Skt. *devá-* 'deity', Lt. *dīvos, deus*, pIE **deiu̯o-* (§76.III, §114, §143.III). See also *daivadāna-*. *daivā* npm. XPh 36, 38, 39.

daivadāna- sb. 'sanctuary of false divinities' (§147.I, §160.Ib): *daiva-* + *dāna-* (in derogatory sense, 'den', acc. to Hz. AMI 8.75, ApI 131). *daivadānam* asm. XPh 37f (written *-dᵃavᵃmᵃ* in second copy, cf. §51, Lg. 13.293).

daug- vb., see *haduga-*.

dauštar- sb. 'friend': NPers. *dōst*, Skt. *joṣṭár-* 'loving'; agent-noun (§154.II) to root *dauš-*, Av. *zaoš-* 'enjoy', Skt. *juṣ-*, Lt. *gustat* 'tastes', NEng. *choose*, pIE **ĝeus-* (§88). *dauštā* nsm. (§124.5, §186.I) DB 4.56, 69, 74; DNb 7, 8, 12; DSj 4.

dacara-, see *tacara-*.

dāta- sb. 'law': Av. *dāta-*, NPers. *dāt*; nt. ptc. to ²*dā-* (§122, §242.II). See also *Vahyazdāta-*. *dātam* nsm. DNa 21; DSe 20°, 37; XPh 18f. *dātā* isn. (less probably absn., §172) DB 1.23; XPh 49, 52. [*d*]*ātā* npm. DNb 58.

datasa, KT's reading, with first and third characters uncertain, DB 4.71f; read *utava*, q.v.

Dātuvahya- sb. (§164.V) 'Datuvahya', father of Megabyzus (§163.Ib): Elam. *da-ad-du-man-ia̯*, Akk. *za-'-tu-'-a*; cf. Hz. AMI 1.84n. *Dāt*[*u*]-*vahyahyā* gsm. DB 4.85.

Dādarši- sb. 'Dadarshi', (1) an Armenian, (2) a Persian, satrap in Bactria: Elam. *da-tur-ši-iš*, Akk. *da-da-ar-šu*. Deriv. of *darš-* 'dare', with reduplication; Skt. *dádhr̥ṣi-* 'bold' (§30, §76.III, §152.I, §164.IV). *Dādaršiš* nsm. DB 2.29, 31f, 48; 3.13, 15. *Dādaršim* asm. DB 2.33, 38, 44.

¹*dan-* vb. 'flow': Skt. *dhán-vati. danu*[*vatiy*] DZc 9 (or *danu*[*taiy*] mid., Wb. KIA 104, after alternative suggestion of Bthl. AiW 683); §216, §216.n1.

²*dan-* vb. 'be acquainted with', see *xšnā-*.

dāna-, in *apadāna-, daivadāna-*: Skt. *dhána-m* 'container, receptacle'; from OP ²*dā-* + suffix *-na-* (§147.I).

¹*dar-* vb. 'hold; (intrans.) dwell': Av. *dar-*, Skt. *dhr̥-*, Lt. *fir-mus* 'firm', Lith. *darýti* 'to make', pIE **dher-* (§76.III, §122). See also *Upadarma-, Dārayavau-, duruva-, Vidarna-*. Present stem *dāraya-* and conj., §215. *dārayāmiy* 1st sg. (§226.I) AmH 5f; AsH 11, 14; DB 1.26; DPh 4f; DNb 14; DH 4. *dārayatiy* DNd 2 (reading certain, acc. to Wb.'s marginal note to AbkSGW 29.-142). *dāraya*ⁿ*tiy* 3d pl. (§232.I) XPh 23f, 24f. *adāraya* imf. (§228.II) DB 1.85; 2.9; 3.23; DNa 41; DSe 20f°; XPh 19; *adāraiya* DNa 22 (§48; Wb. AbkSGW 29.33, cf. Kent, JAOS 35.347n; wrongly Hz. ApI 132, as passive). *adā*[*rayat*]*ā́* imf. mid. with passive meaning DB 4.90f (§235.II; JAOS 62.268). *adaršiy* 1st sg. aor. mid. (§218.I, §233.V) DPe 8. *adāriya* imf. pass. (§220, §228.II) DB 2.75, 90.

ham- + *dar-* 'get hold of, obtain': *hamadārayaiy* 1st sg. imf. (§233.III) DB 1.26.

²*dar-* vb. 'be angry', see *dartana-*.

daraniya- sb. 'gold': Av. *zaranya-* Ars. Phl. *zarēn*, NPers. *zarr*, Skt. *híraṇya-m*, pIE **ĝhl̥-enio-* (§32, §66.II, §88, §126, §144.IV), cf. NEng. *gold*. See also *dāraniyakara-*. *daraniyam* nsm. DSf 35. *daraniyam* asm. DSf 49f. But Gk. δᾱρεικός, a Persian gold coin, is from the name of Darius (Bv. BSLP 30.1.59), and not from a short form of *daraniya-* (as taken by Mt. Gr. §129, Hz. ApI 134–5).

dāraniyakara- sb. 'goldsmith': NPers. *zargar* 'goldsmith'; *daraniya-* with vriddhi, + *kara-* 'maker' (§126, §143.V, §160.Ia; Kónig, Burgbau 65; Hz. AMI 3.73–4; Kent, JAOS 53.21). *dāraniyakarā* npm. DSf 49 (on Frag. Theta, Scheil 21, plate 11, see §44; König, Burgbau, Tafel 5; Kent, JAOS 53.21, against 51.195–6).

Dārayavaʰu- sb. 'Darius' (I, son of Hystaspes, king 522–486 B.C.; II, son of Artaxerxes I, king 426–04 B.C.): Elam *da-ri-ia̯-ma-u-iš*, Akk. *da-ri-ia̯-muš*, Gk. Δᾱρεῖος (by haplology for **Δᾱρειαῖος*; Keiper, Acta Sem. Phil. Erlangen, 1.253). From pAr. **dhāraiat-*, ptc. to root in OP *dar-* (§162, §240), + pAr. **u̯asu* asn. 'the good' (§153.I), see OP *vau-*: 'He who holds firm the good' (Hz. Arch. Hist. Iran 40, ApI 255, 267, takes as hypocoristic of **dāraya-vahu-manah-* 'Holder of Good Thought'; this is rejected by Nyberg, Rel. 361).

Dārayavauš nsm. (§118.IV, §124.2) DB 1.1, 4, 6, 9, 11, 13, 17f, 20f, 24, 27, 35, 44, 48, 61, 71, 73, 81, 83, 90; 2.1, 5, 8, 11, 13f, 18, 29, 37, 42f, 49, 57, 64, 70, 78, 91, 92; 3.1, 9, 10f, 19f, 21, 29, 40, 49, 53, 54, 64, 69, 75, 76, 83; 4.1, 2f, 31, 33, 36, 40, 43, 45, 50, 53, 57, 59, 61f, 67, 69f, 72, 76, 80, 86, 88; 5.1, 14, 18, 20, 30, 34°; DBa 1, 4f, 9, 14; DPa 1;

DPb; DPd 4f, 5, 12; DPe 1, 5f, 19; DPh 1, 3f; DNa 8, 15, 30f, 40, 47f; DNb 5; DSa 1, 3; DSb 1f°; DSc; DSd 1°, 3°; DSe 8, 14, 30f°, 41°, 49f; DSf 5f, 8, 55; DSg 1, 3; DSi 1, 3; DSj 1, 2, 5; DSk 1, 3f; DSl 1; DSm 1, 3°; DSn 1°; DSo 2f; DSq 2; DSt 7°; DSy 1; DZa; DZb 1; DZc 4, 7; DE 12; DH 1, 3; XPc 11; XPf 16f, 30, 33; XPg 6; XSa 2, XV 17; D²Sa 2; D²Sb 1°, 3°; A²Sa 3; Wa 2f; Wb 1; Wc 2; Wd 2; SDa; SDb. *Dārayavahauš* as nsm. XPf 25 (§51; Lg. 9.39).

Dārayavaum asm. DPd 2; DNa 5; DNb 4; DSe 5°; DSf 3f; DSn 2; DSp 1f°; DSt 5°; DZc 3; DE 7; XPf 22f; D²Sa 2f.

Dārayavahauš gsm. (§118.IV, §124.2) DB 3.58f; DPc; DPd 10; DPi; DNc 1f; DNd 1; DZc 3; XPa 9f; XPb 19; XPc 8f, 14; XPd 13; XPe 3; XPf 13f, 17; XPh 11; XPj; XPk; XSc 2°; XE 19, XV 14f; A¹Pa 16. *Dārayavauš* as gsm. XPf 28 (§51; Lg. 9.39); (§313.II) A²Sb, A²Sd 2, A²Hb, A³Pa 13f, 14, 17, 18. *Dārayavaušahyā* gsm. (§57) A¹I; A²Sa 1, 1f, 2f, 3; A²Sc 0 bis; A²Hc 9f, 10 (as nom., §313.I), 13, 14 (as nom.). *Dārayavašahyā* gsm. (§52.VI, §57) A²Ha 2, 2°, 4, 4°.

dāru- sb. 'wood': Av. *dāuru-*, Skt. *dā́ru-*, cf. Gk. δόρυ 'spear'. *dāruv* (§181) nsn. DSf 41, in phrase *asā dāruv* 'ebony', lit. 'stone wood' (§308.-n1), so called because of its hardness; but also probably *asā* because of the assonance translated Akk. *aban* 'stone', cf. Hebr. *eben* 'ebony', Gk. ἔβενος, from Egyptian *hbnj* 'ebony' (J. Duchesne-Guillemin, BSOS 10.925-7 [1942], noting that acc. to Hdt. 3.97 the Egyptians paid a tribute of ebony logs to the Persian King). Not to be normalized *dāruva* to root ¹*dar-* and the phrase taken as 'copper' (Scheil 21.30; Kent JAOS 51.208, 53.18-9), or as 'iron' (Bv. BSLP 30.1.60; who also suggests that *dāruva* may be an adj. referring to some kind of tree); not *asā* + instr. *dāruv* 'window frames of wood' (König, Burgbau 64-5); not *asā sāruva* 'lead' (Hz. ApI 299), to Av. *srva-* 'lead' (Bthl. AiW 1649), for the slight traces do not confirm initial *sᵃ*. [*dār*]*uv* asn. DSf 51 (so Hinz, Orientalia, soon to appear, not [*išmal*]*uv*, see Lex. s.v.).

darga- adj. 'long': GAv. *darəga-*, LAv. *darəγa-*, NPers. *dēr*, Skt. *dīrghá-*, pIE **dḷgho-*, cf. Gk. δολιχός, Lt. *longus* (§31, §68, §101, §143.III, VI). *dargam* asn. as adv. 'for a long time' DB 4 56, 75.

dartana- (or perhaps *zartana-*, with Med. *z*) sb. 'anger': Av. *zarəta-* 'enraged', Skt. *hr̥ṇité* 'is angry' (§34, §147.V, §238). [*da*]*rtanayā* lsn. DNb 13f (conj. of Kent, JNES 4.46-7; cf. §238.n1).

darš- vb. 'dare': GAv. *dərəš-* 'deed of violence', Skt. *dhr̥ṣ-nóti* 'dares', NEng. *dare* (§76.III, §117). See also *Dādarši-*, *daršam*. *adaršnauš* imf. §30, §84, §210.I, §228.III) DB 1.53.

daršam adv. 'mightily': asn. to adj. *darša-* (§143 I), to root *darš-* (against this, Hz. ApI 135-6) DB 1.50 (MB Gr. §366; wrongly Kent, JAOS 35.336-42); 4.37; DNb 14, 15, 50.

dasta- sb. 'hand': Av. *zasta-*, NPers. *dast*, Skt. *hásta-*, pIE **ĝhosto-* (§88, §116, §145). See also *dastakarta-*. *dastayā* lsm. DB 4.35. *dastaibiyā* idm. (§189) DNb 41.

dastakarta- adj. 'handmade': *dasta-* + ptc. *karta-* (§160.Ic), to *kar-* 'make'. [*dasta*]*kartam* (restored after the Elam., Wb. ZDMG 91.85, Hz. ApI 136-8) nsn. as sb. 'handiwork', DSe 42f.

Daha- adj. 'Dahian'; pl., a province of the Persian Empire: Akk. *da-a-an*, Gk. Δάαι (§76.V; Lg. 13.298; Hz. AMI 8.72). *Dahā* npm. XPh 26.

dahyu- sb. 'land, province, district': GAv. *dahyu-*, LAv. *dahyu- daiŋhu-*, NPers. *dih* 'village', Skt. *dásyu-* 'stranger, demon' (§124.2, §153.IV, §166). Decl., §183.II. See also *visadahyu-*.
dahyāuš nsf. AmH 5, 8f (as lsf. §314b); DB 1.59, 2.28, 53, 59, 72; 3.9, 11, 20, 23, 66, 75, 79f; 5 4, 13f, 29f; DPd 6. *dahyāuš-maiy* DB 4.39. *dahyāum* asf. (§53, §72) AsH 8, 11, 13; DPd 15, 18; DNa 53. *dahyāvam* (§124.VI) XPh 33, 58f. *dahyauvā* (*dahyuvā* Wb.) lsf. (§48, §124.2, §137) DB 1.34.
dahyāva npf. (§124 7) DB 1.13, 17, 18, 23, 41; 2.6°, 4.33, DPe 7, 14, DNa 17, 39; DSe 15f, 32f; DSm 5f°; XPh 15. *dahyāva* apf. DB 1.21, 47, 67; 4.92; XPh 31, 35. *dahyūnām* gpf. DB 1.2; DBa 3; DPa 4; DPe 3; DNa 10; DSb 6f; DSe 9°; DZb 2f°; DZc 5; DE 15, XPa 7f; XPb 15; XPc 7; XPd 10f; XPf 10f; XPh 8f; XSc 2°; XE 15; XV 11f; A¹Pa 11f°; A²Sc 3f; Wb 5; Wc 6; Wd 6. *dahyūv-nām* (§23.II) DPh 2; DH 1f. *dahyušuvā* lpf. DB 1.35.

DHum (§42) asf. DSf 58; DSj 6°. *DHyaum* (§53) A³Pa 26. *DHnām* gpf. DSa 2; DSd 1; DSf 6; DSg 1°; DSi 1°; DSk 2; DSm 2°. *DHyūnām*

DSy 2; XPj; A¹I; D²Sb 1; A²Sa 1; A²Sd 1; A²Ha 1°; A²Hc 8; A³Pa 11.

¹*dī-* vb. 'see': Av. ²*dā(y)-* 'see' (Bthl. AiW 724), NPers. *dīdan*, Skt. *dhī-* 'think'. *dīdiy* 2d sg. imv. (§65, §129, §209, §218.II, §237.I) DNa 41; DNb 57.

²*dī-* vb. 'take by force (a thing from a person, 2 acc.), deprive (a person of a thing, 2 acc.)': Av. *zināiti* 'harms' (*zyā-*, Bthl. AiW 1700), Skt. *jināti* 'oppresses', *jáyati* 'conquers' (§88), cf. Gk. βιά 'violence'. *adīnam* 1st sg. imf. (§210.II, §226.II) DB 1.59. *adīnā* imf. (§210.II, §228.II) DB 1.44f, 46, 66. *dītam* asm. past ptc. pass. (§242.I) DB 1.50.

-di- encl. pron. 'him, them', usually with masc. antecedent: Av. *di-* (Bthl. AiW 684); starting by wrong division of *pasāvad-im* etc., where *-im* is acc. to **is*, Lt. *is*, and extended (§195.II; Caland, KZ 42.173; Mt. MSLP 19.53–5, Gr. §166); on competition with pron. *-ši-*, see Bv. Gr. §345.

-dim asm. (§195.II) in *pasāva-dim* (with fem. antecedent) DNa 33; *anu-dim* DNb 16, 18; *avaθā-dim* DNb 17; *hau-dim* DSf 32.

-diš apm. (§195.II) in *tyā-diš* DB 1.65 (with collective sg. masc. antecedent); *naiy-diš* DB 4.73, 78; *paribarāhᵃ-diš* DB 4.74; *vikanāhᵃ-diš* DB 4.77; *avaθā-diš* DB 5.17, 33; *ava-diš* DNa 21, DSe 20°, XPh 19; *utā-diš* DNb 46f (with nt. antecedent); *hau-diš* DSs 6° (with antecedents of different genders). Written as separate word in *drauga diš* DB 4.34 (with fem. antecedents); *pasāva diš* DB 4.35; *avaθā diš* DB 4.36.

daiy DB 5.11, as separate word, properly *v'iyᵃ* with wrongly inserted divider following; read *viy-amarda* with Wb. ZfA 46.55, see under *mard-* (not apm. with Kent, JAOS 62.273; not gen.-dat. sg. with Wb. KIA 73n, Bv. Gr. §345, Gray AJP 53.69).

-diy emphatic encl. particle: Av. *zī*, Skt. *hi*, Gk. encl. -χι in ναί-χι 'yes indeed', οὐ-χί 'not at all', pIE *ĝhi* (§88, §191.I). *ufraštā-diy* DB 4.69 (JAOS 35.351-2; not pron. apm., with Bv. BSLP 31.2.63-4, Gr. §345); hardly *vašnā-[di]y* XPg 7f (despite Lg. 9.320; see under *apiy*); *jᵛva-diy* A²Sd 3 (JAOS 51.229).

didā- sb. 'wall, stronghold, fortress': NPers. *diz*, pIE *dhiĝhā-*, cf. Skt. *dehí-* 'wall', Gk. τεῖχος, NEng. *dike*, *ditch* (§76.III, §88, §143.IV, §166). Cf. also *paradayadām*. *didā* nsf. DB 1.58; 2.39, 44; 3.61, 72; DSe 46; DSf 42. *didām* asf. DB 2.78; DSe 48°; DSf 54.

dipi- sb. 'inscription': Elam. *tup-pi*, Akk. *duppu* (§152.I): borrowed from Sumerian *dup-* (Bv. Gr. §282; hardly contamination of Iran. **ripi-* = Skt. *lipi-* 'smearing, writing', with Sum. *dup-*, as taken by Pisani, Riv. Stud. Or. 14.320, as Skt. *lipi-* 'writing' indicates writing with ink rather than engraving on stone). *dipi[š]* nsf. DB 4.90, 91f. *dipim* asf. DB 4.42, 48, 70, 73, 77, 89; XV 22, 24. *dipiyā* lsf. (§179.V) DB 4.47.

dug- vb., see *hadugā-*.

Dubāla- sb. 'Dubala', a district in Babylonia: Elam. *du-ib-ba-+* (§6, §107). *Dubāla* nsm. DB 3.79.

dūra- adj. 'far (in time or space)': Av. *dūra-*, NPers. *dūr*, Skt. *dūrá-* (§148.I). See also *dūradaša*, *duvaišta-*. *dūraiy* lsn. as adv. 'afar, far away, far and wide' (GAv. *dūire*, LAv. *dūire*, Skt. *dūré*; §65, §191.III) DNa 44. *dūraiy apiy* DSe 11, DZc 6, DE 18, XPa 9, XPb 18, XPc 8, XPd 13, XPf 13, XPh 10, XE 18, XV 14, A¹Pa 14f°, A²Hc 17. *dūraiapiy* DNa 12, *dūrayapiy* DNa 46 (§48, §136).

dūradaša adv. 'from afar', with preceding *hacā*: *dūra-* + adv. *-dā* as in *avadā* + abl. *-ša* as in *avadaša* (§135, §191.II; JAOS 54.37). DSf 23.

duruj- vb. 'lie, deceive': Av. *druj-* 'lie' (*draog-*, Bthl. AiW 767), pres. *družaiti*, sb. *druxš* 'principle of evil, devil', Skt. *drúhyati* 'deceives', Gm. *trügen*, pIE *dhrugh-* (§76.III). See also *drauga-*. *adurujiya* imf. (§101, §103.IV, §113, §128, §132.1, 2, 3, §214, §228.II) DB 1.39, 78; 3.80; 4.8, 10f, 13, 16, 18, 21, 24, 26f, 29; DBb 2f; DBc 2f; DBd 2; DBe 3f; DBf 1f; DBg 2f; DBh 2f; DBi 2f; DBj 2f. *adurujiyašanⁿ* 3d pl. imf. (§214, §218.I, §232.III) DB 4.34f. *duruxtam* nsn. past ptc. pass. (§103.IV, §122, §128, §132.1, 3, §242.I) DNb 52, 55f; asn. DB 4.44f, 49f.

duruva- adj. 'firm, secure': Av. *drva-*, Skt. *dhruvá-*; deriv. to root in OP ¹*dar-* (§122, §128, §150). *duruva* nsf. DB 4.39.

duvaišta- adj. 'very long, very far': superl. to *dūra-* (§156.III, §190.II, §191.III; MB Gr. §275), cf. Skt. *daviṣṭhá-* with slightly different formation.

duvaiš[*ta*]*m* asn. as adv. 'for a long time' DPe 23 (cf. remarks s.v. *hyā*).

duvara- sb. 'door': Av. *dvar-*, Skt. *dhvar-*, Gk. θύρᾱ, Lt. *forēs*, NEng. *door*, Lith. *dvãras* 'courtyard', pIE **dhu̯or- dhur-* and its extended forms **dhu̯oro-* etc.; see also *duvarθi-*. *duvarayā-maiy* lsn. (§136) DB 2.75, 89f.

duvarθi- sb. 'portico, colonnade': *duvar-* 'door' + *varθi-* 'cover, protection', to root *var-* 'cover', with haplology (§34, §129, §152.IV, §160.Ia; Bthl. AiW 766). *duvarθim* asn. XPa 12.

duvitāparanam adv. 'one after the other, in succession', a meaning agreeing with Elam. *šamakmar* 'ex ordine': *duvitā* (§191.III, §204.II), MPers. *dit* 'one or other of two' (Bthl., quoted by Tm. Lex. 102), cf. OP *duvitīyam* 'a second time', Skt. *dviṣ* 'twice', Lt. *bis*, + *paranam* 'before, previously' (Tm. l.c., and Vdt. Stud. 1.8). This is better than Tm.'s 'long aforetime', adv. *duvitā* 'long', GAv. *daibitā*, Skt. *dvitā* (cf. OP *duvaištam*), + *paranam* (as above); also than KT's *duvitāparnam* 'in two lines', containing the cognate of Skt. *parṇá-* 'wing' (supported by Wb. ZDMG 61.724-5, KIA 10-1, and by Hz. AMI 1.112n). DB1.10; DBa 17.

duvitīya- adj. 'second': GAv. *daibitya-*, LAv. *bitya-*, Skt. *dvitī́ya-*, pIE **du̯iti̯o-* (§76.III, §144.II, §204.II). See also *duvitāparanam*. *duvitīyam* asn. as adv. 'a second time', DB 2.37f, 57, 3.77; as inner obj., 'a second (uprising)', DB 3.24 (not *duvitīya-ma udapatatā* 'was second to rise up from me', as Bthl. AiW 964 takes it, since *udapatatā* nowhere else takes an expression of the person against whom uprising is made).

duš- insep. prefix 'ill': Av. *duš-*, Skt. *duṣ-*, Gk. δυσ- (§76.III); in *dušiyāra-*, *duškarta-*.

dušiyāra- sb. 'evil year, bad harvest, famine': *duš-* + *yār-* 'year' made thematic, Av. *yār-*, Gk. ὥρᾱ 'season', NGm. *Jahr* (§140.VII, §143.II). *dušiyāram* nsn. DPd 19f. *dušiyārā* absn. DPd 17.

duškarta- adj. 'ill-done', opposite of *naiba-* (Hz. ApI 143-4): *duš-* + *karta-* 'done, made', past ptc. pass. to *kar-*. *duškartam* nsn. DSe 31f; XPh 42.

draug- vb., see *duruj-* and *draujīya-*.

drauga- sb. 'the Lie', the evil force opposed to Ahuramazda, Avestan *Druǰ*: Av. *draoga-*, NPers. *durōγ*, Skt. *drógha- droha-* '(malicious) injury', pIE **dhrougho-*, cf. NGm. *Trug* 'deceit', and OP *duruj-*, *draujana-*, *draujīya-* (§70, §76.III, §101, §103.IV, §106, §122, §128, §132.2, 3, §143.I, V). *drauga* nsm. DB 1.34, 4.34; DPd 20. *draugā* absm. DB 4.37; DPd 17f.

draujana- adj. 'deceitful', i.e. 'adherent of the Lie': deriv. of *drauga-* (§101, §132.2, §147.II), cf. GAv. *drəgvant-* 'adherent of the *Druǰ*' (Hz. ApI 140-1). *draujana* nsm. DB 4.38, 63, 68. *draujanam* asm. DNb 12.

draujīya- vb. 'regard as a lie', denom. to *drauga-* (§217). [*drau*]*jīyāhy* 2d sg. subj. (§222.II, §227.I) DB 4.43.

drayah- sb. 'sea': Av. *zrayah-*, NPers. *daryā*, Skt. *jráyas-* 'expanse', pIE **ǵrei̯os-* (§88, §113, §128, §156.II). Decl., §185.I. See also *paradraya*. *draya* asn. DB 5.23; DPe 15; DZc 10. *drayahyā* lsn. (§136, §251A; wrongly taken as gen., Hz. ApI 141-3) DB 1.15, DPe 14, DSe 28°; *drayahiyā* (§27) XPh 23.

naiy adv. 'not': Av. *nōiṯ*, Phl. *nē*, Skt. *ned*; from pIE **ne*, Skt. *na*, Lt. *ne-scio* 'I don't know', + **id*, asn. of pron. *i-*, Lt. *id*, OP *id-am*, etc. (§69, §84, §191.I, §291.II, §292a). DB 1.32°, 48, 49 ter, 52, 53, 71, 91°; 2.21, 24, 31, 51, 84; 3.15, 86; 4.44, 47 bis, 51, 55, 58, 63 bis, 63f, 64°, 65 bis; 5.16°, 31; DPd 11; DNb 7f, 12, 13, 21, 23, 36, 40; DSe 36, 40 bis, 43°; DSj 3; XV 22. *nai-maiy* (§136) DB 4.64. *nai-mā* DNb 8, 10, 19. *nai-pati-mā* (§133) DNb 20. *nai-šim* DB 4.49. *naiy-diš* (§136) DB 4.73, 78.

naiba- adj. 'beautiful, (religiously) good', replacing GAv. *vahu-* 'good', and opposite of *duškarta-* (Hz. AMI 8.68, ApI 266-7): NPers. *nēv* 'brave, good' (§11, §75.V, §143.III). *naibā* nsf. DPd 8. *naibam* nsn. XPa 13, 16; XPg 4; XV 20. *naibam* asn. DSe 32°; DSi 4°; DSp 2f°; XPh 43.

naucaina- adj. 'of cedar': NPers. *nōž*, *nōžān* 'pine cone'; therefore *naucaina-* 'pine-cone-shaped' (§147.III), appropriate to the cedar (König, Burgbau 53-4; Hz. AMI 3.58). *naucaina* nsm. DSf 30f.

naθ- vb. 'perish', causative (§123.2, §215) 'injure, destroy': Av. *nas-*, Skt. *naś-*, Gk. νέκυς 'corpse', Lt. acc. *nec-em* 'destruction', *nocet* 'harms', pIE **neḱ-* (§87).

vi- + *naθ-* caus. 'injure, harm': *vināθayatiy* (§215) DNb 17f. *viyanāθaya* imf. (§122, §123.2, §215) DB 4.66. *vināθayāⁿtiy* 3d pl. subj. (§222.II, §232.I) A²Sa 5°, A²Ha 7° (conj. Kent). *vināθayaiš* opt. (§215, §223.II, §228.III) DNb 20, 21. *vinastahyā* gsn. past ptc. pass. as sb. (§93, §122, §242.II) DNb 18.

Nadiⁿtabaira- sb. 'Nidintu-Bel', a Babylonian rebel: Elam. *nu-ti-ut-be-ul*, Akk. *ni-din-tú-ᵘᵘbēl* (§75.V, §76.V, §107). *Naditabaira* nsm. DB 1.77, 92f; 2.1; 4.12; DBd 1. *Naditabairam* asm. DB 1.80, 84; 2.4, 5. *Naditabairahyā* gsm. DB 1.85, 89, 95.

napāt- sb. 'grandson': Av. Skt. *napāt-*, Lt. *nepōs*, pIE **nepōt-* (§75.I, §110, §142). *napā* nsm. (§124.5, §188.I) AmH 4; DB 1.3; DBa 4; A¹Pa 16°.

Nabukudracara- sb. 'Nebuchadrezzar', son of Nabonidus; name assumed by the rebels Nidintu-Bel and Arkha: Elam. *nab-ku-tur-ra-sir*, Akk. *nabu-kudurri-uṣur* (§32, §33, §75.V, §128, §163.-VI). *Nabukudracara* nsm. DB 3.80f, 89; 4.14, 29f; DBd 3f; written *Nabukuracara* (§52.VI) DBi 5f. *Nabukᵘdracara* (§22) DB 1.78f, 84, 93.

Nabunaita- sb. 'Nabonidus', last king of the New Babylonian Empire, 556–39. B.C: Elam. *na-bu-ni-da*, Akk. *nabù-na'id*; Gk. Λαβίνητος (Hdt. 1.74, etc.). *Nabunaitahyā* gsm. DB 1.79. *Nabunaitahya* (§36.IVb) DB 3.81; 4.14, 30; DBd 5f; DBi 7f.

nāman- sb. 'name': Av. *nāman-*, NPers. *nām*, Skt. *nā́man-*, Lt. *nōmen*, pIE **nōmen-*, cf. Gk. ὄνομα, NEng. *name* (§109, §110, §155.III). See also *Anāmaka-*.

nāmaⁿ, suffixless lsn. used with masc. and nt. generic nouns to denote specification (§112, §187, §251C, §312): DB 1.28, 30, 36, 37, 74, 77, 92; 2.8f, 9, 14°, 19, 22, 29, 33, 49, 65, 79, 82, 95; 3.5, 12, 13, 22 bis, 31, 34, 44, 51, 56, 78, 84; 4.8, 10, 12f, 15f, 18, 20, 23, 26, 29, 83 bis, 84 bis, 85, 86°; 5.5, 8, 27; DSe 45°; DSf 31, 46; DZc 9; XPf 18, 19; A²Hc 14f; A³Pa 19, 20; Sa 2f.

nāmā, either asn. **nāmă* or lsn. *nāmāⁿ* (with lengthened grade), specialized for similar use with fem. generic nouns because of similarity of ending (§67.II, §187, §249L, §312; cf. Tm. Lex. 105, with lit.; not with Foy, KZ 35.11, 37.505, IF 12.172n, nor with Debrunner, IF 52.153): DB 1.58, 58f; 2.27f, 39, 44, 53, 59, 72; 3.11, 23, 61, 66, 72, 79; 5.4°.

nay- vb. 'lead': Av. *nayeiti*, Skt. *náyati*. Conj., §213. *anaya* imf. DB 2.88; 3.88°; 5.12. [*a*]*nayaⁿ* 3d pl. imf. (§232.II) DB 5.28. *anayatā* imf. mid. as pass. (§235.II) DB 1.82, 2.73; 5.26°. Some or all of these are possibly *ānay-*, from *ā* + *nay-*.

fra- + *nay-* 'lead forth, provide': *frānayam* 1st sg. imf. (§226.II) DB 1.87.

nar- sb. 'man': Av. Skt. *nar-*, Gk. ἀνήρ, cf. Lt. *Ner-ō*; in *ūv-nara-* (§142).

nāv- sb. 'ship': Skt. *nā́us*, Gk. ναῦς, Lt. *nāv-is*, pIE **nāv-* (§142). See also *nāviyā-*. [*nāva*] npf. (§183.IV) DZc 11 (supplied by Tm. Lex. 52).

navama- adj. 'ninth': Av. *naoma-*, Skt. *navamá-*, pAr. *navama-* remade from pIE *neu̯eno-* after pAr. *daśama-* 'tenth' (§149.II, §204.IV), cf. Lt. *nōnus*. *navama* nsm. DB 1.10; DBa 16f.

nāviyā- fem. adj. as sb., 'navigability', i.e. 'impossibility of fording the river on foot': Av. *nāvaya-* 'navigable', Skt. *navyà-*, adj. to *nāv-* 'ship' (§144.V). Hardly collective, 'collection of ships, flotilla', and certainly not lsf. to *nāv-*, 'on shipboard'; cf. König, RuID 70–1, and esp. Kent, JAOS 62.269–71 (with lit.), 63.67. *nāviyā* nsf. DB 1.86.

nāh- sb. 'nose': Av. *nāh-*, Skt. *nās-*, Lt. *nārēs*, NEng. *nose*, pIE **nās-* (§110, §142). *nāham* asm. (§118.I, §185.IV) DB 2.74, 88f.

ni- prep. and verbal prefix 'down': Av. *nī*, Skt. *ni-*, pIE **ni*; in adv. *nipadiy*, and with verbs *ar-, kan-, çay-, paiθ-, yam-, stā-, had-*.

nij- verbal prefix 'away': sandhi form of pIE **nis-* before voiced stops, generalized, cf. Av. *niš-*, Skt. *niṣ-* (§120); with verb *ay-* 'go'.

nipadiy phrasal adv. and prep., 'on the track of, close after': prep. *ni-* + loc. *padiy*, to *pad-* 'foot' (§76.III, §136, §140, §191.IV). *nipadiy* adv. DB 2.73; prep. with acc. DB 3.73.

nipišti- sb. 'impression': deriv. of *ni-* + *paiθ-* (§152.III). [*nip*]*iš*[*tiyā*] lsf. DB 4.90 (conj. of Kent, JAOS 62.268).

niyāka- sb. 'grandfather': Av. *nyāka-* (§146.-III); cf. *apaniyāka-*. [*ni*]*yāka* nsm. DSf 13; [*nºyā*]*kama* (§22; for *-kam-maiy*, §41, §52.I, §130, §138.I) asm. A²Sa 4.

niyašādayam, see *had-*.

Nisāya- sb. 'Nisaya', a district in Media: Elam. *nu-iš-ša-įa*, Akk. *ni-is-sa-a-a* (§116). Perhaps from *ni-* 'down' + *sāya-*, to root Av. *si-* *say-* 'lie', Skt. *śī-*, Gk. κεῖται 'lies', pIE **ḱei-*. *Nisāya* nsm. DB 1.58.

nīšādayam, see *had-*.

nūram adv. 'now': Av. *nūrəm*; from pIE **nŭ* 'now' (Av. *nū*, Skt. *nŭ*, Lt. *nu-nc*, NEng. *now*) + final of (pAr.) **dūram* 'long' (§148.I), cf. *dūraiy*. DB 4.53.

pā- vb. 'protect': Av. *pā-*, pres. *pāiti*, Phl. *pātan*, Skt. *pā-*, pres. *páti* (ablaut, §122). See also *xšaçapāvan-*. *apayaiy* 1st sg. imf. mid. (Bv. BSLP 33.2.151-2; Kent, Lg. 9.42; §71, §214, §233.III; wrongly to Skt. *pī́-* 'swell', Wb. ZfA 41.320-1) XPf 39. *pādiy* 2d sg. imv. (§208, §237.I) DPe 21f. *pātuv* (§208, §237.II) AsH 12, 14; DPd 16; DPh 10; DNa 52; DSe 50; DSf 57; DSj 6°; DSn 2°; DSs 7°; DSt 8°; DH 8; XPa 18, 20; XPb 28; XPc 12, 15; XPd 18; XPf 45, 48; XPg 13; XPh 57; XSc 5°; XV 25f; A¹Pa 22f; D²Sa 3; A²Hb°; A²Hc 19. *pāⁿtuv* 3d pl. imv. (§237.II) A²Sa 5°; A²Sd 4; A²Ha 6°; A³Pa 25. *pāta* nsm. past ptc. pass. (§242.II) DPe 22.

pati- + *pā-* mid. 'protect one's self against', with *hacā* + abl.: *patipayauwā* (§28; not wrongly written, despite MB Gr. §69) 2d sg. imv. mid. (§71, §214, §237.III) DB 4.38.

paiθ- vb. 'cut, engrave, adorn': Av. *paēsa-* 'adornment', Skt. *piśáti* 'cuts, adorns', Gk. ποικίλος 'variegated', OCS *pĭsati* 'to write', pIE **peiḱ-*, cf. Lt. *pingit* 'embroiders, paints' (Wb. AfOF 7.42). Cf. also *nipišti-*, *paišiyā-*, *Paišiyāuvādā-*, *pisa-*. *apiθa* imf. DSf 54 (§211; cf. König, Burgbau 72). [*ap*]*i*[*θ*]*i*[*ya*] imf. pass. (§220) DB 4.91 (JAOS 62.268). [*p*]*ištā* nsf. past ptc. pass. (§242.I) DSf 42 (Bv. BSLP 30.1.63; König, Burgbau 71; not [*d*]*ištā* with Hz. ApI 121-5].

ni- + *paiθ-* 'engrave, inscribe, write': *niyapaišam* 1st sg. aor. (§92, §102, §130, §218.I, §226.II) DB 4.71. *nipaištanaiy* inf. (§93, §122, §238) XV 24f. *nipištām* asf. past ptc. pass. (§93) XV 22f. *nipištā* npf. XPh 31. *nipištam* nsn. (§122) DB 4.47, 47f; DNb 57°; DSe 52.

paišiyā- sb. 'script, written text': deriv. of *paiθ-* (§89, §144.V). See also *Paišiyāuvādā-*. *pai*[*š*]*iyā* nsf. DB 4.91 (conj. of Kent, JAOS 62.268).

*Paišiyā*ʰ*uvādā-* sb. 'Paishiyauvada': Akk. *pi-ši-'-ḫu-ma-du*. Perhaps, with Justi, IFA 17.107, 'Pasargadae', from *paišiyā-* 'writing' + ʰ*uvādā-* 'abode' (§72, §89, §126, §127, §142, §166, §166.I): 'Home of the Archives and Sacred Writings' (on Pasargadae, cf. also König, RuID 66; but Hz. ApI 275-6, modifying his view in AMI 1.86n, takes prior element to be *pati-*, *pati-* becoming *paši-*, with epenthesis; Bthl. AiW 907-8 normalizes *Piši-* after the Akk., but gives no etymology). *Paišiyāuvādām* asf. DB 3.42. *Paiši*[*yā*]*uvādāyā* absf. DB 1.36f.

pa[*camām*] adj. 'fifth', asf.; wrong restoration of Wb. at DB 5.3 (cf. Kent, JNES 2.109).

pat- vb. 'fly': Av. *pat-aiti*, Skt. *pát-ati*, Gk. πέτεται, Lt. *petit* 'seeks', pIE **pet-*.

ud- + *pat-* 'rise up, rebel' (cf. Bv. TPS 1945.64-66): *udapatatā* imf. mid. (§84, §213, §235.II) DB 1.36, 38, 74, 78; 2.10, 14f; 3.24, 79.

patiy adv., prep., prefix (§140.I, §191.I): Av. *paiti*, Gk. (dial.) ποτί, pIE **poti*, cf. pIE **proti* in Skt. *práti*, Gk. Hom. προτί, classical πρός (cf. Lg. 20.9-10).

(1) Adv. 'thereto, again': DB 2.37, 43, 57; 3.64, 77. *pati-maiy* (§136) DNb 32f. *nai-pati-mā* (§133, §136) DNb 20. *yadi-patiy* (§136) DNa 38. *tya-patiy* XPa 15; XPf 40f.

(2) Prep. (§271) with acc.: DB 5.2 'during'; DNb 22 'against' (Hz. ApI 273 reads *par*[*s*]*aiy* 'in court', sb. to root *fraθ-*); postposed DB 2.62 'on'. Encl., with acc. 'during' DB 1.20 (§133, §136); with inst. 'near, at' DB 2.16°, 3.26; with loc. 'on, upon' DB 2.76, 91; 3.52, 92. Bv. BSLP 42.2.70 takes all these as adverbs except DB 2.62, DNb 22.

(3) Prefix with verbs *avahya-*, *ay-*, *xšay-*, *jan-*, *pā-*, *fraθ-*, *ā-bar-*, *zbā-*; prior element in nouns *patikara-*, *Patigrabanā-*, perhaps *Pātišuvari-* and *Paišiyāuvādā-*, and in phrasal adv. *patipadam*; cf. also *patiš*, *patišam*.

patikara- sb. 'picture, (sculptured) likeness': Phl. *patkar-*, NPers. *paikar-*; *pati-* + *kara-* to root *kar-* (§143.V). *patikaram* asm. DSn 1°. *patikarā* apm. DB 4.71, 73, 77; DNa 41.

Patigrabanā- sb. 'Patigrabana', a town in Parthia: Elam. *pat-ti-ig-ràb-ba-na*; from *pati-* + root *grab-* + suffix (§33, §103.IV, §147.I). *Patigrabanā* nsf. DB 3.4f.

patipadam phrasal adv. (§191.IV) 'on its base, in its own place': *pati-* (§136, §140.I) + acc. *padam* (see *pada-*; §76.III, §122). DB 1.62.

patiš prep. with acc. 'against': *pati-* + adv. *-s*, cf. Lt. *ex*, *abs*, *ops-* in *os-tendō*, *sups-* in *sus-tineō*, Skt. *ni* and *niṣ*, Gk. ἀπό ἄψ, ἀμφί ἀμφίς. See also *patišam*. DB 1.93; 2.33, 38, 43f, 52f, 58, 67; 3.36, 43, 65.

patišam adv. 'in addition': extension of *patiš*, cf. for formation Osc. *per-um* 'without' to (Lt.) *per*, and for meaning Gk. πρὸς δέ 'and besides', Lt. *atque* from *ad-que* 'and thereto' (OP *patiy*, Gk. πρός, Lt. *ad* agree in marking something as an addition). *patišam* DB 4.89 (*pᵃ* probable but not certain KT); [*pat*]*išam* DB 4.90 (restoration of Konig, Klotho 4.45; see also Kent, JAOS 62.267-8).

Pātišʰuvari- adj. 'Patischorian' (§167): Elam. *ba-ut-ti-iš-mar-ri-iš*, Akk. *pa-id-di-iš-ḫu-ri-iš*, Gk. (pl.) Πατεισχορεῖς. Perhaps pAr. **patı-*, with vriddhi (§126), + **syāra-* '(of the plain) before the Hvara Mts.' (§117), with combination (§140.VI) of sandhi forms (so Hz. ApI 183-4, who however disregards the ă in the penult of the OP). *Pātišuvariš* nsm. DNc 1.

paθi- sb. 'path, way' (§76.II, §152.I, §179.-III): Av. *paθ- paθā-*, Skt. *panthan- path-*. *paθım* asf. DNa 58.

pad- sb. 'foot': Av. Skt. *pad-*, Gk. ποδ-, Lt. *ped-* (§142); in *nıpadiy*, cf. also *pada-*, *pāda-*, *pasti-*.

pada- sb. 'footing, step, station': Av. *paδa-* 'foot (as measure)', Skt. *padá-* 'step, footstep, place', Gk. πέδον 'ground'; extension of *pad-* (§143.-II). In *Garmapada-*, *patipadam*; see also *pad-*, *pāda-*.

pāda- sb. 'foot': LAv. *pāδa-* 'step, pace', Skt. *pádа-* 'foot', Gt. *fōtu-*, extension of stem in pIE nom. **pōd-s*, acc. **pōd-m̥*, seen in Gk. Dor. πώς (§76.III, §122, §126, §143.II). Cf. also *pad-*, *pada-*. *pādaibiyā* idm. (§189) DNb 41.

par- vb. 'communicate': Av. ⁴*par-* 'hindurch-, hinubergehen' (Bthl. AiW 851), Gk. πείρω 'I pierce (as with a spit)', Gt. *faran* 'to travel'. *parta*[*mtaiy*] nsn. past ptc. pass. (§242.I) DNb 54 (dubious conj. of Kent, Lg. 15.167, 173-4).

¹*para-* adj. 'later', possibly in *hyāparam* (q.v.): Av. *para-* 'farther', Skt. *pára-* 'distant', Gk. πέραν 'beyond'.

²*para* prep. with acc. 'beyond' (§32, §63.I): Av. *parō* 'before', Skt. *purás* 'before', Gk. πάρος 'before'; DPe 15; DPh 5; DH 4f. See also *paradayadām*, *paradraya*.

parā postpos. with acc. 'along', and verbal prefix 'forth' (§132.3): Av. ²*parā* 'before', Skt. *purā́* 'before, formerly', Gk. παρά 'alongside'; in *avaparā* and with *ay-*, *ar-*, *gam-*, *bar-*.

parauvaiy lsn. as sb. 'in the east': *pᵃrᵃu*[*vᵃ*]*iyᵃ* DPe 15, a misreading for *pᵃrᵃ : dᵃrᵃ yᵃ* (uninscribed space between *rᵃ* and *yᵃ*) = *para : dra ya*; see under *paradraya*.

paradayadām sb. asf., perhaps 'pleasant retreat' (§55.II, §143.IV): A²Sd 3. Possibly miswritten *pᵃrᵃdᵃyᵃdᵃamᵃ* for *pᵃrᵃidᵃidᵃmᵃ* = *paridaidam*, Av. *pairıdaēza-* 'Umwallung, Ummauerung' (Bthl. AiW 865), borrowed in Gk. παράδεισος 'park', cf. JAOS 51.229; or for *pᵃrᵃdᵛdᵛdᵃamᵃ* = *paradıdām*, from ²*para* 'beyond' + *didā-* 'wall' (q.v.), as 'that which is beyond or behind the wall' (cf. Scheil 21.93; Bv. BSLP 30.1.67 *j'vadıy paradayadām* 'paradis de vie').

paradraya phrasal adv. 'across the sea' (§44, §191.IV): ²*para* 'beyond' + acc. *draya* 'sea'. DNa 28f; DSe 29°; XPh 24. *paradraıya* (§48) A?P 24 (Hz. ApI 142). As two words, *para draya* DPe 15 (Cameron, JNES 2.307-8).

parana- adj. 'former': deriv. (§147.II) of stem in OP ²*para*, *parā* (cf. Bthl. AiW 854), Av. ²*parā*, *parō*, Skt. *purā́* 'formerly' (hardly to be normalized *parna-*, with MB Gr. §267, to Gt. *faírneis* 'old'). See also *duvıtāparanam*. *paranam* asn. as adv. 'formerly' DB 1.51, D²Sb 3.

pariy prep. and prefix 'around, about': Av. *pairi*, Skt. *pári*, Gk. περί, Lt. *per* 'through', pIE **peri* (§64, §75.I, §113, §140.I). Prep. with acc. 'about' DB 1.54. Prefix with *ay-*, *bar-*; cf. also *pariyana-*.

pariyana- sb. 'superiority': deriv. (§147.II) of *pariy*, in meaning seen in Av. *pairi* 'vorne, über ... hin', Skt. *pári* as prefix 'much, excessively', cf. Gk. περισσός 'excessive' (otherwise Hz. ApI 273, Sen 250). *pariyanam* nsn. DNb 52.

paru- adj. 'much, many': Av. *pouru-*, Skt. *purú-*, Gk. πολύς, Gt. *filu*, pIE *p̥lu-* (§63.I, §107). See also *paruzana-*. *paruv* nsm. (§114, §127, §140.I) DB 4.49; DSf 56 bis. *parūnām* gpm. DSf 4, 5; DE 9, 10; XPa 5 bis; XPb 9, 10; XPc 4f, 5; XPd 6f, 7f; XPf 6, 7; XPh 5, 6; XE 9f, 11; XV 7, 8; A¹Pa 7°, 8°; A²Hc 6 bis. *parūnām* gpf. DPe 4. *parūvnām* (§23.II) gpm. DNa 6, 7; DSe 6, 7; A³Pa 6, 7.

paruva- adj. 'being before in time or place' (§35.II): Av. *paurva-*, Skt. *pū́rva-*, pIE *pr̥ŭos* (§68, §150), cf. Gk. Ion. πρώϊος 'early'. See also *paruviyata*, *paruviyaθā*. *paruvā* npm. 'former' DB 4.51. *paruvam* asn. as adv. 'formerly' DB 1.9; DBa 15f; DSe 43°, 47; XPh 36, 39; *paruvam-ciy* DB 1.63, 67, 69.

paruviyata, adv. with preceding *hacā*, 'from long ago': *paruviya-* (i.e. *parvya-*, deriv. of *paruva-*), Av. *paouruya-*, Skt. *pūrvyá-*, + adv. suffix *-taʰ*, Av. *-tō*, Skt. *-tas*, Gk. *-τος*, Lt. *-tus* as in *funditus*, pIE *-tos* (§191.II). Cf. also *paruviyaθā*. DB 1.7, 8, 45; DBa 11, 12.

[*paruv*]*iyaθā* adv. 'at first attempt': *paruviya-* (see *paruviyata*) + adv. suffix *-θā*, Av. *-θa*, Skt. *-thā* (§191.II). DSj 3 (conj. of Brandenstein, WZKM 39.49–51; cf. note ad loc.).

paruzana- adj. 'having many men, or many kinds of men' ('having men of all tongues', Wb. ZfA 44.165, after the Akk.): *paru-* 'many' + *zana-* 'man' (§9.III, §88, §120, §161.IIa). *paruzanānām* (§140.I) gpf. DE 15f; XE 15f; A¹Pa 12°. *paruvzanānām* (§23.II) XPb 15f; XPd 11. *paruv zanānām* (§23.II, §44) XPa 8; XPc 7; XPf 11; XPh 9; XV 12.

Parga- sb. 'Parga', a mountain in Persia: Elam. *par-rak-qa*, NPers. *Purg* (§30). *Parga* nsm. DB 3.44.

partara- sb. 'battle' (as in Elam. and Akk. versions): extension of *-r/n-* stem (§30, §148.I, §154.I), cf. Av. *pəšana-* 'battle', Skt. *pŕ̥tana-* 'battle, army', to root in Av. *pərət-ənte* 'they fight' (Bv. TPS 1945.63–4; not agency noun 'fighter, foe' as taken by Wb. KIA 90–1, Bv. Gr. §277; not *paratara-* 'foe', with Wackernagel, KZ 59.29–30, as compar. to [Skt.] *pára-* 'distant' = RV 'enemy'). *partaram* asn. DNa 47.

Parθava- (§29.n2, §31) adj. 'Parthian', also masc. as sb. 'Parthia', a province of the Persian Empire: Elam. *par-tu-ma*, Akk. *pa-ar-tu-ú*, Gk. Παρθία. Extension (§150) of stem seen with vriddhi in *Pārsa-*, but with dialectal difference in the θ/s (§9.VI, §87).

(1) 'Parthian': *Parθava* nsm. DN iv; A?P 4. *Parθavaibiš* ipm. DB 2.96.

(2) 'Parthia': *Parθava* nsm. DB 1.16; 2.7, 92; DPe 15; DNa 22; DSe 21°; DSm 8°; XPh 20. *Parθavaiy* lsm. DB 2.94°, 96°; 3.5, 10.

parna-, see *duvitāparanam*, *parana-*.

¹*parsa-* vb., see *fraθ-*.

²*parsa-* sb. 'court', only in Hz. ApI 273; for his *pa*[*r*]*saiy* lsm. DNb 22, see under *patiy*.

Pārsa- adj. 'Persian'; also masc. as sb., 'Persia', a province of the Persian Empire: Elam. *par-sin*, Akk. *pa-ar-su*, Gk. Πέρσης, Περσία (§9.VI, §87, §126, §143.III). See also *Parθava-*.

(1) 'Persian': *Pārsa* nsm. DB 1.49; 2.18, 19, 49; 3.13, 26, 31, 32, 56, 84; 4.16, 26, 83, 84 bis, 85 bis, 86; 5.8°; DPe 22; DNa 13, 46; DN i; DSe 12f; DZc 7; XPh 12; A?P 1. *Pārsam* asm. DB 2.81; 3.2, 29f; DPe 21. *Pārsahyā* gsm. DNa 13f, 43; DSe 13; XPh 12. *Pārsā* ism. DPe 8.

(2) 'Persia': *Pārsa* nsm. AsH 3 (for loc., §52.I); DB 1.14, 41; 2.7; DPd 6f; DSm 6°. *Pārsam* asm. AsH 8f; DB 1.46; 3.33, 34; 4.9, 28; DZc 12. *Pārsam-cā* DB 1.66. *Pārsā* ism. XPa 14 (here 'Persepolis', acc. to Cameron, by letter; §166, §166.I). *Pārsā* absm. DNa 18, 46f; DSe 17°; DZc 7f, 10; XPh 16. *Pārsā* for lsm. AmH 2 (§56.V, §314b; wrongly Hz. AMI 4.132–4, 8.17–9, as instr. of extent); for nsm. AmH 5 (§53; not nsf. adj., as taken by Hz. AMI 8.20–1, 34). *Pārsaiy* lsm. DB 1.2, 34; 2.9°; 3.23, 24, 28, 34, 52, 53, 77; DBa 2.

pasā prep. 'after', temporal with acc. and local with gen. (Bv. BSLP 33.2.153): Av. *pasča*, NPers. *pas*, Skt. *paścā́*, isn. to stem in Lith. (dat.) adv. and prep. *páskui* 'behind, later, after' (Foy, KZ 35.26); pIE *po* as in Lt. *po-liō, positus*, Gk. ἀ-πό, + *sqʷē*, inst. to root noun from *seqʷ-* 'follow', Av. *hacaite*, Skt. *sácate*, Gk. ἕπεται, Lt.

sequitur (§105; Uhlenbeck, Etym. Wtb. d. altind. Spr., s.v. *paccá*). The *s* in *pasā* is OP for Med. *šc*, Av. *sč*, from pAr. *śc* (Bv. Gr. §114; otherwise Mt. Gr. §114). Less probably pAr. **pas* (Lith. *pàs* 'at, to') from the same **po* + adv. -*s* as in OP *patiš*, + -*cā* isn. of stems in -*añc*-, for -*acā* (from **-ņcā*) by influence of contracted forms like Skt. *prācá* (**pra-acā*) to *prāñc*- (**pra-añc*-) 'forward', cf. similar analogical form in Skt. adv. *nīcá* 'downward' (for **ni-acā*) to *nyañc*-. Hardly from **pas* (as above) + -*ā* after its opposite *parā* 'before' (Bthl. AiW 879). Direct cognation with Lith. *pãskui* is eliminated by the second and third etymologies; with Av. *pasča*, Skt. *paścá*, by the third. *pasā* with gen. DB 3.32; with acc. XPf 31 and in *pasāva* (q.v.).

pasāva phrasal adv. (§191.IV) 'after that, afterwards': *pasā* + asn. *ava* (§131). DB 1.27, 30, 32, 33, 34°, 35f, 40, 43, 46, 54, 72, 73f, 75, 79, 82, 83, 86, 91, 94; 2.1, 3, 4, 12, 16, 19, 21, 27, 31, 32, 47, 49°, 51, 52, 62, 64, 67, 71, 72, 81, 84f, 94; 3.1, 4, 9, 12f, 15, 20, 25, 29, 33, 36f, 41, 50, 59, 70, 73, 75, 81, 84, 86, 90f°; 4.5, 35, 91; 5.3, 6, 9, 10f, 13, 21°, 23, 25°, 29; DSe 48; DSf 25; DZc 10; XPh 36; XSc 3; XV 23; A¹Pa 21°; D²Sb 4°. *pasāva-šim* DB 2.76, 90. *pasāva-šaiy* DB 2.88. *pasāva-dim* DNa 33. *pasāva-maiy* XPh 32.

pasti- sb. 'foot-soldier': Skt. *patti-*, from pIE **ped-* 'foot' (OP *pad-*) + suffix -*ti-* (§85, §152.III; Wb. Grab 40, Hz. ApI 94–8). *pastiš* nsm. DNb 43, 45.

pitar- sb. 'father': Av. *pitar-*, NPers. *pidar*, Skt. *pitár-*, Gk. πατήρ, Lt. *pater*, Gt. *fadar*, pIE **pəter-* (§63.II, §75.I, §76.I, §154.II); see also *hamapitar-*. *pitā* nsm. (§36.II, §124.5, §186.II) DB 1.4 bis, 5 bis, 6; 2.93; DBa 5, 6, 6f, 7, 8; DSf 12, 58; XPa 15; XPc 12; XPf 16, 17, 19, 23, 31, 33, 42; XPg 7; XSa 2; XV 18; A¹Pa 20f; D²Sb 4°. *piça* gsm. (§78, §124.5, §186.II) XPa 20; XPc 14; XPf 35, 38, 47.

Pirāva- sb. 'Nile' (§75.V, §124.II, §166.VI): *Pirāva* nsm. DZc 9, in naming phrase, anacoluthic for abl. after *hacā*; either 'Ivory River', as deriv. adj. to *piru-* 'ivory', or possibly plural 'The Tusks' (JAOS 51.209).

piru- sb. 'ivory' (§75.V, §153.I): Elam. *pi-ru-š*, Akk. *pīlu-*, with cognates (or borrowings) in Eastern Asiatic languages (Przyluski, BSLP 27.3.220–2; Scheil, Rev. d'Assyr. 24.120; Bv. BSLP 30.1.62; König, Burgbau 66; Hz. AMI 3.67–8). *piruš* nsm. DSf 43.

piθ-, vb., see *paiθ-*.

pisa- sb. 'raft': perhaps originally 'cut material', from root *paiθ-* (§143.III). *pisā* ism. or isn , with collective meaning (§255), DB 5.24.

piša- or *paiša-*, vb. stem, see *paiθ-*.

Putāya- adj. 'man of Put, Libyan' (§75.V, §76.V, §144.III); pl., 'Libya', a province of the Persian Empire (Cameron, JNES 2.308–9): Elam. *pu-ú-ti-ia-ap*, Akk. *pu-u-ṭa* (Lg. 13.299, 15.165). *Putāya* nsm. A?P 27. *Putāyā* npm. DNa 29f; DSe 29°; XPh 28.

puça- sb. 'son': Av. *puθra-*, Ars. Phl. *puhr*, NPers. *pus*, Skt. *putrá-*, Osc. *puclo-*, pIE **putlo-* (§64, §75.I, §78, §148.III). *puça* nsm. AmH 3; AsH 4; CMb 2°; DB 1.3, 28, 39, 53, 74, 78, 79; 2.9; 3.25, 79, 81; 4.9, 14, 28, 30, 83, 84° bis, 85 bis, 86; DBa 3; DBb 6; DBd 6; DBh 7; DBi 8f; DPa 5; DPb; DPe 5; DPh 2; DNa 13, 14; DSa 2; DSb 10; DSc; DSd 2; DSe 12, 13; DSf 7; DSg 2°; DSi 2°; DSj 2°; DSk 3; DSm 2°; DSy 3; DZb 5f; DZc 6; DE 20; DH 2; XPa 10; XPb 20; XPc 9; XPd 14; XPe 4; XPf 14; XPh 11, 12; XPj; XPk; XSc 2; XE 20; XV 15; A¹Pa 15f; A¹I bis; D²Sb 2°; A²Sa 1, 2 bis, 3 bis; A²Sb; A²Sc 0° bis; A²Sd 2; A²Ha 2°, 3, 3°, 4, 4°; A²Hc 10, 11, 12, 13f, 15; A³Pa 13, 14, 15, 16, 18, 19, 20; Wa 7; Wb 8; Wc 9; Wd 9; Sa 8°. *pucā* npm. XPf 28; as nsm. A²Hb (§53; with -*ā* after *napā*, acc. to Brd. WZKM 39.92).

farnah- sb., see *Vidafarnah-*.

fra- prefix 'before, forth' (as prep., not found in OP): Av. *frā*, Skt. *pra*, Gk. πρό, Lt. *prŏ-fessus*, Gt. *fra-*, pIE **pro* (§33, §61, §75.II, §106, §132.3). Found with verbs *aiš-*, *jan-*, *nay-*, *var-*, *mā-*, *sā-*, *haj-*; in nouns *framātar-*, *framānā-*, *Fravarti-*; in phrasal adv. *fraharavam*; with suffixes and extensions, in *fratama-*, *fratara-*, *fraθara-*, *fravata*, *fraša-*.

fratama- adj. 'foremost': *fra-* + superl. suffix -*tama-*, Av. *fratəma-*, Skt. -*tama-* (§190.III). *fratamā* npm. DB 1.57; 2.77; 3.48f, 51, 74, 90°, 91.

fratara- adj. 'prior, further': *fra-* + comp. suffix -*tara-*, Av. *fratara-*, Skt. adv. *pratarám*, Gk. πρότερος (§106, §190.III). *fratara* nsm. DNb 38 (Sen 249 needlessly takes as error for *frataram*).

frataram asn. XPg 11; adv. 'previously' DB 3.26, A¹Pa 21.

fratarta DB 3.26, incorrect reading for *frataram* (Cameron).

fraθ- vb. 'ask, examine, investigate, punish': Av. *fras-*, Skt. *praś-*, Lt. *precor*, pIE **preḱ-*, with inchoative present **pṛḱ-sḱe-*, OP *parsa-*, Av. *pərəsaiti*, NPers. *pursaδ*, Skt. *pṛcchátí*, Lt. *poscit*. Cf. also *ufrašta- ufrasta-*. *parsāmiy* 1st sg. (§30, §97, §130, §212, §226.I) DNb 19. *aparsam* 1st sg. imf. (§122, §132.3, §212. §226.II) DB 1.22; 4.67. *parsā* 2d sg. imv. (§212, §237.I) DB 4.38, 69. *fraθiyaiš* opt. pass. (§220, §223.II, §228.III) DNb 21 (not desid. fut. pass., as taken by Hz. ApI 167).
pati- + *parsa-* 'examine, read' (on meaning, Bv. BSLP 31.2.71-2): *patiparsāhy* 2d sg. subj. (§222.-II, §227.I) DB 4.42. *patiparsātiy* subj. (§222.II) DB 4.48.

fraθara- adj. 'superior': *fra-* + variant compar. suffix *-thara-* seen in Av. *fraθara-* (§149.I, §190.III; Wb. ZfA 41.319; Bv. 33.2.150-1, 34.1.33-4, Hz. AMI 4.126-7, 8.39-40, ApI 166-7), cf. superl. *-thama-* in Skt. *prathamá-* 'first'. Cf. also *uraθara-*. *fraθaram* asn. XPf 26f, 37.

Frāda- sb. 'Frada', a Margian rebel: Elam. *pir-ra-da*, Akk. *pa-ra-da-*'; perhaps thematic noun-stem (§141) to *fra-* + *²dā-*, with vriddhi (§126), cf. Av. *frād-* 'to further, increase' (Bthl. AiW 1012), but more probably hypocoristic to a compound name (§164.III; Bthl. AiW 1013) of which the prior part was the participial stem to the same compound verb (§162), cf. Av. adj. *frādaṱ.gaēθā-* 'prospering the household', sb. *frādaṱ.fšav-* 'Promoter of flocks' (name of a divinity; Bthl. AiW 1013-4). Not with Sen 52 (*fra-* + OP **ad-* 'drive', Av. *azaiti*, Skt. *ájati*, Lt. *agit*), nor with Justi, INB 101 (*fra-* + *had-* 'sit', with loss of intervocalic *-h-*). *Frāda* nsm. DB 3.12; 4.23; DBj 1.

framātar- sb. 'master, lord' ('giver of judicial decisions', acc. to Hz. ApI 150-4): *fra-* + root *mā-* + agent suffix *-tar-* (§154.II). *framātāram* asm. (§124.VI, §186.I) DNa 7f; DSe 7; DSf 5; DE 11; XPa 5f; XPb 11; XPc 5; XPd 8; XPf 7f; XPh 6; XE 11; XV 9; A¹Pa 8°; A²Hc 7. *framatāram* (§52.III) A³Pa 8.

framānā- sb. 'command' ('judgment, decision', acc. to Hz. ApI 144-50): Phl. *framān*, NPers. *farmān*; *fra-* + *mā-* + suffix *-nā-* (§128, §147.I), cf. Skt. *pramāṇa-m* 'measure, standard'. *framānā* nsf. DNa 57; DNb 28; DSj 3°. *framānāyā* isf. DNb 37.

fravata adv. 'forward, downward': Phl. *frōt*, NPers. *farōd farō*; from **frava-*, extension of *fra-* as in Gk. πρῶτος 'first' from **proṷa-*, + *-tos* as in *amata* (§191.II; JAOS 51.204, 53.15; Bv. BSLP 30.1.59; hardly with Kònig, Burgbau 51; not identical with Skt. isf. *pravátā* 'downhill'). DSf 23f, 28.

Fravarti- sb. 'Phraortes', a Median rebel: Elam. *pir-ru-mar-ti-iš*, Akk. *pa-ar-ú-mar-ti-iš*, Gk. Φραόρτης: identical either with Av. *fravaši-* 'guardian angel, soul', from *fra-* + *var-* 'protect' + *-ti-* (§31, §152.III) as 'Protection', or with Av. *fraorəti-* 'Sichbekennen zu', from *fra-* + *var-* 'choose (religiously)' + *-ti-* (Bthl. AiW 991, 992, 976; Nyberg Rel. 334-5, prefers second view); as man's name, probably hypocoristic of a longer compound (§164.II). *Fravartiš* nsm. DB 2.14, 66, 71, 73; 4.18; DBe 1f. *Fravartim* asm. DB 2.17. *Fravartaiš* gsm. DB 2.69, 93.

fras- vb., see *fraθ-*.

fraša- adj. 'excellent' ('tauglich', König Burgbau 48, Brd. WZKM 39.37): Av. *fraša-* 'directed toward, useful', formed on adv. *fraša* to *frānk-*, Skt. adv. *prācá* to *prāñc-*, from *pra-* + *añc-* (Bthl. AiW 1006-7); the irregular *-š-* for *-s-* of *šy* may be a contamination of **frasa-* and **frašya-* (otherwise Bthl. IF 2.266-7; borrowed from Avestan acc. to Hz. ApI 162). Hz. ApI 156-65 (recanting derivation from *fra-* + *xšāy-* 'shine', 'brilliant', AMI 3.1-11) takes as deriv. of *pra-*, through an idiom of racing or fighting, as 'extra (certamen), hors (concours)', and therefore 'incomparable, supreme'. Cf. also Hz. RHRel. 113.26; Bailey, BSOS 6.595-7; Kent, Lg. 15.169. *frašam* nsn. DSa 5, DSj 6 (see *frašta-*, for reading). *frašam* asn. DNb 2; DSf 56, 56f; DSo 4°; DSs 1°.

frašta DSa 5, DSj 6: discussed by Bv. BSLP 30.1.63-4, Gr. §103, Gray AJP 53.67, Brd. WZKM 39.20-1; but *frašam θadayātaiy* and not *frašta θadayāmaiy* (§54.II) should be read in both passages (Hz. AMI 3.9-10, ApI 156-8). See under *fraša-*.

fraharavam, phrasal adverb (§191.III), 'in all': *fra-* (§140.I) + asn. *haravam* with variant orthography (§22, §26), to *haruva-*. DB 1.17.

baug- vb. 'free': Av. *baog-*, NPers. *boxtàn*; in *Āθiyābaušna-*, *Bagabuxša-*.

Bāxtri- sb. 'Bactria', a province of the Persian Empire: Elam. *ba-ak-ši-iš, ba-ik-tur-ri-iš*, Akk. *ba-aḫ-tar*, Gk. (nt. pl.) Βάκτρα (§9.I, §79, §103.III). OP *ĭ*-stem, for older *ī*-stem (§152.II), seen in Av. *bāxδī*. *Bāxtriš* nsf. DB 1.16; DPe 16; DNa 23; DSe 22°; DSm 9°; XPh 21. *Bāxtriyā* lsf. DB 3.13f, 21. *Bāxtriyā* absf. DSf 36.

bag- vb., see under *baga-, bāji-*.

baga- sb. 'god': Av. *baga-* 'lot, good fortune', Skt. *bhága-* 'dispenser (of good fortune)', Gk. -φαγος 'eater', OCS *bogŭ* 'god', pIE **bhago-* (§101, §122, §143.I, V, VI); cf. Hz. ApI 105–10. See also *Bagābigna-, Bagabuxša-, Bāgayādi-, bāji-*. *baga* nsm. AmH 6; AsH 6; DNa 1; DNb 1; DSe 1°; DSf 1°; DSs 1°; DSt 1; DZc 1°; DE 1; XPa 1; XPb 1; XPc 1; XPd 1; XPf 1; XPh 1; XE 1; XV 1; A¹Pa 1°; A²Hc 1; A³Pa 1, 25. *bagāha* npm. (§10, §119, §172) DB 4.61, 63. *bagānām* gpm. AsH 7; DPd 1f; DPh 9; DSf 9; DSp 1°; DH 7; XE 2; XV 2; A²Hc 2. *bagaibiš* ipm. DPd 14f, 22, 24; DSe 50f°; DSt 8; XPb 28f; XPc 12f, 15; XPd 18; XPg 13f; XSc 5°; XV 26; A¹Pa 23°. *BGıbıš* (§42) ipm. D²Sa 3.

Bagābigna- sb. 'Bagabigna', a Persian, father of Hydarnes: Elam. *ba-qa-pi-ig-na*; from *baga-* 'god' + *ā-bigna-*, ptc. in *-na-* of an unidentified verbal root, cf. perhaps Skt. *bíja-m* 'seed' (§75.III, §103.IV, §160.Ic, §243). *Bag[ā]bignah[yā]* gsm. DB 4.84f.

Bagabuxša- sb. 'Megabyzus', an ally of Darius against Gaumata: Elam. *ba-qa-bu-uk-ša*, Akk. *ba-ga-bu-ki-šu*, Gk. Μεγάβυζος. From *baga-* 'god' + deriv. of root *baug-* 'free' (§102, §151): 'God-freed' (§160.Ic). *Ba[gab]uxša* nsm. DB 4.85.

Bāgayādi- adj. 'Bagayadi', seventh month, Sept.–Oct.: Elam. *bagiyātiš*, Akk. *tašrītu*. From *baga-* 'god', with vriddhi (§126, §165), + *yad-* 'worship', with lengthened vowel (§126, §165) and formative *-i-* (§152.I): 'God-Worship Month' (§159, §161.Ia), probably referring to Mithras, since Phl. and NPers. call this month *Mihr* '(Month of) Mithras' (Justi, ZDMG 51.247; Bthl. AiW 952–3). *Bāgayādaiš* gsm. DB 1.55.

bāji- sb. 'tribute': NPers. *bāz*; deriv. (§152.I, §165) of root seen in Skt. *bhága-* 'portion, dispenser', OP *baga-* 'god', the verb being Skt. *bhájati* 'apportions', Av. *bag-*, Phl. *baxtan* (§101, §122, §123, §126). *bājim* asf. DB 1.19; DPe 9f; DNa 19; DSe 18; XPh 17.

bātugara- sb. 'drinking cup, saucer': if genuine (§55.II; JAOS 56.215; Schaeder, SbPAW 1935. 489–96), from *bātu-* 'wine' (§153.I; etymology uncertain, but Hz. ApI 114 quotes βατιάκη from Athenaeus, bk. xi, page 784a, as the Persian word for 'phiale, cup') + *-gara-* (§143.I) 'devouring, drinking' (§160.Ia), cf. Av. *aspō.garō* 'horse-devouring', Skt. *aja-gará-* 'goat-swallower, boa constrictor', Gk. δημο-βόρος 'people-devouring', Lt. *carni-vorus* 'flesh-eating', from root in Av. *gar-* 'devour', Skt. *giráti*, Lt. *vorat*, pIE **gᵘer-*. Bv. JAs. 228.233–4 suggests, and Hz. AMI 8.9–17, ApI 113–5, accepts cognation rather with Skt. *galati* 'drips', *gālayati* 'pours', as 'wine-pourer', cf. Lt. *libāre* 'pour (as an offering to the gods)', and NPers. *piyāla* 'drinking cup', from **pati-gāra-*. *bātugara* nsm. (§56.V) A¹I.

baⁿd- vb. 'bind': Av. *band-*, Skt. *bandh-*, Gt. *bindan*, pIE **bhendh-*. See also *badaka-*. *basta* (NPers. *bast*) nsm. past ptc. pass. (§67, §85, §120, §122, §132.1, §242.I) DB. 1.82; 2.75, 90; 5.26. *bastā* apm. DB 3.88°.

baⁿdaka- sb. 'subject, servant' (cf. König, RuID 64): Phl. *bandak*, NPers. *bandah*; deriv. (§146.II) of OP **baⁿda-* 'bond, fetter', Av. *banda-*, Skt. *bandhá-*, to pIE root **bhendh-* (OP *baⁿd-*; §39, §75.III, §111, §122, §132.1). *badaka* nsm. DB 2.20, 30, 49f, 82; 3.13, 31, 56, 85; 5.8. *badakā* npf. DB 1.19.

Bābiru- sb. (*Bābairu-* because of Pali *Bāveru-*, MB Gr. §80) 'Babylon', a city (§56.III, §166); 'Babylonia', a province of the Persian Empire; by transfer, 'Babylonian': Elam. *ba-pi-li*, Akk. *bab-ilu, bab-ilāni* 'gate of the god(s)', Gk. Βαβυλών (§75.V, §107). See also *Bābıruviya-*. *Bābiruš* nsm. DB 1.14, 80; DPe 10f; DNa 26; DSe 25f°; DSm 7°; XPh 22; as ethnic (§56.III), DN xvi, A?P 16. *Bābırum* asm. DB 1.83f, 91 bis; 2.2, 3, 3f; 3 82, 84, 87; 4.15, 30. *Bābirauš* absm. (§168, §182.III) DB 2.65. *Bābirauv* lsm. DB 1.78, 81;

2.5, 6; 3.79, 83, 92; 4.2; DBd 7f; DBi 11 (written *Bāb^arauv*, §22); DSf 33 as loc. with *yātā*, 33 as abl. with *hacā* (hardly a real abl., corresponding to Av. *-aoṯ* despite Hz. AMI 3 55n, Kent JAOS 53.16).

Bābiruviya- adj. 'Babylonian': deriv. (§144.-III) to preceding. *Bābiruviya* nsm. DB 1.77, 79; 3.81; 4.13; DSf 29f. *Bābiruviyam* asm. DB 3.86. *Bābiruviyā* npm. DB 3.78; DSf 53f. *Bābiruviyā* apm. DB 3.88.

bar- vb. 'bear, lift up, esteem': present stem *bara-*, Av. *baraiti*, NPers. *baraδ*, Skt. *bhárati*, Gk. φέρει, Lt. *fert*, Gt. *baíriþ*, pIE **bhere/o-* (§213). See also *ubarta-*, *ušabāri-*, *Gaubaruva-*, *bara-*. *baraⁿtiy* 3d pl. (§122, §232.I) DB 5.22f (written *b^ara^ta^ya*, §22); DNa 42. *abaram* 1st sg. imf. (§61, §75.III, §226.II) DB 1.22; 4.66. *abara* imf. (§40, §84, §228.II) DB 1.25, 55, 88, 94; 2.25, 34f, 40, 45, 54, 60, 68, 86, 97°; 3.6, 17, 37, 45, 62, 67 (written *ar^ar^a*, §54.II), 87; 4.61, 62; DNa 50f; DSf 19°, 32; XPh 33, 45. *abaraⁿ* 3d pl. imf. (§10, §40, §84, §106, §232.II) DPe 10; DSe 18°; DSf 34. *abarahaⁿ* 3d pl. imf. (§10, §218, §232.III) DNa 19f; XPh 17 (written *ab^ar^an^a*, §54.I). *abaraⁿtā* 3d pl. imf. mid. (§10, §236.II) DB 1.19. *abariya* imf. pass. (§35.I, §220, §228.II) DSf 23°, 31f, 35, 36, 38f, 40, 43, 45. *abariyaⁿ* 3d pl. imf. pass. (§220, §232.II) DSf 41, 47. *baratuv* imv. (§237.II) AmH 11°; DPd 14; DSk 5. *bartanaiy* inf. (§238) DNb 47.

ā + bar- 'perform': *ābaratiy* (§213, §228.I) DNb 25. Cf. also Hz. ApI 110–1, who refers to *ā-bar-* certain other forms listed above as augmented forms of uncompounded *bar-*.

pati- + ā + bar- 'bring back, restore': *patiyābaram* 1st sg. imf. DB 1.68 (but *-ā-* perhaps only by influence of *parābartam*, JAOS 62.275; §53, §206c).

parā + bar- 'bear away, take away': *parābara* imf. DB 1.71, 96. *parābartam* nsn. past ptc. pass. (§242.I) DB 1.62, 67f.

pari- + bar- 'protect, preserve' (cf. Hz. ApI 112–3): *paribarāmiy* 1st sg. (§226.I) DNb 17. *paribarāhy* 2d sg. subj. (§27, §136, §222.II, §227.I) DB 4.78; *paribarāh^a-diš* (§27, etc.) DB 4.74. *paribarā* 2d sg. imv. (§237.I) DB 4.72, 88.

fra- + bar- 'proffer, grant': *frābara* imf. AmH 7; AsH 9; DB 1.12, 25, 60f; DPd 3f, 7f; DPh 8; DNa 33; DSf 11; DSm 3°; DSp 2°; DSs 6; DZc 4; DH 7; A²Hc 18f, 20.

bara- sb. 'bearing, bearer': Av. *-bara-*, Skt. *-bhara-*, Gk. -φορος, pIE **bhoros* (§32, §122, §143.I, VI), to root *bar-* 'bear', in *arštibara-*, *takabara-*, *vaçabara-*; also *bāra-* 'borne by, rider of', with vriddhi (§122, §126, §143.I), in *asabāra-*, cf. *ušabāri-*. See Hz. ApI 95.

bard- vb. 'be high': Av. *barəz-* 'high', *barəzant-* 'lofty', NPers. *burz* 'high', Skt. *bṛhánt-* 'lofty', OHG *berg* 'mountain', pIE **bherĝh-*; in *Bardiya-*, *baršan-*, probably in *brazman-*.

Bardiya- sb. 'Smerdis', brother of Cambyses (§164.III): Elam. *bir-ti-i̯a*, Akk. *bar-zi-i̯a*, Gk. Σμέρδις (§29.n2, §30). Deriv. (§144.IV) of OP *bard-* 'be high' (§75.III): 'The Exalted'. *Bardiya* nsm. DB 1.30, 32, 39, 52f; 3.25, 35, 54; 4.9, 27, 82; DBb 4f; DBh 5. *Bardiyam* asm. DB 1.31 bis, 51.

baršan- sb. 'height, depth' (§31): Av. *barəzan-* (Bthl. AiW 950); deriv. of OP *bard-* (§75.III, §155.I; Scheil 21.26; König, Burgbau 51; Hz. AMI 3.57; Bv. Gr. §312; Kent, JAOS 51.204, 53.15). *baršnā* ism. (§96, §120) DSf 26, 26f.

bav- vb. 'become, be': present stem *bava-* (§213), Av. *bavaiti*, Skt. *bhávati*, Gk. φύει 'grows', Lt. *fuī* 'I was', Lith. *búti* 'to be', NEng. *be*, pIE **bheu-*. See also *būmi-*. *bavatiy* (§122, §228.I) XPh 55, 56. *bavaⁿtiy* 3d pl. (§232.I) DNb 14 (*bauvatiy* in 2d copy, Hz. ApI 115; cf. §48). *abavam* 1st sg. imf. DB 1.28, 60, 72; 4.5; 5.4°; DSm 6°; XPf 35, 36f; XPh 30; XSc 4°. *abava* imf. (§228.II) DB 1.32, 33, 34, 40, 48, 77, 80; 2.16f, 17, 80, 94; 3.10, 11, 20, 27, 28, 76, 82, 83; 5.5, 14°, 30; DSf 25; XPf 26. *abavaⁿ* 3d pl. imf. (§112, §232.II) DB 1.76; 2.7, 93; 3.78, 4.34. *bavātiy* subj. (§222.II, §228.I) DNa 43, 45f; DNb 59 (Lg. 15.74; confirmed by photograph, JNES 4.44). [*biy*]*ā* 2d sg. opt. (§114, §218.II, §223.I, §227.II) DB 4.69. *biyā* opt. (**bhu-ii̯ēt*, Bv. Gr. §232, comparing Av. *buyāṯ* from **bhu-i̯ēt*; but Bthl. Gdr. IP 1. §143 takes as **bhu-ī-i̯ēt*, = Lt. *fīet*, which may be either non-thematic opt. or thematic subj.; §114, §122, §208, §218.II, §223.I, §228.II) DB 4.56 bis, 58, 59, 74f, 75, 78f, 79°.

bigna-, in *ā-bigna-*, see *Bagābigna-*.

būmi- sb. 'earth (= world or ground)': Av. *būmī-*, NPers. *būm*, Skt. (RV) nom. *bhū́mī bhū́miṣ*; deriv. of root *bhav-* (see *bav-*) in grade *bhū-*, cf. Skt. aor. *ábhūt*, Gk. ἔφυ (§11, §65, §152.IV, §179.-III).

būmim asf. DNa 2, 32; DSe 2°; DSf 1; DSt 2; DZc 1f; DE 2; XPa 1; XPb 2; XPc 1; XPd 2; XPf 2; XPh 1f; XE 3; XV 2f; A¹Pa 2°; A²Hc 2. *būmām* asf. (§55.I) A³Pa 2. *būmiyā* lsf. (§179.II) DNa 11f; DSb 9; DSe 10; DSm 5; DSs 2°, 3°; DZb 4; DZc 6; DE 17f; XPa 9; XPb 17; XPc 7f; XPd 12; XPf 12, 25; XPh 10; XPj; XE 17; XV 13; A¹Pa 13°; A²Sc 4°; Wb 7; Wc 8; Wd 8.

BU nsf. (§42) DSf 24, 28. *BUyā* lsf. DSd 2°; DSf 7, 15, 16, 18, 24°; DSg 2; DSi 2, 4; DSj 1°; DSy 2; D²Sb 2; A²Sa 1; A²Sd 2; A²Ha 2; A²Hc 9, 17; A²Pa 11.

brātar- sb. 'brother': Av. *brātar-*, NPers. *birādar*, Skt. *bhrátar-*, Gk. φράτηρ 'clan-brother', Lt. *frāter*, OCS *bratrŭ*, Gt. *broþar*, pIE *bhrāter- (§62, §75.III, §128, §154.II). *brātā* nsm. (§124.5, §186.II) DB 1.29f, 39f.

brazmaniya- adj. 'prayerful, reverent' (cf. Kent, Lg. 21.223–9), with *braz-* rather than *barz-* (§33; cf. Elam. *pir-ra-aṣ-man-ni-ia*, Akk. *bi-ra-za-man-ni-i*): deriv. (§144.IV) to pAr. antecedent of Skt. *bráhman-* 'religious devotion, prayer', cf. identical Skt. deriv. *brahmaṇyá-* 'religious', to pIE root *bherĝh-* (see OP *bard-*; §75.III, §95, §120, §155.III; Henning, TPS 1944.108–18). For other views, see Kent, Lg. 13.301; Hartmann, OLZ 40.145–60; Nyberg, Rel. 367, 478; Hz. AMI 8.69, ApI 116–8 (to Av. *barəg-* 'to welcome', *barəg-* 'rite', *barəxδa-* 'beloved'; wrongly, since this would give OP *bragman-*); Christensen, Essai sur la démonologie iranienne 40–1; Henning, BSOS 10.506; Abayev, Iranskie Yazyki 1.134; Scherman, JAOS 65.141–3 n.23. Cf. also O. M. Dalton, Treasure of the Oxus 94–5. On form and meaning of Phl. *brahm brahmak*, see Henning, TPS 1944.-108–18. *brazmaniya* nsm. XPh 41, 51, 54 (hardly *brazmanīy* isn. modifying *artā*; also not *-niy* apn. 'divine' with Sen 155, nor adn. in elliptic dual with Pisani, see under *arta-*).

mᵃ, of dubious meaning, Se 1; taken by Justi, IFA 17.112, to be an abbreviation for OP *māraka* 'seal', NPers. *mārah*.

ma-, stem of 1st person pron. in obl. cases of sg.; see *adam*.

mā conj. 'not', in prohibitions etc.: Av. Skt. *mā*, Gk. μή, pIE *mē (§109, §191.I, §292b). With subj.: DNb 55 (*mā-taiy*), 58. With opt.: DB 4.59, 69, 79°; DPd 18, 19 bis, 20; XPh 39. With inj.: DB 4.54; DPe 21; DNa 58, 59, 60; DNb 52 (*mā-taiy*). With imv.: DNb 60. With lost verbs: DNb 57, DSq 4 bis; with restored subj. A²Sa 5° bis, A²Ha 7, 7°. See also *mātya*.

mā- vb. 'measure': Av. Skt. *mā-*, Lt. *mētior* 'I measure'.

ā + mā- 'extend': *āmātā* npm. past ptc. pass. (§242.II) 'noble' DB 1.7; DBa 11.

fra- + mā- 'command' ('decide, judge', acc. to Hz. ApI 154–6; 'plan,' Hinz, ZDMG 95.233–5); see also *framātar-*, *framānā-*. *frāmāyatā* imf. mid. (§214, §235.II) XPg 5. *framātam* nsn. past ptc. pass. (§242.II) DSf 19f°, 56.

mauθ- vb. 'flee': meaning established by Elam. and Akk. versions (Husing, KZ 38.258); probably to Skt. *muṇṭhate* 'flees' (Jn. JAOS 38.122). *amuθa* imf. (§211) DB 2.2, 71; 3.41f, 71.

Maka- sb. 'Maka', a province of the Persian Empire (lit. on location given in JAOS 56.217–8): Elam. *ma-ak-qa*, Akk. *ma-ak*, cf. Gk. pl. Μάκαι (§99, §132.2, §144.III). See also *Maciya-*. *Maka* nsm. DB 1.17; DPe 18.

magu- sb. 'Magian', member of a priestly order of Media: Elam. *ma-ku-iš*, Akk. *ma-gu-šu*, Gk. Μάγος (§153.I). Uncertain material on meaning and etymology, König, Klotho 4 chap. 12, and RuID 66. *maguš* nsm. DB 1.36, 44, 46, 64, 66, 70f; 4 8; DBb 2. *magum* asm. DB 1.50, 54, 57, 73; 4.81.

Maciya- adj. 'Macian'; pl., name of a province of the Persian Empire: deriv. of *Maka-* (§99, §113, §132.2, §144.III). *Maciya* nsm. A?P 29. *Maciyā* for nsm. (§56.III) DN xxix. *Maciyā* npm. DNa 30; DSe 23f; XPh 25.

mātar- sb. 'mother': Av. *mātar-*, Skt. *mātár-*, Gk. Dor. μάτηρ, Lt. *māter*, pIE nom. *mātē, stem *māter- (§154 II): in *hamātar-*.

mātya conj. 'lest, that not, not': *mā* 'not' + conj. *tya* (§133, §292b). *mātya-mām* (§133) DB 1.52. *mātya* DB 4.43, 48, 71.

maθišta- adj. 'greatest', equal to 'crown prince' in XPf (Speiser ap. Kent, Lg. 9.40–1; Hz. ApI 254–8): Av. *masišta-*, NPers. *mahist*, Gk. μήκιστος 'longest' (radical vowel after that in μῆκος 'length'); superl. to pIE *mak̂-ros, Gk. μακρός, Lt. *macer* 'thin', pIE root *mak̂- (§87) 'be long and slender' + superl. suffix *-isto-* (§117, §156.III,

§190.II), Gk. -ιστο-, Av. -ıšta-, Skt. (with aspiration) -iṣṭha-. *maθišta* nsm. AsH 6f; DB 2.13, 24; 3.70; DPd 1; DPh 9; DSf 9; DSp 1°; DH 7; XE 2; XV 1f; A²Hc 1. [*maθ*]*išta*-[*šām*] DB 5.27. *maθištam* asm. DB 2.20, 83; 3.12, 31, 57, 85; 5.6, 8, 12, 28f; XPf 32.

Māda- (§166.III) adj. 'Median'; masc. as sb. 'Media', a province of the Persian Empire: Elam. *ma-da*, Akk. *ma-da-a-a*, Gk. pl. Μῆδοι.

(1) 'Median': *Māda* nsm. DB 1.49; 2.14°, 16, 18, 82; 4.18; DN ii°; A?P 2. *Mādam* asm. DB 2.21, 82; 3.30. *Mādā* npm. DSf 50, 54f. *Māda*[*ibı*]*š* ipm. DB 2.23. *Mādaıšuva* lpm. DB 2.23.

(2) 'Media': *Māda* nsm. DB 1.15°, 41; 2.7; DPe 10; DNa 22; DSe 21°; DSm 8°; XPh 19. *Mādam* asm. DB 1.47; 2.22, 28f, 48f, 63, 65 bis; 3.32f; 4.20. *Mādam-cā* DB 1.66f. *Mādaıy* lsm. DB 1.34, 59; 2.15, 17, 22f, 28, 66 bis, 72, 92; 3.77; DBe 10f.

¹*man-* vb. 'think': Av. *man-yete*, Skt. *mányate*, Gk. μέμονα '(I have thought of,) I desire', Lat. *memını* 'I remember', pIE **men*-. See also *manah-*. *maniyaiy* 1st sg. mid. (§214, §233.II) DNb 38. *amaniyaiy* 1st sg. imf. mid. (§214, §233.III) DSl 3f. *maniyāhaiy* 2d sg. subj. mid. (§131, §222.II, §234.I) DB 4.39 (*man*[...]); DPe 20 (*manıyāhay*, §27, §52.II); DNa 38 (*maniyā-*[...]); XPh 47 (*maniyāiy*, without the *h*ᵃ: §27, §52.VI, Lg. 13.302; Hz. AMI 8.66, ApI 243–4). *maniyā*[*taiy*) subj. mid. (§222.II) DB 4.50.

²*man-* vb. 'remain': Av. *man-*, iterative pres. *mānaya-* (§123, §215), Gk. μένω, Lt. *maneō*; probably specialization of pIE **men-* 'think' (see ¹*man-*) in meaning 'remain thinking'. *amānaya* imf. DB 2.48, 63; *amānaiya* (§48) DB 2.28.

manaʰuvin- adj. 'mindful, wılful, hot-tempered': from *manah-* + *-ụin-* (§155.V), cf. Lg. 15.170, JNES 4.47 (Hz. ApI 242 otherwise, wrongly). *manauviš* (remade from -*vī*, §187) nsm. DNb 13.

manah- sb. 'thinking power, power of will' (Jn. Iran. Rel. §70; Kent, JNES 4.45–7, 232): Av. *manah-*, Skt. *mánas-*, Gk. μένος 'courage', pIE **menos *menes-* (§124.4, §156.II). Decl., §185.I. See also *manauvin-*, and *-maniš-* with reduced grade in second syllable, in *Ardumanıš-*, *Haxāmaniš-*, perhaps *Imaniš-*. *manaš-cā* (§105) asn. DNb 32. *manahā* isn. (JNES 4.45; wrongly gen., Hz. ApI 240–2 and Sen 235) DNb 14.

māniya- sb., probably 'personal property' in the houses; nt. adj. as collective sb., from *māna-*, GAv. *dəmāna-*, LAv. *nmāna-* 'abode, house' (§126), extension of root seen in Skt. *dáma-* 'house', Gk. δόμος, Lt. *domus*. For varying views, see Tm. Lex. 116, with lit.; Gray, JAOS 21.17, 33.281–3; Bthl. AiW 1168; MB Gr. §261; Fay, JAOS 34.330–1. *māniyam-cā* asn. DB 1.65.

+*mamaita*, see *Atamaita-*.

mayūxa- sb. 'doorknob': Skt. *mayúkha-* 'peg', perhaps to Skt. *mi-* (pres. *minóti*) 'fix (as in the earth)' (§100, §143.III); cf. Hz. ApI 258–9. *mayūxa* nsm. DPi; XPi.

mar- vb. 'die': Av. *mar-*, pres. *miryeite* (§122, §214), Skt. *mriyáte*, Lt. *moritur*, pIE **mer-*. See also *uvāmaršiyu-*, *marīka-*, *marta-*, *martiya-*. *amarıyatā* imf. mid. (§35.I, §235.II) DB 1.43.

marīka- sb. 'person of lower rank, subject', as shown by Akk. ᴸᵁ*gal-la* 'menial': contracted (§23.I) for **mariyaka-*, deriv. of stem in Skt. (Vedic) *márya-* 'young man, stallion', cf. Skt. *maryaká-* 'little man (said of a bull among cows)', Phl. *mērak* (from **maryaka*), Gk. μεῖραξ 'boy, girl' (from **merıak-*); ultimate root pIE **mer-*, OP *mar-* (§122, §146.III). Cf. Hz. ApI 251–3, Bv. TPS 1945.43–4. *marīkā* vsm. DNb 50, 55, 59°.

Māru- sb. 'Maru', a town in Media (cf. Kònig, RuID 71): Elam. *ma-ru-iš*, Akk. *ma-ru-*'. *Mā*[*ru*]*š* nsm. DB 2.22.

Mārgava- adj. 'Margian': adj. to *Margu-*, with vriddhi (§126, §143.II, V, VI). *Mārgava* nsm. DB 3.12; 4.24. *Mārgavaibiš* ipm. DB 3.16.

Margu- sb. 'Margiana', a province of the Persian Empire: Elam. *mar-ku-iš*, Akk. *mar-gu-*', Gk. Μάργος, Μαργιάνη (§31, §153.I). See also *Mārgava-*. *Marguš* nsm. DB 2.7; 3.11. *Margum* asm. DB 4.25. *Margauv* lsm. (§114) DB 4.25; DBj 5f.

marta- ptc. as adj. 'dead': Av. *mərəta-*, NPers. *murd*, Skt. *mṛtá-*, Gk. βροτός (for **βρατός*, with vowel assimilation), Lt. *mort-uos* (after *vī-vos* 'living'), pIE **mṛtos* (§30, §109, §122, §242.I); see OP *mar-*, and cf. Hz. ApI 249–51. *marta* nsm. XPh 48, 55. *martahyā* gsm. DB 5.20, 36.

¹*martiya-* adj. as sb. 'man': -*i̯o-* extension of pIE **mortos*, Av. *marəta-* 'mortal, man', NPers. *mard*, Skt. *márta-* (§31, §106, §122, §242.II), cf. -*i̯o-* extension in Av. *mašya-*, Skt. *mártya-* (§144.IV). See also *umartiya-*, ²*Martiya-*.
   martiya nsm. DB 1.21, 36, 48, 74, 77; 2.8, 14, 79; 3.12, 22, 70, 78; 4.38, 65, 68; 5.5°, 7°; DNa 46; DNb 16, 19, 21, 24; XPh 51. *martiyā* vsm. DNa 56. *martiyam* asm. DB 3.57; DNa 3; DNb 12, 22; DSe 3; DSf 2, 16f; DSs 2f; DSt 3°; DZc 2; DE 4f; XPa 2; XPb 4f; XPc 2f; XPd 3f; XPf 3; XPh 3; XE 5; XV 4; A¹Pa 3f°; A²Hc 3f; A³Pa 3f. *martiyahyā* gsm. DNa 4, 44; DNb 3; DSe 4f; DSf 3; DSs 5°; DSt 4f°; DZc 2f; DE 6; XPa 3; XPb 6; XPc 3; XPd 4f; XPf 4f; XPh 4; XE 7; XV 5; A¹Pa 5°; A²Hc 4f; *martihyā* A³Pa 4f (§52.VI; hardly phonetic, as taken by Morgenstierne, Acta Or. 1.253). *martiyā* npm. DB 1.57f; 4.80, 82; DSf 47, 49, 51, 52, 54. *martiyā* apm. DB 2.77; 3.48, 50, 74, 90, 91. *martiyānām* gpm. DB 4.87f. *martiyaibiš* ipm. DB 1.56f.

²*Martiya-* sb. 'Martiya', a Susian rebel: Elam. *mar-ti-i̯a*, Akk. *mar-ti-i̯a*; same as ¹*martiya-*, specialized as man's name (§163.Ib, §164.III; but cf. HK Iran. Eigenn. 13–4, Phil. 66.183–4, ApKI 1.54, 2.26). *Martiya* nsm. DB 2.8; 4.15; DBf 1. *Martiyam* asm. DB 2.12f.

mard- vb. 'crush': Av. *marəd-* 'destroy', Skt. *mr̥d-* 'rub, crush', Lt. *mordet* 'bites', pIE **merd-* (Foy, KZ 35.48). See also *Marduniya-*.

vi- + mard- 'destroy': *vimardatiy* (§30, §213) DSe 40f. *viyamarda* imf. (written *viya : marda*, §44; cf. also §52.IV, §228.II, and Lex. s.v. -*di-*) DB 5.11.

Marduniya- sb. 'Mardonius', father of Gobryas: Elam. *mar-du-nu-i̯a*, Gk. Μαρδόνιος; perhaps deriv. to **marduna-* 'vintner' (§144.IV, §147.-II, §153.I, §164.IV), cf. NPers *mul* 'wine', Skt. *mr̥dvīkā-* 'grapevine' (Bthl. AiW 1151; otherwise Justi, INB 195), which possibly contains root *mard-* 'crush (the grapes in the wine-making)'. *Marduniyahyā* gsm. DB 4.84.

mav- vb. 'send': cf. Lt. *moveō* 'I move'. [*am*]-*āvatā* imf. mid. as pass. (§213, §235.II) DB 4.92 (dubious conj. of Kent, JAOS 62.269).

Mazdāh- adj. 'wise' (§156.I, §160.Ia): regularly compounded in *Auramazdāh-* (q.v.); both parts declined, but without an intervening worddivider, in *Aurahya Mazdāha* (§185.IV) XPc 10.

maškā- sb. '(inflated) skin'; NPers. *mask*, Akk. *maš-ku-u* 'skin', Aram. *maškā*: borrowed from Semitic (§99, §109, §117, §143.IV; see MB Gr. §101). *maškāuvā* lpf. (§72) DB 1.86.

māha- sb. 'month': Skt. *māsa-*, pIE **mēso-*; extension (§143.II) of pIE **mēs-*, seen in Av. *māh-*, NPers. *māh*, Skt. *mās-*, cf. also Lt. *mēnsis*, Gk. μήν, Gt. *mēna*, OHG *māno*, Lith. *ménuo*, all meaning 'moon' or 'month'. *māhyā* gsm. DB 1.37f, 42, 56, 89, 96; 2.26, 36, 41, 47, 56, 61f, 69, 98; 3.8, 18, 39, 46f, 63, 68, 88 (for **māhahyā*, with contraction of -*āhah-* to -*āh-*, with Gray, AJP 21.13–4; rather than the usual interpretation as lsm. to stem *māh-*; §131, §165.n1, §185.IV).

miθah- sb. (§156.II) 'evil', the opposite of *rāšta-*: Av. *miθahya-* 'evil', *miθaoxta-* 'falsely spoken', Skt. *mith-* 'to meet (as friend or antagonist), engage in altercation'; cf. Hz. ApI 259–61, Kent Lg. 15.169–70, and *hamiçiya-*. *miθa* asn. DNb 7, 9, 11.

Miθra- sb. 'friend'; as deity, 'Mithras': El. *mi-iš-ša*, Akk. *mi-it-ri*; Av. *miθra-*, NPers. *mihr* 'sun', Skt. *mitrá-* 'friend' (§9.VI, §33, §49c, §78, §148.III). Cf. *Vaumisa-* and probably *hamiçiya-*. *Mit[ra]* nsm. A²Hb; *M'tra* (§22) A²Sd 4, A²Ha 6; *M'θra* A²Sa 5, A³Pa 25. As gen. (§313.II), *M'tra* A²Ha 5°, *M'θra* A²Sa 4.

muθ- vb., see *mauθ-*.

Mudrāya- adj. 'Egyptian'; pl., also a province of the Persian Empire, 'Egypt'; masc. sg. as sb., 'Egypt', a province: Elam. *mu-iṣ-ṣa-ri-i̯a*, Akk. *mi-ṣir* (§6, §76.V).
   (1) 'Egyptian': *Mudrāya* nsm. A?P 19. *Mudrāyā* npm. DSf 50f, 52, 55.
   (2) 'Egyptians', as province: *Mudrāyā* npm. DPe 11f.
   (3) 'Egypt': *Mudrāya* nsm. DB 1.15, 2.7°; DNa 27; DSe 26°; DSm 7°; XPh 23. *Mudrāyam* asm. DB 1.32, 33, DZc 8. *Mudrāyā* absm. DSf 41; DZc 11f. *Mudrāyaiy* lsm. DZc 9.

ya- rel. pron. 'who, which', generalized by encl. -*ciy* (cf. Hz. ApI 355–6): Av. Skt. *ya-*, Gk. ὅς, pIE **i̯o-*. See also *yātā*, *yaθā*, *yadā-*, *yadiy*, *yaniy*, *yāvā*. *ya-ciy* nsn. (§105, §130, §197) DNb 57. *ya-ciy* asn. DNb 35, 36.

Yautiyā- sb. 'Yautiya', a district in Persia: Elam. *i̯a-ú-ti-i̯a-iš*, Akk. *ι-ú-tι-i̯a. Yautιyā* nsf. DB 3.23.

yaud- vb. 'be in commotion', present stem *yauda-*: Av. *yaoz-* 'boil up' (§88), pres. *yaoza-* (Hz. AMI 8.67, ApI 362-5); not to Av. *yaod-* 'fight', Skt. *yudh-*, because of the difference in the present stem (Av. *yūiδyeiti*, Skt. *yúdhyatι*; JAOS 58.116). *ayauda* imf. (§213) XPh 31f (not *āyauda* nsm. 'rebellion', as taken by Henning, BSOS 10.505, which is refuted by Akk. version). *ayaudaⁿ* 3d pl. imf. (§232.II) DSe 33°. *yau[daⁿ-tιm]* asf. pres. ptc. act. (§190.I, §240) DNa 32.

Yauna- adj. 'Ionian'; pl., also a province of the Persian Empire; masc. sg. as sb., 'Ionia', a province: Elam. (*i*)-*i̯a-u-na*, Akk. *i̯a-ma-nu*, Gk. Ἰωνίᾱ.

(1) 'Ionian': *Yauna* nsm. A?P 26. *Yaunā* npm. DSf 33f, 48; as nsm. (§56.III) A?P 23.

(2) 'Ionians', as province: *Yaunā* npm. DPe 12f; DNa 29; DSe 27f°; DSm 10°; XPh 23.

(3) 'Ionia': *Yauna* nsm. DB 1.15; DNa 28; DSm 8°. *Yaunā* absm. DSf 42f.

yāumani- adj. 'trained, skilled': adj. to **yauman-*, with vriddhi (§126, §152.I, §155.III), from root seen in Skt. *yā́uti* 'harnesses, fastens', cf. Hz. ApI 365-6 (not with Sen 249, 'agile', from **yāuman-aina-*, fem. *-ī*). See also *ayāumani-. yāumaιniš* nsm. (with epenthesis, §127; Lg. 15.173) DNb 40.

yauviyā- sb. 'canal' (§48): NPers. *ǰoi* 'watercourse, canal', cf. perhaps Skt. (Vedic) *yavyā̀* isf. 'stream, river'; perhaps deriv. (§144.V) of root *ay-/ι-/yā-* 'go' (JAOS 62.271). *yauviyā* nsf. DZc 10. *yauvιyām* asf. DZc 8f, 12.

yakā- sb. (§6, §143.IV) a kind of wood (oak, Scheil 25.28, but if so, not cognate, Bv. BSLP 30.1.61; Afghan cypress, König, Burgbau 54-61; mulberry, Wb. AfOF 7.42; teak, Hz. AMI 3.61-2; certainly not 'timber' in general, as taken by Gray, AJP 53.68). *yakā* nsf. DSf 34.

yaciy, see *ya-*.

yātā conj. and prep.; perhaps *yā* isn. or *yāt* absn. of *ya-* + *-tā* as in *cιtā*, q.v. (wrongly Sen 11).

(1) Conj. (§294) 'until': DB 1.25, 54, 69; 2.28, 48, 63; DNa 51; DNb 23; DSf 24; XPh 45f. 'when' DB 4.81. 'while' DB 2.6; 3.77. 'as long as' DB 4.51.

(2) Prep. with loc., 'unto': DSf 32, 34.

(3) Double prep., *yātā ā*, with abl. (not with acc., as taken by Schwentner, ZII 6.173), 'unto': DPh 6, 7; DH 5, 6.

yaθā conj.: GAv. *yaθā*, LAv. *yaθa*, Skt. *yáthā*; rel. *ya-* + adv. Suffix *-thā* (§76.II, §113). It takes a verb in the indic, except that the pres. subj. shows future time in temporal clauses (DNb 28f); details of syntax, §295.

(1) 'as': DB 1.23 (*yaθā-šām*), 63, 67, 69; 4.35, 52; 5.17°, 29, 33°; DNa 37; DSj 3; DZc 11°, 12.

(2) 'as well as', comparing clauses: DNb 39 (wrongly Hz. ApI 362).

(3) 'when': CMb 3; DB 1.31, 91°; 2.22, 65; 3.34, DNb 28f (*yaθā-maiy*); DSi 3; XPf 25, 32 (*yaθā-maiy*), 36; XPh 29 (*yaθā tya*).

(4) 'after', with prec. or foll. *pasāva·* DB 1.27, 33, 72, 73; 2.32, 52; 3.3; 4.5; 5.3, 23°; DNa 31f; DSf 25; XSc 3°.

(5) 'that', introducing object clause: DB 4.44.

(6) 'so that', introducing result clause: DB 1.70; DSe 35, 39.

(7) 'because': DB 4.63.

yad- vb. 'reverence, worship', usually middle: Av. *yazaite*, Skt. *yájatι*, Gk. ἅζεται, pIE **i̯aǵ-* (§88, §113). See also *Āçιyādιya-, āyadana-, Bāgayādi-, ²yadā. yadataiy* mid. (§213, §235.I) XPh 53. *ayadaιy* 1st sg. imf. mid. (§233.III) DB 5.16, 32; DSf 18°; DSk 5; XPh 40f. *ayadiya* imf. pass. (§220) DB 5.16°, 32. *ayadiyaⁿ* 3d pl. imf. pass. (§220, §232.II) XPh 36, 40. *yadātaiy* subj. mid. (§222.II, §235.I) DB 5.19, 34f. *yadaiša* 2d sg. opt. mid. (§223.II, §234.II) XPh 50. *yadιyaišaⁿ* (§220, §223.II, §232.III; written *yᵃdᵃiyᵃιšⁿ*, §55.I; cf. Hz. AMI 8.67, ApI 357-8) 3d pl. opt. pass. (Ogden ap. JAOS 58.325; not *yadiyaiš* 2d sg. opt. mid. with Wb. Symbolae Koschaker 196, nor fut. pass. with Hz. AMI 8.67, ApI 357-8) XPh 39.

¹*yadā-* conj. 'where': GAv. *yadā*, Skt. *yadā́*; probably rel. nt. pAr. **i̯ad* + postpos. *ā. yadā-tya* XPh 35f (§133, §296; cf. *yaθā tya* XPh 29); *yadāyā* XPh 39 (perhaps error in writing, §55.I; but cf. Hz. AMI 8.66, ApI 358, Nyberg Rel. 477-8).

²*Yadā-* sb. 'Yada', probably 'Anshan' (as shown by the Elam. translation 3.3 *an-za-an.mar*, read by Cameron; cf. §166.n2): not an abstract *yadā-* 'loyalty', to root *yad-* (q v.), as commonly taken (wrongly also Foy, KZ 35.43; Husing, OLZ

8.513-6; Hz. ApI 244-9; Nyberg, Rel. 477-8). *Yadāyā* absf. (§141, §175) DB 3.26.

yadiy conj. 'if, when': Av. *yeiδi*, Skt. *yádi*: perhaps pAr. nt. rel. *$\ast\underset{\circ}{i}ad$ + deictic -*i*. Syntax §297.
(1) 'if', with subj.: DB 4.38f, 54, 57, 72f, 77; DPe 19, 22; DNa 38 (*yadi-patiy*); DNb 29 (*yadi-vā*; cf. Hz. ApI 359); XPh 47 (*yadi-maniyāiy*; §44, §52.VI); with opt., DNb 20f; with pres ind., DNb 25 (*yadi-vā*).
(2) 'when', with imf. ind., DB 1 38, DSf 14; 'whenever', with pres. ind., DNb 38f, 39.

yāna- sb. 'favor, boon': Av. *yąnā-*; deriv. of *yam-*, probably *ya-* from *$\underset{\circ}{i}m$-, with lengthening and suffix -*na-* (§147.I). *yānam* asm. DPd 21, 23°; XSc 4°.

yaniy conj. 'where, whereon': lsn. *ya^hmi* (= Skt. *yásmi-n*, Av. *yahmy-a* 'where') to relative stem *ya-*, with -*n-* after isn. **yanā*, cf. isn. *tyanā* to *tya-* (hardly *yanaiy*, loc. formed on stem *yana-* extracted from isn. **yanā*, as taken by Bthl. AiW 1262; not miswritten for *tyanaiy*, as taken by Müller, WZKM 7.112; other theories in Tm. Lex. 120 s.v.). Syntax §296. XV 22.

yam- vb. 'stretch, reach out': Av. *yam-* pres. *yasaiti*, Skt. *yam-*, pres. *yácchati*, OP pres. *yasa-*, pIE *$\ast\underset{\circ}{i}m$-sk̑e-*. See also *yāna-*.

ā + yam- 'reach out for, (mid.) take as one's own': *āyasatā* imf. mid. (§97, §215, §235.II) DB 1.47; 3.4, 42f.

ati- + yam- 'reach beyond, present, read aloud to': [*a*]*tīya*[*si*]*ya* (§23.I, §140.III, §220) imf. pass DB 4.91 (conj. of Kent, JAOS 62.268; for -*ī-*, cf. *nīyasaya*, below).

ni- + yam- 'reach out and down; (caus.) set down': *nīyasaya* imf. caus. (§23.I, §140.III, §215) DNb 5, 46, 49 (Jn. JAOS 38.123-4; MB Gr. §199; Johnson, Gr. §478b; Hz. ApI 359-61).

yāvā conj. 'as long as', isn. of **yāva-*, extension of pIE rel. *$\ast\underset{\circ}{i}o$-*, pAr. *$\ast\underset{\circ}{i}a$-*, cf. Skt. *yávat*, Av. *yavata*, Gk. ἕως (from *$\ast\underset{\circ}{i}\bar{a}\underset{\circ}{u}os$); hardly from* *yāva^t* *ā* = GAv. (Ys. 43.8) *yavaṯ ā*, with contraction (Wackernagel, KZ 46.275-80). With subj. to show future time (§298): DB 4.71, 74, 78; 5.19, 35°.

raucah- sb. 'day': Av. *raočah-* 'light', Phl. *rōč*, NPers. *rōz*, Skt. *rócas-* 'light', pIE **leuqos* (§70, §107, §156.II), cf. Gk. λευκό-s adj. 'light'. *rauca* nsn. (§119, §185.I) DB 3.8. *rauca-pati-vā* (§99, §133) asn. DB 1.20. *raucabiš* ipn. (§119, §185.I) DB 1.38, 42, 56, 89f, 96; 2.26, 36, 42, 47, 56, 69f, 98°; 3.18f, 39, 47, 63, 68, 88f.

rautah- sb. 'river' (§166): NPers. *rōδ*, Skt. *srótas-* 'current, river', pIE **sreutos* (§118.II, §156.II) to root **sreu-* 'flow'; perhaps same as Av. *θraotah-*, with sandhi initial (Bthl. Gdr. IP 1.§87.-n2, AiW 800). *rauta* nsn. anacoluthic in naming phrase (wrongly gen.-abl. to stem *raut-*, Mt. MSLP 19.56-7, MB Gr. §167, §316) DZc 9.

Raxā- sb. 'Rakha', a town in Persia: Elam. *rak-qa-an* (§100). *Raxā* nsf. DB 3.34.

raxθatuv DNb 60, imv. of vb. of unknown etymology and uncertain meaning (§76.II, V, §103.III, §213, §237.II), perhaps 'inflict punishment upon', cf. Akk. version (Lg. 15.174; see also Hz. ApI 284-5).

ra^nga- sb. 'speed, haste': Av. *rang-* 'leicht, flink werden' (Bthl. AiW 1511), Skt. *ráṃhate* 'hastens, speeds', *ráṃhas-* nt. 'speed, quickness' (for further connections, see Uhlenbeck, Wrtb. d. altind. Sprache 241). *ragam* asn. (or asm.?) as adv. (§143.I, §191.III) DB 4.44, perhaps with development to 'eagerly' or 'confidently'.

Ragā- sb. 'Rhages', a district in Media: Elam. *rak-qa-an*, Akk. *ra-ga-'*, Gk. Ῥάγης, now Rai near Teheran. *Ragā* nsf. DB 2.71f. *Ragāyā* absf. DB 3.2f.

raθa- sb. 'wagon' (§76.II, §143.III), see *uraθa-*.

¹*rad-* vb. 'leave': Skt. *rah-*, pres. *rahati* 'separates, leaves', to pIE **reĝh-*, Av. *razah-* 'isolation', or to pIE **redh-*, NPers. (through Ars. Phl.) *rahaδ* 'he gets free from'; Fr. Muller, WZKM 11.203-4; Foy, KZ 37.564-5; Bthl. AiW 1505; MB Gr. §192.

ava- + rad- 'leave, abandon': *avarada* 2d sg. inj. (§213, §224, §227.II, §237) DNa 60.

²*rad-* vb. 'direct' Av. *raz-*, Skt. *rāj-* 'reign', Lt. *regō* 'I direct, rule', pIE **reĝ-*; in *uradana-*, *rāsta-*.

rādiy postpos. (§133) 'on account of', with gen.: NPers. *rā*, encl. postpos. as in *či-rā* 'why', also particle of various uses, often affixed to direct object for clarity; also OCS *radi*, postpos. with gen., 'on account of'; loc. sg. of *rād-* (§188.III), to root in Skt. *rādh-* 'effect, complete' (not to

²*rad-*, pIE **reĝ-*, with Hz. ApI 280). DB 4.54; DNb 9, 10f; also in *avahyarādiy*, q.v.

ram- vb. 'be at peace', with prefix *ā*, in *Ariyāramna-*, q.v.

rasa- present stem of vb., see *ar-*.

rāsta- adj. 'straight, right, true', with nt. as sb.; ptc. of ²*rad-*: Av. *rāšta-*, Turfan Phl. *rāšt* 'true', Lt. *rēctus* 'straight', pIE **rēk̂to-* (§93, §93.-n1-2, §106, §122, §126, §242.II). Cf. *arštā-*. *rāstām* asf. DNa 59. *rāstam* nsn. DNb 11; asn. DNb 7.

... *rtaiyaiy*, see *vart-*.

Labanāna- (or *Labnāna-*) sb. 'Lebanon' (§6, §107), a mountain in Syria famous for its cedars. *Labanāna* nsm. DSf 31.

-vā encl. conj. 'or' (§133, §291.III); *-vā ... -vā* 'either ... or ...': Av. *vā*, Skt. *vā*, pIE **u̯ē*, cf. Lt. *-ve*. *xšapa-vā rauca-pati-vā* DB 1.20. *hya-vā* DB 4.68. *imai-vā* DB 4.71, 73, 77. *yadi-vā* DNb 25, 29.

vaina- present stem of vb. 'see (mid.) seem': Av. *vaēna-*, NPers. *bīnaδ*, Skt. *véda* 'knows', *vindáti* 'finds', Lt. *videt* 'sees', *vidētur* 'seems'; pAr. **u̯aidna-*, pIr. **u̯aina-* (§69, §83.I, §130, §210.III; Reichelt, Aw. Elmb. §157). See also *Vidafarnah-*. *vaināmiy* 1st sg. (§226.I) DNb 36, 36f, 39, 40. *avaina* imf. DB 2.76, 90; DNa 32. *vainataiy* mid. as pass. (§235.I) DNb 2; XPa 16. *vaināhy* 2d sg. subj. (§37, §222.II, §227.I) DB 4.70, 73, 77; DNb 29. *vaināt̃iy* subj. (§222.II) DSj 5°. *vaināta̰iy* subj. mid. as pass. (§222.II) DNb 35.

vaʰu- adj. 'good' (§11, §153.I); nt. as sb. 'the good, (religious) goodness': Av. nsm. *vaṅhuš*, nsn. *vohu*, Skt. nsm. *vásuṣ*, nsn. *vásu*, pIE **u̯esu-*; in *Dārayavau-*, *Vaumisa-*, *Vahauka-*, *Vahyazdāta-*.

Vaʰumisa- sb. 'Vaumisa', a Persian officer of Darius: Elam. *ma-u-mi-iš-ša*, Akk. *ú-mi-is-sı*, Gk. (Plutarch) Ὤμισης; cpd. of *vaʰu-* and *miθra-* 'friend' (§49c, §78, §148.III): 'Friend of the Good' §160.-Ib; cf. MB Gr. §51). *Vaumisa* nsm. DB 2.49, 51, 62. *Vaumısam* asm. DB 2.53, 58.

vaxš- vb. 'grow', see *Uvaxštra-*.

¹*vaj-* vb. 'be strong': Skt. *vaj-*, *ójas-* 'strength', Av. *aojah-*, Lt. *auget* 'increases': perhaps in *āθahavaja*, q.v.

²*vaj-* vb. 'put out (eyes)', cf. JAOS 62.274: etymology uncertain (dubious equations by Foy, KZ 35.39, and by Bv. Origines 7). *avajam* 1st sg. imf. (§213) DB 2.75, 89.

vaçabara- sb. 'bowbearer' (JNES 4.233): *vaça-* 'bow' (§78, §148.III; uncertain connections in Wb. AbkSGW 29.1.42, and in Bv. Gr. §105) + *bara-* (§160.Ia), to *bar-* 'bear'. *vaçabara* nsm. DNd 1.

van- vb. 'overpower, pack down': Av. *van-* 'superare', pres. *vanaiti* (Bthl. AiW 1350 ¹*van-*; cf. JAOS 53.15–6, Wb. AfOF 7.41, Hz. ApI 346–7), Skt. *vánati* 'desires, gets by effort', Gt. *winnan* 'suffer', NEng. *wın*. *avanıya* imf. pass. (§220) DSf 25, 29 (not *akaniy*, as read by Scheil 21.26; Konig, Burgbau 32; Hz. AMI 3.49, 54; Schaeder, Ung. Jrb. 15.562).

vayam pron. nom. pl. 'we', see *adam*.

Vāyaspāra- sb. 'Vayaspara', father of Intaphernes: Elam. *mi-iš-par-+*, Akk. *mi-is-pa-ru-ʼ*. Acc. to Foy, KZ 35.63, *vayat-* 'weaving' (§162, §240), with vriddhi (§126), + *spāra-* 'shield' (§116, §143.III), 'Man of the Wicker Shield' (§163.Ib); cf. Av. *spāra-dāšta-* if 'having shield in hand' (epithet of Aši; the meaning is inappropriate, and the etymology is therefore rejected by Bthl. AiW 1358–9). *Vā[ya]sp[āra]hyā* gsm. DB 4.83.

var- vb. 'cover, protect; (mid.) choose, convince': Av. *var-*, pres. *vərənav-* (¹*var-*, ²*var*, ⁴*var-* of Bthl. AiW 1360-3, and perhaps ³*var-*, are reducible to one root as to form and meanıng), Skt. *vr̥ṇóti*, Gt. *warjan* 'ward off', Lt. *operıt* 'covers' (from **op-u̯er-*); OP pres. *varnava-* (§30, §210.I), thematic. See also *duvarθi-*, *Fravartı-*. *varnavataiy* mid. (§235.I) DNb 23. *ava[navatā]* imf. mid. (§235.II) DSf 17 (Hz. AMI 3.43; Kent, JAOS 53.11). *varnavātaiy* subj. mid. (§222.III) DB 4.49. *varnavatām* imv. mid. (§237.IV) DB 4.42, 53.

vāra- sb., see *Uvārazmī-*.

varka- sb. 'wolf', see *Varkāna-*.

Varkāna- sb. 'Hyrcania', a district southeast of the Caspian Sea (§166.I): Elam. *mi-ir-qa-nu-ı̯a-ıp* 'the Hyrcanians', Phl. and NPers. *Gurgān*, Gk. Ὑρκανία (§30, §99, §107); 'Wolf-Land', deriv. of pIE **u̯l̥q̯u̯o-*, Av. *vəhrka-*, Skt. *vŕ̥ka-*, Lith. *vilkas*, Gt. *wulfs* (§143.III): see also *Varkazana-*. *Varkāna* nsm. DB 2.92f.

Varkazana- adj. 'Varkazana', eighth month, Oct.-Nov.: Elam. *marqašanaš*, Akk. *araḫsamna*. From *varka-* 'wolf' (§143.III) + *zana-* 'man' (§9.-IV, §88, §120): 'Month of the Wolf-Men' (§161.-IIb). [*Varkazanahya*] gsm. DB 3.88, restored after the Elam. (see Wb. KIA 56-7; the first and the third *a*'s may have been long).

varga- sb., see *haumavarga-*.

vart- vb. 'turn', trans. in active, refl. or intrans in middle: Av. *varət-*, Skt. *vṛt-*, pres. *vártati vártate*, Lt. *vertit*, Gm. *werden* 'become', pIE *u̯ert-*. [*va*]*rtaiyaiy* 1st sg. mid caus. (§31, §48, §215, §233.II; JAOS 62.275, 63.67-8) DB 4.44 (Cameron's reading; not *upa-* + *ā* + *vart-*, [*upāva*]*rtaiy* with dittography in -*tᵃiyᵃiyᵃ*, as proposed by Tm. Vdt. Stud. 1 30-1, Lex. 122; for other restorations, see Gray JAOS 23.60-2, Bthl. WZKM 22.69, Wb. ZDMG 61.728, HK Phil. Nov. 3.103, ApKI 1.61, 2.28).

vard- vb. 'work': Av. *varəz-*, Gk. ϝέργον 'work', Gm. *Werk*, pIE *u̯erĝ-*; in *Artavardiya-*.

vardana- sb. 'town': Av. *vərəzāna-*, LAv. *varəzāna-* 'community', Skt. *vṛjána-* 'enclosed space', pIE *u̯ṛĝeno-* (§30, §147.I), to root *u̯erĝ-*, Skt. *vṛj-*, Gk. ἔργω 'I enclose' (discussion of etymology, with variant view, see Hall, Lg. 12.297-9). *vardanam* nsn. DB 1.92; 2.9°, 22, 66, 95f; 3.5, 22, 34, 51f; DSe 45f.

vasiy adv. (§191.III) 'at will, greatly, utterly'; as indecl. sb., 'much': Sas. Phl. *vas*, NPers. *bas*; loc. of root-sb. *vas-* (§9.VI, §87, §142), to pIE root *u̯eḱ-*, GAv. *vasəmī* 'I wish', Gk. (Cretan) ϝεκών 'willing'; unless properly *vasaiy* (§97), loc. of thematic stem *vasa-* (*u̯eḱ-sḱe-*, acc. to MB Gr. §114), from the present-tense stem of the same root. See also *vašnā*. DB 1.34, 51, 89, 95; 2.26, 36, 41, 46, 55, 61, 69, 98°; 3.7, 18, 39, 46, 63, 68, 4.46, 56, 75; 5.25°; DNb 26f; DSe 31°, 43; XPa 13; XPf 26, 37; XPg 3f; XV 19.

vašdāsaka, uncertain word in Sc, probably a man's name (§163.VII).

vašna- sb. 'will, favor': Av. *vasna-*; deriv. (§96, §147.I) of root *vas-* 'wish', see under *vasiy* (Mt. MSLP 17.354-6; Hz. ApI 349.52; stem *vašna-* acc to Bthl. AiW 1893 and MB Gr. §267, and not *vasan-* with Sen 5). *vašnā* ism. AmH 7; AsH 10; DB 1.11, 13f, 18, 22, 26, 59f, 68, 70, 88, 94°; 2.3°, 25, 35, 40, 45, 54, 60, 68, 86, 97; 3.6, 17, 37f, 45, 62, 67, 87; 4.4, 6, 41, 46, 52, 60, 88; 5.16, 32; DPd 4, 9, DPe 6; DNa 16, 35, 49; DNb 6, 47; DSa 4; DSd 3°; DSe 15, 34, 42; DSf 12, 21°; DSfv 55f; DSi 4; DSj 5; DSl 2; DSm 5; DSo 3°; XPa 11, 16; XPb 26; XPc 10; XPd 16; XPf 34, 43; XPg 2f, 7f (*vašnā*[*pi*]*y* §139, with Bv. BSLP 34.1.33, rather than *vašnā*[*ci*]*y* Lg. 9.229-30), XPh 14, 33, 36f, 44; XSa 1; XV 18f; A¹Pa 18°; D²Sb 4°; A²Sa 4°; A²Sd 3; A²Ha 5; A²Hc 16.

vazraka- adj. 'great': NPers. *buzurg*; deriv. of **vazra-*, Av. *vazra-* 'club', Skt. *vájra-* 'Indra's thunderbolt', pIE *u̯eĝro-*, to root *u̯eĝ-* 'be strong', Skt. *vajati*, Lt. *veget* (§9.III, §88, §120, §128, §143.II, §146.II, §154.I). For -*zra-*, cf. Bv. Origines 15; against *vazarka-* and *vazṛka-*, cf. W. Henning, GN 1932.224.An8, and Schaeder, SbPAW 1935.489.n1. *vazraka* nsm. AmH 1, 7; AsH 1, 6; CMb 1°; CMc°; DB 1.1; DBa 1; DPa 2; DPb; DPd 1; DPe 1f; DPh 1; DNa 1, 8f; DNb 1; DSa 1; DSb 3; DSc; DSd 1; DSe 1°, 8°; DSf 1°, 6, DSg 1°; DSi 1°; DSj 1; DSk 1; DSm 1; DSp 1°; DSs 1°; DSt 1; DSy 1; SZb 1; DZc 1, 5; DE 1, 13; DH 1; XPa 1, 6; XPb 1, 13, 23; XPc 1, 6, 10; XPd 1, 9, 15f; XPe 1f; XPf 1, 9; XPg 2; XPh 1, 7; XPj; XSc 1°; XE 1, 13; XV 1, 10; A¹Pa 1°, 10°, 18°; A¹I; D²Sa 2; D²Sb 1°; A²Sa 1; A²Sb; A²Sc 2; A²Sd 1; A²Ha 1; A²Hb; A²Hc 1, 7f; A³Pa 1, 9; Wa 4f; Wb 2; Wc 3; Wd 3; SXa 2; AVsa. *vazrakam* asn. DSf 11; DSm 4; DZc 4. *vazrakāyā* lsf. DNa 12; DSe 10f, DZb 4; DZc 6; DE 18; XPa 9; XPb 18; XPc 8; XPd 12; XPf 12f; XPh 10; XE 17f; XV 13f; A¹Pa 13f; A²Hc 17.

vah- vb. 'dwell', see *āvahana-*.

Vahauka- sb. 'Vahauka', father of Ardumanish: Elam. *ma-u-uk-qa*, Akk. *ú-ma-aḫ-ku*. Hypocoristic of name beginning *vaʰu-* 'good', with guna in second syllable and suffix *-ka-* (§146.II, §153.I, §164.III); cf. Bthl. AiW 1394-5. *Vahau-*[*kah*]*y*[*ā*] gsm. DB 4.86.

vāhara- sb. 'spring time', see *Θūravāhara-*.

vahyavˈšdāpaya (§22), uncertain word in Sd, probably a corrupt writing of a man's name (§163.VII).

Vahyazdāta- sb. 'Vahyazdata', a Persian rebel: Elam. *mi-iš-da-ad-da*, Akk. *ú-mi-iz-da-a-tú*. From *vahyah-* 'better' (§120, §156.III), Av. *vaṇhah-*, Skt *vásyas-*, comp. of OP *vaʰu-* (§190.II), + *dāta-* 'law': 'Follower of the Better Law (=

the true faith)' (§161.IIa). *Vahyazdāta* nsm. DB 3.22, 35, 41, 54, 60, 70f; 4.26, DBh 1f. *Vahyazdātam* asm. DB 3.27f, 48, 50. *Vahyazdātahya* (§36.-IVc) gsm. DB 3.38f, 46.

vi- prefix 'away, apart': Av. *vī*, Skt. *vi*; with verbal roots *kan-, jan-, tar-, naθ-, mard-*, and perhaps in sbb. *Vidarna-, Vīvāna-, Vištāspa-*, and adj. *Viyaxna-*.

viθ- sb. 'house, royal house, royal clan, court' (JNES 4.232): Av. *vīs-* 'Herrenhaus', Skt. *viś-* 'house, dwelling', Gk. οἶκος 'house', Lt. *vīcus* 'village' (§22, §87, §114, §142). Decl., §188.IV, V. *viθam* asf. AsH 12f; DPe 24; DPh 10; DNa 53; DSe 51; DSt 9°; DH 8; XPh 58; A²Hc 20. *vi̯θam* asf. DB 1.69, 71. *vi̯θā-patiy* isf. (Foy, KZ 35.37–8, 37.556; Hz. ApI 352–4) DB 2.16°; 3.26. *viθiyā* lsf. CMb note: DPc; DPi; DNb 30; DSg 3°; XPi°; XH; A¹I. *vi̯θi[yā]* DB 4.66. *vi̯θbiš-cā* ipf. (§87, §188.V) for apf. (§252.I) 'houses' DB 1.65 (Tm. Lex. 125–6, for various views; Gray, JAOS 33.281–3; Morgenstierne, Acta Or. 1.248–9; wrongly Sen 23, with ablatival meaning).

viθa- adj., probably 'royal, of the royal family', to *viθ-* 'royal house' (§143.II: Tm. Lex. 125; MB Gr. §282); but possibly 'all', the same as *visa-* 'all', because of the Akk. translation (Wb. KIA 81n.). *viθaibiš* ipm DPd 14, 22, 24.

Vindafarnah- sb. 'Intaphernes', a Persian, ally of Darius against Gaumata: Elam. *mi-in-da-par-na*, Akk. +-*in-*+-+-*na-*', Gk. Ἰνταφέρνης; from *vindat-* 'finding' (§111, §162, §211, §240; cf. OP *vaina-*, §83.I), Skt. *vindáti* 'finds', + *farnah-* 'glory' with Med. *f-* (§9.II, §9.n2, §118.IV; borrowed as Aram. *-farna*), Av. *xᵛarənah-* 'royal splendor', pIE *su̯el-nos* (§29.n2, §31, §107, §156.-II), cf. Gk. σέλας (*su̯el-n̥s*) 'brightness', Skt. *svàr* 'sun': 'Finder of the Glory' (Foy, KZ 35.5n; Mt. MSLP 17.107–9, MB Gr. §104; Morgenstierne, Acta Or. 1.249–50; Andreas ap. Lentz, ZII 4.288; Bv. BSLP 31.2.72–6). Otherwise on *farnah-*, Bailey, Zoroastrian Problems 1.77, esp. 1–3, 73–7: originally 'a thing obtained or desired', whence 'good thing(s), welfare, fortune', from pAr. *su̯ar-*, Av. *xᵛar-* 'get, take, esp. take food'. *Vidafarnā* nsm. DB 3.84, 86, 88; 4.83.

Vidarna- sb. 'Hydarnes', a Persian, ally of Darius against Gaumata: Elam. *mi-tar-na*, Akk. *ú-mi-da-ar-na-*', Gk. Ὑδάρνης. Perhaps *vi-* 'apart' + *dar-* 'hold', as 'Support, Security' (§31, §147.I, §164.II, IV), cf. Av. *vi-dar-* 'hold apart, support', *-darana-* 'stronghold, place of resort' (Bthl. AiW 692), Skt. *vi-dhṛ-* 'carry, hold apart, support', *vidharaṇa-* 'checking, supporting'; so Justi, INB 491 (hardly to Skt. *vidīrṇa-* 'torn apart', with Bthl. AiW 1443); possibly hypocoristic to a compound (§164.III). *Vidarna* nsm. DB 2.19, 21; 4.84.

Viyaxna- adj. 'Viyakhna', twelfth month, Feb.–March: Elam. *mi(ya)kannaš*, Akk. *addāru*; perhaps *vi-* + unidentified element (§103.III, §126, §147.I, §165), though Cameron, Pers. Treas. Insc. 45, notes that the more common Elam. transcriptions indicate rather *Vīyxana-* (cf. §23.I), perhaps from *vi* + *xan-* = Skt. *khan-* 'dig' (cf. OP *kan-*) as 'Digging-up (month)', appropriate to the agricultural activities of Feb.–March. *Viyaxnahya* (§36.IVa) gsm. DB 1.37; 2.98; 3.68.

Vivāna- sb. 'Vivana', a Persian, satrap in Arachosia: Elam. *mi-ma-na*, Akk. *ú-mi-ma-na-*'; possibly from *vi-* + root *van-* (§126, §143.I, §164.-II, IV), 'Conqueror, Winner' (hardly *vivahana-*, connected with Av. *vī-vah-vant-* the father of Yima, Skt. *vivásvant-*, §131; despite Bthl. AiW 1452, Hz. AMI 1.83.n2). *Vivāna* nsm. DB 3.55, 73. *Vivānam* asm. DB 3.58, 60, 65, 71.

visa- adj. 'all': OP (Med.) *vispa-*, Av. *vīspa-*, Skt. *víśva-*, pAr. *u̯íśu̯a-* (§90) for pIE *u̯íḱo-* (OCS *vìsĭ* 'all') after *-u̯a-* in (Skt.) *sárva-* (see OP *haruva-*; §150). See also *visadahyu-*, and cf. *viθa-, vispa-*. *visahyā* gsm. DSa 5; DSj 6. *visam* nsn. DSj 4°; DSl 5. *visam* asn. DNa 49; DSf 21; DSi 4°; XPa 16; XPb 25f; XPf 42; XPh 44.

visadahyu- adj. 'of or for all countries or provinces' (§161.IIa): borrowed in Elam. *mi-iš-ša-da-a-hu-iš* and (with Med. *vispa-*) Akk. *u-'-iš-pi-da-a-'-i*; *visa-* 'all' + *dahyu-* 'country, province'. *visadahyum* asm. (§53, §183.II) XPa 12.

vispa- adj. 'all': Median (§9.III, §90) for OP *visa-*, q.v. See also *vispazana-*. *vispā* absn. A²Sa 5°; A²Sda 4, A²Sdc 4 (*vi̯āspā* db, §55.I); A²Ha 6°.

vispazana- adj. 'containing all (kinds of) men' (§161.IIa): borrowed in Elam. *mi-iš-ša-da-na*, from the OP form *visadana-*: Med. *vispa-* 'all' + Med. *zana-* 'man, human being' (§9.III, §88, §90). *vispazanānām* gpf. DNa 10f; DSe 9f; DZc 5.

Vištāspa- sb. 'Hystaspes', father of Darius: Elam. *mi-iš-da-aš-ba*, Akk. *uš-ta-as-pa*, Gk. Ὑστάσπης. Prior element *višta-* perhaps ptc. of (Av.) *vaēs-* 'come in ready for action' (Bthl. AiW 1326), Skt. *viś-* 'enter', second part *aspa-* 'horse': 'Having ready horses' (§9.II, §9.n2, §93, §161.IIa, Lg. 21.55–8; current etymology unlikely: *višta-* ptc. of *vi-* + *had-* 'sit, settle down', Skt. *vi-ṣad-* 'sink, despond', giving meaning 'Having spiritless horses', which would be an ill-omened name; and this ptc. would be OP *višasta-* or the equivalent of Skt. *viṣaṇṇa-*, not *višta-*; also wrongly Husing, OLZ 15.537–41, who takes prior part as a reduced form of *vahišta-* 'best'). *Vištāspa* nsm. DSf 13; XPf 17f, 20. *Vištāspa* (§22) DB 1.4; 2.93, 94, 97; 3.4, 7; DBa 5. *Vištāspam* asm. DSf 57f°. *Vištāspam* (§22) DB 3.2, 3. *Vištāspahyā* gsm. DPa 4f; DPb; DPe 4; DPh 2; DNa 12f; DSc; DSd 2; DSf 7; DSg 2; DSi 2; DSj 1°; DSm 2°; DSy 2f; DZb 5; DZc 6; DE 19f; DH 2; XPf 18f; A²Hc 14; Wa 5f; Wb 7f; Wc 8f; Wd 8f. *Vištāspahyā* (§22) DB 1.2f, 4; DBa 3, 5f; DSa 2; DSb 9f; DSe 11f; DSk 2; A²Sa 3; A²Sc 0°; A²Ha 4°, A³Pa 18f, 19.

Višpauzāti- sb. 'Vishpauzati', a town in Parthia; Elam. *mi-iš-ba-u-za-ti-iš*. *Viš[pa]uz[ā]tiš* nsf. DB 2.95.

sā- vb. 'erect, build': probably from pIE *ḱyā-*, Av. *spā-* 'throw, throw away, set down', Ars. Phl. *pari-sp* 'wall' (§90; Bv. Gr. §113, cf. König, Burgbau 49–50; wrongly Bv. BSLP 30.1.-66–7).

fra- + *sā-* 'erect, build': *frāsah[ya]* s-aor. pass. (§218.I, §220) DSf 27 (1st sg. act. *frāsaha[m]* is possible, as proposed by Kent, JAOS 53.15, and approved by Schaeder, Ung. Jrb. 15.562.n2).

Saka- adj. 'Scythian' (§116, §143.III); masc. sg. as sb., 'Scythia' as province or district; masc. pl. also as name of the province, often with modifiers (cf. JNES 2.304-5; for other discussion, cf. A. Hermann, AfOF, Beiheft 1, Festschrift Oppenheim 157–64 [1933], and J. Kluge, Klio, Beiheft 41, Saka-Studien [1939]). Elam. *sa-ak-qa*, Akk. *gi-mi(r)-ri*, Gk. Σκύθης, Σκυθία. See also *Sakā-*. Probably 'dog' in good sense, = 'guardian of the flocks', pIE *ḱyon-*, Med σπάκα 'dog' (Herod. 1.110), cf. Van Windekens, Beitr. z. Namenforschung 1.98–102.

(1) 'Scythian': *Saka* nsm. DBk 2. *Sakā* npm. as nsm. (§56.III) DN xv; A?P 14, 15, 24. *Sakā* npm. DB 5.31. *Sakā* apm. DB 5.22°, 25. *Sakaibiš* ipm. for abpm. (§252F) DPh 5; DH 4.

(2) 'Scythians', a province of the Persian Empire: *Sakā* npm. DPe 18; DNa 25, 25f, 28; DSe 24°, 25°; XPh 26 bis.

(3) 'Scythia': *Saka* nsm. DB 1.16f; 2.8.

Sakā- sb. 'Scythia', fem. of preceding, as sb. *Sakām* asf. DB 5 21f.

siⁿkabru- sb. 'carnelian': Elam. *ši-in-qa-ab-ru-iš*, Akk. *ṣi-in-ga-+-ru-ú* (§6, §75.V, §116, §153.I; JAOS 54.57–8). For meaning, cf. Bleichsteiner, WZKM 37.101–3; Konig, Burgbau 62–3; Kent, JAOS 53.18, 54.37–8; 'cinnabar', Hz. AMI 3.64–5, ApI 303–5; 'serpentine', Gray, AJP 53.68–9. *sikabruš* nsm. DSf 37f.

Sikayaʰuvati- sb. 'Sikayauvati', a fortress in Media: Elam. *ši-ik-ki-ú-ma-ti-iš*, Akk. *sik-kam-u-ba-at-ti-'*. Possibly *sika-yas-vatī-*, fem. adj. derived from θikā- (q.v.; also §9.I, §87, §152.II, §156.III, §157); therefore 'Fort Rubble' from a wall of broken stones and mortar. Cf. Hz. AMI 3.55–6. *Sika[ya]uvatiš* nsf. DB 1.58.

siyamam adj., asm. for nsm., 'made of silver', A¹I; characters clear, but word dubious (§55.II, §56.V, §116, §149.I). Apparently for NPers. *sīm* 'silver', from Phl. *asēm*, borrowed from Gk. ἄσημον '(unstamped) silver', NGk. ἀσῆμι 'silver'; but this seems anachronistic. Hz. ApI 296–9 (also AMI 7.2–3, 8.10–7) normalizes *saiymam*: against authenticity of the inscription, cf. Schaeder, SbPAw 1935.489–96.

Sugda- Suguda- sb. 'Sogdiana', a province of the Persian Empire: Elam. *šu-ug-da*, Akk. *su-ug-du*, Gk. Σογδιανή (§22, §103.IV, §116, §128). *Sugda* nsm XPh 21. *Suguda* (§128) DB 1.16; DNa 23; DSe 22°; DSm 9°. *Sugᵘda* (§22) DPe 16. *Sugdam* asm. DPh 6; DH 5. *Sugudā* absm. DSf 38.

skauθi- adj. 'poor, weak, lowly': Turfan Phl. 'škvh; cf. §6, §116, §152.I, §190.IV, JAOS 56 219–20, 58.324; Bv. JAs. 223.244–5, Hz. ApI 305–10. Initial *sᵃ* is clear in photographs of DNb. *skauθiš* nsm. DNb 8f. *skauθim* asm. DSe 39f; miswritten *škaurim* DB 4.65. *skauθaiš* gsm. DNb 10.

Skuⁿxa- sb. 'Skunkha', a Scythian rebel: Elam. *iš-ku-in-qa* (§100, §111, §116). *Skuxa* nsm. DB 5. 27; DBk 1f.

Skudra- adj. 'Skudrian'; masc. as sb., 'Skudra', a province of the Persian Empire, probably Thrace and Macedonia (cf. JNES 2.305): Elam. *iš-ku-ud-ra*, Akk. *is-ku-du-ru* (§116).
(1) 'Skudrian': *Skudra* nsm. A?P 25.
(2) 'Skudra': *Skudra* nsm. DNa 29; DSe 29°; DSm 10°; XPh 27 (written *Skudrā*; see §51, Lg. 13.298).

stā- vb. 'set; (mid.) stand': Av. *stā-*, Skt. *sthā-*, Gk. ἵστημι, Lt. *sistō stō*, pIE **st(h)ā-* (§76.II, §116, §122, §132.2–3). See also *upastā-*, *stāna-*. *aʰištatā* imf. mid. (§27, §64, §117, §122, §209, §235.II) DB 1.85.

ava- + stā- 'set down, place, restore': *avāstāyam* 1st sg. imf. (§214) DB 1.63, 66, 69.

ni- + stā-, generalized *ništā-* (§117, §140.VI), 'enjoin, command' (cf. Altheim, ZII 3.37; Hz. ApI 315–8): *niyaštāyam* 1st sg. imf. (§140.III, §214) DB 3.91; DZc 8, 11; XV 23f. *niyaštāya* imf. DSn 1; XPh 50; XV 21; *nīštāya* (§23.I, §140.-III) XPh 52f.

stāna- sb. 'place': Av. *-stāna-* in cpds., NPers. *-stān*, Skt. *sthā́na-*; deriv. of root *stā-* (§116, §122, §132.2–3, §147.I). See also *ardastāna-*. *stānam* asn. XV 20f.

staᵐb- vb. 'revolt': NPers. *sitamb-* 'revolt', perhaps also Skt. *sta(m)bh-* 'fasten, hold up, oppose' (Wb. AbkSGW 29.1.34; Mt. JAs. 1911.637; MB Gr. §202). *stabava* 2d sg. inj. (§216, §224, §227.II, §237) DNa 60.

stūnā- sb. 'column': Av. *stū́na-* masc., *stūnā-* fem., NPers. *sutūn*, Skt. *sthū́ṇā-* (§147.I). *stūnā* npf. DSf 45 (wrongly nsf. collective, Hz. AMI 3.68–9). [*stūnā*] apf. DSg 3°. *stūnāya* uncertain form, perhaps lsf. (for *-āyā*, §52.III, §176, §255; hardly adj. asm., with Hinz, ZDMG 95.250; wrongly Kent, JAOS 51.227–8) D²Sa 1, A²Hb.

spāda- sb. 'army': GAv. *spāda-*, NPers. *sipāh*, Anglo-Indian *spahi*; in *Taxmaspāda-*, cf. *spāθmaida-* (76.V, §83.II, §116, §143.III). Possibly from pIE **ḱyā-* 'swell, be great' (Gray, Lg. 25. 377–8; cf. §90).

spāθmaida- sb. 'camp, war', meaning shown by Akk. version: cf. *spāda-* 'army' (§83.II), Av. *hamaspaθmaēdaya-* name of a diety and of his festival (Hz. ApI 310–5). *spāθmaidayā* loc. sg. DNb 30f.

Sparda- sb. 'Sardis', a province of the Persian Empire: Elam. *iš-par-da*, Akk. *sa-par-du*, Gk. Σάρδεις (§31); with **śy-*, seen in Lydian *Śfard-* (MB Gr. §52; Hz. AMI 3.63–4). See also *Spardiya-*. *Sparda* nsm. DB 1.15; DPe 12; DNa 28; DSe 27°; DSm 7°; XPh 22. *Spardā* absm. DPh 7f; DSf 36; DH 6.

Spardiya- adj. 'Sardian': deriv. (§144.III) to preceding; cf. JAOS 54.40, Hz. AMI 3.37. *Spardi[ya]* nsm. A?P 22. *Spardiyā* npm. DSf 49, 52.

-ša- and *-ši-*, encl. pron. of 3d person: pIE **so- *sĭ-*, Ar. **sa- *sĭ-* and **ša- *šĭ-* acc. to sandhi, pIr. **ha- *hĭ-* and **ša- *šĭ-* (§117; decl., §195), Av. gen.-dat. sg. *hē šē*, acc. sg. *hīm*, acc. pl. *hīš*, Skt. *sīm* etc. Sg. forms may refer to pl. antecedents, and the OP forms make no distinction for gender.

-šim acc. sg. with sg. masc. antecedent, DB 1.50 (as abl., see *hacā*), 59 bis, 83, 96; 2.13°, 75, 76, 90 bis; 3.74; 4.49; 5.13, 27. *-šim* with fem. sg. antecedent, DNa 36; XPh 34. *-šim* with sg. nt. antecedent, DB 1.62. *-šim* with pl. nt. antecedent, DB 4.6.

-šaiy gen.-dat. with sg. masc. antecedent, DB 1.57; 2.30°, 50, 74, 74f, 77, 88, 95°; 3.14, 48, 51, 74, 90°, 91°; DPd 3; DNb 26; DSp 2°. *-šaiy* with sg. nt. antecedent, DSf 23°.

-šām gen. pl. with masc. antecedent, DB 2.13, 20 bis, 27, 37, 42, 47, 56, 62, 83 bis, 98; 3.8, 19, 31, 40, 47, 57 bis, 64, 69, 85 bis; 5.8°, 12°, 15, 27°. *-šām* with fem. antecedent *dahyāva*, DB 1.14, 19, 23; DNa 18, 20, 36f; DSe 17°, 19°; XPh 16, 18.

-šiš acc. pl. with masc. antecedent, DB 3.52.
-ša abl. sg., as suffix to ablatival adverbs *avadaša*, *dūradaša*, perhaps *avaθāša-tā* (Bthl. BB 14.247, AiW 170–1, despite Bv. Gr. §325; wrongly Foy, KZ 35.29–30).

šarastibara, see *arštibara-*.

-ši-, see *-ša-*.

šiyāta- adj. 'peaceful, happy (on earth)': GAv. *šyāta-* 'joyous', LAv. *šāta-*, Lt. *quiētus* 'quiet' (§104): past ptc. pass. to Av. *šyā-* 'rejoice' (§242.II). See also *šiyāti-*, with further remarks on meaning. *šiyāta* nsm. XPh 47, 55 .

šiyāti- sb. 'welfare, peace (on earth), happiness (also after death)' (Hz. AMI 3.40, 8.68–9, RHRel. 113.26–7, ApI 318–22): LAv. *šāti-* 'joy', also in queen's name (Gk.) Παρύσατις, Lt. *quiēs quiēt-is* 'quiet' (§104, §152.III, §179.III); see also *šiyāta-*. For 'happiness after death', see JNES 7.108 with notes 10 and 11. *šiyātiš* nsf. DB 5.20°, 36°; DPe 23. *šiyātim* asf. DNa 4; DNb 2f; DSe 4°; DSf 3; DSs 4°; DSt 4°; DZc 2; DE 5f; XPa 3; XPb 5f; XPc 3; XPd 4; XPf 4; XPh 3; XE 6; XV 5; A¹Pa 4°; A²Hc 4; miswritten *sāyatām* (§55.I) A³Pa 4.

šiyav- vb. 'set forth, go': GAv *šyav-*, LAv. *šav-*, NPers. *savád*, Skt. *cyávati*, Gk. σεύω 'I start quickly after, chase, cause to chase', pIE **qi̯eu-* (§104). *ašiyavam* 1st sg. imf. (§213) DB 1.84, 91; 2.3, 65; 5.21. *ašiyava* imf. DB 1.33 bis, 41, 80; 2.2f, 17, 22, 32, 51f, 72, 85, 95°; 3.4, 16, 28, 32, 33, 42, 59f, 72, 73f, 82, 87; 5.9; XPf 33f. *ašiyavaⁿ* 3d pl. imf. (§232.II) DB 1.76.

škaurim, see under *skauθi-*.

štā-, see under *stā-*.

zana- sb. 'human being': Av. *zana-*, Skt. *jána-*, Gk. γόνος 'child, offspring', pIE **ĝono-* (§88, §143.I); in *paruzana-*, *Varkazana-*, *vispazana-*.

zam- sb. 'earth': Av. nom. *ză*, Gk. χαμαί 'on the earth', Lt. *humus* 'earth', Lith. *žėmė*, pIE **ĝhem-* (§11, §142, §143.II), cf. **ĝdhem-* in Skt. *kṣam-*, Gk. χθών; in *Uvārazmī-*, *uzma-*.

[*za*]*rtanayā* with Med. *z-*, alternative restoration for [*da*]*rtanayā*; see *dartana-*.

Zazāna- sb. 'Zazana', a town on the Euphrates above Babylon: Elam. *za-iz-za-an*, Akk. *za-za-an-nu* (§120). *Zazāna* nsm. DB 1.92.

zūrakara- sb. 'evil-doer' (§143.V, §160.Ia): *zūrah-* 'evil' (§105, §119, §120) + *kara-* 'doer' (§99, §122), to vb. *kar-*. *zūrakara* nsm. DB 4.64, 68.

zūrah- sb. 'deceit, wrong': Av. *zūrah-*, NPers. *zūr* 'lie', cf. Skt. *hváras-* 'crookedness, deceit, trap' (§9.IV, §88, §120, §156.II); see also *zūrakara-*. *zūra* asn. DB 4.65.

Zūzahya- sb. 'Zuzahya', a town in Armenia: Elam. *su-iz-za*, Akk. *zu-ú-zu* (§120). *Zūzahya* (all characters visible acc. to Cameron) DB 2.33.

zbā- vb. 'call' (Lg. 19.226–7; Hz. AMI 8.67, ApI 367): Av. *zav-* and *zbā*, pres. *zbaya-*, Skt. *hū-* and *hvā-*, pres. *hvaya-*, pIE **ĝhu̯ā-* (Med. *zb-*, §9.VI, §91, §120); see also *hazāna-*.

pati- + *zbaya-* 'proclaim' (used of prohibitions only, Bv. BSLP 42.2.70): *patiyazbayam* 1st sg. imf. (§214) XPh 38.

Zraⁿka- adj. 'Drangian'; masc. as sb., 'Drangiana', a province of the Persian Empire: Elam. *sir-ra-an-qa*, Akk. *za-ra-an-ga*, Gk. (Hdt.) Σαράγγαι, (Polybius) Δραγγήνη, (Strabo) Δραγγιᾱνή, (Arrian) Ζαράγγαι (§9.I, §33, §88, §120, §128; cf. MB Gr. §119).

(1) 'Drangian': *Zrakā* for nsm. (§56.III) A?P 9.

(2) 'Drangiana': *Zraka* nsm. DB 1.16; DPe 15f; DNa 24; DSe 23°; DSm 8°; XPh 20.

ha- insep. prefix (§204.I), anteconsonantal (§132.1): Av. *ha-*, Skt. *sa-*, Gk. ἁ-, Lt. *sem-*, pIE **sm̥-*, zero-grade of pIE **sem-* 'one', Gk. εἷς ἕν (from **sem-s *sem*); in *hakara-*, *hadā*. See also *ham-*, *hama-*.

hainā- sb. 'army': Av. *haēnā-*, Phl. *hēn*, Skt. *sénā-* (§118.I, §147.I). *hainā* nsf. DPd 19. *haināyā* absf. DPd 16f.

hauv pron. 'this one', pron. adj. 'this' (§11, §263): pIE nsm. **so*, nsf. **sā*, Av. *hō* (from **so-s*), *hā*, Skt. *sa-s sā*, Gk. ὁ ἡ 'the', + particle **u*, Skt. *u* 'also', seen in Gk. πάν-υ 'altogether', οὗτος 'this' from **so-u-tos*, probably also in OP *u-tā* 'and'. OP *hăuv* shows the regular contraction of *ă-u* (§118.IV, §196); but **sāu*, with *ā* by analogy of the fem., was generalized as masc.-fem. in Av. *hāu*, Skt. *a-sáu*. See also *hawvam*, *hya*.

hauv pron. nsm. AsH 8, 14; DB 1.36, 38, 41, 47, 47f, 74, 76, 78, 81; 2.10, 14, 16°, 17, 19, 24, 93f; 3.23f, 26f, 28, 55, 71, 79, 80, 82, 83; 4.8°, 9, 10, 12, 13, 15, 16, 17, 18, 20, 21, 22, 24, 25, 26, 28, 29°, 30; 5.26°; DPd 2; DSf 9, 9f, 30, 31, 38, 39; DSp 1°; XPh 54; XV 18, 21. *hauv-maiy* DB 2.79. *hau-maiy* DSf 10. *hau-šaiy* DPd 3; DSp 2°. *hau-dim* DSf 32. *hau-diš* DSs 6°.

hauv nsf. (§196) DB 5.4f; *hauv-maiy* DB 3.11; *hauv-taiy* DNa 57; *hauv-ciy* DPe 23f.

hauv adj. nsm. DB 1.82, 92°; 2.21, 27, 66, 71; 3.3, 35, 41, 54, 59, 70, 91°; 5.9°.

haumavarga- adj. 'hauma-drinking' or 'hauma-preparing' (§160.Ia): Elam. *u-mu-mar-qa*, Akk. *ú-mu-ur-ga-'*, Gk. Ἀμύργιοι. From *hauma-* (§149.I), Av. *haoma-*, Skt. *sóma-* name of a plant, also a drink prepared from the juice of its crushed stems, to root Av. *hau-*, Skt. *su-* 'press', + *varga-* (§31, §143.I), of unknown connections. *hauma-*

vargā npm. DNa 25; DSe 24f°; XPh 26; as nsm. (§56.III), A?P 14.

hauvam pron. 'he', nsm. DB 1.29: *hauv* (q.v.) + *-am* from *adam, tuvam*, etc. (§48, §137, §196). Cf. MB Gr. §158.

hakaram adv. 'once' (§191.III, §204.I): Av. *hakərət* 'once', Skt. *sakŕ̥t*, cf. Gk. ἄ-παξ, Lt. *sem-el*; *ha-* (q.v.) + **kr̥t* 'time' (cf. Lith. *kar̃tas* 'time'), remade to *-karam* after *kara-* 'maker' (Hz. ApI 181). Cf. also Bv. Gr. §323. *hakaram-ciy* DNb 34f.

*ha*ᵐ*karta-* (§140.V) ptc. adj., nt. as sb., 'co-operation': *ham-* + *karta-* 'done', past. ptc. pass. to *kar-*. [*ha*]*kartahyā* gsn. DNb 16f (Kent, JNES 4.42–3; not *karr̥pahyā* or [*u*]*karr̥tahyā*, with Hz. ApI 233–5; not [*ha*]*karr̥tahyā*, with dittography of *rᵃ*, with Kent, Lg. 15.170).

Haxāmaniš- sb. 'Achaemenes' (§161.Ib), founder of the Achaemenian dynasty: Elam. *ha-ak-qa-man-nu-iš*, Akk. *a-ḫa-ma-ni-iš-'*, Gk. Ἀχαιμένης. From *haxā-*, LAv. nsm. *haxa*, Skt. nsm. *sákhā* 'friend', + *maniš-*, with reduced grade of vowel in ultima (§63.II, §124.4, §156.IV, §185.III, n1), otherwise identical with *manah-* (q.v.). See also *Haxāmanišiya-*. *Haxāmaniš* nsm. DB 1.6; DBa 8. *Haxāmanišahyā* gsn. (§57, §185.III; cf. Hz. AMI 4.133, 8.31–4) AmH 3f.

Haxāmanišiya- adj. as sb. 'Achaemenian': adj. to preceding (§144.III, §159, §185.n1; hardly *-šya-* from *-tya-*, as suggested by MB Gr. §262, cf. Hz. AMI 4.133, 8.31–4). *Haxāmanišiya* nsm. AsH 4; CMa 2; CMb 2°; CMc°; DB 1.3; DBa 4; DPa 5; DPb; DPe 5; DPh 3; DNa 13; DSb 11; DSd 2; DSe 12; DSf 7f; DSg 2; DSi 2°; DSj 2; DSk 3; DSm 2; DSy 3; DZb 6; DZc 6f; DE 20; DH 2; XPb 20f; XPc 9; XPd 14; XPe 4; XPf 14f; XPh 12; XPj; XPk; XSc 2; XE 20; XV 15f; A¹Pa 16°; A¹I; D²Sb 2; A²Sc 1; A²Sdb 2; A²Ha 5; A²Hb; A²Hc 15; A³Pa 20f; Wa 7f; Wb 8f; Wc 9f; Wd 9f. *Hāxāmanišiya* (§53) XPa 10f. *Haxāmanišᵃya* (§22) DSa 2f; A²Sda, dc 2. *Haxamānᵃšiya* (§22, §51) A²Sa 3. *Haxāmanišiyā* npm. DB 1.7; DBa 10.

*Ha*ᵐ*gmatāna-* sb. 'Ecbatana', a royal residence in Media: Elam. *ag-ma-da-na*, Akk. *a-ga-ma-ta-nu*, Gk. (Hdt.) Ἀγβάτανα, (Aesch., Aristoph.) Ἐκβάτανα, NPers. *Hamadān*. Probably deriv. of *ha-gmata-* (q.v., under *gam-*; §103.-IV, §147.II): 'City of Gatherings'. *Hagmatānaiy* lsm. DB 2.76, 77f.

hacā prep. 'from': GAv. *hacā*, LAv. *hacā*, Skt. *sácā* 'with' (on meanings, see Fay, JAOS 31.403–12): instr. sg. of thematic root-noun to pIE **seqᵘ-* 'follow', Av. *hačaite*, Skt. *sácate*, Gk. ἕπεται, Lt. *sequitur*, Gr. *saíhvan* 'see' (§99). Syntax §271.

(1) With abl.: DB 1.36, 40, 61; 2.64; 3.2, 26; 4.37; DPd 11, 16, 17 bis; DPe 20; DNa 18, 46, 52; DSe 17, 38; DSf 31, 34, 35°, 35, 36, 38, 39, 41, 42, 43, 44; DZc 7, 10, 11; XPh 16, 57; A²Sa 5°; A²Sda 4 (*hašā* dc 4, §49b); A²Ha 6°. *hacā-ma* DB 1.19, 23; 2.6, 12, 16, 93°; 3.27, 78, 81; 4.92; DPe 9; DNa 20; DSe 19°; XPh 18.

(2) With loc. form as abl.: DPh 7; DSf 33, 44; DH 5.

(3) With instr. form as abl.: DPh 5; DH 4.

(4) With ablatival adverbs: *hacā avadaša* DB 1.37; 3.42, 80; DSe 47f°; DSf 47. *hacā paruviyata* DB 1.7, 8, 45; DBa 11, 12. [*hacā-ci*]*y dūradaša* DSf 23.

(5) With preceding encl. pron. in acc.: *-šim hacā* DB 1.50 (Bang, ZDMG 43.534; Bv. BSLP 31.2.64–5).

(6) With anacoluthic naming-phrase in nom.: *hacā Pirāva nāma rauta* DZc 9.

*ha*ⁿ*j-* vb. 'hang': Skt. *sañj-* 'fasten', pres. *sájati*.

fra- + *ha*ⁿ*j-* 'hang out' for display (Foy, KZ 35.39), namely the rebel's skin, stuffed with straw (König, RuID 73–4; wrongly 'imprison', Sen 45): *frāhajam* 1st sg. imf. (§213) DB 2.78.

had- vb. 'sit': Av. *had-*, Skt. *sad-*, Lt. *sedet*, NEng. *sit*. See also *hadiš-*, and possibly *Vištāspa-*.

ni- + *šad-* (§117), caus. *ni-šādaya-* (§76.III, §122, §123.2, §132.2–3, §215) 'set down, establish': *niyašādayam* (§226.II) 1st sg. imf. DNa 36. *nīšādayam* (§23.I, §140.III) XPh 34f (cf. Hz. AMI 8.65, ApI 180–1).

hadā prep. with instr. 'with': GAv. *hadā*, LAv. *haδa*, Skt. *sahá*, pIE **sm̥-dhe* (§11, §67, §76.-III); Ar. **sa-* (see OP *ha-*) + adv. suffix *-dhe* as in *idā* etc. Syntax §270.I. DB 1.56, 93; 2.1f, 21f, 23, 67, 71, 85, 85f, 95°, 96; 3.5, 15, 16, 33, 36, 41, 71, 73, 86; 5.9°, 10°, 21, 24, DPd 14, 22, 24°; DPe 8; DSe 50; DSt 8°; XPb 28; XPc 12,

15; XPd 18; XPg 13; XSc 5°; XV 26; A¹Pa 23; D²Sa 3.

hadaxaya, uncertain word (§163.VII), Sb 1.

hadiš- sb. 'seat, abode, palace': Av. *haδiš-*; deriv. of *had-* 'sit'; for suffix cf. *Haxā-maniš-* to root *man-*, sb. *manah-*, and Skt. *sádas-*, Gk. nsn. ἕδος (§63.II, §76.III, §117, §122, §132.2–3, §156.IV, §185.III). *hadiš* nsn. DSf 22, 27; A²Sd 3. *hadiš* asn. DSj 5°; XPc 11; XPd 16f; XSa 2; XSc 3°; A¹Pa 19°; D²Sb 3°, 4°; A²Sc 5.

haᵐdugā- sb. 'record, statute': *ham-* + *dugā-*, from OP root *daug-*, Skt. *duh-* 'milk, press out', pIE *dheugh-* (§76.III, §140.V, §143.IV, V; Bv. BSLP 30.1.73–4, Gr. §260; otherwise König RuID 67–8, Hz. ApI 188–90); formation like Lt. *fuga*, Gk. φυγή 'flight'; for meaning, cf. NEng. *press* (sb.), *express*, *imprint*. *hadugām* DB 4.55, 57; DNb 23f.

haduᵇbānam, see *hazāna-*.

hanatā- sb. 'old age, lapse of time': abstract (§145) formed on *hana-* 'old', Av. *hana-*, Skt. *sána-*, Gk. ἔνος, Lith. *sěnas*, pIE *seno-* (§143.III), cf. Lt. *senex* 'old man'. *ha[natāyā]* isf. DSe 46 (conj. of Kent, JAOS 54.46, based on the Akk. version).

hapariya-, false interpretation of *apariyāya*; see *pari-* + *ay-*, under *ay-* 'go'.

ham- insep. prefix, 'together, with', like Lt. *com-* and Gk. σύν (with neither of which it is cognate): Av. *ham-*, Skt. *sam-*; originally identical with the numeral *sem-* 'one', q.v. under *ha-* (§132.1, §204.I). Found as prefix in *ha-karta-*, *Ha-gmatāna-*, *ha-dugā-*, *ham-arana-*, *ha-miçiya-*, and with verbs *gam-*, *taxš-*, *dar-*, perhaps with *kam-* (see under *amaxamatā*). See also *hama-*.

hama- adj. 'one and the same': Av. *hama-*, Skt. *samá-*, Gk. ὁμός, pIE *somo-* (§109, §143.II); deriv. of pIE *sem-* 'one', cf. *ha-* and *ham-*. Decl., §203.III. See also *hamātar-*, *hamapitar-*. *hama* nsm. 'unamimous' or asn. as adv. 'altogether' DB 4.92; asn. as adv. DB 4.90 (§191.III; JAOS 62.268–9). *hamahyāyā* gsf. formed on gsm. *hamahyă* (cf. *ahyāyā* to *a-*), DB 4.4, 41, 45, 52, 60.

hamātar- adj. 'having the same mother (as another person, specified)' (§161.IIa): *hama-* + *mātar-*, with haplology (§129). *hamātā* (§62, §124.5, §186.II, §186.n1) DB 1.30.

hamapitar- adj. 'having the same father (as another person, specified)' (§161.IIa): *hama-* + *pitar-* 'father'. *hamapitā* nsm. (§124.5, §186.II, §186.n1) DB 1.30.

hamarana- sb. 'battle': Av. *hamarəna-*, Skt. *samárana-*; sb. to verbal cpd. *ham-* + *ar-* (§32, §140.V, VI, §147.I; cf. Hz. ApI 182–4). See also *hamaranakara-*. *hamaranam* nsn. DB 2.27, 37, 42, 47, 56, 62, 98; 3.8, 19, 40, 47, 64, 69. *hamaranam* asn. DB 1.90, 93, 94, 96; 2.23, 33, 34, 38, 39, 44, 45, 53, 54, 58, 59, 67, 67f, 70, 85, 96; 3.5, 16, 36, 37, 43, 44, 60, 61, 65, 66; 5.10°. *hamaranā* apn. 4.5f, 32.

hamaranakara- sb. 'battle-maker, warrior': *hamarana-* + *kara-* 'maker', from root *kar-* (§160.Ia). Cf. also *ušhamaranakara-*. *hamaranakara* nsm. DNb 34.

hamiçiya- adj. 'rebellious', as sb. 'rebel': deriv. of *ham-* (or *ha-*) + *miça-* 'friend' (see *Miθra-*), as (pl.) 'conjurati', σύνορκοι' (§78, §144.IV, §148.III; MB Gr. §261, cf. Justi IFA 18.36; hardly first element neg. *a-*, 'unfriendly', remodeled to *ham-* by association with *ham-arana-* 'battle', as suggested by Pisani, Riv. Stud. Or. 19.96). Less probably the second element is *miθ-* of *miθah-* (so taken by Hz. ApI 184–6), with suffixes *-ro-* and *-iya-*. *hamiçiya* nsm. DB 1.40, 80; 2.16, 31, 51, 79, 94; 3.27, 81f. *hamiçiyam* asm. DB 2.26, 35, 41, 46, 55, 61, 84, 87, 97f; 3.7, 18, 63, 68; 4.9f, 12, 15, 17f, 20°, 23, 25f, 28, 30f; asn. DNb 36, 39. *hamiçiyā* npm. DB 1.76; 2.32, 38, 43, 52, 57f, 93 (§189.n1); 3.65, 78. *hamiçiyā* apm. DB 4.34. *hamiçiyaibiš* ipm. DB 3.6. *hamiçiyā* nsf. DB 3.11; 5.5. *hamiçiyā* npf. DB 2.6f; 4.33f.

Haraiva- sb. 'Arīa', a province of the Persian Empire: Elam. *ḫa-ri-ịa*, *ḫar-ri-ma*, Akk. *a-ri-e-mu*, Gk. Ἄρειοι; cf. Skt. *saráyu-* 'air, wind, also a certain river in India', to root in Skt. *sárati* 'flows'. See also *Harauvati-*. *Haraiva* nsm. DB 1.16; DPe 16; DNa 22f; DSe 21°; DSm 9°; XPh 21.

Haraʰuvati- adj. as sb, 'Arachosia', a province of the Persian Empire: Elam. *har-ra-u-ma-ti-iš*, Akk. *a-ru-ḫa-at-ti*, Gk. Ἀραχωσίᾱ; Skt. *sárasvatī* nsf. 'rich in waters', from root *sar-* 'flow', nt. sb. *sáras-* 'pond, lake', + adj. suffix *-vant-*, fem. *-vatī* (§118.IV, §152.II, §156.II, §157). Decl., §179.V. See also *Harauva-*, *Harauvatiya-*. *Harauvatiš* nsf. DB 1.17; DPe 17; DNa 24; DSe 23°; DSm 10°;

XPh 20. *Harauvatim* asf. DB 3.55. *Harauvatiyā* absf. DSf 44f. *Harauvatiyā* lsf. DB 3.56, 72, 76.

*Hara*ʰ*uvatiya-* adj. 'Arachosian': deriv. of preceding (§144.III). *Harauvatiya* nsm A?P 10.

haruva- adj. 'all': Av. *haurva-*, Skt. *sárva-*, Gk. Ion. οὖλος, Att. ὅλος, pIE **soluos* (§26, §35.II, §107, §114, §118.I, §150). Decl., §203.II. See also *fraharavam, haruvadā*. *haruva* nsm. DB 1.40, 80. *haruva-šim* DB 2.75, 90. *haruvahyāyā* lsf. formed on gsm. **haruvahyă* as stem (cf. *hamahyāyā, ahyāyā*), DSf 16, 18. *haruvahyāya* (§36.-IVb) DSb 8.

haruvadā adv. 'everywhere': *haruva-* + adv. suffix *-dā* as in *avadā* (§191.II). DB 4.92° (conj. of Kent, JAOS 62.269, after the Elam. version).

hard- vb. 'send forth': Av. *hərəzaiti* 'releases, shoots', Skt. *sṛjáti sárjati*, MHG *selken* 'drizzle', pIE **selĝ-*.

ava- + *hard-* 'abandon', Skt. *ava-sṛj-* 'let loose, abandon': *avahar[da]* imf. lacking augment (§30, §52.IV, §213, §228.II), DB 2.94 (*-har[ja]* Tm. Vdt. Stud. 1.22, Lex. 70, corrected to *-har[da]* CS 21, Johnson IV 50, which is accepted by Bv. BSLP 31.2.69, Gr. §129; Wb. ZDMG 61.726 proposed *avahar[ta]*, nsm. ptc. pass. of *ava-* + cognate of Skt. *sar-* 'flow', approved by Morgenstierne, Acta Or. 1.249, but this is less likely, since there is an object acc.).

harbānam, see *hazāna-*.

Haldita- sb. 'Haldita', an Armenian, father of Arkha: Elam. *hal-ti-da* (§6, §107). *Halditahya* (§36.IVb) gsm. DB 3.79.

hašiya- adj. 'true': Av. *haiθya-*, Skt. *satyá-* (§80, §118.I): deriv. (§144.IV) of (Skt.) *sat-*, weak grade of pres. ptc. (Skt.) *sant-* (§240) to root pIE **es-* 'be' (Skt. *as-*, OP *ah-*), pIE **sṇt-i̯o-*. Possibly in *Āθiyābaušna-* (Hz. ApI 191-3). Cf. Lt. *absent-em, prae-sent-em, īn-sont-em*. *hašiyam* asn. DB 4.44.

hazāna- sb. 'tongue', graphic for *hizāna-* (§27), with OP *z* = Med. *zb* from IE *ĝhu̯* (§91, §120): Av. *hizvā-* varying with *hizū-*, Skt. *jihvā́-* perhaps to pIE root **ĝhu̯ā-* (see OP *zbā-* with Med. *zb*), with *i*-reduplication, and then, in Iranian, dissimilation of the initial (NPers. *zabān* 'tongue', from a dialect with *zb*, has anaptyctic *a*). OP stem identical with Av. *hizvā-* (*-zv-* for *-zb-* by influence of collateral *hizū-*) extended by a suffix which perhaps spread from the gen. pl. (§143.IV, §147.II; cf. Lommel, KZ 50.261). *h*ᵃ*zānam* (reading established by Cameron) asm. (§124.VI, §187) DB 2.74; previous reading and emendations: *harbānam* with *r*ᵃ *b*ᵃ *n*ᵃ damaged, KT; *h*ᵃ*zbānam* Mt. MSLP 19.58-9; *uzbānam* Wb. ZDMG 61.726; *had*ᵘ*bānam* Lommel KZ 50.260-2 accepted by Bv. Gr. §129, cf. Kent Lg. 19.226-7.

*Hi*ⁿ*du-* sb. 'Sind', a province of the Persian Empire, on the upper Indus River; Elam. *hi-in-du-iš*; Av. *hindu-*, Skt. *síndhu-* 'stream, the Indus, country around the Indus' (§27, §111, §118.V, §153.I). See also *Hiduya-*. *Hiduš* nsm. DPe 17f; DNa 25; DSe 24°; DSm 10°; XPh 25. *Hiduv* lsm. as abl. (§251D), DPh 7; DSf 44 (*h*ᵃ*id*ᵃ*uv*ᵃ; not *h*ᵃ*id*ᵃ*av*ᵃ = *Hidāva* as taken by Scheil 21.18, König Burgbau 34, Bv. Gr. §318); DH 5f.

*Hi*ⁿ*duya-* adj. '(man) of Sind': deriv. to preceding (§27, §144.III). *Hiduya* nsm. A?P 13.

hya nsm., *hyā* nsf., rel. pron. and def. art.; cf. similar forms in Skt. (Vedic) *syá-s syā́* 'this': contamination of demonst. Av. *hō hā*, Skt. *sa-s sā*, Gk. ὁ ἡ, pIE **so *sā*, with relative stem pIE **i̯o-*, see under ¹*tya-*; cf. also *hauv, hyā, hyāparam*. Decl., §198; syntax §261, §262.

(1) rel. 'who, which': *hya* nsm. DB 1.21, 22, 49, 51, 84, 93; 2.13 (*hya-šām*), 18, 21, 23, 31, 51, 66, 84, 95 (*hya-šaiy*); 3.15, 30, 35, 54, 58, 70, 86, 89°; 4.37, 38°, 41, 48°, 65, 66, 68, 68°, 68 (*hya-vā*), 70, 82, 87; 5.18, 34°; DPa 5f; DNa 1, 2, 3, 3f, 5; DNb 1, 2, 3, 16, 17; DSe 1, 2, 3°, 4°, 5°; DSf 1, 2°, 2, 3°, 3, 38, 40, 43, 58°; DSj 5; DSs 1°, 2, 4°, 5°; DSt 1°, 2°, 3°, 4, 5°, 10°; DZc 1 bis, 2 bis, 3 bis; DE 2, 3, 4, 5, 7; XPa 1, 2 bis, 3 bis; XPb 2, 3, 4, 5, 7; XPc 1, 2 bis, 3, 4; XPd 1, 2, 3, 4, 5; XPf 1, 2, 3, 4, 5, 23; XPh 1, 2 bis, 3, 4, 46, 51; XE 3, 4, 5, 6, 7; XV 2, 3, 4 bis, 6; A¹Pa 1°, 2°, 3°, 4°, 5°; A¹I (for gsm., §56.V); A²Hc 2, 3 bis, 4, 5; A³Pa 1, 2, 3, 4, 5. *hyā* nsf. DPd 8; *hya* as nsf. (§52.III) AmH 6.

(2) def. art. 'the': *hya* nsm. AsH 6; DB 1.39, 44, 46, 53, 64, 65, 70, 79 bis, 85; 2.16, 25°, 27, 35, 40, 46, 55, 60, 87, 3.17, 25, 26, 32, 38, 45, 62, 67, 81; 4.9°, 14, 27, 30°; DBb 2,.5; DBd 5; DBh

LEXICON

6; DBi 7; DBk 2; DPd 1; DPh 9; DSe 39; DSf 9, 12, 13, 29, 30, 32, 37, 39; DSp 1°; DH 7; XPc 11; XPf 30; XPg 7; XSa 2; XE 2; XV 1, 18; A¹Pa 20°; D²Sb 4°; A²Hb; A²Hc 1. *hyā* nsf. DB 1.8; DBa 12; DNa 56 (on *hyā* DPe 22, see *hyā*, below).

hyā absn. of preceding as adv., 'from this time on' (§191.III, §198; Bthl. IF 12.127n, AiW 1844); not nsf. making an attributive adj. of the following adv. (Foy, KZ 37.561; Mt. MSLP 19.- 55), nor 3d sg. opt of *ah-* 'be' (Thumb ap. Tm. Lex. 70; Hz. ApI 64). DPe 22.

hyāparam phrasal adv. 'later than this, after this': probably abl. *hyāᵗ* + *aparam* (§84, §191.III, §198; Foy, KZ 35.10, 37.500; Kent, Lg. 20.8–9), hardly *param* (Bthl. BB 14.246, AiW 1844), cf. *hyā duvaištam* DPe 22f; hardly asn. *hyaᵗ* + *aparam*, with crasis (Mt. MSLP 19.55, Bv. Gr. §339). DB 3.43, 64f.

NUMERALS (§43, §251C, §252D, §262.II; Lg. 19.228–9)

𐏑	I	DB 1.36, 74, 77; 2.8°, 14, 75°, 79, 89; 3.8, 12, 22, 57, 78; 4.7, 10°, 12°, 15, 18, 20, 23, 26°, 28; 5.5°, 7°.		𐏒𐏒𐏒	XV	DB 2.56.
				𐏒𐏒𐏒	XVIII	DB 2.41.
				𐏒𐏒𐏒	XIX	DB 4.5.
𐏑	II	DB 1.96; Wa 1.		𐏒	XX	DSf 26°.
𐏒	V	DB 3.47.		𐏒𐏑	XXII	DB 2.98°; 3.88.
𐏒	VII	DB 3.68.		𐏒𐏒	XXIII	DB 1.17; 3.18.
𐏒	VIII	DB 1.9, 2.36; DBa 14.		𐏒𐏒	XXV	DB 2.69.
𐏒	IX	DB 1.10; 42; 2.47; 4.7, 32; DBa 17.		𐏒𐏒	XXVI	DB 1.89.
				𐏒𐏒	XXVII	DB 2.26.
𐏒	X	DB 1.56.		𐏒𐏒	XL	DSf 26.
𐏒	XII	DB 3.39.		𐏒𐏒𐏒	LX	Wd 1.
𐏒	XIII	DB 3.63.		𐏑𐏒	CXX	Wc 1.
𐏒	XIV	DB 1.38.				

DEFECTIVE PASSAGES

CMb	large parts of lines 3 to end.
DNb 58	+++++ verb.
DNb 58f	++++++*ātiy*/*ā* nom. 'anyone' + loc. 'in obedience'.
DNb 60	+++++ +++++ +++++*ina*:
DSe 45	++++ name of the *vardanam*.
DSm 11f	end of the line, and continuation.
DSn 1f	+++...|...+++*na*
DSo 1f	+++++ +++++ +++++*našᵃ* |*tam* :
DSq 1–4	parts of all lines.
A²Sc 6	*ta* +++++
A²Sc 7	first part of line.
A²Sc 8	entire line, and continuation.
Sb	line 2 entire; part of line 3.

ADDENDA

The gold tablets bearing the inscriptions AsH (pages 107 and 116) and A²Hc (pages 114 and 155) were exhibited at The Asia Institute in New York City during the winter of 1949–50; they were purchased in January 1950 by the Iranian Government, and after being exhibited at the Boston Museum of Fine Arts, are to be returned to Iran and placed in the Archaeological Museum at Teheran.

On the inscription DSf (pages 110 and 142), G. Goossens has an interesting discussion of the foreign artists and artisans, in La Nouvelle Clio 1.32–44, esp. 36–8 (1949).

The most recent and best account of the religion of Darius and his successors is given by J. Duchesne-Guillemin, in his volume entitled Zoroastre, pages 105-33 (Paris, 1948).

We await with eager anticipation the publication by Cameron of his reading of DB (see page 108), as yet delayed by his academic work. His publication will doubtless show important changes in the text (given above, pages 116–35), in addition to those which he generously communicated to be used in the present volume (see page 118); new readings in 4.90–92 will be of special interest. Further, many characters which we have indicated by italics as entirely lost, will certainly have proved to be legible to him with his new methods (see page 118) and his extremely careful scrutiny and recording.

CPSIA information can be obtained
at www.ICGtesting.com
Printed in the USA
BVHW01s0950230518
517003BV00027B/54/P